Narratology and Interpretation

Trends in Classics – Supplementary Volumes

Edited by
Franco Montanari and Antonios Rengakos

Scientific Committee
Alberto Bernabé · Margarethe Billerbeck · Claude Calame
Philip R. Hardie · Stephen J. Harrison · Stephen Hinds
Richard Hunter · Christina Kraus · Giuseppe Mastromarco
Gregory Nagy · Theodore D. Papanghelis · Giusto Picone
Kurt Raaflaub · Bernhard Zimmermann

Volume 4

Walter de Gruyter · Berlin · New York

Narratology and Interpretation

The Content of Narrative Form
in Ancient Literature

Edited by

Jonas Grethlein
Antonios Rengakos

Walter de Gruyter · Berlin · New York

∞ Printed on acid-free paper which falls within the guidelines of the ANSI to ensure permanence and durability.

ISBN 978-3-11-048236-2

Library of Congress Cataloging-in-Publication Data

Narratology and interpretation : the content of narrative form in ancient literature / edited by Jonas Grethlein and Antonios Rengakos.
  p. cm. — (Trends in classics, supplementary volumes ; 4)
Includes bibliographical references and index.
ISBN 978-3-11-021452-9 (hardcover : alk. paper)
  1. Narration (Rhetoric) — History. 2. Greek literature — History and criticism. I. Grethlein, Jonas, 1978— II. Rengakos, Antonios.
PA3003.N37 2009
808—dc22
                                                           2009008858

Bibliographic information published by the Deutsche Nationalbibliothek

The Deutsche Nationalbibliothek lists this publication in the Deutsche Nationalbibliografie; detailed bibliographic data are available in the Internet at http://dnb.d-nb.de.

© Copyright 2009 by Walter de Gruyter GmbH & Co. KG, D-10785 Berlin

All rights reserved, including those of translation into foreign languages. No part of this book may be reproduced or transmitted in any form or by any means, electronic or mechanical, including photocopy, recording or any information storage and retrieval system, without permission in writing from the publisher.

Printed in Germany
Cover Design: Christopher Schneider, Laufen
Printing and binding: Hubert & Co. GmbH & Co. KG, Göttingen

Contents

Introduction 1

I. Ancient Predecessors of Narratology

Stephen Halliwell
The Theory and Practice of Narrative in Plato 15

Richard Hunter
The *Trojan Oration* of Dio Chrysostom and Ancient Homeric
Criticism 43

René Nünlist
Narratological Concepts in Greek Scholia 63

II. Narratology – New Concepts

Irene de Jong
Metalepsis in Ancient Greek Literature 87

Egbert J. Bakker
Homer, Odysseus, and the Narratology of Performance 117

Deborah Beck
Speech Act Types, Conversational Exchange, and the Speech
Representational Spectrum in Homer 137

Jonas Grethlein
Philosophical and Structuralist Narratologies – Worlds Apart? . 153

III. Narratology and the Interpretation of Epic and Lyric Poetry

Evanthia Tsitsibakou-Vasalos
Chance or Design? Language and Plot Management in the *Odyssey*. Klytaimnestra ἄλοχος μνηστὴ ἐμήσατο 177

Marios Skempis – Ioannis Ziogas
Arete's Words: Etymology, *Ehoie*-Poetry and Gendered Narrative in the *Odyssey* 213

Lucia Athanassaki
Narratology, Deixis, and the Performance of Choral Lyric. On Pindar's *First Pythian Ode* 241

Georg Danek
Apollonius Rhodius as an (anti-)Homeric Narrator: Time and Space in the *Argonautica* 275

Evina Sistakou
'Snapshots' of Myth: The Notion of Time in Hellenistic Epyllion 293

Theodore D. Papanghelis
Aeneid 5.362–484: Time, Epic and the Analeptic Gauntlets .. 321

IV. Narratology and the Interpretation of Tragedy

Francis Dunn
Sophocles and the Narratology of Drama 337

Marianne Hopman
Layered Stories in Aeschylus' *Persians* 357

Seth L. Schein
Narrative Technique in the *Parodos* of Aeschylus' *Agamemnon* . 377

Anna A. Lamari
Knowing a Story's End: Future Reflexive in the Tragic Narrative of the Argive Expedition Against Thebes 399

Ruth Scodel
Ignorant Narrators in Greek Tragedy 421

V. Narratology and the Interpretation of Historiography

Christos C. Tsagalis
Names and Narrative Techniques in Xenophon's *Anabasis* ... 451

Nikos Miltsios
The Perils of Expectations: Perceptions, Suspense and Surprise
in Polybius' *Histories* 481

Christopher Pelling
Seeing through Caesar's Eyes: Focalisation and Interpretation . 507

Chrysanthe Tsitsiou-Chelidoni
History beyond Literature: Interpreting the 'Internally
Focalized' Narrative in Livy's *Ab urbe condita* 527

Philip Hardie
Fame's Narratives. Epic and Historiography 555

List of Contributors 573

Bibliography 577

General Index 617
Passages Index 623

Introduction

1

In the last two decades, a technical analysis of narrative, as outlined by Genette, Bal and others,[1] has become increasingly popular in the field of Classics. De Jong's groundbreaking study of 'narrators and focalizers' in the *Iliad* has inspired narratological readings of other genres as well as prompting further studies of epic.[2] Narratology has proven itself to be a highly apt tool with which to explore the complex structures of the ancient novel.[3] Hornblower has shown that concepts such as 'anachrony' and 'embedded focalisation' can help us to elucidate the sophisticated narratives of ancient historians and so paved the way for Rood's monograph length study of Thucydides.[4] The application of narratology has also been extended beyond prose-narratives: even before de Jong's study of the *Iliad*, Hurst and Köhnken had explored the temporal structure of epinicean poetry;[5] now we also have a full study of the narrator in Archaic and Hellenistic poetry by Morrison.[6] Furthermore, scholars such as Goward, Barrett and Markantonatos have applied a narratological approach to Greek tragedy.[7] The project to write a history of Greek literature from a narratological point of view has already produced two door-stop volumes, *Narrators, Narratees, and Narratives in Ancient Greek*

---

[1] See, e.g., Genette (1972) 1980; Chatman 1978; Bal (1985) 1997. All these approaches are discourse-oriented, i.e. they focus on the mediation of a story in a discourse. Although the works of Calame 1996 and Edmonds 2004 illustrate that there have been attempts to apply story-oriented narratologies (e.g. that of Greimas, Bremond) to classical texts, the influence of this branch of narratology has been significantly smaller.
[2] De Jong (1987) 2004. On Homer, see, e.g., Richardson 1990; Rabel 1997; Alden 2000. Fusillo's narratological study of Apollonius Rhodius' *Argonautica* (1985) predates de Jong's *Iliad*-monograph.
[3] Winkler 1985; Fusillo 1989; Morales 2005.
[4] Hornblower 1994; Rood 1998.
[5] Hurst 1983; 1985; Köhnken 1983.
[6] Morrison 2007.
[7] Goward 1999; Barrett 2002; Markantonatos 2002.

Literature and *Time in Ancient Greek Literature*, and a third volume to focus on space and narrative is in preparation.

Narratological theory has however, in the meanwhile, moved on. Whereas most Classicists are still busy exploring the avenues opened by the application of the structuralist models developed in the 1960s and 70s, in literary theory the singular 'narratology' has given way to a plurality of 'narratologies'.[8] Many approaches including feminism, cultural history and postcolonial studies have developed their own specific narratologies, and in a wide range of disciplines, notably history, psychology and philosophy, the paradigm of narrative has inspired new fields of research.[9] At the same time, attempts have been made to widen the breadth of subjects covered by narratology so as to include in it not only genres such as drama and lyric, but also oral conversation and other media, especially film, art and music.[10] While many of these interdisciplinary and intermedial narratologies still rely on traditional structuralist concepts, some scholars have ventured to set narratology on a new footing. Cognitive studies, in particular, have presented themselves as an attractive starting point for scholars who try to move from the text to the act of reception, one of the most advanced concepts being Fludernik's *natural narratology*.[11]

The 'explosion of activity in the field of narrative study'[12] has not been met with unqualified enthusiasm. Besides denouncing the abuse of 'narratology' as a fashionable label for all kinds of readings that scarcely treat of narratological matters, scholars have expressed their anxiety that the interdisciplinary and intermedial enlargement would lead first to the dilution of narratology and ultimately to its dissolution.[13] A

---

8 For surveys, see Nünning 2003; Fludernik 2005. On the 'new narratologies', see also Herman 1999.

9 The seminal article for feminist narratology is Lanser 1986; Nünning 2000 charts a cultural historical narratology; Bhaba 1994 is important for postcolonial narratology. White 1973 established the paradigm of narratology in history; in psychology, see Bruner 1986; Straub, 1998; in philosophy, see Ricoeur 1984–1988 (for an early predecessor, see Schapp (1953) 1976).

10 See in general Wolf 2002 and the contributions to Ryan 2004; Meister 2005. On a narratology which embraces both literary narratives and oral story-telling, see Fludernik 1996; Herman 2004. Chatman 1978 is a pioneering study for a narratology of film. On narratology and music, see Kramer 1991; Neubauer 1997; on narratology and figurative art, Dieterle 1988; Steiner 1988.

11 Fludernik 1996. For another approach see Jahn 1997.

12 Herman 1999, 1.

13 See, e.g., Meister 2003.

new debate has started which raises pressing questions such as whether narratology should be defined by its object or character as a discipline or what the relationship between abstract theoretical reflections and the analysis of particular narratives ought to be.[14]

The editors of this volume at once share the concerns of traditional narratologists, while at the same time they are fascinated by the results of some of the new lines of inquiry. It seems that narratology can make significant contributions to other approaches through a clear profile rather than through lending its name to fashionable labels. Technical analysis of narrative ought not however to be an end in itself, but needs to be made fruitful for interpretation. For example, observing that the Homeric epos contains a dense net of anachronies does not in itself merit much attention, but does become worth our time, if, say, the impact of the temporal organisation on the recipients' perception of the plot is explored, or if it is linked to the discussion of how we are to place Homer between orality and literacy. We therefore suggest adhering to narratology in the singular and using it as a heuristic tool for interpretation.[15] Narratology thus defined will not deliver fully developed interpretations, but rather present observations which, though without claim on objectivity, are sufficiently formal to enrich various readings.

If we follow this conception of narratology, then combining it with other approaches emerges as a crucial step. Given that, especially in the field of Classics, many studies in the tradition of structuralist narratology content themselves with the task of classification and that, on the other hand, most works of the new narratologies have little to say on narrative structures, one of the major challenges of the moment is to open up new paths following which the technical analysis of narrative can be made fruitful for other approaches such as feminist and New Historical studies.[16] On the same principle, it is well worth exploring the interface of narratology with theories such as reader-response and speech-act as well as the potential of close textual analysis for psychology, philosophy and other disciplines. Although the categories provided by traditional narratology are not at all concerned with history, they can nevertheless

---

14 See, for example, the papers in Kindt – Müller 2003b.
15 See Kindt – Müller 2003a, who argue for a heuristic concept of narratology against autonomist, contextualist and foundationalist approaches.
16 See, for example, Bender's examination of modes of narrativization and their role for the rise of the penitentiary in the eighteenth century (Bender 1987).

be used for diachronic analysis alike and thereby open the door to a historical narratology,[17] which is a project of particular interest to Classicists.

In accordance with these reflections, this volume aims at drawing out the subtler possibilities of narratological analysis for the interpretation of both ancient Greek, and in three cases, Latin texts. The contributors explore the heuristic fruitfulness of various narratological categories, several combining them with other approaches: Linguistics (Beck) and performance studies (Bakker) are shown to have important contributions still to make to structuralist narratology. In other papers, narratology is put together with studies in deixis (Athanassaki, Schein), reader-response theory (Hopman; Miltsios), cognitive psychology (Scodel), landscape studies (Danek), the biography-of-goods approach (Papanghelis) and etymology (Ziogas and Skempis; Tsitsibakou-Vasalos) as well as Ricoeur's philosophy of time (Sistakou, Grethlein). A brief synopsis of the individual chapters concludes this introductory chapter.

2

Narratology as a discipline is the fruit of the second half of the twentieth century, but narrative had already been the object of inquiry in Antiquity. The first section assembles three papers which through exploring texts of very different provenance highlight the variety of ancient approaches to narrative. Halliwell challenges the notion that Plato presents a comprehensive 'embryonic narratology' in *Republic* 3. In linking the reflections on narrative discourse with Plato's own narrative practice, Halliwell demonstrates that there are not only tensions between the tripartite typology of *lexis* in 392–4 (plain, mimetic, mixed) and the normative typology laid out in 394–8, but that the model proposed by Socrates fails to do justice to the complexities of Platonic dialogue as well as epic narrative. Read from this perspective, the narrative itself enables Plato to express the complexity of narrative which it is impossible to theorize fully.

In the *Trojan Oration*, Dio Chrysostomus argues that Paris was the lawful husband of Helena, that Hector killed Achilles and that the Greeks did not capture Troy. Hunter reads the speech as an artful exploration of the limits and purposes of poetic myth that touches on many of

---

17 Examples for diachronic narratological studies are Wolf 1993; Fludernik 1996.

the core issues of narratology. He demonstrates the breadth of questions discussed by Dio, including the anastrophic character of the narrative, in terms of modern narratology its anachronies, and elaborates on Dio's relationship to earlier Homeric criticism and his use of it. What emerges from this analysis is a Dio who sets up a sophisticated game with Homer as well as with Homeric criticism which in turn openly invites criticism of the same kind as that which it itself brings against the Homeric poems.

Nünlist brings to our attention that it is not only technical treatises, but also scholia that explore narratological issues. Examples from the scholia on Homer illustrate that the 'ancient critic at work' reflected on questions of time, voice and focalisation. While the scholia do not develop a theoretical and terminological framework and therefore ought not to be seen as a narratological theory *avant la lettre*, it is nonetheless striking that even complex phenomena such as embedded focalisation were noted and drew comments.

A second section brings together four papers which concentrate on theory, either by putting forth a narratological concept that is new in Classical studies or by using other approaches to overcome deficiencies of current narratological studies or by bringing structuralist narratology into a dialogue with narratology in other disciplines. Metalepsis, i. e. the blurring of the hierarchy of narrative levels, is a much discussed phenomenon in modern fiction. De Jong contributes to the project of a historical narratology by exploring the use of metalepsis in early Greek literature. She examines in particular the figure of *apostrophe*, that is references to the narrative at the level of the action, the blending of narrative voices and the merging of the worlds of the narrator and the narrated at the end of narratives. While in modern fiction metalepses often serve as an 'anti-illusionistic device', de Jong makes a strong case that in early Greek literature metalepses tend to increase the authority of the narrator and the realism of the narrative.

Bakker notes that traditional narratology fails to do justice to narratives such as the Homeric epics the composition and reception of which take place alike in the very act of performance. In his 'narratology of performance', he argues that the virtual absence of free indirect discourse is due to the fixed setting of performance, suggests the term of 'projected indexicality' which takes into account the diachronic dimension of performance, and challenges the value of a sharp distinction between narrator and character speech in the case of orally performed poetry. As the *Odyssey* illustrates, the boundaries between the characters' ἔπη and the bards' ἀοιδή become easily blurred. Like de Jong's paper, Bakker's approach also underscores the importance of a historical narratology that goes beyond the unhistorical frame of traditional narratology.

Beck's argument brings narratology into a profitable dialogue with linguistics. Her test case is the relationship between direct and indirect speech in the Homeric epics. While traditional narratological studies have noted that indirect speeches in Homer are relatively unimportant and are mostly used for orders, Beck observes that, even if not to the same extent, orders nonetheless dominate direct speeches too. In applying the concept of 'expressivity' which addresses the degree of emotional involvement of the speaker, she argues that indirect speeches are often chosen where expressive features do not exist or do not matter. The concept of 'move' which elucidates the way in which particular utterances operate in context sheds further light on the position of indirect speeches in conversations.

In the last paper of the second section, Grethlein outlines an approach which combines Ricoeur's philosophical narratology with Genette's taxonomy. More specifically, the refiguration of time in narrative, a rather vague concept in *Time and Narrative*, can be elucidated by the transformation of a *fabula* into a *sjuzet*, which shapes the tension between expectation and experience at the levels of action and reception. This model is then applied to Herodotus and Thucydides who have similar views of human being in time, but present them in rather different narrative modes. It is finally suggested that the double refiguration of time contributes to the appeal of narrative across cultures and that the different reading experiences offered by Herodotus' and Thucydides' *Histories* illustrate the basic tension between enacting and distancing human temporality in narrative.

While most narratologists have used examples from modern novels to illustrate their models, the dissemination of their theory in the field of Classics started from the study of Homeric epic. The third section of this volume presents papers which explore new avenues in the narratological study of Homer or tackle later epic and other poetic genres the narrative forms of which have not yet been given the attention due to them. In her reading of the *Odyssey*, Tsitsibakou-Vasalos shows that the study of etymology and narratology can complement one another. It has not gone unnoticed by scholarship that Orestes' revenge for his father's murder is evoked as a foil to Telemachus' coming of age in the *Odyssey*. Tsitsibakou-Vasalos argues that a dense net of etymological links underscores and enriches the juxtaposition of Odysseus' return to Penelope with the murderous reception of Agamemnon by Clytaemnestra. The term μνηστή, in particular, used as an epithet for ἄλοχος and, as Tsitsibakou-Vasalos suggests, figuring as the second part of the name Klytaemnestra, links the two stories while encapsulating through etymologies the indeterminacies of female characters which stand at the core of the plot of the *Odyssey*.

The link between etymology and narratology is also explored by Skempis and Ziogas who examine the narrative dynamics of (para-)etymologies of the name Arete in the *Odyssey*. Not only does 'Arete', through the association with ἀράομαι and -ῥητος, establish links between different segments of the text and fulfil pro- and analeptic functions, but it also evokes the genre of *Ehoie*-poetry and so brings out the juxtaposition of genders more sharply through a play with different genres. On this argument, in which narratology intersects with gender and genre studies as well as with an etymological reading, *Ehoie*-poetry provides a channel for inter-gender communication and enables Odysseus to complete his *nostos*.

In studies of Greek lyric poetry, much attention has lately been paid to deixis, a concept which has some elements in common with narratology, besides place and person also time. Athanassaki demonstrates that the narrative category of frequency can enhance our understanding of deictic indications that delineate performative contexts in lyric poems. In particular the notion of (pseudo-)iterative narratives proves helpful for conceptualizing the polysemy of deixis as an expression of dissemination through re-performance. Athanassaki's test case, Pindar's *First Pythian*, features both choral and sympotic performances which establish a complex reflection on song reception and survival through re-performance.

Narratologists have paid much more attention to time than to space. Danek shows that the differences between Homer and Apollonius Rhodius are due not so much to a different management of narrative time – Zielinski's laws can, with important modifications, be applied to the epics of both – as to different treatments of space. To demonstrate this, Danek goes beyond narrative and draws on recent studies which have elaborated the differences between orientation through landmarks and a more complex two-dimensional spatial sense. While the first two books of the *Argonautica* follow a one-dimensional line through space, book 3 plays with multiple storylines. Danek argues that this is made possible not by an innovative treatment of time, but by the introduction of triangular movements which seem to be absent from Homeric epic.

Most Hellenistic epyllia are limited in length and focus on single episodes. Sistakou uses the term 'snapshot' to shed light on the genre's peculiar temporal form in readings of three examples. In the Callimachean *Hecale*, Theocritus' *Little Heracles* and the *Europa* of Moschus, the generic tendency to focus on minor moments and to freeze time converges with a focus on different aspects of time, notably age, memory and man's ephemeral nature. Sistakou demonstrates that, despite the differences, the three texts all explore the tension between objective and phenomenological time (Ricoeur) and so illustrates the way in which time in narrative can be linked to the general notion of time.

A paper dealing with Latin literature complements the third section. In his examination of the funeral games in *Aeneid* 5, Papanghelis combines the narratological analysis of order with anthropological studies that have investigated 'biographies-of-goods'. The temporal structure of the funeral games for Anchises are far more complex than their Homeric model, those for Patroclus in *Iliad* 23. Both the narrative and the speeches set up a *panopticon* in which the present of the games refracts the past as well as the future. Papanghelis elaborates in particular the narrative significance of Eryx' gauntlets which evoke a mythical past and can also be interpreted at a metapoetic level.

Tragedy has been as tempting as it has proved difficult for narratologists. While there is no narrator, the speeches and songs of characters and chorus contain narratives and somehow mediate a story. A survey of recent attempts to apply narratology to drama leads Dunn to the conclusion that, while the absence of a narrator makes it impossible to develop a comprehensive narratology of drama, there is nonetheless room for a strategic narratology of drama which focuses on situations with a narrating agent. Dunn borrows from Chatman the term 'slant' to describe the frame with which internal playwrights such as Athena in *Ajax* provide Greek tragedy. While such internal playwrights cannot be found in all tragedies, the chorus, which presents a specific 'angle' on the dramatic action, is a feature common to all. In a reading of Sophocles' *Electra*, Dunn demonstrates the way in which the slant of the tutor and the angle of the chorus shape the audience's perception of the dramatic action.

Hopman's paper illustrates that narratological models other than Genette's, in this case Greimas' actantial model, in combination with a reader-response approach can be a powerful tool with which to shed new light on much discussed questions. In her reading of Aeschylus' *Persians*, Hopman distinguishes two storylines, first the 'war story', the Persians' defeat at Salamis, which is the object of embedded narratives, and second the 'πόθος story', the Chorus' desire to be reunited with the Persian soldiers, which forms the action played out on stage. While many interpretations of *Persians* have focused on static juxtapositions such as that of East with West, Greimas' narratological model lets Hopman trace the development of the actantial position of the Chorus which first opposes Xerxes and is then, in the end, joined by him in the mourning of the dead. It is this intersection of 'war' and 'πόθος stories', Hopman argues, that allowed the Athenian audience to project their own emotions on their enemies.

Aeschylus' tragedies stand out by virtue of long narratives in the choral songs. Schein examines the arguably most complex example of choral lyric in extant Attic tragedy, the *parodos* of *Agamemnon*, charting it on the 'sliding scale' of choral song which ranges from direct comments on the action to general reflections. While the introductory anapaests are imbued with the specific identity of the chorus as citizens of Argos, the lyric part draws on the traditional communal authority of choruses. In combining narratology with deixis, Schein explores in particular the intricate narrative structure and the vagueness of the temporal and spatial deixis in this ode.

Lamari presents a fresh look at both Aeschylus' and Euripides' plays on the Argive expedition against Thebes, arguing for it to be seen as a highly complex dialogue between the authors which plays with 'future reflexivity'. Just as Aeschylus seems to have written *Eleusinians* after *Seven* although it deals with earlier events, Euripides composed *Phoenician Women* as a 'prequel' to a play staged earlier, *Suppliants*. Although one may have doubts about whether such 'bookish' interpretations do fully justice to the performance culture of fifth-century Athens, the chiastic play with mythological time and the time of performance reveals an interesting aspect of tragedy's manifold relation to time.

Scodel draws on the concept of 'Theory of Mind' which recent cognitive literary studies have developed, and with its help discusses narrative unreliability in Greek tragedy. The distinction of three axes of reliability, those of fact, ethic and knowledge or perception, allows Scodel to explore three cases: narrators, who are aware of their own perceptual limits, such as the Phrygian in *Orestes*; narrators who recognize their limits, but nonetheless attempt to interpret events, for example Tecmessa in *Ajax*; and narrators whose limits are important within a narrative strategy. In this last and most interesting case, the understanding of the plot would require explanations which are not provided by the narrator. For example, the numerous blanks in the narratives of Io in *Prometheus Bound* and the *exangelos* in *Oedipus Rex* force the audience to reflect intensely upon the events which actually took place.

The final section is devoted to historiography, with one paper crossing the borderline to biography. While the papers of Tsitsibakou-Vasalos and Skempis and Ziogas have explored the intersection of narratology and etymology in Homeric epic, Tsagalis argues that proper names serve important narrative functions in Xenophon's *Anabasis*. According to his paper, names establish links between distant sections and produce dramatic effects. Even the use of anonymous characters, patronymics and periphrastic denomination seems to bear narrative significance.

While historians have extensively used and discussed Polybius as a source, literary aspects of his work have found little attention, if we leave aside complaints about his awkward style and endless sentences. In Miltsios' paper, the combination of narratology with reader-response-theory proves a fruitful strategy for elucidating Polybius' underappreciated narrative artistry. Close readings of select passages show the ways in which Polybius plays with the cognitive gap between characters and narratees to create dramatic irony and suspense of anticipation as well as of uncertainty.

Pelling explores the relevance of focalisation for narrative interpretations and representations of the past. Caesar affords a particularly interesting test case, not only because of his power and failure in the end to control history which raise the question whether his role is expressed by the prominence of his focalisation in narrative or not, but also since his life is the object of biography as well as of historiography. In comparing the accounts of Caesar by Cassius Dio, Appian, Plutarch, Suetonius and Velleius, Pelling demonstrates how differently focalisation can be handled and how its use encourages specific interpretations of history.

At the end of the volume stand two papers treating Latin texts. Tsitsiou-Chelidoni examines internally focalized narratives in Livy's *Ab urbe condita*. She follows Genette in distinguishing narratized, transposed and reported speech and explores the artful use of all three forms of internal focalizations to make the narrative vivid, to give it a strong mimetic dimension and to render it plausible. Her close readings of select passages lead Tsitsiou-Chelidoni to a general reflection on the value of narratology which needs to be complemented by further interpretation, but can then yield rich fruits for our understanding of ancient texts.

Hardie examines the use of *fama* in the narratives of Roman epic and historiography. *Fama*, which signifies not only fame, the product of narrative, but also the process of narrating, can shift between inside and outside of the text. Tacitus in particular exploits artfully the possibilities which are based on *fama's* ambivalence towards focalization. Narratives concerning *fama* too play a special role in beginnings and endings where they allow the balancing of closure with openness.

As previous works have amply demonstrated, the strength of narratology lies in its ability to analyze the form of narrative. This is of particular value for the study of ancient Greek and Latin literatures which reveal a high awareness of form. Form is often crucial to the creation of meaning. In combination with other approaches, narratology can help to elucidate the *content of the form*, more specifically the meaning generated by narrative structures, and thereby deepen our understanding of ancient texts. It is our hope that the papers assembled in this volume illustrate some ways in which this can be done as well as inspiring new explorations.

Jonas Grethlein
Antonios Rengakos

Heidelberg – Thessaloniki,
January 2009

I. Ancient Predecessors of Narratology

The Theory and Practice of Narrative in Plato

Stephen Halliwell

All narrative discourse, from the simplest to the most sophisticated, imposes a perspectival structure on temporal experience. To that extent, all narrative can be categorised and analysed, as the powerful tools of modern narratology have demonstrated, in terms of the operation of a number of variable features of discursive form and focus. But because narrativity is so ineliminable from the fabric of human awareness, its ramifications have a tendency to outreach the scope of systematic codification. The fluidity and open-endedness of consciousness, memory, and imagination are entangled with, but also partly resistant to, the organising configurations of narrative. This tension generates a complex web of possibilities whose very richness gives narratological methods much of their *raison d'être* and interest. At the same time, however, it provides reasons to question whether narrative, in all its shapes and sizes, could ever be comprehensively theorised.

Since the present chapter is concerned with some of the relations between the theory and practice of narrative in Plato, it may be fruitful to start with an illustration taken from one of the most intriguingly designed narrative constructions to be found anywhere in the Platonic corpus, the opening of the *Theaetetus*. The main body of the dialogue is framed (or, more strictly, half-framed, since the work ends without a return to the opening interlocutors) by a conversation between two Megarians, Euclides and Terpsion. Euclides recounts to his friend that he has just returned to town after a chance encounter with the Athenian Theaetetus, who had been seriously wounded in battle against the Corinthians and was being taken home to his native city. Euclides goes on to explain how, after leaving Theaetetus (and after urging him in vain to stay and recuperate at Megara), his mind flooded with thoughts of a philosophical discussion in which Theaetetus had once participated with Socrates, shortly before the latter's death, and of which Euclides

---

I am very grateful to Professors Antonios Rengakos and Jonas Grethlein for inviting me to contribute to the stimulating Thessaloniki narratology conference in December 2007. I thank my fellow participants for discussion of my paper.

had received lengthy descriptions, on several occasions, from Socrates himself. So fascinated was Euclides by what he was told about this discussion that he had reconstructed it over a period of time in writing, turning it into a dramatic dialogue whose accuracy he had checked and corrected in direct consultation with Socrates. That written account is presented as the main substance of the *Theaetetus* itself: Euclides agrees to Terpsion's request to hear the dialogue, which is read to them by Euclides' slave.

In formal terms, therefore, Plato's *Theaetetus* comprises a conversation between characters who then listen to the recital of a reconstructed version of a previous conversation between several other characters. As with the more commonly cited but in some ways less remarkable opening of the *Symposium*, this layered or 'parenthetic' construction is notable for its literary intricacy and self-consciousness: there is an obvious *mise-en-abyme* effect in the fact that Plato's dialogue largely consists of (an oral presentation of) Euclides' own dialogue. But this compositional structure, which can be analysed from various angles as a narrative strategy, sets up a depth of perspective whose psychological expressiveness and emotional resonance are less easy to fix or delimit. It is immediately after saying farewell to Theaetetus (and at a place which for some of Plato's readers may have had mythological associations with death),[1] and in a spontaneous surge of highly charged recollection, that Euclides starts to remember Socrates – in particular, his prescience of a future he did not live to see: 'I recalled and marvelled at how prophetic Socrates was about Theaetetus, among many other things' (*Tht.* 142c). This memory is in turn tied up with the degree to which Euclides had been captivated by Socrates' accounts of his first conversation with Theaetetus, a response which had motivated his decision to produce a written version of that conversation. The literary layers of Plato's dialogic composition are matched, in other words, but also expanded by the layers of associative memory revealed by Euclides' remarks to his friend Terpsion. And there is a further element to this aspect of the work. The text invites its readers to suppose (and some of the earliest readers

---

[1] It is possible, though not certain, that Erinus/-um, *Tht.* 143b1, is the same place as the Erineus, at Eleusis, mentioned at Paus. 1.38.5; cf. Frazer 1898, 502. If so, Plato may have expected some readers to be familiar with the legend that this was the spot where Hades returned to the underworld with Persephone. The nature of such a suggestion will not seem far-fetched to anyone who recalls *Phdr.* 229b-c.

are likely to have known this independently) that the historical situation depicted in the dialogue's introduction was the occasion of Theaetetus's death.[2] Obviously telling in this regard is Euclides' description of how, when he came across Theaetetus being carried along, he found him 'alive, but only barely so', and suffering from debilitating dysentery as well as his wounds (142b). In the dialogue's 'real time', then, as Euclides and Terpsion listen to the reenactment of an episode from Theaetetus's adolescence, Theaetetus the man is dying: the talented young mathematician lives again in the (philosophical) imagination, preserved in Euclides' and/or Plato's text, even as his adult self as citizen-soldier brings about his destruction. But does the juxtaposition of Theaetetus's youthful promise with his fatal wounds and sickness (and his desperate need to get home, 142c2) cast a retrospective poignancy over his life? Or does it, instead, allow a kind of philosophical redemption or 'overcoming' of his death? In this and the other respects I have mentioned, the introduction of the dialogue has a potential significance which 'spills', as it were, over the framework of its own literary form and creates for its readers opportunities for reflection (on the imagined lives of Socrates, Theaetetus, Euclides, and Terpsion) which are not susceptible of theoretically neat definition.[3]

I have chosen a few details from the start of the *Theaetetus* as a convenient way of highlighting questions of narrative form and significance which are of much wider consequence for the reading of the Platonic dialogues. In the context of a collective project on the value of narratology for the interpretation of ancient texts, the particular interest of Plato stems from a combination of two circumstances. One is the fact that in the well-known stretch of *Republic* Book 3 (392c-8b) where Socrates, with some rather faltering help from Adeimantus, proposes a set of principles with which to analyse and evaluate poetic *lexis* (here signifying the presentational form or mode of discourse, *logos*), narratologists have been prepared to identify at least an embryonic 'theory of narrative' and the earliest known ancestor of their own critical methods.[4]

---

2   The dramatic date is probably 391 rather than 369: see Nails 2002, 274–8, 320–1.
3   For further discussion of the dialogue's frame, with emphasis on the way in which it suppresses an authorial explanation on *Plato*'s part (producing a 'narratological asymmetry' between him and Euclides), see Morgan 2003.
4   *Lexis* should not here be translated as 'diction' (i.e. word choice), *contra* e.g. Shorey 1937, 225 etc., Morgan, K. 2004, 358; Bers 1997, 13 blurs the point. Note the conjunction and virtual synonymy of *lexis* and *diēgēsis* at

The other is the far more diffuse fact that Plato's own procedures as a writer make extensive and, as we have already glimpsed, elaborate use of various types of narrative structure, thus prompting questions about the relationship between narrative theory and practice in the dialogues. Can we use the 'theory' advanced by Socrates in *Republic* 3 (and said by him, as we shall see, to be applicable to more than poetry) to test Platonic writing itself? If so, with what results? If not, why not? One of my goals in the present chapter is to suggest that both separately and in combination these two circumstances – the 'embryonic narratology' of *Republic* 392c-8b, and the narrative self-consciousness of Plato's own writing – are more difficult to assess than is sometimes appreciated. The nature of this difficulty can throw light on issues which remain worth the consideration of anyone concerned with theoretical models of narrative, as well as being of basic importance for the reading of Plato's work itself.

Before embarking on a close reexamination of *Republic* 392c-8b, it may be helpful to provide some preliminary orientation. First of all, a warning about terminology, though one with conceptual implications as well. Throughout my discussion, unless otherwise signalled, I shall employ 'narrative' to designate what Plato's text, at 392d and subsequently,[5] treats as the genus *diêgêsis*, roughly equivalent to temporally plotted discourse. This means, among other things, that I diverge from the common modern practice of equating 'diegesis' with what Socrates counts at 392d as one particular species of that genus, i.e. 'plain' or 'single-voiced' *diêgêsis* (ἁπλῆ διήγησις).[6] It also means that it

---

396b11; at 396c6 *lexis* is used more loosely to denote 'speech' or 'utterance' as opposed to action (cf. 5.473a). For narratological responses to *R*. 392c ff., see e.g. Genette (1972) 1980, 162–73, de Jong (1987) 2004, 2–5, Laird 1999, 48–78.

5 397b2 appears an exception. But as this is the last of *seventeen* uses of διήγησις and cognates at 392d-7b and is out of line with the preceding sixteen, there is a case for emendation (with addition of either ἁπλῆς or ἄλλης: for the latter cf. 396e6, where Adam unnecessarily emends to ἁπλῆς). 397a2, where the main mss. have διηγήσεται, need not be an exception to the generic sense: on the logic of the sentence, see Slings 2005, 47.

6 Modern narratological usage of 'diêgêsis' etc. has, of course, several variants, complicated by the French distinction between 'diégèse' and 'diégésis': see e.g. Genette (1983) 1988, 17–18. But it remains an error to use 'diegesis' *tout court* for one species rather than the genus when paraphrasing *R*. 392c-4c, as do (among many) Chatman 1974–5, 312, Prince 1988, 52, s.v. 'mimesis', Genette (1972) 1980, 164, Murray 1996, 168, Bers 1997, 11. Cf. Kirby 1991,

is not here a requirement of 'narrative' (or *diêgêsis*) *per se* that it should have a 'narrator': in the terms of Socrates' classification, drama is itself a species of narrative/*diêgêsis*, i.e. wholly mimetic *diêgêsis* (cf. 394c1). My present terminological usage is intended to maximise a scrupulous attention to the details of this section of the *Republic* and thereby to assist in drawing out both the subtleties and the problematic features of the argument. In pursuing this aim, I shall attempt to develop the following four lines of thought, all of which could profitably be taken further than I have the space to do here.

(1) If there is anything like a 'theory of narrative' to be found at *Republic* 392c-8b, it is itself necessarily embedded in the practice of Platonic writing: i.e., it is a representation of the joint efforts of Socrates and Adeimantus to arrive at such a theory. Since, in my view, there is no reliable hermeneutic for tracing a monologic authorial stance (about anything) within Platonic dialogue, 'theory' and 'practice' of narrative in Plato are therefore – here and elsewhere – inextricable. This means, more specifically, that one should not extract a conception of narrative from the text and treat it as though it had independent, free-standing Platonic authority. I shall adhere closely to this injunction in what follows, a procedure which distinguishes my approach from most existing treatments of the subject.

(2) In the passage of *Republic* 3 in question, Socrates' classification of the formal possibilities of narrative is more intricate and in some respects uncertain than is often realised; it calls for careful, cautious explication. In particular, I shall contend that the tripartite typology of *lexis* at 392c-4c – which divides the genus 'narrative' (*diêgêsis*) into two main forms, 'plain' (or 'single-voiced') and 'mimetic' (ἁπλῆ διήγησις and διήγησις διὰ μιμήσεως), with alternation between the two constituting a third, compound form (literally narrative 'by means of both', δι' ἀμφοτέρων)[7] – has a further, second-order and normative typology overlaid on it at 394d-8b. This produces considerable convolutions in the scope of the supposed 'theory' contained in the text.

---

118. In Halliwell 2002, 54 n. 42 an unfortunate misprint has omitted the word 'not' before 'equivalent'.

7 Plain or single-voiced narrative (for the translation of ἁπλῆ cf. n. 17 below): 392d, 393d, 394b. Mimetic narrative: 392d, 393c, 394c-d, etc.; this mode is also called 'mimesis' *tout court*, μίμησις, μιμεῖσθαι, at 393d, 394e, etc. (but n.b. the *wider* sense of mimesis earlier in Book 2, at 373b: cf. Halliwell 2002, 51 n. 35). Compound narrative: 392d, 394c, 396e.

(3) The ramifications of 392c-8b are complicated further when we read this section in the light of the lengthy preceding discussion (at 2.376e-3.392c) of the kinds of poetic stories or discourses (*muthoi*, 'stories' or 'myths', being treated, broadly speaking, as 'false' and/ or 'fictive' *logoi*, λόγοι ψευδεῖς, 376e-7a) which Socrates proposes as (un)suitable for the education of the Guardians of the ideal city under imaginative construction. If it is justifiable to find at least an emergent 'theory of narrative' at *Republic* 392c-8b, that theory ought to count, then, as part of a larger (though, as I shall stress, incomplete) 'theory of discourse' as adumbrated at 376e-98b. But there are a number of difficulties in the relationship between these two stages of argument, difficulties which have received insufficient attention in the scholarly literature but which affect the boundaries of the concept of 'narrative' itself and involve a less than fully integrated dialectic between different ways of interpreting the meaning(s) of narrative texts. Although I shall touch further on this side of the architecture of the dialogue in the later parts of my paper, its implications should be borne in mind throughout.

(4) Any attempt to use *Republic* 392c-8b (even more so, 376e-398b) as the source of criteria with which to frame an assessment of Plato's own practice as a writer needs to face up to several stiff challenges. In addition to the fundamental consideration (see [1] above) that this passage of Book 3, whatever its theoretical possibilities, is itself *part* of the practice of Platonic writing, these challenges include what I hope to show is the significant fact that Socrates' primary schema of plain, mimetic and compound *diêgêsis*, though used later in antiquity to produce classifications of Platonic dialogue form,[8] is insufficient to cope with the degree of diegetic variety found in Platonic writing and therefore cannot be taken as a comprehensive or definitive typology.

---

8   The classifications in question (there were others too, but based on different criteria) occur at Plu. *Mor.* 711b-c, a bipartite scheme of 'diegematic' (διηγηματικός, i. e. introduced by what *R*. 392d calls ἁπλῆ διήγησις) and 'dramatic' works; D. L. 3.50, a tripartite scheme of 'dramatic', 'diegematic', and 'mixed' (δραματικός, διηγηματικός, μεικτός); Procl. *in R*. 1.14.15–15.19 Kroll (similarly tripartite, but using the terms δραματικός/μιμητικός, ἀφηγηματικός/ἀμίμητος, μικτός). For the broader adaptation and extension of these formal categories in ancient criticism, see Haslam 1972, 20–1, Janko 1984, 128–30.

Having given this overview of the direction of my argument, I turn first to some of the problems raised by Socrates' classification of poetic (and, more obliquely, prose) *lexis* into plain, mimetic and compound forms or species of *diêgêsis*. As I proceed, I will use these problems as a reference point for some comparisons with Plato's own wider practices in the dialogues. It will be clear from what has already been said that my approach makes it imperative to refer to 'Plato' only as author of the text and to avoid the question-begging though standard procedure – 'Plato argues', 'Plato supposes', etc. – of treating him as though he were himself an omnipresent voice audible *within* the dialogue.

The typology of *lexis* put forward by Socrates at 392c-4c addresses 'narrative' in a conceptually broad rather than a formally narrow sense. The term *diêgêsis* (and equivalently, though only in passing as it were, the noun ἀπαγγελία, literally 'reporting', and the verb ἀπαγγέλλειν)[9] is used to denote narrative in this broad, generic sense as discourse keyed to a temporal framework of events: 'is it not the case that everything said by storytellers or poets is narrative of past, present or future events?' (ἆρ' οὐ πάντα ὅσα ὑπὸ μυθολόγων ἢ ποιητῶν λέγεται διήγησις οὖσα τυγχάνει ἢ γεγονότων ἢ ὄντων ἢ μελλόντων; 392d) – a question, we need to note for future reference, which indicates that the analysis applies to narrative in prose as well as verse.[10] It is important that in dividing the genus *diêgêsis* into single-voiced, mimetic and compound forms, Socrates defines the first of these not as third-person narrative without qualification but as comprising utterances by 'the poet himself' (393a-d, etc.). The account of Chryses' first approach to the leaders of the Greek army at *Iliad* 1.12–16 is a case in point: in these lines, on Socrates's definition, 'the poet himself speaks' (λέγει ... αὐτὸς ὁ ποιητής, 393a). By automatically equating a (primary or work-framing) third-person narrative with the voice of the poet, Socrates might seem to be sustaining a premise of authoriality which was active in

---

9 See 394c2, 396c7, matching up, respectively, with the use of διήγησις, διηγεῖσθαι in the surrounding analysis. In other contexts, both terms, διήγησις and ἀπαγγελία, could easily refer to third-person narrative alone, but Socrates is not following general usage (hence Adeimantus's uncertainty at 392d).

10 See 378c-d for a further indication that the critique as a whole, and therefore implicitly the analysis of *lexis*, applies also to prose (oral) storytelling; cf. 390a1–2 ('in prose or poetry', ἐν λόγῳ ἢ ἐν ποιήσει). λογοποιοί at 392a13 also probably refers to prose-writers, despite the application of the related verb to poets themselves at 392a. See my text below for the broadest indication of all, at 397c, that the principles at stake are not confined to poetry.

the earlier part of the critique of poetry, i.e. the broader discussion of discourse at 2.376e-3.392c, where formulations of the type 'the poet says' were used in paraphrasing passages from Homeric and other texts. But I shall argue later that there is a difference between that earlier premise — which is a *global and supra-textual* principle of ethical responsibility for the expressive content of poetic works — and the present, intra-textual definition of the plain or third-person narrative mode as communication in the voice of 'the poet himself': hence the fact that in the earlier stages of the discussion, as we shall see, formulations of the type 'the poet says' were *not* restricted to passages covered by Book 3's definition of plain or single-voiced narrative. Moreover, that definition itself conspicuously ignores the possibility (formally recognised, according to some scholars, in Aristotle's *Poetics*)[11] of a primary narrator who is neither a character in the narrative nor the author of the work. As it happens, that possibility is one which is never found in Plato's own dialogues; but then nor is the 'author-as-narrator' type which for Socrates is paradigmatically exemplified by Homeric epic. In this latter respect, it looks as though Plato, unlike Xenophon, deliberately shields his work from being read as direct authorial testimony.[12] Platonic dialogues with a framing narrative in 'compound' mode (there is no instance of a frame entirely in 'plain' mode) always ascribe the role of primary narrator to an identifiable individual, either Socrates himself (*Charmides*, *Lysis*, *Republic*) or someone else (Cephalus in *Parmenides*).[13] But that last point can in turn be converted back into a further observation on Socrates' typology: namely, that it makes no allowance for works

---

11 See de Jong (1987) 2004, 5–8 and (somewhat differently) Lattmann 2005, esp. 36–43, 46–7, on Arist. *Po.* 3.1448a21–3, 23.1460a5–11: interpretation of both these passages, however, remains vexed.

12 Cf. Morgan, K. 2004, 359: 'The Platonic narrator is never Plato'. Xen. *Mem.*, *Oec.* and *Smp.* all begin with direct first-person statements which invite ascription to the author himself; in the second and third of these works there are also claims (however historically questionable) of eye-witness testimony. Plato's presence at Socrates' trial, inserted as a 'dramatic' detail at *Ap.* 34a, 38b (overlooked by Morgan ibid.), is obviously a different literary procedure altogether; cf. the pointed reference to his *absence* from Socrates' death-bed scene at *Phd.* 59b.

13 Morgan, K. 2004, 364 wrongly counts the *Symposium* as having a 'narrative' rather than 'dialogical' frame, but then (365) refers to its 'opening conversation' (cf. her n. 16, which obscures the point). Vegetti 2007, 457 n. 42 wrongly describes the *Republic* itself as 'la *mimesis* di una *diegesis* socratica': in the terms of *R.* 392d, it is, of course, a compound *diêgêsis*.

framed by narratives in the voice of a character either involved directly in the events narrated (as with the *Republic* itself) or reporting an account derived from other persons so involved (Cephalus in *Parmenides* being a sort of halfway house between these two things).[14]

Despite its apparent claim (392d) to be applicable to narrative discourse in general, then, Socrates' typology is not only incomplete (ignoring three of the four main kinds of primary narrator, i.e. *every* kind other than the author-as-narrator type) but also doubly out of alignment with Plato's own practice in this regard. It puts heavy emphasis on a category (the author-as-narrator) which is not found in Plato's texts, and at the same time it fails to encompass practices of narrative framing which Platonic dialogues *do* exploit. So the typology is far from comprehensive, and Plato could hardly have thought that it was. This limitation is obviously in part a consequence of the fact that the typology is slanted towards a particular purpose, evaluation of the narrative forms or modes employed in two main kinds of Greek poetry, Homeric epic (and early hexameter poetry in general) and Attic drama: these are the only genres from which quotations are taken in this stretch of the dialogue.[15] It is true that 394c shows that Socrates intends the typology to be applicable to existing poetry more broadly, not just to epic and drama: he says that cases of unvarying, single-voiced narrative (here again equated with the voice of 'the poet himself') are exemplified 'especially in dithyramb', and that the compound mode occurs 'in many other places' (presumably including narrative elegy) as well as in epic.[16] But the absence of direct examples of any poetry

---

14 Contrary to what is sometimes said, e.g. by de Jong – Nünlist 2004, 545), there is no case of a Platonic dialogue framed by a 'narrative' (i.e. either plain or compound *diēgēsis*, as opposed to a framing conversation) in the voice of a 'disciple' of Socrates who himself either participated in or witnessed the recalled dialogue. *Parmenides* fails this test twice over: the primary narrator was not present at the main dialogue recalled, and Cephalus is not in any case a disciple of Socrates.

15 The only genres quoted at *any* point in the critique, in fact, are 'epic' hexameters (including the unknown verse at 379e2 and Hesiod fr. [dub.] 361 M-W at 390e3) and tragedy.

16 As regards dithyramb, Socrates can be taken to be referring both to the predominant use of 'plain' narrative for the telling of myths and to the general prominence of the poet's first-person voice (e.g. in invocations to the Muses or in other self-conscious comments on the performance of song): both features can be seen in the fragments of Pindar's dithyrambs. But elements of mimetic speech were found in at least some 'modern' dithyrambs: see Timotheus *Persae*

other than epic and drama in the course of 392c-8b leaves no doubt about the dominant focus of the discussion and helps to account for the corresponding simplification of the scheme. That does not, of course, make the poet-narrator model of third-person narrative uncontroversial even for Homer, though Socrates makes it sound as if it were. One could press this point in either (or perhaps both) of two ways: one, which is not really my concern here, by comparing Socrates' procedure with wider Greek cultural assumptions about the poet's presence in his work; the other, which I have already touched on and will return to later, by trying to correlate Socrates' emphasis with the larger understanding of authorial responsibility which can be tracked in the critique of poetic discourse (*logoi*) from 376e onwards. But whichever of those strategies one adopts, one must also recognise that Socrates' interpretation of plain or single-voiced narrative (used either alone or within the compound mode) as essentially a vehicle of authorial 'speech' is not adequate to cope with all the varieties or nuances of narrative presentation, including those employed in the *Republic* itself. In fact, we can say that his explication of ἁπλῆ διήγησις is designed above all to stamp it as 'single-viewpoint' narrative,[17] thereby suppressing the various ways (only too familiar to Plato himself as writer) in which non-mimetic narrative can achieve more complicated effects of perspective than are easily attributable to a unitary authorial voice. But this suppression serves a larger purpose, as will become clear later on, in relation to the overall concern of the argument with the dangers of psychic multiplicity in poetry.

These considerations can be reinforced by examining the other major component of Socrates' typology, 'narrative through mimesis' or 'mimetically enacted narrative', διήγησις διὰ μιμήσεως, including its contribution to the compound mode. Socrates defines mimetic narrative in terms of the direct representation of character speech: the agents' 'spoken words', ῥήσεις (393b, 394b), and the 'exchanges' or dialogue (ἀμοιβαῖα, 394b) between them.[18] It is not without significance, how-

---

791 col. iv.150–61 *PMG*, *Scylla* 793 *PMG* (registered in Aristotle's complaint about Odysseus's lament, *Po.* 15.1454a29–31), and cf. ps.-Arist. *Probl.* 19.15, 918b18–19. Note also the possibility of a connection with dithyramb in Socrates' later complaints about highly 'mimetic' music at 397a: cf. Zimmermann 1992, 123–4, Hordern 2002, 38–9.

17 Part of the force of ἁπλῆ, 'plain' or 'single', in the nomenclature of the typology depends precisely on a contrast with the 'double' (διπλοῦς) or 'multiple' (πολλαπλοῦς) voices of mimesis: see esp. 397e; cf. de Jong (1987) 2004, 3–4.

18 The term ἀμοιβαῖα is *hapax legomenon* in Plato: I note that nowhere in the discussion of poetry in *R.* Books 2–3 do we find the regular terms for conversa-

ever, that here too he preserves traces of an authorial presence by making the poet 'speak *as*', or take on the guise of, each character.[19] Once again, Socrates' construal of his categories is designed to cope with the kinds of poetry on which his sights are chiefly fixed; so wholly mimetic narrative, unsurprisingly, is drama (394b-c), while compound narrative is principally epic. If the exposition of these formal options seems deliberately rudimentary, that is in part for dramatic reasons: Socrates, like a schoolteacher, is guiding an Adeimantus who has some difficulty grasping the essentials (392d). But in treating Homeric epic as comprising a framework of author-narrative which introduces and separates a sequence of character speeches (392e-3c), Socrates creates the impression that at any particular juncture plain and mimetic narrative are either-or and exhaustive alternatives. This means that at the level of classification he disregards, among other things, the degree of formal (and more than formal) narrative intricacy which arises with an embedded story on the scale of Odysseus's Phaeacian *apologos* in *Odyssey* 9–12, even though that part of the epic was cited several times for other purposes earlier in *Republic* 3 itself.[20] In the case of the Phaeacian narrative the voice of a character becomes so sustained as in effect, on Socrates' terms, to displace 'the poet himself' as the controlling narrator. What's more, contained within this supplementary or secondary narrative framework are numerous speeches on the part both of Odysseus himself and of other characters he interacts with or encounters. At two points, in addition, we are given the speeches of characters in narratives embedded at one further remove within Odysseus's story, reporting occasions on which Odysseus himself was not present: the speech of Poseidon to Tyro at *Odyssey* 11.248–52, where Odysseus momentarily functions

---

tion and dialogue, διάλογος, διαλέγεσθαι. Since these terms are elsewhere used for Socratic dialogue itself (e.g. *R.* 1.336b, 354b), and therefore by implication for the dominant form of Plato's own writings, this avoidance tacitly masks the relationship between Socrates' taxonomy and the work in which it appears.

19   See the various formulations at 393a ff.: they cluster round the idea of the poet speaking 'as someone else', ὡς ἄλλος τις *vel sim.*

20   See 386c (Achilles' notorious words of disillusionment in Hades, here 'deleted' or censored yet quoted again by Socrates at 7.516d!), 386d, 390a-b (twice). Quotations from and allusions to *Odyssey* 9–12, especially the 'Nekyia', occur in several other Platonic works: for their importance in the early sections of *Protagoras*, see Segvic 2006, though at 248 she gives a simplified compression of the thesis of Halliwell 2000.

as an 'omniscient' narrator,[21] and the exchange between Helios and Zeus at 12.377–88, for which Odysseus quotes his source (see below). The general consequence of Socrates' silence about such things is that he effectively screens out the possible multiplicities of layering in which narrative voices can be inserted. Yet it is not immediately easy to see why he should underestimate the intricate variations of mimetic and compound narrative forms, since the anxieties he will go on to express about these forms at 393c ff. will centre precisely on discursive multiplicity and its implications for the soul. We shall therefore have to keep this question in mind when we reach that ensuing stage of the discussion.

Before that, it is worth underlining that Socrates' omissions or silences as regard the possible complexities of narrative form happen to stand in an interesting relationship, once again, to the practices of Plato's own writing. The position of Odysseus within his *apologos* to Alcinous is closely comparable to that of Socrates himself in the *Republic*.[22] Both Odysseus and Socrates, as 'internal' narrators, present elaborate accounts within which they quote both their own and others' direct speech. Both, moreover, include subordinate narratives at one remove. In the *Republic*, indeed, Socrates does this to a greater extent than Odysseus and with a wider range of variant techniques. Occasionally this may reflect relatively ordinary conversational chains of transmission: Socrates reporting Cephalus quoting the aging Sophocles' witty rejoinder about his quiescent libido (329b-c) perhaps falls under this heading (which is not to deny that the passage has a larger resonance for the themes of the dialogue). But the complexity of the narrative form of the *Republic*, and the consequent layering of Socrates' voice as narrator, goes much further than that. One example of this is the long speech early in Book 2 in which Adeimantus sets his own statements in a sort of counterpoint with the direct speech of more than one hypothetical interlocutor (imagined, furthermore, in conversation with both self

---

21 Note here that the function of 'omniscient narrator' has no place in Plato's own dialogues. Morgan, K. 2004, 363–4 is misleading on this point: her examples illustrate Socrates' strong readings of others' behaviour/psychology, but nothing which 'borders on omniscience'.

22 Socrates invokes the *apologos* ironically as an anti-model for the myth of Er at 614b: this is the very point, of course, at which Socrates *ceases* to be an Odysseus-like internal narrator. On larger thematic comparisons/contrasts (beyond my scope here) between the Platonic Socrates and Odysseus, cf. Hobbs 2000, esp. 195–6, 239–40.

and others, 365b-6b), and also repeats to Socrates, as a composite 'quotation', the sentiments which Adeimantus and Glaucon had previously put to their mentor (366d-7a): so in this last passage, by a kind of narrative loop, Socrates (as primary narrator) is quoting Adeimantus in the act of quoting Adeimantus himself back to Socrates. (Whose voice, let alone whose point of view, are we hearing in such a context? The question admits no stable answer.) Other examples of the *Republic*'s narrative complexity include Glaucon's recounting of the fable of Gyges' ring at 2.359c-60b; the extemporised speech which Socrates imagines himself making to the citizens of Callipolis as part of the myth or story (*muthos*) of the so-called 'noble lie' (3.415a-c); the passage of Book 5 where Socrates overlays on his (reported) conversation with Glaucon an imaginary conversation with a 'lover of sights and sounds' who denies their view of beauty, in the process producing a kind of blurring of voices which resists clear-cut formal analysis;[23] and the section of Book 8 where Socrates begins his account of defective constitutions by positing a quasi-Homeric invocation to the Muses and then conjecturing their reply in lengthy direct speech (545d-7b).

These examples illustrate the layered multiplication of voices which sometimes occurs within the narrated dialogue (i.e. the compound *diêgêsis*) of the *Republic* itself.[24] Even so, they do not represent the work's full range of narrative techniques, which encompass also the myth of Er's extraordinarily extended *oratio obliqua* (an option not given any prominence in Book 3's taxonomy of *lexis*), embedded in which are further diegetic variations, including indirect discourse 'nested' *within* indirect discourse.[25] But if such formal intricacies partly parallel some

---

23 476e ff. The blurring occurs when the conversation, after starting with Glaucon playing the part of the imaginary interlocutor, becomes indistinguishable from an exchange between Socrates and Glaucon themselves; the difference between the two conversations is eventually reasserted at 479a, but it then becomes blurred again in the same way as before, and there is no further reference to the hypothetical interlocutor.

24 Some examples of narrative complexity in other dialogues are documented in the interesting treatment of secondary and embedded narratives in Morgan, K. 2004, 368–76.

25 The myth of Er is framed in what I would call foregrounded *oratio obliqua*, as opposed to the 'background' *oratio obliqua* of, say, the *Symposium*: cf. Halliwell 2007, 449–50, with Tarrant 1955 for a useful conspectus of sustained passages of indirect speech in Plato. The myth of Er's framework incorporates direct speech (615d-16a, 617d-e), nested indirect speech (614d, 619b, 620d), nested

of the practices of Homeric narrative omitted by Socrates' typology, there is another, somewhat different point of contact between one part of Odysseus's *apologos* and the nature of Plato's own writing. Odysseus explains that his version of the conversation between Helios and Zeus is derived from information given him by Calypso, who had heard it in turn from Hermes. One need not broach here the larger issues raised by the functions of human and divine narrators in the *Odyssey* in order to notice that this provides a precedent for the way in which, in works like *Parmenides*, *Symposium* and *Theaetetus*, Platonic narrators draw attention to the multiple stages through which their accounts have reached them from other sources. Taking all these factors into consideration, then, we come back round to the striking but usually overlooked conclusion that the variants omitted from Socrates' typology of diegetic *lexis* happen to coincide to a considerable degree with narrative possibilities and complications exploited in Plato's own work. Despite its stated applicability to narrative discourse in general, the typology of *diêgêsis* renders the operations of Platonic writing itself anything but transparent.[26]

I would like here to comment briefly on a further aspect of the asymmetry between Book 3's typology and Plato's own writerly practices. This concerns what we call Platonic 'myth', including the *Republic*'s own myth of Er as well as, arguably, such passages as the Cave analogy. I mentioned just above some of the intricacies of narrative form which can be found in Platonic myths, but there is a broader comparative observation which deserves to be added. Socrates' diegetic typology, and indeed his entire critique of poetry in Books 2–3, uses the vocabulary of *muthos* (μῦθος, μυθολογεῖν, μυθολόγος, μυθολογία) to demarcate a corpus of narrative material and a set of mythologic activities which the ideal city would need to regulate. The same terminology is often, though not invariably, found in Plato to describe those passages which are now typically classified as Platonic myths: the myth of Er is a case in point (10.621b8). Socrates' discussion in *Republic* 2–3 treats

---

free indirect discourse (619c), and intruded commentary by Socrates (616d, 618b-19a, 619d-e).

26 See, however, the shrewd but I think inconclusive attempt of Blondell 2002, 232–45 to argue that the *Republic* itself does (partly) practise what Socrates preaches about mimesis in Book 3.

muthoi as narrative or discursive units (a subset of *logoi*: 2.376e)[27] in their own right, but it makes no allowance for *muthoi* which occupy a place within a larger discursive or textual context. It is true that Socrates acknowledges the existence of external (i.e. social) contexts or occasions of performance: in particular, the recounting of myths by adults to children in early upbringing (esp. 2.378c-d), the general learning and assimilation of poetry within an educational framework, and the recitation/acting of epic and drama within institutional settings.[28] But he nowhere indicates that an act of 'myth-telling' (μυθολογία), rather than being a free-standing or self-contained text/performance, might itself be part of a larger discourse. Yet this is always the status of myth-telling in Plato's own works. All Platonic myths are speech acts (and perhaps 'speech genres' too) which occur within a larger, overarching framework of dialogue. Whatever else one makes of any passage of *muthologia* in the dialogues, it must matter that each instance is positioned within such a framework: it is told by the voice of a particular speaker to a particular audience, at a particular juncture in a discussion, for particular (though not necessarily self-evident) reasons. In short, *muthologia* within Plato's own writing always has more than discrete narrative 'content' and 'form': it is also partly constituted by the discursive circumstances or conditions in which it is presented. Yet Socrates' typology in *Republic* 3, precisely by focussing analytically on seemingly self-contained features of narrative structures, obscures the possible importance of such larger circumstances. Where poetry is concerned, this seems not to matter to Socrates' method, since he proceeds on the assumption (signalled at 377c-d) that everything is equally *muthos*. But that does not alter the fact that if one compares Socrates' procedure and assumptions with Plato's own general practices as writer, one is struck by a fundamental gap between the two. The Platonic Socrates remains silent about some of the very things which are most distinctive of the work of his own author.

---

27 Contrast e.g. *Phd.* 61b for the idea of poetry as quintessentially *muthoi* rather than *logoi*: on fluctuating Platonic formulations of the relationship between *muthos* and *logos*, cf. Halliwell 2007, 452–5.

28 The discussion in Book 3 leaves the nature of such institutions within Callipolis somewhat vague. But organised recitation/performance by the young Guardians is clearly if cautiously presupposed at 3.395b-6e (note the use of ῥήτωρ, 396e10, for 'public reciter'); cf. Halliwell 2002, 52 n. 37. Burnyeat 1999, 271–3, with some strain, thinks Socrates' concern is more with the *writing* than the performing of plays.

If the incompleteness of the tripartite schema developed by Socrates at 392c-4c creates more than one possible conundrum for readers of Plato's text, another set of interpretative challenges is introduced by the fact that what initially looks like a formally or technically *descriptive* typology turns into a set of psychologically and ethically *normative* principles. An alternative formulation of this point is to say that at 394d-8b Socrates starts to superimpose a second-order typology of discursive form, *lexis*, onto his first-order typology.[29] One preliminary observation worth making on the transition which starts at 394d (and which, in the larger scheme of 376e-98b, is actually a *reassertion* of the normative over the descriptive) is that Socrates professes to be uncertain where the argument might lead: 'I myself really don't yet know [sc. everything that is at stake], but we must go in whatever direction the argument, like a wind, may carry us' (394d). This uncertainty is the sort of detail many Platonic scholars treat as a frill (if they notice it at all). But those convinced that there are no frills in Plato will be inclined to take it as a dramatic cue to recognise that any attempt to prescribe a set of principles for the relationship between discursive content and form (between 'what should be said', ἃ λεκτέον, and 'how it should be said', ὡς λεκτέον: 394c, cf. 392c) is likely to prove difficult and insecure.

One thing seems clear enough, however. Socrates' concern with 'form' revolves around what he sees as the intrinsic potential of mimesis (*qua* dramatised narrative or the use of direct discourse) to induce *psychic multiplicity*. As soon as he poses the question whether the Guardians in Callipolis should be 'skilled in mimesis' (μιμητικοί, 395e), he reinvokes his earlier principle that each of them needs 'to practise one thing well, not many things'; and the quadruple repetition of πολλά, 'many things', at 394e-5b establishes the thematic note emphatically. It is true that Socrates risks confusing matters by stressing that even particular species of mimesis (such as tragedy and comedy) are, from the point of view of poets and performers, separate practices; the same person, he thinks, cannot be good at more than one of them (395a). But it soon becomes evident that it is psychological multiplicity as a consequence of engage-

---

29 Cf. Giuliano 2005, 43–58 for an alternative analysis of the stages of argument at 392c-8b; he finds a more tightly interlocked chain of reasoning than I do, as well as a more straightforward match with Plato's own writing.

ment in unrestricted mimesis which lies at the heart of his anxieties.[30] If we focus on the argument's immediate extrapolations from its typology of narrative form, what seems most pertinent is that Socrates takes every mimetic utterance, unlike cases of plain or single-voiced narrative, to involve strong psychological assimilation to another mind – first on the part of the imaginatively creating poet (see esp. 393c), then on that of the performer or 'reciter', though this part of *Republic* 3 stops short of extrapolating all the way to the experience of audiences of poetry. The argument therefore entails that different narrative forms are not simply technical alternatives for the telling or presentation of stories: for Socrates, they have differential *expressive* capacities to embody the points of view and mental processes of agents or characters in the story. The crux of the matter here can be exposed by glancing back at Socrates' brief illustration of how to rewrite the early stages of the *Iliad* (1.12–42) into 'plain narrative', stripping it of all mimesis (393d-4a). If we think of narrative point of view purely in terms of 'information' about individuals' reactions, it is unclear why plain narrative cannot in principle achieve the same effects as mimesis.[31] Socrates' short example does, after all, convey information about the viewpoints of the agents – Chryses' fear (before and after his request for the return of Chryseis), the respect felt for the Trojan priest by the Greek army/leaders as a collective unit, and the anger of Agamemnon – both through narrative statement and through (free) indirect discourse.[32] What's more, Socrates stresses the cursory, 'unpoetic' nature of the illustration, leaving us free to imagine (or remember) how much more elaborate and powerful the use of 'plain narrative' might be in the hands of a real poet

---

30 For a larger perspective on this point and its implications for the role of imagination in aesthetic experience, see Halliwell 2002, 72–97. I cannot accept the claim of Brisson 1998, 69–70 that Book 3's critique deems mimesis 'intolerable' on grounds of 'illusion' or of 'confusion … between reality and discourse'.
31 Genette (1972) 1980, 166 is misled by Socrates' illustration into equating mimesis with 'maximum of information' and (plain) *diêgêsis* with the opposite; but there can be no *necessary* correlation between the two modes and the quantity of information conveyed: it is easy to find examples of 'informationally' thin direct speech and richly detailed single-voiced narrative. Bal (1985) 1997, 37, perhaps influenced by Genette in this respect, garbles the point of Socrates' illustration.
32 Narrower usage of 'free indirect discourse' implies absence of speech tags ('he said' etc.): that would not apply to most of Socrates' rewriting of the passage. But in a looser usage the term might cover ἐσέβοντο καὶ συνῄνουν, 'they showed him respect and approval', which corresponds to the indirect discourse of *Il.* 1.22–3. On the scope of 'free indirect discourse', cf. Prince 1988, 34–5.

(or, equally, of a fine prose writer). Agamemnon's abuse of Chryses is presumably an instance of the sort of behaviour Socrates does not want to be offered to the young Guardians of Callipolis in mimetic narrative. Yet he seems happy to think of them having an account of it in plain narrative: the 'de-mimeticised' version preserves the king's threat of violence (including scorn for Chryses' priestly office) and an indication, admittedly less explicit than in Homer, of Chryseis's future as a concubine. Why then in principle should there be such a big difference between the two narrative modes?

Socrates' answer is that mimesis is habit- and character-forming (395d), because for poets and actors at least it is a kind of enactment that shapes the soul and the self on the 'inside'. The same is not true, he supposes, of plain narrative, presumably because even for a reciter or performer of such passages there remains a psychological distance from the characters, who are described and as it were observed, not impersonated or *internalised*. Part of the underpinning of this position is a larger thesis about the 'developmental psychology', so to speak, of childhood and early adulthood: an important philosophical issue in its own right but one which must be left aside here. In any case, Socrates noted at several points in the first part of the critique of poetry (378d, 380c, 387b) that his case does not apply exclusively to children, and this ought to hold good for the discussion of narrative form as well. But we need now to confront the often neglected fact that Socrates' view of mimesis has two sides to it which do not stand in an entirely fixed or static relationship. On the one hand, he sees mimesis (again, principally from the point of view of actors or reciters) as an especially potent form of narrative in the *immediacy* of its impact and the directness of the psychological assimilation (or self-likening, 393c) which it involves: in this regard, mimesis induces the mind to 'mould' itself (a Gorgianic trope) into a particular identity.[33] But Socrates also dwells on the tendency of mimesis to multiply narrative voices and thereby to encourage *fragmentation* of the soul/self. The first of these aspects, as Socrates appreciates, is ethically ambiguous: where 'good' characters (i.e. good role-models for the Guardians) are concerned, the power of mimesis is positively valuable. But a core concern for unity of soul makes the

---

33 The language of 'moulding' (ἐκμάττειν) and 'shaping into moulds' (ἐνιστάναι εἰς τοὺς τύπους) at 396d-e picks up and extends Socrates' original concern with the 'soft', 'plastic' malleability of the young mind at 2.377b. Gorgias uses the lexicon of psychological 'moulding' (τυποῦσθαι) in *Helen* (B11 DK) 13, 15.

psychically fragmentative, multiplicatory tendency of mimesis suspect to Socrates in a more diffuse way. That is why, when he tries to get Adeimantus' agreement to a definition of two 'species' (εἴδη) or paradigms of narrative practice (396b ff., i.e. what I have called his second-order typology of *lexis*), the weight of his normative emphasis falls on selective use of mimesis, not its total elimination: he certainly deems it permissible, *au fond*, where 'good' characters are represented, but wants to limit its availability for impersonation of bad characters.

Before pressing a supplementary question about this position, we need to notice an element of complexity and even equivocation in Socrates' statement of his principles. At 396c-e he says:

(1) the decent or moderate person will be willing to recite/perform a mimetic presentation of a good character (taking on the persona of that person, ὡς αὐτὸς ὢν ἐκεῖνος, 396c7)
    (1a) *especially* (μάλιστα) when such characters are depicted as acting well, but
    (1b) *less so* (ἐλάττω δὲ καὶ ἧττον, 396d1–2), yet by implication still to some extent, when such characters are acting less well (under the influence of disease, sexual passion, drunkenness or 'some other mishap'); and
(2) the decent person will be unwilling to recite/perform *seriously* (σπουδῇ, 396d4; cf. 397a3) the mimetic presentation of bad characters, *except*
    (2a) 'briefly', when such characters do something good, or
    (2b) the performance is undertaken 'for the sake of play' (παιδιᾶς χάριν, 396e2).

The qualifications in that statement – qualifications frequently omitted in scholarly references to the passage – are arresting but hard to elucidate or quantify. In particular, (1b) is of indeterminate scope, though it clearly blocks the inference that the only appropriate models of mimesis are ethically *perfect* characters and it seems to leave room for at least some kinds of tragic and comic scenarios.[34] Equally, (2b) posits an exception

---

34 On this last point cf. Giuliano 2005, 52–4. That mimesis is restricted to ethically perfect characters is wrongly claimed by Gastaldi 1998, 368; Janaway 1995, 98 similarly fails to do justice to ἐλάττω δὲ καὶ ἧττον (see (1b) in my text) by saying that the good narrator will 'draw the line at enacting scenes in which a good man is less than perfect'. It is mistaken to suggest, as Morgan 2003, 106 does, that at 392c-8b 'direct discourse' or mimesis *per se* 'is morally

whose implications are left wholly unelaborated but which could be far-reaching. Would it be acceptable to participate in *any* mimesis provided one did so in a spirit of detached make-believe, holding back from or resisting emotional engagement? If so, what is the alternative or modified psychology that lies undeclared by this invocation of 'play', a term used deprecatingly by Socrates at *Republic* 10.602b to characterise poetic mimesis in general? These are difficult questions to which no one has yet proposed fully cogent answers.[35] What matters for my immediate purposes is that what is usually paraphrased by modern interpreters as an uncompromising set of restrictions on the permissibility of mimetic narrative is actually hedged around in a way which conveys something less than definitive prescriptiveness. This impression is underlined, I think, when the discussion enters its final phase. Here, having set up his two narrative species or paradigms (εἴδη), one predominantly using the single-voiced mode ('with a relatively small portion of mimesis in a long discourse', 396e7), the other predominantly or exclusively using the mimetic mode (397b1–2), Socrates proceeds, as with his original tripartite schema of narrative forms, to allow for 'mixture' or 'blending' of the two (συγκεραννύντες, 397c). But he does not elaborate on what he understands by this last possibility, which is doubly perplexing: for one thing, the two species have just been defined as entailing a sharp *ethical*, not just a formal, contrast (396b-7b), so it is not easy to see what it could mean to blend the two without compromising (or refining) the definitions themselves; for another, Socrates calls both species 'unmixed' (ἄκρατος, 397d2), even though he has explained that each of the two will involve some degree of combination of plain with mimetic narrative (i.e., each will be precisely a compound or mixed form according to the *original* tripartition at 392d).[36] When, moreover, Adei-

---

reprehensible', or that 'imitation is dangerous and bad' *tout court*, Annas 1981, 95.

35 Ferrari 1989, 118–19 offers one interesting line of interpretation, though perhaps making too much of the idea of 'satirical' mimesis. It is pertinent that the phrase παιδιᾶς χάριν ('for the sake of play'), or something very like it, occurs in a number of other Platonic passages, including the famous critique of writing at *Phdr.* 276d (applicable, arguably, to Platonic dialogues themselves). See also esp. *Plt.* 288c (decorative and mimetic art in general), *Criti.* 116b (ornate architecture on Atlantis), *Lg.* 8.834d (equestrian and related contests).

36 Genette (1972) 1980, 162 n. 2 (where the reference should read '397d') erroneously conflates this later use of 'unmixed' with the terms of the earlier tripartition; Genette (1983) 1988, 18 correspondingly and misleadingly glosses mimetic narrative as 'impure – that is, *mixed*' (his italics). Among the more careful

mantus declares his own preference for 'the unmixed mimetic impersonator of the good character' (τὸν τοῦ ἐπιεικοῦς μιμητὴν ἄκρατον, 397d), one could be forgiven for wondering whether he is referring exactly to the first of the species which Socrates had outlined: Adeimantus's wording hardly sounds as though it corresponds to 'a relatively small portion of mimesis in a long discourse' (396e7). The upshot of all this, I suggest, is that after the second-order typology at 396b-7d has been superimposed on the original formal typology of 392c-4c, we are left not so much with a clear-cut taxonomy as with guidelines for a spectrum or sliding scale of narrative styles (each of them marked by an interplay between character, situation, tonal nuances, and diegetic form). And we are left to puzzle out for ourselves where particular genres, and, more importantly, individual works in those genres, are to be placed on that spectrum.

The gap between Socrates' impetus towards a decisive set of precepts for narrative form and the complex adjustments for which he makes provision at 396c-e is only heightened by his curious hint at 397c that selection of diegetic mode has to be made not only by poets but by 'all who say anything' (πάντες ... οἵ τι λέγοντες). It is arbitrary to restrict this phrase, which has attracted less comment than one might have expected, to public speakers, though it must include them.[37] The phrase ostensibly embraces *all* discourse, at least all discourse with a narrative component – all *diêgêsis* of past, present or future (392d), which is, of course, a very large proportion of human discourse in general. If that is right, Socrates is asserting that all narrators, not just poets, face choices at every moment about how they present their accounts, and that they cannot avoid orientating themselves in relation not just to the formal alternatives of 'plain'/third-person and 'mimetic'/first-person narrative, but to all the consequences that these options bring with them for psychological perspective, emotional engagement or distance, and ethical evaluation. Yet Socrates neither develops his more general hint nor, so I have maintained, brings his critique of poetic narrative possibilities to an unequivocal conclusion. Another way of

---

    treatments of the terminological/conceptual twists at 394d-8b are Blondell 2002, 236, Ferrari 1989, 118, Janaway 1995, 97–100.

37 Murray 1996, 181 takes the reference to be to public speakers. Vegetti 2007, 473 is one translator who favours the broader interpretation ('chiunque si esprima con discorsi'); cf. Giuliano 2005, 44–5. There is a connection with the similarly broad and vague clause at 396c1, 'whenever he [sc. the good man] has to say anything', ὁπότε τι δέοι αὐτὸν λέγειν.

putting that point is to say that Plato does not, after all, give Socrates a fully fledged 'theory' of narrative. He gives him only a set of partial intuitions and incomplete arguments which converge on the legitimacy of probing at various levels (psychological, ethical, and ideological) the workings of voice, point of view, and other expressive aspects of form in any narrative discourse which has the power to shape and influence cultural patterns of experience.

This drives us back to a question which has often been posed but which eludes any easy answer. What is Plato's relationship as writer to the analysis of narrative which he places in Socrates' mouth? Two considerations which have figured in my reading of the passage matter greatly here: one, that Socrates' first formal typology (392c-4c) happens to omit or downplay possibilities (including the role of a primary narrator other than the author himself) which are important in Plato's own writing; the other, that the normative extrapolations which Socrates draws from that typology and which produce a further, second-order typology of *diêgêsis* (394d-8b) lay down some strong criteria but also introduce an element of flexibility into the perception of how narrative form can or should be employed for desirable ends. Between them, these considerations mean that *Republic* 392c-8b does not, as it stands, provide a ready-made yardstick by which to judge Plato's own writing. In particular, it is unjustifiably reductive to suppose, as is often done, that the passage articulates a generalised aversion to mimetic narrative *per se* and therefore stands in *prima facie* conflict with Plato's own general practice. The relationship between Socrates' arguments and the nature of the work in which they occur is a problem for any reflective reader of the *Republic*, especially since Socrates himself calls the thought-experiment of 'founding' the ideal city in words an exercise in *muthos* (376d) and thereby brings it within his own category of prose *muthologia* (392d). But it is not a problem that can be stated in terms of simple contradiction.

The problem becomes profound (in extent and difficulty), I suggest, when we take into account the less than consistent alignment between the presuppositions which appear to inform the two halves of the critique of poetry, i.e. the analysis of poetry as, in turn, *logoi* and *lexis* (and/or as 'what should be said' and 'how it should be said', ἅ λεκτέον and ὡς λεκτέον): approximately, that is to say, as 'discursive content' and 'discursive form'.[38] I shall have to limit myself here to a few compressed

---

38 *Pace* Laird 1999, 48–60 (but note his caution on 61–2), this distinction cannot

claims about the earlier stages of the critique (376e-92c). In the first place, the discussion of poetic *muthoi* (a subset, remember, of *logoi*) seems scarcely to recognise the existence of diegetic form. Thus in Book 2 Socrates can use the formulation 'the poet says' (*vel sim.*) even when quoting from character speeches (though usually without mentioning that fact): cases in point are 379d-e (*Iliad* 24.527 ff., Achilles speaking; see below), 380a (Aeschylus fr. 154a.15–16 *TrGF*, Niobe speaking). In other words, in this phase of his analysis he largely ignores the presence or absence of mimesis as later defined at 392d ff.: consider especially, in this connection, the string of seven Homeric quotations in quick succession at 386c-7b, three of them from character speeches, four in the narrator's voice, but without any markers of that difference.[39] Even when Socrates does occasionally register the dramatic identity of a speaker, this does not always seem to impinge on his method of criticism: see for instance the citation at 383a-b of a speech by Thetis (Aeschylus fr. 305) whose attack on Apollo's truthfulness is held against the poet himself; and note Socrates' revealingly unqualified assertion that 'when someone/anyone says such things about the gods, we shall be offended…'. One consequence of the factors just noted is a general impression that Socrates holds poets authorially responsible (i.e. ethically, not just causally) for what is 'said' in their work, *regardless* of the narrative form employed. When he adduces the special status of divine and heroic characters who, he assumes, possess an implicitly religio-ethical valorisation as 'exceptional' and 'renowned' figures (ἐλλόγιμοι, ὀνομαστοί) within the culture's 'inherited conglomerate', Socrates refers equally to what such figures say or to what we are told about their behaviour.[40] Diegetic form appears not, at this stage of the argument, to have any significance in its own right.

be equated with a narratological separation of 'story' (as raw or abstracted events) and 'narrative' (as their ordered disposition in a text), or 'histoire' and 'récit', 'fabula' and 'story' (or any other equivalent pair of terms). Although Socrates comes close to such a distinction in the *lexis* part of his analysis, especially when 'rewriting' the Chryses episode of *Iliad* 1 at 393d-4a, the larger *logoi/lexis* distinction is trickier: *logoi*, as indicated in my text, covers aspects of discourse which extend beyond narrativity.

39 I draw attention to some of the complex implications of these patterns of quotation in Halliwell 2000, 111–12.

40 For the relevance of heroic and semi-divine status, see esp. 387d-8a, 388e (ἀξίους λόγου), 390d, with the application of the principle to the cases of Achilles and Priam at 388a-b. Cf. Socrates' use of the story of the Iliadic Achilles as a positive paradigm at *Ap.* 28b-d.

But we can go further than this. In the first part of the critique Socrates seems not primarily to be concerned with 'narrative' as such, *qua* the plotting of particular events in time, but with *general(isable) propositions* (it is tempting to say 'messages') which he takes to be embodied in and expressed by narrative poetry – propositions, that is, such as 'gods are capable of evil, conflict and deceit' (cf. 377e-83c), 'death is the ultimate negation of everything' (cf. 386a-8b), 'good people are not always happy' (cf. 392a-c). It is such propositions (and elements of a potential 'worldview'), whether explicit or implicit, which he treats as the core of a work's communicative effect and to which his understanding of authorial responsibility chiefly applies. This notion of authorial responsibility is textually 'global', covering everything, it seems, in the composition and 'telling' of a *muthos*. It accordingly needs to be distinguished from the narrower notion of the voice of 'the poet himself' which in Book 3 Socrates identifies with plain or single-voiced *diêgêsis*, though that is not to deny that in reading the critique as a whole, in sequence, some of the force of the global paradigm of authoriality might be felt to carry over, *a fortiori*, into the detection of the poet's voice in the 'plain' narrative mode. What is most remarkable about the global premise of authorial responsibility in the first half of the critique of poetry is that in disregarding diegetic form it also appears to override dramatic psychology and in the process converts the viewpoints of characters into those of the poet himself. Perhaps the most striking instance of this is at 379c-d, where Socrates speaks scornfully of the *poet* 'making a foolish error about the gods' (περὶ τοὺς θεοὺς ἀνοήτως ἁμαρτάνοντος καὶ λέγοντος) by saying that "Two jars stand on Zeus's floor...", as though Homer himself were necessarily endorsing the sentiments expressed by Achilles to Priam. Some readers of the *Republic* have been ready to jump to the conclusion that in passages such as this 'Plato' allows theological and moral concerns to erase any awareness of context or characterisation. But there is a double-sided problem with this inference. On the one hand, such a charge against Plato involves making the same hermeneutic mistake (by automatically equating the words of a character with the beliefs of the author) as Socrates seems to make in Plato's text.[41] On the other hand, it is inconceivable that

---

41 Gould 2001, 315, in ascribing to Plato a failure to distinguish between author and narrator, unwittingly does the same thing himself. More generally, Gould resists what he sees as Plato's commitment to 'simple univocality of meaning'

Plato himself, as the highly self-conscious writer of dialogues which contain many opposed and sometimes eristically antagonistic viewpoints, could have supposed that every author, whether in poetry or prose, necessarily subscribes to everything which he makes his characters say. Why then, we are left to wonder, does he show Socrates apparently resorting to such a supposition without any qualms?

It is hard to escape a sense of tension, or at the very least of incomplete harmonisation, between the models of 'poetics' (or meta-poetics) which Socrates adopts, and largely takes for granted, in the two blocks of argument at *Republic* 376e-92c and 392c-8b. In the first case, Socrates operates with an understanding of *logoi* as essentially the dominant or cumulative meanings (allegedly) conveyed by particular passages or entire works. He regards poets as globally responsible for these *logoi* and as lending them a kind of expressive endorsement even where they put them into the mouths of characters. To that extent, he analyses 'what should be said' in poetry in a manner which not only is ostensibly independent of diegetic form but even appears to make consideration of such form redundant. The meanings Socrates finds communicated by the texts he cites can in that sense be described as 'supra-narrative' propositions, even though they are conceived of at the same time as 'schemata' or 'patterns' (τύποι, e.g. 379a) which inform whole classes of story, such as those of conflict between gods (377e-8d). In the second half of the critique, by contrast, he develops a typology of diegetic form – an intricate two-stage typology, as I tried to show earlier – which gives central prominence to the difference between first- and third-person narrative presentation, thereby distinguishing what is said by 'the poet himself' (now *qua* internal narrator, not as creator of the whole work) from what is said by characters or agents in the narrative and stressing the importance of how that distinction is handled by the choices of the writer. That is not to say that the two parts of the critique could not in principle be better harmonised than they are: even a passage such as 379c-d (cited above), which seems to erase the difference between plain narrative and mimesis, might be taken to depend on the silent assumption that the force of the 'two jars' passage is objectionable in part because of Homer's decision to attribute the thought it contains to the *Iliad*'s chief hero, and at a juncture of supreme dramatic intensity in the structure of the poem. Here and elsewhere, Plato expects

---

(316, cf. 333–4), but he fails to bring to the *Republic* the open-minded hermeneutic which he thinks appropriate for Homer and drama.

readers to have the knowledge to fill out for themselves the contexts from which Socrates often abruptly plucks his material (386c-7a is strongly suggestive in this respect).

But even if harmonisation of the two halves of the critique could be to some degree improved by spelling out tacit premises about speakers and circumstances, it would remain the case that Socrates evaluates poetic (and, more obliquely, prose) narrative from more than one perspective. It is part of the underlying momentum of the passage as a whole that we are shown how narrative (broadly construed) is open to questioning and interpretation on multiple levels. Although Socrates constructs a critical framework within which ethical (and 'theological')[42] considerations trump all others, including those of factual 'truth' (see 378a2), this is not in itself sufficient to integrate all the strands of his argument, since we saw earlier that in his treatment of *lexis* Socrates acknowledges more than one way in which narrative form might be handled with a view to ethical ends, not least in the hints of variable permutations of character, situation, and tone at 396c-e. And here there is an important factor to be added from Plato's own writing. However uncertain we may feel about the applicability of Socrates' normative appraisal of diegetic form to the workings of Platonic dialogue itself, it is impossible to deny that Plato permits ethically discrepant, sometimes harshly discordant, voices to be sounded mimetically in parts of his work. A minimal inference from this is that either Platonic practice is less than seamlessly continuous with the position which *Republic* 3 ascribes to Socrates, or that *Republic* 3 itself cannot be taken to offer a comprehensive set of principles for the correlation of narrative form with ethical viewpoint.

But to that inference we can and must add a salient paradox. Principally because of its preoccupation with designing a system of education for the Guardian class of Callipolis, the discussion between Socrates and Adeimantus lays down principles for minds which, while capable of responding to, and being influenced by, poetic stories and characters, are assumed to be largely incapable of independent critical judgement.[43] But Plato's own dialogue, by contrast, presupposes readers who are capable not only of following and engaging with dialectical argument, but

---

42 The term θεολογία occurs, uniquely in Plato, at 379a5–6.
43 This is explicit in the well-known remark about allegorical interpretation at 2.378d: 'for the young person is not able to judge (κρίνειν) where there is allegorical significance (ὑπόνοια) or not'.

also of tracking closely the narrative-cum-dramatic form in which the argument unfolds. Plato's own practice relies, therefore, on readers who have a more sophisticated sensitivity to the possibilities of narrative form than the audiences of poetry posited by Socrates' proposals. If, moreover, we recall once again that Plato's own practice is also in certain respects different from – and less straightforward than – the parameters which Socrates works with at 392c-4c, we have double grounds, I submit, for concluding that the typology of diegetic form and function in *Republic* Book 3 cannot be a complete 'Platonic' theory of narrative. Its interpretation paradoxically calls for a richer narrative (and conceptual) 'competence' than Socrates' *prima facie* thesis envisages.

I have been arguing in this paper that there is no fully integrated theory of narrative, let alone anything we can call 'Plato's theory' of narrative, to be found at *Republic* 3.392c-8b, and that the difficulties we encounter in pursuing the implications of this stretch of the text are deepened when taken in conjunction with the larger critique of poetic (and more than poetic) discourse at 2.376e-3.392c. If I am right, the interest of Plato for narratology, as well as for the history of poetics in general, consequently lies not in the possibility of systematising certain views expressed in the dialogues into a putatively authorial theory. It lies, rather, in the challenge of coming to terms with the counterpoint between possibilities of 'theory' and 'practice' in the fabric of the works themselves and with the unresolved puzzles to which this counterpoint gives rise. Plato's own writing, which is the only place where we can hope to find 'Plato' at all, embodies a cumulative recognition that the scope and operations of narrative, whether in a wider or narrower sense of that category, will always exceed and outrun any attempt to theorise them.

The *Trojan Oration* of Dio Chrysostom and Ancient Homeric Criticism

Richard Hunter

In the *Trojan Oration* Dio argues, allegedly before a Trojan audience, that the Homeric Trojan narrative is a complete misrepresentation of 'what really happened': Helen was in fact properly given in marriage by Tyndareus to Paris (i. e. he, not Menelaos, was the successful suitor), Hector killed Achilles not vice versa, Troy was not captured by the Greeks, and so on. Critical discussion[1] of the *Trojan Oration* has largely centred on the decidedly problematic state of the text, which certainly contains both interpolations and alternative versions of various passages (even if not to the extent argued for by von Arnim (1898)),[2] on the reflections of ancient Homeric criticism in Dio's strictures on the poet,[3] and on the generic affiliations and purpose of the speech. Much remains, however, to be done on these and other aspects of the speech (as, for example, its historical context). I hope that, despite the limited nature of my concerns in this paper, some sense of Dio's overall strategy will also emerge.

If the whole project of the *Trojan Oration* is in one sense a distortion of a recurrent theme of ancient Homeric criticism – the skilfulness and quality of Homer's 'lies' (cf., e.g., Aristotle, *Poetics* 1460a18–19, Horace, *AP*

I am grateful to Jessica Wissmann, the audience at the Thessaloniki conference and the Editors for helpful criticism and to Michael Trapp for allowing me to see an unpublished paper on the *Trojan Oration*.

1   The best modern introductions to the *Trojan Oration* are Kindstrand 1973, 141–62 and Saïd 2000, 176–86, both with guides to earlier bibliography; I am indebted to both of these discussions. See also Lemarchand 1926, 35–56, Desideri 1978, 431–4, 496–503, and Szarmach 1978. For a brief account of the lively place that this oration has held in scholarly debate over the centuries cf. Swain 2000, 18–19; Kim 2008 is a helpful account of closely related issues in *Oration* 61.
2   My approach to Dio 11 in this paper will be a cautious unitarianism.
3   Cf. Vagnone 2003, 17–18. Montgomery 1902 remains a useful collection and Vagnone's commentary gathers a certain amount of material; there is much more to be done. I have not seen Jouan's 1966 Paris thesis on *Oration* 11.

151–2) – it is often noted that some of Dio's criticisms have a distinctly modern ring to them: Dio as a neo-analyst *avant la lettre*.[4] Thus attention is often directed to claims in the essay such as that 'Patroclus is all but a substitute (ὑπόβλητος) whom Homer has put in the place of Achilles' (102), a view with a significant hold on many modern scholars. Other critical strategies almost look like parodies of modern concerns. The observation (21) that Homer could tell of what happened between Zeus and Hera on Mt Ida in *Iliad* 14, despite the enveloping cloud in which Zeus hid them, is not just a joke about omniscient narration, but turns Zeus' words ('no one will see us ...') at 14.342–5 into a witty authorial excuse by Homer himself for the decent 'veil' which is drawn over what follows, a kind of epic *cetera quis nescit?*.[5] In 108 Dio's Homer has lost control of his false narrative and so describes Achilles' pursuit of Hector and the latter's death 'as in a dream'; the narrative 'most closely resembles strange dreams (τοῖς ἀτόποις ἐνυπνίοις)'. Dio may be picking up the similarity of Athena's deceptive appearance to Hector (22.226–47) to a dream, though it is more likely that his likeness (προσέοικε) echoes one of Homer's, namely the famous dream simile of 22.199–201 describing the pursuit, which was athetised by Aristarchus and said by a scholiast to be 'without value in expression and thought' and to devalue Achilles' swiftness, and which is certainly by any standards ἄτοπον. If so, Dio has taken a simile describing action in the text and applied it to an understanding of the surrounding narrative context as a whole; modern critics who privilege metaliterary self-reference in the understanding of (particularly) Hellenistic and Roman epics will here recognise a kindred spirit. We have perhaps a similar phenomenon in the following chapter when Dio describes Homer's narrative of the funeral games in Book 23 as πάνυ γελοίως; this is most probably explained as, once again, a re-direction of a feature of the narrative itself, namely the rôle of laughter (cf. 23.784, 840).

What may be more interesting than these individual examples is that the *Trojan Oration* as a whole questions the limits and purposes of poetic myth. Is there such a thing as the 'irreducible core' of a myth, however many details may be changed; Dio 11 may make us think of Aristotle's note that, in a comedy, 'Orestes and Aegisthus can become friends and go off at the end, and no one is killed by anyone' (*Poetics* 1453a37–9).

---

4   Cf. esp. Seeck 1990.
5   Dio's διηγεῖται ... τὴν συνουσίαν is suitably ambiguous; the narration of the συνουσία is anything but detailed. On the *Nachleben* of this passage of the *Iliad* cf. Hunter 2006, 311 and 2008b, 893–4.

The *Trojan Oration* is normally connected with the 'Homeric games' which imperial authors love to play (Diktys of Crete etc),[6] or with Dio's concern elsewhere for the revision of myth in accordance with the εἰκός and the πιθανόν,[7] but the antecedents of Dio's revisionist tale have deep roots. Dio is concerned not just with Homer's untruths, but also with the process by which poetic myth arises, and much of *Oration* 11 is best understood against the background of ancient critical discussions, such as that in Book 1 of Strabo, which are concerned not just with whether or not Homer 'got his facts right', but with how elaborated poetic versions of 'history' arise, whether through misunderstanding, rationalisation, 'mythologisation' (e.g. 1.2.36), the creation of symbolic genealogies (e.g. 1.2.10) or any other of the many representational modes open to a poet. As for Homer's veracity, for Strabo poetry contains material drawn from all of ἱστορία, διάθεσις ('rhetorical presentation') and μῦθος (1.2.17); there is much in Homer which is indeed 'as it happened/is', but there is also much which elaborates with poetic licence upon 'starting-points', ἀρχαί (1.2.9) or ἀφορμαί (1.2.40), drawn from history, and which we can use as 'traces (ἴχνη) of historical people and events' (1.2.14). 'To invent everything (πάντα πλάττειν) is neither plausible nor in the Homeric manner', proclaims Strabo (1.2.17, cf. 1.2.9, 13), and, moreover, 'a man would tell more plausible lies if he mixed in a bit of truth as well' (1.2.9). There is very little here with which the Dio of *Oration* 11 would disagree; it needed but a small tilt of the balance to subvert,[8] not just Homer, but the whole tradition of criticism in praise of Homer. It is in that small tilt that the apparent modernity of some of Dio's observations most strikes home. Poetic myth is a recollection of 'real events' but told for particular purposes and with a particular spin aimed at particular contemporary audiences; it is thus not created *ex nihilo*, but neither is it a trustworthy record. Moreover, Homer stood in a particular relationship to his material:

> ... There were no other poets or prose writers who had recorded the truth, but Homer himself was the first who had undertaken to write of these events; he was composing many generations after the events, when both those with knowledge of them and their descendants had disappeared and all that was left was a faint and weak tradition (ἀμαυρᾶς ... καὶ ἀσθενοῦς ἔτι φήμης ἀπολειπομένης), as is to be expected in the matter of events which are very ancient ...
>
> Dio Chrysostom 11.92

---

6   Cf., e.g., Cameron 2004, 136–7.
7   Cf., e.g., Ritoók 1995.
8   Cf. below p. 52–3.

Here then is a Homer not very far from how some modern scholarship imagines him; that the Trojan story had, at least at first, been preserved within the élite families who claimed personal connection with the Trojan expedition is also an idea which the modern study of oral narrative would certainly recognise.[9]

Dio does not explain the misrepresentation of history merely by Homer's desire to gratify a Greek audience,[10] but also suggests ways in which widely-held distortions of the truth may arise. Of particular interest is the account of Paris' successful wooing of Helen, where Dio may have drawn *inter alia* on the *Catalogue of Women* ascribed to Hesiod;[11] thus, for example, Agamemnon works to secure Helen for Menelaos (46), just as he does in the *Catalogue* (fr. 197.4–5 M-W = fr. 105.4–5 Hirschberger). Be that as it may, Dio sets the whole episode within the context of Mycenean *Realpolitik* with a vividness which may well also owe not a little to Dio's experience of such negotiations in the contemporary world. Agamemnon marries Clytemnestra in order to negate the potential threat to his kingdom from Clytemnestra's powerful brothers (46), and Tyndareus awards Helen to Paris in order to become allied to the strongest power in Asia (51), a decision which in turn increases Agamemnon's disquiet about possible Asian interference in Greek affairs (62). The report of the speech which Paris made to persuade Tyndareus and the Dioscuri (49–50) is a masterful parody of the kinds of arguments which we know were in fact employed in interstate relations; I will comment briefly on just two related details. Paris adduces in his favour the fact that he is the heir to Priam's power and wealth; to any ordinary reader of Homer, such as Herodotus (cf. 2.120.4), this would be plain nonsense – Hector was very obviously to be Priam's successor.[12] We can therefore see Paris' claim as one more indication of how erroneous was Homer's story, or – in my view, more probably – we can treat it as a simple untruth, and one not easy to unmask, told by Paris to bolster his case. This example may then form the background to a consideration of Paris' further claim that 'he was dear to the gods and that Aphrodite had promised him the finest of all marriages'. It is possible to see here either a motif borrowed from *Oration* 20

---

9 Cf. further below p. 49 on chs. 145–6.
10 Cf. further below p. 50–1.
11 Cf. Cingano 2005, 133–4.
12 Cf. the bT-scholium on *Il.* 22.229b 'one may suspect that Hector is the oldest of the sons of Priam'.

in which the Judgement is a daydream of Paris as he herds his flocks (20.19–23) or a motif designed to produce a narrative which combines the Judgement with the story of the wooing which Dio tells, but as Dio also casts scorn on the whole idea of the Judgement, such scholarly ingenuity would probably be wasted; there are, of course, inconsistencies and apparent contradictions elsewhere in the speech, and the proper strategy with which to deal with them is in fact an important interpretative issue,[13] but the present case at least admits of a fairly straightforward answer. It seems likely that what we have here is another rhetorical improvisation by Paris, designed to impress a family which already prided itself on its divine connections. In this case, however, we are dealing with a rhetorical improvisation which was to have a very long *Nachleben*, for it was to be taken up and become part of the canonical Judgement story. This is one way, so Dio teaches us, that 'myths' arise. That Dio does not spell this out for us, but rather forces us to reason it out for ourselves, is of a piece with his account of what followed Paris' winning of Helen.

After the departure of Paris and Helen, Agamemnon, who had his own political and military reasons for fearing an over-powerful Asia with a direct connection to Greece (62), gathers the unsuccessful suitors together; naturally enough, like all (good) politicians, he does not openly express fears for his own grip on power, but rather goes for the moral high ground: 'all the other suitors have been treated outrageously (ὑβρισθῆναι) and Greece with contempt (καταφρονηθῆναι)', he declares (62); it is Paris and Priam who are αἴτιοι, not Tyndareus (63), and Agamemnon succeeds in making each suitor feel 'that his own *gamos* had been taken away' (64). In Agamemnon's moral language, allied to his promise of lucrative plunder from a city of unimaginable wealth whose people were 'corrupted by τρυφή' (63), lies in fact the origin of the story of Paris as the seducing adulterer, not as a successful suitor. Few things distort the memory of 'what really happened' (38) more quickly than moral indignation, particularly where the self-esteem of nations is involved. Be that as it may, Dio's account of why the suitors in fact agreed to the foreign military adventure (64) has an alarmingly familiar ring to it: the disastrous decision to 'invade' Troy was an explo-

---

13 Cf. further below, Vagnone 2003, 136. Whether or not Homer knew the story of the Judgement was of course debated in antiquity (cf., e.g., the scholia to *Il.* 24.23), but Dio does not obviously make use of this debate.

sive cocktail of patriotism, wounded male pride and commercial calculation:

> Some [of the suitors] were angry when they heard what Agamemnon had to say and they thought that what had happened was in fact a disgrace to Greece, but others thought that the campaign would yield benefits, for it was widely believed that Asia was a land of great things and surpassing wealth.
>
> Dio Chrysostom 11.64

Whatever modern parallels might strike us, it is in these chapters hard not to recall Thucydides' account of why the Athenians decided in favour of the ultimately disastrous expedition to Sicily (6.24); if Dio is indeed recalling that pattern, then the textual memory reinforces the accuracy of the revolutionary account he offers: in this particular also, the Sicilian expedition (which we know happened as Thucydides describes it) echoed the Trojan expedition (the truth of which we are now learning for the first time).[14]

In setting himself to correct Homeric narrative, Dio stands of course in a very long tradition, but it is Herodotus who occupies the principal position in that tradition. Just as Dio's alleged source is 'a very old Egyptian priest at [with a very probable emendation] Onouphi' (37) and the ultimate source is Menelaos himself (38, 135), so too Herodotus' source for his revision of the Homeric story is explicitly 'the priests' whose own source is (again) Menelaos (2.118.1); Herodotus' question to the priests, 'whether the Greek story about Troy was nonsense or not' (ibid.), is essentially the subject of Dio's speech. Dio and Herodotus, of course, part company on what the true story behind Homer's fiction actually was, but Dio's imitation of Herodotus is in fact quite close.[15] Just as Herodotus finds evidence in the Homeric text that Homer himself knew of the alternative (and truer) version but rejected it on poetic grounds (2.116), this too is a strategy which Dio borrows for his Homer (136); both authors of course draw on arguments from probability to make their case. The adoption of a Herodotean voice, though not one as explicit as in some imperial Greek texts, marks Dio's speech in particular ways. It is not a simple matter of the ambiguous reputation which Herodotus en-

---

14 Modern scholarship too is, of course, interested in the relation between the Greek expedition to Troy and Thucydides' account of the Sicilian expedition, cf., e.g., Kallet 2001, 97–112.

15 The device of an 'aged Egyptian priest' as informant is not, of course, limited to Herodotus; students of Dio 11 regularly refer to Plato, *Timaeus* 21e-2b.

joyed as both historian and purveyor of untruths, for elsewhere Dio rehearses a Thucydidean declaration of his own concern for truth and most men's lack of concern, even where contemporary matters are involved (145–6, cf. Thuc. 1.20). Most men, says Dio, echoing his earlier account of Homer, 'listen only to φήμη' and subsequent generations accept whatever they have been told (146, cf. Thuc. 1.20.1). In these chapters Thucydides contrasts his own narrative with the work of both poets, who exaggerate the importance of their subjects, and *logographoi* (including Herodotus?), whose concern is with providing an attractive tale for their hearers (1.21.1);[16] Dio's account of how poetic myth is created is thus much indebted for its intellectual framework to these chapters, but it is also a radical critique of them.

In chapter 38 Dio ascribes the Egyptian preservation of a true account not just to the quality of their informant (Menelaos) but also to the fact that the Egyptians preserve written records; this is a familiar fact of the Greek ethnography of Egypt, but in the *Trojan Oration* it is made to do special work:

> The priest said that they had written down all of previous history, some on the temples,[17] and some on pillars. Some things were remembered only by a few, as the pillars had been destroyed, and much that was written on the pillars was disbelieved on account of the ignorance and lack of interest of subsequent generations. The material concerning Troy was among the most recent written accounts, because Menelaos had come to Egypt and recounted everything as it had happened (ἅπαντα ὡς ἐγένετο).
>
> Dio Chrysostom 11.38

The basic distinction between oral memory and the written record goes back (at least) to the same programmatic chapters of Thucydides, but whereas Thucydides projects the distinction forward (his history will be 'useful' both because of the pains he has taken to establish the truth and because his history has been composed primarily for written reception rather than for recitations), Dio projects it backwards. The Egyptian written records make up for the fact that Homer had only φήμη to go on (cf. above). What, however, our memory of these Thucydidean chapters does is humorously to undermine Dio's (and Herodotus') reliance upon the autopsy of Menelaos, for Thucydides makes ex-

---

16 Cf. further below p. 51. In *Oration* 18 Dio echoes this chapter of Thucydides in praising the enjoyment to be gained from reading Herodotus: 'you will think that the work has a mythic rather than a historical character' (18.10).
17 This seems more likely than 'in the temples'.

plicit that the reports which an eyewitness offers are determined by each witness' 'prejudice or memory' (1.22.3). How reliable a witness do we imagine Menelaos was, when judged by these Thucydidean criteria? According to Herodotus, Menelaos told the Egyptians τὴν ἀληθείην τῶν πραγμάτων (2.119.1), just as Dio says that he told them ἅπαντα ὡς ἐγένετο (38) and 'concealed nothing' (135); who, however, is to say? Written records are only as good as the information on which they are based; if the Egyptians can laugh because the foolish Greeks have been deceived by one man (Homer), then how much wiser are the Egyptians who also put their faith in a single witness, albeit an eye-witness (37–8). The *Trojan Oration* is thus a reflection not just upon the creation of poetic myth, but also upon the creation of the 'history' which lies behind the myth.

Herodotus was of course 'the prose Homer',[18] and in adopting a Herodotean voice and in retelling the story of Troy Dio is setting himself up precisely as an alternative Homer; he can even imagine a scenario in which the Argives would drive him out for being an 'anti-Homer' (5, cf. 9), just as the ideal poetic imitator (such as Homer) was to be escorted out of Plato's republic (*Rep.* 3.398a). The *Trojan Oration* is to be delivered at more than one location around the Greek world (6), just as the standard view of Homer (15–16) is that poverty forced him to hawk his poems around the Greek world, and common sense, as well as the familiar *Lives* of Homer, suggests that he will have recited καθ' ἡδονήν for the audiences from which he hoped to gain support (15). As an anti-Homer, Dio protests (too much) that he will not seek to gratify (χαρίζεσθαι) his audience (11) and even claims that the *Trojan Oration* will not be 'to the liking' (πρὸς ἡδονήν) of his Trojan audience (6); well, perhaps ... Here, as so often, we hear distorted echoes of ancient Homeric criticism. An aspect of the question of where Homer's sympathies lay is a repeated concern in the scholia with the fact that the poet does not want openly to favour (χαρίζεσθαι) the Greek side;[19] Dio overtly twists this scholarly idea in ch. 82 in which Homer 'shows an empty favouritism for Menelaos' (κενὰς αὐτῶι χαρίζεται χάριτας) by giving him a 'laughable victory' over Paris when his sword broke (*Il.* 3.361–8). Here too Dio can combine the traditions of Homeric criticism and historiography. For Dio, Homer was able to distort 'histo-

---

18 So first in the 'Pride of Halicarnassus', *SGO* 0/12/02 (v. 43).
19 Cf. bT-scholia to *Il.* 4.13, 11.116–17, 364; for the issue in general cf. Richardson 1980, 273–4, with earlier bibliography.

ry', not just because of the faintness of the surviving traditions, but because his mass audiences were largely uneducated (τοὺς πολλοὺς καὶ ἰδιώτας) and he gave them what they wanted to hear, namely exaggerated Greek success and heroism; in this state of affairs, even those who knew the truth kept quiet and did not refute (ἐξελέγχειν) his claims (92), and it is (again) not hard to think of modern parallels for such a situation. Be that as it may, behind Dio's argument lies (again) Thucydides 1.21.1 where the historian contrasts himself with the poets who also exaggerated their subjects (ἐπὶ τὸ μεῖζον κοσμοῦντες, cf. Dio's description of Homer βελτίω ποιῶν τὰ τῶν Ἑλλήνων, 92) and the 'logographers' whose compositions aimed at being pleasing to their audiences rather than true; Thucydides also notes that what these performers reported about the distant past was in any case 'beyond verification' (ἀνεξέλεγκτα). Dio's argument picks up and lightly recasts Thucydides' criticism of 'the many' who are simply not interested in taking pains to discover the truth (1.20.3).

One aspect of Dio as a new (and anti-) Homer, and of Dio's appropriation of the tradition of epic criticism, to which there is space here merely to allude, is the possibility that Dio has composed the *Trojan Oration* in such a way as to make it open to some of the same modes of criticism as the Homeric poems themselves. Critics have rightly found it easy enough to discover inconsistencies in the revisionist history which Dio offers, and the normal explanations of textual doublets, often arising from the conflation of alternative versions of the same passage (presumably originally from different versions of the speech), and of Dio's typical habits of composition must both contain elements of truth, however much, in extreme form, they may resemble some modern approaches to the text of Homer himself.[20] Nevertheless, Paris' reference to a promise made to him by Aphrodite, for example, which I have interpreted above as a rhetorical improvisation by Paris, could be seen as a sign that even the 'true story' of what happened contained within itself indications of rival versions, just as – as we have seen – both Herodotus and Dio later in the *Trojan Oration* find indications in the Homeric text of the rival (and truer) versions. For both Herodotus and Dio, Homer knows what he is doing in such cases; with regard to Aphrodite's promise to Paris in Dio, however, Seeck suggests that what we have is a 'Relikt des Mythos' which survives in Dio's version 'eher versehen-

---

20 Cf., e.g., Kindstrand 1973, 142–3.

tlich';[21] perhaps, however, we should give Dio the same benefit of the doubt which he himself gave Homer. As the Platonic Socrates in very 'sophistic' mode claims to expose inconsistencies in Homer (Plato, *Hippias Minor* 369e–71e) and as Isocrates depicts 'worthless sophists' sitting around swapping what they thought were smart ideas about Homer and the other poets (*Panathenaicus* 18), so Dio, who actually envisages that 'the wretched sophists' will get to work on his speech to refute it (ἐξελέγχειν 6, cf. 14),[22] has played an amusing game by giving these critics material to work with.

Dio and Homer are alike in another way also. If Homer turned the truth completely upside down (36 ἀναστρέφειν ἅπαντα, 92 πάντα τὰ πράγματα ἁπλῶς ἀνέτρεψε), Dio does the same to received tradition, which many would take as the same thing as 'truth'. Here too Dio picks up and distorts an aspect of Homeric criticism. An important idea in the ancient admiration for Homeric narrative technique is ἀναστροφή, a concept which is used in two related ways. It may refer to the way in which the *Iliad* tells the story of a short and climactic period of the war, but through prolepeses and analepses and other modes of expansion, Homer manages to include the whole story of the war; important statements of this idea occur, for example, in the b-scholia to 1.8–9 and to 2.494–877.[23] ἀναστροφή may also refer to the way in which the outcome of a single narrative may be adumbrated first, and then the speaker will go back to explain the causes and course of the narrative.[24] More generally, and with particular reference of course to the model of the *Odyssey*, ἀναστροφή denoted any mode of narration in which the order (τάξις) of events and the order of the telling were not coincident (the issue, in other words, from which all modern narratology takes off). The technique was clearly practised at a relatively early stage of ancient

---

21 Seeck 1990, 99.
22 Von Arnim excised the reference to 'sophists' in 6 (cf. von Arnim 1898, 168–9), and it must be admitted that the construction is not well paralleled. Nevertheless, it can hardly be without significance that Dio's overturning of the established Trojan story, i.e. an argument for the ἥττων λόγος, is itself a very 'sophistic' undertaking (cf. Plutarch, *De malignitate* 5, 855e). Dio is certainly having it both ways.
23 Cf., e.g., Richardson 1980, 267; Rengakos 2004, 291–2. Meijering 1987, 138–48 collects much ancient material on narrative τάξις. See also Nünlist, this volume.
24 Cf., e.g., bT-scholia to *Il.* 11.671–761, 13.665b, Porphyry on *Il.* 12.127–54 (= I 176–8 Schrader).

rhetorical education; in his account of the preliminary exercise of διήγημα, Aelius Theon identifies five possible narrative orderings (middle-beginning-end, as in the *Odyssey*, end-middle-beginning, middle-end-beginning, end-beginning-middle, beginning-end-middle).[25] What Dio has done is to take a much praised feature of Homeric narrative and, so to say, confused two senses of ἀναστροφή, so that Homer's ἀναστροφή now becomes a total 'subversion' of events, rather than a particular way of ordering them in the telling. For Dio, Homer's motive for behaving in such a way was his desire to please his audience and, sitting perhaps only apparently paradoxically alongside this, his contempt for them (35, 92); for criticism sympathetic to Homer, of course, ἀναστροφή was also a result of the poet's relationship with his audience, but in this case a cause and symptom of Homer's unique power to engage them and to hold their attention.

'Anastrophic' narrative (of all forms) calls attention to itself because it differs from the 'natural' order imposed by chronology. The bT-scholia on *Il.* 2.494–877 note that κατὰ τάξιν narrative, i. e. where the order of events and the order of the telling are coincident and which is elsewhere called κατὰ φύσιν narrative,[26] is characteristic of post-Homeric poetry (νεωτερικόν) and prose-writing and that it is not appropriate for poetic dignity (σεμνότης). Such narrative which starts ἀπὸ τῶν πρώτων and proceeds ἐπὶ τὰ ἐφεξῆς (Eustathius, *Hom.* 7.42–4) was, as is well known, believed to be characteristic of 'cyclic', rather than Homeric, epic, a judgement much influenced by Aristotle's views on the preferred structures for epic and tragic plotting and of Homer's superiority to other epic poets.[27] Nowhere, of course, is this subject more prominent than in discussions of how Homer's poems begin; Horace's view of the matter in the *Ars Poetica* is too well known to require discussion (*AP* 136–47). Unsurprisingly, this critical rhetoric is also very familiar to Dio:

> Though he set himself to tell of the war (ἐπιχειρήσας τὸν πόλεμον εἰπεῖν) between the Achaeans and the Trojans, [Homer] did not straightaway begin at the beginning, but at some random point (ὅθεν ἔτυχεν). This is what virtually all liars do: they entangle and twist (ἐμπλέκοντες καὶ περιπλέκοντες) and do not want to tell their story in sequence (ἐφεξῆς).
>
> Dio Chrysostom 11.24

---

25 Theon, *Progymnasmata* 86.9–87.12 Spengel (= pp. 48–9 Patillon-Bolognesi).
26 Cf., e.g., Theon, *Progymnasmata* 86.32 Spengel (= p. 49 Patillon-Bolognesi), Eustathius, *Hom.* 7.9–10, 42–4.
27 Cf., e.g., Hunter 2001, 105–19; Vagnone 2003, 120–1; Rengakos 2004.

We may here be reminded of the answer given in the Underworld by the Lucianic Homer, when asked – a notorious critical question – why he began the *Iliad* with μῆνις, that this opening just occurred to him without any planning (Lucian, *VH* 2.20). Be that as it may, Aristotle famously praises Homer because he did *not* 'set himself to compose a poem about the war in its entirety (μηδὲ τὸν πόλεμον ... ἐπιχειρῆσαι ποιεῖν ὅλον), though it had a beginning and an end' (*Poetics* 1459a31–3); if the similarity of Dio's phrasing to that of Aristotle is coincidental, there is no doubt from where Dio's critical apparatus ultimately derives. Homer *should have* been a cyclic poet, like Horace's *scriptor cyclicus* who announced his subject as *fortunam Priami ... et nobile bellum* (*AP* 136), or a historian, like Thucydides who 'wrote the history of the war between the Peloponnesians and the Athenians' (1.1.1). This 'natural narrative' (κατὰ φύσιν, 25) is characteristic of those who 'wish to set forth the events as each thing happened (ὡς ξυνέβη ἕκαστον) and who report the first thing first, the second thing second, and then all successive events (τἄλλα ἐφεξῆς) likewise' (25); those who want to tell the truth, in other words.

Dio's mode of attack on Homer here is indebted to more than one overlapping intellectual tradition. We are, for example, constantly reminded of the tactics of a forensic orator in denigrating his opponent, subjecting his account to *elenchos* and exposing flaws in his argument.[28] More specifically, however, it was recognised as long ago as Eustathius[29] that Dio's procedure owes much to the rhetorical exercise of ἀνασκευή, in which mythical narratives and other stories were proved to be obvious falsehoods. Theon identifies the arguments to be employed in such an attack as 'unclarity (ἀσαφές), improbability (ἀπίθανον), inappropriateness (ἀπρεπές), defectiveness (ἐλλιπές), excessiveness (πλεονάζον), unusualness (ἀσύνηθες), inconsistency (μαχόμενον), ordering (τάξις), inopportuneness (ἀσύμφορον), unevenness (ἀνόμοιον), falsehood (ψευδές)',[30] and he gives an example of how one would go about disproving the story of Medea's killing of her children;[31] examples of these arguments are easy enough to find in *Oration* 11, and there can be no

---

28 Cf. Classen 1994, 322–4.
29 Cf. Eustathius, *Hom.* 460.10–12; there is a fuller (and more recent) treatment in Mesk 1920–1.
30 Theon, *Progymnasmata* 76.20–25 Spengel (= p. 36 Patillon-Bolognesi); cf. also 93.5–94.11 Spengel (= pp. 57–9 Patillon-Bolognesi).
31 94.12–95.2 Spengel (= pp. 59–60 Patillon-Bolognesi).

doubt that Dio was indebted, and wished to be seen to be indebted, to this tradition.

Finally, we may note another tradition in which the great writers of the past were exposed to serious criticism. Dio 11 has been compared to Plutarch's attack upon Herodotus,[32] but we may rather think of a more scholastic model, such as Dionysius of Halicarnassus' sharp criticism of Thucydides in his essay devoted to the historian. Dionysius certainly is not as harsh with his subject as Dio is with Homer – he goes out of his way in fact to emphasise the historian's virtues and the truth of what he reported is not at issue – but there are nevertheless interesting analogies. No full treatment is possible here, but we may note that Thucydides' arrangement of his narrative by summers and winters leads to a loss of continuity (τὸ διηνεκές) and imposes unreasonable demands upon his readers (*Thuc.* 9);[33] historical narrative should be 'straightforward and free from interruptions' (εἰρομένη καὶ ἀπερίσπαστος). Related to this is another aspect of τάξις and οἰκονομία: Thucydides made wrong choices about where to begin and end. The proper beginning, the κατὰ φύσιν ἀρχή (*Thuc.* 12.1), is from the point where 'there would be nothing (relevant) preceding', but Thucydides did not begin from 'the cause which was true and which seemed to him true' (*Thuc.* 10); it is indeed a question of nature:

> At the beginning of his enquiry into the causes of the war he should first have reported the true cause in which he himself believed; for nature demanded that prior events should have precedence over (ἄρχειν) later ones and true things be stated before false ones, and the introduction to his narrative would have been far more powerful if it had been arranged in this manner.
>
> Dionysius of Halicarnassus, *Thucydides* 11.1

Dionysius' essay gives us a glimpse into a world of narratological discussion which Dio knew well and which has made a significant contribution to *Oration* 11; from one perspective we may say that Dio has replicated some of these arguments, while adding a consideration of why his author chose to proceed in this way. For Dio, of course, Homer's motives were not respectable.

---

32 Both works start from (different versions of) the topos of how literature deceives, and both authors claim (as did Plato, *Rep.* 10.595b-c) simply to be standing up for truth (Dio 11.11, Plutarch, *De malignitate* 1, 854f).

33 Cf. also *Letter to Pompeius* 3; this was obviously a standard scholastic charge against Thucydides, cf. Theon, *Progymnasmata* 80.16–20 Spengel (= p. 41 Patillon-Bolognesi).

There is, then, a lot of evidence to show us that Genette's 'unavoidable *difficulty of beginning*' was an ancient anxiety as well,[34] but let us return to Dio's argument. Where *should* Homer have begun the *Iliad*? Dio has a straightforward answer:

> From where would it have been more appropriate (μᾶλλον ... ἔπρεπεν) to begin than from the outrageous wrong committed by Paris, which resulted in the war, since all readers of the poem would have been angry and been keen to see it accomplished and no one would have pitied the sufferings of the Trojans? In this way Homer would have had a more sympathetic and a more engaged (εὐνούστερον καὶ προθυμότερον) audience.
>
> Dio Chrysostom 11.28

We may object to Dio that Homer's announced subject was not in fact 'the war', but that will cut little ice. Dio's point is that, as an encomiast of the Greek war, Homer would have done his job far better, if he had begun from the beginning. Again Dio appeals to familiar critical arguments, and in fact is able to launch his attack without straying too far from the pattern of ancient praise for Homer. Among the reasons adduced already by the D-scholia on *Iliad* 1.1 as to why the *Iliad* began ἀπὸ τῆς μήνιδος are precisely to heighten the *pathos*, to make the audience 'more attentive',[35] and 'to make his encomia of the Greeks more convincing' by, apparently,[36] highlighting their sufferings and losses at the beginning. As Dio uses Homer to subvert Homer, so he uses Homeric criticism to subvert such criticism. More generally, of course, the quest for the audience's *eunoia* is a fundamental task of any poet, Homer included (cf., e.g., scholia to *Il.* 2.485–6); it is important to rouse the audience's indignation (cf., e.g., the T-scholium to *Il.* 17.205a). Dio's argument is in fact very reminiscent of a well known bT-scholium to *Il.* 6.58–9; Agamemnon urges Menelaos not to spare any Trojan, including unborn children, and the scholiast notes that audiences are revolted by such unfitting savagery, which is why, for example, tragedians do not put such murderous acts on the stage. There are, however, defences against such criticism, and it is within this tradition that Dio takes his stand:[37]

---

34 Genette (1972) 1980, 46 (his italics), cf. Hunter 1993, 122–3.
35 Cf. further below p. 60–1.
36 There are uncertainties about the text here.
37 I have discussed certain other aspects of this scholium in Hunter 2005b, 179–83.

> If these verses had been spoken before the breaking of the oath, they would be rightly criticised. Since, however, they come after the oaths and their transgression, Agamemnon is not hateful. The listener almost wants the whole race of oath-breakers to be wiped out; he is almost angry on behalf of the gods.
>
> bT-scholium to *Il.* 6.58–9

'Pity' is, of course, a prominent motif in ancient discussion of the *Iliad* (as, of course, in the *Iliad* itself): 'Homer ends the *Iliad* in the highest degree of pity' observes the bT-scholium on *Il.* 24.776, adding that this was the origin of the forensic practice of placing the appeal to the audience's pity last in one's speech.[38]

It is no surprise – Dio can have it both ways – that the defective end of the *Iliad* also tells its own story; Homer missed his poetic chance by not describing the sack of the city (which did not, of course, actually happen):

> If he had wanted to tell of the greatest and most fearful things, all forms of suffering and catastrophe, and moreover what everyone most of all was longing to hear (ἐπόθει ἀκοῦσαι), what greater or more powerful subject did he have than the capture of the city?
>
> Dio Chrysostom 11.29

Behind this question lies less the language of 'pity and fear' from Aristotle's *Poetics* than Gorgias' famous description of the effect of poetry (principally tragedy?) in the *Helen*:

> Those who hear poetry feel the shudders of fear, the tears of pity, the longings (πόθος) of grief. Through the words, the soul experiences its own reaction to successes and misfortunes in the affairs and persons of others.
>
> Gorgias, *Helen* 9 (trans. D.A. Russell)

Dio's point in chapter 29 is not that what a Greek audience would indeed have most 'longed' to hear was the deserved sufferings inflicted upon oath-breaking Trojans, but that descriptions of terrible suffering, such as accompanies the sack of cities, bring their own form of 'pleasure', an idea most famously expressed in this passage of Gorgias. The audience's 'desires' are another critical motif familiar in the Homeric scholia,[39] but here the idea is used to show that, even *qua* poet (let alone truth-teller), Homer did not do much of a job.

---

38 Cf. also the scholia to *Il.* 22.337, 370, 24.161–2, 309, 504, 776, Richardson 1980, 274–5.
39 Cf. the scholia to *Il.* 2.6c, 20.443, 24.85.

Dio's extended description of the sack of the city in chapters 29–30 is explicitly a prose version of Priam's piteous appeal to Hector at *Il.* 22.60–71, a version in which the rhetorical αὔξησις of the theme is another illustration of what an opportunity Homer passed up;[40] the Homeric scholia, of course, take a different view and praise the *enargeia* and spare power of the verses. The links between this Homeric passage and other early epic poetry are rightly a subject of great interest,[41] and one which takes its cue from the scholia ('though Homer did not write of the sack of Troy, he nevertheless described its sufferings [παθήματα] ... he foreshadows the capture of Troy'), but it is clear that Dio is (once again) expressing the view that Homer should have been a 'cyclic poet', for behind the description of the sack in *Aeneid* 2, as behind Euripides' *Trojan Women*, lie (at least) the *Iliou Persis* and the *Little Iliad* of Lesches; unsurprisingly, these chapters of Dio share many motifs, not just with *Aeneid* 2,[42] but also with Pausanias' famous description of Polygnotus' painting of the sack of Troy, a painting for which Pausanias sees Lesches' poem as an important source (Paus. 10.25–7). It is of some interest that these chapters of Dio are strongly reminiscent also of Polybius' famous strictures against Phylarchus' description of the sufferings of the Mantineans in chapters which gave rise to a very lively modern debate about 'tragic history':

> [Phylarchus] says that, after they had surrendered, the Mantineans endured such misfortunes ... as to cause all Greeks to reflect and weep. In his eagerness to move his readers to pity and rouse their emotions, he brings on clinging women, their hair dishelleved and their breasts exposed, and men and women weeping and lamenting along with their children and aged parents as they are led away.
>
> Polybius 2.56.6–7 = *FGrHist* 81 F53

As is well known, Polybius' objection is (basically) that such writing, which aims at the *ekplêxis* of the audience (Polybius 2.56.10, cf. Dio 11.30), is appropriate to poetry, particularly tragedy, not to historiography; the apparent similarity in these descriptions between some Hellen-

---

40 Verses 60–8 have in fact been interpolated into the text of chapter 32, perhaps from a misplaced marginal note. Vagnone (2003) *ad loc.* notes that Dio will also have had Euripides, *Troades* 1260–1332 in mind; Dio presumably knew that passage, but there are no obvious verbal echoes; cf. further below.
41 Cf., e.g., Anderson 1997, 29–38.
42 *Aeneid* 2.313 *exoritur clamorque uirum clangorque tubarum* is very like Dio 11.30 (the sounds of the sack) βοὴν ἢ κτύπον χαλκοῦ, but very little should (presumably) be hung on this.

istic historiography and the narratives of cyclic epic is a piece of literary history not without interest,[43] but what is important here is that Polybius' view of the proper functions of poetry chimes with Dio's criticism of Homer: in failing properly to describe the sack of Troy he was failing properly to perform his rôle as a poet.

The choice of where to begin and end is, of course, a matter of planning. How much 'forward planning' went into the *Iliad* and the *Odyssey* which we possess is a matter which students of the poems still rightly discuss, for it is connected (*inter alia*) with the issue of how the poems were actually composed. The ancient scholarship which is reflected in the scholia, however, was in little doubt; the scholia 'assume that the poet has a clear idea from the beginning of the direction in which his narrative is moving'.[44] The idea of Homeric οἰκονομία and of narrative preparation are fundamental to the scholiastic view of Homer; already in the *Iliad* the poet is preparing for the *Odyssey*,[45] just as in *Iliad* 3 he is laying the groundwork for details of *Iliad* 24.[46] Unsurprisingly, Dio takes a different view, and once again it is one with a strikingly modern resonance. For Dio, Homer did not know where his poem was going to go when he set out, and important narrative decisions were made 'as the poem proceeded' (35); one merely has to look at the opening verses to see that (36). Later we learn that the major shift was (roughly) with what we call Book 16, when things start to go the Greek way again and Patroclus emerges as a principal character (92). What should be stressed here, however, is that Dio's subversion of a tenet of ancient Homeric criticism raises (still) important general questions about the assumptions of that criticism.

'Homer gave thought not just to what he should say, but also to what he should not' (bT-scholium to *Il.* 1.44a, cf. Horace, *AP* 149–50). The selection of what features and episodes to highlight is a crucial part of the good poet's art.[47] Like Horace, Dio too links Homeric selectivity with poetic licence, or 'lying' to give it its more straight-

---

43 Cf. esp. Walbank 1960. Such set-piece descriptions (ἐκφράσεις) were a standard school exercise, cf. Theon, *Progymnasmata* 119.23 Spengel (= p. 68 Patillon-Bolognesi) for ἅλωσις.
44 Richardson 1980, 268; pp. 267–9 of Richardson's discussion are all relevant here.
45 Cf. the scholia to *Il.* 2.260a, 10.252–3a, 260.
46 Cf. scholium to *Il.* 3.261–2b.
47 Brink's (1960) note on *AP* 148 collects much relevant material.

forward name (*atque ita mentitur, sic ueris falsa remiscet*); for Dio, however, Homeric selectivity in fact proves Homeric untruthfulness:

> Those who tell lies usually behave like this. They tell some parts of the story and linger over them, but what they most want to conceal they do not offer freely nor when the listener is paying attention, nor do they put it in the place belonging to it, but where it may most escape notice.
> Dio Chrysostom 11.26

Liars not only leave things out, they also try to slip things past their audience when they are not paying full attention. Here Dio not only makes use of the very familiar idea of 'poetic licence', but he also (once again) picks up and 'spins' ideas from the critical tradition. The scholia frequently note how Homer or his characters do or say things λεληθότως;[48] in some of these cases the meaning of this adverb is really no more than 'implicitly', but the language of τὸ λανθάνειν is a powerful and polyvalent one in ancient Homeric criticism. Thus, for example, Duris of Samos criticised the famous simile of *Il.* 21.257–62, in which Achilles' pursuit by the river is compared to a man clearing an irrigation channel for a stream, because (in modern terms) the vehicle hardly corresponded 'in noise and threat' to the tenor;[49] readers, however, 'do not notice' this because they are distracted by the picture of horticultural irrigation. So too, when Dione uses a low (ταπεινόν) word (παππάζουσιν) as she consoles her daughter at *Il.* 5.408, this λανθάνει because the speaker is not a male god or hero, but a mother talking to her daughter (bT-scholia *ad loc.*). Examples could be multiplied,[50] but what is important is that this common language of secrecy and deceit opened the way to a potent charge. Of particular interest here are the few cases where the poet λανθάνει 'slips things by' the audience whose attention is focused elsewhere (cf. bT-scholia to *Il.* 16.395–8, 22.375b). Dio's mode of argument was almost ready-made here, for the idea of variations in the audience's attention is also important in the scholia;[51] Homer, for example, began the *Iliad* in the

---

48 Cf. the scholia to *Il.* 1.242, 2.106b, 5.39, 6.358, 11.116–17, 251, 506, 13.365b, 712–21, 24.3, 249–51. The idea of doing things without being noticed appears, of course, in a number of critical contexts (cf., e.g., Aristotle, *Rhetoric* 3.1404b18).
49 Ge-scholium on *Il.* 21.257–62 = *FGrHist* 76 F89.
50 The language and ideas of τὸ λανθάνειν have in fact a wide spread in ancient literary and stylistic criticism, cf., e.g., 'Longinus', *On the Sublime* 17.
51 Cf. the scholia to *Il.* 11.218, 604c, 711b, 13.665b, 15.556–8, 610–14b, 16.112–13.

way he did in order to ensure the audience's attention (AT and bT-scholia on 1.1). In the scholia the idea of the poet's control over the audience's attention is part of a proper critical concern with the architecture of a long and complex poem; in Dio it is a sign of a much more dubious phenomenon.

Dio's *Trojan Oration* thus opens a window upon nearly every important issue in ancient narratology. If the speech has not recently attracted the attention it deserves, that may be in part the result of the obvious and obviously knowing humour which plays over the speech at every level; to borrow a famous phrase, Dio 'cannot be serious' (can he?). Modern narratology, by contrast, has generally been characterised by a proper scholarly seriousness and intellectual commitment to the patterns it has done so much to reveal. If, however, Dio's claim is that Homer shows us how easy it is to make people believe the opposite of the truth, he also shows us that narratology can have exactly the same bewitching power.

Narratological Concepts in Greek Scholia

René Nünlist

In a way, the goal of this paper is a modest one: it attempts to show that the corpus of Greek scholia has interesting things to say on the topic of literary criticism in general, and, focusing on the subject of the conference and hence the present volume, on narratological questions in particular.

As a general rule, scholia are not at the centre of classical scholarship. They are a marginal phenomenon indeed. If considered at all, they are mostly made use of in one of the following four ways: (1) as a source for fragments of lost poets and authors; (2) as a quarry for variant readings and other questions related to textual criticism; (3) as a dictionary which helps to understand the meaning of difficult words and phrases; (4) as a commentary which provides factual information, mostly *Realien* of some kind. Conversely, literary criticism in the scholia is of limited importance in contemporary scholarship. This is surprising because there is, after all, a considerable interest in the principles of ancient literary criticism as such. But the focus is either on the origins of literary criticism in, say, Aristophanes, Plato, etc., or the emphasis is on the relevant 'technical' treatises such as Aristotle's *Poetics* or Pseudo-Longinus' *On the Sublime*, to name only two.[1] Needless to say, these are important questions, and scholars have made valuable contributions to the knowledge of ancient literary criticism. However, the frequent absence of scholia from these discussions is striking and, as this paper attempts to prove, unjustified.[2] For the scholia are apt to complement and expand the picture gained by studying the treatises. Not the least important factor here is the fundamental difference between treatises and the corpus of scholia. The treatise normally develops a model of interpretation, which is then illustrated by means of relevant passages; but the number of passages dis-

---

[1] Focus on origins, e.g., Ford 2002, Ledbetter 2003; on individual treatises, e.g., Halliwell 1986 on Aristotle's *Poetics*, Russell 1964 on Pseudo-Longinus, etc.

[2] The most important exceptions in the last three decades are the seminal article by Richardson 1980 and the dissertation of Meijering 1987. On older literature see Nünlist 2009.

cussed in a treatise is bound to be relatively small. Conversely, the scholia discuss hundreds of passages, but they rarely give an explanation of the methodological model(s) on which their interpretation is based. It is *a priori* likely that a careful examination of the scholia can shed light on the models of the treatises and *vice versa*. Put in general terms, treatises provide the models and the scholia indicate how they are applied to the actual texts. However, in the individual case it is not easy to determine the exact relationship between treatise and scholia and to answer, for instance, the question whether a scholion is influenced by a treatise (or 'school' of interpretation) and, if so, which. Very often questions such as these either must remain open or can be answered tentatively only. Given the complementary relationship between treatises and scholia, the latter give modern readers the opportunity to see, as the title of my recent book has it, *The Ancient Critic at Work*.[3] What is more, chances are that the highly heterogeneous corpus of scholia contains traces of concepts for which there is no immediate equivalent in the extant treatises. Obviously, these traces are of particular interest in light of the prevalent emphasis on studying the treatises and will be given due weight in what follows. More generally, the paper's focus on scholia is an attempt to even out the balance and should not be taken as an implicit argument that the scholia are more important than the treatises. The same holds true for the preferred treatment of narratological questions, which is due to the topic of the present volume and not indicative of a corresponding preference in the extant scholia.[4]

---

[3] Nünlist 2009. The present article draws on and repeatedly refers to the more extensive treatment in the book, which discusses substantially more examples from the scholia, adduces more parallels from sources other than scholia and provides more references to and discussion of relevant literature. In the book and *a fortiori* in the present article preference is given to secondary literature that discusses the relevant phenomenon in light of and with explicit reference to ancient scholarship.

[4] For concepts of literary criticism other than narratology see Nünlist 2009, esp. Chapters 5 to 19. On how to use and read scholia in general see now Dickey 2007.

1. Order

Narrative texts regularly contain forward and backward references. The text indicates what happened before (i.e., flashback) or what will happen later (i.e., foreshadowing). Strictly speaking, such references are a breach of a purely chronological sequence of the events narrated. In the wake of Gérard Genette ((1972) 1980, esp. 39–40), it is now common to refer to these references as 'analepsis' (for references to what happened before) and 'prolepsis' (for references to what will happen later). Ancient scholars are fully aware of this narrative device.[5] With regard to prolepsis, the scholia most often discuss it by means of the term προαναφώνησις and its verbal cognate προαναφωνέω ('to announce beforehand'). An example, chosen almost at random, is the note on the passage early in book 2 of the *Iliad* where the Homeric narrator exposes the futility of Agamemnon's hope to take Troy immediately by announcing many hardships instead (*Il.* 2.38–40):

> ἡ προαναφώνησις ἐγερτική. πείθεται δὲ ὀνείρῳ Ἀγαμέμνων σφαλλόμενος ὑπὸ Διός.
>
> The prolepsis is stirring. But Agamemnon, deceived by Zeus, trusts the dream.
>
> (sch. bT *Il.* 2.39b *ex.*)[6]

The term προαναφώνησις is the most frequent but by no means the only term used by ancient scholars to mark instances of prolepsis. Alternatives include the term προέκθεσις ('exhibition in advance') or verbal expressions such as προλέγω, προαπαγγέλλω or προαναφθέγγομαι (all roughly meaning 'to mention beforehand').[7] From today's perspective perhaps

---

5 To be fair, this is one of the concepts of literary criticism in scholia that received quite some attention from modern scholars, esp. Duckworth 1931, Meijering 1987, 204–9. On the topic in general see Nünlist 2009, Chapter 1.
6 Not unlike his modern successors, this anonymous critic combines several points in his note: one about formalism (here: prolepsis) and one about psychology (here: reader response). For more on the latter see Nünlist 2009, Chapters 5 and 6.
7 προέκθεσις: e.g. sch. bT *Il.* 15.601–2 *ex.* (on the eventual παλίωξις of the Greeks), προλέγω: e.g. sch. b *Il.* 17.453–5a[2] *ex.* (ditto), προαπαγγέλλω: e.g. sch. bT *Il.* 3.301–2 *ex.* (on Zeus 'not yet' fulfilling the prayer), προαναφθέγγομαι: e.g. sch. bT *Il.* 16.71–2 *ex.* (on the river battle in *Iliad* 20). The first of these terms, προέκθεσις, has its roots in rhetorical theory (cf. Ps.-Hermog. *Meth.* 12, p. 427 Rabe), which is a common phenomenon; see Meijering 1987; Nünlist 2009.

the most intriguing terms are προλαμβάνω ('to anticipate') and the cognate noun πρόληψις.[8] One wonders whether Genette was aware of the fact that, in a way, he *re*introduced a centuries-old term in his *Discours du récit* of (1972) 1980.[9]

Moving on to the counterpart 'analepsis', a first observation is quantitative in nature. Although this narrative device as such tends to be more frequent in narrative texts than prolepsis, it is less often commented on in the extant scholia.[10] The second difference concerns terminology, in that there is virtually no terminological consistency in the scholia that identify instances of analepsis. Most of the time they simply point out the other passage to which the analepsis refers and thereby establish a connection between the two passages without using a specific term (e.g. sch. A *Il.* 9.19*b* Ariston.). This lack of a commonly accepted term for 'analepsis' has important methodological consequences in general. A strict focus on the technical vocabulary (in the scholia and elsewhere) is bound to miss relevant material. The technical vocabulary is of course very important, but it can be equally instructive simply to look at what the individual scholia say. As a consequence, to search the corpus by means of an index or the electronic TLG should not be the one and only method to answer one's questions because ancient critics often give a periphrastic description of the phenomenon under consideration. In the case of analepsis, an exclusive focus on technical vocabulary could lead to the mistaken conclusion that ancient critics do not discuss the device.

Returning to the actual treatment of analepsis in the scholia, it is noteworthy that, in addition to simply connecting the two relevant passages, ancient scholars also seem to make a distinction that is roughly comparable to Genette's pair of terms 'repeating analepsis' and 'completing analepsis'. 'Repeating analepsis' does not provide new information, whereas 'completing analepsis' does (Genette (1972) 1980, 51–61). The former can be found referred to by means of the rhetorical term ἀνακεφαλαίωσις (lit. 'recapitulation').[11] Completing analepsis, on the other hand, is described as a form of 'filling the gap'. The verbs

---

8 E.g. sch. bT *Il.* 15.610 *ex.* (on Hector's imminent death).
9 In this he is preceded by Kraut 1863.
10 In this particular case, such a quantitative point can be made in spite of the general cautionary remarks about statistics expressed at the end of the paper.
11 E.g. sch. AbT *Il.* 1.366*a/b ex.* (Achilles gives Thetis a summary of what happened).

used are, for instance, ἀναπληρόω or συμπληρόω.¹² Another way of referring to completing analepsis is to say that the narrator did not describe the event when it was taking place, but refers to it afterwards as one which took place beforehand. The Greek phrase for this is τοῦτο γινόμενον μὲν οὐ παρέστησεν, ὡς γενόμενον δὲ παραδίδωσι (the poet 'did not present the event as one which is taking place, but refers to it as one which took place previously').¹³ The relevant scholion is of additional interest because it derives from the Augustan critic Aristonicus and is therefore likely to represent the view of Alexandria's master literary critic Aristarchus himself.

The concept 'analepsis' recurs in another context. Apparently, ancient readers had been wondering why Homer did not narrate the entire Trojan war, but covered only a small fraction towards the end of the war.¹⁴ The answer they found was that, unlike his competitors, Homer selected the climactic phase of the Trojan war for his subject matter and incorporated the antecedents by means of analepsis. The expression used in this connection is ἐξ ἀναστροφῆς, that is to say, 'in inverse order':

> θαυμάσιος ὁ ποιητὴς μηδ' ὁτιοῦν παραλιμπάνων τῆς ὑποθέσεως, πάντα δ' ἐξ ἀναστροφῆς κατὰ τὸν ἐπιβάλλοντα καιρὸν διηγούμενος, τὴν τῶν θεῶν ἔριν, τὴν τῆς Ἑλένης ἁρπαγήν, τὸν Ἀχιλλέως θάνατον· ἡ γὰρ κατὰ τάξιν διήγησις νεωτερικὸν καὶ συγγραφικὸν καὶ τῆς ποιητικῆς ἄπο σεμνότητος.

> The poet is admirable: he omits no part of the story, but narrates all events at the appropriate moment in inverse order, the strife of the goddesses (sc. Hera, Athena and Aphrodite), the rape of Helen, the death of Achilles. For chronological narrative is typical of later (i.e. post-Homeric) epic poets and of historians and lacks poetic grandeur.
> (sch. b Il. 2.494–877 ex., p. 288 Erbse)

The term ἀναστροφή implies that an analepsis (such as the one, for instance, of Paris' judgment in Il. 24.29–30) is in breach of the 'correct'

---

12 ἀναπληρόω: e.g. sch. bT 4.251b ex. (the passage complements the introduction of the Greek commanders in the Catalogue); συμπληρόω (τὴν ὑπόθεσιν): e.g. sch. bT Il. 9.328 ex. (on Achilles' earlier raids into the Trojan hinterland).
13 Sch. A Il. 8.230a Ariston. (cf. sch. A Il. 12.211a Ariston.). In the Homeric passage (Il. 8.228–35) Agamemnon encourages the despondent Greek army by reminding them of how each of them had sworn right before the actual beginning of the war that he could take on a hundred Trojans or even two-hundred.
14 E.g. sch. bT Il. 1.1b ex., also Arist. Po. 1459a30–7 or Horace's famous phrase *medias in res*, which had better be called *ultimas in res* (cf. Quint. 7.10.11). See also Hunter, this vol.

chronological order, a phenomenon which Genette calls 'anachrony' ((1972) 1980, 35–6). Essentially the same idea is expressed by the phrase ἀνατρέχειν ἐπὶ τὴν ἀρχήν (e.g. sch. bT *Il.* 11.769 *ex.*): the narrator (or, in a speech, the character) so to speak 'runs back to the beginning' of the Trojan war. The passage in question (*Il.* 11.769–90) refers to the moment in the prehistory of the Trojan war when Nestor and Odysseus came to Peleus' house in order to enlist Achilles as an ally.

As mentioned before, prolepsis is more often treated in the scholia than its counterpart analepsis, although the latter is more frequently found in the texts themselves. A possible explanation for this imbalance is the fact that prolepsis is apt to create suspense among the audience, a topic the scholia have a great deal to say about in general (Nünlist 2009, Chapter 5). In this connection, it is worth discussing two ramifications of prolepsis. The first ramification is the distinction between explicit prolepsis and what is called a 'seed' (Genette (1972) 1980, 76–7). Explicit prolepsis, on the one hand, anticipates in so many words what is going to happen. A 'seed', on the other, is a piece of information the full meaning of which becomes apparent only later. The literary device is particularly at home in detective novels where, for example, the inobtrusively inserted piece of information becomes the decisive clue that eventually leads to the conviction of the murderer. This narrative device again is not unknown to ancient scholars, the term for it being σπέρμα ('seed').[15] This is a remarkable instance of terminology coming full circle. Genette's original French term was 'amorce' (lit. 'bait'), which was rendered by Jane Lewin in the English translation as 'seed'. It seems improbable that she was aware of the terminological coincidence.

The second ramification of prolepsis concerns the creation of false expectations. This phenomenon is often referred to by modern scholars as 'misdirection', and Jim Morrison has devoted an entire book to 'Homeric Misdirections', in which he also draws attention to relevant scholia, for instance (1992, 132 n. 22):

---

15 E.g. sch. b *Il.* 2.761–5 *ex.* (the mention of Eumelus' horses is a seed of the chariot race in *Iliad* 23), sch. T *Il.* 15.64c *ex.* (on the seed of Patroclus' death in *Il.* 11.604). Incidentally, a scholion on this passage itself (sch. bT *Il.* 11.604c *ex.*) speaks of a prolepis (ἀναφώνησις, here equivalent to προαναφώνησις) and praises its brevity, which is indicative of the difficulty to differentiate between an explicit but brief prolepsis and a seed. Similarly, sch. T *Il.* 15.64c *ex.* (*Did.?*) tellingly speaks of 'putting merely a seed' (σπέρμα μόνον τιθείς).

ὁ μὲν ἀκροατὴς δεινὰ ἐλπίζει ἐπὶ τῇ παρόδῳ τῶν θεῶν, οἷα καὶ πρώην γέγονεν, ὁ δὲ ἀνακόπτει τὸ προσδοκώμενον, θέαμα δὲ ἀντεισάγει τὴν ἀλαζονείαν Ἕκτορος, τὴν αἰδῶ Ἑλλήνων, τὴν σπουδὴν Μενελάου καὶ Ἀγαμέμνονος, τὴν Νέστορος δημηγορίαν.

> Due to the arrival of the gods (sc. Athena and Apollo) the reader expects terrible things (sc. to happen immediately), as has happened before already, but he (sc. Homer) thwarts the expectation; instead he introduces as a spectacle: Hector's boasting, the reluctance of the Greeks (sc. to accept the challenge), the eagerness of Menelaus and Agamemnon, Nestor's speech.
> (sch. bT *Il.* 7.29 *ex.*)

Previous divine interventions on the human plane induce the reader to expect nothing good when Athena and Apollo arrive on the scene in *Il.* 7.17–43. However, the Homeric narrator appears to have created this expectation not least in order to frustrate it by means of retardation. The narrative in book 7 first continues with a number of scenes that are carefully listed in the second part of the scholion. As in previous examples, the note combines formalism with psychological interpretation.

All in all, the various terms and concepts, together with the relevant examples, show that ancient critics had a well-established and differentiated notion of and interest in questions of narrative structure and coherence that are not unlike the ones which modern narratology discusses under the general rubric 'order' (e.g. Genette (1972) 1980, 33–85).

2. Time

The scholia on analepsis above implicitly testify to an ancient interest in questions of chronology and temporal sequence. An explicit interest in temporal phenomena can be documented, for example, by the notes that discuss the question of simultaneous events.[16] This is hardly surprising if one takes into account that Aristotle explicitly draws a distinction between a dramatic and a narrative text (*Po.* 1459b22–7): whereas it is impossible for a playwright to present two scenes which are taking place simultaneously in two different locations, this is perfectly possible in a narrative text.[17] Thus the topic 'simultaneous events' nicely illustrates the point made at the beginning of this paper about the complementary

---

16 Cf. Lundon 2002; Nünlist 2009, Chapter 2, esp. 79–83.
17 By the way, if modern scholars had given due weight to this passage, the bibliography on the alleged absence of simultaneous scenes in Homer might be shorter.

relationship of treatises and scholia: Aristotle so to speak provides the theory, the scholia give actual examples. In one of the relevant passages (the night expeditions of Diomedes and Odysseus, on the one hand, and of Dolon, on the other) the specific question concerns the chronology of the respective preparation and execution. They are narrated one after the other (*Il.* 10.180–298, 299–339), but the assumption is that 'in reality' they are taking place simultaneously:

ἡ διπλῆ, ὅτι οὐχ ὡς ἡ τῶν ἐπῶν ἔχει τάξις, οὕτω καὶ τὰ πράγματα· οὐ γὰρ προεληλυθότων ἤδη τῶν περὶ Ὀδυσσέα καλεῖ τοὺς προβούλους ὁ Ἕκτωρ, ἀλλὰ καθ' ὃν καιρὸν καὶ ὁ Ἀγαμέμνων· οὕτω γὰρ καὶ ἑαυτοῖς συμπεσοῦνται οἱ ἀπεσταλμένοι.

The *diplê* (= wedge-shaped sign in the margin), because the order of the text does not correspond to that of the events. Hector does not summon his counsellors after Odysseus and Diomedes have already set out, but at the same time as Agamemnon. And so it comes about that the parties dispatched will run into one another. (trans. Lundon)

(sch. A *Il.* 10.299a *Ariston.*)

In other words, narrative sequence does not correspond here to a sequence of events; the latter are in fact simultaneous. The wider background of this particular interpretation is one of the comparatively rare occasions where the scholia actually do provide a theoretical discussion of their methodological principles. It is probably no coincidence that this explanation comes from a papyrus commentary and not a marginal scholion in the mediaeval manuscripts – a healthy, if sobering, reminder of how much may have been lost in the course of the textual transmission. The note deals with the chronology of the events in *Iliad* 2 but has a strong generalising component too:

δεῖ δὲ νοεῖν ὅ[τ]ι κα[τ' αὐ]τὸν τὸν χρόνον τοῦ ὀνείρου ἔτι κ(αὶ) αὕτη ἀπέσταλται. ὁ δὲ ποιητὴς διηγηματικὸς ὤν, [ο]ὐ δυνάμενος ἅ<μα> πάντα εἰπεῖν, τὰ κατὰ τὸν <αὐτὸν> χρόνον πραχθέντα παρὰ μέρος εἴρηκεν.

'It must be noted that she (sc. Iris) too was sent out at the very time of the dream (sc. *Il.* 2.6–16), but the poet, narrative poet that he is and thus unable to recount all things at once, has related events that took place at the same time one after the other.' (trans. Lundon)

(sch. pap. *Il.* 2.788, p. 169 Erbse, suppl. Lundon)

The note reflects the views of Aristarchus, who appears to have recognised that, on account of the fact that a narrative text is by necessity linear, it cannot but recount simultaneous events in linear succession. Literal simultaneity is impossible in a narrative text (excepting modern experiments such as *Finnegan's Wake* or *Zettels Traum*). Consequently, Aristarchus and other critics would point out a considerable number of passages where, they argue, successively narrated events must be assumed to be taking place simultaneously. The method, if not all the examples or conclusions, is essentially the same as Zielinski's 1899–1901 more than two millennia later.

There is one particular type of simultaneous events that deserves special attention. In book 6 of the *Iliad* Hector leaves the battlefield and goes back to the citadel in order to encourage the female population to pray on behalf of the Trojan army. Hector leaves the battlefield in line 118 and he arrives at the Skaian gates in line 237. The intervening 118 lines are covered by the encounter of Diomedes and Glaucus which ends in the famous exchange of armor. Ancient and modern Homerists are in agreement that the Diomedes-Glaucus-scene is assumed to cover the time that Hector takes to get from the battlefield to the citadel. The scholia's phrase for this is τὸ διάκενον ἀναπληρόω ('to fill the gap', e.g., sch. bT *Il.* 6.237a *ex.*), which is of course a temporal gap. In modern scholarship the same device is referred to as 'Deckszene' ('covering scene') or as 'fill-in technique' (e.g. de Jong 2001, xiv). A modern novelist is unlikely to have a problem with the idea of Hector leaving the battlefield in line 118 and arriving at the citadel in the next line, that is, with the narrative skipping the actual journey. But Homer's narrative technique is different, and ancient scholars single out a number of relevant passages.[18]

Sch. A *Il.* 10.299a *Ariston.* (quoted above) argues that the sequence of the narrative does not correspond to the sequence of the 'actual' events. Similarly, ancient scholars came to discuss the relationship between the duration of the narrative and that of the events described by it. A case in point is the chronology of the events in *Iliad* 11–16. In *Il.* 11.611–15 Achilles sends Patroclus to Nestor in order to find out whether the wounded warrior is indeed the doctor Machaon. Having arrived at Nestor's tent, Patroclus declines the offered chair because, he says, he is in a hurry (11.648–54). Why, then, some readers seem to have asked, do we get Nestor's long narrative about his achievements as a young man (*Il.* 11.656–803)? Why does Patroclus not return to Achilles until book 16 (sch. bT *Il.* 15.390 *ex.*, quoted below)? And how can Nestor – heaven forbid! – dare to keep drinking in his tent for such a long time, namely until the beginning of book 14 (sch. D

---

18 Sch. bT *Il.* 2.53b *ex.*, bT *Il.* 7.194 *ex.*, bT *Il.* 11.619–43 *ex.*, etc., see Nünlist 2009, 83–7.

Il. 14.1)?[19] The last question, in particular, might be apt to confirm the reservations of those modern scholars who opine that exegetical scholia tend to be little more than the ramblings of literal-minded readers. However, more is at stake here, as an examination of the relevant scholia will show:

> πῶς δὲ ἐπιλαθόμενος Ἀχιλλέως τοσοῦτον χρόνον διάγει; ἢ οὐ πολὺς μὲν χρόνος, τὰ δὲ γεγονότα ποικίλα ἐν ὀλίγῳ καιρῷ.
>
> Why is he (sc. Patroclus), having forgotten Achilles, spending so much time? Or, the duration (sc. of his absence) is not actually long, but many different things happen in a short period of time.
>
> (sch. bT *Il.* 15.390 *ex.*)

The second part of the scholion shows awareness of the distinction between, in modern terms, story time (*erzählte Zeit*) and narrative time (*Erzählzeit*).[20] Since many different things happen more or less simultaneously and in multiple locations, the critic argues, it takes (narrative) time to give an account of them, but the story time remains unaffected by this. Essentially the same argument underlies a note on Patroclus' medical treatment of Eurypylus on his way from Nestor back to Achilles (*Il.* 11.806–12.2, cf. 15.390–405):

> εἰ δὲ ἐπιμηκεστέρα γέγονεν ἡ ἐπιμέλεια, μὴ θαυμάσῃς· διαφόρους γὰρ πράξεις ἐν ἑνὶ λέγειν καιρῷ ἀδύνατον.
>
> Do not be surprised if the treatment (sc. of Eurypylus by Patroclus) is of greater length. For it is impossible to recount different actions at one and the same time.
>
> (sch. AbT *Il.* 12.1–2*a ex.*)

Both scholia argue against an equation of story time and narrative time. The duration of the latter is not automatically indicative of the former, especially not when many different things are happening in multiple locations. Even if some ancient readers were genuinely disconcerted, for example, by Nestor's apparent lack of self-control – but could sch. D *Il.* 14.1 (quoted in n. 19) not be formulated thus for didactic purposes?

---

19 Sch. D *Il.* 14.1: ἐζήτηται δὲ πῶς ὁ Νέστωρ ἐπὶ τοσοῦτον πίνει χρόνον, ἀρξάμενος ἀπὸ τῶν ἐσχάτων τῆς Λάμβδα. ('Question: how could Nestor have been drinking for such a long time, having begun at the end of book eleven?')

20 To clarify, story time (*erzählte Zeit*) is the time span, for example, of the 51 days that cover the *Iliad* from Chryses' arrival until Hector's burial, whereas narrative time (*Erzählzeit*) refers to the time it takes to perform (or read) the almost 16,000 lines of the poem. Cf., e.g., Genette (1972) 1980, 87–8.

–, their mistake, the equation of story time and narrative time, was readily exposed by others who pointed out the difference.[21]

3. Voice

Modern critics regularly distinguish between 'first-person narrative' and 'third-person narrative'. An example of the former is *Robinson Crusoe* ('I was born in the year 1632') or *Moby Dick* ('Call me Ishmael'), an example of the latter is Jane Austen's *Emma* ('Emma Woodhouse, handsome and clever…'). Strictly speaking, this terminology is not entirely satisfactory because the decisive factor is not whether the narrator uses the first or the third person. Decisive is whether the narrator is himself/herself a character in his/her own story, that is, whether he/she is part of his/her own narrative universe.[22] However, for the purpose of this paper it will do little harm to stick to the traditional terms 'first-person narrative' and 'third-person narrative', the main reason being that ancient scholars seem to have made a similar distinction. Unfortunately, the evidence is slim and not immediately clear. The argument rests on the interpretation of an intriguingly difficult scholion on Pseudo-Lucian:

> καὶ ποτὲ μὲν ὡς ἀπὸ πρώτου προσώπου δραματικῶς, ποτὲ δὲ ὡς ἀπὸ τρίτου ἀφηγηματικῶς, ὅπερ πολὺ παρὰ Πλάτωνι τῷ φιλοσόφῳ ἐστιν εὑρεῖν.
>
> Now as if (?) from the first person in the dramatic mode, now as if (?) from the third <person> in the narrative mode, as it is often found in the philosopher Plato.
>
> (sch. Luc. 58.2, p. 224 Rabe)

Not untypically of this kind of source material, the text of the scholion has reached posterity in abbreviated form and requires a good deal of interpretation. It seems clear, though, that a distinction is being made between 'as if from the first person', on the one hand, and 'as if from

---

21 It remained for modern narrators to toy with the deliberate confusion of narrative time and story time, for example: 'It is about an hour and a half's tolerable good reading since my uncle *Toby* rung the bell, when *Obadiah* was order'd to saddle a horse, and go for Dr. *Slop*, the manmidwife; – so that no one can say, with reason, that I have not allowed *Obadiah* time enough, poetically speaking, and considering the emergency too, both to go and come; – tho', morally and truly speaking, the man, perhaps, has scarce had time to get on his boots.' (L. Sterne, *Tristram Shandy*, vol. 2, ch. 8)
22 Genette (1972) 1980, 243–5, who therefore distinguishes between homo- and heterodiegetic narrators.

the third person', on the other. The former is called 'dramatic', the latter 'narrative'. The distinction between 'dramatic' and 'narrative' has parallels elsewhere (see below). It is, however, necessary first to analyse the passage which the scholion actually comments on.[23] It is the opening of Pseudo-Lucian's *Encomium of Demosthenes*, a text which begins with a more or less open imitation of the narrative situation in texts such as Plato's *Republic, Charmides* and *Lysis*: a short opening narrative explains how the first-person narrator ran into another character. Their subsequent dialogue is then quoted in direct speech, which is regularly punctuated by the narrator's remarks 'and I said' or 'and he said'.[24] At this point a sceptic might be inclined to stop any further attempt to bring this scholion into connection with the distinction between first-person and third-person narrative. He/she might argue that all the scholion meant to say is that there is an alternation between 'what I said' (that is, as if from the first person) and 'what he said' (that is, as if from the third person). This narrative situation is often found in Plato. Period. Such an objection may well be right. Its main weakness is that it does not account for the fact that the scholion illustrates a first pair of opposing concepts, 'first *versus* third person', with a second pair, 'dramatic *versus* narrative'. More appears to be at stake in this fascinating scholion.

A good starting point is indeed the distinction between δραματικῶς ('dramatic') and ἀφηγηματικῶς ('narrative'), which is known from other sources. In essence it originates with Plato's famous discussion in *Republic* book 3 (393d–394d), where he distinguishes three types of literary art: (1) pure narrative, which does not contain speeches, (2) pure drama, which does not have a surrounding narrator-text, (3) a mixture of the two. Plato's model proved to be highly influential, and it per-

---

23 Careful examination of the text that is commented on in the scholion is generally advisable (Dickey 2007, 142), especially in the case of scholia that presuppose much information without spelling it out, as they tend to do.
24 'While I was walking on the far side of the Porch – on the left as you go out – shortly before noon on the sixteenth of the month, I was met by Thersagoras who will perhaps be known to some of you ... Now, when I saw him still coming towards me, I said, "Where's Thersagoras the poet going? And where's he come from?" – "I've been at home" he said, "and I've come here." – "For a stroll?" said I. – "Of course," said he, ...' (Ps.-Lucian, *Dem. Enc.* 1)

vades ancient discussions of the topic.[25] One of the side effects is a considerable terminological variety, as the following table illustrates:

Pure Narrative	Drama	Mixture
ἀφ-/διηγηματικόν	μιμητικόν	μικτόν
ἀπαγγελτικόν	δραματικόν	ἐξ/δι'
ἀμίμητον		ἀμφοτέρων
διεξοδικόν		

In the present context the individual terms need not be discussed in detail.[26] It is, however, worth emphasising that μιμητικόν and δραματικόν are synonyms in this model.[27] In addition to the terminological variety, one can also see extensions and adaptations of the Platonic model, for example, by applying the terms not only to entire texts, but also to parts of texts. Consequently, it is not uncommon to see the speeches of a 'mixed' text referred to as μιμητικόν and the narrator-text as διηγηματικόν (examples below). It is, therefore, fair to assume that the distinction between 'speech' and 'narrative' is relevant to the interpretation of the scholion on Pseudo-Lucian. This said, the reference to Plato at the end of the scholion remains a puzzling factor. Its relevance does not immediately become clear. In this connection it will be worth remembering that there is evidence for an ancient categorisation of Plato's dialogues as being either 'dramatic' or 'narrative'.[28] The former group of dramatic dialogues will have included purely dialogic texts such as *Euthyphro*, *Crito*, or *Phaedrus*, whereas the latter will have comprised texts such as the *Republic*, *Charmides*, or *Parmenides*, which all have a framing narrative. The scholion's reference to Plato probably needs to be read against the backdrop of this bipartition. This interpretation has a flaw, though. The framing narratives of Plato's narrative dialogues are actually *first*-person narratives, not third-person narratives. And so is the very

---

25 On the passage from Plato see also Halliwell, this volume, who agrees that this is how it has been understood by ancient and modern readers, though he argues that this is a simplification.
26 For discussion and references see Nünlist 2009, Chapter 3, esp. 94–9.
27 This reflects the narrower, 'Platonic' meaning of μίμησις ('imitation', 'impersonation' and hence 'speech'), as opposed to the broader, 'Aristotelian' meaning ('imitation' in the general sense of 'representation in art'). Needless to say, a heterogeneous corpus such as the scholia contains attestations of both meanings. The present account is restricted to cases where μιμητικόν refers to 'drama' or 'speech' and ἀμίμητον to 'pure narrative'.
28 Cf. Plut. *quaest. conv.* 711b–c, D.L. 3.50.

text to which the scholion refers, Pseudo-Lucian's *Encomium of Demosthenes* (cf. n. 24). This creates a difficulty, but not a fatal one.

The wider context in which Plato introduces the tripartition 'narrative-dramatic-mixed' (*R.* 393d–394d) expresses his objections to what ensues from direct speech (μίμησις). It forces the poet to slip into the role of the character whom he impersonates or 'mimes', to which Plato takes exception. At the beginning of *Iliad* 1, for example, Homer speaks as if he were the priest Chryses (*Il.* 1.17–21). And when he refers to himself, he obviously does so in the first person ('I, Chryses'). Conversely, in Plato's 'purely narrative' rewriting of the same passage, Chryses and the other characters are continuously referred to in the third person. Read against this backdrop, it seems likely that ὡς ἀπὸ πρώτου προσώπου ('as if from the first person') and ὡς ἀπὸ τρίτου προσώπου ('as if from the third person') refer to this distinction. Consequently, the two forms are described as δραματικῶς ('dramatically', i.e., in direct speech) and ἀφηγηματικῶς ('[purely] narrative') respectively because in speeches characters speak 'as if from the first person', whereas (purely) narrative texts are written 'as if from the third person'. This, I submit, is a satisfactory interpretation of the scholion as such and one that testifies to an ancient distinction which in a way adumbrates the distinction between first- and third-person narratives. It is true, though, that the specific application of the concept to Pseudo-Lucian's *Encomium of Demosthenes* and, indirectly, Plato is less than fortunate.

Indirect support for the suggested interpretation comes from a group of scholia that reflect a similar distinction, this time between narratives in the second and third person respectively:

ἀπὸ τοῦ πρὸς αὐτὸν λόγου εἰς τὸν περὶ αὐτοῦ μετέστη.

He (sc. Pindar) went over from the narrative addressed to him (sc. the victor) to the one about him.

(sch. Pi. *N.* 7.106a)

That is to say, there is a transition in the Pindaric ode from second-person narrative ('to him') to third-person narrative ('about him'). Similar transitions are commented on in scholia on various Greek poets.[29] An-

---

29 E.g. sch. A *Il.* 17.681b *Ariston.*, sch. E. *Or.* 333, p. 133.10–11 Schwartz (more examples in Nünlist 2009, 110–12). Terminologically and conceptually such notes are indebted to the communication model of Aristotle (*Rh.* 1358a37–b2), who distinguishes between the speaker (ὁ λέγων), the addressee (πρὸς ὃν λέγει) and the subject matter (περὶ οὗ λέγει).

other scholion on Pindar is of particular interest because of its terminology. The text that is commented on is the opening of *Pythian* 11:

προοιμιάζεται δὲ κατὰ τὸν προσαγορευτικὸν λόγον καὶ οὐχὶ κατὰ τὸν διηγηματικόν· πρὸς γὰρ αὐτὰς ἀποτείνεται, οὐχὶ δὲ περὶ αὐτῶν λέγει.

He (sc. Pindar) gives a proem in the 'apostrophic' mode and not in the narrative <mode>. For he addresses them (sc. Semele and Ino, the daughters of Cadmus) and does not speak about them.

(sch. Pi. *P.* 11 inscr. b)

The distinction between second-person narrative and third-person narrative is here referred to by what seems to be standard terminology. The expression for second-person narrative, προσαγορευτικὸς λόγος ('apostrophic/addressing speech'), resembles the ancient term for 'vocative case', προσαγορευτικὴ πτῶσις, which is bound to occur in a piece of second-person narrative. The term διηγηματικός is of course the same as the word for '(pure) narrative' (cf. above). In Greek (and other Western) narrative literature third-person narrative is the prevalent mode, which can therefore count as the default type of narrative literature in general. Taken together with the scholion on Pseudo-Lucian, it seems clear that ancient scholars had at their disposal the concept of a narrative in the first, second or third person respectively.

It has been mentioned above that the terms διηγηματικόν and μιμητικόν can refer to the narrator-text and speeches respectively. One of the recurrent phrases has it that the narrator ἀπὸ τοῦ διηγηματικοῦ ἐπὶ τὸ μιμητικὸν μεταβαίνει, that is, 'he makes a transition from narrator-text to speech' (e.g. sch. bT *Il.* 4.303b *ex.*). This type of transition is of course extremely common in the Homeric epics. As a result, it is commented on in no less than seven Iliadic scholia.[30] On the one hand, this is a considerable number. On the other, the *Iliad* contains 678 speeches, that is to say, 678 transitions from narrator-text to speech. From that perspective seven scholia looks like a small number. Chances are that the phrase ἀπὸ τοῦ διηγηματικοῦ ἐπὶ τὸ μιμητικὸν μεταβαίνειν has a more restricted meaning than simply the transition from narrator-text to speech. And this is indeed the case, as the following scholion shows:

λείπει τὸ 'τάδε λέγων'. εἴωθε δὲ μεταβαίνειν ἀπὸ τοῦ διηγηματικοῦ ἐπὶ τὸ μιμητικόν.

---

30 Sch. bT *Il.* 1.17 *ex.*, bT *Il.* 4.303b *ex.*, bT *Il.* 6.45–6 *ex.*, A *Il.* 15.346 *Nic.*, T *Il.* 15.425–6 *ex.*, A *Il.* 23.855a *Ariston.*, bT *Il.* 23.855b *ex.* For the argument Nünlist 2009, 102–6.

> 'Saying this' is missing. He (sc. Homer) is wont to make transitions from narrator-text to speech.
>
> (sch. bT *Il.* 23.855*b* *ex.*)

This anonymous critic comments on the fact that the relevant line lacks the speech introduction that regularly precede Homeric speeches (e. g. 'He uttered winged words and addressed him/her'). *Iliad* 23.855 does lack such an introduction, and so do the other passages where the phrase occurs in the scholia (de Jong (1987) 2004, 11). The conclusion is that the phrase does not simply describe any transition from narrator-text to speech, but the abrupt, unmarked transition. Obviously, this is the type of transition that is most likely to cause difficulties for a reader and is therefore deemed noteworthy. All the other transitions to speech are far too common to be commented on explicitly. At the same time the scholia on unmarked transitions are indicative of the fact that ancient scholars had a clear notion of Homeric speech introductions and their purposes.[31] The same holds true for their observation of stylistic and other differences between narrator-text and speech (see below).

Returning to the difference between first-person and third-person narrators, the following distinction is commonly made in modern criticism. A third-person narrator can have unlimited access to, for instance, the hidden thoughts of his characters because he does not enter his own narrative universe. He can, in other words, be omniscient, and most third-person narrators in ancient Greek texts are in fact omniscient.[32] Conversely, a first-person narrator cannot, by definition, be omniscient. He does, however, have the option of making use of his *ex eventu*-knowledge, the knowledge from hindsight. Following the lead of Spitzer ((1928) 1961, 448–9), critics would make a distinction between 'erlebendes Ich' (experiencing I) and 'erzählendes Ich' (narrating I). 'Experiencing I' means that the first-person narrator recounts the events as he experienced them at the time, that is to say, *without* making use of his *ex eventu*-knowledge. A 'narrating I', on the other hand, does make use of his *ex eventu*-knowledge. The distinction between 'experiencing' and 'narrating I' is not made as such in ancient literary criticism, but the scholia do comment on Odysseus making use of his *ex eventu*-knowledge in the *Apologues*. For example, in the narrative of his encounter

---

31 This understanding extends, among other things, to the way in which speech introductions have an influence on how the audience understand the subsequent speech; see Nünlist 2009, 316–18.
32 Cf. the relevant chapters and the index s.v. in de Jong – Nünlist – Bowie 2004.

with the Cyclops, Odysseus recounts that he expected Polyphemus to be wild and lawless (*Od.* 9.213–15). Strictly speaking, he could not have known this before he actually met him. However, the scholion on the passage argues that this is not really an inconsistency:

προληπτικῷ γὰρ τρόπῳ χρῆται, ἃ μετὰ ταῦτα ἐν ἀρχῇ τιθείς.

For he (sc. Odysseus) makes use of an anticipatory mode, putting at the beginning the things which he learned only afterwords.
(sch. HQT *Od.* 9.229)

Odysseus makes, in other words, use of his *ex eventu*-knowledge and thereby overcomes the limitations in knowledge that normally obtain to the narrator of a first-person narrative. Essentially the same point is made in other scholia on the *Apologues*.[33] While these notes are primarily concerned with the question of apparent or real inconsistencies in the text of the *Odyssey*, it is nevertheless clear that their solutions presuppose a distinction that resembles the one between 'experiencing' and 'narrating I'.

From a systematic point of view, a narrator's omniscience (or lack thereof) is more a question of focalisation than of voice.

4. Focalisation

This last section of the paper can be brief because the main points have already been made elsewhere.[34] A short summary will suffice: ancient scholars regularly consider the question of who the speaker is, for example, the narrator or one of his characters. Consequently, a reference to the so-called λύσις ἐκ τοῦ προσώπου (lit. 'solution from the character <speaking>') often allows them to prove that alleged contradictions and inconsistencies are merely apparent because the speaker is not the same in each case (e.g. sch. A *Il.* 17.588a Ariston.). The examination of the different viewpoints also has them discuss the question as to whether or not there are instances of 'paralepsis' (the narrator intruding upon the focalisation of his characters).[35] Next, ancient critics observe that the Homeric narrator and his characters have categorically different

---

33 Cf. sch. Q *Od.* 12.240 and the implication of sch. HQV *Od.* 10.108; see in general Nünlist 2009, 125–6.
34 Cf. Nünlist 2003, revised and expanded in Nünlist 2009, Chapter 4.
35 E.g. sch. bT *Il.* 6.377 *ex.*, sch. T *Il.* 10.220b *ex.*

ways of referring to the same thing (e.g. the city of Corinth or sunrise and sunset), which is indicative of a difference in conceptualising the world.[36] Another difference concerns their respective treatment of similes and epithets. The last point is worth quoting. A papyrus commentary on book 21 of the *Iliad* contains, among other things, the following note:

ὁ Σιδώνιός φησιν ὅτ[ι] ὁ πο[ι]ητὴς ἐξέ[πε]σεν εἰς τὴν διηγη[μ]ατικὴν κατασκε[υ]ὴν μιμητικῶν ὄντων τῶν λόγω[ν.

The Sidonian (i.e. Dionysius of Sidon, second half of the second cent. BC) says that the poet fell into the style of the narrator, although the words are part of a speech.

(sch. pap. *Il.* 21.218, p. 98 Erbse)

The note is indicative of a stylistic distinction between narrator-text and speech which, Dionysius argues, is not observed in the passage under consideration.[37] The relevant line (*Il.* 21.218) comes from the speech of the river Skamander, where he describes his own bloodstained flow as ἐρατεινὰ ῥέεθρα ('lovely waters'). The crucial factor is the epithet 'lovely', as can be gathered from scholia that argue along similar lines (e.g. sch. bT *Il.* 6.377 *ex.*). Ancient scholars appear to have held the view that – in the terminology of Parry – ornamental and generic epithets belong to the domain of the narrator, not that of the characters. Passages such as *Il.* 21.218 contradict this principle, as pointed out by Dionysius. Modern scholars are likely to emphasise other differences between narrator-text and speeches in Homer, for example, the virtual absence of judgmental language from the narrator-text.[38] It is, nevertheless, remarkable that ancient scholars made a categorical distinction between narrator-text and speech. In doing so, they collected examples of 'narrator language' and 'character language' respectively. The method, if not the actual examples, is essentially the same as that of their modern successors.

Arguably the most surprising point is the recognition that a concept which looks so distinctly modern, namely 'embedded focalisation' (representation of a character's viewpoint in the narrator-text), is in fact part

---

36 Corinth: e.g. sch. A *Il.* 2.570a[1] *Ariston.*; sunrise/sunset: e.g. sch. A *Il.* 7.422 *Ariston.*
37 As often, the note is triggered by an apparent or real exception to a general 'rule'. The concern with narrative rules and exceptions testifies to systematic research on the part of ancient commentators (Nünlist 2009, 11).
38 E.g. Griffin 1986, de Jong 1988, 1997b.

of ancient scholars' arsenal too.[39] What is particularly neat about this discovery is the fact that one of the scholars in question can actually be identified. His name is Nicanor (second cent. AD), the author of a book on how to punctuate the Homeric epics, often neglected or scorned. However, the relevant scholion is further proof that one had better not treat him as a mere 'Kommagärtner' (lit. 'comma gardener', i.e., bean counter).

5. Envoy

A summary and selective paper such as the present one is unlikely to gain much from an even more summary conclusion. Instead it seems preferable to conclude with a few general remarks on the purpose of the paper and the book on which it draws:

(1) To open another season of 'chasing the πρῶτος εὑρετής' is *not* among its goals.
(2) Equally avoided are two notions that are popular with some classicists. They attempt either to defend modern approaches by pointing out their possible adumbrations or precursors in antiquity ('if it's good enough for Aristarchus, it's good enough for me') or to use the same material in order to discredit modern approaches ('this new theory doesn't teach us anything we classicists didn't know already'). Neither of these positions seems particularly helpful. What is more, they both entail the risk of glossing over significant differences between then and now and imposing on our ancient predecessors notions that are essentially foreign to them. The paper's focus on narratological concepts should not be seen as a self-contradiction. The focus itself is determined by the general topic of the conference for which the paper was written. The implication is not that narratological questions take a privileged position among the many concepts of literary criticism that can be found in the scholia (as exemplified in *The Ancient Critic at Work*). The focus on narratology could be seen as an invitation to provide evidence of similarities. However, the preceding account mentions similarities and dissimilarities alike. Among the latter, the most important one is perhaps worth repeating here. Much of the theoretical and

---

39 A crucial witness is the two interpretations of *Il.* 18.246−8 that are considered in sch. A *Il.* 18.247−8 *Nic.*, see Nünlist 2003, 65−6, 2009, 128−9.

terminological framework that modern narratology provides is absent or remains implicit. The scholia do not contain a narratological theory *avant la lettre*. But some of the reading strategies and questions/solutions show similarities that are remarkable and therefore worth pointing out.

(3) More generally, the idea is to bring the scholia (back) to the attention of modern literary critics who are interested in the methods of their ancient predecessors because scholia are an invaluable source of ancient reading strategies. Hopefully, the preceding account will have given readers a sense of what they can gain from extending their research beyond the standard treatises such as Aristotle's *Poetics*; not least so because one sometimes gets a more immediate insight into the study of ancient critics. Moreover, it should have become clear that modern scholars should not limit themselves to studying the relevant technical vocabulary. Ancient critics often give a periphrastic description of a particular phenomenon for which others may or may not have a technical term.

(4) The transmission of Greek scholia is the victim of goddess Τύχη in more than one respect, which cautions against generalising statements about the corpus as a whole, statistical comparisons ('notes on X are three times more frequent than notes on Y') or arguments from silence. This said, the transmission of the scholia is of course not entirely random. It can be no coincidence that the extant scholia on Homer (the *Iliad*, in particular) are especially rich. This state of affairs is reflected in the prominent position that Homeric scholia take in this paper. It is, nevertheless, not a paper on Homeric scholia specifically. Several concepts either have been or could have been documented by scholia to authors other than Homer. In the latter case, preference was given to Homer because the epics are so well known that the individual passage requires little contextualisation to be understood.[40]

(5) Finally a word on terminology. Readers may have noticed the absence of the word 'scholiast'. Not only does it have a derogatory ring, it also conceals the fact that the scholars in question often drew on sources of the highest quality and, no doubt, contributed many good ideas of their own. It is true that not all scholia are equally illuminating or fascinating. An inevitable characteristic of

---

[40] The reader will find numerous scholia to authors other than Homer discussed and referred to in Nünlist 2009.

a heterogeneous corpus such as the scholia is that brilliant flashs of genius and sheer stupidity can clash in immediate juxtaposition. However, to use the latter in order to discredit the corpus as a whole is methodologically questionable.

II. Narratology – New Concepts

Metalepsis in Ancient Greek Literature

Irene de Jong

1. Introduction. Why narratological terminology?

The concept of metalepsis, which forms the basis of this paper and which I will introduce shortly, derives from one of the central figures in narratology, Gerard Genette, who has devised a detailed model for analysing narrative texts.[1] In the course of setting up this model Genette introduced numerous terms, some of them his own coinage: analepsis, prolepsis, paralepsis, paralipsis, etc. Although sometimes frowned upon as 'jargon', these terms allow us to analyse literary texts in clear and unequivocal terms, much in the way that linguists are wont to proceed, or heuristically to open up new roads of interpretation.[2] As an example of the first benefit of narratological terminology, I point to the new history of Ancient Greek narrative, *Studies in Ancient Greek Narrative*, which is currently being written under my direction. The departure point of this literary history is not author and work, but rather narratological concepts. The first volume deals with the narrator and the narratee, from Homer to the novel, and the second volume with aspects of time, such as prolepses and analepses.[3] It is only when all the collaborating authors employ the *same* terms that, instead of comparing apples and oranges, we can make true comparisons or even detect points of contact between different texts in the first place.

The present paper is an example of the second or heuristic value of narratological terminology: having been alerted to the existence of something called metalepsis, I began to look for instances in Ancient

---

I wish to thank audiences in Edinburgh, Thessaloniki, Groningen, and Paris, and the members of the Amsterdam Hellenistenclub for their valuable comments and suggestions, and Mrs. B. Fasting for the correction of my English.
1 See Genette (1972) 1980, (1983) 1988.
2 See Genette's own defense of the use of technical jargon: 'Le "jargon" technique a du moins cet avantage qu'en général chacun de ses utilisateurs sait et indique quel sens il donne à chacun de ses termes' (1982, 11, n. 1).
3 See de Jong – Nünlist – Bowie 2004 and de Jong – Nünlist 2007.

Greek literature, and came up with a surprisingly large number of examples.

2. Metalepsis

The term metalepsis, lit. 'sharing', appears in ancient rhetoric, where it refers to a particular status of a juridical case, or to figures of speech such as metonymy or metaphor, when one word is used for another.[4] It was Genette who in his *Narrative discourse* ((1972) 1980) adopted the term and gave it a narratological use. In order to understand this term, we must first recall one of the basic principles of narratology, the distinction between the levels of text, story, and fabula:[5] when we read a narrative *text*, we are dealing with a narrator who recounts to his narratees a series of events, the story. The *story* is a focalized, i.e., filtered, coloured, and often temporally disordered version of the events of the fabula. The *fabula* consists of the events in their – reconstructed – chronological order and 'pure' form.

The level of the text is fundamentally different from the levels of story and fabula, that is to say, the narrator and his act of narration belong to a different time and place, a different universe than the characters in the story and fabula.[6] Even a first-person or internal narrator tells about his former self at a different (later) time and often in a different place. For example, in Homer's *Iliad* we are dealing with an external narrator, 'Homer', who tells us in a certain place (where?) and at a later time (when?) about the acts of heroes from the past in Troy and Ithaca. In J. D. Salinger's *The Catcher in the Rye*, we are dealing with an internal narrator, Holden Caulfield, who tells in a mental asylum at a later time about events in the life of the character Holden Caulfield, from the past up until the present.

---

4   Status: Hermagoras *Stat.* 2.16, Quint. *Inst. Orat.* 3.6.83–4; figure: Trypho *Trop.*, ed. Spengel 1856, 195, Quint. *Inst. Orat.* 8.6.37, Choerob. *De Figuris*, ed. Spengel 1856, 247 (I owe the latter reference to Dr. D. Sieswerda). For a discussion of the history of metalepsis as a rhetorical term, see Wagner 2002, 235–7.
5   This three-layered model derives from Bal (1985) 1997.
6   The only exception is the – extremely rare – form of simultaneous narration: a narrator, like a sports reporter, recounting events which are happening at that very moment and in that very place. See Genette (1972) 1980, 218–19.

So much for the fundamental distinction between the level or universe of the narrator and the level or universe of the events and characters. The levels text versus story and fabula are in a hierarchical relation: the narrator tells about characters, but of course the characters do not know that they are the subject of a story: they simply act or undergo events.

Armed with these basic insights into narratology, let us now return to metalepsis, as defined by Genette, and later adopted by a number of other scholars.[7] This term means that the principal distinction between, or hierachy of, levels has been broken down or violated: the narrator enters ('shares') the universe of the characters or, conversely, a character enters ('shares') the universe of the narrator.[8] Let me explain this phenomenon by means of a number of examples:

1a Ch. Brontë, *Shirley*, ch. 1
You shall see them, reader. Step into this neat garden-house on the skirts of Whinbury, walk into the little parlour – there they are at dinner ... you and I will join the party, see what is to be seen, and hear what is to be heard. At present, however, they are only eating; and while they eat we will talk aside.

The narrator and his narratees enter the world of the characters.

1b L. Sterne, *The Life and Opinions of Tristram Shandy*, V. 5
In this attitude I am determined to let her [Mrs. Shandy] stand for five minutes: till I bring up the affairs of the kitchen ... to the same periode ...

---

7 Studies on metalepsis include: Genette (1972) 1980, 234–7, (1983) 1988, 58–9, McHale 1987, Herman 1997, Wagner 2002, Fludernik 2003a, Genette 2004, Pier – Schaeffer 2005.

8 Genette (1972) 1980, 234–5: 'any intrusion by the extradiegetic narrator or narratee into the diegetic universe (or by diegetic characters into a metadiegetic universe, etc.), or the inverse'; Genette (1983) 1988, 88 'that deliberate transgression of the threshold of embedding...: when an author (or his reader) introduces himself into the fictive account of the narrative or when a character in that fiction intrudes into the extradiegetic existence of the author or reader, such intrusions disturb, to say the least, the distinction between levels'; McHale 1987, 119: 'violation of the hierarchy of narrative levels'; Herman 1997, 132: 'the interplay of situations, characters or events occupying diegetic levels that are *prima facie* distinct'; Fludernik 2003a, 383: 'the move of existents or actants from any hierarchically ordered level into one above or below (also possibly skipping intermediate levels)'.

Here the narrator freezes the events on the fabula level in order to gain time for his own narration, in other words he forsakes his fictional role of the one recounting *what has happened,* and instead reveals his real role as the *inventor* of the events recounted: he is the one who makes characters do what they do. The characters are only puppets on a string handled by the narrator. This theme is employed at great length in, e.g., Diderot's *Jacques le fataliste,* where the narrator is constantly telling us how he might have given his story a different direction.

1c J. Cortazar, *Continuity of Parks (Continuidad de los Parques)*
A man reads a novel in which a killer, approaching through a park, enters a house in order to murder his lover's husband – the man reading the novel.

Here the universes of the main story, a man reading a novel, and the embedded story, the novel he is reading, mingle and start interfering with one another.[9]

1d S. Milligan, *Puckoon,* ch. 1
He eyed them [his legs] with obvious dissatisfaction. After examining them he spoke aloud: 'Holy God! Wot are these den? Eh?' He looked around for an answer. 'Wot are dey?' he repeated angrily. 'Legs.' 'Legs? LEGS? Whose legs?' 'Yours.' 'Mine? And who are you?' 'The Author.' 'Author? Author? Did you write these legs?' 'Yes.' 'Well, I don't like dem. I don't like 'em at all at all …'.

This is perhaps the most radical form of metalepsis, when a character converses with his own author.

1e A. Robbe-Grillet, *Dans le labyrinthe* (transl. R. Howard)
[the narrator describes a picture of a bar-room scene] At the right hand side several groups of drinkers are seated around tables … A little before … a young boy is sitting on the floor … Somewhat separated … three soldiers are sitting at a small table … The contrast between the three soldiers and the crowd is further accentuated by a precision of line, a clarity in rendering, much more evident in their case than in that of other individuals the same distance from the viewer. The artist has shown them with as much concern for detail and almost as much sharpness of outline as if they were sitting in

---

[9] The same procedure is used, e.g., in M. Spark, *The Comforters* (the heroine, Caroline Rose, finds out that she is a character in a novel, and reluctant to become involved in a fictional plot, she decides to become a writer and write her own story); John Barth's *Giles Goat-Boy* (the hero meets a woman who is reading the novel *Giles Goat-Boy*, in fact the very scene in which a man meets a woman who is reading, etc.).

the foreground ... the soldier shown full face has been portrayed with a wealth of detail that seems quite out of proportion to the indifference it expresses ... He has finished his drink some time ago. He does not look as if he were thinking of leaving. Yet, around him, the cafe has emptied. The light is dim now, the bartender having turned out most of the lamps before leaving the room himself ... It is the child which speaks first: 'Are you asleep?'

What we see here is a narrator who first clearly describes a picture, referring several times to its status as work of art ('the artist has shown', 'the soldier has been portrayed'). But then the picture seems to start to come alive, a temporal dimension creeps in ('some time ago', 'now', the bartender leaves), and finally the characters in the painting start to speak. Later it will turn out that the soldier in the picture is also the main character in the story.[10] This kind of merging of two worlds is a favourite expedient not only in novels, but also in drama and film, as in, for example, Woody Allen's *Purple Rose of Cairo*.[11]

I have culled most of these examples from the studies on metalepsis which have appeared so far.[12] These studies have basically done three things: 1) distinguished between different forms of metalepsis, 2) discussed its effects, and 3) explored its historical dimension. The variation in the forms of metalepsis is reflected in the five different examples given above. As for its effect, opinions differ: according to Genette, metalepsis 'produces an effect of strangeness that is either comical or phantastic'. McHale suggests that metalepsis lays bare the fictionality of fiction, and adds that the device, which shows fictional characters as puppets in the hands of their authors, may function as a metaphor for us mortals, who are puppets of fate or history. Wagner likewise stresses that the effect of metalepsis is to reveal the constructedness of literary texts (their textualisation), while Genette 2004 refers to a 'ludic pretense of belief' on the part of the reader, instead of the normal

---

10 Interestingly, Lethcoe 1965 suggests that we are in fact dealing with the figments of the mind of a feverish (indeed dying) soldier who is looking at a picture in his hospital room and begins to 'enter' the picture. This reading thus provides a realistic explanation for the metalepsis.
11 Genette 2004, in particular, discusses many examples of metalepsis in film and drama, making it clear that it is not only a narratological concept but that it may be applied to other texts in which the worlds of characters and author/audience meet. In my paper I will concentrate on metalepsis in narrative texts.
12 See n. 7.

'suspension of disbelief'.[13] Fludernik, however, remarks that while metalepsis *may* have the effect of undermining the mimetic illusion and realistic expectations of a novel, it is not *necessarily* an 'anti-illusionistic device' (2003a, 392). This will turn out to be a very important observation when discussing metalepsis in Ancient Greek literature.

This brings me to my third point, the historical dimension. Can we actually expect to encounter metalepsis in ancient texts? The first examples put forward by Genette were derived largely from postmodern novels (Robbe-Grillet, Cortazar), although he does mention some examples from earlier novels, which however are well-known for their meta-reflective or self-conscious nature, such as Laurence Stern and Diderot. The idea that metalepsis belongs mainly to the modern or postmodern era was reinforced by the chapter on metalepsis in Brian McHale's study *Postmodernist fiction*. He discusses examples from John Barth, Pynchon, Brooke-Rose, Garcia Marquez, and Calvino, and on p. 120 remarks that 'postmodern examples could be multiplied'. Both Wagner and Fludernik, however, provide examples from earlier texts, such as Cervantes and Sidney's *Arcadia*, pushing the history of the device back several centuries. In the course of her paper Fludernik even – tantalizingly – remarks: 'Metalepsis is not an exclusively postmodern device. It has a long history reaching back to the Renaissance and, *possibly, to antiquity*.' (2003a, 393, my italics).

In his recent study of metalepsis Genette does indeed discuss one example from antiquity, the description of Achilles' new shield in *Iliad* 18, where the figures on the shield come alive, move and speak, much like those in the picture at the beginning of Robbe-Grillet's *Dans le labyrinthe*, example 1e.[14] In a 2005 French volume on metalepsis, Rabau comes up with another ancient example – which strictly speaking is no real example and yet belongs to the same sphere of the mixing of narrator and characters:

---

13 Genette (1972) 1980, 235; McHale 1987, 123; Wagner 2002, 239 ('les métalepses, dans leur diversité, ont toutes en commun le fait de signaler l'essence construite du récit, c'est-à-dire le procès de textualisation'), 250 ('la capacité de dénudation du médium littéraire'); Genette 2004, 24–5 ('La métalepse ne serait donc plus une simple figure (traduisible), mais bien une fiction à part entière, à prendre ou à laisser... fiction certes, mais fiction de type fantastique, ou merveilleux, qui ne peut guère attendre une pleine et entière suspension d'incrédulité, mais seulement une simulation ludique de crédulité.').

14 I discuss the Shield as an instance of metalepsis in a forthcoming paper in a volume on ekphrasis, edited by M. Fantuzzi and M. Paschalis.

(2) Lucian, A true story II, 15
(the narrator arrives on the Isle of the Blessed, the Elysian fields, and there sees how the blessed dead eat):
Ἐπὶ δὲ τῷ δείπνῳ μουσικῇ τε καὶ ᾠδαῖς σχολάζουσιν· ᾄδεται δὲ αὐτοῖς τὰ Ὁμήρου ἔπη μάλιστα· καὶ αὐτὸς δὲ πάρεστι καὶ συνευωχεῖται αὐτοῖς ὑπὲρ τὸν Ὀδυσσέα κατακείμενος.
During dinner they pass their time with poetry and song. For the most part they sing the epics of Homer, who is there himself and shares the revelry, lying on a couch above Odysseus.[15]

In this paper I will present many more passages which in my view may be considered examples of metalepsis. I will start with four forms of metalepsis of which I have found more than one example, and end with a rest category of incidental instances. Most of the examples derive from early Greek literature, but there are occasionally examples from Hellenistic and Imperial times. I suspect that there are in fact many more examples to be found in these later periods, but I will leave it to the specialists to collect and discuss them more systematically.

3. Metalepsis in Greek Literature 1: apostrophe in narrative texts

A first, relatively straightforward example of metalepsis is the use of apostrophe in a narrative text: when a narrator *turns away* from his normal addressee, the narratee, to address one of his characters, thereby entering the narrated world.[16] The Homeric epics provide numerous examples, e.g.:

(3) *Iliad* 16.692–3
Ἔνθα τίνα πρῶτον, τίνα δ' ὕστατον ἐξενάριξας,

---

15 Very similar confrontations between Homer and his characters in Philostr. *Her.* 25.45 and 43.15.
16 The term 'apostrophe' derives from rhetoric, cf. e.g. Quint. *Inst. Orat.* 4.1.69, 9.2.38–9. It refers to a speaker 'turning away' from his normal audience to another, second audience, which may consist of the opponent (in a trial), absent persons, living or dead, or things (fatherland, building, etc.). The Quintilian concept is discussed in Franchet-d'Espèrey 2006. In the modern definition of e.g. Cuddon (1976) 1991, the aspect of turning away has disappeared: 'a figure of speech in which a thing, a place, an abstract quality, an idea, a dead or absent person, is addressed as if present and capable of understanding'. Indeed, in English, French, and German the word 'apostrophe' is used for any solemn address.

> Πατρόκλεις, ὅτε δή σε θεοὶ θάνατόνδε κάλεσσαν;
> Then who was the first, and who the last that you killed,
> Patroclus, when the gods called you to your death?

The narrator addresses Patroclus on many other occasions (8 x) and Menelaus as well (7 x), while Melanippus and Achilles are apostrophied once, and Apollo twice; in the *Odyssey* it is only Eumaeus who is apostrophied, no fewer than 15 times.

Scholars are divided on the evaluation of these apostrophes. We can divide their interpretations into three groups. 1) The apostrophe is merely a metrical expedient to fit in certain names (Matthews 1980); this may be true for the largely formulaic speech-introductions featuring Eumaeus, but it does not seem to tell the whole story. A variant of this interpretation is the suggestion by Yamagata 1989 that the apostrophes are either ready-made expressions which the poet has borrowed from dialogue (where vocatives of course are at home) or, in the case of Patroclus and Eumaeus, new coinages, which allow him to use their stock epithets ἱππεύς and συβώτης. 2) The apostrophe is used by the narrator only in connection with certain characters, who are vulnerable but loyal, in order to give expression to his sympathy (scholia, Parry 1972, Block 1982, Martin 1989, 35–6,[17] Kahane 1994, 104–13). This works for Patroclus and Eumaeus, but is less convincing for Achilles, Apollo, and Menelaus. 3) The apostrophe is a marked way of speaking, employed to call attention to a turning point in the narrative (Mackay 2001).[18] Again this interpretation works in most but not all instances.[19]

---

[17] In fact, Martin goes further than Parry and Block. He contends that the apostrophes of Patroclus in Book 16 suggest that 'Homer himself sees his death through the eyes of Achilles, his alter ego, ... who most often addresses Patroklos in the course of the poem'. In my view, it is not narratologically sound to call Achilles the 'focalizer of narration' in Book 16, as Martin does. There is no indication that Achilles is witnessing what is happening to Patroclus; on the contrary, cf. 18.5–15.

[18] Block 1982, 8 also notes that the apostrophe occurs at 'emotional junctures', and cf. Franchet-d'Espèrey 2006, 179: 'L'apostrophe a alors cette valeur de mise en relief'.

[19] The explanation works for the apostrophes of Menelaus in 4.127, 146 (his wounding, which means a reopening of hostilities), 7.104 (in combination with 'if not'-situation, to mark his near death), 17.679, 702 (he has to give up the defence of Patroclus' body); of Patroclus, all in book 16 (they underscore his climactic role as Achilles' stand-in, and more specifically mark the steps leading to to his death); of Apollo in 15.365–6 (destroying the wall

Looking at the apostrophe in terms of metalepsis leads me to the following interpretation. Taking all the instances together, the sum effect of the apostrophe is to add to that vital characteristic of Homeric epic, *enargeia*: the events are presented in such a way that they seem to take place before the eyes of the narratees. Addressing characters directly is as 'enargetic' as the many speeches, when the narratees seem to actually hear the characters, impersonated by the narrator.[20] Moreover, the metaleptic apostrophe also adds to the authority of the Homeric narrator's story: his characters are real, since they can be addressed.

We might even go one step further. The two apostrophes of Apollo very much resemble the 'Du-Stil'[21] typical of hymns:

(5) *Iliad* 15.365–6
ὥς ῥα σύ, ἤϊε Φοῖβε, πολὺν κάματον καὶ ὀϊζὺν
σύγχεας Ἀργείων, αὐτοῖσι δὲ φύζαν ἐνῶρσας.
So you, Eïan Apollo, smashed the result of the exertion and toil
of the Greeks and started a panic among them.
For which compare:
(6) *Homeric hymn to Apollo* 119–21 (ed. M. West 2003)
ἐκ δ' ἔθορε πρὸ φόωσδέ, θεαὶ δ' ὀλόλυξαν ἅπασαι.
ἔνθα σὲ, ἤϊε Φοῖβε, θεαὶ λόον ὕδατι καλῷ
ἁγνῶς καὶ καθαρῶς ...
And he sprang out into the light, and all the goddesses gave a yell.
And there they washed you in clear water, Eïan Apollo,
in pure and holy fashion ...

In the case of hymns, the 'Du-Stil' is entirely natural, since hymns are like prayers: its singer(s) address(es) the god, who is supposedly present or at least able to hear the hymn wherever he is.[22] The two apostrophes

---

around the Greek camp which has been fought over for books); and of Achilles in 20.2 (he is about to return to battle for the first time after his *menis*). I agree with Mackay (and Yamagata), however, that the apostrophe of Eumaeus is a mere formula which has lost its apostrophic impact through repetition. The apostrophes of Menelaus in 13.603 (death of Pisander) and 23.600 (he is pleased with Antilochus' pacifying gesture), of Melanippus in 15.582 (attacked by Antilochus), and of Apollo at 20.152 (gods seat themselves around Ares and Apollo) cannot convincingly be interpreted as marking vital points.

20 For the importance of *enargeia*, see e.g. Ford 1992, 54–6. For a discussion of many linguistic markers which suggest *enargeia*, see Bakker 1997.
21 The term derives from Norden (1913) 1996, 149–60.
22 For the 'Du-Stil' of cultic hymns, sung by choruses, see Bremer – Furley 2001, 1–64. The more literary rhapsodic Homeric hymns contain only remnants of this 'Du-Stil' in their salutations at the end of the poems (e.g., *h.Cer.* 490–4: 'So come, *you* that preside over the people of fragrant Eleusis,

of Apollo in the Homeric epics may thus have been borrowed by the narrator from a hymnic context. In the case of the apostrophes of *mortal* characters, finally, I wonder whether this phenomenon might be linked to the Homeric narrator thinking of his heroes as 'semi-divine', ἡμιθέων γένος ἀνδρῶν (12.23).[23]

Turning now to the individual instances, I contend, with Mackay, that the metalepsis involved in apostrophe creates pragmatically marked moments: for an instant, the distinction between the – temporal and spatial – universes of the narrator and the narrated world collapses.[24] Such pragmatically marked passages are generally inserted by the narrator at vital (cf. interpretation 3) and/or emotional (cf. interpretation 2) points in the story. In this respect the apostrophe is comparable to Muse-invocations and narratorial questions of the type 'there whom first and whom last did he kill?', which likewise mark vital points in the story.[25] Indeed in the case of example 3 we even find the two devices, apostrophe and narratorial question, combined, in order to mark this dramatic moment of Patroclus' success just prior to his death.

At this point it may be instructive to note that apostrophe also occurs in *speech*, e. g.:

(4) *Odyssey* 24.191–3
    Τὸν δ' αὖτε ψυχὴ προσεφώνεεν Ἀτρείδαο:

---

and seagirt Paros and rocky Antron, Lady, bringer of resplendent gifts in season, mistress Deo, both *you* and your daughter, beautiful Persephone: be favorable and grant comfortable livelihood in return for my singing.'). The *Hymn to Apollo* is unique in that second-person forms also occur *in the course of* the narrative body of the hymn.

23 Yamagata 1989, 97 also points to a possible origin of the apostrophe of Apollo in hymns, but uses this connection as an argument in favour of apostrophe as an oral-formulaic device. Cf. also Fraenkel 1950, 698 (at the end of his discussion of A. *Ag.* 1470 f.), who speaks of the 'secularization of this originally hieratic form of address'.

24 Cf. Mackay 2001, 18: 'Normally, the narrator is addressing his narrative to his listeners. Suddenly, he turns aside to address one of his characters and instantly breaks down the otherwise clear divisions between his story and the context in which he is telling it, between the here-and-now of his performance and the there-and-then of his tale'; Franchet-d'Espèrey 2006, 179: 'elle [la rupture creée par l'apostrophe] correspond à un télescopage entre énonciation et énoncé ... L'apostrophe fait émerger le narrateur et, avec lui, le niveau de l'énonciation. Seulement, l'allocutaire, lui, c'est-à-dire le personnage, n'est pas dans la situation d'énonciation, il appartient à l'énoncé.'

25 For an inventory and discussion of Muse-invocations and narratorial questions, see de Jong (1987) 2004, 45–51.

'ὄλβιε Λαέρταο πάϊ, πολυμήχαν' Ὀδυσσεῦ,
ἦ ἄρα σὺν μεγάλῃ ἀρετῇ ἐκτήσω ἄκοιτιν.'[26]
Him [Amphimedon] answered the ghost of Agamemnon:
'Blessed son of Laertes, Odysseus of many devices,
indeed you won yourself a wife endowed with great virtue.'

We find ourselves in the Underworld, where one of the suitors, Amphimedon, has just told Agamemnon how they were killed by Odysseus. Answering Amphimedon, Agamemnon turns away from this addressee in front of him and addresses absent Odysseus. The apostrophe is a clear expression of Agamemnon's emotion.[27] Interestingly enough, two of the three instances of apostrophe in Homeric speech have an eulogistic nature (ὦ μάκαρ Ἀτρεΐδη: *Il.* 3.182, ὄλβιε Λαέρταο πάϊ: *Od.* 24.192), which again points to a possible hymnic origin of the device.

I conclude that this form of ancient metalepsis, the apostrophe, differs greatly from most of its modern counterparts in both function and effect: it is neither 'anti-illusionistic' nor 'comical' but, on the contrary, adds to the authenticity of the story and the admiration for the semi-divine heroes, which is inherent in that story. At the individual level it is a pragmatically marked utterance which may be employed to highlight emotional or crucial events.

Other instances of metaleptic anastrophe in narrative (con)texts are: S. *El.* 100–2 (Agamemnon); E. *Alc.* 583–7 (Apollo); *Tro.* 840–5 (Eros), 799–807 (Telamon), 820–5 (Ganymedes); *IT* 1250–7 (Apollo); *Ph.* 818–21 (Earth); *IA* 573–89 (Paris); *El.* 1160–1 (Agamemnon); A. R. *Arg.* 4.445–9 (Eros), 1199–1200 (Hera), 1383–7a (Argonauts), 1485–9 (Canthus), 1673–5 (Zeus), 1706–9 (Apollo); Theoc. 22.85, 131–2, Call. *Jov.* passim (Zeus), *Cer.* 72–190 (Artemis), *Del.* 27–55 (Apollo), 106–7, 215–17 (Hera).[28]

---

26 Other examples are: *Il.* 3.182–3 (Priam, standing with Helen and the Trojan elders on the walls of Troy, addresses Agamemnon, who is on the Trojan plain before them) and 11.816–18 (Patroclus, seeing the wounded Eurypylus, addresses the Greeks and laments their fate).

27 For a different interpretation of this apostrophe, see Tsagalis 2003, 47–8 ('it is not so much the soul of Agamemnon that speaks, but the poet of the *Odyssey* who is actually addressing its main hero, Odysseus, whose omnipresent identity is notionally in the Underworld').

28 This list is far from complete, since there is no systematic study of apostrophe in Greek narrative. It is interesting to note that the majority of instances concern gods, which strengthens the thesis of a hymnic background of apostrophe. Thus Hunter 1993, 16, n. 68 speaks in connection with A. R. *Arg.* 4.445–9 of a 'hymnal flavour'.

4. Metalepsis in early Greek literature 2: characters announce the text in the text

I turn now to what may be considered more or less the reverse of apostrophe, where it is not the narrator who turns to one of his characters and, as it were, enters the narrated world, but one of the characters who enters the world of narration. In ancient Greek literature we find (I think) no instances of characters conversing with their narrator/author, such as we saw in *Puckoon*. But there are some interesting passages where characters 'announce' the text in which they themselves figure, e.g.:

(7) *Iliad* 6.357–8:
'οἷσιν ἐπὶ Ζεὺς θῆκε κακὸν μόρον, ὡς καὶ ὀπίσσω
ἀνθρώποισι πελώμεθ' ἀοίδιμοι ἐσσομένοισι.'
'(Hector, you have to fight hard because of Paris and myself),
on whom Zeus set a vile destiny, so that even hereafter
we shall be subjects of song for men of future generations.'

Helen's statement is a special variant of the more general notion which is often voiced by Homeric characters, that they hope to gain *kleos*, so as to be heard of even by later generations; cf. e.g. Hector in *Il.* 22.304–5. Thus most scholars have interpreted this passage, and a handful of comparable ones, from the point of view of the characters, regarding them as a consolatory motif. In a paper dating from 2006, however, I argued that passage 7 can also be interpreted metaleptically: it is impossible for the narratees not to think of the *Iliad* itself when hearing Helen's words; she would thus be 'referring to' the very text the Homeric narrator is recounting at that moment.[29] Again, the effect of this metalepsis is not phantastic nor does it destabilize the realism of the story. Rather it enhances its status and authority: the *Iliad* is anticipated in the heroic past itself, by one of the characters involved.

My examples of this type of metalepsis, i.e., a character in a text announcing that text, include *h.Ap.* 3.299: the people of Delphi built a temple for Apollo, 'to be a theme of song for ever'; Hdt. *Hist.* 7.220: Leonidas stayed in Thermopylae, because 'if he remained, he would

---

29 See de Jong 2006b, 195–8, where also more literature, to which should be added Grethlein 2006a, 143–4.

leave a name of great renown';[30] E. *Tro.* 1242–5 (Hecuba): 'if Troy had not been destroyed, we would not have been sung about, providing subjects of song to the Muses of later men';[31] X. *An.* 6.5.24 (Xenophon to his troops): 'it is sweet by saying or doing something noble and courageous now to create a lasting memory of oneself', A. R. *Arg.* 4.1143: the Argonauts cover the marriage bed of Jason and Medea with the Golden Fleece, 'so that the wedding should be honoured and become the subject of song'; Longus *Daphnis and Chloe* 2.27: the god Pan announces that Love intends to make a story out of Chloe.[32] Variants are found in E. *Alc.* 445–54: the chorus announces that the death of Alcestis will become the subject of song, whereas in fact Euripides' play portrays her as coming back to life; Theoc. 12.11: the speaker announces that he and his lover might become a subject of song for generations to come, and then immediately quotes that song. For a more recent example we may think of Shakespeare's *Julius Caesar:* '(Cassius:) How many ages hence shall this our lofty scene be acted over in states unborn and accents yet unkown.'

5. Metalepsis in Greek literature 3: blending of narrative voices

The next group of metalepsis passages concerns the blending of narrative voices. In order to make clear what I mean by this, I will start with a relatively easy and well-known example. In the *Odyssey* the Homeric narrator thrice presents a song by the singer Demodocus. Rather than turning him into a secondary narrator by quoting his words in direct speech, as he does in the case of the story-teller Odysseus in books 9–12, the narrator presents Demodocus' songs in indirect speech. In the case of the long song about Ares and Aphrodite, the dependent construction is quickly given up in favour of the independent one:

---

[30] Cf. Pelling 2006b, 93, 97: '[Helen] famously thinks of herself as the object of song, of course including Homer's own songs, just as Leonidas is inextricably linked with the Herodotus text that will ensure that his glory does not fade'.
[31] Thus far, commentators have connected Hecuba's words to the *Iliad*, but in my view they refer equally to the *Troades* itself.
[32] Cf. Morgan, J. 2004, *ad loc.:* 'the story (or myth) to be made out of C is, of course, the book we are reading'.

(8) Homer *Odyssey* 8.266–70
αὐτὰρ ὁ φορμίζων ἀνεβάλλετο καλὸν ἀείδειν
ἀμφ' Ἄρεος φιλότητος ἐϋστεφάνου τ' Ἀφροδίτης,
ὡς τὰ πρῶτ' ἐμίγησαν ἐν Ἡφαίστοιο δόμοισι
λάθρῃ· πολλὰ δὲ δῶκε ...
Striking his lyre he started to sing beautifully
about the love-affair of Ares and Aphrodite,
how they mingled in love for the first time in Hephaestus' house
in secret. And he [Ares] gave many things ...

This is nothing unusual. It is the result of what Slings has called the 'downslip' principle, the tendency, especially observable in oral or aural texts, to change from a complex to a simpler sentence structure.[33] Main clauses being easier to handle than subordinate infinitive constructions, the narrator abandons the dependent construction in favour of an independent one. We could conclude our interpretation here, and simply declare ourselves satisfied with this technical, linguistic explanation.

However, due to the change from a dependent construction to an independent one, we can no longer determine whether we are hearing the primary narrator, 'Homer', or the reported narrator,[34] Demodocus: their voices merge.[35] It is only at the end (some hundred lines later) which, as Richardson remarks, comes 'somewhat as a jolt', that we are reminded that the song was Demodocus' after all: ταῦτ' ἄρ' ἀοιδὸς ἄειδε περικλυτός (367). I am inclined to see this merging of voices as a conscious metaleptic move. The question which then presents itself is whether its effect is that 'the bards within the story are images of [Homer] himself' and that 'the songs they sing are his own songs' (Richardson 1990, 86); or rather that the voice of Demodocus is 'allowed to intrude into the discourse of the present', that his song is 'appropriated by the *Odyssey* of the present' and '"becomes" the *Odyssey*' (Bakker

---

[33] Slings 2002, 53–4, where he gives as examples of downslip: 'from part to whole, from paraphrasis to the entity that is paraphrased, from indirect to direct speech, from infinitive to finite verb, from subordinate clause to main clause, and from marked case (dative, genitive) to unmarked case (accusative, nominative).'

[34] I speak of reported narrator when dealing with a narrative which is presented in indirect speech; see de Jong (1987) 2004, 108–110.

[35] Cf. Richardson 1990, 86: 'Demodokos's voice and his own blend quite naturally into each other'; Bakker 1999, 13: 'we have here a curious blend of Demodokos, the poet of the past, and Homer, the poet of the present'.

1999, 13[36])? In other words, does Homer become Demodocus or does Demodocus become Homer? It would seem that the Homeric narrator here manages to have his cake and eat it: blending his own voice with that of a famous singer of the past (one of whose stories is, moreover, explicitly authenticated by the eyewitness Odysseus himself), he increases the authority of his own story and at the same time indicates that his own song is just as good as a song of the heroic past.[37]

A similar, and more daring, instance of metalepsis, in which the voices of primary and reported narrator blend, is found in the famous, highly complex proem to Hesiod's *Theogony* (68–75, ed. M. West 1966):

(9) αἱ τότ' ἴσαν Ὄλυμπον, ἀγαλλόμεναι ὀπὶ καλῇ,
ἀμβροσίῃ μολπῇ· περὶ δ' ἴαχε γαῖα μέλαινα
ὑμνεύσαις, ἐρατὸς δὲ ποδῶν ὕπο δοῦπος ὀρώρει
νισομένων πατέρ' εἰς ὅν· ὁ δ' οὐρανῷ ἐμβασιλεύει
αὐτὸς ἔχων βροντὴν ἠδ' αἰθαλόεντα κεραυνόν,
κάρτει νικήσας πατέρα Κρόνον· εὖ δὲ ἕκαστα
ἀθανάτοις διέταξε νόμους καὶ ἐπέφραδε τιμάς.
ταῦτ' ἄρα Μοῦσαι ἄειδον...

They next went to the Olympus, delighting in their sweet voice,
with heavenly song. The dark earth rang round
them as they sang, and from their dancing feet came a lovely thud
as they went to their father. He is king in heaven,
holding thunder and the smoking bolt,
after he had defeated his father Cronus. He well appointed, each separately,
their ordinances to the immortals and assigned them their privileges.
Those things the Muses sang ...

When we hear or read lines 71b and further, 'He is king in heaven ...', we naturally ascribe them *to the narrator*, who continues from 'as they went to their father'. It is not until 75, on hearing the typical closing phrase ταῦτ' ἄρα Μοῦσαι ἄειδον, that we realize that lines 71b-5 must represent *the Muses*' song.[38] Their singing had been indicated by ἀγαλ-

---

36 He bases this mainly on the presence in 8.367=83=521 of ταῦτα (instead of the distancing ὥς).

37 It should be noted that in the case of the third song, about the Wooden Horse, the primary narrator does return to the dependent, indirect speech construction on several occasions (514, 516).

38 Cf. Wilamowitz 1916, 468; Lenz 1980, 164–6; Thalmann 1984, 137, Bakker 1999, 11, n. 28. Some scholars make ταῦτα refer to earlier points in the proem: Aly 1913, 26–7, to 35 (36–67 being an interpolation); Büchner 1968, 24–37, to 52; Verdenius 1972, 249 (who takes τότε in 68 as referring back to 10, στεῖ-

λόμεναι ὀπὶ καλῇ, ἀμβροσίη μολπῇ, and ὑμνεύσαις, but no song had been marked grammatically by an indirect speech construction (such as we have at the beginning of Demodocus' song, example 8).

What might the intended effect of this metaleptic move be? The Hesiodic narrator has just proudly recounted how he was initiated into the art of singing by the Muses themselves (22–35). Blurring the boundaries between his song and theirs seems to subtly hint at how well he has learned their trade. Indeed, if we look at the three references to songs by the Muses in this proem – which I take to be manifestations of the same theogonic song, sung on different occasions – we see an interesting pattern:[39] in 11–21 we hear about the song omnitemporally sung by the Muses on the Helicon, as once overheard by the shepherd Hesiod;[40] in 44–51 about the song omnitemporally sung by the Muses on the Olympus, as known to the by now omniscient narrator Hesiod; in 71–75 about the song as sung for the first time by the Muses after their birth, now almost appropriated by the narrator Hesiod himself. All of this leads up to 109–13, a summary announcement of the song

---

χον) to 11–21 (22–67 being a digression). No interpreter of Hesiod's proem would nowadays consider 36–67 an interpolation, while in the other interpretations the scope of anaphoric ταῦτα is extremely – for an aural poem, unacceptably – long, while the twofold hymnic structure of the proem (with clear caesura at 35) is ignored, for which see the next note.

[39] The structure of the proem to the *Theogony* has been the subject of much debate; for an overview of scholarship see West 1966 *ad* 1–115 and Clay 2003, 49–80. For an understanding of the structure, I found Minton 1970, Lenz 1980, 123–207, and Thalmann 1984, 134–65 most helpful. The proem consists of a combination of a hymn (1–104), comparable to the Homeric hymns (*Th.* 1 Μουσάων Ἑλικωνιάδων ἀρχώμεθ' ἀείδειν ~ *h.Hom.* 11.1 Παλλάδ' Ἀθηναίην ἐρυσίπτολιν ἄρχομ' ἀείδειν; *Th.* 104 χαίρετε, τέκνα Διός, δότε δ' ἱμερόεσσαν ἀοιδήν ~ *h.Hom.* 11.5 χαῖρε, θεά, δὸς δ' ἄμμι τύχην εὐδαιμονίην τε), and a Muse-invocation (105–15), such as we find at the beginning of *Iliad* and *Odyssey* (*Th.* 105 κλείετε δ' ἀθανάτων ἱερὸν γένος αἰὲν ἐόντων ~ *Il.* 1 μῆνιν ἄειδε, θεά...). The hymn consists of two movements (1–34 and 36–104): the narrator begins by indicating the Muses as his subject, then goes on to describe their typical activity, but instead of the customary narrative paradigmatically illustrating that typical activity (cf. e.g. *h.Ven.* 5.45 ff., where the story about Aphrodite falling in love herself illustrates her power as the goddess of love), he inserts a narrative on how the Muses taught him to sing. With line 35 he breaks off this story and at 36 starts hymning anew, again indicating the Muses as his subject, and then proceeds with a narrative of their birth and journey to Zeus' palace on the Olympus, and a description of their power.

[40] Cf. Méautis 1939, 575; Minton 1970, 367–9. According to Lenz 1980, 152–3, the Muses sing for themselves and are not overheard by mortals.

to be sung by Hesiod himself together with the Muses: the *Theogony*. We see how the narrator gradually takes over the initiative from the Muses: from their casual audience he turns into a professional colleague, who, with superior self-confidence, enlists their co-operation.[41]

I move on to a comparable but even more complex instance of the blending of narrative voices, which is found in Pindar:

(10) *Nemean* 5.25–39 (ed. Snell-Maehler 1980)

αἱ δὲ πρώτιστον μὲν ὕμνη- 25
σαν Διὸς ἀρχόμεναι σεμνὰν Θέτιν
Πηλέα θ', ὥς τέ νιν ἁβρὰ
Κρηθεῒς Ἱππολύτα δόλῳ πεδᾶσαι
ἤθελε ...,
ψεύσταν δὲ ποιητὸν συνέπαξε λόγον, 29
... τὸ δ' ἐναντίον ἔσκεν· ... 31
... ὁ δ' εὖ φράσθη κατένευ-
σέν τέ οἱ ...
Ζεὺς ἀθανάτων βασιλεύς, ὥστ' ἐν τάχει 35
ποντίαν χρυσαλακάτων τινὰ Νη-
ρεΐδων πράξειν ἄκοιτιν,
γαμβρὸν Ποσειδάωνα πείσαις, ὃς Αἰγᾶθεν ποτὶ κλει-
τὰν θαμὰ νίσεται Ἰσθμὸν Δωρίαν·
ἔνθα νιν εὔφρονες ἶλαι
σὺν καλάμοιο βοᾷ θεὸν δέκονται,
καὶ σθένει γυίων ἐρίζοντι θρασεῖ. 39

[the narrator recounts how the Muses sang at the wedding of Peleus and Thetis] And, after a prelude to Zeus, they first sang of august Thetis and Peleus, how the elegant daughter of Cretheus, Hippolyta ... sought to snare him [Peleus] by a trick ... and made up a false tale (viz. that Peleus was courting her) ... But the reverse was true ... (Peleus rejects Hippolyta's avances) And ... Zeus ... observed it well and promised to him [Peleus] ... that he would soon make a sea nymph, one of the Nereids ... to be his bride, after persuading their brother-in-law, Poseidon, who often goes from Aegae to the famous Dorian Isthmus, where joyous crowds receive the god to the sound of the pipe and compete with the bold strength of their limbs.

---

41 My analysis complements that of Thalmann (1984) 138–9, who notes a progression in the *contents* of the Muses' songs, and concludes: 'they [the Muses' three songs] are essentially the same song ... The song for which he finally asks their aid (ll. 104–15) combines the subjects of their performances and uses motifs and phrases from all the previous descriptions. The Muses' gift to the mortal poet, the *Theogony* itself, is the human realization of the divine song.'

We see the same phenomenon as in Homer (example 8): the beginning of the Muses' song is marked by the primary narrator, Pindar, by a verb of singing ('they first sang of Thetis and Peleus ...') and by an indirect speech construction ('... how elegant Hippolyta sought to snare him'); from 'she put together a false tale' onwards, however, the dependent construction is given up in favour of an independent one, and the voices of the primary narrator and the reported narrators, the Muses, begin to merge. The difference with Homer (and Hesiod) is that there is no closing remark, 'those things the Muses sang'. As Young (1968, 84, n. 2) notes, 'it is impossible to distinguish where the song of the Muses ends and the poet's narrative resumes', Personally, I would suggest that in line 37, with 'Poseidon often going to the Isthmus', we enter an omnitemporal world, which forms the transition, in customary Pindaric fashion, to the present of the narrator ('where joyous crowds receive'), who by now has again completely taken over from the reported narrators, the Muses. Pfeijffer, in his commentary on this ode, goes much further: the absence of a closing tag 'conveys the suggestion that the remainder of the ode, including the praise of Pytheas and his family, is part of the song of the Muses.... By creating the illusion that the Muses are still singing when the victories are mentioned, the Aeginetan chorus performing the present ode merges with the chorus of the Muses'.[42]

No matter where we place the end of the song of the Muses, the effect of the metaleptic move is comparable to that in Hesiod: the mortal narrator proudly showing his close collaboration with the Muses.[43] It also reinforces the much sought-after alligning of the heroic world of the past and the present of the aristocratic victors: the Muses seem to be singing at the celebration of the athlete.

At this point, there is a methodological issue to be addressed: how can we be sure that we are dealing with a conscious metaleptic move on

---

42 Pfeijffer 1999a, 72–3, and cf. 79–80, 85–6, 142. In this interpretation, *Nem.* 5.40–54 would be an instance of metaleptic fade-out; see my section 6 below.

43 Cf. Pfeijffer 2004, 230, 'a specimen of proud self-consciousness'. Stern 1971, 173 also notes the 'subtle merging' of narrative voices, which he interprets – not convincingly, in my view – as 'a revitalization of the ode which parallels the revitalization of Peleus: both descend to a nadir, but by a specifically stressed contact with divinity, both also succeed in rescuing themselves from that depth. To this extent the merging of Pindar and the Muses into a unit represents exactly the same thing as the marriage of Peleus and Thetis ...'.

the part of Pindar, rather than a simple instance of downslip? Here I would point out that, when he so wishes Pindar is perfectly capable of having a reported narrator tell a story from beginning till end in *oratio obliqua*. An example is found in *Nemean* 1, where in line 61 the seer Tiresias is quoted as prophesying the life of Heracles, a prophecy which continues until line 74, the very end of the poem, and which is marked as indirect speech throughout. In other words, no change is made to an independent construction, nor is there any merging of the voices of primary and reported narrator.[44]

Other examples of the third type of metalepsis, i.e., the merging of the voices of primary and reported narrator, are *h.Pan* 19.27–47: nymphs sing 'about the gods and above all Pan, how …'. From 31 onwards the dependent construction is abandoned in favour of an independent one and the voices of primary narrator and reported narrators, the nymphs, blend; Pi. O. 13.61–92: the reported narrator Glaucus begins to recount the story of his father Bellerophon in indirect speech, but in 66 we change to an independent construction and the voices of reported and primary narrator begin to merge, until the primary narrator Pindar breaks off the tale in 92; A. R. *Argon.* 1.496–512: the song of Orpheus is presented in indirect speech, with the verb of speaking being repeated more than once, but from 507 onwards we are dealing with an independent construction, while in 512 the song is capped by an unmistakable reference to its singer Orpheus; A. R. *Argon.* 2.705–13: once more a song of Orpheus, about Apollo, is represented in indirect speech, but in 708 an apostrophe of the god is inserted, so that it is impossible to decide whether it is voiced by Orpheus or by the primary narrator Apollonius;[45] Theoc. 7.83–9: from 72 onwards we are dealing with a representation by Lycidas in indirect speech of a song by Tityrus, but the sudden apostrophe of Comatas at 83–9 seems to be voiced by Lycidas himself.[46] Closely comparable are cases

---

44 Cf. 61: φράζε; 66: φάσε; 69: ἔνεπεν. Cf. also *I.* 8.31–45, where a reported narrator, Themis, is first quoted in indirect speech, which in 35a becomes direct speech, which in 45–45a is capped by attributive discourse.
45 For both Apollonian examples, cf. Hunter 1993, 149 ('in the final six verses of the song, our uncertainty as to whether the words are those of Orpheus or of the poet increases; the mingling of voices, our uncertainty as to "who speaks", is crucial. Orpheus and the poet have become one'); 150–1 ('in fact it is not possible to distinguish the voices here').
46 Cf. Hunter 1999, 72–3: 'the direct address to Komatas in 83–9 fuses Tityros' song with a personal intrusion by Lykidas … into that song'.

where *direct* speeches by characters are not capped, but imperceptibly merge into the story of the primary narrator: Pi. *O.* 7.34 ff.: Apollo's oracle to Tlapolemus is indirectly quoted but merges into a story by the Pindaric narrator about the birth of Athena;[47] B. *Ode* 3.76 ff.: Apollo speaks to Adrastus, but gradually, in lines 85, 87, 92?, the narrator takes over again;[48] in B. *Ode* 3.10–14 it is not clear who is voicing the *makarismos* of Hiero, the narrator or characters in the story of his victory. A variant appears in B. *Ode* 20.1–3, which starts with 'Once in Sparta the blonde (daughters) of the Lacedaemonians sang a song *such as this* …'.[49]

6. Metalepsis in Greek literature 4: fade-out

My last type of metalepsis features the merging of the world of the narrated and the world of the narrator at the end of narratives, for which reason I speak of fade-out. An example is:

(11) Bacchylides *Paian/Dithyramb* 17.128–32 (ed. Snell-Maehler 1970)
      ἀγλαό-
  θρονοί τε κοῦραι σὺν εὐ-
  θυμίαι νεοκτίτωι
  ὠλόλυξαν, ἔ-
κλαγεν δὲ πόντος· ἠίθεοι δ' ἐγγύθεν
νέοι παιάνιξαν ἐρατᾶι ὀπί.
Δάλιε, χοροῖσι Κηΐων
φρένα ἰανθείς
ὄπαζε θεόπομπον ἐσθλῶν τύχαν.
(When Theseus resurfaces from the sea after a miraculous dive) the splendid-throned maidens cried out
with new-founded joy,
and the sea rang out; and nearby the youths

---

47 Cf. Young 1968, 84, n. 2: 'there is no clearly marked break, but Apollo's oracular response becomes Pindar's myth imperceptibly'.
48 Cf. Führer 1967, 59–60; Pfeijffer 2004, 231–2: 'this trick of merging the primary and secondary narrators contributes to the encomiastic aims of the ode. For the suggestion is conveyed that the praise of Hieron is sanctioned by divine authority'.
49 Cf. Zimmermann 1992, 104: 'Auf alle Fälle wird durch das Ineinandergreifen der mythischen und aktuellen Zeitebene … erreicht, dass im Ritus, in der Aufführung des Chorlieds, der Mythos zu Aktualität wird und gleichzeitig die Gegenwart ihren Wert, ihre Bedeutung und ihre Deutung im Gesang des Chores aus dem Mythos erhält'.

raised a paean with lovely voice.
God of Delos, rejoice in your heart
at the choirs of the Ceans
and grant a heaven-sent fortune of blessings.

The maidens and youths are the seven Athenian girls and boys who accompany Theseus on his dangerous mission to Crete to bring tribute to the Minotaur, i. e. to be sacrificed to this monster. So far the entire song has dealt with the sea-voyage of Theseus and the young Athenians to Crete, during which Theseus fights a verbal duel with Minos, which ends with an athletic trial for Theseus, his dive into the sea. Against all odds, he survives the trial and the maidens and youths start singing a song of gratitude. When at this point the words 'God of Delos, rejoice in your heart' resound, the hearers of the poem will assume they are hearing the beginning of the paean of the young Athenians. Only in the course of the sentence does it become clear that the words must be connected with the chorus of the Ceans which sings Bacchylides' poem at the Delian festival. The worlds of narrated and narrator merge, the metalepsis serving to bring together past and present and to show the continuity between myth and actuality.[50]

The same device is found, in a highly complex form, in the *Hymn to Apollo*, which also brings us back to the subject of apostrophe:

(12) *Homeric hymn to Apollo* 146–76 (ed. M. West 2003)
ἀλλὰ σύ, Δήλῳ, Φοῖβε, μάλιστ' ἐπιτέρπεαι ἦτορ,
ἔνθα τοι ἑλκεχίτωνες Ἰάονες ἠγερέθονται
αὐτοῖς σὺν παίδεσσι γυναιξί τε σὴν ἐς ἀγυιαν·
οἱ δέ σε πυγμαχίῃ τε καὶ ὀρχηστυῖ καὶ ἀοιδῇ
μνησάμενοι τέρπουσιν ὅταν καθέσωσιν ἀγῶνα.   150
φαίη κ' ἀθανάτους καὶ ἀγήρως ἔμμεναι ἀνήρ,
ὃς τότ' ἐπαντιάσει', ὅτ' Ἰάονες ἀθρόοι εἶεν·

---

50 Cf. Snell 1932, 10–11; Käppel 1992, 177; Zimmermann 1992, 85 ('Der Jubel der Knaben und Mädchen ... wird zum Gebet des Chors ... *ohne dass durch inhaltliche oder metrische Signale die beiden Ebenen durch eine Zäsur getrennt würden*'; my italics); Maehler 1997, 210 ('der Paian, den die athenischen ἠΐθεοι anstimmen ... übergeht in den Paian des Chores aus Keos, der bis hierher den "Chor" der ἠΐθεοι gleichsam dargestellt hatte: die Mythenerzählung mündet in die Gegenwart der Aufführung ein'). Snell, followed by Rösler 1975, mentions as a parallel Sappho 44, where the embedded myth (and the poem itself) ends with a bridal song being sung at the wedding of Hector and Andromache. Assuming that Sappho's poem also was a bridal song, he concludes that the songs of the past and present merge. The identification of *Ode* 44 as a bridal song is contested, however, and I hesitate to call this an instance of metalepsis.

πάντων γάρ κεν ἴδοιτο χάριν, τέρψαιτο δὲ θυμόν
ἄνδρας τ' εἰσορόων καλλιζώνους τε γυναῖκας
νῆάς τ' ὠκείας ἠδ' αὐτῶν κτήματα πολλά.   155
πρὸς δὲ τόδε μέγα θαῦμα, ὅου κλέος οὔποτ' ὀλεῖται,
κοῦραι Δηλιάδες Ἑκατηβελέταο θεράπναι·
αἵ τ' ἐπεὶ ἂρ πρῶτον μὲν Ἀπόλλων' ὑμνήσωσιν,
αὖτις δ' αὖ Λητώ τε καὶ Ἄρτεμιν ἰοχέαιραν,
μνησάμεναι ἀνδρῶν τε παλαιῶν ἠδὲ γυναικῶν   160
ὕμνον ἀείδουσιν, θέλγουσι δὲ φῦλ' ἀνθρώπων.
...
ἀλλ' ἄγεθ' ἱλήκοι μὲν Ἀπόλλων Ἀρτέμιδι ξύν,   165
χαίρετε δ' ὑμεῖς πᾶσαι· ἐμεῖο δὲ καὶ μετόπισθε
μνήσασθ', ὁππότε κέν τις ἐπιχθονίων ἀνθρώπων
ἐνθάδ' ἀνείρηται ξεῖνος ταλαπείριος ἐλθών·
'ὦ κοῦραι, τίς δ' ὕμμιν ἀνὴρ ἥδιστος ἀοιδῶν
ἐνθάδε πωλεῖται, καὶ τέῳ τέρπεσθε μάλιστα;'   170
ὑμεῖς δ' εὖ μάλα πᾶσαι ὑποκρίνασθαι ἀφήμως·
'τυφλὸς ἀνήρ, οἰκεῖ δὲ Χίῳ ἔνι παιπαλοέσσῃ,
τοῦ πᾶσαι μετόπισθεν ἀριστεύουσιν ἀοιδαί.'
ἡμεῖς δ' ὑμέτερον κλέος οἴσομεν ὅσσον ἐπ' αἶαν
ἀνθρώπων στρεφόμεσθα πόλεις εὖ ναιεταώσας·   175
οἱ δ' ἐπὶ δὴ πείσονται, ἐπεὶ καὶ ἐτήτυμόν ἐστιν.

But it is in Delos, Phoebus, that your heart most delights,
where the Ionians with trailing robes assemble
with their children and wives on your avenue,
and with their boxing, dancing, and singing
they take heed of you and give you pleasure, whenever they seat the gathering.
A man might think they were immortal and unaging
who came along then when the Ionians are all together:
he would take pleasure in the beauty of the whole scene, and be delighted
seeing the men and fair-girt women
and swift ships and the people's piles of belongings.
And besides, this great wonder, the fame of which
 will never perish,
the Maidens of Delos, servants of the Far-shooter,
who after first hymning Apollo, and
then in turn Leto and Artemis,
take heed of the men and women of old
and sing a song, and charm the mass of people ...
But now, may Apollo be favorable, together
with Artemis,
and I salute you all (girls): take heed of me, also in future,
whenever a long-suffering stranger of earthliving
mortals comes
here and asks: 'Maidens, which is your favorite singer

who visits here, and who do you enjoy most?'
Then you must all answer with one voice (?):
'it is a blind man, and he lives on rocky Chios;
of him all his songs are forever best.'
And we will carry your reputation wherever we go
as we roam the cities of men, and they will believe it,
since it is true.

The scholarly debate on this passage is vast, the main topics being the identity of the blind singer from Chios and the structure of the hymn, whether it is a unity or a conflation of two originally separate hymns, a Delian and a Pyhtian one.

Occupied by these questions, scholars have paid less attention to what actually happens in this little scene. Let us take a closer look. Thus far, the hymn has been devoted to the birth of Apollo, and then, in the lines immediately preceding our passage (140–5), the narrator recounts how Apollo is wont to visit all kinds of places throughout the world (omnitemporal narration).[51] His favorite destination is Delos, at the time when the Ionians gather there for their yearly festival in his honour (146–55: omnitemporal narration).[52] The festival is first focalized by the god, who 'delights' in what he sees (146–50). But then something special happens: the focalization passes from Apollo to 'a man' who looks at the spectacle of the assembled Ionians and is likewise 'delighted' (151–5). These lines have led to strange interpretations: Jacoby and Dornseiff take the man to be the narrator himself, who – since he is blind – cannot actually see the beauty of the scene he is describing, and must be narrating something he can only picture mentally.[53] West assumes that the *Hymn to Apollo* was composed by the rhapsode Cynae-

---

51 Janko 1981, 18 notes that 'the end of the myth is carefully blurred', but considers 140–2 as past and still part of the myth, and 143–5 as past or present. In view of ἄλλοτε μέν ... ἄλλοτε δέ in 141–2, I would be inclined to consider ἐβήσαο as a gnomic aorist and ἠλάσκαζες as iterative imperfect, and take the whole section 140–5 as omnitemporal. Miller 1986, 57, too, points to the 'explicitly generalizing force' of ἄλλοτε ... ἄλλοτε, but then refers to 'the ostensibly historical ἐβήσαο and ἠλάσκαζες.' Cf. also Förstel 1979, 113: 'Obwohl die Verse [141–2] noch die allgemeine Situation der Geburtserzählung berücksichtigen, führen sie doch über die begrenzte Zeit und Örtlichkeit, in der sie spielt, hinaus ins zeitlich und räumlich Unbestimmte und zeigen durch diese Verallgemeinerung die Tätigkeit des Gottes ins Typische abstrahiert'.
52 Cf. the iterative subjunctive ὅταν ... καθέσωσιν (150); the optative ὅτ' ... εἶεν (152) is triggered by the potential optatives φαίη, etc.
53 Jacoby (1933) 1961, 177; Dornseiff 1933, 15 ('eine ergreifende Stelle').

thus, who, however, wanted to pass it off as the work of the blind singer Homer. Lines 151–5 must prove his thesis: it would never have occurred to a blind man to describe the festival, and where we do find such a description, with numerous references to seeing, this signals to the audience of the hymn that this text is not really by the blind singer Homer.[54]

These interpretations fail to appreciate that we are dealing here with the 'anonymous witness' device, which in fact occurs quite frequently in Greek literature,[55] starting with Homer, e.g.

(13) *Iliad* 4.539–44
Ἔνθα κεν οὐκέτι ἔργον ἀνὴρ ὀνόσαιτο μετελθών,
ὅς τις ἔτ' ἄβλητος καὶ ἀνούτατος ὀξέϊ χαλκῷ
δινεύοι κατὰ μέσσον, ἄγοι δέ ἑ Παλλὰς Ἀθήνη
χειρὸς ἑλοῦσ', αὐτὰρ βελέων ἀπερύκοι ἐρωήν·
πολλοὶ γὰρ Τρώων καὶ Ἀχαιῶν ἤματι κείνῳ
πρηνέες ἐν κονίῃσι παρ' ἀλλήλοισι τέταντο.
Then no-one who came close to the action could make light of it,
a man who still unhit and still unstabbed by the sharp bronze
wheeled at the battle's centre, Athena leading him
by the hand and keeping him safe from the flying weapons.
For many Trojans and Greeks were lying that day
with their heads down in the dust next to each other.

Thus the man in line 151 of the *Hymn to Apollo* is not the narrator (and hence not the blind singer from Chios) but an anonymous witness. What is the function of this anonymous witness? It would seem that the narrator, wanting to make the point that the assembled Ionians 'seem to be immortal and ageless', could not use the focalization of Apollo (who presumably would never call mortals immortal), and yet wanted a more authoritative focalizer than himself. For this reason, he introduces, in Miller's words, a 'hypothetical observer from outside the pan-Ionian community ... whose testimony carries conviction because it is independent of ethnic or cultic allegiances' (1986, 58).

In 156 the narrator takes over from the anonymous witness and himself focalizes the highpoint of the festival, the amazing chorus of

---

54 West 1999, 368–72.
55 See the index of de Jong – Nünlist – Bowie 2004. The regular nature of this device is overlooked by Jacoby (1933) 1961, 177, who says that it is not epic, Miller 1986, 55, who only gives a parallel from Isocrates, and West 1999, 371, who calls it 'not a traditional motif'.

the Maidens of Delos (156–64). I am inclined to take τόδε in line 156 as deictic rather than cataphoric; this would then be the first signal that we are moving from the omnitemporal narrated world to the world of the narrator.[56] It turns out that he finds himself in the presence of the Maidens of Delos, *about* whom he has been singing so far. Indeed, another deictic marker, ἐνθάδε at 168, will confirm that the narrator finds himself on Delos.[57] At first glance it may seem surprising that a hymnic solo-singer should draw such lavish attention to a different (choral) form of singing. But, as Miller rightly remarks, this is in fact in keeping with the over-all encomiastic purposes of the hymn, since the remarkable talents of the girls are clearly the result of their being servants of Apollo (157).[58] Moreover, the narrator's praise of the girls will be followed in 171–3 by their praising *him*; the fact that this praise of himself comes from such excellent singers and connoisseurs makes it all the more powerful.

In 166 the narrator even starts apostrophizing the Maidens, no longer narrating about them in the third person but addressing them directly. From the omnitemporal we have now definitely moved to the *hic et nunc* of the moment of narration (and performance).[59] He starts by sal-

---

56 I have found only a few parallels for such a (possible) deictic in the narrator-text of a Homeric hymn: *h.Cer.* 480 (ὄλβιος ὃς τάδ' ὄπωπεν ἐπιχθονίων ἀνθρώπων), *h.Hom.* 6.20 (ἐν ἀγῶνι|... τῶιδε), *h.Hom.* 13.3 (τήνδε ... πόλιν).

57 In itself the reference of ἐνθάδε at 168 is not specified, but the repetition of ἐνθάδε at 170, in a speech addressed to the Maidens of Delos, makes clear that 'here' means on Delos (cf. also earlier ἐνθάδε at 80, in a speech by Delos). In later reperformances of the hymn at other places (which the narrator himself alludes to at 174–5) this deixis *ad oculos* will become deixis *am Phantasma*. Note that the 'Pythian part' of the *Hymn to Apollo* also contains numerous instances of ἐνθάδε, which all occur, however, in speeches (247, 249, 258, 287, 289, 366, 381). To my surprise these deictics (and cf. also those of the previous note) are not discussed by commentators and have never been connected to the vexed question of the circumstances of composition of the Homeric hymns.

58 Miller 1986, 59–60. For a rather strained (antagonistic) interpretation of the relation between hymnic narrator and the Deliades, see Burkert 1987. Others, e.g., Förstel 1979, 404–5 and Clay 1989, 51–2, assume that the narrator-poet of the *Hymn to Apollo* also led the chorus of the Delian girls, either as dancing accompaniment to his own solo-singing or in other, choral songs.

59 Janko 1981, 14–15, refers to 'prolongation' ('at the end of the Myth a few lines may be devoted to bring it up to the present time'), but does not distinguish between omnitemporal present and present of the narrator. According to West 1999, 370, Cynaethus 'claims to be reciting verbatim a hymn composed

uting them, employing the salutation typically found in the epilogue of Homeric hymns (χαίρετε δ' ὑμεῖς πᾶσαι ≈ καὶ σὺ μὲν οὕτω χαῖρε, Διὸς καὶ Μαιάδος υἱέ: *h.Herm.* 579).[60] Addressing the girls thus in the manner of gods, the narrator confirms what was said at 151 about all the Ionians, that they seem to be 'immortal and ageless', and makes clear that 156–64 has been a kind of 'hymn' to the Delian girls. He then makes a request, which again resembles the typical requests of hymnic epilogues: ἐμεῖο δὲ καὶ μετόπισθε μνήσασθ' ≈ (χαίρετε, τέκνα Διός) καὶ ἐμὴν τιμήσατ' ἀοιδήν (*h.Hom.* 25.6).

What he means by μνήσασθ' is worked out – in a unique expansion of a hymnic request and an equally unique 'dialogization' of an apostrophe – in a hypothetical dialogue between an anonymous man[61] and the Maidens of Delos (167–73): if this man asks them who their favorite singer is, they must answer that it is the blind man from Chios.[62] As in 151–5, the narrator introduces an anonymous witness – here even an interlocutor – in order to suggest objectivity. As καὶ μετόπισθε (166) indicates, he envisions this dialogue *in the future*, which explains the μνήσασθ': when asked this question, they must *recall* the narrator and answer... The use of this verb in relation to himself, while it is typically used in connection with gods and heroes (cf. 150, 160, and 546),

---

by Homer many generations earlier and addressed to an earlier Delian audience', and hence there is no apostrophe of persons present.

60 I am much indebted to Miller 1979, whose analysis of 166–76 as an epilogue to a 'hymn' to the Deliades (comprising the typical elements salutation-request-promise), and 166–78 as a whole as transitional, in my view is highly convincing.

61 Incorrectly Dornseiff 1933, 9 ('wie liebenswürdig stellt sich der Chier das Frage-und Antwortspiel vor, dass *er* sich mit den delischen Sängerinnen wünscht', my italics). Miller 1986, 62 rightly refers to a 'hypothetical dialogue between them [Deliades] and a third party'. His suggestion that the reference to the stranger as 'much-suffering' establishes a motive for his quest, in that he is looking for the 'sweetest' singer, who will assuage his griefs, is ingenious but perhaps a bit far-fetched. A more mundane explanation of the epithet would be that the poet of the *h.Ap.* adapted the following line from the *Odyssey*: πολλοὶ δὴ ξεῖνοι ταλαπείριοι ἐνθάδ' ἵκοντο (19.379).

62 I do not agree with Clay (1989, 51) that μνήσασθ' (166) 'can only mean "include me in your song"'; thus μνησάμενοι at 150 does not have this specific meaning and see also *LfgrE* s.v. I am likewise not convinced by the suggestion of Clay 1989, 52 (and others, listed in her footnotes) that the dialogue would be 'a playful display of his comprehensive mastery of the art by imitating a choral performance within the framework of his hexameter poem'. Rather I would suggest that it shows that, like the Deliades, he 'knows how to mimic all people's voices' (162).

seems to be a subtle means of self-elevation. Projecting this dialogue into the future also hints that his fame will be eternal, a point which is then made explicit in the praise which he places in the mouths of the girls at 173: 'all of his songs remain supreme ever afterwards (μετόπισθε)'. The narrator then promises – in a variant of the typical hymnic epilogue element of the promise – that, in return, he will spread the *kleos* of the girls both in the future and all over the world. The idea is, of course, that he will do so by singing his *Hymn to Apollo*, including as it does in lines 156–64 a 'hymn' on the Delian girls (note in particular ὅου κλέος οὔ ποτ'|ὀλεῖται at 156).[63]

I conclude that *h.Ap.* 146–67 is a complex instance of metaleptic fade-out: first the narrator introduces into the narrated world a hypothetical witness, then links this world to his own world via deictic τόδε, then directly addresses characters who belong to both the narrated world and his own world, the Maidens of Delos, and finally even makes these apostrophied characters speak. The effect of the metaleptic blurring of the boundaries between narrated world and world of narrator is that not only the mortal Maidens of Delos, but even the mortal singer-narrator himself partakes of the encomiastic atmosphere of the hymn. The narrator manages to squeeze in a forceful plug for his own work, in the context of a 'hymn' to the Maidens of Delos, which forms part of a hymn to Apollo.[64]

Other examples of this type of metalepsis include: *h.Ap.* 544–6 and *h.Hom.* 7.55–9: the absence of a capping formula makes it appear as if the narrator's salutation *chaire* responds directly to the speeches of Apollo and Dionysus respectively.[65] A counter-example, *h.Ven.* 291, where we do find a speech capping between the speech and the *chaire* suggests that the metalepsis in these two passages is intentional.

---

63 The same observation in Clay 1989, 52, who defends a Panhellenic nature of the Homeric hymns. However, her suggestion that οἴσομεν is in fact an instance of the encomiastic future contradicts her own interpretation, since such futures refer to the actual performance of a text, whereas for her thesis she needs future performances (in other places than Delos). I note that Pfeijffer 1999b has actually demolished the existence of an encomiastic future = present. οἴσομεν would fall into his category 2b ('reference to a specific moment beyond the performance of an ode').
64 Cf. Miller 1979, 186, n. 44: 'The poet of the hymn ... develops the full tripartite pattern in such a way that ... he is also advancing a claim to preeminent stature in his art – a claim that can only enhance the value of the present hymn as a tribute to Apollo's glory'.
65 See Führer 1967, 57–8.

7. Metalepsis in Greek literature 5: varia

In the previous sections I discussed four types of metalepsis which occur with some regularity in Greek literature. I am convinced that the number of examples in these four groups can and will be augmented. New types of metalepsis may also be identified. In this last section I discuss two incidental instances of metalepsis. The first would provide an ancient parallel to my example 1b from Laurence Sterne, the narrator displaying his actual role as the creator – rather than the reporter – of the story:

(14) *Iliad* 22.326–9:
τῇ ῥ' ἐπὶ οἷ μεμαῶτ' ἔλασ' ἔγχεϊ δῖος Ἀχιλλεύς,
ἀντικρὺ δ' ἁπαλοῖο δι' αὐχένος ἤλυθ' ἀκωκή·
οὐδ' ἄρ' ἀπ' ἀσφάραγον μελίη τάμε χαλκοβάρεια,
ὄφρα τί μιν προτιείποι ἀμειβόμενος ἐπέεσσιν.
There godlike Achilles drove in with his spear as Hector charged him,
and the point went right through his soft neck:
but the ash spear with its weight of bronze did not cut the windpipe,
in order that Hector could still speak and answer Achilles.

The narrator here 'orchestrates' the wounding of Hector by Achilles in such a way as to allow the dying hero a last speech. Aristarchus, with characteristic acumen, noted the anomalous procedure employed here, and athetised line 329 as being 'ridiculous' (γελοῖος). The (Arn/A, bT) scholia coming to Homer's defence note that the poet sometimes treats accidental events as if they were designed, and adduce *Od.* 9.154–5 ('nymphs sent goats, in order that my companions could eat') and 12.427–8 ('a southern wind came on, in order that I would have to retrace my course until Charybdis'). These parallels are not apt, however, since they are voiced by Odysseus as secondary narrator, who is of course free to interpret *accidental* incidents in terms of gods helping humans or nature harming humans. In the case of Hector's fatal wounding no gods are involved, and I would not hesitate to consider this a – unique – sleight-of-hand on the part of the narrator Homer.[66]

---

[66] This form of metalepsis, a narrator revealing himself creator rather than reporter, will become much more common in Latin literature, e.g. Virgil *Ecl.* 6.45–6: *et fortunatam, si numquam armenta fuissent, Pasiphaen nivei solatur amore iuvenci*, 'Now he [the secondary narrator Silemus] *solaces* Pasiphae – happy one, if herds had never been! –, with her passion for the snowy bull' (in-

My second example is comparable to example 1a, a narrator physically entering the scene of the story:

(16) Philostratus, *Vita Apollonii* 8.1
 Ἴωμεν ἐς τὸ δικαστήριον ἀκροασόμενοι τοῦ ἀνδρὸς ἀπολογουμένου ὑπὲρ τῆς αἰτίας, ἡλίου γὰρ ἐπιτολαὶ ἤδη καὶ ἀνεῖται τοῖς ἐλλογίμοις ἡ ἐς αὐτὸ πάροδος,...
 Let us go to the law-court to listen to the man [Apollonius] pleading his cause; for it is already sunrise and the doors have been opened to admit the celebrities.

The narrator, who belongs to a later time than that of the story he recounts (cf. 1.2–3), invites his narratees to join him and 'go to' the scene of the action.

8. Conclusion

In this paper I have argued that the narrative device of metalepsis, the transgression of the boundaries between narrative universes or the subversion of the hierarchy of narrative levels, which has thus far been discussed by scholars mainly in connection with examples from modern and postmodern novels, also occurs in ancient texts. A major difference between modern and ancient examples of metalepsis is that the latter are for the most part serious (rather than comic) and are aimed at increasing the authority of the narrator and the realism of his narrative (rather than breaking the illusion). The study of metalepsis in ancient narrative is a prime example of what Fludernik 2003b recently referred to as diachronic or historical narratology. In my view, classicists have an important task to fulfil in the writing of a history of European story-telling, which might well be the desired outcome of such diachronic narratology.

---

stead of 'he *tells about* Pasiphae's passion for the snowy bull', cf. earlier *canebat, refert, adiungit*). For a full discussion of this device, see Lieberg 1982.

Homer, Odysseus, and the Narratology of Performance

Egbert J. Bakker

Narratology, the formal study of narrative discourse, has without doubt been an important impulse for the study of Greek literature, and has brought major advances in our understanding not only of the genre of epic, but also of historiography as well as other literary forms with a narrative component, such as tragedy and oratory. The paradigm has provided an indispensable heuristic framework that has revealed important features of well-known texts that would otherwise have remained unexplained or gone unnoticed. Narratology has been especially important in the case of Homer and epic poetry. In particular the work of Irene de Jong has brought observations to the fore that would otherwise have remained hidden under scholarship focusing on oral poetry and formulaic diction.[1]

But narratology – or rather we should say 'classical narratology'[2] – has a number of (partly self-imposed) limitations. As a branch of structuralism looking at narrative as an idealized scientific object, it is uninterested in the historical and social contexts in which narrative functions and is presented. For the study of Homer, the subject of the present chapter, a dimension that is particularly relevant in this regard involves what could be called historical situatedness and the social and generic pragmatics of narrative. Awareness of historical situatedness is to study narratives against the background of the conventions of a culture's major narrative genres, particularly the media by which they are pre-

---

1 On Homer, De Jong (1987) 2004, 2001a; on drama, De Jong 1991.
2 The original ('classical') structuralist conception of Genette (1972) 1980 on which De Jong's work is ultimately based (mediated through the work of Bal [1985] 1997), has come to be modified and reformulated in the wake of postmodernism, with 'subjective' and 'agentive' functions (as, e.g, the role of the reader or the 'narratee') by and large replacing the more 'objective' functions in the original model. For some modern developments of narratology, see, e. g., Fludernik 1996, Herman 2003, and Pier 2004. See also the Introduction to this volume.

sented, which may differ from culture to culture and from period to period. No one would deny that there are important differences between Homer and *Madame Bovary*.

The comparison between archaic Greek epic and narratives meant to be received in reading, such as the nineteenth-century novel, points up important differences in the 'pragmatics of fiction.' What is fictional in narratology and in the novel (i.e., the narrator and the narratee), becomes embodied in epic, and we may ask what actually happens when a story is told by a real narrator to a real audience. What are the communicative conditions under which the narrator tells his story? What are the assumptions of the audience? What kind of role does the narrator play and with how much authority, if any, is that role invested? In terms of written literature these are questions that pertain to the publication of the literary work and its reception, areas that are commonly seen as outside the purview of narratological analysis. But when publication and reception are phenomena subject to cultural and historical conditions, it may not be so easy to keep them out of the picture, especially when publication and reception are intimately bound up with the storytelling event itself.

Indeed, publication and reception can be the very essence of the storytelling event. When narrative is an act, a performance, the work's publication *is* its telling. An adequate account of Homeric narrative has to address the question of performance, and a narratology of epic has to be, if epic is to be studied in terms of its original reception, a narratology of performance. Note that this concept of performance does not imply the absence of writing or of any written text, as in the older literature on oral poetry, where performance is the moment of the song's (formulaic) *composition*.[3] As a storytelling event, performance is much more than an act of composition and not at all incompatible with the existence of a written text. Communicative primacy, however, resides in the performance, and not in the written text. That text, in other words, is a recording of the speech of the storytelling event and the performance, conversely, is more than a mere act of recitation.[4]

In what follows I will introduce three aspects of a narratology of performance that is designed for the study of Homer, in order of presentation: (i) narrative syntax and historical situatedness; (ii) projected indexicality in performance; and (iii) *mimesis* and direct speech. The

---

3   Lord 1960, 13 ff.
4   Bakker 1997a, 18–32.

chapter will close with a discussion of a number of narrative features of the *Odyssey* that cannot be adequately accounted for in traditional narratology.

1. Narrative Syntax and Historical Situatedness

Gustave Flaubert, famously, was put on trial for the alleged obscenity of *Madame Bovary*. An important aspect of this encounter between literature and law was the author's pioneering use of *style indirect libre*.[5] In this mode of narrative representation, a character's thought (or 'point of view,' or 'focalization' as the narratologist would say) is mediated through the voice of the narrator. The character does the thinking or seeing, and the narrator the saying.[6] This narrative mode was apparently not readily understood by Flaubert's contemporary audience, a detail that confronts us with the historical dimension of narrative syntax: *style indirect libre* (i.e., free indirect discourse or embedded focalization) is not something that can be taken for granted; not all stories in all periods and cultures have it and a literary culture may be unfamiliar with it.

Style indirect libre is characterized by a blending of the deictic perspective of the narrator with that of characters in the story. Let us take a simple case:[7]

She still had a lot to do. Tomorrow was Christmas.

The combination of a future temporal adverbial with past tense is typical of the deixis of modern narrative, in which free indirect discourse or embedded focalization is a naturally occurring process with its own grammar. Tense and person (solid underline in the example) will adjust to the perspective of the narrator (who refers to another person than himself and to another time than his own writing/telling moment); but temporal adverbials (dotted underline), indeed adverbs in general,

---

5   LaCapra 1982.
6   See, e.g., Hamburger 1957; Leech–Short 1981, 325–336; Banfield 1982, 65–108, 158; Ehrlich 1990, 6–26; Chafe 1994, 195–196.
7   Adaptation of 'Aber am Vormittag hatte sie den Baum zu putzen. Morgen war Weihnachten' from Alice Berends' *Die Bräutigame der Babette Bomberling* (Berlin 1915, S. Fischer), cited and discussed by Hamburger 1957, 33. The sentence is discussed with reference to French and Ancient Greek by Steinrück 1999, 324–325. See further below.

readily convey the perspective of the character in the story.[8] The narrator has unrestricted access to that perspective, and indeed, the whole point of the story is the creation of the character's mind, thought, and perception as the principal means to gain access to the fictional story world; the narrator gains access to the character's mind, without actually voicing the character's words. A kind of ecstasis takes place: the narrator leaves his own self and lodges himself in another self that thinks and acts in another time and place.

The syntax of this narrative operation differs from language to language. Ironically, French, the language of Flaubert, is apparently incapable of using *demain* in a translation of the sentence just mentioned; instead, it has to use *le lendemain*, a temporal adverb that conveys not the character's temporal vantage point but the narrator's.[9] The syntax of *style indirect libre* also differs from age to age. In Greek it is slow to develop, if it develops at all to anything similar to what we see in the modern European languages. The Swiss scholar Martin Steinrück claims that in Greek a use of the temporal adverb for 'tomorrow,' αὔριον, does not occur until Athenaeus:

> καὶ ἐς αὔριον παρεκάλει συνδειπνῆσαι.
>
> And he called on him to dine with him tomorrow.
> (Athen. 4.29.13–14).[10]

I have not verified this claim, but I am confident in asserting that Homeric narrative has no *style indirect libre*. The 'embedded focalization' that does occur is, as Irene de Jong has shown, a matter of the use of an emotionally charged term that usually occurs in the speech of characters but that occasionally can be used in the narrator text to convey a character's point of view. An example is

> Αἴαντ' αὖθ' ἑτέρωθεν ἐϋκνήμιδες Ἀχαιοὶ
> εἰς Ἀγαμέμνονα δῖον ἄγον κεχαρηότα νίκῃ.
>
> Ajax, on the other side, the well-greaved Achaeans,
> they led him to illustrious Agamemnon, rejoicing at his victory.
> (*Il.* 7.311–312)

---

8 Hamburger 1957, 32–34; Chafe 1994, 249–258.
9 Steinrück 1999, 324.
10 Steinrück 1999, 326.

This is the end of the duel between Hector and Ajax, which ended undecided, so there is no victory from an objective point of view. De Jong is probably right in thinking that νίκη here reflects Ajax's perspective.[11]

But cases such as this one remain relatively isolated and are sometimes open to alternative interpretations. No systematic grammar of free indirect discourse is detectable in Homer. Nor is the principal medium of Homeric narrative conducive to what comes so easily to the authors of the modern novel. In performance, the narrator does not so much enter the mind of the character, as in modern fiction; rather, the perspective of the character can intrude in the discourse of the narrator.

Style indirect libre remains an elusive phenomenon in Greek grammar and narrative; it never really takes off. The closest to anything similar to what we see in the modern novel is Thucydides' war narrative. Just as Flaubert, Thucydides can use tense, the imperfect tense to be precise, to convey an 'internal' point of view, a vantage point from *within* the story that does not necessarily coincide with the point of view of the historian-narrator in the present. But this strategy usually does not set up anyone's individual mind as means of access to the historical events; rather, it draws the reader into the past as part of the historian's strategies to achieve vividness. When Thucydides presents historical events focalized through the participants in the action, the perspective is often that of a *collective* self, e.g., what the Athenians thought in a particular situation, as an instrument for the historian to express his sense of historical causation. Thucydides is the first to use temporal deictics, νῦν in particular, to convey a temporal vantage point other than that of the narrator. But as far as I can see, this happens only in indirect discourse, carried by infinitives rather than finite verbs, as in the following extract, from the description of the naval battle in the harbor of Syracuse:

πολλὴ γὰρ δὴ ἡ παρακέλευσις καὶ βοὴ ἀφ' ἑκατέρων τοῖς κελευσταῖς κατά τε τὴν τέχνην καὶ πρὸς τὴν αὐτίκα φιλονικίαν ἐγίγνετο, τοῖς μὲν Ἀθηναίοις βιάζεσθαί τε τὸν ἔκπλουν ἐπιβοῶντες καὶ περὶ τῆς ἐς τὴν πατρίδα σωτηρίας <u>νῦν, εἴ ποτε καὶ αὖθις</u>, προθύμως ἀντιλαβέσθαι.

And there was an enormous amount of exhorting and shouting on the part of the boatswains on either side, both as to battle technique and to increase the urge to win; to the Athenians they cried out to force their way out and for

---

11 De Jong (1987) 2004, 101–102. See also Grethlein 2006a, 231. De Jong discusses free indirect speech elsewhere in this volume.

> the survival of their fatherland, <u>now, if ever again</u>, to hold on ferociously to the chance.
>
> (Thuc. 7.70.7)[12]

Constructions such as these have not (yet) emancipated themselves from the syntax of indirect discourse and verbal complementation. This indirect discourse is not yet 'free' or *libre*; it is still bound. But Thucydides seems a highly innovative narrator, pushing Greek grammar into new narrative directions.

I use temporal modifiers such as 'not yet' or 'still' deliberately to suggest a developmental framework that reflects the increasing 'writtenness' of Greek narrative when we move from Homer to the historians. The lack of a grammar of indirect speech, let alone *free* indirect speech, is a sign of the extent to which Homeric narrative is steeped in performance.[13] When narrative is a real life storytelling event, with a 'me/us-here-now' firmly in place, it is much more difficult for narrators to relinquish their time, place, and self and to get lodged in another self at another time and place while still talking in their own voice. It is much more natural to adopt wholesale a character's deictic vantage point, by way of *mimesis*, on which more later.

Thucydides' narrative, by contrast, has a high degree of 'writtenness' by many accounts, not just the narratological one. It is one of the most readerly discourses ever to have been produced by an ancient Greek writer, aiming at usefulness for each generation anew. Its narrative is fictional in being able to speak to ever new generations of readers in the future. Thucydides' text can speak to the future, as Thucydides' self can travel to the past.[14]

2. Projected Indexicality in Performance

Thucydides is of course not alone in Greek literature in his insistence on the endurance of his achievement. Homeric narrative is about endurance too, but not through a projected series of encounters of future readers with a text; the endurance of Homer is predicated on the poetics of performance. Performance is of course the face-to-face interaction of a narrator with an audience in real time and in the real world. The

---
12 Bakker 1997b, 40–41; 2005, 163.
13 Bakker 2005, 174–175.
14 On Thucydides' writing, see Bakker 2006a, 109–129.

idea of the oral presentation of a narrative need in itself not worry the narratologist or require a narratology of its own. After all, a story that has been presented orally can be read and analyzed as a written narrative, and, conversely, modern novelists can recite their own work, reading it out aloud without changing the fictional communication that inheres in the text.

Homeric performance, by contrast, is much more than the mere declamation or recitation of the story of the *Iliad* or *Odyssey*. That recitation is built into the very fabric of its narrative contract. Unlike the modern recital of a novel or poem, performance as the vehicle of a *tradition* is never a one-time event; nor is it the rendition of a story that is seen as preexisting as text the telling event. The event *is* the story. And the performance-event is what it is, crucially, by being not unique or notionally isolated. Any given performance is never the first or the last one. If performance as mode of publication is the means for the epic poem to travel in time and space – two dimensions that are essential for its survival – then performance means in practice always *re*-performance.

Re-performance, the 're-use' of narrative statements that are shaped in narrator-audience interaction, involves a peculiar referential phenomenon that I propose to call 'projected indexicality.' In discourse linguistics, indexicality is a property of statements that contain so-called *indexicals*, demonstrative or deictic elements like 'I,' 'you,' 'now,' or 'here.'[15] The referentiality of such elements is very different from normal referential expressions, such as proper names; they come to designate anything or anyone specific only in a concrete context of utterance, when the 'I' is the speaker that the addressee is actually listening to, the 'now' the actual moment when the verbal transaction takes place, and the 'here' the actual place of the speech event. So utterances like 'I like it here,' or 'Tell me what you think!' are indexical because the 'I,' the 'you,' and the 'here' are meaningful only in the context in which the utterance takes place.

Now when a given statement is not only uttered or performed (as in any ordinary conversation or narration), but also *meant to be performed*, that is, meant to be *re*performed, the indexicality of the phrase, its inbuilt 'hereness,' and 'nowness,' is projected. Whoever utters, performs, it will complement its referentiality. I propose 'projected indexicality' as an important feature of panhellenic poetics, in which poems and per-

---

15 See, e.g., Levinson 1983, 54–96 and, for Greek in particular, Felson 2004.

formances are supposed to travel in time and place, thus extending, and projecting, the indexicality of their constitutive utterances.

Typical moments of projected indexicality in Homer occur in the invocations of the Muses in the *Iliad*:

ἔσπετε <u>νῦν μοι</u>, Μοῦσαι, Ὀλύμπια δώματ' ἔχουσαι ...

Sing <u>now to me</u>, Muses who hold Olympian dwellings ...
(Hom. *Il.* 2.484; 11.218; 14.508; 16.112)

And, of course, in the Muse invocations in the first lines of the times, especially the *Odyssey*:

Ἄνδρα <u>μοι</u> ἔννεπε, Μοῦσα, πολύτροπον, ὃς μάλα πολλά ...

Sing <u>to me</u>, Muse, the man, the one of many turns, who very much ...

The 'now' (νῦν) of the Muse invocations is very different from Thucydides' internally represented 'now' of the Athenian commanders in the harbor of Syracuse in the extract above. This 'now' is not represented in the tale as a displaced, a shifted deictic center; it is not a now *in* the text, but the now *of* the text, the inbuilt projected now of the performance-event that is actualized in each new reperformance. This νῦν μοι is the moment at which the epic tradition itself comes to be embodied in the person of the performer. Narratology would call him the 'Homeric narrator' and consider him a fiction, a narrative function. But when we look at Homer as poetry in performance, this narrator becomes Homer, the essence and voice of the entire tradition, a voice that can be this voice only by sounding in various places and at various times. Each time the νῦν μοι or other projected indexicals in the narrative are uttered, the actual 'me' and the actual 'now' are different, depending on the performer and the time and place of performance. But that variable external deixis ensures the stability and durability of the νῦν μοι in the text, which is the hereness and nowness of Homer in performance.

The concept of projected indexicality, then, cuts across, or goes beyond, a distinction that is dear to the narratologist, the distinction between real life, historical *author* and fictional *narrator*, with the former being irrelevant for narratological analysis. In a narratology of Homeric performance, the biographical, the external 'I' and the fictional, the internal 'I' collapse in the typical deixis of the performance.

Projected indexicality, I suggest, is also what pertains to the deictic references to "this city" in the *corpus theognideum*:

Κύρνε, κύει πόλις ἥδε, δέδοικα δὲ μὴ τέκηι ἄνδρα
εὐθυντῆρα κακῆς ὕβριος ἡμετέρης. (Th. 39–40)

Kurnos, this *polis* is pregnant; I fear that it may beget a man who will be the chastizer of our bad *hybris*.

Κύρνε, πόλις μὲν ἔθ' ἥδε πόλις, λαοὶ δὲ δὴ ἄλλοι,
οἳ πρόσθ' οὔτε δίκας ἤιδεσαν οὔτε νόμους (Th. 53–54)

Kurnos, this *polis* may still be a *polis*, but its people is different; those who first knew neither justice nor laws....

On a reading of these extracts as one-time compositions, the deictic expression πόλις ἥδε refers to an unnamed city in which a fictional adviser addresses a fictional *erômenos* about a generic political situation. Some might prefer to think of a poet, an author, addressing his *erômenos*, in which case the *polis* in question would be archaic Megara, the city with which Theognis was traditionally associated. But it is hard to see how any poet would express himself in these terms about the concrete political situation in his city. I think it is more likely that the wording, rather vague, but specific enough to apply to the particular political problems of the time, is meant to make sense in a whole range of *poleis*. So πόλις ἥδε and ἄνδρα, even the vocative Κύρνε, are projected indexicals, applying to whatever city forms the backdrop of the given symposium in which the song was performed, whatever citizen was likely to be suspected by the aristocratic drinking companions of having tyrannical aspirations, and whatever adolescent happened to be the singer's *erômenos* at the time. Theognis, self-consciously panhellenic in aspirations and scope (cf. 237–254), has built-in indexicality that turns any city into the actual context that motivates the poem's admonitory speech acts. This poetry is self-staging, self-contextualizing, made, not *in*, but *for* performance.

3. *Mimesis* and Direct Speech

The idea of projected indexicality proposed here is substantially not very different from the conception of Homeric performance put forward by Gregory Nagy, in which the old distinction between the *aoidos*, the creative oral poet, and the reciting rhapsode is left behind in favor of a conception in which the rhapsodic reenactment of Homer in performance is the essence of the tradition. But the terminology is different. Nagy calls the μοι in ἔσπετε νῦν μοι, Μοῦσαι or in ἄνδρα μοι ἔννεπε, Μοῦσα the *mimesis* of Homer, whereby the rhapsode does not so much *represent*

Homer; rather, he *becomes*, he *is* Homer.'[16] Nagy is concerned with the same issues that I have called the narratology of performance; but I would not use the term *mimesis* here. 'Homer' is not a character to be impersonated, like Achilles. Homer is not a character from the past who comes into the present; Homer *is* the present. At the same time, Homer is far less specific and explicitly individualized than Achilles or any speaking character in the poems. Irene de Jong's narratological analyses have clearly demonstrated that the language, the vocabulary, of Homer (or of the narrator in her terminology) is different from that of the characters, an important feature of Homeric narrative that was being neglected in scholarship focusing predominantly on the oral-formulaic features of Homeric poetry.

And yet, from the standpoint of the performer who presents his 'one man show' at festivals and other gatherings, 'Homer' and Achilles (or any character) are related to each other as different *roles* to be played.[17] Telling the epic story in performance is switching between the *indexical* role of 'Homer' and the *mimetic* roles of the characters, between embodying the tradition and impersonating the epic characters.

The difference between this approach in terms of performance roles and the narratology of written narrative is significant. In the narratology of written narrative it is customary to speak of an opposition between narrative and character speech, or 'direct speech.' But the term 'direct speech' is problematic in the perspective I am developing. 'Direct speech' is meant to make sense, of course, both as a term and as a phenomenon, in opposition to 'indirect speech:' no distortion takes place as the speech is not presented in the voice of the narrator or subordinated syntactically. Underlying this conception is a literate notion of 'quotation,' the idea that someone else's words are repeated literally, exactly as they were uttered, without change and with the originally intended meaning left intact, as indicated in writing through inverted commas. But in the performance perspective the speech of the 'quoting' narrator is no less 'direct speech' than that of the characters. There is nothing that is not framed in theater or performance. What happens when Achilles or Odysseus begin to speak is not a withdrawal of the fictional narrator or an act of quotation, but the performer shifting from one role into anoth-

---

16 Nagy 1996, 60–62.
17 See also Nagy 2003, 36–38 on the relation between *rhapsoidos* and *hypokrites*, 'actor'.

er, from narrator to character and from indexical 'I' to mimetic 'I,' the impersonation of Odysseus or Achilles.

More important than terms, however, is a general conception of narrative. The idea of direct speech as akin to quotation is, in spite of the pretense of semantic integrity and freedom of the quotee's words, essentially a hierarchical conception, since the quoter is in charge and the quotee's words come to be inserted in the framework of the quoter's discourse. There may be no syntactic subordination, but there is semantic or conceptual subordination. As the sociolinguist Deborah Tannen has argued for conversational storytelling, 'direct speech,' or 'reported speech,' is never 'direct,' or 'reported' in the sense of undistorted.[18] It is impossible not to alter the words of someone else one 'quotes'; these words become one's own. The narrator can hide or yield the floor to a character only in writing, where his voice is fictional just as the character's. On the stage of orally performed narrative, whether in formal performance or in informal conversational settings, no voice, neither the narrator's nor the character's, is fictional, and representing the speech of others is one aspect of the multifarious nature of storytelling as a speech event.

4. Homeric *Enargeia* and the Audience

In the case of Homer specifically, to question the hierarchical relation between narrator and character (or, when a character tells a story, between *primary* narrator and *embedded* narrator), has some further important consequences. Again, the narratological distinction between 'narrator' and 'character' has produced important insights into the differences between the two discourse modes. But the performance perspective yields observations that narratology does not, or cannot, or does not want to, take into account. I have recently argued that the famous 'vividness' (*enargeia*) of Homeric narrative, which creates the illusion to the audience that they are spectators watching the epic events rather than listeners hearing of them through the poetry's words is at least partly achieved through the narrator (performer) using markers of 'evidentiality' that are typically used by speakers who interact with the physical en-

---

18 Tannen 1989, 98–133.

vironment around them.[19] A good example is the use of the deictic pronoun οὗτος in the following example:

οὗτοι ἄρ' ἡγεμόνες Δαναῶν καὶ κοίρανοι ἦσαν.

These then were the leaders and the lords of the Danaans.

(*Il.* 2.760)

The demonstrative οὗτος is much more common in the speech of characters than in the speech of the narrator, and that is to be expected, since οὗτος is inherently dialogic: in using it, the speaker situates the thing pointed at as close to the listeners, or otherwise readily accessible to them. In interactive speech, the use of οὗτος conveys that the thing or person pointed at is perceptually shared between speaker and interlocutor; οὗτος signals 'presence.'[20] In the extract just cited the persons 'pointed at' with οὗτοι are of course the assembled Achaean leaders and their contingents that have just been enumerated in the Catalogue of Ships. They are now set up as 'present' in the performance. The Catalogue follows on the famous address of the Muses which contains, as we saw, the projected indexical phrase with ἔσπετε νῦν μοι, Μοῦσαι. The deictic phrase in *Il.* 2.760 shows that the audience is part of the communication between the performer and the Muses, and since οὗτοι is a projected indexical, it includes all audiences, up to and including ourselves. In speaking to his audience, Homer models his speech on that of the characters in the tale as they speak to each other and interact with their environment.[21]

5. *Epos* and *Aoide* in the *Odyssey*

But there are further ways in which the relation between the narrator *of* the tale and the characters *in* the tale in Homer is more complicated than would seem in ordinary narratological analysis. In epic traditions, *performance* traditions, there can be a special relation between narrator and character: poet-performers can identify strongly with their principal hero, a special empathy that can have all sorts of narratological conse-

---

19 Bakker 2005, chs. 5–9.
20 Bakker 2005, 75–78.
21 Other deictic elements in Homeric narrative discourse taken from (and more frequent in) the discourse of characters include the particle ἄρα and the augment of the verb, see Bakker 1993, 15–25; 2005, 114–135.

quences for the tale. For the *Iliad*, Richard Martin has argued that there is a special bond between Homer and Achilles.[22] I propose in the remainder of this chapter to discuss Homer and Odysseus in the *Odyssey* in this regard.

Let us first look at the terms for speech and performance in Homeric Greek. The most important terms in Homer for what for the narratologist is character speech are *muthos* and *epos*; only the second is important for my present purposes.[23] Within Homer, the word ἔπος is used for what characters say to each other, speech *within* the poem, whereas the speech *of* the poem, or the language of the performance itself, is always referred to as ἀοιδή. But when we look at the epic tradition from outside, the term for 'epic' as genre is not ἀοιδή, but ἔπος, the term that epic itself uses for 'character speech.' In other words, the term for the whole from outside is the same one as the term for the part from inside.[24] This peculiar lexical situation should alert us to the peculiar relation between narrator speech and character speech in Homer. For the generic term for 'epic' is, within epic, not the term for what Homer says, but the term for what Achilles and Odysseus say. The language of the heroes is not exactly subordinated, embedded, or represented: it takes center stage, even ousting the language of the narrator when it comes to typifying epic as a genre. Epic, at least Homeric epic, in other words, subverts the hierarchical relation between narrator and character, between representing and represented.

This is nowhere more glaringly clear than in the *Odyssey*. This poem pushes the lack of a hierarchical relation between a primary narrator who 'quotes' and characters or secondary narrators who are 'quoted' to the point at which outright competition – and at the same time strong assimilation – between the narrator and the character occurs. The character is of course Odysseus, whose story, the *Apologue* of Books 9–12, can for its sheer length alone hardly be called 'subordinated' to any matrix narrative. The poem uses Odysseus' narrative, a matter of *epos*, to typify itself in its proem, the onset of *aoidê*. The proem does not single out events from Homer's own narrative to get the poem started, such as, for instance, 'Muse, tell me of the man who completed his *nostos*, disguised as a beggar, and of the Suitors of his wife, who perished because of their own *atasthaliai* when Odysseus made them meet the day

---

22 Martin 1989, 231–239, with parallels from African performance traditions.
23 On these two words, see Martin 1989, 1–42.
24 See Bakker 2006b, 2–4.

of their doom, when he killed them all in his *megaron*.' Instead, of course, all the elements selected for inclusion in the proem are from *epos*, the tale, not of Homer, but of Odysseus: the wanderings, the sufferings on the high seas, the Cattle of the Sun, and the *atasthaliai*, the culpable recklessness, not of the Suitors, but of the Companions. In other words, the poem is presenting itself in a way that suggests that the narrative of its main character Odysseus is more typical of the poem than the narrative of Homer himself. Character speech, *epos*, seems to win out over narrator speech, *aoidê*, and inset tale seems to eclipse the matrix story.

The impact of *epos*, Odysseus' narrative, is such that *aoidê* has to reassert itself by means of explicit references to the proem after the hero has finished his tale and the matrix story resumes:

ὡς ἡ ῥίμφα θέουσα θαλάσσης κύματ' ἔταμνεν,
ἄνδρα φέρουσα θεοῖς ἐναλίγκια μήδ' ἔχοντα,
ὃς πρὶν μὲν μάλα πολλὰ πάθ' ἄλγεα ὃν κατὰ θυμὸν
ἀνδρῶν τε πτολέμους ἀλεγεινά τε κύματα πείρων,
δὴ τότε γ' ἀτρέμας εὗδε, λελασμένος ὅσσ' ἐπεπόνθει.

Thus running lightly, it cut through the swellings of the sea,
carrying <u>a man</u> with thoughts similar to the gods,
<u>who</u> earlier <u>had suffered many woes in his spirit</u>,
<u>living through wars of men and the painful waves</u>;
but then he slept undisturbed, forgetful of all that he had suffered.
(*Od.* 13.88–92)

The metrical localization of ἄνδρα, the modifier μάλα πολλά in a digressive relative clause attached to it, and the essential phrase πάθ' ἄλγεα ὃν κατὰ θυμόν, the sufferings on the high seas, are all unmistakable reminders of the beginning of the poem:

Ἄνδρα μοι ἔννεπε, Μοῦσα, πολύτροπον, ὃς μάλα πολλὰ
πλάγχθη, ἐπεὶ Τροίης ἱερὸν πτολίεθρον ἔπερσε·
πολλῶν δ' ἀνθρώπων ἴδεν ἄστεα καὶ νόον ἔγνω,
πολλὰ δ' ὅ γ' ἐν πόντῳ πάθεν ἄλγεα ὃν κατὰ θυμόν,
ἀρνύμενος ἥν τε ψυχὴν καὶ νόστον ἑταίρων.
ἀλλ' οὐδ' ὣς ἑτάρους ἐρρύσατο, ἱέμενός περ·
αὐτῶν γὰρ σφετέρῃσιν ἀτασθαλίῃσιν ὄλοντο,
νήπιοι, οἳ κατὰ βοῦς Ὑπερίονος Ἠελίοιο
ἤσθιον· αὐτὰρ ὁ τοῖσιν ἀφείλετο νόστιμον ἦμαρ.

(*Od.* 1.1–9)

The beginning of the poem, in fact, is happening anew. It is as if Homer is reoccupying the floor that he had to yield to a competitor, who is now silent, finally, sleeping the deepest sleep of his life. The hero's forgetting 'all that he had suffered' becomes the reverse of his remembering, i.e., telling, enacting his sufferings. In other words, the hero's forgetting becomes the necessary condition for the poet's remembering and the continuation of the tale.

But conversely, the hero models the beginning of *his* tale on the beginning of the poet's matrix story:

Ἰλιόθεν με φέρων ἄνεμος Κικόνεσσι πέλασσεν,
Ἰσμάρῳ· ἔνθα δ' ἐγὼ <u>πόλιν ἔπραθον</u>, ὤλεσα δ' αὐτούς·
ἐκ πόλιος δ' ἀλόχους καὶ κτήματα πολλὰ λαβόντες
δασσάμεθ', ὡς μή τίς μοι ἀτεμβόμενος κίοι ἴσης.
ἔνθ' ἦ τοι μὲν ἐγὼ διερῷ ποδὶ φευγέμεν ἡμέας
ἠνώγεα, τοὶ δὲ μέγα <u>νήπιοι</u> οὐκ ἐπίθοντο.
ἔνθα δὲ πολλὸν μὲν μέθυ πίνετο, πολλὰ δὲ μῆλα
ἔσφαζον παρὰ θῖνα καὶ εἰλίποδας ἕλικας βοῦς.

From Ilion the carrying wind took me to the Kikones,
to Ismaros; there <u>I sacked the city</u>, and destroyed them all;
taking their wives and many possessions from the city,
we divided it all, so that no one was cheated of his fair share.
There I urged that we be fleeing with swift foot;
but they, <u>fools</u>, they would not listen.
Then much wine was drunk and many sheep
they slaughtered and many cattle with rolling gait and curvy horns.

(*Od.* 9.39–46)

Just as the epic as a whole, this story begins with the sack of a city (πόλιν ἔπραθον picks up the proem's Τροίης ἱερὸν πτολίεθρον ἔπερσε); and both proems talk of a situation in which the hero is contrasted with his companions, who are in both cases characterized as νήπιοι in indulging in the consumption of meat that they should not have eaten. An entirely new performance has started, in dialogue with the one that started earlier. In this new performance the audience comes face to face with the hero himself.

Now narratology relies on a distinction between *fabula* and *story*, 'fabula' being the causally related chain of events that underlies the narrative, and 'story' the articulation of the fabula into narrative discourse.[25] The idea is that the story may recount the events of the fabula in sequence or out of sequence, or embedded, told by another narrator as a flashback or as a flashforward (analepsis and prolepsis). For the narratologist, Odysseus' tale is such a flashback, a manipulation of the 'natu-

---

25 E.g., De Jong (1987) 2004, 31–33; for a critique of such a 'dualist' conception of narrative, see Smith 1981.

ral' sequence of events in the fabula. In telling his tale, the narratologist's reasoning goes, Odysseus retroactively and out of sequence fills the gap that the primary narrator did not cover, the chain of events from the sack of Troy to the hero's arrival on Calypso's island.[26]

I think such an account does little justice to the narrative complexity of the *Odyssey*; it also does little justice to Odysseus himself, who is much more than an 'embedded' or 'secondary' narrator who is hierarchically subordinated to Homer, the narrator of the matrix story. Odysseus' tale is not subordinated to Homer's; both are performances in their own right, complementing each other, reacting to each other, even competing with each other.

Epos, the hero's tale, in fact, takes on unmistakable features of *aoidê* when the teller is confronted, as if he were a poet, with the unmanageable dimensions of his subject, the catalogue of heroines he saw in the Land of the Dead:

> πάσας δ' οὐκ ἂν ἐγὼ μυθήσομαι οὐδ' ὀνομήνω
> ὅσσας ἡρώων ἀλόχους ἴδον ἠδὲ θύγατρας
> πρὶν γάρ κεν καὶ νὺξ φθῖτ' ἄμβροτος.
>
> There is no way I could tell or name them all,
> All those I saw who were consorts or daughters of heroes;
> before <I could do this>, the immortal night would have dwindled away.
> (*Od.* 11.328–330; cf. 517)

As many Homerists have seen, these lines are built on the same formulaic pattern as the invocation of the Muses in the *Iliad* at the beginning of the Catalogue of Ships:

> πληθὺν δ' οὐκ ἂν ἐγὼ μυθήσομαι οὐδ' ὀνομήνω.
>
> Their multitude, there is no way I could tell or name <them all>.
> (*Il.* 2.484)

I would argue that the similarity is more than a mere matter of formulaic composition in performance. The Odyssean lines either consciously recall the famous Iliadic moment, or at least they instantiate epic's fundamental expression of the poetic, i.e., human, condition, subject as it is to time and physical limitations. The lines are the backdrop for Alkinoos' famous compliment, in which he states that the skill of Odysseus in telling his story is professional-grade, as if he were a real *aoidós*:

---

26 De Jong 2001a, 221.

σοὶ δ' ἔπι μὲν μορφὴ ἐπέων, ἔνι δὲ φρένες ἐσθλαί,
μῦθον δ' ὡς ὅτ' ἀοιδὸς ἐπισταμένως κατέλεξας.

Upon you is comeliness of *epea*, in <you> are noble *phrénes*;
and the tale, as an *aoidos* you have most expertly told it in all its detail.
(*Od.* 11.367–368)

A few books later the swineherd Eumaios, another appreciative audience for Odysseus, goes even further, when he describes not Odysseus' technical narrative skills, but the enchanting effects that Odysseus' narrative had on him:

ὡς ὅτ' ἀοιδὸν ἀνὴρ ποτιδέρκεται, ὅς τε θεῶν ἒξ
ἀείδῃ δεδαὼς ἔπε' ἱμερόεντα βροτοῖσι,
τοῦ δ' ἄμοτον μεμάασιν ἀκουέμεν, ὁππότ' ἀείδῃ
ὣς ἐμὲ κεῖνος ἔθελγε παρήμενος ἐν μεγάροισι.

As when a man looks at an *aoidos*, who starting from the gods
sings having learned *epea* full of longing to mortals
And they long insatiately to hear him whenever he sings:
This is how that man enchanted me sitting next to me in my hall.
(*Od.* 17.518–521)

The hero's tale of his Wanderings, then, is much more than a flashback or filling in of a temporal gap in the matrix tale; it is also much more than a series of 'folktales' that have come to be imported somehow into the story of Odysseus' return. The hero's tale about his Wanderings is a complementation of Homer's tale of the *nostos* of Odysseus and each tale enriches the understanding of the other. Both tales revolve around a central crime, the consumption of forbidden meat, by the hero's Companions on Thrinakia when they slaughter the Cattle of Helios, and the Suitors as they are depleting the resources of livestock in Odysseus' palace. In both tales the hero has to deal with a mysterious and desirable female, goddess or woman, who resides on an island.[27] So instead of one of the two tales being subordinated to the other there is a continuous and mutually enriching dialogue between the two. Both tales shape each other as Homer and Odysseus vie for prominence in the performance, but are both working toward a common goal.

Many students of the *Odyssey* have noticed the pervasive self-reflexivity of the *Odyssey*, working with the passages that I have quoted as well as others. This kind of observation sits uncomfortably with the ap-

---

[27] See Louden 1999, 1–30; Nagler 1996. The question of eating in the two intertwined stories is the subject of a monograph in preparation (Bakker, forthcoming.).

proach to Homer as 'oral poetry,' which would consider self-reflexivity a 'literary' feature. I think that 'performance' as a critical paradigm emphasizing the importance of performer-hero interactions across the generations goes a long way toward resolving the conflict. There is something between Homer and Odysseus, the hero who becomes a poet in a poem in which a poet becomes a hero (*Od.* 8.483). The mimetic role of the hero that the performer must play begins to interfere with the indexical role he has to play as 'himself.' Poet and hero are engaged in an interaction that conventional narratology cannot cope with. The well-known but enigmatic phrase that rounds off the (first) proem comes into full play here:

τῶν ἁμόθεν γε, θεά, θύγατερ Διός, εἰπὲ καὶ ἡμῖν.

From some point onwards starting from these events, tell us too, goddess, daughter of Zeus.

(*Od.* 1.10)

The personal pronoun ἡμῖν has been taken by most commentators as referring to 'the poet and his audience;' I would agree, provided we read the phrase with projected indexicality: the deictic ἡμῖν means 'us here now,' performer and audience at the occasion of the telling of the tale. But what about καί ('<to us> *too*')? 'Too' with respect to whom or what? We may think, as most have done, of an inclusion of the poet and his audience into what the 'goddess,' i.e., the Muses, already knew.[28] But we may also think of a relation between the poet (and his audience) and Odysseus, an inclusion in what Odysseus already knew: 'to us, too' – in addition to Odysseus. This makes sense, because the events mentioned in the proem, as we already saw, are the adventures of Odysseus as told by Odysseus. The as yet unknown and unnamed hero, the generic ἄνδρα whose name is being withheld, is set up as a source of knowledge and information of which the present performer and his audience want to be part, through the intervention of the Muse. Homer the performer needs to gain access to the world of Odysseus the hero.

If read in this way, the proem sets up Odysseus as a privileged source of knowledge, the one who was there, did it, and saw it. Odysseus' tale, told in the first person singular, is typologically the tale of the shaman who returns from his trip in the otherworld and tells of his adventures

---

28 Another solution proposed is to see the present performance as included in the sum total of all the previous performances. See also Nagy 1997, 188 n. 74.

there.[29] The shaman, who has a privileged access to the other side of things and the poet who has a privileged access to the Muses' vision of the past, are natural counterparts. The one tells in the first person, the other in the third person. Odysseus and Homer, in fact, together make up the ultimate performer of the epic tale. The one is an eyewitness in a privileged position; the other is assisted by the Muses in overcoming the disadvantages of his position. Together they encompass all the important features of a performer practicing in a highly evolved tradition of epic poetry that is very much aware of and ready to reflect on its own medium of transmission and reception.

But Odysseus' privileged position has also its dangers. Someone who has seen so much, endured so much, and traveled so far and so long, needs much time to tell his story. We saw this theme already in Odysseus' words to the Phaeacians about the enormity of his narrative task; Odysseus utters similar words in Eumaios's hut, where he tells another tale:

ῥηϊδίως κεν ἔπειτα καὶ εἰς ἐνιαυτὸν ἅπαντα
οὔ τι διαπρήξαιμι λέγων ἐμὰ κήδεα θυμοῦ,
ὅσσα γε δὴ σύμπαντα θεῶν ἰότητι μόγησα.

Easily hereafter even for a full year
I would not be finished telling of the sorrows of my heart,
all, in their totality, that by the will of the gods I have toiled.
(*Od.* 14.196–198)

It is interesting to compare these words of Odysseus with the famous Homeric *recusatio* in *Iliad* 2, of which the beginning (*Il.* 2.484) was cited earlier. Homer cites human cognitive limitations, such as a failing voice, failing lungs as reason for his *recusatio*; Odysseus, on the other hand, cites lack of time, an equally human constraint. If left unchecked, he would make time stand still for his audience. In other words, in the *Odyssey* ἔπος, the hero's tale, poses risks to ἀοιδή, the tale of the poet; it could go on forever and so crowd out the poet's tale. Odysseus's performance has the potential to preempt Homer's, taking the stage and never leaving it. But that would be a fatal error, for without Homer, Odysseus would not complete his *nostos*. The two performances, in fact, not only complement each other; they need each other. Without Homer, Odysseus would never be able to complete his *nostos* and enjoy the *kleos* that comes from being sung in *aoidê*. But, conversely, without

---

29 Bakker 2006b, 14–18.

Homer having Odysseus as a sparring partner telling his tale, there would be no ἀοιδή. Homer wouldn't have had any song to sing.

Speech Act Types, Conversational Exchange, and the Speech Representational Spectrum in Homer

Deborah Beck

This paper outlines a method for studying how speech is represented in the Homeric poems. In brief, traditional narratology does not provide sufficiently nuanced tools for understanding a) how speeches in Homeric epic are distributed among direct speech, indirect speech, and speech mention, or b) the effect(s) of these different modes of representation in the narrative texture of the poems. Attempts to understand speech representation from a traditional narratological standpoint have therefore fallen short and have not explained fully either that there is a speech representational spectrum in Homeric epic, or how it works as a tool for constructing the narratives in the poems. This paper proposes to deepen and broaden the insights about Homeric speech representation that narratology has offered by adding relevant ideas and concepts from linguistics to the speech representational spectrum devised by narratologists. First, it briefly describes how the concept of the speech representational spectrum has developed in narratology, and what the current emphases of narratology are in relation to speech representation. Next, it defines several linguistic concepts and applies them to Homeric speech representation. In studying Homeric speech representation, it is necessary to know what *speech act type*[1] is being represented to make sense of

---

I would like to thank Jonas Grethlein and Antonios Rengakos for inviting me to the Thessaloniki conference, which was enormously stimulating; for their wonderful hospitality while the conference was in progress, which must have involved a truly Herculean logistical effort but which showed no trace of any such effort while the conference was in progress; and for their editorial help with the transition from conference paper to this volume. It has been a great pleasure to participate in this conference from start to finish. Among the other conference participants, I would especially like to thank Christopher Pelling for his apposite questions and Irene de Jong, not only for all the work she has done to bring narratology to a classical audience but also for pointing out areas for improvement in my paper.
1   Risselada 1993, 23 defines a speech act as 'the verbal action which a speaker performs by means of an utterance.' Her discussion provides a clear and concise overview of the relationship among various terms that are commonly used to

how it is represented. *Expressivity*, a blanket term for the subjective features of an utterance, most accurately captures the differences between direct and non-direct modes of speech representation. The *move* of a given utterance, a way of describing both speech act type and how individual utterances are linked together to form conversational exchanges, is also related to how Homeric speeches are represented. Finally, a short conclusion notes some of the lines of argument that this framework implies.

1. Narratological approaches to speech representation

The speech representational spectrum that I apply to the Homeric poems divides speech representation into three large categories basically identical to the ones de Jong uses in *Narrators and Focalizers*: namely, direct speech, indirect speech, and speech mention (equivalent to de Jong's speech-act mention ((1987) 2004, 114–15)).[2] I base these categories on linguistic and grammatical criteria because these are relatively objective features, and because in practice, these are the ways that speech is presented in the *Iliad* and *Odyssey*: direct speech consists of a verb of speaking and an independent clause; indirect speech uses a verb of speaking to govern a dependent clause, usually an infinitive but sometimes a subordinate clause governed by ὡς; and speech mention uses a verb of speaking with either no object or with an accusative object like ἀγγελίη. Genette 1980 takes a similar approach, using the terms reported (direct), transposed (indirect), and narratized discourse (speech mention; 171–73).[3]

On the other hand, influential treatments of speech representation have put forward a more nuanced, spectrum-oriented approach. These include McHale 1978, followed by Rimmon-Kenan (1983) 2002, 110–14, and Fludernik 1993, 280–91. Fludernik argues elo-

---

talk about speech acts. She notes later on that speech act theory '(more or less tacitly) assume[s] that the units by means of which verbal interaction takes place are single sentences' (50), even though in practice this is rarely the case.

2   This mode is also called 'narrative report of speech act' by some scholars, e.g. Leech – Short 1981, 323–24.

3   Although he is characterized by Fludernik 1993, 283 as a proponent of a scalar model, I do not agree with that. It seems to me that his presentation in the citation just given very clearly lays out three distinct modes of speech representation.

quently for a spectrum-based typology partly on the grounds that the 'ideal trinity' approach does not account for many modes of speech representation that actually occur in narrative (280–81). This issue does not apply to a situation in which one's goal is to understand a specific text rather than to create a typology that is as powerful and wide-ranging as possible. Moreover, speech representation in Homer for the most part tends to fall into clear categories rather than at multiple points along the kind of spectrum that Fludernik describes. The most extensive study of speech representation in Latin literature (Laird 1999, 86–101) disclaims linguistic criteria as a legitimate way of classifying speech representations, but it seems to me that the system Laird comes up with instead – particularly his use of the term free direct speech – is sufficiently subjective in its implementation as well as idiosyncratic in relation to previous work on speech representation that it causes as many problems as it solves.[4]

Current directions in narratological research, however useful they may be for other texts, generally do not provide fruitful approaches to Homeric speech representation. Narratological work on speech representation in particular focuses mainly on modes in which some kind of boundary crossing or blurring between narrative levels or voices seems to take place. This is particularly true of free indirect speech,[5] which in addition to featuring the blurring of the voices of the narrator and a character has also attracted a lot of interest insofar as it supposedly characterizes and was invented by modern literary fiction.[6] Although – contrary to popular belief[7] – there are examples of free indirect speech in Homer,[8] they are rare and generally do not function in the same way

---

4   Unlike most scholars working on speech representation, Laird does not use 'free direct speech' to mean the direct speech analogue of 'free indirect speech.' This is unnecessarily confusing, given the widespread use of this term to mean something other than what Laird uses it to mean.
5   Fludernik 1993 is a particularly comprehensive recent study of free indirect speech.
6   Claimed in e.g. McHale 1978 but disputed by Fludernik 1993, 84–95 and Collins 2001, 135–36.
7   See e.g. de Jong (1987) 2004, 269 n. 41, where she asserts that modes of speech representation other than the three she focuses on are 'irrelevant' to Homeric epic.
8   One of the most striking is the end of Cleopatra's emotional plea to Meleager, where her description of the sufferings of a captured city is rendered in free indirect speech (*Iliad* 9.593–94).

that modern examples of free indirect speech do.[9] While Homeric speech representation is well worth studying, its noteworthy features generally do not line up well with the aspects of speech representation on which narratologists tend to concentrate. Moreover, what one might call the recent 'second wave' of narratology has moved into different issues after a period of gloom and *aporia* in the 1990s:[10] the table of contents in the recent *Blackwell Companion to Narrative Theory* (Phelan – Rabinowitz 2005) contains no chapter on speech representation and no entry for it in the index.

Homerists working within a narratological framework, the most prominent of whom is of course Irene de Jong, have seen non-direct[11] forms of speech as unimportant because they are comparatively rare in relation to direct speech: they are used for representing orders and peripheral speeches.[12] While these characterizations are true as far as they go, they need a broader context that relates the norms of non-direct speech more closely to the norms of direct speech. This approach leads to a more meaningful understanding of what non-direct speech positively contributes to Homeric narrative. Conversely, it gives us a clearer view of why direct speech predominates so heavily in the Homeric poems and what effect that has on the poems' audiences as they interact with the poems. Rather than claiming that indirect speech is mainly used for orders (also true of direct speech), it is more accurate to say that non-direct speech tends *not* to be used for certain kinds of speech act types. The question that naturally follows from this is, why not, and what does that mean? Moreover, the claim that indirect speech is used for unimportant or peripheral speech is backwards. Rather, speeches can become unimportant because they are represented with indirect speech. Again, the question is: what characterizes a speech that is cast into the background in this way? What does that tell us about Homeric narrative?

---

9 Primarily because they represent mainly speech rather than thought, as free indirect speech does in modern literary fiction.
10 Indicated quite starkly in the title of a 1990 article by the prominent narratologist Mieke Bal: 'The Point of Narratology.'
11 A collective term for indirect speech and speech mention.
12 Richardson 1990, 71–74 and 77–78 associates indirect speech with orders and peripheral speeches; de Jong (1987) 2004, 114–18 argues that indirect speech is 'the exception to the rule of direct speech.' In her view, it is used to summarize, usually because the speech in question is unimportant for some reason, and for speeches that take place before the main story of the poem.

2. Linguistics and speech representation

Let me now turn to various linguistic concepts that will provide the tools to make more nuanced and illuminating statements about the relationship between the various modes of speech representation in Homeric poetry, namely speech act type, expressivity, and move. The speech act type 'order' is part of the larger speech act category of directive, which is any speech act that tries to get the addressee to do something.[13] Other kinds of speech acts[14] include assertives (statement of fact, e.g. the famous 'the cat is on the mat'); interrogatives (invites the addressee to take a position on a statement of fact: 'is the cat on the mat?'); and emotives[15] (assumes a fact and expresses the speaker's emotion about this: 'I wish the cat were on the mat!,' which presupposes that the cat is *not* on the mat, although it does not make this explicit). The various kinds of directives – not just orders, but also pleas and supplications, prayers, proposals, requests, threats, and warnings – are the most common speech act type in Homeric epic in both direct speech and non-direct speech, although they are more predominant in non-direct speech than they are in direct speech. 56% of direct speech consists of directives in the *Iliad*, and 41% in the *Odyssey*.[16] 87% of non-direct speech consists of directives in the *Iliad*; the analogous figure in the *Odyssey* is 62%. Meanwhile, emotives and interrogatives are essentially absent from non-direct modes of speech representation. Expressivity can explain both the lack of emotives and interrogatives in non-direct speech and the differences between directly quoted and non-directly represented directives (or assertives).

Linguistics-oriented research gives us the notion of expressivity, a tool to describe in a quantitative manner what exactly direct speech

---

13 A directive is any speech act whose goal is to get the addressee to do something (Searle 1976, 11). Henceforward, the term 'directive' means the broad category of such speeches, while 'order' refers specifically to a directive whose proposed action primarily benefits the speaker and which does not offer – or does not seem to offer – the addressee the option not to comply.

14 This typology follows Risselada 1993; see in particular 37. An influential contrasting perspective on speech acts, which does not consider interrogatives a separate category, can be found in Searle 1976.

15 More usually called 'expressives', but I have changed the name to 'emotive' to avoid confusion with the way 'expressive' is used in this paper.

16 These figures and all subsequent figures, unless noted, are taken from Beck 2008. They are percentages of speech 'moves' that contain directives rather than individual speeches, a concept I will explain in detail below.

conveys that non-direct speech does not and more importantly, what effect this has in a narrative. Expressivity is a somewhat slippery catch-all term covering the features of an utterance that make it the speech of a particular person with feelings about what he is saying.[17] What distinguishes linguistically oriented discussions of expressive features from what a narratologist might say about (for example) focalization is primarily their focus on understanding the *vehicles* for conveying emotions and judgments rather than the specific emotions or judgments conveyed. Moreover, expressive elements may convey nothing more than that a particular speaker *is* the speaker (such as first-person forms) without implying any additional feeling on the speaker's part. Besides first and second person forms, expressive elements also include exclamations like ὤ μοι, vocatives,[18] and language that contains evaluations, emotions, and reasoning by the character speaking (Fludernik 1993, 228).[19]

Emotive speeches and expressive features in other types of speeches are not found in non-direct speech forms.[20] Some expressive features are impossible in non-direct speech,[21] of which the most common in Homeric poetry are exclamations like ὤ μοι and vocatives. Other expressive features, however, like the reasons that characters offer to justify or explain the directives they give, can appear in non-direct speech but in

---

17 Benveniste 1971, 224 coins the term 'subjectivity' for 'the capacity of the speaker to posit himself as "subject"'; that is, to shape his utterance according to his own emotions and perceptions. Most other scholars use the term 'expressive' for those features of language and speech that are related to or depict the consciousness of the speaker (e.g. Banfield 1982 *passim*; Fludernik 1993, esp. ch. 4; and Collins 2001, 35, who identifies expressivity with emotion).

18 Names seem like objective facts, but they are not: which among various possible forms of address a speaker chooses for his addressee may convey important information about his feelings toward that person, as Achilles' vocatives for Agamemnon in *Iliad* 1 make clear (on which see Friedrich 2002).

19 Her focus in her chapter about expressivity is primarily on linguistic and syntactical indications of expressivity, such as hesitation, repetition, emphatic preposing of words, and so on.

20 Two exceptions occur in *Iliad* 24: 24.102 mentions but does not quote Hera's greeting to Thetis, and 24.720–22 describes the lamentation of the professional mourners (ἀοιδούς, 720) who accompany the women of Hector's family. The emotional involvement of these professionals – if any – bears no relationship to what the women feel in the directly quoted laments that end the poem.

21 Banfield 1982, 30–32 gives exclamations and 'repetitions and hesitations' (32) as non-embeddable expressive elements. She lists vocatives separately as a different kind of non-embeddable element.

practice do not. Interrogatives, which require an answer, are very rare.[22] Only directives and assertives, the types of speech that can most comfortably exist without conversational interchange and without expressive elements, regularly occur in non-direct speech modes. This suggests that the interchange of conversation itself has an expressive value in Homeric poetry, and indeed, an unjustly ignored argument by Samuel Bassett asserted many years ago that the kinds of speech that appear in non-direct forms are those which are 'outside of the dialogue' (Bassett 1938, 106).

The lack of expressivity that characterizes non-direct speech occurs with directives in specific kinds of social and narrative contexts: the emotions of the speaking character toward his addressee(s) are either non-existent (in the sense that the two have no emotional relationship) or else not the most important thing at that particular moment in the narrative. Sometimes the narrator uses the low expressive quality of non-direct speech to cast a particular speech as peripheral. Non-direct speech does not just passively reflect an objectively obvious lack of importance in non-direct speeches. It regularly makes speeches unimportant in comparison to speeches nearby in order to shape a conversation or a scene.

To consider a couple of examples, speeches to people whose entire function is to receive and carry out directives are rarely quoted directly: heralds (particularly when being ordered to summon an assembly), maids and/or servants performing household chores, and charioteers are all regular addressees of indirect speech. Named servants, however, like Eumaeus and Euryclea in the *Odyssey*, have significant relationships with the main characters and play active roles in the unfolding drama, and these characters very rarely speak or get addressed indirectly. Arete's speeches to her maids represent the norm of speech representation for servants. Such speech usually occurs after a conversation of some sort between major characters and is represented non-directly. So, after Odysseus makes his appearance in the Phaeacian palace and is welcomed

---

22 Each poem has two non-direct questions: *Il.* 6.238 (εἰρόμεναι with accusative objects) and 13.365 (ἤτεε with accusative); *Od.* 17.70 (ἐξερέεινον with internal accusative) and 17.368 (ἀλλήλους τ' εἴροντο τίς εἴη καὶ πόθεν ἔλθοι [they asked each other what man he was, and where he came from]).

by Alcinous, at *Odyssey* 7.334–38, Arete gives a series of instructions to her maids for arranging a place to sleep for their visitor.[23]

ὣς οἱ μὲν τοιαῦτα πρὸς ἀλλήλους ἀγόρευον,
κέκλετο δ' Ἀρήτη λευκώλενος ἀμφιπόλοισι
δέμνι' ὑπ' αἰθούσῃ θέμεναι καὶ ῥήγεα καλὰ
πορφύρε' ἐμβαλέειν, στορέσαι τ' ἐφύπερθε τάπητας
χλαίνας τ' ἐνθέμεναι οὔλας καθύπερθεν ἕσασθαι.

So now these two were conversing thus with each other,
but Arete of the white arms told her attendant women
to make up a bed in the porch's shelter and to lay upon it
fine underbedding of purple and spread blankets above it
and fleecy robes to be an over-all covering.

Arete gives more orders to her maids at *Odyssey* 8.433–34, again following a directly quoted speech and again represented indirectly. In both cases, the maids represent a tool for accomplishing something that major characters talk about in direct speech in the preceding conversation. They generate no interest on their own account. Euryclea, in contrast, is the addressee of twenty directly quoted speeches and no indirectly represented speeches. Many of these directly quoted speeches are directives from Telemachus or Penelope, and so Euryclea is still discharging the usual functions of a maidservant.[24] But at the same time, she is a full participant in conversations with the people who give her orders rather than – as with Arete's maids – simply a way to accomplish some activity that her mistress has in mind.

Similarly, exhortations to troops in battle may appear either as direct speech, in which the speaker appeals in a direct emotional way to his troops, or non-directly with less or no expressive content. For example, Hector's speech to his troops at *Iliad* 11.285–91 includes vocatives, imperatives (both general commands and ones specific to the situation), and a rationale for the directive being given.

Τρωσί τε καὶ Λυκίοισιν ἐκέκλετο μακρὸν ἀΰσας·
'Τρῶες καὶ Λύκιοι καὶ Δάρδανοι ἀγχιμαχηταί,
ἀνέρες ἔστε φίλοι, μνήσασθε δὲ θούριδος ἀλκῆς.
οἴχετ' ἀνὴρ ὤριστος, ἐμοὶ δὲ μέγ' εὖχος ἔδωκε
Ζεὺς Κρονίδης· ἀλλ' ἰθὺς ἐλαύνετε μώνυχας ἵππους

---

23 Greek quotations are from the Oxford Classical Text of Allen and Monro; translations are by Richmond Lattimore (1951 [*Iliad*] and 1967 [*Odyssey*]).
24 For example, compare Telemachus' instructions to her when he is preparing for his expedition, directly quoted at *Odyssey* 2.349–60, with Arete's instructions to her maids about Odysseus' bed.

ἰφθίμων Δαναῶν, ἵν᾽ ὑπέρτερον εὖχος ἄρησθε.'
ὣς εἰπὼν ὄτρυνε μένος καὶ θυμὸν ἑκάστου.

He called out in a great voice to Trojans and Lykians:
'Trojans, Lykians and Dardanians who fight at close quarters,
be men now, dear friends, remember your furious valour.
Their best man is gone, and Zeus, Kronos' son, has consented
to my great glory; but steer your single-foot horses straight on
at the powerful Danaans, so win you the higher glory.'
So he spoke, and stirred the spirit and strength in each man.

In contrast, an exhortation in non-direct speech is simply one deed the troops' leader performs in battle. We see this at *Iliad* 5.494–96 when Hector responds to a rebuke from Sarpedon with a series of actions, first jumping down from his chariot with his armor and brandishing his spear (5.494–95) and then also exhorting the Trojans (5.496, ὀτρύνων μαχέσασθαι). Thus, a particular kind of directive, such as 'order to servant' or 'exhortation to troops' is represented differently in different contexts to achieve different kinds of expressive effects.

Within one conversation or scene, non-direct speech can be used to represent just one of a series of speeches exchanged between two named individuals to de-emphasize that speech in favor of direct speeches nearby. The moment when Achilles calls for Patroclus to find out what is happening on the battlefield in *Iliad* 11 (602–606) represents a crucial turning point in the story, beginning the sequence of events that ultimately leads to the death of Patroclus. προσέειπε appears here as a speech mention to introduce Achilles' first speech to his companion.

αἶψα δ᾽ ἑταῖρον ἑὸν Πατροκλῆα προσέειπε,
φθεγξάμενος παρὰ νηός· ὃ δὲ κλισίηθεν ἀκούσας
ἔκμολεν ἶσος Ἄρηϊ, κακοῦ δ᾽ ἄρα οἱ πέλεν ἀρχή.
τὸν πρότερος προσέειπε Μενοιτίου ἄλκιμος υἱός·
'τίπτέ με κικλήσκεις, Ἀχιλεῦ; τί δέ σε χρεὼ ἐμεῖο;'

At once he spoke to his own companion in arms, Patroklos,
calling from the ship, and he heard it from inside the shelter, and came out
like the war god, and this was the beginning of his evil.
The strong son of Menoitios spoke first, and addressed him:
'What do you wish with me, Achilleus? Why do you call me?'

This is the only occurrence of προσέειπε as a non-direct form of speech representation out of nearly two hundred instances of this verb in the Homeric epics.[25] In contrast, Patroclus' response to Achilles' summons

---

25 For additional instances of a participial form of φθέγγομαι with a common verb

is quoted directly, and he is described with the adjective πρότερος, implying that he was the first to speak. In fact, he was only the first to be quoted directly, and his speech – just one verse in which he asks why Achilles has called him – is no more or less important or interesting than Achilles' request that precedes it. By using both speech mention and direct speech in one conversation, the narrator presents Patroclus as the 'first' speaker although in fact he is responding to a summons. This mode of representation implies that in a larger sense, Patroclus actively takes the initiative in his own doom.[26] The representation of speech here, in fact, serves an analogous function to the narrator's unusually expressive aside in verse 604. In this conversation, speech mention de-emphasizes one speech in order to make another speech more prominent. Because both speeches appear to be equally important (or unimportant) from an objective point of view, we can see this effect particularly clearly in this conversation.

This exchange between Patroclus and Achilles, in which an initial speech – very unusually – is represented non-directly, but the responding speech and the rest of the conversation are represented directly, brings out another difference between non-direct and direct modes of speech representation. Non-direct speech usually represents speeches that react to a previous speech or are not part of a conversational interchange rather than speeches that begin an exchange. This brings us to the idea of the *move*. A 'move' is essentially a speech act in a conversational context:[27] 'speech act' defines a particular utterance as a directive, assertive, and so forth in terms of particular linguistic and grammatical features of the utterance, whereas 'move' concentrates on how a particular utterance operates in its context. Kroon defines a move as

> the minimal free unit of discourse that is able to enter into an exchange structure ... A move usually consists of a central act (which is the most im-

---

of speaking to introduce a direct speech, see *Il.* 24.169–70 (προσηύδα ... φθεγξαμένη); *Od.* 14.492 (φθεγξάμενος ... πρὸς μῦθον ἔειπε); *Od.* 21.192 (φθεγξάμενος ... προσηύδα).

26 Nagy 1974, 293–94 connects Patroclus' doom with the expression 'equal to Ares,' which describes Patroclus both here (ἶσος Ἄρηϊ) and at 16.784 (ἀτάλαντος Ἄρηϊ).

27 My discussion of 'move' derives mainly from Kroon 1995, 58–95. Other useful discussions include Edmondson 1981 (uses many different descriptive terms for moves so that his terminology becomes unwieldy and hard to apply outside the specific context in which he first developed it, for describing classroom interactions); Risselada 1993, 49–62 (less extensive than Kroon, but more helpful on how a move can spread over several individual speeches).

portant act in view of the speaker's intentions and goals) and one or more subsidiary acts, which also cohere thematically with the central act (1995, 66).

Moves do not map exactly onto individual speeches. A given speech may consist of one move, or it may include multiple moves, such as a reaction to a previous move and then an initiation of a new exchange within the ongoing conversation. Sometimes the same move may extend over several speeches.

The same basic categories apply to moves as to speech acts (a move can be directive, assertive, interrogative, or emotive) but the interactive perspective of move terminology entails a second dimension. Moves are classified both by what they are trying to do and by where they are in the interactional structure of the exchange in which they occur. So, a move can be initiating, reactive, or non-preferred, depending on whether it begins a new topic or theme (initiating), responds satisfactorily to a topic begun by a previous move (reactive), or somehow objects to or refuses to go along with the previous move (non-preferred).[28] Non-preferred moves are both reactive and initiating at the same time.[29] Most often one initiating and one reactive move form an exchange, but from time to time a reactive move itself elicits a reaction[30] or two different speakers react to the same initiating move.[31] While all of these move types are found in direct speech in Homeric epic, non-direct speech consists predominantly of either directives that receive no verbal response (i.e. are not part of a conversational exchange) or, less commonly, of reactive moves. In the *Iliad*, there are 91 non-direct representations of speeches. Only eight of these, including this conversation between Patroclus and Achilles in *Iliad* 11, use indirect speech for an initial move that has a reactive move following it. Most of these exchanges

---

28 Kroon 1995, 91 provides a helpful table of each type of move (assertive, directive, and interrogative, which she calls 'elicitation') as initiating moves and the expected reactive moves in response to each one.
29 This is the most context-dependent category of the three: a refusal to follow a directive is a reactive move if the refusal is not challenged by the person who issued the directive, but non-preferred if it leads to a discussion of the refusal.
30 For instance, after Helen identifies Odysseus (*Il.* 3.200–202) in response to a question from Priam (192–98), Antenor talks about him at length in a second reactive move (204–24).
31 As when Idaeus orders Ajax and Hector to cease their duel in *Il.* 7 (279–82, initiating), to which Ajax and Hector each react individually (284–86 and 288–302 respectively).

that start with a non-direct initiating move relate in some way to the death of Patroclus.[32] In other words, the function of directing attention by means of combining direct and indirect speech appears mainly in connection with a central story line in the *Iliad*. The concentration of this technique around a thematically prominent and meaningful part of the story suggests that the technique specifically highlights that theme by – for example – drawing out the complexities of who is responsible for Patroclus' death at the moment when the train of events leading to his death is seen to begin. This effect would not be possible if these conversations followed the usual pattern for speech representation by the main narrator and appeared entirely in direct speech.

3. Norms of speech representation within character-speech

Homeric narratologists – like other narratologists – have not seen the speech representation contained within character speech as a tool for studying speech representation at the level of the main narrator. Traditionally these are seen as two separate phenomena because they occur on two different narrative levels, but in poems that contain as much direct speech as the Homeric epics, we cannot reach a full understanding of 'speech representation' if we omit speech represented by characters from consideration. Speech representation in the poems overall comprises both speech represented by the main narrator and speech represented by characters, although this paper focuses mainly on speech represented by the main narrator.

Expressivity and various features associated with conversation – questions and initiating moves, in particular – rarely appear in non-direct speech that is reported by the main narrator. Characters, in contrast,

---

32 Initiating moves in non-direct speech where a reactive move is also represented are found at *Iliad* 6.238 (Trojan women to Hector, followed by another non-direct speech), 7.185 (the Greeks identifying whose lot has been chosen for the duel with Hector, followed by non-direct), 11.602 (our passage, followed by direct speech), 11.646 (Nestor to Patroclus, followed by direct speech), 13.365 (back story on a dead warrior, followed by non-direct speech), 19.304 (the Greeks beg Achilles to eat, followed by direct speech), 23.39 (the Greeks try to arrange a bath for Achilles, followed by direct speech), 23.203 (the winds invite Iris to sit down, followed by direct speech). Our passage is the only one where non-direct speech is followed by direct speech and the context is not a directive being refused.

have a quite different speech representational spectrum from the main narrator. Indirect speech rather than direct speech is the norm: characters in the *Iliad* quote directly just twenty times out of a total of 272 speeches they represent; in the *Odyssey*, direct speech is more common, since characters often use it to tell their own stories, but non-direct speech is nonetheless more common (out of 386 speeches represented by characters, 126 are direct speeches). Moreover, when characters quote the conversations of others, they are more likely than the main narrator to use non-direct speech for this purpose. Whereas the main narrator of the *Iliad* includes just two conversational exchanges that are represented in non-direct speech in the entire poem, Odysseus gives five of these in his narrative in *Odyssey* 9–12.[33] Characters are more inclined to mix different modes of speech representation within a given exchange and even within a single speech, as we see in a conversation that appears in non-direct forms at *Odyssey* 10.14–18.

> μῆνα δὲ πάντα φίλει με καὶ ἐξερέεινεν ἕκαστα,
> Ἴλιον Ἀργείων τε νέας καὶ νόστον Ἀχαιῶν·
>   initiating question
> καὶ μὲν ἐγὼ τῷ πάντα κατὰ μοῖραν κατέλεξα.
>   reactive assertive
> ἀλλ' ὅτε δὴ καὶ ἐγὼν ὁδὸν ᾔτεον ἠδ' ἐκέλευον
>   initiating directive
> πεμπέμεν, οὐδέ τι κεῖνος ἀνήνατο, τεῦχε δὲ πομπήν.
>   reactive assertive

> A whole month he [Aeolus] entertained me and asked for everything
> of Ilion, and the ships of the Argives, and the Achaians'
> homecoming, and I told him all the tale as it happened.
> But when I asked him about the way back and requested
> conveyance, again he did not refuse, but granted me passage.

In verses 14–15, Aeolus asks an initiating question that is represented with speech mention. In Odysseus's reply, spanning verses 16–18, there are two different moves that follow Aeolus' initiating move. First, at verse 16, we find a reactive assertive move represented with speech mention: Odysseus tells the story that answers Aeolus' question. Next, he gives an initiating directive at verses 17–18. If this were a speech represented by the main narrator, this directive would immedi-

---

33 10.14–18, 10.109–111, 10.311–13, 11.234 (which, unusually, puts the reactive move first and the initiating move second), 12.34–35.

ately follow the reactive move as part of the same speech.[34] Here the directive is given partly as speech mention (ὁδὸν ᾔτεον, 17) and partly as indirect speech (ἐκέλευον πεμπέμεν, 17–18). This is a rare instance of a non-direct speech that contains more than one move, and Odysseus's speech represents the two moves with two different speech modes.

These norms of character-represented speech can throw the different norms of speech represented by the main narrator into relief. Indeed, several types of speech representation that are supposedly absent from the poem when we study only the main narrator's approach to speech representation do in fact occur in character-reported speech. These include: free indirect speech, where the voice of both the narrator and the speaker of the speech being reported seem to merge (found, e.g., at a highly emotional moment in Phoenix' crucial story of Meleager to Achilles in *Iliad* 9); indirect speech as a common and important way of representing speech; and non-direct forms of speech representing conversational exchange. This tells us that such modes of representation are within the compass of the poems overall. They are not simply absent, but *omitted* from speech represented by the main narrator.

4. Conclusions and future directions

This general framework leads to a wide range of specific lines of inquiry that I will merely sketch in here. Filling out the narratological model of a speech representational spectrum with linguistic concepts from pragmatics and speech act theory gives us an enriched perspective on how speech is represented in the Homeric poems. We can see more clearly that there are times when non-direct speech accomplishes narrative goals better than direct speech, rather than characterizing it as a fallback option when for some reason the default option of direct speech is not necessary. These may include highlighting a nearby directly quoted speech, as in the previously discussed conversation of Patroclus and Achilles in *Iliad* 11; characterizing a speech as more of an action than a speech, as with servants performing the orders of a master or mistress; or the representation of secrecy or privacy, as with surreptitious reports

---

34 E.g. Telemachus' speech to Aegyptius at *Od.* 2.40–79, where he first answers Aegyptius' question about who has called the Ithacans to assembly and then gives a directive to the assembled group.

given to Penelope about Telemachus' journey while the suitors revel about her.[35] It makes more sense to see direct speech, indirect speech, and speech mention as complementary parts of a speech representational spectrum, each member of which has a role to play in the poems overall, than to call direct speech a 'default' option.[36] Direct speech, the complement of non-direct speech, is bursting with expressive features, even in apparently brief and colorless directives that seem to lack emotional content. Direct speech occurs as often as it does in Homeric epic because the poems put a premium on this expressive capacity. This perspective gives us a new way both to understand the overall shape of the Homeric speech representational spectrum and to evaluate individual examples of speech representation within the Homeric poems. Non-direct speech is more worthy of our attention than has been previously realized, and direct speech merits study for some hitherto unnoticed reasons.

Moreover, the norms of character speech give us a powerful context for evaluating the norms of the main narrator's typical patterns of speech representation. The speech representational possibilities of the poems overall include the norms not only of the main narrator, but the very different tendencies of character-narrators in the *Iliad* and the again different behavior of character-narrators in the *Odyssey*. In other words, the speech representational spectrum of the main narrator represents a sub-section of the complete range of speech representational possibilities in the poems overall. Why does the main narrator avoid certain modes of representation? What is the effect of the way that characters represent speech? How do the two interact? The framework this paper proposes leads the way to a comprehensive approach to speech representation that not only answers these questions individually, but relates them to each other in a powerful, unified view of speech in the Homeric poems overall.

---

35 At *Odyssey* 16.337–39, a herald arrives in the palace to bring Penelope the news that Telemachus has returned home, as well as some unspecified further details about his trip and future course of action. Both direct quotation and non-direct representation are used to represent the herald's speech in such a way as to affirmatively conceal the content of the speech.

36 Collins 2001, 51 points out that 'the notion of default modes is at best an oversimplification and often an illusion; putatively 'basic' modes have pragmatic rationales.'

Philosophical and Structuralist Narratologies – Worlds Apart?

Jonas Grethlein

For a while, it looked as though narratology along with its structuralist agenda and scientific aspirations would be swept away by the anarchic force of deconstruction. However, narratology has not only survived the Dionysiac reign of poststructuralism, but has come to bloom a second time and now more splendidly than the first. It is striking though that many of the 'new narratologies' barely consider specifically narrative features. As pointed out in the introduction to this volume, it is a major challenge to go beyond the all too easy recourse to trendy labels and to establish links between traditional narratology and approaches such as cultural history and feminism as well as disciplines including psychology and philosophy. Such dialogues, rare as they are, promise rich rewards for both sides: whilst narratology stands in prospect of overcoming some of its technical sterility, its partners have the chance to ground their explorations with solid textual analysis.

A particularly intriguing case is the relationship between philosophy and traditional narratology. On the one hand, it is hard to imagine worlds more different than the lofty realms of philosophical speculation and the depths of narratological fieldwork. On the other, they have categories in common which are central to both. Most prominently, time, which has attracted much attention from philosophers since the Presocratics, has emerged as crucial to narratological studies. Is it possible to bridge the gap and make philosophy and structuralist narratology enter a dialogue? In this paper, I argue for a cross-fertilization between Ricoeur's philosophical and Genette's structuralist narratologies with time as the connecting link. More specifically, the use of Genette's taxonomy allows us to refine Ricoeur's approach to time and narrative (1). I will illustrate my model through a brief look at the works of Herodotus and

---

I wish to thank the participants of the conference for a lively discussion and in particular Carolyn Dewald, Francis Dunn, Chris Pelling and Antonios Rengakos for their helpful comments.

Thucydides (2), the discussion of which will lead me to a tentative suggestion for an anthropology of narrative (3).

1. The reconfiguration of time in narrative: Ricoeur and Genette[1]

In the three monumental volumes of *Time and Narrative*, Ricoeur tries to define time in terms of narrative.[2] He shows that a pure phenomenology of time, as traced by Husserl and Heidegger, is bound to fail as phenomenological and cosmic times cannot be reconciled. There is always a gap between time as experienced by human beings and the objective time that Heidegger calls 'vulgar' time.[3] Instead, Ricoeur suggests taking narrative as a poetic answer to the *aporiai* of the phenomenology of time: narrative reconfigures time and doing so creates historical time which mediates between phenomenological and cosmological time.[4] Ricoeur argues that the reconfiguration of time takes place in the reciprocal interweaving of historical and fictional narratives.[5] Historical narratives contain fictional elements whereby phenomenological time is inscribed into cosmological time. At the same time, cosmological time is inscribed into phenomenological time through historical elements that pervade fictional narratives.[6] Thus, Ricoeur sees a strong

---

1   This section relies on the fuller argument in Grethlein 2006a, 180–204.
2   Ricoeur 1984–1988, I-III. For a more extended summary of the work, see Grethlein 2006a, 188–192. It is striking that Ricoeur's work is often referred to in general form, but that the actual reception of *Time and Narrative* and engagement with its argument is rather scarce. For possible reasons, see Polti 1997. Ricoeur 1980 is an illuminating pre-stage of the link between time and narrative as established in *Time and Narrative*, in which not the juxtaposition of cosmological and phenomenological times, but Heidegger's threefold analysis of time provides Ricoeur with a starting point.
3   Ricoeur 1984–1988, III, 11–96.
4   Ricoeur 1984–1988, III, 99 f.
5   Ricoeur 1984–1988, III, 142–192.
6   Ricoeur 1984–1988, III, 192: 'The interweaving of history and fiction in the reconfiguration of time rests, in the final analysis, upon this reciprocal overlapping, the quasi-historical moment of fiction changing places with the quasi-fictive moment of history. In this interweaving, this reciprocal overlapping, this exchange of places, originates what is commonly called human time, where the standing-for the past in history is united with the imaginative variations of fiction, against the background of the aporias of the phenomenology of time.' However, Ricoeur also notes that the narrative approach does not

link between narrative and time, namely 'that between the activity of narrating a story and the temporal character of human experience there exists a correlation that is not merely accidental but that presents a transcultural form of necessity. To put it another way, time becomes human to the extent that it is articulated through a narrative mode, and narrative attains its full meaning when it becomes a condition of temporal existence.'[7]

While Ricoeur's thesis, that narrative reconfigures human time, is striking and unveils a crucial aspect of narrating, his description of the reconfiguration remains rather abstract and does not really deal with narrative *qua* narrative. The three forms through which phenomenological time inscribes itself into historical narratives, namely the calendar, the succession of generations and the trace,[8] are not specifically narrative, and the 'imaginative variations on time' which add the historical aspect to fictional texts are explicit reflections on time and temporality.[9] I suggest that the reconfiguration of time in and through narrative can be specified by the use of the tools of narratology.

Yet, before we turn to Genette's taxonomy, it is helpful to reconsider the notion of time. Ricoeur views time in the tension between time as objective and as experienced. Another approach to time that takes into account both the phenomenological and the cosmological aspects of time, but directs the focus on the perception of this tension in the human consciousness, has been put forward by Reinhart Koselleck. Based on his examination of changing temporalities around 1800 CE, Koselleck defines historical time as the tension between the horizon of expectations ('Erwartungshorizont') and the space of experiences ('Erfahrungsraum').[10] Guided by previous experience, we direct expect-

---

give a simple answer to the question of what time is (261): 'The reply of narrativity to the aporias of time consists less in resolving these aporias than in putting them to work, in making them productive'.
7 Ricoeur 1984–1988, I, 52. For a creative reading of Ricoeur's reflections on time and narrative, see White 1987, 169–184, who suggests that narratives have temporality as a second referent at Ricoeur's level of metaphoric reference. This interpretation, however, erases the distinction between fiction and history that Ricoeur is eager to maintain and replaces the idea of reconfiguration with reference. Cf. Grethlein 2006a, 191 f.
8 Ricoeur 1984–1988, III, 104–126.
9 Ricoeur 1984–1988, III, 127–141 discusses Wolf's *Mrs. Dalloway*, Mann's *Zauberberg* and Proust's *À la recherche du temps perdu* as examples of the 'imaginative variations on time'.
10 Koselleck 1985. For a critique of this model, see Schinkel 2005.

ations to the future which are either fulfilled or disappointed by new experiences which, in turn, not only form the background to new expectations, but also retroactively transform the memory of previous expectations and experiences. While the relationship between expectations and experiences differs from culture to culture,[11] the very tension between them seems to have a transcendental character and defines human temporality.

Koselleck's definition of historical time which can be traced back to Augustine's reflections on time and is indebted to Heidegger's emphasis on the future in *Sein und Zeit* allows us to draw on the framework of classical narratology in order to refine Ricoeur's thesis of the reconfiguration of time in narrative.[12] The tension between expectations and experiences is reconfigured at two levels in narrative. First, the reception of narratives has, as Jauß made clear,[13] the character of an experience. For example, when we read a novel, we build up expectations about the development of the plot which in the further process of reading either come true or not. The temporal dynamics of reading can be further specified by Sternberg's definition of narrativity: 'I define narrativity as the play of suspense/curiosity/surprise between represented and communicative time (in whatever combination, whatever medium, whatever manifest or latent form).'[14] Sternberg's three 'master strategies' signify different forms of the tension between expectation and experience. Suspense is based on the expectations about the future (prospection), curiosity directs the expectations to a past, yet unknown experience (retrospection) and surprise marks the disappointment of an expectation (recognition).

It is, however, important to add that, although reading is an experience, this experience differs from real-life experiences. As absorbed as we can get by narratives, the experiences in our reception always remain within the frame of 'as-if'.[15] Even with the strongest suspension of dis-

---

11 In Grethlein 2006a, 97–105, I compare the view of the tension between expectations and experiences in the *Iliad* with the construction of time in Historicism.
12 See book 11 of the Augustine's *Confessiones*. On Koselleck's indebtedness to *Sein und Zeit*, see Grethlein 2006a, 27 f.
13 Jauß 1982b.
14 Sternberg 1992, 529.
15 Iser 1991 harks back to Vaihinger's category of 'as-if' in his literary anthropology and models the relation between fiction and reality on the notion of 'Spiel'.

belief, there remains some distance, and while characters with whom we identify are being tortured or killed we are still lying comfortably on the sofa. The reception of narrative therefore allows us to repeat the temporal structure which characterizes our existence, namely the tension between expectation and experience, without the strains of real life ('ein von lebensweltlicher Pragmatik entlastetes Widerspiel'[16]).

The comparison of readers with characters leads me to a second level. Narratives not only unfold in time, but narratives also deal with characters in time.[17] The time span represented by narratives varies widely, but nonetheless nearly all stories deal with temporal proceedings in which the characters have expectations and experiences.[18] Thus, the reconfiguration of time in narrative is twofold. The reception doubles, albeit in the frame of the 'as-if', the tension between expectations and experiences at the level of the action.[19] The doubling of prospection, retrospection and recognition creates a dynamic interplay between the levels of the reception and the action, as the expectations of the readers may be identical with or differ from those of the characters.[20] As we see, narrative invites us to view in the form of an experience (which, however, takes place in the 'as-if') the tension between expectations and experiences as it unfolds in a particular story with particular characters.

It is now time to show that this reconfiguration of time can be elucidated by a technical examination of narrative. A founding idea for classical narratology is the Russian Formalists' distinction between 'fabula' and 'sjuzet', between the story in simple temporal and chronological sequence on the one hand and its artistic presentation in narrative on the other.[21] Needless to say, the 'fabula' is only a construct,[22] and yet, it is

---

He also conceptualizes the reception of fiction as play (468–480). See also Suttrop 2000.
16 Iser 1991, 404. In Grethlein 2006a, 199–201, I argue that the way narrative plays with expectations and experiences helps to complement Iser's literary anthropology in so far as it goes beyond the negativity of his model and demonstrates that literary fiction reconfigures the temporal structure of experience.
17 On the distinction between narrative time and narrated time, see Müller 1968, 247–268.
18 In this context, it is interesting to note that Bruner 1986, 16–19 emphasizes the central role of the characters' intentions for narrative.
19 An important aspect of this is highlighted by Kermode 1967, who demonstrates that the function of the ending in fiction mirrors its central place in life.
20 For another recent approach to the dynamics of reading, see Lowe 2000 with the criticism in Grethlein 2006a, 196–199.
21 A similar distinction, 'story-plot' was coined by Forster who, however, attributes causality to the level of 'plot'. Cf. Sternberg 1978, 10–13.

heuristically a most valuable category for alerting us to the fact that the same events can be presented in rather different ways.[23] In what has proven to be a most, if not the most, influential taxonomy of classical narratology, Genette identifies three categories in which a 'fabula' is transformed into a 'sjuzet': 'tense', the shaping of time through order, duration and frequency; 'mood', the selection of information and its presentation through focalization; and 'voice', the narratorial instance.[24]

Genette's system may not be as objective as it presents itself to be – Sternberg, for example, has argued that it privileges anachronies over chronology[25] – but it is nonetheless a taxonomy that lends itself to the sober analysis of texts without offering much of an interpretation of the data. We can note that the *Iliad* is told by a heterodiegetic narrator and that it is full of anachronies, some of them given from the narrator's perspective, others focalized by characters, but these observations are not yet an interpretation of the *Iliad* and it is one of the greatest challenges for narratological readings of particular texts to make the technical analysis fruitful for the interpretation.

Here, I would like to suggest that the technical analysis of narrative not only provides data that can stimulate our understanding of particular passages, but that it also allows us to refine Ricoeur's thesis that narratives reconfigure time. More specifically, Genette's categories of 'tense', 'mood' and 'voice' enable us to elucidate the character of the experiences of characters and readers. Shifts in perspective and focalization give the readers insights into the expectations at the level of the action as when speeches or representations of the characters' interior lives inform the readers about their plans. The handling of narrative time shapes the expectations of the readers themselves. Particularly prolepses which can range from explicit statements to vague references and even implicit patterns instill in the readers expectations about the future development of the plot. Perspective, focalization and time taken together determine the relation between the characters' and readers' experiences. For example, prolepses that are imparted to the readers directly by the narrator privilege them over the characters. In this case, the readers are saved the disappointment of expectations that awaits the characters. On the other

---

22 The narrative form of reality as argued for by Carr 1986 makes it doubtful that reality and narrative can be separated so clearly.
23 See Chatman 1978, 37 and also Culler 1980.
24 Genette (1972) 1980.
25 Sternberg 1990, 908 f.

hand, a narrator can conceal something that is known at the level of the action and thereby put the readers in a worse-informed position than the characters and excite their curiosity. To sum up, through the examination of the way in which 'tense', 'mood' and 'voice' shape the tension between expectations and experiences at the levels of action and reception, Genette's narratology can help us to refine Ricoeur's thesis that narrative reconfigures time.

2. The reconfiguration of time in Herodotus and Thucydides[26]

I would now like to illustrate my model for the reconfiguration of time in narrative by discussing examples taken from Herodotus and Thucydides. Genette originally developed his taxonomy for fictional literature, but he later pointed out that it could also be applied to non-fictional narrative. Recent works in the field of Classics have proven the fruitfulness of a narratological approach to the artful accounts of ancient historians.[27] Nonetheless, it is important to keep in mind the distinctive features of historiographical writing. While the attempt to represent past reality is the most striking, albeit heavily debated, aspect that distinguishes historical from fictional writing, another point is more pertinent to the approach taken here. The frame of 'as-if' is not limited to the reception of fictional narratives, for the balance between absorption and distance in the readers is not affected by the veracity or fictionality of the narrative. At the same time, the focus on the past seems to limit the tension between expectations and experiences that can emerge in the reception, as the events narrated become known. This point, however, needs to be qualified in two regards. First, many of the ancient narratives that we classify as fictional deal with mythical stories with which ancient readers and audiences were familiar and which they considered to constitute part of their past. Second, cognitive research has shown that recipients who know a plot can nonetheless feel some kind of suspense arising from it, the so-called 'anomalous suspense'.[28]

---

26 For a fuller discussion, see Grethlein forthcoming a.
27 See Genette (1991) 1992, 65–93 on the application of his taxonomy to non-fictional texts. Groundbreaking studies for the application of narratology to the ancient historians are Dewald 1987; Hornblower 1994. For Herodotus and Thucydides, see also Rood 1998; de Jong 1999; 2001b; Rengakos 2006a; b.
28 Cf. Gerrig 1989a; b. See also the discussion of this question by Miltsios in this volume.

If we add that the readers of historical works are not necessarily informed of all the details,[29] then it makes good sense to discuss the reconfiguration of time in historical narratives. Herodotus and Thucydides afford an interesting test-case, because they combine a similar assessment of human temporality as revealed at the level of the action with distinct modes of presentation.

a) Herodotus

Let us begin with Herodotus: the Croesus-logos, placed prominently at the beginning, sets the tone of the *Histories* and starts the series of rulers who will rise and fall in the course of it. The Croesus-logos itself has an interpretive frame in the encounter of the Lydian king with Solon, in which the wise Greek points out (1.32.1–9):

> Croesus, when you asked me about men and their affairs, you were putting your question to someone who is well aware of how utterly jealous the divine is, and how it is likely to confound us. Anyone who lives for a long time is bound to see and endure many things he would rather avoid ... No two days bring events which are exactly the same. It follows, Croesus, that human life is entirely a matter of chance ... It is necessary to consider the end of anything, however, and to see how it will turn out, because the god often offers prosperity to men, but then destroys them utterly and completely.[30]

Not only is the content of Solon's message confirmed by its echo of the proem in which Herodotus himself emphasizes the changeability of men's happiness (1.5.4), but the account of Croesus' life which follows also reads like an illustration of his very words.[31] In spite of and, in the end, because of the various cautionary measures which Croesus takes, he first loses his beloved son, then ruins his empire and finally falls into the hands of Cyrus. Although Croesus takes pains to inquire about the future, particularly through the consultation of oracles, these events strike him most unexpectedly.[32]

---

29 Cf. de Jong 1999, 244 f. on Herodotus and his readers.
30 See Harrison 2000, 38 f. with references to parallels and scholarship. Mikalson 2003, 147–153 emphasizes the poetic origin of the reflections which he strictly distinguishes from popular religion.
31 See in particular Croesus' reference to his encounter with Solon when he is on the pyre (1.86).
32 Stahl 1975 emphasizes the role of surprise in the Croesus-logos.

Modern historians are very cautious in their assessments of the thought processes of historical agents, because it is hard, if not impossible, to get access to their consciousness through the sources that we usually have at our disposal. Herodotus, on the other hand, like most other ancient historians, has no scruples about giving detailed and in-depth accounts of the interior lives of his characters.[33] Time and again, he makes Croesus the focalizer and reports his unexpressed expectations as well as his utterances, often marking them as futile through anachronies. In some cases, the perspective shifts from the character to the narrator for the prolepses, for example in the transition from the Solon scene to the following narrative when Herodotus marks out Solon's reflections as being significant for Croesus, 1.34.1:

> After Solon's departure, the weight of divine anger descended on Croesus, in all likelihood for thinking that he was the happiest man in the world.

While here the authorial prolepsis contrasts with the expectation of the character, in other cases true prolepses already exist at the level of the action where they are most often misunderstood or ignored. Most prominently, the Delphic oracle predicts that Croesus, should he attack Persia, will destroy an empire (1.55.2). Here, the art of mantics provides the characters with a glimpse of the future, but assuming 'that he would destroy Cyrus' empire' (1.54.1), Croesus brings about his own ruin. Later, the narratorial voice explicitly marks the misunderstanding (1.71.1): 'Due to his misunderstanding of the oracle, Croesus invaded Cappadocia on the assumption that he would depose Cyrus and destroy the Persian empire.'

In addition to prolepses, there are analepses which hark back to the expectations that were directed to current experiences, some of them given from the narrator's perspective, others focalized by characters. For instance, Herodotus comments on the death of Croesus' son, Atys (1.43.3):

> Since it was a spear that hit him, he fulfilled the prophecy of the dream ...
> (ὁ μὲν βληθεὶς τῇ αἰχμῇ ἐξέπλησε τοῦ ὀνείρου τὴν φήμην...)

The actual event appears in a participle, while the main verb marks it as a fulfilment of the dream and thereby establishes an analepsis which points out that, despite the warning of the dream, Atys' death comes

---

33 Rengakos 2006b, 184 f. points out that internal focalization is a borrowing from the epic tradition.

unexpectedly for Croesus. Paradoxically, Atys is killed by the guardian, Adrastus, whom Croesus had given him to prevent the fulfilment of the dream. Here, the analepsis is given by the narrator, but not much later in the narrative Croesus himself looks back when he addresses Adrastus, who accidentally killed Atys, 1.45.2:

> You are not to blame for the terrible thing that has happened to me; you were just an unwitting instrument. Responsibility lies with one of the gods, who even warned me some time ago about what was going to happen.

The number of examples could easily be enlarged, but I hope those given will suffice to demonstrate how the shaping of narrative time and the use of shifts in perspective and focalization throw into relief the tension between expectations and experiences at the level of the action. If we turn from the experiences of the characters to the reception, the examples discussed reveal that, in addition to the familiarity with the basic data of past events, prolepses and changes in perspective well prepare the readers for the development of the plot so that the reading experience contains little surprise.

At the same time, it is important to notice that the foreshadowing tends to be vague. To start with the first prolepsis of Croesus' disaster, Herodotus mentions the oracle given to Gyges that in the fifth generation his crime will be punished (1.13). Since Gyges is followed by Ardys, Sadyattes, Alyattes and Croesus, circumspect readers learn that Croesus will fall victim to divine retribution, but what form the punishment will take remains open. The explicit prediction that 'the weight of divine anger would descend on Croesus', made by Herodotus after Croesus' encounter with Solon (1.34.1), alerts the readers to a forthcoming downfall – but again, the exact character and extent of the retribution are not specified. In the subsequent narrative, there are no prolepses that anticipate the death of Croesus' son, and the reader has to wait until 1.71.1 to receive an explicit narratorial foreshadowing of Croesus' defeat against Cyrus. Thus, while the prolepses privilege the readers over the characters, they are vague enough not to interfere with the forms of epic suspense that de Jong and Rengakos have found in the Herodotean narrative.[34] The vagueness of the foreshadowing combined with, for example, retardation even contributes to creat-

---

34 De Jong 1999, 242–251 adduces 'prolepses, connaissance, identification, conflit/contraste' as suspense-creating devices; Rengakos 2006b examines suspense that is established through retardation, misdirection and dramatic irony.

ing suspense as it makes the readers desire to learn how the known end will come to pass.

The readers are also prepared for the further development of the plot through devices that are not really grasped by Genette's taxonomy, but nonetheless fulfill a proleptic function.[35] For example in the digression on Athenian and Spartan history (1.56–68), Herodotus reports an oracle that was given to the Spartans when they consulted the Pythia about whether or not to invade Arcadia: 'I will give you the dance-floor of Tegea; you can caper there/ and measure out her beautiful plain with a rope.' (1.66.2). The Spartans took this as a prediction that they would own Tegea and consequently attacked. They were, however, defeated and the oracle was fulfilled by their working the Tegeans' fields as slaves. This oracle is strongly reminiscent of the one given to Croesus: asked if a neighbor ought to be attacked, the Pythia gives an oracle which is taken as the confirmation of victory, but then turns out to have predicted defeat. The similarity is highlighted by the adjective κίβδηλος, which is applied to both oracles, the only two occurrences of the word in the meaning 'deceptive' in the *Histories* (1.66.3; 75.2). The parallel marks Croesus' misunderstanding of his oracle and so draws attention to the looming defeat at the hands of Cyrus. The foreshadowing is only implicit and requires an attentive reader, but nonetheless it is worth pointing out that here an analepsis fulfills a proleptic function.

The principle of analogy that underlies the indirect prolepsis just discussed figures prominently in the *Histories* at different levels. As scholars such as Regenbogen, Immerwahr and Cobet have pointed out, the pattern of the rise and fall of eastern rulers structures the abundant narrative.[36] This 'corset' contains a set of smaller patterns. For instance, time and again 'wise advisors' warn the Eastern monarchs before they set out on their fateful expeditions.[37] Croesus is warned by Sandanis and, indirectly, by Solon, and after his downfall he serves as advisor to Cyrus and Cambyses. Darius ignores good advice given by Artabanus, Coes, Gobryes and Megabazus, and his son Xerxes neglects warnings by Artabanus and Demeratus. In the same vein, laughing comes to

---

35 De Jong 1999, 242 gives a list of implicit forms of prolepsis: 'la nature, amerces, conventions narratives, doublet, mise en abîme'.
36 Regenbogen 1930; Immerwahr 1966; Cobet 1971. See also Corcella 1984 on analogy in Herodotus.
37 Bischoff 1932; Lattimore 1939.

stand for unjustified self-assurance[38] and the crossing of rivers frequently signifies a transgression.[39] The rejected warning, the despotic laughter and the crossing of geographical boundaries indicate not only a hybristic action, but also signal to the readers the impending downfall. Such patterns are similar to prolepses in that they prepare the readers for the further development of the plot. Yet, the information is even vaguer here than in narratorial prolepses – how and when the disaster will occur is not specified – and thus leaves the process of reading its dynamics.

It can be concluded that the reconfiguration of time in the *Histories* establishes a strong discrepancy between characters and readers. The temporal organization of the narrative combined with the use of perspective and focalization emphasizes on the one hand the disappointment of expectations at the level of the action, and, on the other, safely guides the readers through the narrative without major surprises, while at the same time maintaining suspense as to the exact character of the further development. The gap between characters and readers comes to the fore in the numerous signs and oracles that play a double role at the levels of action and reception. Being part of the action, signs and oracles are frequently misunderstood and simultaneously serve as prolepses at the level of the reception. The force of contingency that Herodotus deploys in his narrative is not only distanced from the readers through the "as if" of the reception, but also contrasts with the safety of the reading experience.

b) Thucydides

As is well-known, the gods who figure prominently in Herodotus' narratives are more or less absent from Thucydides' *History*. Nonetheless, Thucydides also emphasizes human short-sightedness and the failures of even well-planned enterprises. As in Herodotus, men's expectations are often crossed by chance, the prominence of which is nicely grasped in Cornford's summary of the Pylus-episode:

> The fleet, bound as it was for Sicily, with instructions to call on the way at Corcyra, where it was urgently needed, would never have put in at Pylos, if a storm had not 'by chance' driven it to shelter ... It was owing to the accidental continuance of bad weather that from sheer want of something to do 'an impulse seized' the soldiers to fortify the place ... They had time to

---

38 Lateiner 1977; Flory 1978.
39 Immerwahr 1954, 28; Lateiner 1989, 129 f.; Munson 2003, 9–11.

finish it because the Lacedaemonians at home were just then celebrating a festival ... Just when reinforcements and a supply of arms are urgently needed by the extemporized garrison, a couple of piratical craft come bearing down the wind from the north. They turn out, oddly enough, to be Messenians with forty hoplites aboard and – how very fortunate! – a supply of spare arms.[40]

While at Pylus chance favours the Athenians and has them make an unhoped for coup, their expectations are harshly disappointed by the disaster of the Sicilian expedition which I shall use in the following to illustrate the reconfiguration of time in Thucydidean narrative.[41] We will see that the disappointment of expectations is as prominent as in Herodotus, but that the shaping of time, perspective and focalization leads to a rather different reading experience.

Let us start at the end: the final battle in the harbor of Syracuse in which the Athenian armada is devastatingly defeated. Borimir Jordan demonstrates that a series of motives and verbal echoes links this final blow to the hopeful departure of the army from Peiraeus.[42] As in a ring-composition, two spectacular harbor-scenes enclose the Sicilian expedition. The links to the pompous farewell scene are even more obvious in the Athenian departure after the battle.[43] After referring in passing to the high hopes that had inspired the departure (7.75.3; cf. 6.31.6), Thucydides remarks in more detail (7.75.6 f.):[44]

> The general degradation and equal apportionment of misery, although this lightened the load somewhat (in that many were sharing), were not on that account regarded at the same time as easy to bear, above all because from such splendor and vaunting at first they had reached such an end in humiliation. For this was certainly the greatest reversal for any Hellenic army, since what resulted for these men was that, in comparison with their arriving to enslave others, they were going away fearing that instead they themselves would suffer this, in comparison with the prayers and Paians they sailed off with, they were setting out for home again with contrasting words of ill omen, and they were proceeding as infantry instead of sailors, committed to hoplite rather than nautical arms.

---

40 Cornford 1907, 88 f.
41 In 7.71.7, Thucydides explicitly juxtaposes the Athenian disaster in Syracuse with their experiences at Pylus.
42 Cf. Jordan 2000, 76 f.
43 Cf. Stahl 2003, 192 f.
44 Already the μέγιστον ... τὸ διάφορον contrasts with the μέγιστος διάπλους in 6.31.6.

The analepsis, focalized by the defeated Athenians and spelled out by the narratorial voice, forcefully juxtaposes the current experience with the original expectations and so throws into relief the extent of the disaster. Like Herodotus, Thucydides uses analepses, structural parallels and linguistic echoes to reinforce the tension between experiences and expectations at the level of the action.

If we return, however, to the beginning of the Sicilian expedition, we notice the virtual absence of prolepses to the outcome of the expedition.[45] Whereas Herodotus uses prolepses to emphasize the futility of human planning, Thucydides abstains from drawing attention to the Athenians' blindness through the adumbration of the failure. Strikingly, he indicates the shortcomings of the Athenian expedition more subtly through an analepsis, the Sicilian archaeology, which he introduces as important knowledge that the Athenians ignored in their planning (6.1.1).[46] Thucydides otherwise elaborates on the expectations of the Athenians without explicitly contrasting them with the outcome of the expedition:

> A passion for the expedition afflicted everyone alike, the older men satisfied that either they would get control of the places they were sailing against or a great force could meet with no harm, others with the longing of youth for faraway sights and experiences and as confident of surviving as the masses were of earning money in the military for now and acquiring dominion that would provide unending service for the pay. (6.24.3)[47]

---

[45] See, however, 6.15.4 on Alcibiades: 'The masses, frightened by the magnitude of his license in conducting his personal life and of his aims in absolutely everything he did, whatever it was, developed hostility toward him as an aspiring tyrant, and while he as a public person managed the war with the utmost skill, they as private individuals detested him for his behavior, and by entrusting the city to others they ruined it in short order.' However, this prolepsis does not juxtapose an expectation with an experience and is so vague that it triggered a scholarly debate as to what event Thucydides refers to. On the rarity of prolepses in Thucydides, see Erbse 1989, 45 f. Dunn 2007, 116 emphasizes that Thucydides 'anticipates the future in order to motivate judgment of the episode at hand, rather than to demonstrate a connection between earlier and later events.' On prolepsis in Thucydides, see also, with different emphasis, Rengakos 2006a, 298 f.

[46] Thucydides' digression on the tyrannicide (6.54–59) is an interesting parallel for an analepsis that covers important information the ignorance of which proved detrimental for the Athenians.

[47] See also 6.6.1; 30.2–31.1 and Rengakos 1984, 102, who counts 13 references to the Athenians' goal to conquer Sicily. On the special ambitions of Alcibiades, see 6.15.2.

Thucydides further sheds light on the Athenians' expectations through two speech-triads. In Athens, Nicias first speaks against the expedition, then Alcibiades argues for it, and finally, when the assembly is swayed by Alcibiades, Nicias unsuccessfully tries to deter his fellow citizens from an invasion by elaborating on the supplies that will be required (6.9–23). The arguments put forward by Nicias and Alcibiades receive no evaluation through the narrator and, although Nicias may resemble some of Herodotus' wise advisors, it would be hard to argue that the warner is such an established figure in Thucydidean narrative that the readers would automatically accept Nicias' qualms as predictions.[48] The juxtaposition of the speeches and some correspondences with the narrative convey a rather complex picture of the motives and expectations that prompted the Athenians to invade Sicily.[49]

This picture is further enriched by a parallel set of three speeches held at Syracuse, where Hermocrates warns the Syracusans that the Athenians are on their way, Athenagoras rejects this as rumor, and finally an anonymous general decides to prepare for an attack, but not to send out troops as Hermocrates suggests (6.33–41). The juxtaposition of the two sets of three speeches not only illustrates the similarity between Athens and Syracuse against which Nicias warns the Athenians (6.20.3; later confirmed by the authorial voice in 7.55.2; 8.96.5), but also sheds light on the Athenians' plan. Particularly Athenagoras' considerations of how absurd an attack by the Athenians would be, but also Hermocrates' conviction that the Athenians will be defeated, lend support to the misgivings put forward by Nicias. More specifically, the scarcity of food from which the Athenians would suffer, as mentioned by Hermocrates (6.33.5), and Athenagoras' confidence that the lack of horses and equipment would disadvantage the Athenians (6.37.1 f.) echo points made by Nicias. As many other speech pairs in the *History*, the speeches preceding the Sicilian expedition illuminate the expectations at the level of the action from many perspectives. The following narrative will prove Nicias' general reservation as well as many specific

---

48   A figure similar to Nicias in the *History* is the Spartan king Archidamus, whom Pelling 1991 compares to Herodotus' Artabanus.
49   For example, Nicias' warning that the money promised by the Egestaians may merely exist in their words (6.22) is backed up by a narratorial comment in 6.8.2. On the other hand, Alcibiades may err about the Sicilians' ability to unite against an invading force, but his emphasis on the instability of Sicily is to some extent confirmed by the Sicilian archaeology in which ruptures and conflicts loom large.

warnings right,[50] but, unlike Herodotus, Thucydides does not throw into relief the futility of the Athenian plans through prolepses.

In my section on Herodotus, I noticed that patterns can fulfill a proleptic function. I have already argued that, unlike in Herodotus' narrative, the wise advisor does not establish a pattern in Thucydides' *History*. At a more general level, recent works have elaborated on Thucydides' use of the Trojan War and the Persian Wars as backdrop to his account of the Peloponnesian War and some have even claimed that Thucydides casts the Sicilian expedition in a Herodotean mold.[51] However, as I argue in another paper, references to Homer and Herodotus do not so much present the Peloponnesian War as a repetition of a pattern as much as they shed light on it through a complex set of similarities with, and differences from, the previous wars.[52]

It thus seems that Thucydides limits his readers to the knowledge that the characters have. As far as time is concerned, this point is by and large true, but it needs qualification. First, the Sicilian archaeology provides the readers with knowledge about Sicily that the Athenians ignored. The additional information allows the readers to assess the risk of the expedition better than the characters, but since the information refers to Sicily's history, geography and ethnography, it is something that the Athenians would have known had they done their homework. Second, through shifts in perspective and focalization Thucydides gives his readers insights into both camps. While the Athenians do not know what the Syracusans are thinking and doing and the Syracusans have a hard time figuring out the Athenians' plans, the readers learn about both sides in much detail.

An interesting case in which access to different perspectives combined with adherence to chronology makes for a very gripping narrative is the episode of the financial support that the Egestans promised the Athenians if they were to come to their help. The Athenians were duped into believing that the Egestans actually had the promised money when the Egestans hosted their embassies at the temple of Aphrodite at Eryx, displaying all the dedicated objects in the temple and col-

---

50 For the supply problems predicted by Nicias (6.20.4), see 6.42.1; 48; 71.2; for problems created by the superior Syracusan cavalry, see 6.52.2; 70.3; and as expected by Nicias, other poleis rise against Athens (6.88.8: Corinth; 6.93.2: Sparta).
51 See, for example, Marinatos-Kopff – Rawlings 1978; Rood 1999; Kallet 2001, 85–120; Rogkotis 2006.
52 Grethlein 2008a.

lecting silver and gold to show off at the banquets. When Thucydides first mentions the story, he merely remarks that the Egestans' claims were untrue, but nonetheless believed by the majority of the Athenians (6.8). Here, the narrator goes beyond the perspective of the Athenians and imparts to the readers his knowledge of the simultaneous events in Egesta. Afterwards, he touches upon the story again (6.22; 44.4) and so arouses the readers' interest in the details, but he does not fully report the trick until the Athenians themselves learn of it (6.46).[53]

Notwithstanding his omniscience, Thucydides' reticence with prolepses contributes to the strong mimetic dimension of the *History* which has been remarked upon since antiquity. Following Plutarch's lead, scholars have elaborated on Thucydides' *enargeia*, which comes to the fore in vignettes such as the final battle in the Syracusan harbor, where the focalization through an internal audience gives the readers the feeling of directly witnessing the event.[54] In addition to internal audiences, Thucydides' adherence to chronology as well as his restraint with intrusions into the narrative, apart from a few explicit reflections and some set phrases, give the impression that the narrative unfolds at the same time as the events themselves.[55]

Of course, the Peloponnesian War belongs to the past and the readers know for example that the Sicilian expedition ended in a disaster: the opportunities therefore for surprise, recognition and suspense are limited. Nonetheless, unlike Herodotus, Thucydides does not capitalize on hindsight through the use of prolepses, but his focus on the characters' expectations brings the readers as close to the level of the action as is possible in retrospect. This effect can be further elucidated by Morson's concept of 'sideshadowing'.[56] Morson takes up Bakhtin's reflections on chronotopes and juxtaposes the closed time in narrative to the openness of time in our experience. While in real life the future

---

53 On the effects of this artful unfolding of the episode and the interesting parallel in the Herodotean account of Polycrates' downfall (3.123–124), see Kallet 2001, 69–79. See also Erbse 1989, 43 f. Thucydides' narrative strategy is thrown into relief by the account of the same event by Diodorus 12.84.4 ff., who gives the full story right at the beginning.
54 Cf. Plut. *De glor. Ath.* 347a-c. In modern scholarship, see e.g. Davidson 1991, 24; Walker 1993, 355 f.; Greenwood 2006, 19–41.
55 On the *History*'s temporal structure, see more recently Dewald 2005; Dunn 2007, 111–150. On narratorial interventions, see Gribble 1998 and Rood 2006, 243 f., who gives the narratorial interventions a more prominent role.
56 Morson 1994.

is undetermined, 'in a well-constructed story, everything points (or will turn out to point) to the ending and to the pattern that will eventually be revealed'.[57] This feature of narrative is most obvious in foreshadowing, because it 'involves backward causation, which means that, in one way or another, the future must already be there.'[58] Devices of 'sideshadowing', on the other hand, recreate 'the presentness of the past' through 'cultivating a sense that something else might have happened.'[59]

Morson discusses Dostoevsky and Tolstoy, his prime examples for 'sideshadowing', but the concept applies well to the aspect of Thucydidean narrative that I have just pointed out. The extensive presentation of the characters' thought processes, unevaluated by narratorial prolepses, restores the openness of the present that is easily lost in accounts of the past. The focus on expectations is not the only element of 'sideshadowing' in Thucydides.[60] Two further devices that are well-known from the epic tradition are 'Beinahe'-episodes and counterfactuals. For example, when the Peloponnesians do not succeed in their siege of Plataia, they try to set the city on fire (2.77.4–6):[61]

> And a blaze resulted that was the greatest anyone had ever seen up to that time, of those intentionally set; for in the mountains wood rubbed together by the wind has sometimes started fire and flames by itself. But this was big and came very close to destroying the Plataians after they had survived the rest. A large area of the city inside was unapproachable, and if a wind had come up and carried the fire around it, they would not have escaped. But it is said that what happened now was this, that heavy rain came with thunder from heaven and put out the blaze, and so the danger ceased.

The irrealis in counterfactuals signals to the readers that the alternative version did not take place and the 'Beinahe' of the episode quoted is not extended as the phrase 'came very close to' marks that Plataia did not burn down. Thus, no false expectations are raised, but nonetheless the passage demonstrates the possibility of a very different course and so conveys to the readers the presentness of the past.

---

57 Morson 1994, 7.
58 Morson 1994, 7.
59 Morson 1994, 6 f.
60 See the Thucydides-chapter in Dunn 2007 for an extended examination of presentness in Thucydides from a different angle and with different emphasis.
61 On counterfactuals in Thucydides, see Flory 1988, who compares them with Homeric counterfactuals. He also notes that there are far fewer counterfactuals in Herodotus (47 f.). See also Dover 1988.

To sum up, not only are Herodotus' and Thucydides' *Histories* well-suited to illustrate the twofold reconfiguration of time in narrative, but the examination of experiences at the levels of the action and the reception has revealed striking differences as well as important similarities. Both historians elaborate on the tension between the characters' expectations and experiences and emphasize that human plans are often not realized. The free use of focalization marks a crucial difference from modern historians who do not claim to have direct access to the interior lives of historical agents and, if they are interested in being taken seriously by their peers, do not take the liberty to recreate speeches in accordance with τὰ δέοντα.

While the focus on the characters' attitude to the future aligns Thucydides with Herodotus, their narratives create very different reading experiences. A dense net of prolepses and patterns prepares the readers of Herodotus' *Histories* for the development of the action. Thus, Herodotus makes narrative use of the power of hindsight to create a gap between the characters, who are exposed to unexpected turns, and the readers, who can indulge a safe reading experience. Thucydides, on the other hand, abstains by and large from prolepses and, while his readers know what has happened and thereby are privileged over the characters, Thucydides uses devices of 'sideshadowing' to restore the openness of the past when it was still the present. Retrospect does not allow for much surprise, but the *History* invites its readers to assess the future from the vantage point of a contemporary who has access to various perspectives.

3. Time and the anthropology of narrative

The observation that there are narratives in nearly all cultures and time periods makes it tempting to consider something the very thought of which, thanks to Historicism, old and new, makes most of us shudder, namely an anthropology of narrative. What is it that makes narrative such a ubiquitous phenomenon? In a recent paper, Michael Scheffel suggests:

> Versteht man unter Erzählen im Sinne Dantos in erster Linie das Herstellen von Geschichten, dann dient das Erzählen neben der Erinnerung und Planung von menschlichen Handlungen vor allem der Ordnung von raumzeitlichen Daten und damit der Erklärung und kognitiven Bewältigung von Geschehen. Inmitten der Kontingenz des Faktischen schafft das Erzäh-

len Kohärenz und ermöglicht sowohl die Raum- und Zeiterfahrung des Menschen als auch die Ausdifferenzierung der Identität von Individuen und Kollektiven. Sieht man im Erzählen dagegen in erster Linie den kommunikativen Akt, dann dient das Erzählen vor allem dazu, soziale Beziehungen herzustellen und zu helfen, diese Beziehungen quantitativ zu vervielfältigen und qualitativ zu differenzieren. Zugespitzt formuliert: Qua Struktur nutzt das Erzählen der Orientierung in Zeit und Raum, qua Tätigkeit ermöglicht es die Stiftung und Erhaltung sozialer Gemeinschaften.[62]

I hope that my attempt to combine Ricoeur's ingenious thesis of the narrative reconfiguration of time with Genette's sober analysis of narrative structures in the light of Koselleck's observations on time has helped to elucidate the first aspect mentioned by Scheffel, i.e. narrative's function *qua* structure. I have used examples from Herodotus and Thucydides to illustrate the dual manner in which narrative plays with time. The different reading experiences created by their historical accounts merit some further reflection because they illustrate two complementary aspects of narrative that may contribute to its appeal across cultures and times.

As we have seen, Herodotus' shaping of time, perspective and focalization creates a strong contrast between the power of contingency at the level of the action and the safety of the reading experience. I have focused on the level of the reception, but one could as well discuss the instance of the narrator who controls the openness of time through a net of prolepses and patterns. In the episode discussed in this paper, Solon emphasizes the meaning of the end, a point which has meta-historical significance.[63] Retrospect, the advantages of which the narrative form of the *Histories* fully uses, allows Herodotus to create coherence and find significance where the historical agents, who are in the middle of the process, are lost and grappling to find sense. The control of contingency is reinforced by the specific object of the *Histories*. I have chosen my examples from the programmatic first *logos*, but the same case could be made for the last three books which deal with the Persian Wars.[64] The invasions of the Persians posed an immense threat to

---

62 Scheffel 2004, 131.
63 Cf. Grethlein forthcoming b.
64 It is striking though that Rengakos 2006b illustrates his case for epic suspense in the *Histories* with the last books and I suspect that there are fewer prolepses in the account of the Persian Wars than in the Croesus-logos. A possible explanation for this is that Herodotus could rely on a greater degree of familiarity of his readership with recent Greek events.

Greece. For Herodotus' readers, however, this traumatic experience of vulnerability is transformed into a meaningful account.[65]

While Herodotus gives an account of events that are two or more generations old, Thucydides claims that he began 'his work as soon as the war broke out, expecting that it would be a major one and notable beyond all previous wars' (1.1). It does not matter if we believe this assertion or not, Thucydides' narrative rarely offers the readers glimpses of what lies ahead and makes it difficult to argue for patterns with proleptic functions. I have argued that 'sideshadowing' devices, particularly the focus on the expectations of historical agents combined with the reticence in using prolepses, recreate the presentness of the past. The function of this narrative form is elucidated by Morrison's argument about the engagement of the reader in the *History*. He points out that the multiplicity of perspectives, the authorial reticence and the episodic structure require an 'engaged reader' and suggests linking this to Thucydides' claim that his account is useful. The texture of the *History* challenges the readers 'to engage in the activities of extrapolation, conjecture, and prediction'[66] and thereby has the readers practice the very skills that are at the core of political activity. This may not be the only aspect which prompts Thucydides' claim to usefulness, but it highlights the significance of the reading experience.

Perhaps this comparison of the two founding fathers of Greek historiography not only illuminates an interesting difference, but also indicates a key tension of narrative in general. The reception of narrative takes place in the realm of the 'as-if' which comes with a 'Mischung aus kognitiver Distanz und emotionaler Partizipation'.[67] More specifically, narrative allows us to experience the temporal structure of our existence without the strains of everyday life. While readers of both Herodotus and Thucydides will experience distance as well as participation, the narrative of the Persian Wars rather capitalizes on the distancing, whereas the account of the Peloponnesian War is more pressing in inviting a participatory reading. It may be part of what makes narrative so appealing to human beings beyond cultural boundaries that it allows us

---

65 Other strategies of overcoming the experience of contingency can be observed. In the *Persians*, for example, contingency is projected into the distance of the heroic vagueness and, more importantly, presented in the camp of the others, cf. Grethlein 2007.
66 Morrison 1999, 100.
67 Neumann 2000, 294.

at the same time to enact and to distance the tension between expectation and experience.

III. Narratology and the Interpretation of Epic and Lyric Poetry

Chance or Design?
Language and Plot Management in the *Odyssey*.
Klytaimnestra ἄλοχος μνηστὴ ἐμήσατο

Evanthia Tsitsibakou-Vasalos

The *Odyssey* incorporates details from the Agamemnon tale, which are chosen and placed so that they become signposts, proleptic or analeptic, for the events of the epic's main plot and their thematic significance. The discourse between the *Odyssey* and the so-called *Oresteia* is kept open with a dense network of allusions, parallelisms and contrasts. The embedded microstory of the *Oresteia* emerges at nodal points in the story, anticipates narrative peaks and transitions and heightens the suspense.[1] Even though it narrates events almost contemporary with

---

I would like to express my deep gratitude to Lillian E. Doherty who read my paper at an early stage and offered me generous help and insightful comments. My thanks also go to Jonas Grethlein for his very helpful suggestions.

1 Various functions have been posited for this tale, see: Düring 1945, 95–99, 122 (a continuous *Leitmotiv* … to obtain an effect of contrast, the figures of the saga are used as … a foil to the main plot, as παράδειγμα for other characters); D' Arms and Hulley 1946 (theodicy-moral responsibility, parallel characters and ennobling parochial families); *LfgrE* 1955, 258 s.v. Αἴγισθος (a number of foil stories); Clarke 1967, 10–12 (a *Leitmotiv*, dramatic paradigm, multiplying, clarifying and tightening the plot of the *Odyssey*); cf. Lesky 1967, 15; Davies 1969, 238 (parallel figures and an effective paradeigma for the *nostos* and revenge of Odysseus); Friedrich 1975, 86–87 ('Kontrastparallele'); Sternberg 1978, 67–74 (contextual importance of digressions and analogical relations between the two stories which heighten the reader's suspense); Neschke 1986, 289 ('contraste du récit principal pour mettre en relief les parallèles et les oppositions entre le sort des personnages'); Olson 1990, 57 with n. 1, 70–71 (creation of suspense and irony through deceptive hints and foreshadowings); id. 1995, 24 with n. 2; Katz 1991, 6–7, 41–53, and 192–93 (not just a foil or warning motif, but an alternative narrative structure endowed with authority, 'toward which the *mythos* of the *Odyssey* is drawn'). On the *Oresteia* as a hortatory paradigm for Telemachos see March 1987, 84, 86; de Jong 2001a, 33, 78n and ib. 12–13 with n. 26 (parallelism of major figures, 'a warning to Odysseus, an inspiration for Telemachus, and a vindication of Penelope' [so Clarke 1967, 10]). Schmidt 2001 (unity of the *Atreidenmythos* and the poetic intentions; 'Neuorientierung des Heroischen oder besser Heldischen'; Agamemnon pro-

those of the *Odyssey*, it functions as a mythical *exemplum*. In an effort to highlight its paradigmatic purpose and differentiate the material that pertains to Agamemnon from that of Odysseus, I refrain from using the term *Oresteia*, which may be rather confusing in view of Aischylos' trilogy, and I adopt terms, such as 'Agamemnon-tale' and 'Odysseus-tale', speaking of the *Odyssey* as the 'plot' or the 'story'.[2]

The Agamemnon-tale is focalized by male characters, including Athena, a mediating figure by birth and function.[3] They present their narratees with details of different tone and escalating intensity, serving different purposes each time; scholars have submitted various explanations of the discrepancies of the myth reported in the course of the poem.[4] In the first four books of the *Odyssey*, Telemachos is tutored by substitute parental figures (Athena, Nestor, Menelaos) and given a crash course in coming of age. He is encouraged to espouse the precepts of the tale and, driven by the *kleos* ideology, to claim his paternal property, behaving as Orestes' surrogate; the future avenger of the suitors is trained. Telemachos, seeking his self-identity, his lineage and lost father, will often stumble upon

---

vides the background for the 'Sieg der neuen Heldentugenden', 170–71). Rengakos 2002 examines the function of the 'Telemachy' in the framework of the poem, and the interplay of alternatives on an intratextual and intertextual level, focusing on the 'Spannungsstrategien', among which are retardation, and the recipient's misdirection. Radke 2007, 1–38, esp. 28–38, argues for the sovereignty of the poet vis-à-vis the tradition; the different versions of the tale function as a 'Stoffundus einer souveränen Kompositionstechnik', result from different intentions (31–32) and speech-strategies, serve a specific poetical 'Skopos', and contribute to the narrative unity.

2 By the term 'plot' I mean the selection and arrangement of events within the work as we have it; in this respect plot is the story. In the present study I use the translation of Murray as revised by Dimock (Loeb), occasionally with minor modifications. With a sparing use of e x p a n d e d   s p a c i n g I mark words of major narratological and etymological significance. With *italics* I mark cognate words of thematic importance; with underline I point out synonyms that clarify the underlying etymology and meaning. I attempt to illustrate the parallelism between the individual poetic verses and their prose rendering, marking off the latter with slashes (/). This is not always felicitous since the translators observe the syntactical principles of their native language, bypassing the ancient word-order. In such cases I omit the slashes.

3 On Athena's mediation 'as a female upholder of a male-dominated structure' see Murnaghan 1995, 61–80.

4 On one unified source or contamination of variants, see Düring 1945, 95–99, who stresses the coherent and conscious character of the *Odyssey* as a work of art; Hölscher 1967, 4–5, 12; id. 1990, 302; Lesky 1967, 13–18; Heubeck 1989, 102; Katz 1991, 48–49.

Orestes. *Tele-machos* is called upon to imitate *tele-klytos* Orestes, and establish his heroic worth.[5] In book 11, Agamemnon's death is focalized by the slain hero himself, while Odysseus is forewarned to be circumspect, and avoid the naivety of Agamemnon, if he is to stay alive and reaffirm the integrity of his *oikos* and his *kleos*. Odysseus must embody and reverse at the same time the qualities of Aigisthos, the deceptive model suitor, becoming his double figure and foil. But if he aspires to win back Penelope, he must also conquer the potential 'Klytaimnestra' in her, and adopt the proper strategy, combining manly heroism and feminine weaving of wiles and snares. In *Odyssey* 24, the Agamemnon-tale caps the story of the *Odyssey* in a jubilant manner.

As I hope to show, Penelope and Klytaimnestra almost converge around ἄλοχος μνηστή before they conclusively part around κουριδίη. In both tales, the wedded but wooed wife, ἄλοχος μνηστή, is given a central role as affecting the survival of the heroes and the dispensation of κλέος.[6] Ancient and modern scholars associate μνηστή both linguistically and semantically with words that signify recollection – even if deadly – courtship and steadfastness, i.e. μνάομαι, μνηστήρ, μνηστεύω, μίμνω, μένω, μιμνήσκομαι, and μνῆμα.[7] It is no accident

---

5   Murnaghan 2002, 138, argues that Telemachos' story celebrates Odysseus; 'a new model emerges for Telemachus in the role of Menelaus' (148–51).
6   On *kleos*, its semantics and redefinition in the *Odyssey*, see Katz 1991, *passim*; Segal 1995, 210–21; Schein 1995, 23–25; Foley 1995, 95, 105; Tsagalis 2003, 52–56.
7   On the linguistic kinship of μνηστή, μιμνήσκω, μένω and μνάομαι see: Hsch. μ 1511, *μνηστή· ἡ κατὰ μνηστείαν γαμηθεῖσα ἢ ἡ ἐκ παρθενείας μείνασα νῆστις, ἤγουν ἀπείρανδρος*; so Suda μ 1167. *Et.Gud.* μ 396.23, *μνήστωρ, ἐκ τοῦ μένειν στερρῶς. EM* 589.14, *μνεία. ἀπὸ τοῦ μένω*; 589.16, *μνήμη. παρὰ τὸ μένω ... ὅθεν μνημοσύνη ... καὶ μνῆμα τὸ μνημόσυνον*. On the association of *μνηστή, μνηστεία, μνάασθαι, μνηστεύεσθαι* see sch. *Od.* 1.36, 39 (Ludwich), and 36e, f1., f2., 39e1., e2., f. (Pontani). Chantraine *DELG* s.v. *μιμνήσκω*, 'autre présent: *μνάομαι*, avoir en tête, songer à, rechercher une femme en mariage'; ib. s.v. *μνηστήρ*, 'qui rappelle'; Chantraine posits a 'radical *mnā- qui appartient à l'importante racine *men- de μέμονα ... Tout le système est une création grecque, mais est apparenté à μέμονα, μένος, μαίνομαι, avec une forme *mneə₂- de la racine'. Cf. Frisk *GrEW* s.v. *μιμνήσκω*: 'Die durchgreifende Neugestaltung hat *μιμνήσκω* von dem alten μέμονα und noch mehr von μαίνομαι isoliert'. See id. s.v. *μνάομαι*: 'sich erinnern, gedenken, sinnen ... um eine Frau werben, freien'; ib. s.v. *μνηστή* ('gefeit, vermählt, ehelich, erinnerungswürdig'), πολυμνήστη ('vielumworben, wohl eingedenk, in der Erinnerung haftend'). Schmidt 1993a, s.v. *μνάομαι*, 'gedenken'; vgl. μιμνήσκομαι. Markwald 1993, 235–40, s.v. *μνηστήρ*.

that μνηστή often figures in such collocations, positively or negatively (1.29–39; 4.765–70; 11.177–83; 15.18–32; 24.121–32). Through these clustered cognates, whose etymological import is unmistakable, she is connected with potentially disruptive marital activities, and functions as a sign of anomaly that affects social coherence and stability. The perils signalled by ἄλοχος μνηστή are eventually balanced by κουριδίη and κουρίδιος, whose collaboration releases the deadly tensions inherent in the μνηστή, and restores order. Significantly, the notion of infamous μνηστεία (a term unattested in the epos), the word μνηστή, implicitly coupled with negation of 'remembering' and 'remaining' faithful, as well as deadly contrivance, μήδομαι, are embedded in Κλυται-μνήστρα's name and essence, and serve the requirements of the plot. Once more etymology and narrative interlock, bridging the tales of Agamemnon and Odysseus, and integrating them into the wider, enframing story of the *Odyssey*.

Multiple and often intricate are the techniques by which ancient poets elicit or even impose etymological connections, and exploit their potential in generating narrative. Homeric poetry illustrates a rich gamut of etymological practices, whose function and typology I have discussed in detail elsewhere.[8] A brief outline of them may prove helpful in the present enterprise. Displaying a remarkable flexibility, Homer employs categories of varying degrees of complexity, which range from the simple paronomastic collocations, the epexegeses and analyses of compound words into their constitutional parts, the concatenations of lexical units, such as clustered cognates and synonyms, to the more demanding and elaborate types of narrativized and especially resignified etymologies. The last category implies the rearticulation of the underlying phonetic sequences of mostly compound proper names, and the semantic manipulation of the lexemes produced by this implicit internal reorganization. Significant is the function of clusters of cognates, which mark off the boundaries of their own semantic and lexical communities, and with their incessant flux, they engender and ingrain new subjects, emerging as a significant compositional factor. Relying on such etymological devices, the poet intertwines his themes, and allows them to coalesce into a long

---

[8] On ancient poetic etymologizing see Tsitsibakou-Vasalos 1997–1998; 2000; 2001; 2007, *passim*. In particular, narrativization and contextualization of etymology: 2007, 57–59; rearticulation and resignification of Proper Names: ib. 66–80. On the interaction of etymology and narrative see id. 2004; 2007, 39–40 and *passim*.

narrative, signposted by lexical and semantic structures, and also marked by pronounced repetition, a valuable feature for an orally composed and performed poetry. The poet weaves the web of his story, constantly jogging the memory of his audience, and subtly rendering etymology a mnemonic, literary and narratological tool. The tales of Agamemnon and Odysseus will hopefully clarify further the working of the above preliminary yet cursory remarks, and sustain the argument that etymology underscores narrative.

1. Agamemnon-tale in *Odyssey* 1

This myth makes its debut immediately after the proem, in which the primary narrator of the *Odyssey* invokes the Muses, circumscribes his subject, the character of the homonymous protagonist,[9] the current state of affairs, and presents his narratees with axial themes that pervade the poem (1.1–28). He adumbrates the semiology of *atasthaliai*, a kernel concept which stands for mental and moral mistakes manifested in hybristic deeds, such as unlawful feasting, erotic *peitho* and malignant contrivance as well as coveting and appropriating alien goods, including one's legitimate spouse. The narrator summarizes the obstacles to a successful *nostos*: mental blindness (7), lack of sense (8), and consumption of forbidden food are causally connected with an aborted day of return (νόστιμον ἦμαρ, 7–9). Though yearning for *nostos* and his wife, Odysseus is hindered by Poseidon's wrath and the love forced on him by the infatuated Kalypso (11–15, 49–59). In an overt reversal of gender roles, Odysseus is depicted as a reluctant and suffering partner in love, thus prefiguring the plight of his wife at home. Significantly, the Agamemnon-tale follows immediately thereafter in the character-speech delivered by Zeus (1.29–43):[10]

---

9 Odysseus' name is suppressed (*antonomasia*) until verse 21, but this does not impair his identification: he is the renowned *polytropos*, *ptoliethros*, *polytlas* but also *odyromenos* and *oizyros* hero, who will soon disclose the ancestral hate (*odyssamenos*) imprinted in his name.
10 On this speech and its 'argument function' see de Jong 2001a, 13, 81. Segal 1994, 225, argues that 'viewed narratologically, Zeus can be regarded as an authorial function: the sign of the poet's intention to redefine the inherited material of his tale and stamp it with a moral meaning'. Curiously, Olson 1990, 59–60, divests Zeus' speech of 'any intention of setting the intellectual stage for a Homeric epic ... [Zeus] is simply complaining ... about mortal folly and unreasonableness'. On the significance of the 'warning-motif', and the

μνήσατο γὰρ κατὰ θυμὸν ἀμύμονος Αἰγίσθοιο,
τόν ῥ' Ἀγαμεμνονίδης τηλεκλυτὸς ἔκταν' Ὀρέστης·
τοῦ ὅ γ' ἐπιμνησθεὶς ἔπε' ἀθανάτοισι μετηύδα·
'ὢ πόποι, οἷον δή νυ θεοὺς βροτοὶ αἰτιόωνται.
ἐξ ἡμέων γάρ φασι κάκ' ἔμμεναι· οἱ δὲ καὶ αὐτοὶ
σφῆσιν ἀτασθαλίῃσιν ὑπὲρ μόρον ἄλγε' ἔχουσιν,
ὡς καὶ νῦν Αἴγισθος ὑπὲρ μόρον Ἀτρεΐδαο
γῆμ' ἄλοχον μνηστήν, τὸν δ' ἔκτανε νοστήσαντα,
εἰδὼς αἰπὺν ὄλεθρον, ἐπεὶ πρό οἱ εἴπομεν ἡμεῖς,
Ἑρμείαν πέμψαντες, ἐΰσκοπον Ἀργεϊφόντην,
μήτ' αὐτὸν κτείνειν μήτε μνάασθαι ἄκοιτιν·
ἐκ γὰρ Ὀρέσταο *τίσις* ἔσσεται Ἀτρεΐδαο,
ὁππότ' ἂν ἡβήσῃ τε καὶ ἧς ἱμείρεται αἴης.
ὣς ἔφαθ' Ἑρμείας, ἀλλ' οὐ *φρένας* Αἰγίσθοιο
πεῖθ' *ἀγαθὰ φρονέων·* νῦν δ' ἀθρόα πάντ' *ἀπέτισε'.*

For in his heart he recalled flawless [*amumon*] Aigisthos,/whom far-famed Orestes, Agamemnon's son, had slain./Thinking of (remembering) him he said the following to the immortals:/'It is astonishing how the mortals blame the gods,/for they say that evils spring from us. But they even by themselves,/through their own blind folly, have sorrows beyond that which is ordained,/just as now Aigisthos, beyond that which was ordained,/took to himself the wedded wife of the son of Atreus, and slew him on his return,/though well he knew of sheer destruction, seeing that we told him before,/sending Hermes, the keen-sighted Argeïphontes,/that he should neither slay the man nor woo his wife;/for from Orestes shall come vengeance for the son of Atreus/when once he has come to manhood and longs for his own land./So Hermes spoke, but for all his good intent he did not persuade Aigisthos' heart; and now he has paid the full price for it all (with slight changes transl. Murray rev. Dimock, Loeb).

Zeus recalls and mentions (μνήσατο, ἐπιμνησθείς, 29, 31) the basic features of the tale, namely the fate of ἀμύμων Aigisthos, who seduced Klytaimnestra and killed her husband, thwarting his *nostos*. Aigisthos embodies mental blindness (34) and suffers beyond what was fated or allotted to him (34) for marrying Agamemnon's lawful wife (γῆμ' ἄλοχον μνηστήν, 36). Aigisthos defied the divine warning not to kill the husband nor marry his wife (μνάασθαι ἄκοιτιν, 39) because this will trigger the vengeance of Orestes, when he comes of age and longs for his fatherland. The gods had dispatched Hermes,[11] who in

---

paradigmatic contrasting parallels (foils) in Zeus' speech see Hommel 1955; Hölscher 1967, esp. 7; id. (1989) 1990, 304; Schmidt 2001, 162.

11 Hermes' epithets, ἐΰσκοπος Ἀργεϊφόντης (38), overlap semantically, as suggesting clear vision and revelation; the latter epithet especially suits the context as prohibiting death: sch. bT *Il.* 2.103. *ἀργεϊφόντῃ: ἀργῷ φόνου ... πέπλασται δὲ*

spite of his good intentions, failed to move Aigisthos' *phrenas* (42–43). Despite the divine interdiction, the man committed his crimes and paid all in one for his mental and moral depravity at the hands of Orestes, the τηλεκλυτὸς Ἀγαμεμνονίδης, the legitimate son and heir, who was famed far and wide. The tale is framed as a programmatic case of theodicy: personal moral responsibility and divine dispensation embrace the poem in a ring, which Agamemnon will close, attributing his death to the contrivance of Zeus and the adulterous perpetrators (*Od.* 24.96–97), thus unwittingly confirming Zeus' complaint that mortals blame the gods for the evils they suffer because of their own mental and moral mistakes (1.32–34). Aigisthos is included in the category of those ridden by ἀτασθαλίαι, i.e. by φρενοβλάβειαι, μωρίαι, παράνοιαι, or ἁμαρτίαι and 'thrives in mental blindness',[12] thus emerging as a model suitor, hybristic, defiant of the gods and sound *peitho*, in sum a reprehensible and criminal usurper. If so, what's the meaning of ἀμύμων?

1.1. ἀμύμων Αἴγισθος

The ancient scholars derive ἀμύμων from ἀ-*privativum* + μῶμος,[13] and explain it in terms of beauty, nobility of birth, and blameless or impeccable character; some others reject any characterological interpretations. A most comprehensive picture is drawn by the Odyssean scholia,[14]

τοῖς νεωτέροις τὰ περὶ τὸν Ἄργον. Sch. A(D) ad loc. ἀργῷ καὶ καθαρῷ φόνου ... ὁ Ἑρμῆς ... τὸν Ἄργον ... ἀπέκτεινε. καὶ ἐντεῦθεν Ἀργειφόντης ἐκλήθη. See sch. S *Od.* 1.38, ... καὶ παρὰ τὸ ἀργεννά ἤτοι καθαρὰ φαίνειν τὰ τῆς ψυχῆς ἐνθυμήματα, and sch. *Od.* 1.38 h1., h2., i (Pontani).

12 Sch. *Od.* 1.7 and 34 (Ludwich), παρὰ τὸ ἐν ἄταις θάλλειν. On Ἄτη see sch. AbT *Il.* 19.91; sch. bT *Il.* 19.91c; sch. A *Il.* 19. 94a. Cairns (1993) 131–33, contrasts *aidōs* with *hybris* and *atasthaliē*, 'indeed, these two vices, implying lack of inhibition and failure to respect the *timē* of others, operate as rough antonyms of *aidōs*'.

13 Sch. HPV *Od.* 1.29; sch. HQ *Od.* 19.109; Scholia-D *Il.*1. 92, ἀμύμων: ἀμώμητος, ἀγαθὸς καὶ ἄψογος; similarly sch. bT *Il.*15.463–4; Hsch. α 4176, 4179, and μ 1867, μῦμαρ· αἶσχος, φόβος, ψόγος. On ἀμύμων <ἀ-priv. + μῶμος, or μύω see: Or. 28.11–15~ *Et.Gen.* α 702.3, 758; *Et.Gud.* α 119.5–6, 127.12–13; *EM* 87.32, 95.34; Choirob. *Epim. in Psalmos* 124–21.

14 Sch.*Od.*1.29 (Ludwich), ἀμύμονος Αἰγίσθοιο: ἤτοι καλοῦ πρὸ τοῦ μοιχεῦσαι, ἢ τοῦ κατὰ γένος ἀγαθοῦ. H¹ Mᵃ P QVY. εὐγενοῦς ἢ εὐμόρφου· οὐ γὰρ ἐπὶ τοῦ τρόπου ληπτέον. Mᵃ. κατὰ τὸ εἶδος ἢ κατὰ τὸ γένος, ἢ πρὸ τοῦ συμμιγῆναι τῇ Κλυταιμνήστρᾳ. D. τοῦ πρὶν φρονίμου. M¹. τοῦ ἀμύμονος καὶ τοῦ ἀψόγου, ὅσον κατὰ τὸ πρῶτον, μετὰ δὲ ταῦτα δὲ οὔ. ἢ κατὰ ἀντίφρασιν. Υ, '*amymonos*

where ἀμύμων figures as a term of commendation, the calumny attached to Aigisthos being a *post adulterium* feature. A discordant, yet not influential, voice is heard in sch. Y: 'or it was an antiphrastic use', and also in sch. e. G¹ (Pontani): 'it was an ironic use', κατ' εἰρωνείαν.

Modern scholars consider ἀμύμων 'generic' or 'formulaic' in the Parryan sense,[15] a stock or ornamental epithet. Others regard it as 'the most notoriously inappropriate Homeric adjective' that nonetheless fits well the context,[16] or only superficially a 'contradictory and ill-suited epithet; it has a satisfying Homeric ring' and is 'relevant only to the momentary act'.[17] They all espouse the ancient etymology from ἀ-*priv.* + μῶμος, and render the epithet as 'blameless', 'flawless', 'faultless' or 'handsome',[18] thus exonerating or blotting out Aigisthos' vice, and em-

---

Aigisthou: that is handsome before committing adultery, or noble as regards his *genos*. Of noble descent, or good looking; it should not be taken in respect to his manners. As far as his looks or his *genos* are concerned, or before he mingled in love with Klytaimnestra. Who was prudent in the past. Who was *amymon* and blameless, at first but not after these acts; or *kata antiphrasin*'.

15 See Düring 1945, 96, 'a purely conventional epithet, strangely out of place'; Stanford 1947/1996, 210, accepts ἀμύμων < ἀ-*priv.* + μῶμος, and associates it with 'physical beauty ... Or else it is a careless use of a *formula*'. Whitman 1958, 115, sees a 'traditional intrusion of a formulaic word which is actually not at all appropriate'; it is 'a careless use of formulae' (ib. 335 n. 25).
16 So Combellack 1982, 361, who adheres to 'blameless'; 'the epithet is "generically" unsuitable, but fits the context'. He builds on τότε/φύσει to explain the behavior of Aigisthos (364–65, 372); ib. 368, 'Aegisthus was as blameless as blameless Orestes'. Combellack's analogy (366, 368) between Orestes and Aigisthos is not supported by Zeus' speech.
17 So Vivante 1982, 131, *amymon* 'simply lets us linger on the name'; 'any ... indication of the character's depravity would be out of tune ... "blameless Aegisthus" has its own poetic logic. It is ... characteristic of Homeric expression ... relevant only to the momentary act, quite apart from the narrative and moral ramifications of the story'; ib. 107, *amymon* 'does not have any moral meaning. And yet it lends itself to moral implications' when 'used predicatively'. Adkins 1960, 81 n. 11, considers the epithet a value term belonging to the *agathos*-group, 'even Aegisthus is *amymon* in the social sense ... and ... "courageous", too, for Homer does not represent him as a coward, though he disapproves of his staying at home, iii.263 ff'. See also Nagy (1979) 1999, 257 § 6 n. 5.
18 Parry 1973, 123–24, considers 'blameless' Aigisthos a blatant misuse and solves the incongruity rendering the epithet as 'handsome'; see ib. 115–16, 155, 156–57,164, 'possessing the strong handsome body of a warrior', and the consequent overtones of 'brave'; '"handsome" accounts more satisfactorily than any other for ἀμύμων's course of development', 'beautiful because possessing a strong, well-shaped, well-coordinated body'. Similarly Neschke 1986, 287, 'excellent par sa beauté'; West 1988, 77, 'beautiful, handsome', from which devel-

phasizing his heroic rank and irresistible beauty, even though Zeus denigrates Aigisthos' moral and mental capacity; beauty and genealogical nobility are irrelevant to his immediate argument. Interestingly, Odysseus in the guise of an ugly, old beggar will court his own wife.

Close reading of the poem suggests that *amymon* is not a blunt epithet, employed carelessly and mechanically. It is an ambiguous adjective, meaningfully integrated into the Odyssean ideology and plot. The overlooked yet engaging scholiastic remark, κατὰ ἀντίφρασιν, opens a new interpretive venue, and provides the key to the semantic and functional elucidation of the epithet. The scholiast of the Y manuscript challenges the attachment to the *alpha privativum*, insinuating a process that modern scholarship characterizes as 'reversal of etymology' or 'deformation' by which the poet reverses and belies the intimate connection of name and thing.[19] His comment affects our perception of the first component of ἀμύμων, and leaves room for two equally plausible alternatives, which build upon the potential of *alpha copulativum* or *intensivum*. These options tie in well with the specific Homeric context, and underpin Zeus' argument which requires that Aigisthos be not 'blameless', but on the contrary 'attended by' or 'loaded with' blame for his mischievous acts. This interpretation, capitalizing on the contextual evidence and its pronounced ethography, dispels the overt incongruity of having a paradigmatic seducer and murderer qualified by an epithet of unconditional commendation. Aigisthos ἀμύμων and ἀτάσθαλος, i.e. fraught with blame and beset with mental blindness, foreshadows a major conflict centering on moral and mental integrity, and prefigures the character and destiny of the suitors, who squander Odysseus' property, pursue his wife and pose a deadly threat to his son. Handsome or not (Eur. *El.* 948–49, κάλλει τ' ἀραρώς ... παρθενωπός), Aigisthos initiates a paradigm of narratological significance. With him, ἀμύμων, an evaluative term of social, intellectual and heroic repercussions, starts its long career of semantic and functional redefinition.

Two selective examples illustrate my argument: the suitor Antinoos adumbrates the semantics of μῶμος, concatenating words that signify unrestrained strength and reproach (μένος ἄσχετε, αἰσχύνων, 2.85–86). Eurymachos elaborates on ἀμύμων in a context studded

---

ops the sense 'excellent, expert'; Rutherford 1992, 144, 'the newly accepted translation is "fine", "fair", "excellent"'. Cf. Combellack 1982, 362.

19 On the 'reversal of etymology' see Stanford (1939) 1972, 32, 102; on 'deformation or unnaming' see Higbie 1995, 14–16. See also Louden 1995, 31–33; Tsitsibakou-Vasalos 2001, 24–27; ead. 2007, 80–89 and *passim*.

with terms of heroic worth and value, affirmed or retracted. In the presence of her disguised husband, he addresses Penelope as *periphron* and *koura* of Ikarios (so potentially an unmarried and available girl), and objects to Odysseus' participation in the trial of the bow, since this would heap disgrace upon the suitors; people may reproach them for being cowardly and inferior to her *amymon* husband (21.320–329):

> ἀλλ' αἰσχυνόμενοι φάτιν ἀνδρῶν ἠδὲ γυναικῶν,
> μή ποτέ τις εἴπησι κακώτερος ἄλλος Ἀχαιῶν·
> 'ἦ πολὺ χείρονες ἄνδρες ἀμύμονος ἀνδρὸς ἄκοιτιν
> μνῶνται, οὐδέ τι τόξον ἐύξοον ἐντανύουσιν·
> ἀλλ' ἄλλος τις πτωχὸς ἀνὴρ ἀλαλήμενος ἐλθὼν
> ῥᾳδίως ἐτάνυσσε βιόν, διὰ δ' ἧκε σιδήρου'.
> ὣς ἐρέουσ', ἡμῖν δ' ἂν ἐλέγχεα ταῦτα γένοιτο.

> But we feel shame at the talk of men and women,/that hereafter some base fellow among the Achaeans shall say:/'Truly men far weaker are wooing the wife of a flawless man, and cannot string his polished bow./But another, a beggar, that came on his wanderings,/easily strung the bow, and shot through the iron'./Thus will men speak, but to us this would become a reproach.

Odysseus in the guise of a beggar will enter the bow contest to fulfil Eurymachos' prophetic utterance. He will not only humiliate and extinguish the suitors, but will also regain his wife and house, proving 'blameless' indeed! *Aischynein, kakos, cheiron* and *elenchea* are key-terms of social and moral censure in the Homeric shame culture,[20] and illuminate the semantics of μῶμος and ἀμύμων.

To recap, Zeus focalizes the crime and punishment of Aigisthos, exploiting the ambiguity of ἀμύμων. The concepts conveyed by μῶμος and ἀμύμων are negotiated in the entire poem, and provide a point of contact between the Agamemnon- and the Odysseus-tales. Starting with the paradigmatic yet inadvisable case of Aigisthos, who exemplifies the workings of ἀ-*copulativum* or *intensivum* and μῶμος, and aiming at restoring the integrity of the once *amymon oikos* of Odysseus (1.232), the poet builds a ring, which is coextensive with the poem. Odysseus and Penelope will instantiate the exonerating ἀ-*privativum* and μῶμος; ἀμύμων draws a full cycle, temporal and spatial, before its final disambigua-

---

20 On shame culture see Dodds 1951, 17–18, and ch. 2; Adkins 1960, 48–49, 154–56; Cairns 1993, 27–47, 140, 392. On *cheirōn, aischos, aischros, aischynein* and *elenchea* see Adkins 1960, 40–46; Cairns 1993, 54–60, 65–67, 175, 243–45. Posterity stamps Aigisthos as *aischyntēr* (A. *Cho*. 990).

tion in an outlandish realm, the Underworld; at that point, the two tales will make a clean break, and part for good.

To return to *Odyssey* 1, Zeus' speech is marked by heavy alliteration produced by the words μνήσατο, Ἀγαμεμνονίδης, ἐπιμνησθείς, μνηστήν and μνάασθαι (29–43), and consolidates the central motifs of the poem. Clusters of cognates that signify recollection or oblivion, namely a forceful commemorative function,[21] courtship, and perseverance or wavering, flanked by *kleos*, will prove linguistic and thematic points of contact between the two tales. Zeus combines recollection and *prolepsis* to insinuate details still undisclosed. Although the wedded and wooed wife of Agamemnon lurks unnamed in the background, her name and identity resonate in the passage: Κλυταιμνήστρα emerges as the famous or rather notorious bride (κλυτός + μνηστή) and the object of an ill-starred μνάασθαι. It is no accident that ἄλοχος μνηστή is used only twice in the *Odyssey*, firstly of Klytaimnestra, the protagonist of the Agamemnon-tale (1.36), and secondly of Penelope, the protagonist of the Odysseus-tale (11.177).

1.2. ἄλοχος μνηστή

The atmosphere around ἄλοχος μνηστή is disquieting, as attested by the discourse of Odysseus with his mother in the Underworld. When he queries the desires and designs of his wedded wife as well as her loyalty and perseverance as mother and consort, he uses the words μένει ('remains') and ἔμπεδος ('steadfast') which insinuate the derivation and the semantics of μνηστή, and prefigure the ultimate test by means of the bed 'embedded' in the olive tree.[22] Antikleia pays tribute to Penelope's *kleos*, portraying her as a doublet of Odysseus in steadfastness and suffering (11.181–83): Penelope stays, μένει, in the palace with enduring

---

21 For the function of memory within the ancient commemorative tradition in early Greek poetry and tragedy see Segal 1989. On reconstructive memory and the restoration of relationships see Thalmann 1984, 160–63.
22 *Od.* 11.177–78, εἰπέ δέ μοι μνηστῆς ἀλόχου βουλήν τε νόον τε,/ἦε μένει παρὰ παιδὶ καὶ <u>ἔμπεδα</u> πάντα φυλάσσει, 'And tell me of my wedded wife, of her purpose and of her mind. Does she remain with her son, and keep all things safe?' *Empedon* prefigures the olive tree passage (23.203), which signals 'embedded' conjugal trust and fidelity. On this pun on bed and 'embeddedness' see Zeitlin 1995, 118. On the bed as *sêma* of steadfastness see id. 1995, 118–43; Katz 1991, 181.

mind (τετληότι θυμῷ), and spends wretched (ὀιζυραί) nights and days in tears,[23] thus resuming the linguistic *sēmata* by which she emerges as the perfect match of Odysseus (see n. 9, above). The negativity of μνηστή resurfaces when Penelope as πολυμνήστη prepares to marry, unaware of the deadly trap the suitors have plotted for her son (4.770–71); merriment and mourning embrace πολυμνήστη, creating a climate of discomfort, ambiguity and suspense. The epithet recurs when Odysseus contrives an anomalous festivity and song as well as a sham wedding (23.130–151), with the purpose of concealing the massacre: and one would say, 'very surely someone has wedded the queen wooed by many', the πολυμνήστη βασίλεια (23.149).[24] This appellation crowns a massacre masked as a wedding, and proves the gloomy connotations of both μνηστή and πολυμνήστη. Penelope is pictured as a 'much-remembered', unforgettable Queen of death. At this point the grim implications of her funeral robe, φᾶρος ταφήιον, have been revealed.

The threatening aspects of *mnesteia* resurface in *Odyssey* 15, when Athena urges Telemachos to sail back home to find his mother still *amymon*, and salvage his property because she is preparing to marry Eurymachos (15.10–23). Athena insists on the unpredictable female disposition: women care about their new relatives, and do not remember their former children and *kouridios* husband; μνηστῆρες, μνάομαι and μέμνημαι unite (*Od.* 15.18–23) just before Athena warns Telemachos that the suitors lie in ambush for him (λοχόωσιν, 28–30). The Iliadic strategy of *lochos* is adapted to the Odyssean circumstances: *lochos* characterizes men, sly and cowardly, who covet the *alochos* of another man and her *lechos*. Odysseus will retaliate in a homeopathical manner. The negativity of *mnesteia* culminates when Helen presents Telemachos with a splendid yet inauspicious wedding gift, a *peplos* 'which shone like a

---

23 Antikleia, playing upon *aganos* and *mel-*, clarifies the causes of her death (11.198–203): it was not Artemis with her *aganois beleessin* (199) who killed her, nor disease which took life from her limbs (*meleōn*), but rather the *aganophrosynē* of her son which took her honey-sweet spirit, *meliēdea thymon*. See Doherty 1995: Antikleia exhibits solidarity with Penelope (49–50 n. 40, 81 n. 41, 110), ends her speech with the climactic revelation of mutual grief (110), and is 'permitted to focalize portions of the Nekuia' as 'those who support their male kin loyally' (95, 117). On Antikleia's report as foil to Agamemnon's see Heubeck 1989, 101.

24 See de Jong 2001a, 554, 'the fulfilment of Odysseus' expectation … takes the form of an *actual *tis*-speech'.

star' (ἀστὴρ δ' ὣς ἀπέλαμπεν, 108). She subtly focalizes its gloomy implications (15.125–28):[25]

δῶρόν τοι καὶ ἐγώ, τέκνον φίλε, τοῦτο δίδωμι,
μνῆμ' Ἑλένης χειρῶν, πολυηράτου ἐς γάμου ὥρην,
σῇ ἀλόχῳ φορέειν· τῆος δὲ φίλῃ παρὰ μητρὶ
κεῖσθαι ἐνὶ μεγάρῳ.

'This gift, dear child, I too give you,/a remembrance of the hands of Helen, against the day of your longed-for marriage,/for your bride to wear it. But until then let it lie in your halls in the keeping of your dear mother'.

This passage, especially verse 126, is imbued with a semantic and syntactical ambiguity, which results from three factors: firstly, from the concurrence of two alternative metrical and conceptual cuts;[26] secondly, from the duality of πολυηράτου, which as *loveable* and/or *accursed* (< ἔρως or ἀρά) may refer either to Helen (Ἑλένης) or the wedding (γάμου),[27] and thirdly, from the semantic ambiguity of μνῆμα, which signifies *reminiscence, souvenir* or *grave* (see *Il.* 23.619).[28] The collocation of Helen and the radiant *peplos* evokes her Iliadic double and purple web in which she sprinkled the toils that the Greeks and the Trojans suffered for her sake (3.125–28). The poet posits a worthy authorial archetype of his own poetry[29] as Helen *qua* bard weaves her own story in purple, a luxurious yet ominous dye. The web is double, so is Helen, 'dou-

---

25 On the ominous connotations of the star simile see Tsitsibakou-Vasalos 2004, 43 with n. 41.
26 In verse 126 two caesurae are viable and equally possible: either after the second long (μνῆμ' Ἑλένης), or a masculine caesura after the third long (μνῆμ' Ἑλένης χειρῶν).
27 On the ambiguity of πολυήρατος see Eust. *Od.* 2.94.23–25, Τὸ δὲ πολυηράτου, ἀμφιβολίαν ἔχει. ἄδηλον γὰρ εἴτε πολυηράτου Ἑλένης ῥητέον, εἴτε γάμου πολυηράτου. τοῦτο δὲ ἢ διὰ τοὺς κατὰ τὸν γάμον ἔρωτας ἢ διὰ τὸ εὐκταῖον αὐτοῦ χάριν τεκνογονίας, ἢ καὶ διότι πολλῶν εὐχῶν χρεία τοῖς περὶ γάμους. On its etymology see sch. BQV *Od.* 11.275.5–6, πολυηράτῳ] πολλὰς ἀρὰς καὶ βλάβας ὑπομεινάσῃ παρὰ θεῶν. οὐ γὰρ ἐρασμίῳ; similarly Eust. *Od.* 1.414.20–23. See sch. H *Od.* 15.366, ἣν καταλαβεῖν πολλοὶ εὔχονται, τὴν πολύευκτον.
28 On μνῆμα, see Frisk *GrEW* s.v., 'Andenken, Denkmal, Grabmal'; Schmidt 1993b, s.v., 'Andenken, vgl. μιμνήσκομαι', 'Andenken an das Begräbnis'; on *Od.* 15.126, 'als Andenken an die Hände (Handarbeit) der Hel.', see n. 7, above. Significantly, Helen as author of death, along with polymnestē, figures in the curse uttered by Eumaius (*Od.* 14.64–71).
29 See sch. bT *Il.* 3.126–7, ἀξιόχρεων ἀρχέτυπον ἀνέπλασεν ὁ ποιητὴς τῆς ἰδίας ποιήσεως.

bleness is the distinguishing mark of her entire tradition', while purple is the color of blood and death, and metaphorically of troubled and gloomy thoughts.[30] The presence of Helen, the dangerous weaver, evil-minded bride (*kakomēchanos*, *Il.* 6.344) and authoress of death (*penthos*, *Od.* 23.224), heightens the anxiety aroused by this μνῆμα-gift. The god-sent *teras* of the eagle that snatched a house-bred goose reaffirms the ominous forebodings surrounding this *peplos*. Helen prophesies the *nostos* and vengeance of Odysseus, who is already at his home 'sowing the seeds of evil for all the suitors', μνηστῆρσι κακὸν πάντεσσι φυτεύει (15.160–78).[31] Helen emerges as the doublet of her sister, although she endeavors to conceal the destructiveness embedded in her name, and to polish her tarnished Iliadic image with νηπενθῆ φάρμακα, biased stories (4.219–89) and ambiguous gifts.[32] The potential funeral associations of φορέειν (cf. φορεῖον, *bier*) intensify the ambiguity. Significantly, until this *peplos-mnêma* is worn by Telemachos' wife, it will lie beside his wooed mother; the verb κεῖσθαι is used, among others, for erotic or funereal lying; the woven *peplos* becomes the emblem of a menacing *mnesteia*. Like Helen, its donor, so also Penelope, the temporary recipient in whose name the notion of weaving is imprinted,[33] will

---

30 On Helen's doubleness see Bergren 1983, 79–85, in the *Iliad* and the *Odyssey* she 'is forever double' (82); id. 2008, 23–24, 26, 29. On πορφύρω (of dark rough sea or emotional disturbance) and πορφύρεος (of death or blood), see sch. A *Il.* 14.16a, sch. bT *Il.* 14.16c.; sch. BEPQV *Od.* 4.427; sch. T *Od.* 4.572. Purple, a sign of wealth, anticipates blood and death (A. *Ag.* 910, 957–60). See Whitman 1958, 118 with n. 39.
31 Reworking this Homeric scene in his *Nostoi* (*PMG* 209), Stesichoros lingers on Helen's bridal status (νύμφα) and divination. On this fragment see Tsitsibakou-Vasalos 1993, 27–31.
32 See Bergren 1983, 79–80, 82, 84; id. 2008, 111–30. In A. *Ag.* 681–749, Helen's name accords with her deadly nature; her new kinship proves 'a marriage in the true meaning of the word' (κῆδος ὀρθώνυμον, 699–700). See Fraenkel 1950, 133, 'the double meaning of κῆδος is untranslatable'; the hymenaeal hymn becomes song of much mourning (709–11), and Helen is identified with Erinys bringing tears to brides (749). On Helen's poetic etymologies see Tsitsibakou-Vasalos 2004, 45–48.
33 See sch. HPQ *Od.* 4.797. Ναυπλίου δὲ ῥίψαντος αὐτὴν εἰς θάλασσαν ... ὑπὸ πηνελόπων αὐτὴν σωθεῖσαν οὕτως ὀνομασθῆναι. ἐν δὲ ἐπιμερισμῷ ... *Πηνελόπην* αὐτήν φησι λελέχθαι, παρὰ τὸ *πένεσθαι* τὸ *λῶπος*. Sch. Pi. *Ol.* 9.79d.5–11, ὥσπερ καὶ ἐπὶ τῆς *Πηνελόπης* ... παρὰ τῶν φύντων εἰς τὴν θάλασσαν ἐκριφῆναι, εἶτα ὑπό τινων ὀρνέων πηνελόπων λεγομένων εἰς τὴν χέρσον ἐξενεχθῆναι, καὶ οὕτως ... ὀνομασθῆναι *Πηνελόπην* ἀπὸ τῆς τῶν ὀρνίθων ὁμωνυμίας, καὶ τραφεῖσαν διώνυμον εἶναι τὸ λοιπόν. Eust.

dispense *penthos*; even though a prerequisite for marriage, her φᾶρος ταφήϊον exudes death.³⁴ Helen's *peplos* parallels the *pharos* of Penelope to the extent that it causes death, and becomes 'a metaphor for the song itself'.³⁵

Helen's *quasi*-prophetic language anticipates another famous μνῆμα, the bow by which Odysseus will take revenge upon the suitors. This bow was the beginning of ξεινοσύνης προσκηδέος (21.35), that is, of hospitality attended by κῆδος, a word that signifies *kinship by marriage* and *care* as well as *mourning* and *penthos*.³⁶ The bow lay in Odysseus' halls as a reminiscence and memorial, μνῆμα, of his friend; significantly and ominously, Odysseus wore it (φόρει) only on Ithaka.³⁷ This bow will eventually reveal the duality of κῆδος, bringing death upon the uninvited *xenoi* and aspiring grooms (see n. 87, below). The female *peplos* or *pharos* and the male bow emerge as the gendered emblematic weapons that integrate the Ithakan family and the *Odyssey*.

The funeral ambiguity that embraces μνηστὴ ἄλοχος is unmistakable in *Iliad* 11: Iphidamas is killed by Agamemnon far from his wedded youthful wife (μνηστῆς ἀλόχου … κουριδίης, 242–43) whose charms he

---

Il. 4.831–32.4, παρὰ τὸν *Πᾶνα*, ὅς ἐστι, φασίν, εὑρετὴς ὑφαντικῆς, ἀφ' οὗ καὶ τὸ *πανίον*, ἡ ἀγοραία λέξις. ἐκ δὲ τοῦ *πηνίου* καὶ τὸ *ἐκπηνίζειν* … καὶ ἡ *Πηνελόπη* δὲ ἀπ' αὐτοῦ. Eust. *Od.* 1.65.26–32, *Πηνελόπη* δὲ λέγεται, ἢ παρὰ τὸ *πένεσθαι περὶ λόπος. λόπος* δὲ ἐστὶν ὕφασμα λεπτόν … ἐξ οὗ κατὰ ἔκτασιν, *λώπιον* … ἢ παρὰ τὸ *πηνίον ἐλεῖν*. See Felson 1995, 167 n. 16. Levaniouk 1999, 95–136, suggests that the meaning of Penelope's name resonates with a number of prominent themes (solar, memory, and grief for the husband), expressed as the mournful song of the bird πηνέλοψ (135–36).

34 On the correlation of loom and death, on singing songs or prophetic and magical incantations, and administering drugs by females called *deinē* and *audēessa*, and by Penelope, 'a discreet hypostasis of the same dread goddess', see Nagler 1977; McClure 1999, 65–67, 83–85.
35 Scheid – Svenbro 1996, 116 with n. 13. On Helen's 'storytelling cloth' see Clader 1976, 6–11, 'Helen is both author and subject of her work', she weaves 'the very fabric of heroic epic'. Bergren 1979, 19–34: Helen's web is a reflection of the process of poetic composition. See also Austin 1994, 37–41. Clayton 2004, 34, 123, treats Penelope as 'both a literal and figurative weaver of *mêtis*', 'a figurative bard'.
36 Cf. 'of a loving friendship', transl. Murray rev. by Dimock, Loeb. On κῆδος see n. 32, above.
37 *Od.* 21.40–41, ἀλλ' αὐτοῦ μνῆμα ξείνοιο φίλοιο/κέσκετ' ἐνὶ μεγάροισι, φόρει δέ μιν ἧς ἐπὶ γαίης, '(the bow) lay in his halls at home as a memorial of a staunch friend, and he carried it in his own land'.

did not enjoy despite the gifts he gave for her sake.[38] In *Iliad* 6, the despair of the Trojans and the hostility of Athena also provide the backdrop for the contrasting scene of marital harmony and happiness in peacetime: Priam's sons, most of whom will die in this war, sleep beside their wedded wives (παρὰ μνηστῆς ἀλόχοισι, 245–46).

Meaningful, too, is the use of ἄλοχος μνηστή in *Iliad* 9: Agamemnon, offering rich regalia, invites Achilles to become his son-in-law, his *gambros* (142=284, 146=288). Achilles rejects his gifts and marriage. He refuses to marry any of Agamemnon's three daughters whose names (Chrysothemis, Laodike, Iphianassa) encapsulate the regal and judicial authority of their father. Achilles renounces them along with the other gifts, which include Briseis and a number of beauties whose availability is conditional upon the sack of Troy. Beauty, booty and death, accompanied by Helen, the authoress of doom and unseemly deeds (*ergon aeikes*, *Od.* 23.218–24), mingle insidiously in this passage (9.270–90) to motivate the outburst of Achilles, who challenges the cause of this war, and redefines the conventional values governing marital love (336–43). Entertaining an impressive wordplay, κούρην δ' οὐ γαμέω Ἀγαμέ-μνονος ... οὐδέ μιν ὣς γαμέω (9.388, 391),[39] Achilles negates not only the *gamos* currently proposed to him, but also implicitly the marriage of Agamemnon himself. Achilles' stout heart eagerly seeks love and loyalty and a respectful wife (μοι ... ἐπέσσυτο θυμὸς ἀγήνωρ/ γήμαντα μνηστὴν ἄλοχον ἐϊκυῖαν ἄκοιτιν, 9.398–99), unlike Agamemnon who preferred Chryseis over Klytaimnestra, his legitimate wife (κουριδίης ἀλόχου, *Il.* 1.114), even though Klytaimnestra was no less χερείων in beauty and natural talents of mind and hands.[40] Klytaimnestra will retaliate, exploiting those talents, and choosing a weak (ἄναλκις) and lesser man (χείρων).[41] She will become a foil for the *mnestē alochos* whose

---

38 Grethlein 2006a, 155–56, discusses the dynamics of exchange apropos the tragic 'mors immatura' of Iphidamas, who instead of getting his due in the rich marriage exchange, he himself becomes an object of exchange when Agamemnon strips him off his armor.

39 See Martin 1989, 221, 'The daughter I will not marry of No-marriage'.

40 *Il.* 1.113–15, καὶ γάρ ῥα Κλυταιμνήστρης προβέβουλα/κουριδίης ἀλόχου, ἐπεὶ οὔ ἑθέν ἐστι χερείων,/οὐ δέμας οὐδὲ φυήν, οὔτ' ἄρ φρένας οὔτέ τι ἔργα, 'For in fact I prefer her to Clytemnestra,/my wedded wife, since she is in no way inferior to her,/either in form or in stature, or in mind, or in handiwork'.

41 Hes. fr. 176.5–6, M.-W., ὡς δὲ Κλυταιμήστρη <προ>λιποῦσ' Ἀγαμέμνονα δῖον/Αἰγίσθωι παρέλεκτο καὶ εἵλετο χείρον' ἀκοίτην, 'so too, Clytemestra, leaving behind godly Agamemnon,/lay beside Aegisthus and preferred a worse husband' (transl. Most 2007, fr. 247).

features Achilles has adumbrated, and a foil for Penelope who prefers to die than please the mind of a lesser man (χείρονος ἀνδρός, 20.82). But Achilles' hopes prove illusory as he chooses *aphthiton kleos* (9.413). His life is short and intertwined with *alpha privativum*; he will never share the bed of a μνηστὴ ἄλοχος and ἄκοιτις. The *alpha copulativum* will never attend him; his *gamos* is *agamos* as also that of Agamemnon.

The gloomy career of μνηστὴ ἄλοχος is reaffirmed in the mythical *exemplum* addressed to Achilles by Phoinix: the Aitolian prince Meleager lay beside his *mnestē alochos*, the beautiful Kleopatra (κεῖτο παρὰ μνηστῇ ἀλόχῳ, καλῇ Κλεοπάτρῃ, 556), whose double names, *Kleopatra* and *Alkyone* (9.562), commemorate the *kleos* of her father Idas and the weeping of her mother Marpessa, a woman raped by Apollo, but keeping her vows to Idas (557–64). Kleopatra's virginal and married life is interwoven with *kleos* and *penthos* (563), thus matching the destiny of her husband with the inauspicious name,[42] who will eventually save his besieged city, moved by the supplication of his *mnestē alochos*, but will die cursed by Althaia, his mother with the ironic name. The verb κεῖτο anticipates the funeral outcome and foreshadows Achilles' lying in death (*Od.* 24.40), thus fulfilling the myth's exemplary function.

The above intratextual and intertextual survey has hopefully shown that in the *Iliad* and especially the *Odyssey*, a song pervaded by illicit μνάασθαι, the figure of μνηστὴ ἄλοχος is a vehicle of contradictory values, such as happiness or grief, stability or wavering, indeterminacy, and abiding or faltering memory. As such, it instantiates the conflicts dramatized in the Agamemnon- and the Odysseus-tale. Klytai-mnestra embodies the inauspicious ambiguities inherent in μνηστή both functionally and etymologically, emerging as a negative bridal model and as a foil for Penelope. Few scholars are willing to explore this etymology; Cauer is one of them. He argues that in his *Iphigeneia in Tauris* (ἃ μναστευθεῖσ' ἐξ Ἑλλάνων, 208), Euripides, by the participle μναστευθεῖσα, meant to replace the name of the person, that is, Κλυταιμνήστρα.[43] This passage would provide a felicitous corroboration of the

---

42 Eur. F 517, *TrGF* with *test*. (5:558, Kannicht): Μελέαγρε, μελέαν γάρ ποτ' ἀγρεύεις ἄγραν. See Mühlestein 1987, 45 n. 15, 77, 'der Mann der "vergeblichen Jagd"'. On the relation of Alkyone and the bird halcyon with mourning and solar metaphors see Levaniouk 1999, 102–04, 116–29.

43 Cauer 1921, 26–27, in agreement with Bruhn. So also Bechtel – Fick 1894, 401, Κλυταιμνήστρη zu μνηστήρ, 'Freier'. Room 1990, 99, s.v. *Clytemnestra*, submits '*clytos*, "famous", and *mnesteira*, "bride" or in a more general way 'praiseworthy wooing', with the latter half of her name from *mnesteuo*, "to

derivation of Κλυται-μνήστρα from μνηστή and μνάασθαι, indeed, if only it were possible to confirm the subject of the participle (Iphigeneia or Klytaimnestra?), its exact position in the wider passage, and even its true reading and meaning.[44] Yet this etymology goes back to the *Odyssey*, book 1 (γῆμ' ἄλοχον μνηστήν, 36; μνάασθαι ἄκοιτιν, 39). This is not a 'late etymologizing fantasy',[45] but a genuine poetic etymology serving the ethography and the plot, and behaving no differently from all other instances of ancient etymologizing: it manipulates the sounds of the name and conditions its meaning on the narrative requirements. It is true that modern scholars in their majority opt for κλυτός+μήδομαι,[46] influenced by the two *Nekyiai* and the ancient lexicographers.[47] At the turn of the 19th century, there arose, indeed, a debate about the spelling and derivation of *Klytaimnestra*. On the evidence of the manuscripts of the 10th or 11th century and the vase inscriptions,

---

woo". Wooer she may have been; "praiseworthy' is another matter', Room concludes.

44 See Rank 1951, 50 with n. 56; von Kamptz 1982, 80; Kyriakou 2006, 103–04 with n. 4.
45 So West 1988, 176, in favor of μήδομαι.
46 On *Klytaimnestra*'s derivation from μήδομαι rather than from μνηστή, μνάομαι see Papageorgiou 1910, 1–51, who defends the authenticity of -μήστρη on the evidence of the best manuscripts and vase inscriptions, with the approval of Höfer 1890–94, 1230–1232 s.v. *Klytaim(n)estra*; Kretschmer (1894) 1969, 166–68; id. 1912; Bethe 1921, 890–91 s.v. Klytaimestra; Fraenkel 1950, 52–53; Rank 1951, 49–50, and von Kamptz 1982, 79–80, 210. Fiesel 1928, 58, supports the priority of –μ– on Etruskan evidence. Cf. Schwyzer 1939.1, 448, 'Wunschname auf Grund von *κλυτὰ μήδεται'. Mader 1991, 1460 s.v. *Κλυταιμνήστρη/μήστρη*, wavers between μνηστή and μήδομαι. Kunst 1924–25, 26, argues that at first 'Klytaimestra' had *agathai phrenes* (*Od.* 3.266), so was on a level with Penelope; adducing *Klytomedes* [*Il.* 23.634] as her masculine counterpart, Kunst, seems to point to μήδομαι rather than μνηστή which Katz 1991, 45, attributes to him, '*Klytaimnēstrē* meaning "renowned for being wooed"'; Katz (p. 4) opts for μήδομαι. So Nagy 1974, 260; id. 1979, 37 § 13 n. 3; Harder 1999, 611–12, s.v. *Klytaimestra*; id. 2003, 487–88 s.v. *Clytaemnestra*; Tsitsibakou-Vasalos 2007, 212 n. 499.
47 On *Klytaimnestra*, see *Et. Gud.* κ 329.15–18 Κλυταιμνήστρα, παρὰ τὸ κλυτός καὶ τὸ μήδω, τὸ φροντίζω γίνεται κλυτομνήστρα, ἡ ἔνδοξα φροντίζουσα καὶ τροπῇ τοῦ ο εἰς α καὶ πλεονασμῷ τοῦ ι Κλυταιμνήστρα. *EM* 521.17–21 Κλυταιμνήστρα, παρὰ τὸ κλυτόν, ὃ σημαίνει τὸ ἔνδοξον, καὶ τὸ μήδω, τὸ φροντίζω, γίνεται Κλυτομήστρα, τουτέστιν ἡ ἔνδοξα φροντίζουσα; cf. ib. n. 19, '*melius fortasse* ... καὶ προσθέσει τοῦ ν. *Alioqui enim a* μνήσασθαι *facienda est derivatio*'. Mader 1991, 1460, s.v., considers ἡ ἔνδοξα [sic] φροντίζουσα a wordplay *e contrario* on her bad fame (Hes. fr. 176.2), and -μνήστρη, also *e contrario*, an allusion to *Od.* 1.36 and Hes. fr. 176.6 M.-W.

scholars delete the so-called 'parasitic ν',[48] as a later addition. Yet a much earlier source testifies to the presence of a 'pleonastic ν'.[49] This controversy has been conducted in default of Homer, who weaves his poetic canvas around the implications of Klytaimnestra's complex identity as both μνηστή or object of μνάασθαι, and author of μήδεσθαι. Homer exploits these complementary alternatives in an escalating fashion; neither can raise claims of exclusivity. In the Agamemnon-tale the δολόμητις μνηστήρ and μνηστή emerge as the negative role models against which Odysseus and Penelope will be measured in the story. As I hope to show, etymology proves its interactive character, expanding the literary space of poetry and underpinning the stages of narrative; etymology generates narrative, integrating the Agamemnon-tale into the story through a network of verbal and thematic parallelisms.

Klytaimnestra, for instance, interchanges her diacritical linguistic *sēmata* with her former and new relatives; κλυτός and μήδομαι circulate among them. Orestes vindicates the familial male *kléos* and his κλυτός father, assuming in the process part of his mother's essence and name; κλυτός, a common parental *sêma*, is transferred onto him. As τηλεκλυτός he authenticates his right act. Aigisthos, on the other hand, parallels Klytaimnestra's deception and scheming, and as δολόμητις kills her husband. From this point on, the adulterous and criminal couple will be showered with negative *kleos*, with infamy, for their combined connivance, i. e. for their δόλος, μῆτις and μήδομαι. It is no accident that in a poem obsessed with the notion of craft and

---

48 So Papageorgiou 1910, 33, 'παράσιτον εἶναι τὸ ν'.
49 *Epim. Hom.* 113A 1–6, Dyck 1983, 153, Κλυταιμνήστρης: παρὰ τὸ κλυτόν, ὃ σημαίνει τὸ{ν} <u>ἔνδοξον</u>, καὶ τὸ μήδω, <u>τὸ φροντίζω</u> ... τουτέστιν <u>ἡ ἔνδοξα</u> <u>φροντίζουσα</u>· τροπῇ τοῦ ο εἰς α καὶ προσθέσει τοῦ ι καὶ πλεονασμῷ τοῦ ν, Κλυταιμνήστρα. On the formation of her name and implicitly the date of the *lemma*, see ib. 113A 7–16, with Dyck's assumption that it perhaps comes from Hdn. Περὶ παρωνύμων, and his reference to Hdn. 2.195.4 ('Εκ τῶν Ἡρωδιανοῦ Περὶ παθῶν, *77 = *Epim. Hom.* 421.31 Lentz). On the date of the *Epimerismi Homerici* see Theodoridis 1979, esp. 4, 'Durch die Zitate aus diesen beiden Dichtern [sc. Johannes von Damaskos und Kosmas von Jerusalem] ergibt sich als frühester terminus post quem für die Entstehung der Epimerismen zu Homer das Jahr 750'. See also Dyck 1975, 5; id. 1995, 25–26, 34–40. The above references suggest that the *Epim. Hom.* gleans material dating back to late antiquity and this affects our –ν–.

guile, δολόμητις constitutes an exclusive attribute of Aigisthos and Klytaimnestra![50]

The manipulation of Klytaimnestra's name gives an insight into the nature of her offence: she threatens the archaic male ideology and society, submitting a new sense for κλυτός, κλέος and μῆτις or μήδομαι. The Homeric technique of transference of etymology, by which 'the etymological pointers and lexemes of names are sometimes transferred from the person they naturally etymologize to another, closely affiliated person',[51] intensifies this sense of confusion, blurring the gender boundaries, and insinuating a social and ethical dissolution. Klytaimnestra's linguistic signs hover in the Agamemnon-tale and threaten to invade the Odysseus-tale. Athena alludes to this, urging Τηλέ-μαχος to emulate Orestes τηλε-κλυτός who earned κλέος for killing the δολόμητις murderer of his glorious, κλυτόν, father (1.298–300):[52]

ἦ οὐκ ἀίεις οἷον κλέος ἔλλαβε δῖος Ὀρέστης
πάντας ἐπ' ἀνθρώπους, ἐπεὶ ἔκτανε πατροφονῆα,
Αἴγισθον δολόμητιν, ὅ οἱ πατέρα κλυτὸν ἔκτα;

Or have you not heard what fame the noble Orestes won/among all mankind when he slew his father's murderer,/the guileful Aegisthus, because he slew his glorious father?

It is vital for the males in the story to 'correct' the Agamemnon-tale and restore equilibrium, exploiting the same qualities: assisted by his son, Odysseus will regain his *mnestē alochos* and wealth by wiles and snares, earning eternal *kleos*.

2. Agamemnon-tale in *Odyssey* 3–24

This tale recurs in book 3, clothed in the same significant words of devising ill. Nestor informs Telemachos that Aigisthos 'devised a woeful doom' for Agamemnon (ἐμήσατο λυγρὸν ὄλεθρον, 3.194), but Orestes

---

50 Aigisthos (*Od.*1.300; 3.198, 250, 308; 4.525); Klytaimnestra (11.422). Elsewhere δολόμητις qualifies Zeus and Hermes (*Il.* 1.540; *h.Merc.* 405). Athena, the daughter of *Μῆτις* and *μητίετα* Ζεύς, renders δόλος and *μῆτις*, guile and contrivance, a legitimate strategy. See de Jong 2001a, 111: this epithet 'belongs to the character-language'.
51 Tsitsibakou-Vasalos 2007, 60; on transference of etymology see ib. 60–66, and *passim*; id. 2003. See also Skempis-Ziogas (pp. 219, 220 in this volume).
52 This is the first *prolepsis* of Odysseus' revenge, observes de Jong 2001a, 14.

took revenge, killing Αἴγισθον δολόμητιν (198).⁵³ Athena focalizes the death of Agamemnon who died at the hearth by the guile of Aigisthos and his own wife (ἀπολέσθαι ἐφέστιος … ὑπ' Αἰγίσθοιο δόλῳ καὶ ἧς ἀλόχοιο, 234–35). The manner of his death becomes a proleptic signpost for Odysseus' *nostos* and the fate of the suitors. Eurykleia will bring her mistress the good tidings: Odysseus returned alive to the hearth, the kernel of the archaic life,⁵⁴ and punished all the suitors at his home (ζωὸς ἐφέστιος … τοὺς πάντας ἐτίσατο ᾧ ἐνὶ οἴκῳ, 23.55–57). The Agamemnon-tale once more prefigures the Odysseus-tale, although Eurykleia fails to establish her etymology and her inherited qualities as daughter Ὤπος Πεισηνορίδαο (1.429), failing to convince a female this time, Penelope (23.58–68).⁵⁵ From this point on the Agamemnon-tale is framed by contrivance and Klytaimnestra's escalating incrimination. Athena is the first to hint at the complicity of Klytaimnestra through the syntax and the implications of ὑπό.

Telemachos wonders how Aigisthos, implicitly a lesser man (χειρείων-χείρων), devised the murder of a better man (τίνα δ' αὐτῷ μήσατ' ὄλεθρον/Αἴγισθος δολόμητις, ἐπεὶ κτάνε πολλὸν ἀρείω, 3.249–50). The adjective ἀρείω ironically echoes the adultery of Ares

---

53 The parallelism of Orestes and Telemachos is suggested through clusters of cognates and synonyms (3.193–240) bearing on revenge (τίνω), reputation (κλέος, κλύω, ἀκούω), and Athena's love (φιλέω, κήδομαι). Telemachos closes the capsule of cognates with κηδόμενοι, 240. An ironic parallelism of Agamemnon and Odysseus is revealed when both kiss their fatherland (4.520–23 ~ 13.353–54); the former will be buried in it, the latter will regain it.

54 On the symbolic value of the hearth as 'generatrix of the authority that is kingship', see Nagy 1990b, 143–80. Hearth, *qua* sacrificial altar, is the *locus* of Agamemnon's murder (A. *Ag.* 1056–57, 1310); Aigisthos is the fire in Klytaimnestra's ἑστία (1435). In Soph. *El.*, Aigisthos pours παρεστίους libations (270) in the hearth where he killed the king; in this hearth the king's ghost fixed an ominous heirloom, his scepter ἐφέστιον (419–23); Chrysothemis utters a prodigious oath by the paternal ἑστία (881). In Eur. *El.* 205, 216, Elektra's lowly hearth becomes the seat of recognition and conspiracy.

55 Sch. P *Od.* 1.429. Εὐρύκλεια ἡ εὐρὺ καὶ μέγα κλέος ἔχουσα. Based on the harmony of names, Mühlestein 1987, 40–42 (also 48, 175 n. 5), exploits κλέος, κλύω, and submits for her, 'ihr wird "weitherum *gehorcht*"'. Der Name ist für ihre Funktion als Vorsteherin der Mägde ausgewählt'. He associates (41–42) Ὤψ with ὀψ-, 'voice' ('mit Stimme versehen … der befehlen kann'; cf. von Kamptz 1982, § 66.2, p. 214, 'Auge, Antlitz, Anblick'), and renders Πεισήνωρ as 'der, welcher Männer zu überreden … zu befehlen versteht' (41). See n. 71, below.

and Aphrodite and the cunning of Hephaistos (*Od.* 8.266–366).[56] Nestor's response (3.253–75; 301–12) centers on δόλος and μήδομαι: Aigisthos machinated a deed of great magnitude (μάλα γὰρ μέγα μήσατο ἔργον, 261), and adopted a feminine love strategy, seducing Agamemnon's wife with words (264). At first Κλυταιμνήστρη refused the unseemly deed for she was of prudent mind (ἀναίνετο ἔργον ἀεικές … φρεσὶ γὰρ κέχρητ' ἀγαθῇσι, 3.265–66); ἔργον ἀεικές functions as a proleptic and euphemistic signpost for Agamemnon's murder (11.429–30). Nestor, the paragon of wisdom, is the first to give Klytaimnestra her name and identity, recognizing her duality and the deformation or reversal of both her etymology and character at this pivotal point of transition from sensibility to folly.[57] As soon as the fate of the gods forced her to succumb, Aigisthos disposed of the *aoidos* who protected her chastity, thus thrusting from home the *charis* of civilization and morality. He led her to his home in mutual love; they were both equally willing (τὴν δ' ἐθέλων ἐθέλουσαν, 272). Free will and compulsion play a significant part in Nestor's speech, supplying a link between the Agamemnon- and the Odysseus-tale (see 16.93–96).[58] Aigisthos, he continues, offered the gods gifts, among which were woven objects, ὑφάσματα (274), for having accomplished a great and unhoped for deed (ἐκτελέσας μέγα ἔργον, ὃ οὔ ποτε ἔλπετο θυμῷ, 275), namely the seduction and the murder.[59] This *hapax* generic term, ὑφάσματα, be-

---

56 This song (*Od.* 8.266–366), studded with words bearing on shame, fame (*kleos, periklytos, klytoergos*), and connivance (*byssodomeuōn, dolos, doloeis*), works paradigmatically for the two human couples of the *Odyssey*. Hephaistos, feigning a trip out of town (*metadēmios*), immobilizes (*empedon … menoien*) and traps the adulterous couple in the act. By art and craft the lame god exposes the adultery of his wife and Ares, the exponent of physical masculine strength. Aigisthos eliminates the legitimate yet superior husband (ἀρείω, 3.250) through guile; the *aoidos* drives the lesson home for Odysseus (n. 73, below).

57 Felson 1994, 97, observes that 'Nestor alone gives a nuanced interpretation of Klytaimestra, mitigating her treachery perhaps for the benefit of Telemakhos'.

58 In a passage marked by recollection, suitors and contrivance (*anemnēsas, mnestēras* and *mēchanaasthai*, 3.211–15), Nestor inquires Telemachos whether the suitors plot evils against his will or not (ἀέκητι, ἑκών ~ 16.93–96). On the interplay of free will and compulsion, see Adkins 1960, 19–23.

59 The motif of hope is exploited in Attic tragedy. Aischylos makes a programmatic statement about the γυναικὸς ἀνδρόβουλον ἐλπίζον κέαρ (*Ag.* 11), and reserves the motif for empty hopes or inauspicious premonitions anticipating death (911, 990–1000, 1031–32, 1044–45, 1056–58, 1434, 1668). In the *Cho.* (187, 194, 236, 412, 539, 699, 776), hope is associated with Orestes' life or death. Interestingly, words signifying hope are not attested in the *Eume-*

longs to an imagery that is widely exploited in the poem: the verb ὑφαίνω applies to manual and mental weaving, usually elaborate and crooked. Both aspects are embedded in Aigisthos' ὑφάσματα, as they celebrate the accomplishment of an erotic and murderous weaving. The ominous ὑφάσματα in the Agamemnon-tale mark the reversal of normalcy and evoke Helen's *mnêma*-textile and especially the woven shroud in the Odysseus-tale: Penelope's ταφήιον φᾶρος looms large, a source of anxiety and suspense: whose wedding or death will this eventually crown?

The question haunts the story of Odysseus. Aigisthos' ὑφάσματα and Penelope's φᾶρος provide the threads that hold the fabric of the narrative together, bringing into contact the two tales. Woven items acquire a prodigious potency when the Aischylean Agamemnon shrinks from trampling woven objects, ὑφάς (949) with his feet; at death he lies in a spider's web, ἀράχνης ἐν ὑφάσματι τῶιδ' (1492, 1516), while Aigisthos rejoices at the sight of his enemy, lying dead in the woven robes of the Erinyes, ὑφαντοῖς ἐν πέπλοις Ἐρινύων (1580).[60] Death is prefigured in terms of weaving and bridal offerings are transformed into shrouds. Meanwhile Nestor rounds off the tale, focusing on *dolos* and *mēdomai* (3.301–10):

ὣς ὁ μὲν [Μενέλαος] ἔνθα πολὺν βίοτον καὶ χρυσὸν ἀγείρων
ἠλᾶτο ...
τόφρα δὲ ταῦτ' Αἴγισθος ἐμήσατο οἴκοθι λυγρά,
κτείνας Ἀτρεΐδην, δέδμητο δὲ λαὸς ὑπ' αὐτῷ.
ἑπτάετες δ' ἤνασσε πολυχρύσοιο Μυκήνης,
τῷ δέ οἱ ὀγδοάτῳ κακὸν ἤλυθε δῖος Ὀρέστης
ἂψ ἀπ' Ἀθηνάων, κατὰ δ' ἔκτανε πατροφονῆα,
Αἴγισθον δολόμητιν, ὅ οἱ πατέρα κλυτὸν ἔκτα.
ἦ τοι ὁ τὸν κτείνας δαίνυ τάφον Ἀργείοισι
μητρός τε στυγερῆς καὶ ἀνάλκιδος Αἰγίσθοιο.

So he was wandering there with his ships ... gathering much livelihood and gold;/but meanwhile Aegisthus devised this woeful work at home,/slaying the son of Atreus, and the people were subdued under him./Seven years he reigned over Mycenae, rich in gold,/but in the eighth came as his bane the

---

nides; mortals have fastened their hopes onto the gods and the court of justice. See also Soph. *El.* 186, 856–57, 958–63, 1127–28, 1263, 1281, 1460. Eur *El.* 352, 570, 579, 580.

60 Agamemnon's death is bound with woven cloths: Geryon's *chlaina* (870–73), spread-out items (*petasmasin*, 909), woven sea-dyed objects (*halourgesin*, 946; *hyphas*, 949), vestiments dyed (*heimatōn baphais*, 959–60), or trampled (*patēsmon heimatōn*, 963); cf. *plouton heimatos kakon* (1383); 1580, 1516, 1580. On the function of cloths see McClure 1999, 83–85; McNeil 2005.

noble Orestes/back from Athens, and slew his father's murderer,/the guileful Aegisthus, because he had slain his glorious father./Now when he had slain him, he made a funeral feast for the Argives/over his hateful mother and the craven Aegisthus.

During Menelaos' wanderings (302), Aigisthos contrived evils at home (ἐμήσατο οἴκοθι λυγρά, 303), killed Agamemnon and usurped his throne and wealth. Orestes retaliated upon his return, killing Aigisthos δολόμητις, and offered the Argives a funeral feast for his hateful mother and the valorless, *analkis*, Aigisthos (306–10; cf. 4.333–40). Nestor parallels the two tales, admonishing Telemachos not to wander far from home, or else his mother's suitors will waste his property (3.313–16). Aigisthos and Klytaimnestra surface as models of deceptive and criminal courtship; a feast of death caps their punishment at the hands of a kinsman, Orestes.

In book 4, Menelaos uses the 'speech within a speech device'[61] effectively, reporting the story he heard from Proteus. With a contemptuous and emotionally charged 'other', ἄλλος, Menelaos suppresses the names of the murderous couple, dwelling on their combined deceit: another man surprised and killed his brother unawares and by stealth, assisted by the guile of his destructive wife (ἀδελφεὸν ἄλλος ἔπεφνε/λάθρῃ, ἀνωϊστί, δόλῳ οὐλομένης ἀλόχοιο, 4.91–92; 524–35). Menelaos focalizes the surge of a storm (*thyella*) in the fish-filled sea (*ichthyoeis pontos*) near the house of *Thyestes* and *Thyestiades* Aigis*th*os (515–18), as well as Agamemnon's murder, in a passage marked by the heavy alliteration of θυε-/θυο- (4.524–35):

τὸν δ' ἄρ' ἀπὸ σκοπιῆς εἶδε σκοπός, ὅν ῥα καθεῖσεν
Αἴγισθος δολόμητις ἄγων, ὑπὸ δ' ἔσχετο μισθὸν
χρυσοῦ δοιὰ τάλαντα· φύλασσε δ' ὅ γ' εἰς ἐνιαυτόν,
μή ἑ λάθοι παριών, μνήσαιτο δὲ θούριδος ἀλκῆς.
βῆ δ' ἴμεν ἀγγελέων πρὸς δώματα ποιμένι λαῶν.
αὐτίκα δ' Αἴγισθος δολίην ἐφράσσατο τέχνην·
κρινάμενος κατὰ δῆμον ἐείκοσι φῶτας ἀρίστους
εἷσε λόχον, ἑτέρωθι δ' ἀνώγει δαῖτα πένεσθαι.
αὐτὰρ ὁ βῆ καλέων Ἀγαμέμνονα, ποιμένα λαῶν,
ἵπποισιν καὶ ὄχεσφιν, ἀεικέα μερμηρίζων.
τὸν δ' οὐκ εἰδότ' ὄλεθρον ἀνήγαγε καὶ κατέπεφνε
δειπνίσσας, ὥς τίς τε κατέκτανε βοῦν ἐπὶ φάτνῃ.

Now from his place of watch a watchman saw him, whom/guileful Aegisthus took and set there, promising him as a reward/two talents of gold;

---

61 So de Jong 2001a, 111.

and he had been keeping guard for a year,/for fear Agamemnon should pass by him unseen, and be mindful of his furious might./So he went to the palace to bear the tidings to the shepherd of the people,/and Aegisthus at once planned a treacherous device./He chose out twenty men, the best in the land,/and set them to lie in wait, but on the further side of the hall he bade prepare a feast./Then he went with chariot and horses to summon Agamemnon, shepherd of the people,/his mind pondering a dastardly deed./So he brought him up all unaware of his doom,/and when he had feasted him he slew him, as one slays an ox at the corn crib.

Agamemnon is spied by the human, well-paid *skopos* whom Aigisthos δολόμητις, in defiance of *eüskopos* and death-averting Hermes (1.38 with n. 11, above), had stationed, so as to intercept the returning hero and hinder him from remembering his unrestrained valor (μή ἑ λάθοι παριών, μνήσαιτο δὲ <u>θούριδος ἀλκῆς</u>, 4.527). This phrase, a *hapax* in the *Odyssey*, echoes the *Iliad* (8x) and marks a decisive step: Iliadic martial valor is replaced by Odyssean snares and wiles (δολίην ἐφράσσατο τέχνην, 529). Aigisthos laid an ambush (λόχον), and invited the shepherd of the people to dinner (531–32), pondering offensive schemes (533); he slew him, as one slays an ox at the manger (534–35). Although Homer never mentions the perverse *Thyestean deipna*, he subtly alludes to them here through the striking alliteration of the passage and the ox-simile. Alliteration and simile join forces, subtly re-enacting the suppressed tale, and the internecine feud.[62] The scheming son of Thyestes slaughters his kin as a sacrificial animal, thus blurring the semantic nuances of θύω (*rush, storm, rage/sacrifice*, *LSJ* A, B) and the boundaries between sacred, profane and beastly. This paves the way for the Aischylean vision of Agamemnon's corrupted sacrifice at the hands of his wife.[63] Etymology and narrative combine in a critical moment to underscore the total extinction of the hero with the significant name: Agamemnon's physical annihilation coincides with the reversal of his linguistic *sēmata* the moment he is obstructed from '*remembering* his impetuous valor (i.e. his *menos*)', from '*withholding*', and from acting as 'shepherd of people' (532), 'in a society that conceived of sovereignty

---

[62] On the 'desecrated feast' and its prefigurations see Clarke 1967, 11. Schmidt 2001, 161–62, dwells on the Thyestes story: this motivates the divine forewarning addressed to Aigisthos, and Zeus sets new yardsticks for the internecine vengeance and retaliation.

[63] See Zeitlin 196; id. 1966. In Eur. *El.*, Klytaimnestra and Aigisthos pay for the *sphagiasmos* of the father (203–06), engaged in a sacrificial activity (627, 635–41, 784–85, 795–858, 1132–46).

through a pastoral vocabulary';[64] Aigisthos has usurped the title and the office that goes with it. Caught by surprise and stealth, Agamemnon is prohibited from exercising the qualities that make up his name and essence, in sum, his capacity of ἄγαν μιμνήσκεσθαι, μένειν and μέδειν.[65] This essential nexus is broken at death, and the mighty king is reduced to a mere physical insubstantiality in the Underworld, 'But no longer had he anything of strength or might remaining' (οὐ γάρ οἱ ἔτ᾽ ἦν ἴς ἔμπεδος οὐδέ τι κῖκυς, 11.393). In the second *Nekyia*, Agamemnon will deplore the loss of his signifier and signified.

In the two *Nekyiai*,[66] Agamemnon's ignominious and pitiable death is focalized by the very victim. To start with the first *Nekyia* (*Od.* 11), here Agamemnon exemplifies men suffering a nonheroic death (397–403 = 406–08) by the animosity of a wicked woman (κακῆς ἰότητι γυναικός, 384).[67] Conversing with Odysseus, the slain hero broods over his shameful and bovine slaughter (11.409–412):

ἀλλά μοι Αἴγισθος τεύξας θάνατόν τε μόρον τε
ἔκτα σὺν οὐλομένῃ ἀλόχῳ, οἶκόνδε καλέσσας,
δειπνίσσας, ὥς τίς τε κατέκτανε βοῦν ἐπὶ φάτνῃ.
ὣς θάνον οἰκτίστῳ θανάτῳ.

But Aegisthus brought upon me death and fate,/and slew me with the aid of my accursed wife, when he had bidden me to his house/and made me a feast, just as one slays an ox at the crib./So I died by a most pitiful death.

Agamemnon visualizes the gruesome scene: we were lying about the mixing bowls and the laden tables in the hall, he says; the floor was seething with blood (δάπεδον δ᾽ ἅπαν αἵματι θῦεν, 420). Comparing his comrades to swine slaughtered for a wedding or feast of a rich man (412–15), and masking the massacre into an abhorrent *heortē*, he foreshadows the sham wedding which Odysseus will feign, and the death of the *mnestêres*

---

64 Detienne 1996, 60–61.
65 On Agamemnon's etymology (< ἄγαν μένω, μέδω-μέδομαι, μέμνημαι) see van der Valk 1955, 34–42, s.v.; Tsitsibakou-Vasalos 2007, 43, 81–82, 126, 208–11.
66 On the two 'Nekyiai' as authentic and organic parts of the *Odyssey*, see Bassett 1918; Kullmann 1992, 291–304; Heubeck 1992, 353–56; Tsagalis 2003, 43–66. Clarke 1999, 225–28, does not commit himself, while West 1989 proposes a post dating.
67 See Adkins 1960, 36–37, *kakos* denigrates women who do not possess *aretē* and the 'quiet' virtues. Cf. Yamagata 1994, 211.

(22.309; 24.185), which replicates his own death.⁶⁸ *Analepsis* and *prolepsis* obliterate any temporal divisions, drawing a parallelism between the two tales. Agamemnon will take his revenge even if by proxy, namely Odysseus.

Agamemnon heaps crimes and scorn on Klytaimnestra δολόμητις who killed Kassandra and him even before he saw their son (11.453); her epithet cannot be 'purely traditional'.⁶⁹ There is nothing more dreadful and shameful than the woman who plots death for her *kouridios* husband. Agamemnon showers his wife with canine sexual abuse and disgrace for posterity (11.421–22, 427–30, 432–34, 452–53):

> οἰκτροτάτην δ' ἤκουσα ὄπα Πριάμοιο θυγατρός,
> Κασσάνδρης, τὴν κτεῖνε Κλυταιμνήστρη δολόμητις.

But the most piteous cry that I heard was that of the daughter of Priam,/ Cassandra, whom guileful Clytemnestra slew.

> ὡς οὐκ αἰνότερον καὶ κύντερον ἄλλο γυναικός,
> ἥ τις δὴ τοιαῦτα μετὰ φρεσὶν ἔργα βάληται·
> οἷον δὴ καὶ κείνη ἐμήσατο ἔργον ἀεικὲς
> κουριδίῳ τεύξασα πόσει φόνον …

So true is it that there is nothing more frightful or more shameless than a woman/who puts into her heart such deeds,/like the ugly thing she plotted,/contriving her wedded husband's murder.

> ἡ δ' ἔξοχα λυγρὰ ἰδυῖα
> οἷ τε κατ' αἶσχος ἔχευε καὶ ἐσσομένῃσιν ὀπίσσω
> θηλυτέρῃσι γυναιξί, καὶ ἥ κ' εὐεργὸς ἔῃσιν.

But she with her heart set on utter horror,/has shed shame on herself and on women yet to be, even on her who does what is right.

> ἡ δ' ἐμὴ οὐδέ περ υἷος ἐνιπλησθῆναι ἄκοιτις
> ὀφθαλμοῖσιν ἔασε· πάρος δέ με πέφνε καὶ αὐτόν.

But my wife did not let me sate my eyes even with the sight of my son. Before that it was I myself whom she slew.

Agamemnon narrativizes Klytaimnestra's name, reversing its signified and expressing the emotional and social tension. In a climactic manner, he replaces her originally honorable reputation and sensibility with infamy and deadly scheming (κτεῖνε, ἐμήσατο, τεύξασα φόνον, λυγρὰ ἰδυῖα, πέφνε, αἶσχος). He forewarns Odysseus of the perils lurking at home and issuing

---

68 See de Jong 2001a, 13, 'additions … shifts of accent … and variants (Agamemnon killed during a feast not in bath) … all serve to tailor this embedded story to the particular of the *Odyssey*'.
69 So Düring 1945, 104, apropos δῖα and δολόμητις.

from an unfaithful wife,[70] but makes Klytai-mnestra a foil for Penelope who is wise and knows good thoughts (πινυτή τε καὶ εὖ φρεσὶ μήδεα οἶδεν/... περίφρων, 445–46).[71] Klytaimnestra moves on the fringes of masculinity, and Odysseus draws a comprehensive parallelism of the two infamous women of this family: Helen destroyed many, while Klytaimnestra 'spread a snare' for Agamemnon (δόλον ἤρτυε, 439).

Ironically, only *post mortem* does Agamemnon turn into a schemer and trickster. He advises Odysseus, an exemplary living trickster who has descended into an alien and unnatural place, how to remain alive by hiding his thoughts and words, by reaching his fatherland secretly and by having no trust in women (11.441–43; 454–56).[72] Odysseus recalls Agamemnon's advice when Athena invites him to a concerted scheme against the suitors (μνηστῆρσιν, 13.373, 376), who pursue his godlike wife (μνώμενοι ἀντιθέην ἄλοχον, 13.378). Assisted by Athena in the past, Odysseus had 'loosened the bright headdress of Troy' (387–91). With this metaphor, which blends the erotic and metaphorical nuances of κρήδεμνον, Odysseus launches his private war for love and status, activating his *polykerdēs noos* (13.255), his *polykerdeiai* (24.167), his multiple faces, hidden identities, tricky counsels, wiles and snares.[73]

---

70 Segal 1986a, 169, argues that '*mêtis*, particularly in the sexual realm, is the sinister property of the woman'; female sexuality is associated with guile, trickery, and seduction.

71 Phrases with περίφρων cluster in the second half of the poem, qualifying almost exclusively Penelope (50x) and Eurykleia (4x), a trans-generational surrogate mother figure in whom father and son confide ever since Laertes honored her as much as his wife, ἶσα ... κεδνῇ ἀλόχῳ τίεν (*Od.* 1.432); ἶσα echoes Anti-kleia. She and κεδνὰ ἰδυῖα Eury-kleia (1.428) are given parallel yet contrasted functions. The former is 'heard' in the realm of shadows and futility, yet she provides the emotions that propel Odysseus' heart and *nostos*. The latter, authoritative and dynamic, is 'listened to' (κλύω) in the Upperworld, thus reassuring the κλέος of her masters and herself (see n. 55, above).

72 Scholars discern here a sign of misogyny: Cantarella 1987, 27; Katz 1991, 28–29, 51, 58, 112,194; Felson 1994, 93, 100–07; Doherty 1995, 93 and 22, 68, 100–02 (Agamemnon as spokesman of misogyny). See Pomeroy 1994, 21–22, on *Od.* 24.200–01, 'this generalization is the first in a long history of hostility towards women in Western literature'. On the misogyny in the Aischylean *Oresteia* see Zeitlin 1978.

73 Fighting by stealth and pursuing κέρδεα is sanctioned by Athena and applied by Odysseus who is not ἐπιδήμιος (1.194) but is ποικιλομήτα (13.293), activates his δόλος, μῆτις, ἀπάτη, μηχανᾶσθαι, μερμηρίζειν, μῆτιν ὑφαίνειν, emerging as ἐπίκλοπος and κερδαλέος (13.291–310), ἀγχίνοος and ἐχέφρων, in an effort to regain his *empedon* bed, his wedded wife and his *oikos*.

In the second *Nekyia* (*Od.* 24), the funeral honors offered to Achilles are focalized by Agamemnon, who concludes with bitterness (93–94):

ὣς σὺ μὲν οὐδὲ θανὼν ὄνομ' ὤλεσας, ἀλλά τοι αἰεὶ
πάντας ἐπ' ἀνθρώπους κλέος ἔσσεται ἐσθλόν, Ἀχιλλεῦ.

Thus not even in death did you lose your name, but always/shall you have fair fame among all men, Achilles.

Name, reputation and memory are tantamount to life, even if substitute. Agamemnon focalizes instead his own infamy and anonymity. His non-heroic death (95–97) has effaced both his existence and name; in the Underworld, the heroic values are reduced to mere 'pleasure' (ἦδος, 95). With new awareness, Agamemnon mitigates his former hostility: it was Zeus who contrived a wretched death for him at the hands of Aigisthos and his accursed wife (Ζεὺς μήσατο λυγρὸν ὄλεθρον/Αἰγίσθου ὑπὸ χερσὶ καὶ οὐλομένης ἀλόχοιο, 96–97). In a ring, the Agamemnon-tale returns to the issue of personal responsibility and divine dispensation laid out in book 1.

Meanwhile the slain suitors of the story descend to Hades. One of them, Amphimedon, 'a man of two minds', or 'ruling in two worlds', converses with Agamemnon,[74] and narrates the outcome of their *mnesteia*, framing his 'mirror story'[75] in a cluster of cognates that signify memory, wooing and withstanding (μέμνημαι, μνώμεθα, μίμνετε, 24.122, 125, 132). He starts with Penelope: she contrived a ruse (δόλον τόνδ' ἄλλον ἐνὶ φρεσὶ μερμήριξε, 24.128), and procrastinated, weaving a funeral shroud that shone like the sun or the moon (φᾶρος ταφήιον ... ἠελίῳ ἐναλίγκιον ἠὲ σελήνῃ, 132–48). The duality of this web is subtly radiated by the word *ταφήιον* itself: astonishment (*τέθηπα*) and funeral associations (*τάφος*) converge in her handiwork.[76]

---

[74] Significantly, both men share a similar fate and etymology. On Ἀμφιμέδων see von Kamptz 1982, 84, 208, 'von μέδομαι "sinnen, bedacht sein auf etwas, walten" neben hom. μέδων "Obwalter, Herrscher"'. On Agamemnon and μέδομαι see n. 65, above.

[75] De Jong 2001a, 571.

[76] Stupor, awe and grave/tomb are imprinted in *τάφος*; see sch A(D) *Il.* 9.193. ταφών: ἐκ τῶν τάφων δὲ ἡ μεταφορά. καὶ γὰρ ἡμεῖς ὁρῶντες τοὺς τάφους ἐκπληττόμεθα τὸ μέλλον δεινόν; see sch. *Od.* 16.12; sch. E *Od.* 3.309 and sch. BT *Od.* 4.547. Athena anticipates the duality of *τάφος* (1.181, 260–66), appearing in the guise of Μέντης/Μέντωρ, a figure personifying stoutness (μένω) and memory (μέμνημαι; sch.T *Il.* 7.73a; Eust. *Il.* 3.33.6–10; id. *Od.* 1.109.38–46; Mader *LfgrE* s.v.), and as a *Taphian* king, whose father had allegedly provided Odysseus with deadly medicine. Her departure is attended

The sinister implications of weaving and of the *mnestē* are now foregrounded. In collaboration with his son, Odysseus planned a pitiful death for the suitors; the floor was seething with blood (δάπεδον δ' ἅπαν αἵματι θῦεν, 24.185), while their bodies, gory, uncared for and bereft of the last funeral *geras*, lay in the hall, σώματ' ἀκηδέα κεῖται ἐνὶ μεγάροις (187). The truth shines like the funeral shroud; *βίος*, the gift of ξεινοσύνης *προσκηδέος*, and Athena's loving *κῆδος* for Odysseus and his family have deprived the suitors of their *βίος* and *κῆδος*, namely of their life and funeral honors. Agamemnon has at last taken vicarious revenge,[77] as his counsel (11.440–56) proved vital for Odysseus. This justifies the enthusiastic exclamation of his soul in Hades upon hearing the *mnesterophonia* (24.192–202):

ὄλβιε Λαέρταο πάϊ, πολυμήχαν' Ὀδυσσεῦ,
ἦ ἄρα σὺν μεγάλῃ ἀρετῇ ἐκτήσω ἄκοιτιν.
ὡς <u>ἀγαθαὶ φρένες</u> ἦσαν ἀμύμονι Πηνελοπείῃ,
κούρῃ Ἰκαρίου· ὡς εὖ μέμνητ' Ὀδυσῆος,
ἀνδρὸς κουριδίου· τῷ οἱ κλέος οὔ ποτ' ὀλεῖται
ἧς ἀρετῆς, τεύξουσι δ' ἐπιχθονίοισιν ἀοιδὴν
ἀθάνατοι χαρίεσσαν <u>ἐχέφρονι</u> Πηνελοπείῃ,
οὐχ ὡς Τυνδαρέου κούρη κακὰ μήσατο ἔργα,
κουρίδιον κτείνασα πόσιν, στυγερὴ δέ τ' ἀοιδὴ
ἔσσετ' ἐπ' ἀνθρώπους, χαλεπὴν δέ τε φῆμιν ὀπάσσει
θηλυτέρῃσι γυναιξί, καὶ ἥ κ' εὐεργὸς ἔῃσιν.

Happy son of Laertes, Odysseus of many devices,/truly you won a wife of great virtue [or, with great virtue you won your wife]./How good intellect had blameless Penelope,/the daughter of Ikarios, and how well she remembered Odysseus,/her wedded husband. For this reason the fame for her excellence will never perish,/and the immortals will fashion a graceful song among men on earth for wise Penelope./Not in this manner the daughter of Tyndareos contrived evil deeds,/killing her wedded husband, and hateful will be the song about her among men, and she shed a bad repute/upon women, even upon the one who does what is right.

Agamemnon concludes his own tale, contrasting the fate of the two couples.[78] He encapsulates Odysseus' success in *ὄλβιος*, a common epi-

---

by awe (θάμβησεν, 323–24) and her speech, informed with deadly premonitions (1.251–66), foreshadows the *mnesterophonia*; τάφος proves its doubleness.

77 See Felson 1994, 106 on Agamemnon's vicarious vindication and his pleasure at the outcome of the affairs on Ithaka.
78 See Heubeck 1992, 380, 'Agamemnon's speech acts as the climax of the contrasting treatment of the fates of the two families'. Segal 1994, 108, argues that 'this scene in the second *Nekyia* completes the symmetries and contrasts between Odysseus and Agamemnon, Penelope and Clytaemnestra'.

thet which nonetheless fits the particulars of the story, since the hero has integrated and healed his ὅλον βίον through his βιός and βίη.[79] Agamemnon verbalizes the *homophrosynē* of the Ithakan couple in an ambiguous and evasive context.[80] Language and syntax collaborate to highlight the intricate mingling of the united couple: Odysseus' great *aretē* and *kleos* are connected with those of his wife, whose renown will be everlasting (24.193, 196–97); here the heroizing term *kleos* is reserved only for her, not for Klytaimnestra.[81] Odysseus is deservedly embraced by *kleos* figures, such as Penelope, Anti*kleia* and Eury*kleia* (nn. 55, 71, above). In the person of Penelope, the virtuous ἄλοχος μνηστή of the story, the positive values of ἀμύμων, ἄκοιτις and ἄλοχος are at last reinstated: she is worthy of sharing Odysseus' bed (ἀ-*cop.* + λέχος/κοίτη) as his legitimate and beloved consort,[82] for having proven morally and mentally flawless (ἀ-*priv.* + μῶμος) and for having manifested a virtuous mind (ἀγαθαὶ φρένες) through the trial of the *mnēsteia*. The Ithakan οἶκος is restored and proven ἀμύμων (1.232), and Odysseus' wish to find upon his *nostos* his wife blameless and his friends unscathed in his house is fulfilled (ἀμύμονα δ' οἴκοι ἄκοιτιν/νοστήσας εὕροιμι σὺν ἀρτεμέεσσι φίλοισιν, 13.42–43). The problematic notion of impeccability embraces the poem in a ring. The same is true for memory; Penelope remembered well (εὖ μέμνητ') her *kouridios anēr*, says Agamemnon, playing upon the axial theme of recollection and at the same time upon the sounds of his own name and 'deformed' etymology (nn. 64, 65 above). He was not an object of benign and loving memory, but of a memory

---

79 On the derivation of ὄλβιος from ὅλος-ὁλόκληρος/ὁλαί (= κριθαί)/οὔλιος-οὖλος (= ὑγιής) + βίος see: Ap. Soph. 120.3–4; Hsch. o 512; cf. ib. o 513, 514. Eust. *Il.* 1.633.13–15; *Et.Gud.* o 425.14–15; *EM* 621.21–26. On 'a submerged poetic association' of βίος-βίη see Thalmann 1998, 179–80.
80 On the syntactical ambiguity of *kleos* and *aretē* in this passage see Nagy (1979) 1999, 38; Katz 1991, 20–21; West 1989, 124. On Penelope as moral agent driven by these virtues see Foley 1995.
81 Segal 1989, 336.
82 For the semantic differentiation of ἄλοχος (legitimate wife) and ἄκοιτις (term of affection) see Chantraine 1946–47, 223, 226. Ironically, in tragedy the death of the criminal couple results from the conspiracy of Ἠλέκτρα, inexperienced of the conjugal bed (Soph. *El.* 165, 962–66; cf. 489–94; Eur. *El. passim*), and Orestes, who committed the matricide and matured, activating his ancestral fearlessness (Ἀτρεύς < ἀ-*priv.* + τρέω) and the impetus, ὁρμή, imprinted in his own name (Soph. *El.* 1508–10). On Orestes see Tsitsibakou-Vasalos 2007, 127, 185, 216–221, 223; on Atreus see ib. 82, 172, 174, 205–06, 212.

that struck him at the heart of his essence.[83] The tales of the two heroes are thus sharply contrasted.

Agamemnon is tormented by the recollection of Klytaimnestra's deceitful *mnēsteia* and criminal *mēdesthai*. The Argive κουρίδιος πόσις, the legitimate husband, is overpowered by the craft of a deceitful wife, and reduced to a mere shadow, weak and still emotionally vulnerable, residing in the Underworld. Agamemnon fails to sustain his status as πόσις, and act out its meaning as 'master of the house', and metaphorically as 'irrigating' a woman's womb and procreating children'.[84] Significantly, she did not give him the chance to see his offspring. The Aischylean Klytaimnestra will exploit the grim connotations of πόσις, and, gloating over the corpse of her husband, will exclaim in triumph, οὗτός ἐστιν Ἀγαμέμνων, ἐμὸς/πόσις, νεκρὸς δέ (*Ag.* 1404–05); this ironic collocation negates the existence of authority, vital fluids and vigor.[85] Contrastingly, the Ithakan κουρίδιος ἀνήρ enjoys the fruits of his victory, reaffirming the meaning of ἀνήρ and its inherent relation to accomplishment, preeminence and excellence.[86] In the manner of a skilled *aoidos*, Odysseus makes his deadly *palintonon* bow (21.11, 59) ring like a lyre in Apollo's festival, and taking on the contradictory yet complementary qualities of the god of death and healing,[87] he ironically sends forth a song like a

---

[83] Κλυται-*μνήστρα* qua *μνηστή* is associated with *μιμνήσκομαι*; she fails to 're-member' her husband, or is perhaps beset with the 'memory' of her sacrificed daughter, a detail suppressed by Homer but exploited by tragedy: recollection of the sacrifice, coupled with the illicit *mnēsteia*, arms Klytaimnestra's hand in tragedy. See n. 90, below.

[84] On πόσις παρὰ τὸ ποτίζειν τῇ γονῇ see *Et.Gen.* α 1235; *Et.Gud.* 477. 8–14; *EM* 149. 42–48, 684. 21–24. See Frisk *GrEW* s.v. πόσις, 'Ehemann, Gatte, Gemahl, Herr'; cf. Latin *potis*, 'vermögend, mächtig'. Chantraine *DELG* s.v. πόσις, 'époux, maître de la maison, puissant, qui peut'; on the distinction between *posis* ('époux légitime', 'de valeur juridique plutôt que sentimentale'; cf. Soph. *Tr.* 550) and *anēr* (a rather generic term) see Chantraine 1946–1947, 220–22, 233–34.

[85] Νεκρός, πόσις, ἄκικυς, ἀλίβας and διερός are bound with the presence or absence of humidity and vital fluids; A. frs. 229 (ἰκμάς), 230 *cum test.* (*TrGF* 3: 339–40, Radt), σοὶ δ' οὐκ ἔνεστι κῖκυς, οὐδ' αἱμόρρυτοι φλέβες; Or. 30.14 ~ *Et.Gen.* α 489, ἀλίβας, ὁ νεκρός. παρὰ τὸ μὴ ἔχειν λιβάδα, ὅ ἐστιν ὑγρότητα· οἱ γὰρ ζῶντες ὑγροί, *et al.*

[86] On the derivation of ἀνήρ from ἀνύω/ἀρετή see sch. *Od.* 1.1 f. (Pontani); *Et.Gud.* 144.15; sch. EQ *Od.* 1.1; *Et.Gen.* α 776, 875. 1–7; *Et.Gud.* 145; *EM* 107. 30–51; *Et.Sym.* 1.20.26.

[87] Burkert 1985, 146–48, argues that Apollo's functional ambiguity is crystallized in the image of the bow and the lyre, the unity of which is articulated by He-

swallow heralding the spring (21.405–11): killing the suitors and creating chaos, he reinstates order, conjugal and parental harmony as well as the χάρις of song and civilization in the microcosm of his *oikos*.

Klytaimnestra, the wicked ἄλοχος μνηστή and schemer of the Agamemnon-tale, closes her career exactly as she started it: unnamed yet accompanied by a substitute reversed namegiving conveyed by a hateful song; στυγερός suits her, linked as it is with deadly betrayal, curse and death (cf. Eriphyle, *Od.* 11.326). She sheds an evil fame indiscriminately on herself and all womankind. Hence her *klytos* component is irreversibly equated with infamy and everlasting notoriety. Interestingly, *klytos* qualifies *onoma* (ὄνομα κλυτόν) on two occasions involving Odysseus' false and fictive appellation.[88] The truth is always revealed, and Klytaimnestra is no exception to this rule: she will reap disgrace and death. Posterity will dwell on the ironic value of her name.[89] In Pindar, Ἀρσινόα, Orestes' foster mother, will contrapose her sound mind (ἄρτιος νόος) to the notorious contrivance of Klytaimnestra, the νηλὴς γυνά, rescuing the boy from the strong hands of her pitiless biological mother (*Pyth.* 11.17–26).[90]

---

rakl. (22 B. F51, *VS* D.-K.) as παλίντροπος ἁρμονίη, as 'a fitting together turned back on itself' (146). So also Bierl 1994, 82. On the complex symbolism of the bow, its divergent meanings and the Apollo-like epiphany of Odysseus in the act of killing see Thalmann 1998, 174–80.

88 *Od.* 9.364: *Outis*; 19.183: *Aithon*; cf. also *h.Aphr.* 146: *Otreus*, a fictive father fashioned by Aphrodite during her seductive speech to Anchises, and her attempt to *otrynein* him to making love.

89 A. (*Ag.* 10–11), κρατεῖ ... ἀνδρόβουλον, alludes to Klytaimnestra's androgynous character, and her relation to μέδομαι/μήδομαι (1100–02). His chorus, perverting the meaning of *periphrōn*, showers Klytaimnestra with contempt (*Ag.* 1426–27), μεγαλόμητις εἶ, περίφρονα δ' ἔλακες, 'You are great in your plans, arrogant in your talk' (Collard 1975). Elektra discards the signified of her mother's name, οὐδαμῶς ἐπώνυμον/φρόνημα παισὶ δύσθεον πεπαμένη (*Cho.* 190–91). See Eur. *El.* ἄνακτα ... ἔκανεν, Τυνδαρίς, σὰ λέχεα, κακόφρων κούρα (479–81); ἥτις φρενήρης (1053); εἴθ' εἶχες ... βελτίους φρένας (1061); καλῶς γε σωφρονεῖν παρεῖχέ σοι (1080); ἐξῆν κλέος σοι μέγα λαβεῖν (1084). See Frisk *GrEW* s.v. μήδομαι.

90 March 1987, 90–98, focusing on the artistic evidence and the sacrifice of Iphigeneia, argues that Pindar modelled his *Oresteia* myth not on Stesichoros (see e.g. Mueller-Goldingen 2000, 3–14), but on Simonides (*PMG* 608), the first to mention this sacrifice. Homer keeps silence, the *Kypria* mentions the aborted sacrifice and the deification of the girl, as also Hesiod (fr. 23[a] 17.21–26 M.-W.) and Stesichoros (*PMG* 191, 215). This theory contradicts the textual evidence: (a) the story takes place at Mycenae, πέπλασται ὁ λόγος ... ἐν Μυκάναισι (*PMG* 608.20–21), yet Stesichoros and Simonides locate the royal seat of Agamemnon in Lakedaimon, and Pindar in Amyklai;

Masks fall at last in *Odyssey* 24. With a flashback, Agamemnon focalizes the first contract of love, the time of innocence and maidenhood, when the wives were still *kourai* and daughters of a father. With differing mental dispositions, these *kourai* brought about an unequal destiny on their *kouridios* husband. Penelope is mentioned twice by name and praised both as daughter and wife, in contrast to Klytaimnestra whose name is significantly suppressed. Agamemnon stamps her with a *hapax* periphrasis, *Tyndareou kourē* (24.199), which subtly anticipates the stigma of infidelity imposed by Aphrodite on Tyndareos' daughters (Hes. fr.176.5−6 M.-W.; Stes. *PMG* 223). With this reversion into the ideal value of *kouridios* and *kourē* and the mental reenactment of their wedding, Agamemnon evokes the inauspicious *gamos agamos* of Achilles (*Il.* 9), annuls his own rotten marriage, but ratifies that of Odysseus who is reinstated as *kouridios* beside a virtuous *kourē*;[91] normalcy and equilibrium are restored in the Ithakan palace. The Agamemnon-tale proves an integral part of the *Odyssey*, and contributes to its unity.[92]

3. Conclusions

The indeterminacy of the female characters and the plot depends on the semantic and functional ambiguity of the *mnestē*, who is associated with *mnaomai, menō, mimneskō,* and *mnema*. Klytai-*mnestra* encapsulates the qualities of *mnestē* in her name and essence, but reverses them, reflecting the deadly conflicts dramatized in the two tales. She functions as a dis-

---

(b) the supplement, τούτωι ὁ Σιμω-[νίδης ἂν συμφω-/νοῖτο περὶ τούτου (2−3, with an unusual verb in middle voice) is dubious: who would Simonides agree with and on what? The Stesichorean pretext of Iphigeneia's marriage with Achilles (*PMG* 217) anticipates the motif of her sacrifice, which we can hardly eliminate from the ancient myth without gainsaying Aristotle (*Po.* 14.1453b.21−25; cf. 8.1451a.18−35). Cf. *PMG* 608.10 τὴν σφαζομέν[, and Hes. fr.23 (a)17, Ἰφιμέδην μὲν σφάξαν. If Elektra's etymology goes back to Xanthos (*PMG* 700), to whom Stesichoros is indebted, we may assume with some confidence that a *quasi* tragic version on a copious scale would be in circulation long before Simonides. The text and the method of the papyric commentator do not allow us to elicit the authentic Simonidean version.

91 Katz 1991, 113, 172−82, 193, considers the character problems of Penelope important and functional aspects of the narrative, serving the poem's ideology of exclusivity and the *homophrosynē* by which this ideology is represented. The reunion of Odysseus and his wife after the period of estrangement and alienation is an important aspect of 'the *Odyssey*'s ideology of exclusivity'.

92 Friedrich 1975, 83.

torting mirror of gender values and conjugal virtues, and signposts the anomalies to be amended in the *Odyssey*. As a 'bad woman ... she has no direct voice', and is not allowed to focalize any part of the *Odyssey*,[93] contrasting the Aischylean Klytaimnestra, whose deceptive persuasion depends on the efficacy and power of language, on her hypocritical, boastful and hated *glossa*.[94] The Odyssean *sēmata* of Klytaimnestra will creep into tragedy: with his customary amphibolic dexterity, Aischylos will identify Klytaimnestra with *Mēnis*, who 'dwells' in the house, 'remembers', and rises again and again, seeking revenge for the child.[95] Penelope *qua mnestē* is expected to waver, too, and be ridden by doubts. Her *pharos*, woven and unwoven, is the physical token of her vacillating disposition and loyalty, which nonetheless proves as *empedos* as the emblematic bed. Ἄλοχος μνηστή embodies the marital and social crises that arise in the aftermath of the *Iliad* when the returning heroes engage in domestic wars, waged primarily by stealth. The weaving metaphors accommodate the exigencies of such internal and internecine feuds. 'I weave wiles', *dolous tolypeuō* (19.137) to avoid the *mnestēres*, Penelope says to Odysseus, using a verb by which men also describe the successful *telos* of their wars (*Od.* 1.238; 4.490; 14.368).[96] *Tolypeuō* marks the disillusion of Agamemnon who used to weave wars (24.95; see *Il.* 24.7–8), but now lies in Hades, bereft of glory and name. Men intrude into the female space weaving schemes (μῆτιν ὑφαίνω, 4.678; 9.422; 13.303). Significantly, Klytaimnestra does not

---

93 So Doherty 1995, 112, 117, 177, 190.
94 See March 1987, 81–82, Aischylos will 'exploit the dramatic effectiveness of silence' before Klytaimnestra exhibits her *glossa* (*Ag.* 1228, 1399). McClure 1999, 70–111, notes the polysemy and bilingualism of Klytaimnestra's speech, and her capacity to blend conventional feminine and masculine ways of speaking. In Sophokles, mother and daughter vie in terms of *glossa*; as if a venomous snake, Klytaimnestra is envisaged as 'throwing her tongue' (ἵης γλῶσσαν, 596), while Elektra is accused of spreading rumors with much-tongued noise (πολυγλώσσῳ βοῇ, 641, 798, *loud-voiced cry*, *LSJ*). See Eur.: Elektra's tongue is a true interpreter (*El.* 334) and bitter if attended by evil mind (1014); even Apollo's tongue is not wise (1302).
95 A. *Ag.* 152–53, μίμνει γὰρ φοβερὰ παλίνορτος / οἰκονόμος δολία, μνάμων Μῆνις τεκνόποινος. The ring of crime will close with Orestes, a figure embodying 'rushing' or 'rising' (n. 82, above).
96 Sch. T *Il.* 14.86. b: ἐκτελεῖν. ... ἐξ οὗ καὶ τολύπη τὸ κατε<ι>ργασμένον ἔριον. Sch. bT *Il.* 24.7a. τολύπευσε· εἰς τέλος ἤγαγεν, ἀπὸ τῶν ἐρίων. ἔνθεν τὸ ἐκ πολλῶν πραγμάτων εἰς ἕν τι κεφαλαιοῦν τολυπεύειν λέγεται; sch. EV *Od.* 1.238. ἐπεὶ πόλεμον τολύπευσε· κατειργάσατο, μεταφορικῶς. τολύπη γὰρ εἶδος βοτάνης θανασίμου; sch. V *Od* 4.490.

weave and does not speak either: she only plots, standing in an absolute polarity with the other weaving women of the *Odyssey*. She prefigures the Hesiodic μητέρα [ἣν ὑπερήν]ορα, the overweening mother whom Orestes killed with pitiless bronze,[97] or the Pindaric pitiless woman, νηλὴς γυνά, and the Aischylean fully-fledged woman with the masculine and hoping spirit (*Ag.* 11), who distorts the benign function of woven cloths, turning them into instruments of hideous crime. The quiet or cooperative virtues of the females in the house are metaphorically taken over by warriors who once fought outside; in and out are ominously confused and gender boundaries are blurred. In the end the cunning use of the bow, an heirloom emblematic of self-identity (cf. οὐδέ τις ἄλλος), hospitality and heroic deeds, reconciles the worlds of the *Iliad* and the *Odyssey* as the Odyssean web is finished.

Employing μνηστή and Κλυταιμνήστρα as case study, I hope to have shown that common and proper names, analyzed, manipulated and re-signified in imaginative and meaningful ways, become constituent parts of an action and narrative, which often breaks the audience's or reader's horizon of expectation. It is argued, consequently, that etymology and narratology follow parallel and complementary courses: the former constructs lexical and semantic units the interlacing of which brings forth a coherent and articulate narrative; the latter by explaining the layering of focalization, helps us understand the motivation behind it, how it is that a word can mean different things at different times or to different characters, and how the conflicting meanings embodied in a word can be activated in the course of a narrative.

---

97 So fr. 23(α) 30 M.-W. March 1987, 88, 89 with n. 39, adopts Musso's supplement, ὀλεσήν]ορα.

Arete's Words: Etymology, *Ehoie*-Poetry and Gendered Narrative in the *Odyssey*

Marios Skempis – Ioannis Ziogas

This paper deals primarily with Arete's role in the *Odyssey* and offers a gendered as well as a generic interpretation of this figure's grounding in the narrative. Arete's laconic stance in the so-called Phaiakia has raised controversy over the way in which the queen of Scherie is to be involved in the prime theme of the poem, Odysseus' nostos.[1] It is not only the few and extremely cautious words spoken by Arete that are under discussion in this essay, but also the formalities of further speeches that frame her textual presence and determine her reception by ancient and modern audiences. The first part of this paper tackles the question of whether and to what extent Homer made use of etymological practice in shaping Arete's role in the *Odyssey*. On this ground, we suggest and subsequently analyze the etymological potential of Arete's name and the function of these etymologies in the narrative dynamics of the poem. Our main focus will not be on acknowledging or discovering possible etymological or para-etymological derivations, but examining whether the etymologies suggested are justified by the narrative and how they affect our reading of the *Odyssey*.

1. Etymology and Narratology

Etymological as well as para-etymological practices operated by the narrator in the field of onomastics and denomination are of great significance in interpreting narrative texts, and especially the Homeric epics since, in most cases, the narrator does not consider the meaning of a proper name fixed; on the contrary, there seems to be a constant interplay between primary or explicit meaning established by linguistic derivations and secondary or implicit meaning as this can emerge from con-

---

1   For an assessment of this issue see Hölscher 1960; (1989) ³1990, 122–34; Fenik 1974, 105–30.

text-specific parameters. The semantic flexibility of a proper name and its subsequent potential for multiple interpretations allow it to be inscribed within a set of circumscribed, embedded narratives, all familiar with and subordinate to the main narrative. Of course, etymology as a textual phenomenon can entail a certain amount of poetic subjectivism since it shows how the narrator (either primary or secondary) perceives the meaning of a name and how she/he wishes to project it to her/his narratees, internal and external. Etymologizing, however, serves as a rhetorical device that binds the literary character to the story, 'the events as dispositioned and ordered in the text';[2] it constitutes the means by which characters are embedded in narrative situations, while it may also reflect the *etymon* of the name-bearer as well as her/his ensuing ambiguities. The etymologies of Arete, in specific, as proposed in the following sections, will show that name-etymologizing stipulates manifold relations between narrative segments that are concerned with the name-bearer. In other words, the etymology of a proper name is to be identified as a mechanism formatting narrative structures.[3]

Etymology is compressed narrative, and unpacking the etymological potential of a word is to deploy its narrative force (*uis*).[4] Etymologies are enmeshed in narrative structures, and thus their use calls for a narratological approach. The etymology of a name, in particular, is closely associated with the characterization of a figure. Given that etymologizing is a dynamic process of revealing or constructing the meaning of a name, etymological analyses are crucial to interpreting the traits of characters as they are presented or perceived not only by the primary narrator, but also by the internal narrators. Defining the meaning of a name is a power game.[5] Thus, etymologies can reveal character features, which are real or artificially constructed or representative of class or type.[6]

---

2   De Jong – Nünlist – Bowie 2004, xviii.
3   On the narrative use of name-etymologizing see Calame 1995, 174–85; on speaking names foreshadowing the plot see the analysis of Aristophanes' *Thesmophoriazusae* in Bierl 2001, 276–82.
4   *uis,* the force of the word, means the etymology of a word in Latin.
5   For an illuminating discussion of the power inherent in etymologizing see Struever 1983. Nagy (1979) 1999, 69–93, Peradotto 1990 and Tsitsibakou-Vasalos 2007 have explored the narrative dynamics of etymologizing in the Homeric epics. On etymology and narratology see also Tsitsibakou-Vasalos (this volume).
6   See Phelan 1989, a narratological study of characterization. Phelan distinguishes the mimetic, thematic, and synthetic traits of a character.

As a means of implicit or explicit characterization, the meaning of a name often foreshadows the words and/or acts of a character, or informs the external and internal narratees about the character's past. Thus, etymologies can function as prolepses, anticipating certain character features, or as analepses, recalling marked qualities of a figure. Yet, the etymology of a name is not always confirmed by the narrative, but often negated (a narrativized case of etymologizing *e contrario*), and thus the narrator can misdirect the audience/readers. Anticipating the fulfillment of a name's etymology can also activate a retardation effect or create suspense (*Spannung*).

Etymologies can also form a second narrative level which goes in line with or opposes the main narrative. On the one hand, they may be explanatory in relation to the main plot and the motivation of a character, while, on the other, the implications of an etymological analysis may contrast with the main narrative. In the latter case, etymology transcends the basic narrative structure since the meaning derived from an etymological approach points to an alternative narrative version; or it can result in an independent thematic unit that may further function as a complementary excursus. In other words, etymology can be seen as a second narrative voice, which is sometimes in harmony with and other times in opposition to the plot.

After making these preliminary remarks on the association between narratology and etymology, and establishing etymology as a starting-point for our approach, we may proceed to examine the significance of Arete's name. We shall first deal with the etymology from ἀράομαι.

2. Arete-ἀράομαι

The Arete-ἀράομαι connection has been acknowledged long since by various scholars.[7] The basic argument is that this etymology befits a character who is 'to be prayed to' by Odysseus.[8] Hence, the name 'Arete' fulfills its function in the *Odyssey*. Peradotto, however, objected to the connection between Odysseus' supplication to Arete and the etymology of her name from ἀράομαι.[9] The basis of his objection is that nowhere is this root used of prayers directed to any but divine beings.

---

7   See Stanford 1974 *ad* 7.54; Frame 1978, 79 n. 73; Ahl – Roisman 1996, 58.
8   On the semantics of ἀράομαι and its affiliation with the context of Homeric prayer see Morrison 1991, 147 with n. 8; Lateiner 1997, 246; Pulleyn 1997, 70–6.
9   Peradotto 1990, 108.

His observation is valid, but his conclusion needs reconsideration. We argue instead that this etymological connection contributes to the poet's purpose to present the Phaiakian queen as an elevated, goddess-like figure. So, let us first examine whether our point is justified.

First of all, when the disguised Athene presents Arete to Odysseus, we learn that the Phaiakian people look upon the queen as a goddess (7.71: οἵ μίν ῥα θεὸν ὣς εἰσορόωντες). There are also two formulas used of Arete, which allude to her divine status. The first is the expression θαῦμα ἰδέσθαι (6.306) used for the handicrafts of her spindle.[10] The same formula is used when Odysseus marvels at the harbors, ships, markets, and walls of the Phaiakians (7.45). Arete's works remind us of the semi-divine status that the Phaiakians enjoy. What is more, the formula θαῦμα ἰδέσθαι (6.306; 7.45) used both of Arete's female handicrafts and of constructions that belong to male oriented activities (ships, market place etc.) anticipates the gender juxtaposition between Alkinoos and Arete which is about to follow.

The second formula which might point to Arete's divine status, is φίλα φρονέῃσ' ("she has friendly thoughts", 6.312 = 7.75).[11] This formula is used several times in the *Odyssey* for Athene. In the Phaiakian episode, in particular, the formula refers to the friendly thoughts that Athene has toward Odysseus (7.15; 42). We will see that this formula, referring to Athene's divine support of her protégé, is transferred from Athene to Arete. When Athene, disguised as a young girl, meets Odysseus, she tells him that his safe homecoming depends on the friendly thoughts of the Phaiakian queen:

εἴ κέν τοι κείνη <u>φίλα φρονέῃσ'</u> ἐνὶ θυμῷ,
ἐλπωρή τοι ἔπειτα φίλους ἰδέειν καὶ ἱκέσθαι
οἶκον ἐς ὑψόροφον καὶ σὴν ἐς πατρίδα γαῖαν.

So if she (scil. Arete) has thoughts in her mind that are friendly to you,
then there is hope that you can see your own people, and come back
to your house with the high roof and to the land of your fathers.

(7.75–7)[12]

---

10 This expression is used of divine (*Il.* 5.725; 18.83; 18.377; *Od.* 8.366; 13.108) or godlike works (*Il.* 10.439; *Od.* 7.45).

11 Louden 1999, 11 notes on φίλα φρονέῃσ' at 7.75: 'Elsewhere in Homer this term (and its opposite κακὰ φρονέων) usually describes a deity's attitude toward a mortal.'

12 All translations of the Odyssean passages cited are taken from Lattimore 1999 with occasional slight adaptations, whereas the Hesiodic ones from Most 2007.

At the end of book 6 (6.324–6), Odysseus prayed to Athene and asked to come among the Phaiakians 'loved' (φίλον) and 'pitied' (ἐλεεινόν). Let us examine Odysseus' prayer to Athene and its relation to Arete closer:

αὐτίκ' ἔπειτ' <u>ἠρᾶτο</u> Διὸς κούρῃ μεγάλοιο·
'κλῦθί μοι, αἰγιόχοιο Διὸς τέκος, Ἀτρυτώνη·
νῦν δή πέρ μευ ἄκουσον, ἐπεὶ πάρος οὔ ποτ' ἄκουσας
ῥαιομένου, ὅτε μ' ἔρραιε κλυτὸς ἐννοσίγαιος.
δός μ' ἐς Φαίηκας <u>φίλον</u> ἐλθεῖν ἠδ' <u>ἐλεεινόν</u>'.
ὣς ἔφατ' εὐχόμενος, τοῦ δ' ἔκλυε Παλλὰς Ἀθήνη·
αὐτῷ δ' οὔ πω φαίνετ' ἐναντίη· αἴδετο γάρ ῥα
πατροκασίγνητον· ὁ δ' ἐπιζαφελῶς μενέαινεν
ἀντιθέῳ Ὀδυσῆϊ πάρος ἣν γαῖαν ἱκέσθαι.
Ὣς ὁ μὲν ἔνθ' <u>ἠρᾶτο</u> πολύτλας δῖος Ὀδυσσεύς,
κούρην δὲ προτὶ ἄστυ φέρεν μένος ἡμιόνοιϊν.

And immediately thereafter [Odysseus] prayed to the daughter of great Zeus:
'Hear me, Atrytone child of Zeus of the aegis,
and listen to me now, since before you did not listen
to my stricken voice as the famous shaker of the earth battled me.
Grant that I come, as one loved and pitied, among the Phaiakians.'
So he spoke in prayer and Pallas Athene heard him,
but she did not yet show herself before him, for she respected
her father's brother, Poseidon, who still nursed a sore anger
at godlike Odysseus until his arrival in his own country.
So long-suffering Odysseus prayed, in that place,
but the strength of the mules carried the young girl on, to the city.
(6.323–7.2)

Odysseus prays to Athene and the narrator frames his prayer with the verb ἠρᾶτο at the end of book 6 and at the very first line of book 7. This verb here seems to allude to Arete's etymology from ἀράομαι and functions as an anticipatory echo of the supplication scene that is about to follow (7.139–152). Odysseus' prayer to Athene follows Nausikaa's advice that he should supplicate her mother (Arete's name remaining unmentioned). After Odysseus' prayer, the disguised Athene gives him the same advice: his homecoming depends on the queen (7.75–7). We see that Odysseus' prayer, framed with ἠρᾶτο, is placed between Nausikaa's and Athene's similar advice, that Arete is the key-person to enable the hero's homecoming.[13] To put it in another way,

---

13 Nausikaa's advice (6.303–15): Odysseus should supplicate her mother-ἠρᾶτο (6.323) – Odysseus' prayer-ἠρᾶτο (7.1) – Athene's advice: Odysseus' homecoming depends on Arete (7.53 ff.).

Odysseus' prayer anticipates his supplication to Arete. What is more, the fact that Arete's etymology is anticipated in a prayer to a goddess points to her divine status. Athene hearkens to Odysseus' prayer, but she appears disguised as a girl out of respect for her uncle Poseidon, who is enraged with Odysseus. It turns out that Athene could not help Odysseus straightforwardly. The fulfillment of Odysseus' prayer is to be made through Arete, and that is what Athene does. She delegates the prayer addressed to herself to the Phaiakian queen. Athene is φίλα φρονέουσα (7.15) to Odysseus, but his safe return home depends overtly on the friendly disposition of the queen (7.75–7), not that of Athene. The redirection of Odysseus' plea from Athene to Arete, alluded to by the Arete-ἀράομαι etymology and the parallel φίλα φρονέουσα (7.15 for Athene) and φίλα φρονέῃσ' (7.75 for Arete), elevates Arete's status to a divine level.[14] She is to play Athene's role and she will play this role well. It is interesting in this respect that Athene does not appear openly out of respect for her uncle Poseidon (6.229–30: αἴδετο γάρ ῥα/ πατροκασίγνητον). Arete eventually wants to support Odysseus, but must also respect her husband and uncle Alkinoos (who is her πατροκασίγνητος, the brother of her father Rhexenor). Poseidon also stands in Arete's way since she knows that helping Odysseus is against his will.[15]

The fact that Odysseus' prayer to Athene anticipates the supplication scene and the potential etymology of Arete should not surprise us. Homer often uses this technique in order to achieve effects not stated plainly in the narrative. By using a word alluding to the etymology of a character, the poet invokes this character without mentioning her/him by name. When Odysseus leaves Kalypso's island, for instance, he is washed up naked onto Scherie and faces a difficult dilemma; if

---

14 Beye 1966, 177 notes that Athene's presentation of Arete 'serves to magnify' Arete; see also Rose 1969, 404.
15 Doherty argues that Arete can be seen as braving Poseidon's wrath by helping Odysseus. She compares Tyro's defiance to Poseidon's order that she remain silent (11.251–2) with Arete's cautious silence. By telling Tyro's story, Odysseus is inviting Arete to speak and help him against Poseidon's will. See Doherty 1993; 1995, 125. That Odysseus' adventure in Scherie as well as his encounter with Arete should be set against the theme of Poseidon's wrath against Odysseus is for the first time implied in 7.34–5, where the narrator makes the connection of the Phaiakians with the realm of Poseidon fairly explicit. In this respect, it is also significant that Arete herself descends from Poseidon (7.56–66). On Poseidon and the Phaiakians cf. Reinhardt 1960, 122 ff.; Aronen 2002, 92 f., 99 f.

he rests by the river, he may freeze to death, but if he climbs up the slope to the shady wood and lies down to rest in the thick brushwood, he may become prey to wild beasts. He finally finds a sheltered copse guarded from cold and wild beasts. We see here that the first thing Odysseus must do upon his arrival on a new island after leaving Kalypso ('the Concealer') is to hide and thus secure himself. Odysseus' eager willingness to shun eternal concealment and oblivion is now challenged by his need to be hidden and thus survive. In this passage, the poet alludes to Kalypso by means of her etymology:

> ὡς Ὀδυσεὺς φύλλοισι <u>καλύψατο.</u> τῷ δ' ἄρ' Ἀθήνη
> ὕπνον ἐπ' ὄμμασι χεῦ', ἵνα μιν παύσειε τάχιστα
> δυσπονέος καμάτοιο, φίλα βλέφαρ' ἀμφι<u>καλύψας</u>.
>
> So Odysseus covered himself in the leaves, and Athene
> shed a sleep on his eyes so as most quickly to quit him,
> by veiling his eyes, from the exhaustion of his hard labors.
>
> (5.491–3)

Odysseus now has to cover and shield himself from death, something that Kalypso was also willing to do by granting him immortality. Kalypso is now absent, but at the same time present under cover of her etymology. It is a nice touch that Kalypso is here concealed, true to her name. What is more, her function of concealing passes from Odysseus finally to Athene, who covers his eyes with sleep. ἀμφικαλύψας is the very last word of book 5; a book where Kalypso is a very prominent figure. Athene now takes over her functions as she pours sleep that covers Odysseus' eyes (7.14–7). We see that Athene takes over Kalypso's role and etymology at the end of book 5 and continues to do so in book 7, as she pours mist over Odysseus in Scherie.

Tsitsibakou-Vasalos has recently called the compositional technique at issue 'transference of etymology.'[16] This technique is an indispensable tool in enriching narrative structures, since it 'creates pairs of surrogate or foil figures, forms alliances or enmities, most importantly of mortals and immortals…'.[17] Elaborate cases of transference of etymology contribute to understanding the interaction of characters in the plot, and consolidate the structure of the narrative.

In *Od.* 5.491–3 the technique of transferring the etymology of a character to another functions as a transitional device. This sort of trans-

---

16 See Tsitsibakou-Vasalos 2003, 119–29; 2007, 60–6.
17 Tsitsibakou-Vasalos 2007, 61.

ference is marked by the formula δεινὴ θεός, occurring right after Athene has poured mist to cover Odysseus on his way to Alkinoos' palace (7.41); a characterization applied elsewhere to designate only Kalypso (7.246; 255; 12.449) and Kirke (11.8; 12.150), the initial 'blockers' and eventual 'helpers' of Odysseus' nostos.[18] Furthermore, the motif of the 'dread goddess' is curiously linked in the cases of Athene and Kalypso to female affection (7.42: φίλα φρονέουσα; 7.256: ἐνδυκέως ἐφίλει; 12.450: μ' ἐφίλει): both goddesses show their love towards the hero by covering him. This instance of 'transference of etymology' seems, then, to have a rather ambivalent effect: it does not only point out the occasional similarity of Athene's role to that of Kalypso in terms of covering and sentimental connection to the hero, but also stresses the discrepancy between the two of them since Athene uses the covering device in order to advance Odysseus' nostos, certainly not to block it. On a further level, Athene hands over her role as a recipient of Odysseus' prayer to Arete at the beginning of book 7. We see Odysseus' fate passing from Kalypso to Arete through Athene. The transition is made through Kalypso's and Arete's etymologies (Kalypso – Athene [ἀμφικαλύψας]/Athene [ἠρᾶτο] – Arete).

This transition underscores Arete's divine status. We have already mentioned the parallels between Arete and Athene. There are also similarities between Kalypso and Arete. In Kalypso's first appearance mention is made of the goddess' hearth and weaving (5.59–62). Likewise, in Arete's first appearance, Nausikaa approaches her mother, who sits by the hearth spinning her spindle (6.52–3). Another goddess that Arete shows parallels with is Kirke. Louden pointed out the similarities between Kirke and Arete, commenting on the pattern φίλα/κακὰ φρονέουσα, and argued that Kirke, who is first κακὰ φρονέουσα (10.317), changes her evil thoughts to friendly ones and helps Odysseus to return to his country.[19] She is at first hostile, but after asking who he is (10.325: τίς πόθεν εἰς ἀνδρῶν;) and learning Odysseus' identity, she changes her attitude. Likewise, Arete, first cautious and suspicious, asks about Odysseus' identity (7.238: τίς πόθεν εἰς ἀνδρῶν) and becomes finally φίλα φρονέουσα after Odysseus' account of the heroines he met in the under-

---

18 On the inherent ambivalence of women as 'blockers and helpers' in the *Odyssey* see Foley 1995, 107. Within this context, Beye 1974, 95 speaks of an 'archetype', on which the poet of the *Odyssey* relies in order to fabricate the representation of each individual woman of the poem.
19 See Louden 1999, 6, 11.

world. We see that Arete's role in the *Odyssey* is constantly paralleled with goddesses.

Though presented as if she were a goddess, Arete is definitely not a goddess as far as the *Odyssey* is concerned. However, she appears to flirt with the divinized status acquired by the heroines of Greek cult after their death. In the *Odyssey*, against the contentions of older scholars,[20] the deification of a mortal is possible. In his trip from Ogygia to Scherie, Odysseus' raft is wrecked by Poseidon and finally the hero is saved by the intervention of Ino-Leukothea (5.333–5). Ino-Leukothea enters the list of powerful female figures that save Odysseus and facilitate his homecoming. Her appearance before Odysseus' arrival at Scherie gives us the important information that a mortal woman can become a goddess (τὸν δὲ ἴδεν Κάδμου θυγάτηρ, καλλίσφυρος Ἰνώ,/ἣ πρὶν μὲν ἔην βροτὸς αὐδήεσσα,/νῦν δ' ἁλὸς ἐν πελάγεσσι θεῶν ἐξέμμορε τιμῆς, 'The daughter of Kadmos, sweet-stepping Ino called Leukothea, saw him. She had once been one who spoke as a mortal, but now in the gulfs of the sea she holds degree as a goddess', 5.333–5). Deification of women is also a recurring motif in the *Ehoiai*:[21] Iphimede becomes Artemis Enodia (fr. 23a.22–6 M.-W.) and Phylonoe becomes immortal and ageless (25a.10–2 M.-W.). Fr. 91 probably refers to Ino-Leukothea and her apotheosis (Hirschberger 2004, 79). The deified Ino in the *Odyssey* might point to a motif and a character of the *Catalogue of Women*. Odysseus' deliverance by this heroine preludes the importance of Arete and the *Catalogue of Women* in Odysseus' nostos.

Helen, as she appears in book 4, is another example of a demigoddess. Arthur pointed out that Helen's elevated status in book 4 is related to her semi-divine nature. She also commented on Helen's similarities with Arete and argued that their elevated status is singled out as anomalous. Helen's and Arete's presence in the megaron after the meal and their participation in the reception of a *xeinos* mark them out as exceptional female characters.[22] Arete does not only participate in the recep-

---

20 Wilamowitz 1884; Rohde 1950; Farnell 1921 argued that there is no trace of hero cult in Homer. This view has been challenged by Hack 1929; Hadzisteliou-Price 1973; 1979; Lyons 1997, 7 ff., *passim*.
21 For apotheosis as a recurring motif in the *Catalogue of Women*, see Rutherford 2000, 87–8: Hirschberger 2004, 79; 2008, 122–5.
22 Arthur 1984, 16–19. See also Doherty 1992, 162 ff.; 1995, 76; Wohl 1993, 32–5.

tion of Odysseus, but also declares him as her own *xeinos* (11.338).[23] Another parallel between Helen and Arete is that their exceptional authority seems to be a source of tension with their husbands. It is true that we find a similar implicit, but easily traced conflict between husband and wife both in Sparta and Scherie. Helen's divine descent guarantees Menelaos' immortality (4.569), but her peculiarly high status as a woman is a cause of domestic friction. In short, Arete's parallel with Helen hints at her exceptionally high position. We have reasons to suspect that the queen belongs to the world of the heroines, like Helen and Leukothea, an aspect that Odysseus will later on exploit successfully.

3. Arete-ἄ(ρ)ρητος

Arete's name and the narrative dynamics of its etymology are not exhausted with the Ἀρήτη-ἀράομαι nexus. We suggest that her name is also associated with ἄ(ρ)ρητος ('unspoken,' 'ineffable') and examine whether this hypothesis can be supported by the narrative. Arete's name most likely derives from the adjective ἀρητός.[24] The etymology of this adjective is, however, doubtful; it could derive either from ἀράομαι or be a variant of ἄρρητος.[25] Both etymologies of ἀρητός, from which Arete's name derives, are narrativized in the *Odyssey*.[26]

Let us examine first whether our text suggests a relation between Arete and ἄρ(ρ)ητος. In the beginning of book 6, when Nausikaa,

---

23 A comparison with a similar scene in Nestor's palace reveals that the queen does not join the men, but appears only later sleeping at her husband's side (3.404); see Arthur 1984, 18–9.

24 Eust. *Od.* 1474.43–4; 1567.54–5. Cf. *LfgrE* s.v. Ἀρήτη and Ruijgh 1967, 153 n. 287 on the link of the personal name Ἄρητος to ἀρητός.

25 The adjective ἄρρητος with double ρ must be a later spelling of ΑΡΗΤΟΣ (see Eust. *Il.* 4.10.4 ὅτι δὲ τὸ ἀρητὸν πένθος ἄρρητον τινὲς γράφουσι, δῆλον, καὶ ὡς οὐκ εὐαρεστοῦνται οἱ παλαιοὶ τῇ γραφῇ and the remarks in *LfgrE* s.v. ἀρητός). It is indicative that the double ρ in ἄρρητος was considered superfluous by the ancient etymological dictionaries (*Et. Mag.* 237.42–4 s.v. γογγύζω: Ἢ τὸ γογγρύζω ἀπὸ τοῦ γογγύζω πλεονασμῷ τοῦ ρ, ὡς ῥητὸς ἄρρητος).

26 On ἀρητόν and ῥηθῆναι (ἀεί ῥητόν) see Apion fr. 20 N. with Rengakos 1992, 44; sch. D *Il.* 17.37c; sch. *Il.* 24.741. Furthermore, the Hellenistic poet Aratus, to give an example similar to Arete, puns on his name and the word ἄρρητον, as Peter Bing argued, at *Phaen.* 1–2: ἐκ Διὸς ἀρχώμεσθα, τὸν οὐδέποτ' ἄνδρες ἐῶμεν/ἄρρητον. Callimachus makes the same pun in one of his epigrams (*Ep.* 27.3–4 Pf.: λεπταί/ῥήσιες, Ἀρήτου [...]). See Bing 1990.

after her dream, goes to report it to her parents, the narrator makes clear that she will speak both to her father and her mother:

> Αὐτίκα δ' Ἠὼς ἦλθεν ἐΰθρονος, ἥ μιν ἔγειρε
> Ναυσικάαν εὔπεπλον· ἄφαρ δ' ἀπεθαύμασ' ὄνειρον,
> βῆ δ' ἴμεναι διὰ δώμαθ', ἵν' ἀγγείλειε <u>τοκεῦσι</u>,
> <u>πατρὶ</u> φίλῳ καὶ <u>μητρί</u>· κιχήσατο δ' ἔνδον ἐόντας.
> ἡ μὲν ἐπ' ἐσχάρῃ ἧστο σὺν ἀμφιπόλοισι γυναιξίν,
> ἠλάκατα στρωφῶσ' ἁλιπόρφυρα.

And next the Dawn came, throned in splendor, and wakened the well-robed
girl Nausikaa, and she wondered much at her dreaming
and went through the house, so as to give the word to her parents,
to her dear father and her mother. She found them within there;
the queen was sitting by the fireside with her attendant
women, turning sea-purple yarn on a distaff.

(6.48–53)

However, Nausikaa will not disclose her dream (or her intention to marry), but will ask her father to provide her with a chariot in order to do the laundry by the river. This is a case of misdirection[27] the effect of which is to make Nausikaa's reticence more conspicuous, as de Jong points out.[28] What is more, Nausikaa will not speak in the end to her mother, but only to her father. This is a second misdirection since the anticipation of a speech to the Phaiakian queen is not fulfilled, and, therefore, it is emphasized that the queen is not addressed.[29] Arete's name is not mentioned either. Although the narrator describes her sitting by the hearth and spinning her spindle, she is not introduced by name.[30] We see Arete on stage, but her name remains 'unmentioned'; we expect Nausikaa to speak to her, but Arete is not to be spoken to. Later on, when Nausikaa advises Odysseus to go to Alkinoos' palace

---

27 The poet applies this poetic device in order to manipulate his audience by creating expectations that are eventually not fulfilled; by interspersing false indications that lead to an outcome other than the one that will actually occur. The aim of such strategies is usually to increase the suspense about the way the story unfolds or surprise the audience. On Homeric misdirection see Morrison 1992, de Jong 1997b, 321–2.
28 De Jong 2001a *ad* 6.49–51.
29 It is odd that Nausikaa does not address her mother about washing the clothes since the task of doing the laundry might be more in the jurisdiction of the lady of the house. The subject of Nausikaa's request to her father makes her failure to address her mother more prominent. See Ahl – Roisman 1996, 59.
30 Alkinoos' name, on the other hand, has been mentioned at 6.12.

and supplicate her mother because his return depends on her, Nausikaa mentions Alkinoos' name twice (6.299; 302), but refers to Arete as μητέρ' ἐμήν (6.305). Here the absence of Arete's name is more conspicuous. It makes sense that Odysseus needs to know the name of the queen since he has to supplicate her, but Nausikaa's silence about her mother's name leaves Arete's name still 'unmentioned'.[31] And although one acknowledges the natural way in which Nausikaa refers to Arete as 'mother', her silence does manage to bring about a quite tantalizing retardation effect.[32]

The supplication scene also suggests Arete's etymology from ἄ(ρ)ρητος.[33] When the mist that covered Odysseus disperses, everyone is speechless (7.144: οἱ δ' ἄνεω ἐγένοντο). From all the speechless Phaiakians Odysseus has to address the queen. When Odysseus finishes his supplication, everybody is again silent (7.154: οἱ δ' ἄρα πάντες ἀκὴν ἐγένοντο σιωπῇ) and above all Arete. She now has become 'speechless' from 'unspoken' and will keep her silence for a long time. Ekheneos breaks in and tries to resolve the awkward situation, but he ignores Arete and advises Alkinoos how he should deal with the stranger (7.155–66). Alkinoos follows his advice and commands Pontonoos to pour wine and make a libation to Zeus of the suppliants (7.167–81). Then he speaks to the Phaiakian leaders (7.186). Although Odysseus supplicated Arete, she remains completely unmentioned afterwards.

It is only when the Phaiakian leaders withdraw that Arete breaks her silence. It turns out that she did not speak to Odysseus because what she had to say was not to be spoken publicly. Arete noticed that Odysseus wore the cloak and tunic that she had made herself and that her daughter took to wash. Therefore, she knows that Odysseus most likely met Nausikaa. The fact that he wears these clothes makes him suspicious and

---

31 Later on, after Odysseus will have learned Arete's name and genealogy from the disguised Athene (7.63–78), he will start his supplication to Arete by stating her name and her father's name (Ἀρήτη, θύγατερ Ῥηξήνορος ἀντιθέοιο, 7.146). On the revelation of Nausikaa's and Arete's names, see Olson 1992.

32 In Homeric poetry this sort of retardation in naming a hero constitutes a rather usual poetic technique; cf. Il. 1.307/337 (Patroklos); 1.351/413 (Thetis) – we owe this point to Magdalene Stoevesandt. It is a fact, though, that the interval between the introduction of a figure and its naming lasts in Arete's case unusually long, exceeding the boundaries of a book (6.52–7.54). On retardation technique in the *Odyssey* see Rengakos 1999.

33 On the supplication scene see Pedrick 1982, 138; Crotty 1994, 134; Naiden 2006, 39; Dreher 2006. Newton 1984, views this scene of supplication as a metaphor for 'the ritual of rebirth'.

Arete skeptical to grant him his requests. Her silence is cautious and prudent since she does not reveal her concerns in public and thus tarnish her daughter's reputation (see Besslich (1966) 1990, 61–9). We see now Arete's etymology functioning in a different direction. While Ekheneos and Alkinoos ignored her and left her unmentioned, she herself proves her name to mean a person who knows what and especially when something is not to be spoken. But when the occasion is appropriate, she finally asks Odysseus bluntly:

'ξεῖνε, τὸ μέν σε πρῶτον ἐγὼν <u>εἰρήσομαι</u> αὐτή·
<u>τίς</u> πόθεν εἰς ἀνδρῶν; <u>τίς</u> τοι τάδε εἵματ' ἔδωκεν;
<u>οὐ δὴ φῄς</u> ἐπὶ πόντον ἀλώμενος ἐνθάδ' ἱκέσθαι;'

Stranger and friend, I myself first have a question to ask you.
What man are you and whence? And who was it gave you this clothing?
Did you not say that you came here ranging over the water?

(7.237–9)

Arete's use of εἰρήσομαι, a cognate with ἄρρητος (see Chantraine s.v. 2 εἴρω), is here particularly significant. εἰρήσομαι seems to allude to Arete's name *e contrario*; the queen negates her unutteredness, rendered so far as suppression of her importance by Alkinoos and Ekheneos, and as silence on her own part, and speaks. οὐ φῄς seems to set up a further etymological wordplay on Arete's narrative profile as ἄρ(ρ)ητος as well as an anticipatory echo on οὔτις and Odysseus, especially since Odysseus will not reveal his name to Arete. His name will be also unuttered and hence he will remain very much a 'nobody.'[34] If we acknowledge the Arete-ἄρ(ρ)ητος connection, the narrator's delay to mention Arete's name can be paralleled to Odysseus' long delay in revealing his name to the Phaiakians. Odysseus' movement from anonymity to heroic *kleos* is analogous to Arete's elevation from being an unknown character, probably invented by the poet of the *Odyssey*, to a heroine that finally acquires *kleos* by her place in the *Catalogue of Women* (fr. 222 M.-W.).[35]

---

34 The parallel between Odysseus and Arete on the basis of their names can first be made through Odysseus' epithet πολυάρητος, which is the name that Eurykleia implicitly suggested that Autolykos should give to Odysseus (19.404). Peradotto 1990, 108, 120–42 discusses Arete's name and its relation to Odysseus' epithet πολυάρητος. Note also that Odysseus has been mentioned obliquely as a πολυάρητος θεός by Nausikaa at 6.280. On the implications of the epithet see also Murnaghan 1987, 39–41.

35 ἄρρητος can mean a person without *kleos*. See *LfgrE s.v.* ἄρρητος B2: 'von Menschen ungenannt, ruhmlos', cf. Hes. *Op.* 2–4: ... Δι' ἐννέπετε .../ὅν τε διὰ βροτοὶ ἄνδρες ὁμῶς ἄφατοί τε φατοί τε,/ῥητοί τ' ἄρρητοί τε...

As a character given prominence in the *Odyssey*, she resembles Kalypso. The names of Kalypso ('the Concealer') and Arete ('the Unmentioned') are very suitable to these heroines who rise from concealed anonymity to epic prominence by enabling Odysseus' travel back home; a travel that for him is always a travel from anonymity to heroic fame.

Odysseus, being the master of manipulating his own name, seems to have grasped Arete's connection with ἄρ(ρ)ητος. In his response, he first tells her that what she asks is hard to be spoken. He goes on to say that he will tell her what she asks him, but then he gives an abbreviated version of his wanderings and, what is more, he does not say who he is or where he is from:[36]

'ἀργαλέον, βασίλεια, διηνεκέως <u>ἀγορεῦσαι</u>,
κήδε᾽ ἐπεί μοι πολλὰ δόσαν θεοὶ Οὐρανίωνες·
τοῦτο δέ τοι <u>ἐρέω</u>, ὅ μ᾽ <u>ἀνείρεαι</u> ἠδὲ μεταλλᾷς.

It is a hard thing, O queen, to tell you without intermission,
all my troubles, since the gods of the sky have given me many.
But this now I will tell you in answer to the question you asked me.
(7.241–3)

Odysseus' answer to Arete contains linguistic traits that underpin the proposed Arete-ἄ(ρ)ρητος connection further: the use of ἐρέω and ἀνείρεαι, both cognates with ἄρρητος, invites us to acknowledge a striking and persistent allusion to Arete's name.[37] Odysseus will end his speech to Arete with a ring composition, saying that he spoke, as was asked to do, although he was distressed (7.297: ταῦτά τοι ἀχνύμενός περ ἀληθείην <u>κατέλεξα</u>).

At this point, it is worth mentioning Virgil's adaptation of 7.241–2. Dido asks Aeneas at the end of book 1 of the *Aeneid* to tell her about the ambush of the Greeks, the downfall of the Trojans, and his wanderings (1.753–6). Then everyone is silent (2.1). Aeneas answers to the Phoenician queen more or less as Odysseus answered to the Phaiakian queen:

<u>*infandum*</u>, *regina, iubes renouare dolorem*

'Queen, you are asking to renew an <u>ineffable</u> pain.
(*Aen.* 2.2)

The word *infandum*, emphatically placed at the head of the line, corresponds to the Greek word ἄρρητον. Virgil here alludes to Odysseus' an-

---

36 See Besslich (1966) 1990, 60–1.
37 διηνεκέως ἀγορεῦσαι (7.241) actually recalls the etymology of ἀρητός from ἀεὶ ῥητόν, attested at sch. D *Il.* 17.37c; sch. *Il.* 24.741.

swer to Arete and we suggest that he also alludes, in the subtle way of an Alexandrian poet, to Arete's etymological connection with ἄρ(ρ)ητος. By doing so, he leaves Arete's (but also Dido's) name unmentioned, but at the same time, implied. Virgil manages to hint at the scene he adapts here by means of a witty paradoxical pun; Arete is mentioned by remaining 'unmentioned'.

Turning back to the *Odyssey*, after 8.445 Arete will remain silent and unmentioned until book 11. Her silence does not reduce her importance in the narrative.[38] We argue against scholars who believed that, although Arete is proclaimed to be the key-person for Odysseus' return, her role is afterwards downplayed.[39] Doherty argues convincingly that Odysseus organizes the first half of his apologoi as an attempt to win over Arete.[40] Odysseus realizes that the Phaiakian queen has the power to either facilitate his nostos or keep him in Scherie trapping him in a world of anonymity forever. Arete's ambivalent power resembles that of the goddesses Kalypso and Kirke. All these women threaten Odysseus' nostos but finally offer valuable help. It seems that the queen can decide whether Odysseus will return home or stay marooned in the fictional and isolated Scherie.[41] Odysseus does not seem to have forgot-

---

[38] Arete's name and its etymology from ἄρ(ρ)ητος provide a nice paradox that explains her function and her importance in the *Odyssey*; by remaining unmentioned for a long time, she is present through the etymology of her name. To put it in another way, the etymology of her name evokes her presence through her silence. The emphasis of her importance by means of her withdrawal from the forefront of the narrative resembles Achilles in the *Iliad*, whose absence from the battlefield does not reduce his importance, but rather emphasizes how crucial he is for the war.

[39] Nitzsch 1826–40, 2.138; Thomson 1949, 419; Fenik 1974, 105 ff.; Pedrick 1988, 87.

[40] See Doherty 1992; 1995, 87–160. See also Minchin 2007a, 20–1 = 2007b, 266.

[41] Tsitsibakou-Vasalos suggests an intriguing etymological parallel between Ares and Arete. Ares' etymological relation to ἀράομαι/ἀρά (cf. sch. A *Il.* 18. 521b; Hsch. 7145) suggests that the god is 'a curse, a bane' (*per litteras*). Being a belligerent god, Ares is also ἄρ(ρ)ητος, unpersuaded by words and reason. Thus, Ares shares the same etymological potential with Arete, but while the god of war develops the dark sides of his etymologies in the *Iliad*, the Phaiakian queen activates the positive dynamics of her etymologies in the *Odyssey*. Ares and Arete have a relation of polarity. The Iliadic Ares is a baneful god that defies negotiation, while the Phaiakian queen stands for supplication and persuasion. Arete, the daughter of Rhexenor ('Breaker of Men'), incorporates the semata of Ares, who is a man-slaughtering god (cf. παύσασθαι βροτολοιγὸν

ten Nausikaa's (6.310–15) and Athene's (7.75–7) advice that his safe return to his longed-for fatherland depends on Arete. If he wants to return to Ithaca and claim his *kleos*, he has to talk his way out of Scherie by winning her over. The only way to accomplish that is to speak of his unspeakable woes.

4. Gender and Generic Tension in Scherie

The above section has made apparent Arete's double etymological dynamics, which indicates her centrality in the Phaiakian episode. In the following section we argue that Arete belongs to a generic frame that renders her role in the narrative comprehensible. This generic frame, the so-called *ehoie*-poetry, and its narrative conventions seem to be the point where Arete's semantic multivalence and her prominent role in the gender-system of the *Odyssey* intersect. The Phaiakian episode provides a nice glance at the harmonic cooperation of gender and genre mechanics. We are invited to see how gender roles are performed in an archaic epic context, and to what extent the narrative contributes to the construction of gender identities and inter-gender relationships.[42]

In specific, attention is drawn to the fact that the gender of the narrator (Odysseus) and the narratee (Arete) holds a key position in establishing communication, and consequently that this configuration imposes a certain discourse upon the narrative so that communication can be achieved after all. Moreover, the episode of Odysseus' encounter with the Phaiakians contains an instance of inter-genre transference of a gendered narrative mode, i.e. the stylized narrative patterns of *ehoie*-poetry, within an already explicitly gendered genre. Thus, we are called to observe how the gendered narrative of *ehoie*-poetry works in an epic praising a male hero, and what kind of narrative purposes it serves.

Ἄρη' ἀνδροκτασιάων, *Il.* 5.909), but reverses the qualities of the Iliadic god of war, accommodating the values of the new epic. Note also that Demodokos' song about Ares and Aphrodite (*Od.* 8.266–366) may activate the juxtaposition between Ares and Arete in the Phaiakian episode. In sum, the etymological parallels between Ares and Arete highlight the antithetical/foil relation between the god of war and the Phaiakian queen, and adumbrate Arete's function in the *Odyssey*.

42 For current insights into the relationship of narratology to gender studies see Lanser 1986, Nünning 1994, Prince 1996.

We have already mentioned that Arete's high position makes her comparable to a heroine of the *Catalogue of Women*. Let us examine this point closer. We begin with Athene's presentation of Arete to Odysseus (7.53–77). When the disguised Athene introduces Arete's genealogy, we move from the world of heroic epic poetry, which focuses synchronically on heroes of a certain age and time, to the diachronically oriented catalogue poetry. Athene's language emphasizes this generic shift, and frames Arete and her genealogy within the poetic tradition of the *Catalogue of Women*.

Earlier as well as contemporary Homeric research has curiously overlooked a trait intrinsic to the presentation of Arete in book 7: the fact that Athene's speech makes extensive use of linguistic elements and especially formulas that recall the typical language of the so-called *ehoie*-poetry. To begin with, the explicitly genealogical frame of the narrative that Athene puts forward in order to introduce Arete is to be identified as a distinctive feature of this kind of female-oriented narrative mode. According to the genealogical tree given, Arete's grandmother was Periboia, who is described as a woman of exceptional beauty (7.57: γυναικῶν εἶδος ἀρίστη). This expression, attested hapax in the Homeric epics, constitutes an allomorph of the recurrent Iliadic formula θυγατρῶν εἶδος ἀρίστη[43] and should be semantically associated with γυναικῶν φῦλον … αἳ τότ' ἄρισται ἔσαν in the proem of the Hesiodic *Ehoiai* (fr. 1.1–3 M.-W.) as well as with the introductory section of the Odyssean 'Catalogue of Women' (11.225–7: […] αἱ δὲ γυναῖκες/ […]/ὅσσαι ἀριστήων ἄλοχοι ἔσαν ἠδὲ θύγατρες).[44] Its narrative function is to mark and activate the *ehoie*-genre – a turn made all the more explicit as soon as the genealogy reaches its intended point of reference, Arete. This association of Arete with the semantics of ἀρίστη, mainly addressing beauty and social status, on the one hand urges us to think of a poet suggesting an oblique wordplay – this wordplay might be implied, as Alkinoos asks his wife to fetch the best chest with a clean cloak and a chiton in it for the stranger to use after his bath (8.423–4: δὴ ῥα τότ' Ἀρήτην προσέφη μένος Ἀλκινόοιο·/δεῦρο, γύναι, φέρε χηλὸν

---

43 *Il.* 2.175 (Alkestis); 3.124, 6.252 (Laodike); 13.365 (Kassandre); 13.378 (daughter of Atreids); *hDem.* 146 (Kallidike); cf. also *hVen.* 41: μέγα εἶδος ἀρίστη ἐν ἀθανάτῃσι θεῇσι (Hera). Cf. Meier 1976, 144 with n. 3. On female εἶδος in the Hesiodic *Ehoiai* see Osborne 2005, 10 f.

44 Lyons 1997, 10 f. notes the thematic connection of the two Catalogues in terms of these 'best women' (ἄρισται). See also Irwin 2005, 41.

ἀριπρεπέ', ἥ τις ἀρίστη [Thereupon the king Alkinoos said to Arete:/ 'Come, wife, bring out a magnificent coffer, the best one you have']). On the other hand, the term is followed within the narrative by another superlative, πρώτη, stressing Arete's primary position in the episode (cf. 7.53: πρῶτα).

In addition, the formal elements that directly follow the sequence οἵην ... Ἀρήτην point towards conceiving Arete's entry as a disguised form of an *ehoie*: line 7.66 touches on the union of Arete and Alkinoos, brought forth by the formula 'he made her his wife' (ποιήσατ' ἄκοιτιν). That the formula occurs seven times in the *Ehoiai* in a marriage context is surely indicative of the formula's connection to *ehoie*-poetry.[45] In the following line the theme of Arete's exceptional τιμή is addressed (7.67–8: καί μιν ἔτισ' ὡς οὔ τις ἐπὶ χθονὶ τίεται ἄλλη/ὅσσαι νῦν γε γυναῖκες ὑπ' ἀνδράσιν οἶκον ἔχουσιν ['and (scil. Alkinoos) honored her as no other woman on earth is honored, such women as there are now and keep a house under their husbands']).[46] In the Homeric epics men usually honor men, whereas their respect towards women is expressed only twice in the *Odyssey*, with regard to Arete and Eurykleia. In the case of Eurykleia, we find a slightly similar wording as well as a concise genealogy (1.428–33: τῷ δ' ἄρ' ἅμ' αἰθομένας δαΐδας φέρε κεδνὰ ἰδυῖα/Εὐρύκλει', Ὤπος θυγάτηρ Πεισηνορίδαο,/τήν ποτε Λαέρτης πρίατο κτεάτεσσιν ἑοῖσι,/πρωθήβην ἔτ' ἐοῦσαν, ἐεικοσάβοια δ' ἔδωκεν,/ἶσα δέ μιν κεδνῇ ἀλόχῳ τίεν ἐν μεγάροισιν,/εὐνῇ δ' οὔ ποτ' ἔμικτο, χόλον δ' ἀλέεινε γυναικός ['and devoted Eurykleia went with him, and carried the flaring/torches. She was the daughter of Ops, the son of Peisenor,/ and Laertes had bought her long ago with his own possessions/when she was still in her first youth, and gave twenty oxen for her,/and he favored her in his house as much as his own devoted/wife, but never slept with her, for fear of his wife's anger']).[47] The similarity of the phrasing relat-

---

45 Cf. frr. 23a.31, 33a.7, 85.5, 190.6 M.-W.; frr. 5.59, 6.1, 11.12 Hirschberger. Mureddu (1983) 119 recognizes the formula as a variant of the type (φίλην) κεκλήσῃ/ποιήσατ' ἄκοιτιν. Cf. Dräger 1997, 24.
46 Wagner-Hasel 2000a, 206 and 2000b, 191–3 believes that the exceptional τιμή that Arete enjoys in Scherie is interwoven into the 'soziales Geleit', which in the ritual of guest-friendship rests on the fabrication of signs made from textile. On Arete as hostess see Pedrick 1988, 86–87, 92–3.
47 On the parallel Arete-Eurykleia in terms of τιμή see Wagner-Hasel 2000b, 205. Eurykleia's low social status seems to be a good reason why the alleged formula might have been modified in this case. Eurykleia's moral integrity and the fact that she functions as a surrogate for Antikleia show her to be a rather distorted

ing τίω to a discourse of τιμή is, however, to be found also in the *ehoie* of Alkmene. The diction at Hes. *Eh*. fr. 195.16–7 M.-W. = *Scut*. 9–10 (ἣ δὲ καὶ ὣς κατὰ θυμὸν ἑὸν τίεσκεν ἀκοίτην,/ὡς οὔ πώ τις ἔτισε γυναικῶν θηλυτεράων ['and in her spirit she honored her husband as no other female woman ever yet honored hers']) is strongly reminiscent of *Od*. 7.67–8, although the circumstances of attributing τιμή are not exactly identical.[48] Alkmene was not being honored by her husband like Arete, but honored her husband in a unique manner. It is our contention that the discourse related to female τιμή, as presented in the cases of Eurykleia, Arete and Alkmene, belongs to a fixed concept of an orally transmitted genealogical poetry, the *ehoie*-poetry. The poet of the *Odyssey* must have inherited this concept and the subsequent vocabulary from an allegedly pre-Hesiodic genealogical tradition.[49] Thus, by the time of Hesiod it seems to have been already established as a formula.

These parallels can explain why Odysseus proceeds to relate his encounter with famous heroines and, what is more, why these tales are appealing to Arete.[50] Minchin (2007a, 20–1 = 2007b, 266) has recently argued that Arete responds positively to the tales of Odysseus in *Od*. 11.336–7 and encourages him to continue because she enjoys listening to them. This is true, but Minchin fails to explain why Odysseus' storytelling is so appealing to her as to make her break her protracted silence and retract her cautious behavior concerning Odysseus' reception as a guest. It is, in our view, precisely the well-established nexus based on multiple implicit and explicit allusions to *ehoie*-poetry that helps us to comprehend Arete's approval of the excursus of the 'Catalogue of Women' in the *Odyssey*. As a result, when Odysseus decides

---

image of a noble woman; on this see Skempis (forthcoming). In this respect it should be noted that only Eurykleia and Eumaios out of the slaves of Odysseus are worthy of acquiring a concise genealogical entry by the poet. On this see Higbie 1995, 7 f.

48 Hirschberger 2004, 366 on fr. 91.9–10 and Hunter 2005c, 253 n. 51 note the similarity in poetic expression, but do not comment on the stylization of the formulaic language of the *Ehoiai*. Neitzel 1975 and Cohen 1989–90 do not include the passage in their studies as an example of Homeric reception in Hesiod.

49 On the existence of such a pre-Hesiodic tradition see West 1985, 125; Rutherford 2000, 89–93; Hirschberger 2004, 63, 64 f.; Hunter 2005a, 2; Nasta 2006, 64–8; Arrighetti 2008. Rutherford 2000, 93–6 even believes that an early version of the Hesiodic *Ehoiai* was available to the poet of the *Odyssey*.

50 This point has recently been put forward also by Doherty 2006, 313 f., who nevertheless does not develop her argument on a textual basis.

to interrupt his story right after he has finished reciting the heroines he met in the Underworld, he does not do so randomly, and accordingly, the self-interruption is far from unexpected.[51] Odysseus wants to test the efficiency of the narrative skills he has employed to serve a concrete goal: that of gaining Arete's sympathy by acknowledging the importance of the heroines in the epic universe of the *Odyssey*.

In the light of this generic interpretation we should now turn back to reassess the verse that introduced Arete (7.65–6: ἐν μεγάρῳ μίαν οἴην παῖδα λιπόντα/Ἀρήτην): she was the one and only daughter of Rhexenor, the brother of Alkinoos. The word οἴη not only expresses the genealogical particularity of Arete, but furthermore implicitly marks her uniqueness as a female Homeric character; it designates, to put it in Kahane's words, her 'existence as a heroic one-of-a-kind' (Kahane 1997, 118). Further we suggest that this precise word (οἴην) might be thought of as subjected to a process of semantic fluctuation, fairly equivalent to R. Barthes' famous notion of anchorage and his 'floating chain of signifieds.'[52] Thus, it sets up an allusive interplay with οἵη. Bearing in mind the predominantly genealogical context of Athene's speech so far, a reader would be enticed to see in the pronoun an alluring association with the marker of female genealogical poetry (ἠ') οἵη[53] and subsequently to read the passage as a proper *ehoie*. Against this background, Kahane maintains that 'within the specific discourse of Homeric hexameter there are significant pragmatic links between the word *oios* (alone, on his own) and the word *hoios* (such a…/what a…, as an expression of emotion), [….]. This idea should not surprise us. What Milman Parry termed calembour (more serious than a pun) is a recurrent feature of Homeric poetry: autme//and aute//; omphe//and odme//; demos// (fat) and demos//(people) are some well known examples, all localized (like the rhythm in later poetry) at the end of the verse' (Kahane 1997, 121–2). We suggest that a further instance of this calembour might be the semantic approximation of οἵη to οἴη in Athene's speech.[54]

---

51 For a different view on this matter see Rabel 2002; Graziosi – Haubold 2005, 47; Minchin 2007b, 242.
52 Barthes 1977, 39.
53 On the formula see West 1985, 35; Cohen 1989–90, 60–5; Rutherford 2000, 83–5; Hirschberger 2004, 30 f.; Nasta 2006, 59–64; Arrighetti 2008, 13–4.
54 Cf. the relevant remark in Minchin 1996, 13: 'The connectedness of his material at associative and semantic levels would have been of considerable assistance to Homer as he sang his lists and catalogues'.

Of course, in our case there is no double mentioning of οἴη and οἴη, which would make the phonetic parallelism somewhat explicit, and accordingly, no *ehoie*-formula. That the *ehoie*-formula, however, is not attested in the 'Nekyia',[55] the most straightforward instance of *ehoie*-poetry, can be explained on a narratological basis: Odysseus' apologoi, where the 'Catalogue of Women' is integrated, requires a formulaic expression adapted to Odysseus' first-person narrative of his encounter with the heroines instead of the *ehoie*-formula, which is appropriate to third-person narration.[56] In other words, Odysseus does not need here the formula in order to make the transition to the *ehoie*-poetry.[57] In our view, it is exactly the position of οἴην, appropriated in a passage making extensive use of formulas connected to *ehoie*-poetry and above all introducing a female figure, that effectively triggers the allusive play with the *ehoie*-formula.

The use of variants of the *ehoie*-formula in the *Odyssey* as a means of alluding to the genre of *ehoie*-poetry as crystallized in the Hesiodic *Ehoiai* is not unique. When Telemakhos speaks of his mother to the suitors, οἴη functions as a signpost of poetry related to the *Catalogue of Women*:[58]

Ἀλλ' ἄγετε μνηστῆρες, ἐπεὶ τόδε φαίνετ' ἄεθλον,
οἴη νῦν οὐκ ἔστι γυνὴ κατ' Ἀχαιίδα γαῖαν,

But come on suitors, since there is a prize set before you, a woman such as there is none in all the Akhaian country now.

(21.107–8)

Telemakhos invites the suitors to the bow contest which has Penelope as its prize (ἄεθλον). Note that the wooing of a woman as well as a

---

55   In this respect, Rutherford 2000, 93–4 believes that the *ehoie*-formula might have been 'replaced with a set of formulas amounting to "And I saw:" τὴν δὲ ... ἴδον ..., καὶ ... εἶδον ... and so on' and that 'the Nekuia catches and preserves for us an earlier stage in the development of *ehoie*-poetry'.
56   On the implications of Odysseus' first-person narration in the apologoi see Reinhardt 1960, 58–62; on the arrangement and significance of the apologoi see Most 1989 and Bierl 2007.
57   Nasta 2006, 60 points out: 'Au fil des apparitions Ulysse reprend chaque fois le même tour introductif: (ἴδον .../ ἔσιδον ... εἶδον...) "J'ai vu .../Je vis encore .../Je vis aussi ...". Ailleurs, selon la spécificité des contextes, ἢ οἴη aurait pu fonctionner comme une formule de relance, tout aussi véhémente que l'itération du verbe qui faisait revivre dans *l'Odyssée* un témoignage focalisé par le narrateur'.
58   Cf. Nasta 2006, 63–4.

woman set as the prize of a contest are recurring motifs in the *Ehoiai*.[59] The female excellence of Penelope, who is said to be the best of the Akhaian women, is also thematically associated with the Hesiodic *Ehoiai* (cf. fr. 1.1–4 M.-W.). Thus, the passage quoted above relates Penelope to the most characteristic formula and themes of the *Ehoiai*. Penelope is actually compared to the heroines of the *Catalogue of Women* by Antinoos: ἔργα τ' ἐπίστασθαι περικαλλέα καὶ φρένας ἐσθλὰς/κέρδεά θ', οἵ' οὔ πώ τιν' ἀκούομεν οὐδὲ παλαιῶν,/τάων αἳ πάρος ἦσαν ἐϋπλοκαμῖδες Ἀχαιαί,/Τυρώ τ' Ἀλκμήνη τε ἐϋστέφανός τε Μυκήνη ('to be expert in beautiful work, to have good character and cleverness, such as we are not told of, even of the ancient queens, the fair-tressed Akhaian women of times before us, Tyro and Alkmene and Mykene, wearer of garlands'; *Od.* 2.117–20). Within this context, οἵα seems to set up an allusion to the *Ehoiai*.

However, this generic interplay is not without tension in Scherie. We argue that the undercurrent of the gender conflict in the Phaiakian episode is reflected upon the generic interplay between heroic and *ehoie*-poetry. Arete is a woman who enjoys a higher status than usual (see Arthur 1984, 16–9). Alkinoos honored her as no other woman/wife on earth is honored (7.67–9). Her authority is so strong that she can even resolve quarrels among men (7.74).[60] Nausikaa's and Athene's advice to Odysseus to supplicate Arete further elevate her exceptional status. We contend, however, that her elevated status is a cause of covert tension in Phaiakia. When Odysseus beseeches her, her subsequent silence causes Ekheneos' intervention. Ekheneos ignores her and the fact that Odysseus supplicated her, and addresses Alkinoos. Subsequently, Alkinoos addresses the Phaiakian leaders and also ignores his wife, who is sitting next to him. It also seems that Alkinoos and Arete have constantly opposite attitudes towards Odysseus. While Alkinoos is garrulous and friendly to Odysseus, and offers him Nausikaa's hand, Arete

---

[59] Several episodes of the *Catalogue* develop the motif of the wooing of a woman and the woman is often the prize of a contest. Atalanta's suitors woo her by competing with her in a foot race (fr. 72–6 M.-W.). Sisyphos woos Mestra on behalf of his son Glaukos, promising countless wedding gifts (fr. 43a.21: μυρία ἕδνα). The *Ehoiai* conclude with the lengthy episode of the wooing of Helen (fr. 196–204 M.-W.), which is actually a contest of wealth. On the motif of wooing in the *Odyssey* see Tsitsibakou-Vasalos (this volume).

[60] On the idealized image of Arete as presented in Book 7 see Wohl 1993, 29–32; Latacz 1994, 105–11; Whittaker 1999; Felson – Slatkin 2004, 105 with n. 41; Buchan 2004, 190–3.

is silent and skeptical. Alkinoos is initially enthusiastic, whereas Arete is cautious and suspicious with the stranger. While Alkinoos speaks publicly and makes his offer without knowing the identity of the stranger, Arete speaks in private and asks Odysseus bluntly who he is. Alkinoos offers Odysseus gifts and is confident about his safe return (8.424–32), whereas Arete warns Odysseus that he might be robbed by the Phaiakians on his way home (8.443–5). When Arete has been won over and suggests that the Phaiakians bestow more gifts upon her guest, the gender tension reaches its peak. Arete sees the bond of *xenia* with Odysseus as a personal one (11.338: ξεῖνος ... ἐμός ἐστιν; see Doherty 1995, 80). Thus, she replies obliquely to Ekheneos (7.159–66), who addressed his speech to Alkinoos, using the word ξεῖνος three times and passing over the fact that Odysseus had supplicated Arete and not Alkinoos. Ekheneos now intervenes for a second time. He politely seconds the queen's suggestion, but notes that this business belongs to Alkinoos (11.344–6). Alkinoos agrees with Arete's proposition, yet in seconding her he uses the same formulaic language in which Telemakhos rebuked Penelope: μῦθος/πομπὴ δ' ἄνδρεσσι μελήσει/πᾶσι, μάλιστα δ' ἐμοί· τοῦ γὰρ κράτος ἔστ' ἐνὶ οἴκῳ/δήμῳ (1.358–9 ~ 11.352–3).[61] This is the men's business, not Arete's, who urged the Phaiakians not to make haste to send Odysseus away (11.339: τῷ μὴ ἐπειγόμενοι ἀπο<u>πέμπετε</u>; 11.352: <u>πομπή</u>). Telemakhos utters these words while his authority is seriously questioned. By alluding to book 1, the poet parallels the two situations.[62] Alkinoos of course is not weak like Telemakhos, but the repetition of the lines implies that Arete's intervention might intrude into the male sphere of authority. In book 1, Penelope is excluded from the audience of Phemios' song and retreats to her place after being rebuked. Alkinoos also rebukes Arete (though subtly), but not only has Arete enjoyed Odysseus' stories (unlike Penelope whom Phemios' song grieved), but also Odysseus attempted to win her over by choosing a subject matter and a treatment of his topic that would please her.

---

61 For this formula and possible interpretations of the tensions between Arete and Alkinoos, see Doherty 1991, 151; Wohl 1993, 31–2, 38, 42. Cf. Hektor's answer to Andromakhe in *Il.* 6.492–3, (πόλεμος δ' ἄνδρεσσι μελήσει/πᾶσιν, ἐμοὶ δὲ μάλιστα, τοὶ Ἰλίῳ ἐγγεγάασιν), a passage also pregnant with gender tension; see Rutherford 1991–93, 51; Kahane 2005, 168–71.

62 See Doherty 1992, 166.

Arete belongs to the genre of female ἀρετή, and we know from Hes. *Eh.* fr. 222 M.-W. that she had a place in the Hesiodic *Catalogue of Women*. Within the narrative of the *Odyssey*, Athene's speech to Odysseus contains two pieces of advice; an overt one (that is to beseech the queen) and a covert one (that is that Arete belongs to the genre of the *ehoiai*, and therefore should be treated respectively). Odysseus will exploit the second hint while relating the heroines he met in the Underworld. In order to ingratiate Arete, he will turn to the genre to which Arete belongs.

Let us examine some parallels between Athene's presentation of Arete's genealogy and Odysseus' foray into the 'Catalogue of Women': Odysseus relates at length Poseidon's affair with Tyro. Likewise, Athene mentioned Periboia's affair with Poseidon.[63] Tyro is also referred to as βασίλεια (11.258), a title also given to Arete (7.241; 11.345). Tyro's husband Kretheus was her uncle, according to *Eh.* fr. 30 M.-W. Likewise, Alkinoos and Arete are uncle and niece. The silence motif is also important in Tyro's story (see Doherty 1993). Poseidon asked Tyro that she not reveal their affair (11.251–2). However, Tyro defies his order as she reports her affair to Odysseus. It is striking that Poseidon's words are given in direct speech (*Od.* 11.248–52), although in book 11 women do not speak directly, but their stories are reported in indirect speech by Odysseus. The direct speech stresses Tyro's defiance. The revelation of the affair is against Poseidon's prohibition, and his words, which are supposed to remain concealed, resound in direct speech. Doherty argues that Tyro and Arete, like Odysseus, can be seen as resisting the will of the god Poseidon. Tyro's defiance consists of breaking the taboo of silence, while Arete can also be seen as braving Poseidon's wrath by helping Odysseus (Doherty 1995, 125). By breaking her silence, Tyro guarantees her place in the *ehoie*-poetry. Hence, her name acquires *kleos*. Had she obeyed Poseidon's order, she would remain unknown and unmentioned. Her only escape from anonymity is the fame ensuing from her affair with Poseidon. Therefore, Odysseus' story of Tyro would be targeting Arete's cautious silence. The hint is that Arete should not be afraid of Poseidon, and should speak for Odysseus' cause. Odysseus' return home will guarantee Arete's fame. Since Odysseus features as a poet of *ehoie*-poetry, and Arete belongs to this poetic universe, he is her chance to escape ano-

---

[63] Doherty 2006, 313 points out some parallels between the stories of Tyro and Periboia.

nymity. The epic world of Odysseus has not been incompatible with the world of the heroines. On the contrary, the one guarantees the *kleos* of the other.

As already mentioned, the gender tension in Phaiakia is reflected upon the generic interplay with the *ehoie*-poetry. Ekhenoos is the key-character that connects the gender with the generic tension. In his twofold intervention, he ostentatiously passes over Arete and emphasizes Alkinoos' authority. He is twice referred to as 'hero' (7.155, 11.342: ἥρως Ἐχένηος) by the narrator – a rather peculiar appellative considering the standards of the peaceful Phaiakians, who refrain from any kind of warrior activity.[64] As a character underscoring Alkinoos' authority and undermining Arete's,[65] his characterization as ἥρως may implicitly presuppose an attempted generic shift, which the representative of the heroic world tries here to squeeze out. In this respect, it is significant that these two formulaic references to Ekheneos are carefully placed by the poet after 'Arete's *ehoie*' (7.155–7) and after the 'Catalogue of Women' (11.342–3a) respectively.[66] Ekheneos undermines Arete's power by pointing to Alkinoos' authority and thus exemplifies the undercurrent of conflict between the king and the queen of Scherie.[67] In this way, he seems to react implicitly against *ehoie*-poetry. His reaction points against the potential establishment of powerful female figures like Arete and the women of the Catalogue in the narrative of the *Odyssey*. This would signal a grave 'adulteration' of the heroic poetry by *ehoie*-poetry. Besides, the significant name of Ekheneos, the one

---

64 On the use of ἥρως in Homer see now van Wees 2006, 366–70, who argues against a secular meaning.
65 On this see Doherty 1995, 68 f., 77 f.
66 On the interventions of Ekheneos see the brief remarks in Hölscher (1989) ³1990, 128 and Garvie 1994, 196 *ad* 7.155–6; cf. Heubeck 1989, 98 *ad* 11.342–6, Latacz 1994 and Mori 2001, 93, 111 on the same passage.
67 As far as Arete is concerned, her father's name seems to reveal an analogous semantics of gender conflict, on the condition that one accepts the paternal nomenclature as an *ad hoc* invention by the poet of the *Odyssey* in order to indirectly serve the characterization of Arete: Ῥηξήνωρ (7.63) is the one who 'breaks armed ranks' (cf. *LfgrE* s.v. ῥηξήνωρ: 'men-breaking, shattering (the ranks of) his opponents') and subsequently his daughter displays the same trait, though certainly not on the battlefield. The similar function of Eurykleia's paternal nomenclature (*Od.* 1.429; 2.347; 20.148: Ὦπος θυγάτηρ Πεισηνορίδαο) is treated in Skempis (forthcoming). On the identification of epic women with their fathers see Olson 1992, 4 n. 13.

who 'possesses ships',[68] suggests the Homeric aristocratic ideal, and makes him particularly appropriate to bring up the subject. The emphasis on Ekheneos' age in both instances as γέρων and Φαιήκων ἀνδρῶν προγενέστερος emphasizes the significance of the old counselor's opinion. But one is also inclined to think that this reference may also imply the character's reaction to a lapse of the traditional heroic epic into the thematically diverse genre of the 'Catalogue of Women'.[69] It is a fact that the *Odyssey* significantly refines the epic tradition, in particular the ideal of the Iliadic warrior hero, and consequently reflects on the evolution of the epic genre.[70] We believe that the Phaiakian episode offers a concrete example of this evolutionary tendency inherent in the *Odyssey* by projecting a generic tension between heroic epic and *ehoie*-poetry.

At 11.363–76, Alkinoos says that Odysseus does not seem to be a dissembler or a thief. Thus, he answers obliquely to Odysseus' suggestion that he would be willing to stay for one more year in Scherie, should that be more profitable for him (11.355–61). Alkinoos' attitude to Odysseus is again at odds with that of his wife; while Arete seems willing to shower Odysseus with gifts and delay his escort home (11.339–41), Alkinoos is not at all willing to have Odysseus for one year in Scherie and increase his gifts. Oddly enough, Alkinoos says that Odysseus has surveyed skillfully the story of his own sorrows and of all the Argives (11.368–9). This is of course a strange statement. First of all, Odysseus did not say anything about the sorrows of the Argives, much less about all the Argives. Odysseus has just finished relating his encounter with the heroines, but Alkinoos not only does not praise, but deliberately passes over this part of Odysseus' account. Then, he asks Odysseus to change the subject. Alkinoos dismisses the '*ehoie*-poetry' and asks Odysseus to tell them about his comrades who followed him and died at Troy. We see here that Alkinoos is interested in the Iliadic stories of Odysseus. His request is that Odysseus change genre and move from the female catalogue to the male-oriented heroic poetry. He phrases this request by leaving the *ehoie*-like part of Odysseus' account

---

68 See von Kamptz 1982, 63; Braswell 1982, 133 n. 12; Pedrick 1988, 86–7; Wohl 1993, 29–31.
69 For a different approach cf. Wagner-Hasel 2007, 329 f.: 'der greise Heros Echeneos repräsentiert mit seinem Alter eine Art Körpergedächtnis, in dem ebenso wie in den Geweben der Frauen das Wissen um zentrale Werte der Gesellschaft aufgehoben ist'.
70 For the most recent discussion on this see Slatkin 2005, 316 ff.; cf. Pucci 1995.

completely unmentioned.[71] Alkinoos seems to imply that Odysseus should speak about the heroes who died at Troy, about the epic world that he claims to be a part of, and not about the women of *ehoie*-poetry. Arete's fascination with the account of the heroines and Alkinoos' request that Odysseus change topic and thus genre represent the gender tension reflected upon the generic question.

Hence, our reading proposes an *ehoie*-frame that starts in a rather oblique way with Athene's speech in book 7 and ends more straightforwardly with the 'Catalogue of Women' in book 11. Odysseus' narrative in the 'Nekyia' extols female virtue and particularly motherhood through the long conversation with Antikleia in the Underworld.[72] It is worth noting that *ehoie*-poetry provides a particularly suitable 'vessel' for praising motherhood due to the matrifocal emphasis on the presentation of the genealogies of heroes.[73] Gera is right to acknowledge that Arete is the first of Odysseus' listeners to react to his Catalogue, where the encounter with his dead mother Antikleia is recounted – it seems that the narrative activates Arete's motherly responses.[74] It is also noteworthy that Nausikaa refrains from naming Arete, but refers to her twice merely as 'mother' (6.305; 310), a designation which brings forth the text's accent on Arete in her capacity as a mother. In this respect, it might be no coincidence that Odysseus decides to narrate the meeting with his dead mother, perhaps seeking to create a link with Arete and her position in Scherie. The point seems to be that in his cultural background, i.e. that of an epic hero, one's mother is as highly respected as Arete appears to be in the community of the Phaiakians.

5. Conclusion

The usefulness of the formal references to *ehoie*-poetry lies on creating a codified channel of communication between Odysseus and Arete. This kind of poetry, standing at the heart of an innovative epic, provides a

---

[71] Still, οἷα (11.364) in this context might allude to *ehoie*-poetry.
[72] On the details and implications of this conversation see Combellack 1974, Ahl – Roisman 1996, 126–34, and especially Tracy 1997, 361–3.
[73] Cf. Lyons 1997, 5. On the matrifocal and subsequently matrilineal character of the genealogies in the Hesiodic *Ehoiai* see West 1966, 34 f.; Heilinger 1983, 28. *Pace* Finkelberg 1991, 308, who speaks of an explicit patrilineality in Greek genealogical poetry relying on West 1985, 31–50.
[74] Gera 1997, 48; cf. Louden 1999, 119 f.

heuristic tool for honing inter-gender communication. *Ehoie*-poetry is, however, a code, which is phatically articulated, though left unclassified, unnamed, at times even covert, as in the case of Arete's entry. One sees in the reaction of Ekheneos that this sort of poetry can cause a disruption on the heroic conceptualization of the epic collective and its representatives, i.e. men. Arete's narrativized etymologies and her affinity to genealogical poetry about women in the Phaiakian episode serve to establish a social communication, which transgresses gender and genre. Besides, the two etymologies of Arete's name which have been discussed in this paper exhibit the paradoxical nature of her name's semantics: on the one hand, it claims communication as its basis and, therefore, fosters narrative by suggesting the necessity of her being addressed by Odysseus; on the other, it reveals a character more or less challenging communication since she remains silent most of the time after Odysseus has supplicated her. Yet, in Arete's case, the meaning of her name as well as her generic affiliation with *ehoie*-poetry have a concrete narrative function: Odysseus understands Athene's hint in book 7, i.e. that his safe homecoming depends on a heroine of genealogical poetry, and when the time comes, he veers his narrative to Arete's world, a world of female *arete*. He seems to be aware that his epic nostos passes through *ehoie*-poetry, just as Arete's *kleos* passes through Odysseus' nostos.

Narratology, Deixis, and the Performance of Choral Lyric. On Pindar's *First Pythian* Ode

Lucia Athanassaki

1. Frequency and Deixis

Can studies in deixis and narratology engage in fruitful dialog? Deixis and narratology share an interest in the fundamental questions of time, place, and person.[1] Their take on these issues is different, but points of contact obviously exist. In what follows I will discuss one promising aspect of interaction, namely the interpretative advantage of introducing the narrative category of frequency in the study of the nexus of deictic indications that delineate performance contexts. Pindar's *First Pythian* will serve as my test case, but in the course of my discussion I will adduce parallels from a number of other songs that illustrate the advantages of the dialog between the two interpretative approaches for questions of performance.

A few preliminary remarks on narrative frequency are in order. Unlike questions of order, mood, and voice, which have been central to narrative analyses of choral lyric and in particular of epinicians, which form the largest component of the surviving texts and often display complex narrative patterns, frequency has received little attention.[2] Of

---

Warmest thanks to Antonios Rengakos for his invitation and generous hospitality in Thessaloniki and to Peter Agócs, Ewen Bowie, Ettore Cingano, Bruno Currie, Jonas Grethlein, André Lardinois and Anastasia-Erasmia Peponi for their valuable suggestions and comments on this version.

1   For place/space as a subject of narratological analysis see Bal (1985) 1997, 133–42.
2   The little attention which is paid to frequency does not represent a tendency restricted only to narrative studies of choral lyric. This is Bal's (1985) 1997, 111 assessment of all studies twenty five years after the publication of Genette's work, who had made exactly the same observation; see Genette (1972) 1980, 116. See, however, Tim Rood's recent essay for interesting observations on frequency in the Thucydidean narrative: Rood 2007, 133–37. For narrative analyses in terms of order, mood, and voice in the epinicians, see e.g. Hurst 1983;

Genette's four types of narrative frequency, *iterative narratives*, i. e. narrating once what happened *n* times, are of particular importance for the present discussion.[3] According to Genette, 'every iterative narrative is a synthetic narrating of the events that occur and reoccur in the course of an iterative *series* that is composed of a certain number of singular *units*.'[4] An interesting variant is *pseudo-iterative* narrative, which is a contamination of the single scene (Genette's term is *scène singulative*) by the iterative. According to Genette, these are 'scenes presented, particularly by their wording in the imperfect, as iterative, whereas the richness and precision of detail ensure that no reader can seriously believe they occur and reoccur in that manner, several times, without any variation.'[5] The iterative series on which I will focus are shorter or longer descriptions of, or even allusive references to, performance modes and settings.

Studies of deixis explore the linguistic forms that point intra- or extra-textually to a particular context (*deixis ad oculos*) and imaginatively to contexts which they bring to mind (*deixis am Phantasma*).[6] Various aspects of the celebratory occasion have recently been the subject of a number of essays on deixis and choral lyric, which appeared together in 2004 in a volume edited by Nancy Felson. Through different lines of enquiry these essays have reached a common conclusion, namely the difficulty of reconstructing the original performance context with any degree of certainty on the basis of the textual pointers.[7] One of the difficulties is the use of the same deictic markers for ocular and imaginary deixis.[8] A representative example of conflict of deictic markers is the *Eighth Olympian*, where Pindar uses the same deictic pronoun to point to a comastic procession at Olympia (τόνδε κῶμον, 10) and to orient us to Aegina (τάνδ' ἁλιερκέα χώραν, 25) without any indication that would account for the change of scene.[9] In so far as studies of the nexus of deictics aim at recovering the original performance context

---

Felson 1978 and 1984; Athanassaki 1990, 75–144; Pfeijffer 2004; Nünlist 2007.
3   The other three types are (a) *singulative* narratives: narrating once what happened once; (b) narrating *n* times what happened *n* times; (c) narrating *n* times what happened once; see Genette (1972) 1980, 114–15.
4   Genette (1972) 1980, 127.
5   Genette (1972) 1980, 121.
6   See Felson 2004 with bibliography.
7   See Athanassaki 2004; Bonifazi 2004; Calame 2004, 427–34.
8   See Felson 2004, 264–65.
9   I discuss the effect of the interplay of localizations in the *Eighth Olympian* in Athanassaki forthcoming a.

the finds are negative. For the study of broader issues of performance, however, deictic indeterminacy opens a different line of inquiry, namely the examination of the ramifications of the polysemy of deixis. Studies of the polysemy of deixis are in dialog with a growing body of scholarly work that centers on dissemination through reperformance.[10]

Iterative performance scenes have an effect similar to that of mutually exclusive deictic markers: they destabilize the deictic focus on a given performance context and introduce an alternative setting which features performance as a recurrent event. The fact that different readers opt for one setting as the performance context and consider the other fictive and vice versa shows that iterative narratives function as focus-shifters.

In what follows I focus on the function of iterative scenes of sympotic performance and I examine the interplay of public festival and symposium as performance settings in light of the survival of song through reperformance. I have chosen the *First Pythian* as my test case, because it draws attention to the importance of song reception. In sections II.1 and II.2 I examine divine and human performances focusing on narrative aspect, performance context, and the parameter of audience response for the survival of poetry on the human plane. In section II.3 I examine the politics of sympotic imagery and etiquette. Comparative material is drawn from other songs that Pindar composed for Hieron and his general Chromius, specifically the *First Olympian* and the *First* and *Ninth Nemeans*. In section III I examine the destabilization of the deictic focus on public festival by iterative sympotic scenes drawing comparative material from the odes which Pindar composed for the ruling family of Acragas and in particular the *Sixth Pythian* and the *Second Isthmian*. Section IV offers a summary of my conclusions and a contextualization of the *First Pythian* in its historical background.

2. Pindar's *First Pythian*

The elaborate description of human and divine performance in the opening triad has received much scholarly attention, whereas the concluding sympotic scene has attracted less interest. Scholarly discussion has so far centered on the significance of music for the broad issues of

---

10 See Herington 1985, 41–57; Morgan 1993; Nagy 1994; Athanassaki 2004; Currie 2004; Hubbard 2004; Carey 2007; Morrison 2007; Athanassaki 2009.

cosmic and human order and disorder, which pervade the poem, and on more specific issues such as the identity of performers and mode of performance.[11] My discussion focuses on performance contexts and audiences. Audience response is a dominant theme in the ode, but has remained unexplored. A study of the aspect of the presentation of audience responses sheds light on the regularity with which they are represented as occurring. The frequency of audience reactions bears directly on issues of song reception and survival through reperformance. The identification of performance contexts, which are inscribed in an ode, is important for the assessment of the communicative strategies which a certain composition adopts. In sections II. 2 and II. 3 I examine the communicative strategy of political paraenetic speech in the two different performance contexts which are inscribed in the ode, namely public festival (θαλίαι) and aristocratic symposium.[12]

A clarification on terminology is in order. I borrow Ferdinand de Saussure's distinction between synchrony and diachrony and I use the terms diachrony, diachronic axis etc. with reference to a limitless or limited sequence of identical or similar events which are represented in the

---

11   For the impact of the music on cosmic and human order and disorder, see e. g. Skulsky 1975; Carne-Ross 1985, 101–10; Cingano 1995, 12 f., 20, 327 ff.; Segal 1998 13–18. Brillante 1992 suggests that the opening triad reflects Spartan perceptions and practices. Lines 1–12 and 97–98 have been used as evidence in the debate of the monodic vs. the choral hypothesis; choral hypothesis: see Burnett 1989, 286 and 289 and Carey 1989, 554–55; monodic hypothesis: Lefkowitz 1991, 192–93 and Heath – Lefkowitz 1991, 180 and 186–87.

12   For the distinction between public festival and aristocratic symposium see Murray 1990. Cf. Schmitt Pantel 1990 who underplays the differences between the two and is followed by Vetta 1996. Stehle 1997, 214 n. 5 points out that lack of differentiation between the two ignores the problem of factions within a city. I add that it also ignores the existence of different social classes and their different interests. In an earlier study Vetta 1983, xxv-xxviii observed the distinction between public festival and symposium, but suggested that the symposia at Hieron's court were very big and impressive. The possibility cannot be excluded, but evidence is lacking. The Pindaric odes, i. e. *Olympian* 1, *Nemean* 1 and *Nemean* 9, do not indicate that the symposia of Hieron and Chromius were different from the typical aristocratic symposium and as I argue in section II. 3 it is doubtful that they offer realistic representations. In an interesting forthcoming study Currie uses the term *hestiasis tēs poleōs panēgyreōs* for public commensality keeping thus the distinction between public festival and symposium (Currie forthcoming).

text as repeatedly occurring over time.[13] The events I focus on are divine and human performances. In this scheme every performance, either human or divine, constitutes a synchrony. The sum of all synchronies constitutes a diachrony. If we were to imagine, for instance, the regular reperformance of the *First Pythian Ode* (choral or monodic in Syracuse, Aetna, or elsewhere) each and every reperformance would represent a synchrony and the sum of all synchronies would constitute the diachronical axis of the performance of this particular song, which theoretically could extend into the future for a limited period, e. g. Hieron's lifetime, or infinitely. The première would of course be the *terminus post quem* for a limited or limitless diachrony.

There is an important similarity between human and divine temporality. Divine performances are perceived as eternally recurrent events and in this sense they constitute a limitless diachrony. In Pindar's *Fourteenth Olympian Ode*, for instance, the performance of the Graces in honor of Zeus is represented as an eternally recurrent event (αἰέναον σέβοντι πατρὸς Ὀλυμπίοιο τιμάν, 12). Yet, exactly like human performances, there is a *terminus post quem* for the beginning of divine performances, which is the time of the birth of gods. In William Mullen's succinct formulation,

> In Greek poetry everything has a beginning and nothing has an end – nothing, that is, but the linear span of a mortal's life. Even the *Theogony*, which has so much to say about the endless existence of the gods, assigns to each of them a definite act of beginning, of coming-into-being, the *athanatōn ieron genos aien eontōn* (21) which starts with Chaos and proceeds to Earth in a distinct temporal sequence (*Chaos genet', autar epeita/Gai'*, 116–17). Having been generated in space and time these deathless ones then endure in it forever without any hint of 'last things,' for while there were many beliefs about cyclical world-ages and individual reincarnations, there is nowhere in archaic Greece the suggestion that at some point space and time might disappear altogether.[14]

Thus deities associated with music are represented as staging their musical première soon after their birth. Hermes, for instance, transforms the tortoise into a lyre right after his birth and starts singing of the love of Zeus and Maia and his own birth (*HH to Hermes* 20–61). Right at his birth Apollo declares his love for the lyre, which he will soon play at his

---

13 Saussure 1983, 79–98.
14 Mullen 1982, 210–11.

grand première on Olympus (*HH to Apollo* 131, 182–206 and 1–18).[15] The same is true for the performance of the Muses (*Theogony* 53–74).

It has been pointed out that in Pindar's poetry divine choral performances serve as the ideal paradigm for human performances.[16] Does this paradigmatic function include the limitless diachrony of divine performances? In other words, did Pindar expect his songs to live forever through reperformance? This is the question that the following discussion endeavors to explore.

2.1. Divine performance: the diachronic axis

The *First Pythian* opens with an impressive description of choral performance that places equal emphasis on music and dance:

> Χρυσέα φόρμιγξ, Ἀπόλλωνος καὶ ἰοπλοκάμων
> σύνδικον Μοισᾶν κτέανον· τᾶς ἀκούει
>   μὲν βάσις ἀγλαΐας ἀρχά,
> πείθονται δ' ἀοιδοὶ σάμασιν
> ἁγησιχόρων ὁπόταν προοιμίων
>   ἀμβολὰς τεύχῃς ἐλελιζομένα.[17]   (*Pythian* 1, 1–4)

> Golden lyre, rightful possession of Apollo
> and the violet-haired Muses, to you the footstep listens
>   as it begins the splendid celebration,
> and the singers heed your signals,
> whenever with your vibrations you strike up
>   the chorus-leading preludes.[18]

Some scholars have taken the opening as part of the immediately following description of divine performance.[19] Others have seen it as a reference to the visible human performance in Aetna.[20] The latter view

---

15 For the temporal relation of opening descriptions of Apollo's arrival on Olympus in the Delian and the Pythian parts of the hymn see Bakker 2002.
16 See in particular Mullen 1982, 209–20; Calame 1997, 90.
17 All Pindaric citations are taken from the editions of Snell-Maehler (epinicians) and Maehler (fragments).
18 All Pindaric translations are William Race's; modifications are registered in footnotes.
19 See, for instance, Wilamowitz 1922, 298–99; Kranz 1967, 262–63; Lefkowitz 1991, 192–93; cf. however Lefkowitz 1976, 106.
20 See, for instance, Segal 1998, 12–15; Cingano 1995, 12–13; Brillante 1992, 7–8; Race 1986, 37.

gains support from the second triad where, at long last, the purpose and the context of celebration is introduced (29–40). In the epode of the second triad the speaker voices his expectation for the future renown of Aetna for its victories and melodious festivities and prays to Apollo to grant his wish. The mention of performance and of Apollo in the epode echoes the opening of the ode in ring form:

ὁ δὲ λόγος
ταύταις ἐπὶ συντυχίαις δόξαν φέρει
λοιπὸν ἔσσεσθαι στεφάνοισί ν<ιν> ἵπποις τε κλυτάν
καὶ σὺν εὐφώνοις θαλίαις ὀνυμαστάν.
Λύκιε καὶ Δάλοι᾽ ἀνάσσων
   Φοῖβε Παρνασσοῦ τε κράναν Κασταλίαν φιλέων,
ἐθελήσαις ταῦτα νόῳ τιθέμεν εὔανδρόν τε χώραν.   (*Pythian* 1, 35–40)

   And this saying,
given the present success, inspires the expectation that
hereafter the city will be renowned for crowns and horses
and its name honored amid tuneful festivities.
Lord of Lykia, O Phoebus, you who rule over Delos
   And who love Parnassos' Kastalian spring,
willingly take those things to heart and make this a land of
brave men.

The echoes between the two passages argue in favor of reference to the visible human performance at the opening. As Segal observes, however, the diction in the opening is generalizing, almost abstract, and gives the human performance a metaphorical cast. Through the swift transition to the divine performance at line 6, Segal continues, 'the visible performance blends with its invisible archetype on Olympus'.[21] The description of the performance of Apollo and the Muses at the wedding of Peleus and Thetis in the *Fifth Nemean* offers a good parallel for the fusion of divine and human song: the beginning of the divine performance is clearly demarcated (22), but there is no marker indicating its end. Thus the song of the Muses becomes imperceptibly the epinician singer's own song.[22] The absence of any deictic marker that would anchor the reference either to the human or to the divine plane in the *First Pythian* suggests that Pindar opts for a similar effect.

The mention of the lyre's power to quench the thunderbolt of Zeus clearly marks a shift of focus from the performers to the effect of music and is the first step in the transition to the theme of audience response,

---

21 Segal 1998, 13.
22 For more examples of merging voices in Pindar see Athanassaki 1990, 130–38.

which dominates the first triad. Simultaneously it is the first clear marker that leads the eye to Olympus. The virtuosity of divine performers is of course mentioned, but in passing (12). In contrast, the magic spell that divine performance casts on its audience, individually and collectively, receives elaborate treatment:

> καὶ τὸν αἰχματὰν κεραυνὸν <u>σβεννύεις</u>
> αἰενάου πυρός. <u>εὕδει</u> δ' ἀνὰ σκά-
> πτῳ Διὸς αἰετός, ὠκεῖ-
> αν πτέρυγ' ἀμφοτέρωθεν χαλάξαις,
> ἀρχὸς οἰωνῶν, κελαινῶπιν δ' ἐπί οἱ νεφέλαν
> ἀγκύλῳ κρατί, γλεφάρων ἀδὺ κλάι-
> θρον, κατέχευας· ὁ δὲ <u>κνώσσων</u>
> ὑγρὸν νῶτον <u>αἰωρεῖ</u>, τεαῖς
> ῥιπαῖσι κατασχόμενος. καὶ γὰρ βια-
> τὰς Ἄρης, τραχεῖαν ἄνευθε λιπών
> ἐγχέων ἀκμάν, <u>ἰαίνει</u> καρδίαν
> κώματι, κῆλα δὲ καὶ δαιμόνων <u>θέλ-</u>
> <u>γει</u> φρένας ἀμφί τε Λατοί-
> δα σοφίᾳ βαθυκόλπων τε Μοισᾶν.   (*Pythian* 1, 5–12)

You quench even the warring thunderbolt
of ever-flowing fire; and the eagle sleeps
    on the scepter of Zeus,
        having relaxed his swift wings on either side,
the king of birds, for you have poured
over his curved head a black-hooded cloud,
    sweet seal for his eyelids. And as he slumbers,
he ripples his supple back, held in check
for your volley of notes. For even powerful
    Ares puts aside
his sharp-pointed spears and delights his heart
in sleep; and your shafts enchant
        the minds of the deities as well, through the skill
        of Leto's son and the deep-breasted Muses.

The predominance of present indicative throughout this scene is unmistakable. In light of the belief that divine performance on Olympus is an eternally recurrent event, the present tense denotes customary action.[23] In narratological terms, the detail that characterizes the description of the reactions of specific members of the audience, in particular the eagle, suggests that the scene is pseudo-iterative rather than iterative, i.e. the audience response in this instance is a realization in an iterative

---
23 See Rijksbaron (1984) ³2002, 5 § 3 n. 2 and 10 § 5.3. For an overview of Pindaric and earlier representations of divine performances see Krischer 1985.

series of similar, but not necessarily identical, responses to divine music. In other words, on other occasions different members of the divine audience may experience similar reactions to the same or similar repertoire.[24] What is eternally recurrent is the irresistible appeal of divine performance.

The present tense persists in the immediately following brief mention of the reaction of Zeus' opponents to the song of the Muses, which is also iterative:

ὅσσα δὲ μὴ πεφίληκε Ζεύς, <u>ἀτύζονται</u> βοάν
Πιερίδων <u>ἀίοντα</u>, γᾶν τε καὶ πόν-
    τον κατ' ἀμαιμάκετον,
ὅς τ' ἐν αἰνᾷ Ταρτάρῳ κεῖται, θεῶν πολέμιος,
Τυφὼς ἑκατοντακάρανος· τόν ποτε...   (*Pythian* 1, 13–16)

But those creatures for whom Zeus has no love are terrified
when they hear the song of the Pierians, those on land
    and in the overpowering sea,
and the one who lies in dread Tartaros, enemy of the gods,
Typhos the hundred-headed, whom...

If the antistrophe foregrounds the irresistibility of divine song, the epode highlights a rather unusual side, its inescapability. Zeus' enemies all experience constant terror, both because divine song reaches everywhere on land, at sea, and in the Underworld and because it is eternally reiterated. This is also an instance of a single unit in an iterative series – no longer of pleasure, but of suffering. As in the scene on Olympus, audience response is treated both individually and collectively, but in reverse order. Of all Zeus' foes Typhon is singled out for mention whereby the mythical narrative is introduced.

2.2. The human performance: the diachronic axis

In the magnificent description of the eruption of Aetna, which follows the brief account of the downfall and punishment of Typhon (14–20), we find the first unambiguous temporal and spatial localization on the human level. The transition from the remote past of Typhon's confinement in Tartarus to the present is gradual. It begins with the temporal νῦν (17), which as elsewhere in Pindar covers the wide timespan from

---

[24] See e.g. fr. 70b, 5–23, where Pindar describes the response of different gods to a Dionysiac choral performance.

illud tempus to the present.[25] The eruption of the volcano some nine or six years before the composition of the ode is the first temporal specification before anchoring the narrative in the *hic et nunc* of the performance. The mention of eyewitnesses of the wondrous event of the recent past (τέρας μὲν θαυμάσιον προσιδέσθαι, θαῦμα δὲ καὶ παρεόντων ἀκοῦσαι, 26) paves the way for the demonstrative τοῦτ' ὄρος (30), whereby the speaker's spatial localization in its vicinity becomes explicit. The spatial localization is followed by a temporal indication, i. e. sometime after Hieron's chariot victory in Delphi and his proclamation as Aetnaeus (31–32).[26] Towards the end of this section, which begins with a prayer to Zeus and ends with a prayer to Apollo (29–40) the speaker expresses the wish for Aetna's continuing fame for future horse victories and tuneful festivities.

Thus at the end of the second triad the image of human performance, which was suspended in order to foreground the cosmic impact of divine music, is re-introduced. I have already suggested that the prayer to Apollo to grant the wish for future victories and melodious songs recalls the opening invocation of the lyre, the rightful possession of Apollo and the Muses. The evocation of the opening in ring-form suggests that the opening image is an instance in the series of the wished for future performances. The designation of these performances as εὔφωνοι θαλίαι in the epode is an unambiguous indication that Pindar thinks of public festival as the context of future performances or reperformances (λοιπόν, 37).

Pindar uses the term θαλίαι always with reference to public festival. In the *Seventh Olympian* the celebrations of the Eratids are located in the festivals of the polis (Ἐρατιδᾶν τοι σὺν χαρίτεσσιν ἔχει θαλίας καὶ πόλις, 93–94). In the *Tenth Olympian* songs celebrating victories at the very first Olympic games are sung in the sanctuary amid pleasant festivities (ἀείδετο δὲ πᾶν τέμενος τερπναῖσι θαλίαις τὸν ἐγκώμιον ἀμφὶ τρόπον, 76–77). In the *Sixth Paean* Pindar calls Apollo's sanctuary in Delphi a nurse of crowns and feasts, where Delphian maidens dance and sing in honor of Apollo (στεφάνων καὶ θαλιᾶν τροφὸν ἄλσος Ἀπόλλωνος, τόθι Λατοΐδαν θαμινὰ Δελφῶν κόραι χθονὸς ὀμφαλὸν παρὰ σκιάεντα μελπ[ό]μεναι ποδὶ κροτέο[ντι γᾶν θο]ῷ, 13–18). Still more informative

---

25 See *Olympian* 1.90 and Athanassaki 2004, 334.
26 André Lardinois suggests to me that localization zooms in, comes closer and closer to the place of performance: Cilicia (17) – Cyme (18) – Sicily (19) – Aetna (20).

is the elaborate description of the θαλίαι of the Hyperboreans in the *Tenth Pythian*, where in addition to choral performances, feasts, and crown-processions there is mention of sacrifices:

παρ' οἷς ποτε Περσεὺς ἐδαίσατο λαγέτας,
δώματ' ἐσελθών,
κλειτὰς ὄνων ἑκατόμβας ἐπιτόσσαις θεῷ
ῥέζοντας· ὧν θαλίαις ἔμπεδον
εὐφαμίαις τε μάλιστ' Ἀπόλλων
χαίρει, γελᾷ θ' ὁρῶν ὕβριν ὀρθίαν κνωδάλων.

Μοῖσα δ' οὐκ ἀποδαμεῖ
τρόποις ἐπὶ σφετέροισι· παντᾷ δὲ χοροὶ παρθένων
λυρᾶν τε βοαὶ καναχαί τ' αὐλῶν δονέονται·
δάφνᾳ τε χρυσέᾳ κόμας ἀναδήσαν-
      τες εἰλαπινάζοισιν εὐφρόνως.   (*Pythian* 10, 31–40)

With them Perseus, the leader of people once feasted,
upon entering their halls,
when he came upon them sacrificing glorious hecatombs
of asses to the god. In their festivities[27]
and praises Apollo ever finds greatest delight
and laughs to see the beasts' braying insolence.

And the Muse is no stranger
to their ways, for everywhere choruses of maidens,
sounds of lyres, and pipes' shrill notes are stirring.
With golden laurel they crown their hair
      and feast joyfully.

Such is evidently the context which Pindar indicates for the present and future performances in Aetna. The question that arises is why he opts for an implicit as opposed to an explicit association of the initial reference to choral performance with the festival to which he subsequently points as performance context.

Charles Segal, who drew attention to the subordination of the visible performance to the invisible performance on Olympus, has suggested that 'Pindar mythicizes the performance situation not necessarily because the performance is less real for him but because as heir to a long tradition of choral song he can reflect self-consciously on that tradition.'[28] Segal's insight is worth exploring from a different angle as well, the poet's self-conscious reflection on the conditions of survival

---
27 Race translates θαλίαις as banquets. I have preferred 'festivity': see Slater 1969 s.v.
28 Segal 1998, 15.

and dissemination of choral traditions. This question leads to the examination of the other representations of human performance in the ode and their relation to divine performance.

Before turning to Pindar's representations of human performance it is worth recapitulating the distinctive features of divine performance: (a) choice of diction that points up its repetition in a limitless diachrony and (b) emphasis on audience response, which clearly privileges pleasure, but offers a glimpse into the suffering that song can cause. After an elaborate praise of Hieron, Pindar comes back to these questions in the end of the fourth and the fifth triad. Yet whereas in the first triad he handles the cosmic dimension of these issues, in the final triad he translates them in human terms.

In the fourth and fifth triad (61–100) Pindar explores audience response to encomiastic song tackling the issue from three different perspectives: (a) choice of subject-matter vis-à-vis audience identity, (b) style of presentation, and (c) suitability of subject-matter for the survival and dissemination of song in posterity. In raising these issues Pindar draws attention to the fact that, unlike the impact of divine song, the appeal of human song is not unconditional. It is neither universally nor eternally irresistible or inescapable.[29]

The issue of relativity of the appeal of song comes as a generalizing conclusion to the praise of the military and civic achievements of Hieron and his family, which extends from the second to the fourth triad:

> ἀρέομαι
> πὰρ μὲν Σαλαμῖνος Ἀθαναίων χάριν
> μισθόν, ἐν Σπάρτᾳ δ' <ἀπὸ> τᾶν πρὸ Κιθαιρῶ-
>   νος μαχᾶν,
> ταῖσι Μήδειοι κάμον ἀγκυλότοξοι,
> παρὰ δὲ τὰν εὔυδρον ἀκτὰν
>   Ἱμέρα παίδεσσιν ὕμνον Δεινομένεος τελέσαις,
> τὸν ἐδέξαντ' ἀμφ' ἀρετᾷ, πολεμίων ἀνδρῶν καμόντων. (*Pythian* 1, 75–80)

> I shall earn
> from Salamis the Athenians' gratitude
> as my reward, and at Sparta I shall tell of the battle
>   before Kithairon,
> in which conflicts the curve-bowed Medes suffered

---

29 Another similarity between divine and human song is that they can both reach the Underworld: for human song see e.g. *Olympian* 8.79–84, *Olympian* 14.21–25, *Pythian* 5.98–103 and the discussion of Segal 1985. Interestingly, Pindar does not raise this possibility in this ode.

> defeat;
> but by the well-watered bank of the Himeras I shall pay
>   to Deinomenes' sons the tribute of my hymn,
> which they won through valor, when their enemies were
>   defeated.

Scholars have suggested that Pindar's decision to put Gelon's victory at Himera on a par with the victory of the Athenians at Salamis and of the Spartans at Plataea is a praise strategy to highlight the importance of the Deinomenids's contribution and to remind the mainland Greeks of the Sicilian tyrants' active participation in the struggle of Greeks against the barbarians.[30] The equation of the importance of the three battles, however, is left to inference. The poetic statement is cast in such a way as to privilege a different angle, namely the different preferences of different audiences. In light of the Panhellenic aspirations of epinician poetry the introduction of the parameter of audience preference for certain topics shows the flip side of the coin. It serves as a reminder that the appeal of song is conditional, subject to local bounds. In terms of narrative aspect, the different appeal of different topics to different audiences is presented as a single event.

The conditions under which encomiastic poetry can overcome local and temporal bounds and win the approval of posterity is the subject of the final triad. The first condition is style:

> καιρὸν εἰ φθέγξαιο, πολλῶν πείρατα συντανύσαις
> ἐν βραχεῖ, μείων ἕπεται μῶμος ἀνθρώ-
>   πων· ἀπὸ γὰρ κόρος ἀμβλύνει
> αἰανὴς ταχείας ἐλπίδας,
> ἀστῶν δ' ἀκοὰ κρύφιον θυμὸν βαρύ-
>   νει μάλιστ' ἐσλοῖσιν ἐπ' ἀλλοτρίοις.   (Pythian 1, 81–84)

> If you should speak to the point by combining the strands
> of many things in brief, less criticism follows from men,
>   for cloying excess
> dulls eager expectations
> and townsmen are grieved in their secret hearts
>   especially when they hear of other's successes.

---

30 See Cingano 1995, 17–18; Hubbard 2004, 74–75. In contrast Harrell 2006, 132–33 thinks that Pindar proclaims Hieron a Panhellenic hero 'before the home crowd in Sicily', a 'local audience in a city firmly under the tyrant's control' and concludes that 'we can be sure that this is no coincidence.' Pindar, however, did not compose with an eye only to a single performance and to a local audience, but *sub specie aeternitatis*; see also below n. 53.

Focused and concise diction causes less blame on the part of the audience, which might otherwise feel boredom or envy. The negative formulation of people's reactions brings out the resistance which audiences tend to put up, and therefore the obstacles which songs of praise must overcome in order to be successful.

The addressee of this remarkable indefinite second-person statement can easily be more or less general. Depending on the identity of the targeted audience the statement can serve different purposes. If directed to all members of any given audience, it serves as a means of bridging the distance between *laudator* and audience and of establishing mutual understanding.[31] The speaker winks at his audience, as it were, calling attention to the fact that he understands why they dislike rambling and excessive praise. Simultaneously, the didactic tone of the statement makes it relevant to anybody who has the ambition to engage in effective encomiastic rhetoric, for instance poets and chroniclers, who receive attention a little later. The shift from first- to second-person reference enables the speaker to establish some distance between the song he sings in the *hic et nunc*, namely the encomium of Hieron, and look at it from the broader perspective of the objectives and challenges of encomiastic rhetoric. The distance that the speaker gradually takes from his own song is completed in the epode where he shifts to third-person deixis (94) and meditates on the conditions and channels of survival of encomiastic song in general.

The transition from proper encomiastic style to encomia of diachronic appeal is effected by means of a gnome (85–86) which marks a change of addressee too:

ἀλλ' ὅμως, κρέσσον γὰρ οἰκτιρμοῦ φθόνος,
μὴ παρίει καλά. νώμα δικαίῳ
    πηδαλίῳ στρατόν· ἀψευ-
    δεῖ δὲ πρὸς ἄκμονι χάλκευε γλῶσσαν.

εἴ τι καὶ φλαῦρον παραιθύσσει, μέγα τοι φέρεται
πὰρ σέθεν. πολλῶν ταμίας ἐσσί· πολλοὶ
    μάρτυρες ἀμφοτέροις πιστοί.
εὐανθεῖ δ' ἐν ὀργᾷ παρμένων,
εἴπερ τι φιλεῖς ἀκοὰν ἁδεῖαν αἰ-
    εἰ κλύειν, μὴ κάμνε λίαν δαπάναις·

---

31 For a general second-person reference see Jakob's discussion with bibliography in Jakob – Oikonomidis 1994, 200 *ad* 81–82(b). The advice of course applies to the speaker himself. For the function of this statement as a self-exhortation see Race 1990, 166.

ἐξίει δ' ὥσπερ κυβερνάτας ἀνήρ
ἱστίον ἀνεμόεν {πετάσαις}. μὴ δολωθῆς,
  ὦ φίλε, κέρδεσιν ἐντραπέ-
λοις· ὀπιθόμβροτον αὔχημα δόξας

οἷον ἀποιχομένων ἀνδρῶν δίαιταν μανύει
καὶ λογίοις καὶ ἀοιδοῖς. οὐ φθίνει Κροί-
  σου φιλόφρων ἀρετά.
τὸν δὲ ταύρῳ χαλκέῳ καυτῆρα νηλέα νόον
ἐχθρὰ Φάλαριν κατέχει παντᾷ φάτις,
οὐδέ νιν φόρμιγγες ὑπωρόφιαι κοινανίαν
μαλθακὰν παίδων ὀάροισι δέκονται.
τὸ δὲ παθεῖν εὖ πρῶτον ἀέθλων·
 εὖ δ' ἀκούειν δευτέρα μοῖρ'· ἀμφοτέροισι δ' ἀνήρ
ὃς ἂν ἐγκύρσῃ καὶ ἕλῃ, στέφανον ὕψιστον δέδεκται. (*Pythian* 1, 85–100)

But nevertheless, since envy is better than pity,
do not pass over any noble things. Guide your people
 with a rudder of justice; on an anvil of truth
  forge your tongue.

Even some slight thing, you know, becomes important
if it flies out from you. You are the steward of many
  things;
 many are the sure witnesses for deeds of both kinds.
Abide in flourishing high spirits,
and if indeed you love always to hear pleasant things said
 about you, do not grow too tired of spending,
but let out the sail, like a helmsman,
to the wind. Do not be deceived,
  O my friend, by shameful gains,
  for the posthumous acclaim of fame

alone reveals the life of men who are dead and gone
through[32] both chroniclers and poets. The kindly
  excellence of Croesus does not perish,
but universal execration overwhelms Phalaris, that man
of pitiless spirit who burned men in his bronze bull,
and no lyres in banquet halls welcome him
in gentle fellowship with boys' voices.
Success is the first of prizes;
  and renown the second portion; but the man who
meets with both and gains them has won the highest
  crown.

---

32 This is a modification of Race's translation 'to both chroniclers and poets.' See the immediately following discussion.

The use of second-person deixis persists in the cluster of admonitions that run through the end of the antistrophe (85–92), but their political content makes clear that the speaker no longer addresses the audience, but the *laudandus*. Some scholars have argued that the recipient of political advice cannot have been the experienced tyrant of Syracuse, but the young Deinomenes. On the basis of textual evidence, however, Hieron is the likelier candidate. The fourth triad concludes with the mention of the victory of the sons of Deinomenes, i.e. Gelon and Hieron, at Himera. An associative transition from grandfather to grandson is not inconceivable, but is certainly harsh. I therefore side with those who think that Hieron is the addressee and in the next section I will offer some further arguments in favor of this view in the course of my discussion of the intended effect of the political paraenetic speech, where I will also examine the adaptability of such speech to different performance contexts.[33]

Among the admonitions of the speaker to the *laudandus* is the importance of lavish expenditure for securing everlasting good reputation (90). The adverb αἰεί anticipates the eternal fame through song which emerges in the epode through a cluster of iterative statements. The first of these statements is general: ὀπιθόμβροτον αὔχημα δόξας οἷον ἀποιχομένων ἀνδρῶν δίαιταν μανύει καὶ λογίοις καὶ ἀοιδοῖς. The exact meaning of this passage depends on how we construe the datives. Some scholars take them as indirect objects with the verb, whereas others consider them instrumental. In support of the latter Ettore Cingano adduces an eloquent parallel: παροιχομένων γὰρ ἀνέρων, ἀοιδοὶ καὶ λόγιοι (ἀοιδαὶ καὶ λόγοι edd.) τὰ καλά σφιν ἔργ' ἐκόμισαν (*Nem.* 6.29–30).[34] The common denominator of the two variant formulations is the cardinal role of chroniclers and poets for the preservation of the glory of those who died. Unlike the *Sixth Nemean*, however, where the aorist indicates the mere occurrence of the contribution of

---

33 For a survey of the arguments in favor of Hieron and Deinomenes see Köhnken 1970 who argues in favor of Hieron. See also Race 1986, 48 who, on the basis of Aristotle (*Rhetoric* 1367b37), points out the encomiastic function of the paraenetic speech. According to Race the aim of the paraenesis is to show that Hieron is an ideal ruler; Pindar, however, does not say it explicitly, he only implies it. The use of present participles, Race continues, suggests that Hieron must keep trying. For the encomiastic function of paraenetic speech in general see Pernot 1993, 710–24. For Pindar's influence on later 'kingship theory' see Hornblower 2004, 63–66 with bibliography.
34 Cingano 1995, 361 *ad* 94.

poets and chroniclers in the past, the use of present tense in the *First Pythian* underlines the continuity of their impact. The twofold example of the posthumous fortunes of two rulers, a good and an evil one, serves as the illustration of the continuing impact of commemoration.

Pindar telescopes the channels of the survival of fame through song by means of the negative example of Phalaris. Phalaris, who is surrounded by hateful speech everywhere, is systematically excluded from the sympotic repertoire. This is yet another iterative statement that captures in a nutshell the nature of memory and oblivion which are at stake. Phalaris is not forgotten, for his cruelty lives on in people's hate-talk, but he is permanently exiled from the symposium, the cradle of aristocratic lifestyle and song diffusion. By implication, songs celebrating Croesus are welcome to travel from symposium to symposium thus keeping alive the memory of his kindly excellence.[35]

In the closure of the ode Pindar formulates concisely and in negative terms the topic which Theognis treated elaborately and in positive terms:[36]

σοὶ μὲν ἐγὼ πτέρ' ἔδωκα, σὺν οἷς ἐπ' ἀπείρονα πόντον
 πωτήσηι καὶ γῆν πᾶσαν ἀειρόμενος
ῥηϊδίως· θοίνηις δὲ καὶ εἰλαπίνηισι παρέσσηι
 ἐν πάσαις, πολλῶν κείμενος ἐν στόμασιν,
καί σε σὺν αὐλίσκοισι λιγυφθόγγοις νέοι ἄνδρες
 εὐκόσμως ἐρατοὶ καλά τε καὶ λιγέα
ᾄσονται. καὶ ὅταν δνοφερῆς ὑπὸ κεύθεσι γαίης
 βῆις πολυκωκύτους εἰς Ἀΐδαο δόμους,
οὐδέποτ' οὐδὲ θανὼν ἀπολεῖς κλέος, ἀλλὰ μελήσεις
 ἄφθιτον ἀνθρώποις αἰὲν ἔχων ὄνομα
Κύρνε, καθ' Ἑλλάδα γῆν στρωφώμενος ἠδ' ἀνὰ νήσους
 ἰχθυόεντα περῶν πόντον ἐπ' ἀτρύγετον,
οὐχ ἵππων νώτοισιν ἐφήμενος, ἀλλά σε πέμψει
 ἀγλαὰ Μουσάων δῶρα ἰοστεφάνων·
πᾶσι δ' ὅσοισι μέμηλε καὶ ἐσσομένοισιν ἀοιδὴ
 ἔσσηι ὁμῶς, ὄφρ' ἂν γῆ τε καὶ ἠέλιος.[37]   (Theognis, 237–252)

---

35 Köhnken 1970, 12, n. 1: 'Wer im Gebrauch von Macht und Reichtum Kroisos folgt, wird immer Gegenstand rühmender Lieder sein, wer sich Phalaris zum Vorbild nimmt, wird nie in sie aufgenommen werden.' For Croesus as an exemplary ruler in epinician poetry see also Kurke 1999, 131–42.
36 See Carey 1989, 554–55 who draws attention to the similarities between the two passages in terms of 'survival in song through commemoration at feasts by means of voice and accompaniment.'
37 The citation is taken from West's edition.

> For my part, I have made you wings on which to fly
> across the endless sea and all the earth
> with ease: you'll be at every dinner, every feast,
> and many a man will have you on his lips,
> and lovely lads accompanied by alto pipers
> will sing of you in voices sweet and clear
> and orderly. And when, down in the earth's dark nooks,
> you go to Hades' house of wailing grief,
> not even then in death will your fame fade, but men
> will always cherish your immortal name,
> Cyrnus, as you roam over all the land of Greece
> and all the islands of the teeming sea,
> not riding then on horseback; no, the violet-wreathed
> Muses will speed you by their noble grace.
> Future men likewise, all who have an interest,
> will sing of you, while earth and sun exist. (transl. M. L. West)

Theognis' statement is a clear and precise formulation of the survival of song through reperformance at symposia all over the Greek world. In comparison, the Pindaric reformulation is concise and allusive, but the similarities in imagery and diction evoke Theognis' version and suggest that in Pindar's view too the symposium was one of the venues of survival of encomiastic songs through reperformance.

The most striking difference between the two versions of eternal fame through song is that, unlike Pindar's cautious posture, Theognis asserts the unconditional appeal of his songs. In terms of their survival through reperformance, we have a case of limitless diachrony. In comparison to Theognis' optimistic view, Pindar's model is not only cautious, but more complex as well. The introduction of divine performance into the picture serves as a reminder of the limitations of human performance. The picture of the obstacles that human song must overcome, constructed step by step, gains force from historical precedent, the fortunes of Croesus and Phalaris. It is notable too that unlike Theognis' promise to Cyrnus, Pindar does not even say that Hieron is a second Croesus. He concludes with yet another cautious statement which only implies that the tyrant of Syracuse may prove one of those who achieve such a good fortune.[38]

---

38 For Pindar's cautious praise of Hieron see Race 1990, 166–68. As Jonas Grethlein suggests to me, the concluding statement, being part of the preceding long appeal to Hieron, strengthens the impression that Hieron is not automatically a second Croesus; the tenor is: 'keep trying'. See also n. 33 above.

The descriptions of divine and human performance, symmetrically positioned in the opening and the closure, reflect one another but their trajectories are different. The irresistible appeal of divine performance is an ideal model towards and against which mortals strive, but as Pindar makes clear the path is not without obstacles and success depends on various interrelated factors: poetic virtuosity, the appeal of the personality and the deeds of the *laudandus*, contemporary interest, and posthumous reception. Clearly this is a much more complex picture than the one which Theognis paints to his addressee and the reason must lie in the fact that Hieron was no ordinary aristocrat. Posthumous inclusion in the sympotic repertoire, either through re-performance of old songs or as a source of inspiration of new songs, was unquestionably the ultimate challenge for tyrants. The organization of magnificent spectacles in Syracuse and Aetna was not a challenge for Hieron who attracted the greatest poets of his time to his court and had every means at his disposal to stage splendid performances.[39] Far greater was the challenge of portraying the human side of the tyrant in order to win the approval of the aristocratic circles in the Greek world during his lifetime and after his death. For such an ambitious task the emphasis on Hieron's impeccable sympotic manners was a shrewd and advantageous strategy.

2.3. Turning the symposium inside out

Two of the four epinician odes that Pindar composed for Hieron display a similar strategy in staging the *laudator* vis-à-vis the *laudandus*. In all four epinicians the speaker addresses Hieron, but only in the *First Olympian* and the *First Pythian* does second-person deixis form part of a nexus of indications that produce the effect of proximity between speaker and addressee.[40] The sense of proximity is stronger in the *First Olympian*: there the speaker situates himself at a symposium in Hieron's palace in Syracuse, where he explicitly states that he performs in the presence of the *laudandus*. The effect of proximity is re-enforced by a long con-

---

39 For Hieron's cultural program see Dougherty 1993, 84–91.
40 The shifting of temporal reference and localization in the *Second Pythian* (ll. 3–4 and 67–68 respectively) and the cluster of counterfactual conditions in the *Third Pythian* (ll. 63–76) with regard to the speaker's presence in Syracuse create a certain sense of distance; see D'Alessio 2004, 290 and Athanassaki 2004, 325, n. 22.

cluding speech, where the representation of the relationship of speaker and addressee as *homilia* is filled out by a sustained alternation of self-referential statements and second-person reference. In contrast, in the opening the speaker opts for third-person distal deixis in order to single out the *laudandus*. The initial distance is bridged in the final triad, where distal deixis gives way to proximal second-person deixis. The *First Pythian* displays a similar staging pattern. The long maintained distance between speaker and addressee is bridged in the final triad, where the speaker shifts to second-person deixis. Yet unlike the *First Olympian* where Hieron is the sole addressee, in the *First Pythian* second-person deixis has a double function: the speaker first reaches out to the audience and then turns to the *laudandus*.

A very important difference between the *First Olympian* and the *First Pythian* is the representation of performance mode and setting. Unlike the *First Olympian*, where the speaker situates himself inside Hieron's palace at the moment his turn has come to pick up his lyre and sing at the symposium which is in full swing, the speaker of *First Pythian* conjures up the image of a public festival as the performance setting. Public festival is the context which Wilamowitz posited for the performance of the *First Pythian*:

> So the marvelous poem is something incomparable. Whoever wants to read it correctly must locate himself in Aetna near a place where the mighty peak sticks up to the heavens. Below in the depths rumbles and groans the chained but still dangerous Typhoeus. In the agora of the new city sits the old ruler, its founder. We should think of him in his priestly finery. Next to him the young king, decked out with the marks of his rank, marks of which we admittedly know only the scepter for sure. Round about him an impressive military retinue, but also the citizenry with their chosen officials, a festive gathering of the people. Sacrifices are made, altars blaze, the chorus comes in and sings the song that adds the dedication of art to the dedication of the priests. It is Pindar's song; he does not name himself, he does not say that he has sent it from distant Thebes, but he speaks the words, and the words gain their weight from the fact that he utters them.[41]

Wilamowitz's view is in line with the testimony of the ancient scholiasts who report that Hieron and Chromius celebrated their Panhellenic victories at the festival of Zeus Aetnaeus.[42] To what extent Wilamowitz's imaginative reconstruction corresponds to the actual performance is of course unknown. In outline, however, it cannot be far from reality, if

---

41 Wilamowitz 1922, 298 (my translation).
42 *Scholia vetera in Nem.* 1.7b.

we posit a choral performance at a festival in the newly founded city.[43] Pindar's description of the splendid celebrations of the Hyperboreans in *Pythian* 10 provides a useful model for the *thaliae* which the tyrant of Syracuse had all the means to organize. It is against such a background that I will examine the communicative strategy of the paraenetic speech and the sympotic imagery of the fifth triad of *Pythian* 1.

Sympotic imagery and etiquette are quite prominent in the odes that Pindar composed for Hieron and his lieutenant Chromius. We shall turn first to the *First Olympian*, where the symposium is the dominant theme of the celebratory occasion and the mythological narrative. On the basis of a detailed analysis of the sympotic themes Eveline Krummen has interpreted the sympotic imagery literally and suggested that Pindar composed the ode for sympotic performance in Hieron's palace.[44] Yet whereas it is true that the imagery points to the suitability of the ode for sympotic performance, there are reasons to doubt that Hieron intended to celebrate his most prestigious first victory at the Olympic games privately in his palace in the company of a smaller or larger group of guests and that Pindar composed the song with a sympotic première in mind.[45] We have seen that according to an ancient scholiast, who draws on Didymus, Hieron and Chromius celebrated their Panhellenic victories at the festival of Zeus Aetnaeus. Pindar's reference to *thaliae* in the *First Pythian* points to similar public celebrations. Finally, regardless of the pragmatics of the first performance, the superabundant emphasis on sympotic imagery and etiquette in the *First Olympian* suggests that Pindar's aim must have been broader than the composition of a song to be sung at Hieron's symposium.[46]

In the *First Olympian* Pindar casts speaker and addressee as fellow symposiasts. He attributes the same roles to the protagonists of the mythical narrative, Tantalus and Pelops. Through Pindar's revision of the mythical tradition Tantalus is acquitted of the charge that he served Pelops to the gods. He is punished, however, because he stole the gods'

---

43 For a very similar picture of choral performance at a public festival see Currie forthcoming with a survey of the evidence.
44 Krummen 1990, 155–216.
45 Similar is Carey's view who points out that it 'is inherently implausible that a grand song of praise like this was squandered on an informal gathering', (2007, 205).
46 Through a study of the deictic pattern of the *First Olympian* I have argued that, in addition to Syracuse, Olympia is also a deictic center which in turn indicates the suitability of the ode for performance at Olympia. See Athanassaki 2004.

food and drink and served them to his fellow mortal symposiasts. In so far as sympotic etiquette is concerned Tantalus is clearly an untrustworthy symposiast. Pelops, on the other hand, whose sojourn on Olympus among the gods was impeccable, enjoys divine favor during his lifetime and eternal posthumous honors.[47] As scholars have pointed out, the imagery of the posthumous libations in honor of Pelops is sympotic as well.[48] In the mythical narrative of the *First Olympian* sympotic manners are the touchstone of the *ethos* of the protagonists. Hieron is a protagonist in his own symposium which is invested with the characteristics of the positive model, namely men who sing in turn the choicest of songs, splendor, and hospitality.

Interestingly enough the two odes that Pindar composed for Chromius show a similar emphasis on the symposium. As in the *First Olympian*, the performance of the *First* and the *Ninth Nemean* are also set in a sympotic setting, but neither representation is realistic. In the *Ninth Nemean* the opening performance setting features a joyous comastic procession heading from Sicyon to Aetna (1–5). In the closure of the ode, however, the comasts have by now arrived at Chromius' palace and sing around the crater (48–53). In the *First Nemean* the performer situates himself at the dividing line between open and closed space, namely at the courtyard of Chromius' palace (19–20). At this liminal spot, which affords greater audibility and visibility to the performer than the banquet awaiting him inside the house, he sings of Chromius without forgetting to mention his hospitality and his cosmopolitan banquets.[49]

Through a comparative study of the depiction of the symposium of the *First Olympian* and the *First* and *Ninth Nemeans*, I argue elsewhere in detail that the primary function of sympotic imagery is not to indicate the intended performance context, but to strip Hieron and Chromius of their tyrannical and violent features and attribute to them the characteristics of mild, hospitable, and affable statesmen.[50] For the purposes of the present discussion I will restrict myself to one piece of testimony which is much later, but exemplifies the problems of the tyrant's participation in the symposium. In the fictional dialog between Hieron and

---

47 The mention of Ganymedes' later arrival on Olympus points up Pelops' sympotic duties; see *Olympian* 1.42–44.
48 See e.g. Krummen 1990, 164–65 and Slater 1989.
49 See Athanassaki 2009, ch. 3. 2–3.
50 Athanassaki 2009, ch. 3. 2–5.

Simonides, Xenophon makes the tyrant of Syracuse account for the incompatibility between the role of tyrant and that of symposiast:

> Βούλομαι δέ σοι, ἔφη, ὦ Σιμωνίδη, κἀκείνας τὰς εὐφροσύνας δηλῶσαι ὅσαις ἐγὼ χρώμενος ὅτ' ἦν ἰδιώτης, νῦν ἐπειδὴ τύραννος ἐγενόμην, αἰσθάνομαι στερόμενος αὐτῶν. ἐγὼ γὰρ ξυνῆν μὲν ἡλικιώταις ἡδόμενος ἡδομένοις ἐμοί, συνῆν δὲ ἐμαυτῷ, ὁπότε ἡσυχίας ἐπιθυμήσαιμι, διῆγον δ' ἐν συμποσίοις πολλάκις μὲν μέχρι τοῦ ἐπιλαθέσθαι πάντων εἴ τι χαλεπὸν ἐν ἀνθρωπίνῳ βίῳ ἦν, πολλάκις δὲ μέχρι τοῦ ᾠδαῖς τε καὶ θαλίαις καὶ χοροῖς τὴν ψυχὴν συγκαταμιγνύναι, πολλάκις δὲ μέχρι κοίτης ἐπιθυμίας ἐμῆς τε καὶ τῶν παρόντων. νῦν δὲ ἀπεστέρημαι μὲν τῶν ἡδομένων ἐμοὶ διὰ τὸ δούλους ἀντὶ φίλων ἔχειν τοὺς ἑταίρους, ἀπεστέρημαι δ' αὖ τοῦ ἡδέως ἐκείνοις ὁμιλεῖν διὰ τὸ μηδεμίαν ἐνορᾶν εὔνοιαν ἐμοὶ παρ' αὐτῶν· μέθην δὲ καὶ ὕπνον ὁμοίως ἐνέδρᾳ φυλάττομαι.[51]
>
> (Xenophon, *Hieron* 6, 1–3)
>
> 'But now, Simonides,' he continued, 'I want to show you all those delights that were mine when I was a private citizen, but which I now find are withheld from me since the day I became a despot. I communed with my fellows then: they pleased me and I pleased them. I communed with myself whenever I desired rest. I passed the time in carousing, often till I forgot all the troubles of mortal life, often till my soul was absorbed in songs and revels and dances, often till the desire of sleep fell on me and all the company. But now I am cut off from those who had pleasure in me, since slaves instead of friends are my comrades; I am cut off from my pleasant intercourse with them, since I see in them no sign of goodwill towards me. Drink and sleep I avoid as a snare.

Hieron attributes the incompatibility of the two roles to the radical change in the dynamics of his relationship with his *hetairoi*. The reciprocity of feelings and equality that governed his relations before he became tyrant are lost, because now his *hetairoi* are no longer his friends but his subjects. As a result he perceives no good will on their part and thus the pleasure of sympotic *homilia* is forever lost. At the end of their dialog Simonides points out that the situation is not irreversible provided that Hieron transforms into a mild, generous, and moderate ruler who invests his money, power, and energy in the city and the citizens (*Hieron* 9–11). Pindar is not of course a political theorist, but I suggest that a similar motivation lies behind the representation of Hieron as an affable listener in the *First Pythian*. In what follows, I will examine the communicative strategy of casting the speaker in the role of the tyrant's political adviser at the closure of the ode.

---

51 The citation and translation are taken from Marchant's Loeb edition.

Wilamowitz who, as we have seen, posited a public choral performance before the citizen body of Aetna, thought that the recipient of the political advice could not be the tyrant of Syracuse, but must be his young and inexperienced son, Deinomenes. Moreover, correlating the didactic tone of the closure with Pindar's emphasis on the freedom of the citizens of Aetna in the fourth triad (61–70), Wilamowitz thought that Hieron must have been displeased, for he was in no need of a preacher and his idea of freedom was different from that of the Theban aristocrat. According to Wilamowitz, the consequence of Hieron's annoyance with Pindar was to ask Bacchylides to celebrate his Olympic victory in 468.[52] Why Hieron did not ask Pindar to celebrate his subsequent Olympic victory is an intriguing question, but in light of our evidence the answer must remain open. More promising, in my view, is Wilamowitz's distinction between monarchic and aristocratic mentality.

In this ode Pindar cautiously delimits the appeal of encomiastic song and calls attention to the role of audience response in its posthumous survival. He also foregrounds the sympotic repertoire as a decisive factor for the survival of glorious deeds through song. In Pindar's time political paraenetic speech had had a longstanding sympotic legacy as is clear from the poetry of Alcaeus and Theognis. In this sense, it was a most appropriate medium for painting Hieron's profile in aristocratic colors.[53] Songs casting Hieron in the role of affable listener could stand far better chances than eulogies of appealing to aristocratic circles over which there would be a day when he could have no control. Wilamowitz may well have been right in thinking that aristocratic peer idiom was not particularly welcome at the monarchic court. In such a case the poetic strategy was lost on the tyrant. Yet if Hieron gave his consent for

---

[52] Wilamowitz 1922, 302–304. Interestingly enough Bacchylides chose to sing of the *philophron areta* of Croesus in *Ode* 3 for Hieron's Olympic victory in 468.

[53] For the efforts of the Deinomenids to win the approval of the Panhellenic aristocracy see Kurke 1999, 133–34. For their conformity with the Panhellenic aristocratic dedicatory idiom see Harrell 2002 who, however, asserts that in contrast to the monumental dedications at Olympia and Delphi, whereby the Deinomenids presented themselves as private citizens in accordance with aristocratic custom, the poetry that Pindar and Bacchylides composed for them targeted a local audience. The view that Pindar and Bacchylides composed for local consumption (reiterated in Harrell 2006) fails to account for the Panhellenic aspirations of the epinician poets, frequently and openly expressed, and the Panhellenic diffusion of their songs on which see Hubbard 2004.

the performance of the ode at a public festival in Aetna, it is not unlikely that he had understood the advantages of the poetic strategy for his public image.

The communicative strategy is particularly powerful if, with Wilamowitz, we imagine the performance of the ode by a chorus of citizens in the presence of the older and the younger king, some officials, their fellow-citizens and possibly delegates from other Sicilian cities. Some and possibly all members of the audience surely knew that the song was composed by the Theban poet. During the performance, however, they witnessed their fellow citizens affirming their freedom by giving advice to their king. As Stehle nicely puts it, what mattered was not who had put together the text but the fact that the performers '*affirmed it by speaking the words in public*'.[54] The concluding speech serves as living proof of the divinely fashioned freedom that Hieron bestowed on the city following Dorian law upon its foundation, of which the chorus had earlier sung (τῷ πόλιν κείναν θεοδμάτῳ σὺν ἐλευθερίᾳ/Ὑλλίδος στάθμας Ἱέρων ἐν νόμοις ἔκτισσε, 61–62). The *parrhesia* of the chorus was not obviously spontaneous, but on the poet's part it was a brilliant stroke highlighting the affinities rather than the differences in terms of civic liberties between the people of Aetna and the aristocratic Dorian world.[55] Hieron, who had violently displaced the people of Catane in order to found Aetna, was clearly more in need of good public relations with the rest of the Greek world than the young Deinomenes.[56] For this reason, I think that the aim of the poetic strategy is to promote the benevolent image of Hieron rather than of Deinomenes. But the truth of the matter is that the second-person reference in the last triad is indeterminable.

The ambiguity of the identity of the addressee of the paraenetic speech could easily be resolved by the performers. All that was needed was a gesture or a turn towards Hieron or Deinomenes or towards both.[57] If however we divorce the performance of the song from its original celebratory occasion and consider it as a recurrent event in a

---

54 Stehle 1997, 15.
55 For Pindar's *parrhesia* in the enigmatic final triad of *Pythian* 2 see Stoneman 1984.
56 Diodorus Siculus 11.49. For the grim realities of the foundation of Aetna and Pindar's tendency to mask colonial violence see Athanassaki 2003, 119–22 with bibliography. For population displacements in Sicily under the tyrants see Lomas 2006.
57 For the variety of non-verbal communication see Boegehold 1999.

limitless series, as the examples of Croesus and Phalaris suggest, a new and interesting dimension of the deictic indeterminacy emerges. There is nothing in the final triad to restrict its relevance either to Hieron or Deinomenes. Its message is equally relevant to any tyrant, king, or even high-profile democratic statesman. This is a case where only *deixis ad oculos* can determine the identity of the addressee. If the song is performed in a totally different context, the singer can address the last triad to any qualifying addressee, whereas the first four would have a function similar to that of mythological or historical paradigms. The last triad can also be easily excerpted. We cannot know of course if the poet found this alternative appealing, but he must have been aware of such a possibility from personal experience of sympotic singing.

3. Sympotic performances: The diachronic axis

The *First Pythian* is certainly not the only Pindaric ode which begins by conjuring up the image of performance at a public festival and ends with glimpses of recurrent sympotic entertainment. The closest example is the *Sixth Pythian* which Pindar composed for the chariot victory of Theron's brother Xenocrates in 490. Pindar praises all three Emmenids, but addresses the song to Xenocrates' son, Thrasybulus.

The ode opens with a self-referential description of the chorus' procession to the temple of Apollo and the designation of their song as a treasure-house which is superior to monuments, because it is immune to the uncontrollable force of the elements of nature:

Ἀκούσατ᾿· ἦ γὰρ ἑλικώπιδος Ἀφροδίτας
 ἄρουραν ἢ Χαρίτων
ἀναπολίζομεν, ὀμφαλὸν ἐριβρόμου
χθονὸς ἐς νάιον προσοιχόμενοι·
Πυθιόνικος ἔνθ᾿ ὀλβίοισιν Ἐμμενίδαις
ποταμίᾳ τ᾿ Ἀκράγαντι καὶ μὰν Ξενοκράτει
ἑτοῖμος ὕμνων θησαυρὸς ἐν πολυχρύσῳ
Ἀπολλωνίᾳ τετείχισται νάπᾳ·

τὸν οὔτε χειμέριος ὄμβρος, ἐπακτὸς ἐλθών
 ἐριβρόμου νεφέλας
στρατὸς ἀμείλιχος, οὔτ᾿ ἄνεμος ἐς μυχούς
ἁλὸς ἄξοισι παμφόρῳ χεράδει
τυπτόμενον. φάει δὲ πρόσωπον ἐν καθαρῷ
πατρὶ τεῷ, Θρασύβουλε, κοινάν τε γενεᾷ

λόγοισι θνατῶν εὔδοξον ἅρματι νίκαν
Κρισαίαις ἐνὶ πτυχαῖς ἀπαγγελεῖ.   (*Pythian* 6, 1–18)

Listen! For indeed we are plowing once again
the field of bright-eyed Aphrodite
or of Graces, as we proceed to the enshrined
navel of the loudly rumbling earth,
where at hand for the fortunate Emmenidai
and for Akragas on its river, yes, and for Xenocrates,
a Pythian victor's
treasure house of hymns
has been built in Apollo's valley rich in gold,

one which neither winter rain, coming from abroad
as a relentless army
from a loudly rumbling cloud, nor wind shall buffet
and with their deluge of silt carry into the depths
of the sea. But in clear light its front
will proclaim a chariot victory,
famous in men's speech
shared by your father, Thrasyboulos, and your clan
won in the dells of Krisa.

Immediately after the assertive declaration of the immortality of his song for the Emmenids, the speaker turns to Thrasybulus and affirms the youth's devotion to his father by pointing out that he upholds the precepts which Chiron once gave to young Achilles, thereby introducing the first mythological paradigm (19–27). The second mythological paradigm relates the death of Antilochus at the hands of Memnon in order to save his father Nestor (28–43) and intensifies the idea of filial devotion. I argue elsewhere that the two mythological examples constitute a reconfiguration of the sculptural diptych of the East Frieze of the Siphnian treasury, which would be the sight that any choral procession heading to the temple of Apollo would see on its way.[58] One of the effects of the evocation of the Siphnian monument is to keep the scene of the choral procession in the foreground.

The end of the mythological narrative and the transition to the present marks a change of scenery:

Τὰ μὲν παρίκει· τῶν νῦν δὲ καὶ Θρασύβουλος
πατρῴαν μάλιστα πρὸς στάθμαν ἔβα,

πάτρῳ τ' <u>ἐπερχόμενος</u> ἀγλαΐαν {ἔδειξεν} ἅπασαν.
    νόῳ δὲ πλοῦτον <u>ἄγει</u>,

---

58 Athanassaki forthcoming b. See also Shapiro 1988.

ἄδικον οὔθ' ὑπέροπλον ἥβαν δρέπων,
σοφίαν δ' ἐν μυχοῖσι Πιερίδων·
τίν τ', Ἐλελίχθον, ἄρχεις ὃς ἱππιᾶν ἐσόδων,
μάλα ἁδόντι νόῳ, Ποσειδᾶν, προσέχεται.
γλυκεῖα δὲ φρὴν καὶ συμπόταισιν ὁμιλεῖν
μελισσᾶν ἀμείβεται τρητὸν πόνον.   (*Pythian* 6, 43–54)

Those things are past:
But of men now, Thrasyboulos
Has come closest to the standard of filial devotion,

while approaching his uncle in all manner of splendor.
He uses his wealth with intelligence,
he enjoys a youth without injustice or insolence,
and culls wisdom in the haunts of the Pierians.
And to you, Earthshaker, who rule the paths to horse
       racing,
he keeps close, Poseidon, with a mind you greatly favor.
And his sweet spirit,
in company with his drinking companions,
surpasses the perforated labor of bees.

The song that opens with the scene of a choral procession in progress ends with the image of Thrasybulus at the symposium in the company of his fellow-drinkers. The majority of scholars think that the opening of the song reflects its performance setting, but there are also some who favor the symposium as the locus of performance.[59] If our aim is to reconstruct the first performance, we must decide between the *via sacra* of the Delphic sanctuary and a symposium either in Delphi or Acragas.

Content and form show that, unlike the opening scene which describes a single act in progress, the concluding scene is iterative. Thrasybulus' emulation of his uncle Theron, the intelligent management of his wealth, his modest behavior, his enjoyment of poetry, his love for horse races, and his sweet sympotic manners are all expressed in present tenses and describe the young aristocrat's daily pattern of life at home and abroad. The phrase σοφίαν δ' ἐν μυχοῖσι Πιερίδων (sc. δρέπων) anticipates the entertainment of the sympotic *homilia* which closes the song. The sympotic scene here is a miniature version of the much more elaborate description of sympotic entertainment at Hieron's court in the *First Olympian*:

---

59 In favor of the Delphic sanctuary, see e.g. Bury 1892, 29–30; Wilamowitz 1922, 135–39; Farnell 1932, 183; Burton 1962, 15 and 17; Jakob – Oikonomidis 1994, 287; Race 1997a, 312. In favor of symposium: Boeckh 1821, 297 and 300; Clay 1999, 30–31; Carey 2001, 22, n. 20.

[...] <u>δρέπων</u> μὲν κορυφὰς ἀρετᾶν ἄπο πασᾶν,
<u>ἀγλαΐζεται</u> δὲ καί
μουσικᾶς ἐν ἀώτῳ,
οἷα <u>παίζομεν</u> φίλαν
ἄνδρες ἀμφὶ <u>θαμὰ</u> τράπεζαν. [...] (Olympian 1, 13–17)

[...] He culls the summits of all achievements
and is also glorified
in the finest of songs,
such as those we men often perform in play
about the friendly table. [...]

This is also an iterative description of sympotic entertainment which at the end of the song is also termed *homilia* (εἴη σέ τε [...] ἐμέ τε τοσσάδε νικαφόροις ὁμιλεῖν, 115–16). In addition to the different degree of elaboration, the other important difference between the sympotic versions of the *First Olympian* and the *Sixth Pythian* is that in the Olympic ode the song, which the speaker is about to sing on his lyre, is represented as part of the recurrent sympotic entertainment, whereas in the Pythian ode the performance of the song is situated outside the symposium, on the sacred way of the sanctuary. In the *Sixth Pythian*, the symposium clearly features as an alternative channel. In this sense the *First Pythian* offers a closer parallel in that the scene of public celebration recedes gradually into the background in order to yield the stage to recurrent sympotic performances. But unlike the *First Pythian* where reference is to symposia in general, Pindar here zooms in on symposia where the addressee is present either as guest or host.

Whether the *Sixth Pythian* was first performed as a processional song on the way to the temple of Apollo, as the speaker states in the opening, is impossible to ascertain, but we are on firmer ground with regard to the symposium as a channel for its survival through reperformance. Some twenty years later, after the death of Xenocrates and possibly Theron as well, Pindar composed another song for Thrasybulus, the *Second Isthmian*. In this song, which is full of reminiscences, Pindar stresses the familiarity of the Emmenid houses with comastic revels and songs:

καὶ γὰρ οὐκ ἀγνῶτες ὑμῖν ἐντὶ δόμοι
οὔτε κώμων, ὦ Θρασύβουλ', ἐρατῶν,
οὔτε μελικόμπων ἀοιδᾶν.

οὐ γὰρ πάγος οὐδὲ προσάντης
    ἁ κέλευθος γίνεται,
εἴ τις εὐδόξων ἐς ἀν-
    δρῶν ἄγοι τιμὰς Ἑλικωνιάδων. (Isthmian 2, 30–34)

> And so, your family's houses are not unfamiliar
> with delightful victory revels, O Thrasyboulos,
> nor with songs of honey-sweet acclaim.
>
> For there is no hill,
>   nor is the road steep,
> when one brings the honors of the Helikonian maidens
>   to the homes of famous men.

The diction is here general in order to give an overview of sympotic entertainment at the houses of the Emmenids. The immediately preceding enumeration of victories, however, serves as a reminder of the songs that Pindar and others had composed for them: (a) ll. 12–17 refer to Xenocrates' Isthmian victory in 488, which was celebrated by Simonides.[60] (b) l. 18 refers to Xenocrates' Pythian victory in 490, for which Pindar composed the *Sixth Pythian*. (c) In ll. 19–22 Pindar mentions Xenocrates' victory at the Panathenaea, for which no song has survived. (d) ll. 23–29 refer to Theron's Olympic victory, for which Pindar composed the *Second* and *Third Olympians*. Pindar also composed a sympotic song for Thrasybulus, which has survived (fr. 124), but the date of composition is unknown. In addition to the victory catalog there are numerous verbal echoes that allude to specific Pindaric songs.[61] Regardless of the pragmatics of their first performance, all these songs are now presented as part of the sympotic repertoire.

The picture of sympotic diachronical reperformance is completed in the epode, where Pindar directly links reperformance with the survival of memory of Xenocrates:

> μή νυν, ὅτι φθονεραὶ
>   θνατῶν φρένας ἀμφικρέμανται ἐλπίδες,
> μήτ' ἀρετάν ποτε σιγάτω πατρῴαν,
> μηδὲ τούσδ' ὕμνους· ἐπεί τοι
> οὐκ ἐλινύσοντας. αὐτούς ἐργασάμαν.
> ταῦτα, Νικάσιππ', ἀπόνειμον, ὅταν
> ξεῖνον ἐμὸν ἠθαῖον ἔλθῃς.   (*Isthmian* 2, 43–48)

---

60 The ode has not survived, but see *Scholia vetera in Isthm.* I, inscr. a, 18–21.
61 The phrase εἴ τις εὐδόξων ἐς ἀνδρῶν ἄγοι τιμὰς Ἑλικωνιάδων echoes the phrase σοφίαν δ' ἐν μυχοῖσι Πιερίδων (*Pythian* 6.49). The *hapax* μελίκομπος echoes *Pythian* 6.54 (μελισσᾶν ἀμείβεται τρητὸν πόνον) and the echo offers support to Kurke's suggestion that the reference in the conclusion of *Pyth.* 6 is to this very poem; see Kurke 1990. The description of Xenocrates' legendary hospitality and observance of festivals in ll. 39–42 echoes the diction of *Olympian* 3.39–40 where both Theron and Xenocrates are said to honor the Dioscuri.

> Therefore, since envious hopes
>   hang about the minds of all mortals,
> let the son never keep silent his father's excellence
> nor these hymns, for I truly
> did not fashion them to remain stationary.
> Impart these words to him, Nikasippos,
> when you visit my honorable host.

The use of the participle ἐλινύσοντας in the final line suggests that the *Sixth Pythian*, the poetic treasure-house of songs, was very much on Pindar's mind.[62] The *Second Isthmian* corroborates the view that the function of the concluding iterative sympotic scene in the *Sixth Pythian* is to introduce an alternative performance setting. In terms of the eternal survival of song, however, it is clear that it does not have the confident tone of the earlier ode. Pindar's urge to Thrasybulus to keep the songs going is a reminder that active involvement of the interested parties is required.

Comparison of the *Second Isthmian* with the *First Pythian* shows that Pindar presents Hieron with a far greater challenge. Both songs explore the posthumous survival of fame through song. Yet whereas in the case of Xenocrates Pindar treats the issue as a family matter, in the case of Hieron he sets up a model that breaks free of personal ties of all sort. The human diachronic axis of the *First Pythian* foregrounds the ever changing audiences as the ultimate judge. The reference to Athenian, Spartan, and Sicilian audiences points up the challenge of Panhellenic appeal. The sympotic performance context adds one further parameter, the aristocratic identity of the intended audiences.

4. εὔφωνοι θαλίαι and φόρμιγγες ὑπωρόφιαι: Posthumous prospects

Do tyrants fare well in the symposium? Xenophon's representation of Hieron makes clear that they do not, unless they lose their tyrannical features. Interestingly enough Xenophon chooses for the role of Hieron's political adviser a poet who tried his hand in a variety of genres including epinicians.[63] It seems at first that such a dialog between tyrant

---

62 See also the previous note.
63 For the attractive suggestion that Herodotus' account of the meeting of Solon and Croesus (I. 30–33) served as model of Xenophon's *Hieron* see Gray 1986.

and poet is only possible in Athenian aristocratic fiction long after their death. Yet the message of the *First Pythian* is a subtler version of Xenophon's fictional dialog. The iterative descriptions of divine and human performances, which are symmetrically positioned and mirror one another, frame Hieron's encomium and set the limits for human expectations. The first important message is that only divine song is eternally and unconditionally irresistible. On the human plane the posthumous fortunes of Croesus and Phalaris offer a balanced, but optimistic picture. Thus the second message is that the *ethos* of the tyrant can earn him a place in the entertainment of those who value equality and thrive in competition.[64] In practice, Pindar casts Hieron into the role of affable statesman, a *persona* which enhances his public image in his lifetime and opens up the possibility of his posthumous admission to circles which were not only traditionally hostile to tyrants, but even loved to sing songs directed against tyrants as well. Because of the magnitude of the challenge, however, Pindar does not go so far as to link the fortunes of Hieron explicitly with those of Croesus or even to wish the Sicilian tyrant openly a similar popularity. Thus the diachronic axis of sympotic reperformance only serves to open up a conceivable possibility which the poet could tacitly wish out of personal motives as well, namely the widest possible diffusion of his own songs.

According to Diodorus Siculus (11.49.2), in founding Aetna Hieron expected to enjoy the heroic honors which were accorded to city-founders after their death. The fall of the tyranny shortly after his death in 466 thwarted his plans. The old inhabitants of Catane came back and displaced the settlers of Aetna to Inessa. The displaced people of Aetna probably continued to honor their founder at the new site, but they could obviously not afford the splendor that Hieron must have envisaged when he conceived the plan.[65] In 470 Pindar could not foresee this outcome and could take for granted that Hieron's memory would survive in Sicily through song and cult. Thus the εὔφωνοι Θαλίαι, for which he prays to Apollo, were the expected context for Hieron's posthumous honors as well. Pindar's picture of the honors which the Rhodians accorded to Tlepolemus and the Cyreneans to Battus features sac-

---

64 For the fierce display of equality and relentless competition in the aristocratic symposium see Węcowski 2002.
65 Diodorus Siculus 11.66.4 reports that posthumous heroic honors were accorded to Hieron, but it is not clear whether he has in mind the period between Hieron's death and the expulsion of his colonists in 461 or a broader timespan.

rifices, athletic games, processions, and songs.[66] It is against such a background that Pindar's choices must be interpreted.[67] Reperformance in such a context of the songs, which Pindar composed for Hieron, was not an unreasonable expectation.[68]

If both poet and tyrant took posthumous honors in Aetna for granted, inclusion in the Panhellenic sympotic repertoire was the next step. In such an eventuality, however, the *ethos* had to be sympotic. Pindar could not turn Hieron into Cyrnus or even into Thrasybulus, but he could invest him with the φιλόφρων ἀρετά of a legendary king by casting the speaker into the role of the tyrant's political adviser. The choice of this particular communicative strategy is best explained if the targeted audience was Panhellenic.[69] That despite all effort Pindar did not perceive it as an easy task is obvious not only from his caution in not drawing too close a parallel between Croesus and Hieron, but from his emphasis on the importance of audience reception. In retrospect, however, Pindar's mention of the preferences of Spartan and Athenian audiences seems almost prophetic, for some of his songs for Hieron remained popular in Athens even through the years of radical democracy.[70]

---

66 For the posthumous honors of the mythical founder of Rhodes, Tlepolemus, see *Olympian* 7.77–81 with the discussion of Athanassaki 2003, 112. For the posthumous honors accorded to Battus see *Pythian* 5.93–104, where commemoration of the founder is linked to the Carneia. For the cults of city founders see Malkin 1987, 187–240.
67 Currie 2005, 258–9 suggests that the reference in *Pythian* 2.18–20 is to choruses of Locrian maidens singing in honor of Hieron in partial anticipation of future heroic honors. If he is right, in the poet's and the tyrant's minds Locri would be another venue for the choral reperformances of the songs for Hieron.
68 Bruno Currie draws my attention to the ancient testimony reporting Aeschylus' posthumous honors in Gela, which included reperformance of his dramas at the site of his tomb (*Life of Aeschylus*, 11: εἰς τὸ μνῆμα δὲ φοιτῶντες ὅσοις ἐν τραγωιδίαις ἦν ὁ βίος ἐνήγιζόν τε καὶ τὰ δράματα ὑπεκρίνοντο.)
69 Xenophon's *Hieron* is an extremely eloquent example of the reception of Hieron in Greek aristocratic circles. The importance of song for improving the image of the Sicilian tyrant is succinctly formulated by Arrian (*Anabasis* 1.12.2): ἀλλ' οὐδὲ ἐν μέλει ᾔσθη Ἀλέξανδρος, ἐν ὅτῳ Ἱέρων τε καὶ Γέλων καὶ Θήρων καὶ πολλοὶ ἄλλοι οὐδέν τι Ἀλεξάνδρῳ ἐπεοικότες, ὥστε πολὺ μεῖον γιγνώσκεται τὰ Ἀλεξάνδρου ἢ τὰ φαυλότατα τῶν πάλαι ἔργων. On this passage see Hornblower 2006, 162.
70 The most celebrated example is Aristophanes' parody of an *hyporchema* for Hieron (fr. 105) in the *Birds* (926–30 and 941–45). For the circulation of Pindar's odes in Athens see Irigoin 1952, 14–18 and Nagy 1990a, 382–413.

Apollonius Rhodius as an (anti-)Homeric Narrator: Time and Space in the *Argonautica*

Georg Danek

This paper offers preliminary observations on the structuring of storylines in time and space in the *Argonautica*. Whereas the category of time has always been at the centre of narratological interest, it will be seen that narratologists have more or less disregarded the category of space. For my analysis I will therefore draw on recent studies of spatial orientation and historical geography.

I begin with the category of time. Massimo Fusillo, who wrote one of the first full-length narratological studies on a classical subject,[1] did not show much interest in Apollonius' organisation of storylines. Neither does he in his detailed account of time management pay much attention to Apollonius' relationship with Homer. In recent years, significant progress has been made in our understanding of the intertextual relationship between Apollonius and Homer, thanks above all to Antonios Rengakos' work on Apollonius' meta-literary use of Homeric vocabulary.[2] Thus, most recent scholars aim at understanding Apollonius' relationship to Homer as an intertextual one in every respect, including narrative technique. One goal of future Apollonian studies might therefore be to develop a narratology of intertextuality.

These considerations should guide us also when we study the narrative representation of time and space in Apollonius. We should not content ourselves with looking at how the *Argonautica* is structured in terms of time management just by adopting Genette's narratological model; rather, we should ask how Apollonius adopted Homer's time-structuring devices and used them for his own purposes.

Within the broad field of narrative time management, I will concentrate on issues arising from the use of multiple storylines, i.e. questions

---

I would like to thank Johannes Haubold for helpful suggestions and for correcting my English.
1 Fusillo 1985, referring to Genette (1972) 1980.
2 Rengakos 1994.

of simultaneity vs. successivity.[3] Narratologists have not paid sufficient attention to these problems, despite the fact that we deal here with a favourite topic of Homeric scholarship, familiar to readers under the rubrique of 'Zielinski's Rule'.[4] As this topic has stimulated much interest during the last few years, I start with some preliminary remarks, that enable us to rule out certain misconceptions and to make the problems which Zielinski addressed (and partly created) amenable to a strictly narratological approach.

The most famous and most hotly debated aspects of Zielinski's complex system of rules may be formulated in the following way:

a) Homer presents events that belong to parallel storylines and are narrated by the primary narrator as being successive, i.e. never as being simultaneous.
b) Sometimes events presented as successive can be shown to be simultaneous 'in reality'.
c) It is our duty as Homer's readers to reconstruct the 'real' order of time which lies behind Homer's narrative representation of time.

Against these assumptions, we should remember that:

a) narrators represent events as imagined events,
b) there is no ulterior level of reality beyond the events as they are represented by the narrator,
c) thus, there is no hidden reality for us to uncover behind the narrator's representation of events.

This leads us to conclude:

a) Zielinski was right with his claim that Homer does not represent simultaneous events in parallel storylines,[5]
b) which means that Homer did not imagine those events which he recounts as being simultaneous either,

---

3 Klooster 2007 in his chapter on time in Apollonius spends only a short paragraph on this specific problem: 'Simultaneity and parallel storylines', 69 f.
4 Zielinski 1899–1901. The discussion has been best advanced by Krischer 1971; Patzer 1990; Rengakos 1995. See now Scodel 2008, and, for a summary, de Jong 2007, 30 f.
5 This principle has been recently questioned by several scholars who, however, can adduce only minor 'deviations' from the rule as a whole: See Olson 1995, 91–119; Rengakos 1998; Nünlist 1998. But see Danek 1998b.

c) but imposed artificial restrictions on his own use of possible timelines, including all the further sub-rules, i.e. further restrictions, which need not concern us here.[6]

Starting from this suggestion, I will try to show how Apollonius writes his epic for an audience that is accustomed to this set of rules as it is observed in the Homeric epics; and how, at a superficial level, he keeps very close to these rules, which means that Apollonius does not 'violate' Zielinski's rule, i.e. the 'law of successivity', any more than Homer does.

This may come as a surprise to scholars who have come to the opposite conclusion, namely that Apollonius in his narrative use of time differs significantly from Homer. Most readers of Apollonius will share their opinion, as Apollonius achieves quite different aesthetic effects from Homer, concerning both simple and complex narrative structures. But we shall see that the difference between Homer and Apollonius does not lie so much in his time management as such, as Apollonius does not violate Zielinski's rule any more than Homer does. Instead, I shall try to show that the difference may be located within the category of space, as well as the plurality of his narrator's voices.

But let us start from the beginning. Every reader of Apollonius is aware that through Books 1 and 2 of the *Argonautica* we get a single storyline which is identical with the movement of the Argonauts from their starting point, Iolcus, towards their goal, Colchis. Events are told in chronological order, and space is represented as unilinear, while events lying outside the route (both concerning time and space) are not visited directly but just referenced by the narrator's voice.

Up to this point, nobody would argue that Apollonius breaks Zielinski's rule, as a single storyline cannot include simultaneous events. Even so, we recognize that this way of narrating the story is markedly different from what we are used to in Homeric narrative. In both Homeric epics the narrative starts with a single storyline which immediately splits into two separate strands, and subsequently into many more. With the end of *Iliad* 1, we already have four parallel storylines, and with the end of Book 3, there are no fewer than seven separate storylines which, and this is the important thing about it, can resurface whenever the nar-

---

[6] Neither will we be concerned here with the question as to whether Homer inherited this set of rules from the epic tradition, or developed it by himself. See Danek 1998b.

rator wants them to reappear in the narrative. So what we see is a complex system of bifurcations and ramifications. Time is represented as a continuum, as the primary narrator never looks back in time when he switches to a different storyline.[7] So, of course, different storylines do exist, consisting in different persons staying at different places at the same time; but relevant actions are never represented as taking place simultaneously.

This results in artificial restrictions on how to represent possible storylines, i.e. possible worlds contained within time and space. In a similar vein, Homer visualizes space as one single line which contains several landmarks like beads on a string and which may be split up, at the most, into parallel lines within a plane.[8]

This – specifically narrative – way of representing space can be related to a more general conception of space which is usually associated with archaic Greek culture. According to one theory, the early Greeks did not perceive their geographical space as two-dimensional planes admitting of human coordination in orthogonal systems (surveys), but as pathways following narrow lines through planes and organized by means of landmarks which must be encountered in a specific order (routes), allowing no deviance or short cut, e.g. by crossing a plane along a diagonal.

It has been argued that this way of perceiving and dealing with space corresponds to an early stage of human development: mankind first perceived space through *landmarks*, then through *routes*, and only on the highest level of evolution through *surveys*. As far as their own (linear) movements through space are concerned, most people content themselves with routes, constructed by interconnected landmarks. Men learn to perceive two-dimensional space in its most complete sense only at a certain level of cultural development. Scholars have argued

---

[7] The only exception being when a new person (= new storyline) joins an already established storyline: here the primary narrator may go back in time to report how the new person came to appear in the narrative. Otherwise the use of analepsis is limited to secondary narrators who, however, are bound by further restrictions: see Steinrück 1992.

[8] We can thus explain some notorious problems of Homeric scholarship, for instance the position of the river Scamander in the Trojan plain: the battlefield is represented as a line of possible movements between the Achaean ships and the city of Troy, containing several landmarks which – apart from their symbolic connotations – suggest only a certain distance from Troy viz. the Achaean ships: see Thornton 1984, 150–163.

that within the cultural evolution of the Greeks this last stage can be identified with the development of the first maps, or even world maps, in the late 6th century B.C.[9]

Here as elsewhere, ontogeny reflects phylogeny, which means that we all learn to orient ourselves in space during our first years of childhood: from landmarks via routes to a full perception of space (surveys).[10] Consequently, in every society a certain number of human individuals remains at an earlier stage of evolution than humankind at its culturally most sophisticated, and vice versa: certain exceptional individuals perceive and construct space in its full two-dimensional aspect while most contemporaries still content themselves with finding their way by remembering landmarks along routes. It can be shown that Homer had a clear vision of human actions and movements in two-dimensional space.[11] But for narratorial reasons he usually constricts himself to representing actions and movements in space as taking part along a string of landmarks belonging to one single route. As a consequence, movements belonging to separate storylines are not usually related to one another; but if so, they are plotted as either taking place on the same line at different times,[12] or at different points of the same line, or on parallel lines.[13]

Returning to Apollonius, we realize that his narrator, by keeping to a single storyline in Books 1 and 2 of the *Argonautica*, restricts himself even more than Homer does. Here we find no bifurcations opening up separate storylines at all and, as a consequence, no simultaneous ac-

---

9 See Janni 1984; Gehrke 1998; Brodersen (1995) 2003.
10 Piaget – Inhelder 1948.
11 So far, there have only been preliminary studies of the topic, touching on specific details: Homer's vision of the geography of the Greek mainland and the Aegeis in the Catalogue of Ships (Danek 2004); the plotting of the Aegean in *Od*. 3 and 9 (Danek 1998a, see the index s.v. 'Nostos'); the geography of the Trojan plain (Herzhoff 2008).
12 This is the case in *Il*. 6, where Hector moves along a single route meeting the following landmarks: battlefield – city gate – palace entrance (Hecuba) – Paris' thalamos – Andromache's thalamos – back to the city gate – battlefield. The movements of all other persons run along the same route, only at different times; only Hecuba prolongs the line from the palace to Athena's temple which is located at the top of the city (6.297).
13 I know of no relevant studies on this topic. First results might be achieved through an analysis of the *teichomachia* where the narrator views movements both forward and backward, and sideward, along the battlelines. For first observations on battlefield movements, see now Wenger 2008a and 2008b.

tions in parallel storylines. Thus we may conclude that Apollonius limits his narrator's view of the world in an even more artificial way than Homer does: he writes at a time when fully developed maps did exist and, even if they were not part of everyday cultural life, they were discussed in learned circles like the Museion in Alexandria. Despite all that, Apollonius signals that he views the world he represents in his narrative in the same archaically restricted way as Homer does, indeed, that he does so even more consistently. We can see how Apollonius operates with his own set of restrictions when we look at the few passages in Books 1 and 2 of the *Argonautica* where the single storyline almost, but not quite, splits in two.

Only once on their way from Iolcus to Colchis do the Argonauts lose their way and are driven in a wrong direction which leads them away from their pre-determined pathway (1.1015 ff.: Doliones – Gegeneis – Doliones). But in this case, they are driven back exactly along the same route which they had travelled the day before,[14] and their mistake results in the killing of their previous hosts *per errorem*, including their young king Cyzicus. After the Argonauts have recognized their fatal error, they resume their journey along the same pre-determined pathway.

Only once do we get an actual bifurcation in the Homeric style, in the epsiode of the rape of Hylas by a nymph (1.1187 ff.). It is on this occasion that Heracles is left behind by the Argonauts. However, when Heracles subsequently sets out on his own journey, he does not form the subject of a new storyline; as a character in the narrative, he is literally lost from view, both by the Argonauts within the narrative, and by the narrator and the narratees. At several points later on in the narrative, the narrator will remark that Heracles is still on his way, that he has left traces which can be seen by the Argonauts, etc. But the narrator never sets eyes on him again.[15]

In Book 2, the Argonauts meet the blind singer Phineus who is beset by the Harpyies. When these monsters return to harrass him once more, the Boreads pursue them until the goddess Iris intervenes and puts an end to the chase. Just as the Boreads begin their long journey back (2.295 f., ὑπέστρεφον ἄψ ἐπὶ νῆα/σεύεσθαι, impf.), the Argonauts start to wash the seer (2.301, τόφρα + aor.), make sacrifice, feast

---

14 See Clauss 1993, 160–67.
15 See Rengakos 2004, 296 f., against Gummert 1992, 68–71, who argues that the Heracles storyline may be compared to the absent Achilles in the *Iliad*.

and afterwards wait the whole night for the return of the Boreads. In the meantime, Phineus gives them a detailed prophecy of their future journey and some of the challenges that await them. When he has finished the Boreads arrive and give a precise report of what we already know from the primary narrator's account. Here we have a true bifurcation, i.e. the branching off of a secondary storyline which, however, will soon rejoin the main storyline, as we know from the outset. Time is treated in such a way that no simultaneous actions are reported.[16] Thus, we have a bifurcation of storylines that does not result in separate narrative threads but rather leaves us with a temporary side-line, of which we know from the outset that it will soon rejoin the main storyline.

I would now like to turn to a case of spectacular non-communication between two possible storylines. In *Argonautica* Book 2, Apollon crosses the pathway of the Argo in a very literal sense: he appears from the right on his way from Lycia to the Hyperboreans, steps on the island where the Argonauts are moored, and proceeds on his journey through the air to the left, i.e. across the Black Sea (2.674 ff.). The encounter does not lead to any physical contact, and the Argonauts, after making sacrifice to the god, proceed on their way. Here we get two storylines which are not related either in time or space: while space is articulated precisely through geographical indexing, Apollo's movement is so swift that the Argonauts do not even understand what they have seen. It is as if time stood still for the Argonauts while Apollo passes by at the speed of light. The reader senses that there exists an entire world of actions beyond that of the main narrative: Innumerable different storylines potentially intersect with one another in ways that are beyond our control; yet this entire cosmos remains hidden from the narrator's view and, therefore, the readers' perception, too.

Only on one occasion in Books 1 and 2 of the *Argonautica* is a separate new storyline added to the main narrative:[17] at the end of Book 2

---

16 Most interpreters understand τόφρα (2.301) as pointing back in time. But in combination with the aorist tense ἱρεύσαντο (302), τόφρα must mean 'at this exact moment in time', and not 'during the same period of time'; it goes without saying that τόφρα cannot mean 'at a previous moment in time'. Apollonius may echo the usage of τόφρα in *Odyssey* 3.464.

17 In all other cases the persons whom the Argonauts meet form no separate storyline, as they have no story apart from their meeting with the Argonauts. The Phrixids are the first persons to join the Argonauts on their voyage.

the Argonauts meet the sons of Phrixus who have set off from Colchis to sail to Greece, their father's homeland; they have been shipwrecked and land on the same island where the Argonauts happen to be staying over night. In accordance with Zielinski's Rule, the narrator here retraces his steps to explain where the new storyline comes from,[18] and reports the Phrixids' journey from its beginning up to the moment of their meeting with the Argonauts.[19] What concerns us here is the fact that the Phrixids arrive from exactly the opposite direction, i.e. along the same route which the Argonauts will travel the next day to reach their intended destination, Colchis. So even here, when for the first time two different storylines meet and are represented as two different movements in space, we have only one dimension of space, namely the line of the Argo's pathway.

This observation is crucial for our understanding of how the interrelated systems of time and space are represented in Homer and in Apollonius: in Books 1 and 2 of the *Argonautica* Apollonius represents space as a single line leading from Greece to Colchis. By this method, Apollonius deliberately restricts his perspective on time and space, producing a sense of tunnel vision, a claustrophobic movement along a pre-determined line which allows no departures or alternatives. We get the impression that the narrator's view is strictly limited to a camera's eye installed on top of the mast of the Argo. Anything else that catches the narrator's interest is just referenced by his voice from the off while his main object moves forward and passes by landmarks, objects and peoples.

This preliminary distinction between the 'narrator's view' and the 'narrator's voice'[20] may prove valuable for understanding the main dif-

---

18 Compare the prehistory of Lycaon (*Il.* 21.34–48), or the prehistory of Theoclymenus (*Od.* 15.223–256), both brought in by the narrator at the point where the 'new' person is introduced into the narrative.

19 The flashback contains only the verses 2.1093–7, as can be seen by the synchronization signals: 1097 νήσοιο refers to 1031 νήσου; 1100 ἡμάτιοι to 1032 ἡμάτιοι. Thus the shipwreck of the Phrixids is marked as taking place while the Argonauts are already waiting on the island. *Contra* Fusillo (1985, 261): 'si passa ad eventi che si sono svolti in simultaneità con un tratto già narrato del viaggio argonautico'; similarly Klooster 2007, 71. But Apollonius, by artificially synchronizing the two strands of action, follows good Homeric practice: see Danek 1999.

20 One may think here of similar categories used in point-of-view studies. Cf. Stanzel 1955 ('auktoriale Erzählsituation' vs. 'personale Erzählsituation'). Better results may be achieved by integrating recent film studies, cf. Bach 1997.

ference between Apollonius' narrative technique and that of Homer (as the 'objective narrator' *par excellence*). Those differences concern the categories of both time and space: the Apollonian narrator's view in Books 1 and 2 of the *Argonautica* catches only a single unidirectional movement progressing in time along a single one-dimensional line through space. This produces the illusion of one person's strictly limited perspective on the action, the perspective, moreover, of somebody staying very close to the events. The narrator's voice, on the other hand, comments on this journey by freely moving backward and forward, both in time and space.[21]

So much for Books 1 and 2 of the *Argonautica*. Things change immediately when we come to Book 3. As soon as the Argonauts reach Colchis and moor their ship on the river Phasis, the narrator's view switches to mount Olympus, and we get for the first time a fully fledged scene of the gods. That means that for the first time we see a second storyline which is completely separated from the main line, the pathway of the Argonauts. Storylines will multiply in the course of Book 3, and this tendency might give the impression that we are finally presented with an almost unlimited amount of possible storylines which combine and interact with one another. This sudden proliferation of storylines is made explicit when the Argonauts arrive at king Aietes' palace. The narrator describes the ordering of buildings inside the palace as they are viewed by the Argonauts (and perhaps explained to them by the Phrixids). The narrator enumerates the houses or rooms inhabited by the members of the royal family: Aietes (together with his wife), Apsyrtus, Chalciope, and Medea. With the exception of Apsyrtus, these persons appear in the courtyard immediately afterwards.[22] We will need all of them in the ensuing narrative, as the Argonauts will interact with

---

21 Cf. Klooster 2007, 80: 'Collecting and combining the manifold historical, ethnographical and literary sources that refer to events somehow related to the Argo's journey, Apollonius turns this event into a pivotal point in Greek history.' Klooster is concerned only with time, but his judgement applies to the category of space, as well.

22 Here we catch the difference to the scene of Hector's arrival at the palace (*Iliad* 6), which Apollonius uses as his model: in the *Iliad*, the different storylines are kept separate from one another, as Hector moves on his route from one landmark to the next, interacting with the subjects of the different storylines one after another.

Aietes himself, with both his daughters, Chalciope and Medea, and, later on in Book 4, with his son Apsyrtus.[23]

So we are presented with four potential storylines which we will follow through the course of Book 3: the Argonauts, Aietes, Chalciope, and Medea. Soon we realise that there is even a fifth storyline, the Phrixids, who were added to the main line at the end of Book 2 and who will mediate between the different lines, running to and fro; their storyline will in turn split into that of Argus, on the one hand, and that of his three brothers, on the other hand. In the same way, one or more Argonauts will branch off from the rest of the companions. So we get a complex web of manifold actions occurring in different places, interacting, connecting, splitting up and combining again.

The question arises how the narrator represents the temporal relationship between these different storylines. Most scholars assume that Apollonius represents the events in these storylines as taking place simultaneously. Francis Vian postulates no less than five instances of simultaneous action in Book 3.[24] In each case he assumes that the narrator goes back in time when he switches from one storyline to another and fills in the same section of time once again. If we accept Vian's argument, we would at one point in Book 3 end up with no fewer than four parallel storylines, each represented by the narrator as occuring simultaneously. Vian comments on this result, which is in striking breach of Zielinski's set of rules, in the following way: 'La narration atteint rarement pareille complexité dans l'épopée et même dans le roman grecs.' The same point is made by Richard Hunter who explains most related passages in a similar way,[25] and by Antonios Rengakos.[26]

Contrary to what these critics have argued, it can be shown that even in Book 3 of the *Argonautica* Apollonius never violates Zielinski's rule, and that the apparent differences in the management of storylines

---

23   The non-appearance of Apsyrtus in this scene foreshadows that he will be of no need in the narrative as long as the Argonauts are within the reach of the palace.

24   Vian 1980, 5: 'On sait que chez Homère deux actions ne peuvent se dérouler simultanément en des lieux différents: pendant que l'une s'accomplit, le poète est constraint de mettre en sommeil les autres personnages. Apollonios s'affranchit de cette servitude.'

25   Hunter 1989b, 24 with n. 102.

26   Rengakos 2004, 297: 'Eine ähnliche Komplexität der Handlungsführung erreichen selbst die in dieser Hinsicht vergleichbaren Szenen im 6. Buch der *Ilias* oder im 4. Buch der *Odyssee* bzw. in den Palastszenen des letzten Teiles des jüngeren Epos nicht.'

in Homer and Apollonius must be explained in a different way. To substantiate this claim, I would ideally like to present a careful analysis of the whole of Book 3, concentrating on the use of the Greek verbal aspect system with every single change of scene. But I limit myself here to presenting a detailed analysis of the passage where Vian postulates four parallel storylines with simultaneous actions, 3.572–616.

572 After a long discussion Jason sends the Phrixid Argus from the ship to his mother Chalciope in the palace. With the imperfect προΐαλλε we leave him as he goes on his way, just as we leave Hector on his way from the battlefield to Troy (*Il.* 6.117 f. τύπτε, impf.).

573–5 The Argonauts draw their ship ashore (575 ἐπέκελσαν, aor.).

576 Aietes assembles the Colchians immediately afterwards (576 αὐτίκα ... ποιήσατο, aor.). Hunter (*ad* 3.576) comments: 'Aietes' assembly follows straight on from his dismissal of the embassy in 438. Three simultaneous actions are described: Medea's emotions (443–71), planning by the Argonauts (472–575) and Aietes' plans (576–608).' Contrary to this, we can read Aietes' action as a direct response to the Argonauts' final landing (573–5): Aietes in his speech to the assembly explicitly mentions the ship which, up to that time, has been hidden from the sight of the Colchians. We may take this as an attempt on the part of the narrator to signal a forced synchronism.

579–608 Aietes' address to the assembly is reported in indirect speech (579 στεῦτο – 607 ἀπείλεε, all verbs in the imperfect). Thus the whole assembly scene remains in the background and is marked as not visualized and not represented, but just referenced, by the narrator.

609–615 In the meantime (609 τόφρα) Argos arrives at the palace (609 μετιών, imperfect aspect) and talks to his mother (610 παρηγορέεσκεν, impf.), who has already been considering the situation by herself (612 πρόσθεν μητιάασκε, impf.). Here two situations overlap, both presented in the imperfect tense and thus not focussed by the narrator's view as detailed actions. We may speculate that Chalciope was already pondering events when Aietes started his assembly, that Argus arrives at the palace while Aietes is still speaking, and that Argus and his mother start their discussion while Aietes finishes his speech. But as neither situation is brought into the foreground, no specific actions (nor their temporal relationship) are made visible to the narratees.

616 ff. While this is going on, Medea falls asleep (616 κατελώφεεν, impf.). The narrator has already shifted seamlessly from one background (Aietes) to another (Argus and Chalciope); now he shifts to a third background (Medea) which he will bring into the foreground for presenting a detailed description of Medea's inner feelings, including a dream, a soliloquy and a simile, until finally Chalciope joins her for a dialogue.

The treatment of Aietes will remain symptomatic of the handling of storylines in the rest of Book 3, and indeed in Book 4, too: after his first meeting with the Argonauts, Aietes never gets a direct speech again; instead, we are told about his silent movements to and fro, and there is a second assembly scene at the beginning of Book 4 which once again is reported to us only in indirect speech.[27] The same is true of Apsyrtus who becomes an important agent of the narrative in Book 4, but even there never gets a single direct speech.

Even the treatment of Chalciope follows the same pattern: she participates in fully narrated scenes when she meets the Argonauts, i.e. the representatives of the main storyline (3.253–270), and when she talks to Medea, who represents the second main storyline (3.673–740). Yet, when she plots with her sons, she never gets a direct speech but remains in the background. Thus the narrator does not represent her as the protagonist of an independent storyline but as a person who becomes visible to him only when she comes into contact with one of the two main storylines.

To conclude this section of the argument: Book 3 opens by signalling the possibility of at least four different storylines. Yet, half way through the book we realize that Apollonius represents only two of them (the Argonauts, and Medea) as fully viewed by the narrator while the rest of them (Aietes, Chalciope, as well as the additional Phrixids) are restricted to their roles as intermediaries and interlocutors of the two main parties: their actions are not viewed but only referenced by the narrator.

Medea, we recall, has been stung into action by Eros' arrow: the single storyline of Books 1 and 2 has been supplemented at the beginning

---

27 As is well known, Homer almost completely avoids the use of indirect speech.

of the second half of the *Argonautica* only by the intervention of the gods, which was in turn initiated by the narrator's invocation of Erato as an additional Muse (3.1). It is only the gods who make us see more than the Argonauts moving forward on their pre-determined path. The difference is one of quality as well as quantity because only Eros/Erato allows us to look inside Medea and catch a glimpse of her most intimate feelings.

Taking all this together we see that it is not the category of simultaneity which makes the web of storylines in the *Argonautica* more complex than that of the *Iliad* and the *Odyssey*: neither the greater number of parallel storylines nor the introduction of simultaneous actions can be called innovative compared to Homer. To fully understand how Apollonius' technique works, we must return to the category of space and ask how Apollonius represents the spatial movements of persons acting in separate storylines. For this I will take a closer look at two passages in Book 3.

In 3.159, after the opening scenes on Olympus, Eros sets off to Colchis, to shoot Medea with his arrow. We have already heard that, while the gods plotted on Olympus, the Argonauts have been lying low on board their ship which is anchored in the river Phasis (3.6–7, μίμνον … λελοχημένοι, impf.). Now, Eros leaves the gates of mt. Olympus (3.159 ἐξήλυθεν, aor.). There follows a description of the gates in the present tense (3.160 ἐστι, 161 ἀνέχουσι, 163 ἐρεύθεται); the description of a timeless condition is thus presented in the narrator's voice. Then we switch back to the epic past (3.165, φαίνετο) which means that the narrator's gaze now merges with that of Eros (secondary focalization). Eros scans the world, and gazes more specifically at the cities of men and the streams of rivers. That we are indeed dealing here with Eros' outlook becomes even clearer from the expression ἀν' αἰθέρα πολλὸν ἰόντι (166). It is only now that we realize that Eros has already started his flight through the aether to reach his goal, Colchis: the view from Olympus has merged with Eros' view from mid-aether, as he makes his way to Colchis. Thus our gaze is directed at Eros' goal or, more precisely, his *goals*, for they are yet to coalesce: later on, we will learn that Eros must direct his arrow at Medea from behind Jason's back (3.281 f.). When leaving Olympus, Eros has before his mind's eye a single goal that involves both Medea and Jason. Yet, his goal does not yet exist as a unified situation, because the Argonauts, including Jason, are still waiting on their ship and Jason has not yet joined Medea.

The narrator leaves Eros on his flight in the imperfect aspect (3.166, ἰόντι), and switches back to the Argonauts who are still on board their ship (3.168, λελοχημένοι ἠγορόωντο, harks back to 3.7, λελοχημένοι). This is in perfect accordance with Homeric narrative technique: the narrator has left the Argonauts doing nothing, waiting in the imperfect tense, while the scene on Mount Olympus took place. When we now meet them again they are still lying in wait, although in the meantime they have begun talking (3.168, ἠγορόωντο, impf.). While we listen to Jason's ensuing speech and follow the Argonauts on their way to Aietes' palace, Eros will be on *his* way to Colchis, in the imperfect tense, until the narrator's gaze meets him again at the moment of his arrival at Colchis (3.275).

All this reminds us of how Homer arranges separate storylines in time. Remember, for instance, the famous scene in *Iliad* 6: Hector leaves the battlefield for the city of Troy to meet his mother.[28] The narrator switches back to the battlefield where we witness the famous encounter between Glaucus and Diomedes; after this, he switches back to Hector who is just arriving at the gates of Troy (6.237). A foregrounded scene containing human activity bridges a scene in the background with human inactivity, i.e., in this case, predictable movement.[29]

And yet there is still a crucial difference between Apollonius and Homer: Eros sets out towards a goal which does not yet exist at the moment of his departure. For him to be able to reach his goal, Jason has to make his way from the ship to the palace during his flight. Only then can Eros arrive at what he visualised as his destination when embarking on his journey. This allows us to conclude that it is the twofold goal envisioned by Eros which lies behind the notion of 'the cities of men and the holy streams of rivers' (3.164 f.): Medea is already in the city, but Jason is still on the river.

Thus we are left with a sort of triangle in a plane, with the three pivots Olympus, river, and palace. While Eros makes his way from Olympus to the palace, Jason must make *his* way from the river to the palace. As far as I can see, Homer never portrays such interconnected triangular movements on a plane, as he always visualizes space as one-

---

[28] The narrator turns his gaze away from Hector as he strolls away, mentioning as a last detail his shield rim bouncing on his calves and his neck (6.117). Our last glimpse of Hector is from behind, moving away and fading out.
[29] See already Zielinski 1899–1901, 422.

dimensional lines structured by landmarks, or as parallel lines which separate and re-unite again.

There is a second prominent example of this new technique in Apollonius: Still in book 3, Medea goes from the palace to the temple of Artemis in order to meet Jason; when she arrives there, Jason sets off from the ship after he has been informed by the Phrixids that Medea has already left for the temple (3.913–6); thus we may conclude that the Phrixids (who were told by Argus to do so, 3.825–27) have come from the palace to the ship to deliver this information. So here again, we get a triangle, consisting of the three relevant locations which are interconnected by the movements of three different (groups of) characters: palace, river, and temple.

It would be difficult to produce full evidence for the negative assertion that those triangular relationships in space cannot be found in Homer.[30] Homer, of course, is well aware that human activity in space is organized in such a way as to lead to triangular (or even more complicated) constellations, too. But he avoids representing such complex interrelationships in his narrative and, instead, sticks to his basic system of bifurcation, concerning space, as well as time.[31] I will show how this simple model works in a passage in *Odyssey* 15–16 where within 533 verses no less than eight different storylines are involved – an unusually large number, even for the more sophisticated of the two Homeric epics.

At the end of Book 15 Telemachus arrives from Pylus. He disembarks early in the morning on the shore of Ithaca at Phorcys' harbour, which is known to us from Odysseus' landing in Book 13. He tells his comrades to proceed on their route to the city's main harbour and announces that he himself will join them in the evening after having paid a visit to Eumaeus 15.503–5). The comrades sail towards the town (553 πλέον, impf.) and Telemachus goes inland to Eumaeus' hut where he meets Eumaeus and Odysseus. After a first reception, he sends Eumaeus

---

30 A first systematic reading of the Odyssey confirms my assumption for this epic.
31 At one occasion we even get a narrator's comment on this technique: in the 'Doloneia', Agamemnon tells Menelaus to fetch Aias and Idomeneus, and announces that he himself will join Nestor to meet the sentinels outside the camp. Menelaus asks if he should join him again after having deposited the two comrades with the sentinels. Agamemnon answers: αὖθι μένειν, μή πως ἀβροτάξομεν ἀλλήλοιιν/ἐρχομένω· πολλοὶ γὰρ ἀνὰ στρατόν εἰσι κέλευθοι (*Il.* 10.65 f.). As a narrator's comment, this means: 'Let's stick to the bifurcation scheme; otherwise we get all our storylines mixed up!'

to Penelope to tell her that he has savely arrived, without letting the suitors know it (16.130–134). Eumaeus goes on his way, and in the meantime we witness the recognition scene between Telemachus and Odysseus. The narrator leaves the two of them still plotting and switches to the ship of Telemachus' comrades who are just reaching the city's main harbour (κατήγετο, impf.). The comrades send a herald to the palace to tell Penelope of her son's stay with Eumaeus (16.328–332). The herald meets Eumaeus before entering the palace, they enter the palace together, the herald pronounces openly 'Lady Queen, your son is back' (16.337), while Eumaeus gives her a full account of events standing close to her (16.338 f.).[32] He then leaves the palace to go back to his hut (16.340 f.). The suitors react to the news by stepping out of the *megaron* and plotting in front of the entrance door. At this moment they see the suitors' ship as it enters the harbour (16.351–353). They go down to the shore, are told about the failed assassination attempt, go on plotting against Telemachus, and return to the palace (16.407 f.). There follows a further conversation between the suitors and Penelope, and we leave the palace with Penelope having fallen asleep (16.450 f.). At this moment (16.452, ἑσπέριος) Eumaeus arrives at his hut and gives his report to Telemachus. When Telemachus asks him if the suitors have returned from their ambush, he replies that on his way back, at a landmark named Ἑρμαῖος λόφος, he saw a ship entering the harbour filled with armed men (16.470–475).

This complicated web of criss-crossing storylines contains an explicit comment on the simultaneity of parallel movements by a secondary narrator. Nevertheless, space is still constructed as just two parallel lines running in close proximity to one another (within eyeshot), the first one focussing on the coastal route travelled by the ships, the other one on the route from Phorcys' harbour to Eumaeus' hut and, beyond, across the mountains to the palace. Thus there is no room left for triangular constellations. The complexity of the personal constellations is reduced to Homer's basic system of bifurcations: a single storyline splits into two lines, which may remain separate or re-unite again. Several

---

[32] The striking doubling of the message has not been explained by commentators. Its main function is that the suitors learn from the herald that Telemachus has escaped their ambush but are not informed (like Penelope is by Eumaeus) that he is staying with Eumaeus, and thus cannot even think of ambushing him again before he arrives in the palace, i.e. in a public space. My earlier comments on this scene (Danek 1998a, 322 f.) seem to me much too complicated by now.

protagonists use one and the same route at different times, but there is no 'triangular communication' or 'triangular conflict' visible.

Let us come back to the *Argonautica*. We have seen how Apollonius in Book 3 opens up a wide field of spatial ramifications, while still adhering to the Homeric model of successivity. This twofold strategy will persist in Book 4: new storylines emerge, and spatial ramifications become more and more complicated (e.g. the river Ister dividing into two branches). Nevertheless, Apollonius keeps events in parallel storylines in the background and avoids representing actions which unfold in full view of the narrator as taking place at the same time. In the end, after the Argonauts leave the Phaeacians (4.1223–1781), the narrative is restricted to a single storyline again, concerning both time and space, just as it was in Books 1 and 2. Apollonius deliberately does not keep up the same degree of narrative complexity until the end of the epic.

Apollonius avoids violating the most prominent Homeric 'rules' on how to arrange competing storylines, but still offers something completely different from Homer's narrative technique. Further studies on his narrative use of time and space will no doubt build on these preliminary observations on a fascinating topic.

'Snapshots' of Myth:
The Notion of Time in Hellenistic Epyllion

Evina Sistakou

Apart from the common meaning of 'a photograph taken quickly or at a moment of opportunity', the word 'snapshot' has a second, metaphorical sense: 'a piece of information that quickly gives you an idea of what the situation is like at a particular time' (*Longman Dictionary of Contemporary English*), 'a short description or a small amount of information that gives you an idea of what something is like' (*Oxford Advanced Learner's Dictionary*), 'a glimpse of something; a portrayal of something at a moment in time' (*Wiktionary*). Although the various dictionaries are far from unanimous, certain features of the concept of 'snapshot', as deriving from the abovementioned definitions, are fundamental to the present discussion: the small amount of information, the particular detail that provides an insight into a general situation or background; the (quasi)coincidental choice of subject matter; the focus on a single event; the lack of development in time, the 'freezing' of time; and the emphasis on a particular *moment* within the broader frame of biographical or historical *time*.

In the present paper I will argue that the epyllia focus on particular 'snapshots' highlighting a brief phase within a broader mythical story.[1] It seems that the epylliac 'snapshots' mark a major turning point for an individual (whether a hero or a figure on the margins), thus symbolizing a passage from one stage to another in his life. In highlighting the connection between the function of time within the narrative and the themat-

---

1   *Mutatis mutandis* the same holds true for the Homeric and tragic plots. To mention the most famous examples, the *Iliad* focuses on 51 days out of the 10-year Iliadic war and the *Odyssey* records only the last days of Odysseus' return to Ithaca after his 10-year *nostos*. However, it is not only scale that differentiates the Homeric plots from the epylliac 'snapshots' whose extremely short duration in terms of *fabula*-time is their distinctive feature; it is mainly the lack of a dramatic development, a progressive movement in time, viz of an actual plot, that brings to the fore the antithesis between the grand literature of the past and the modernistic epyllion. Cf. below p. 295–6 and n. 11.

ics of time in certain Hellenistic epyllia, I hope to demonstrate that the temporal strategies employed reflect the broader notion of time in each individual epyllion; a notion of time deriving from the very nature of 'snapshot' which lies at the core of this, peculiarly Alexandrian, poetic genre.[2]

Before moving on to the discussion of particular epyllia, certain delimitations concerning the terminology adopted and the scope of the present approach are necessary. Narratologists mainly distinguish between the content of a narrative (*fabula*), its organization within the narrative (*story*) and its verbal representation (*text*).[3] *Time* is one of the main factors that determine precisely how a fabula might be turned into a story and thence into a narrative text. Time is vital to the structuring of a story, to the making of a plot out of a series of events; between story-time and text-time (which, of course, cannot be measured but only consumed during reading) there is an interrelation on three levels, *order*, *duration* and *frequency*.[4] It is obvious that the handling of time depends on various elements, ranging from the narrative tactics in terms of point of view, arrangement of material, beginning and closure devices to the generic identity and conditions of reception (reading or performance) of a literary text.

Regarded vaguely as a subcategory of epic poetry, the *epyllion* appears to belong to the narrative literary genres; epic narratives of the rhapsodic tradition and lyric narratives focusing upon one episode selected from an extended story have been suggested to be the closest ge-

---

2   Modern approaches to epyllion, though not always radically divergent from the older views expressed by Crump 1931 and Allen 1940, are offered by Gutzwiller 1981, Cameron 1995, 447–53 and Fantuzzi – Hunter 2004, 191–6. For an overview of the research about the epyllion, see Bartels 2004, 3–16.
3   Terms and definitions vary between theoretical schools, Anglo-American New Criticism, Russian Formalism, French Structuralism etc., on which see Lowe 2000, 17 n. 1. For example, while Genette (1972) 1980, 25–9 makes a bipolar distinction between *story* and *narrative*, for Bal (1985) 1997, 5 each narrative entails three different levels, that of *fabula*, *story* and *text*. Bal's tripartite distinction – also adopted in the present paper – is mostly preferred by classicists studying the narratology of ancient texts, see e. g. de Jong 2004a; in Lowe 2000, 17–20 the three categories are renamed as *story-narrative-text* respectively.
4   For this categorization I follow Lewin's rendering of Genette's key terms into English (Genette (1972) 1980, 35). An alternative, and more comprehensive, model is suggested by Bal (1985) 1997 who examines separately the factors of time on the level of *fabula* (duration, chronology and logical sequence) and on the level of *story* (sequential ordering, rhythm, frequency).

neric 'relatives' of the epyllion.[5] Nevertheless, in the poems customarily described as epyllia description and dramatization are equally, or perhaps even more, vital than narration itself.[6] Moreover, a series of devices, such as digressions, i.e. stories framing the main narrative or recounted by the characters themselves, and *ecphrases*, affect the organization of time in the epyllia. Taking into account these generic features, I will attempt to sketch out the main characteristics that, in my opinion, constitute the notion of time in the majority of the poems regarded as epyllia.

What most definitions have in common is the observation that the epyllion is a short hexameter or elegiac poem, concentrating upon one mythical episode.[7] Both the limited length[8] as well as the focusing on a single episode specify not only the function but also the perception of time in epylliac narratives. This episode, which I describe as 'snapshot', is selected from within a broader plot, but has barely any action at all; thus, it remains in itself undeveloped over time.[9] Judging from the surviving poems and fragments (even from summaries), we may infer that the epyllion is apparently based on a unified line of plot, although, in effect, it records only a small phase of this plot. For example, although

---

5   Fantuzzi – Hunter 2004, 193–5. Most scholars, however, call this categorization into question. E.g. Allen 1940, 18 denies that the epyllion is a distinct literary type, since, in his opinion, no two of the poems labelled as such have any basic characteristic in common. Similarly, Cameron 1995, 447–52 casts doubt on the assumption that the epyllion was an autonomous literary genre. On the term 'epyllion' as an invention of 19th c. scholars, see Fantuzzi in *DNP*.

6   Allen 1940, 14 suggests that 'the style of an epyllion can be, in the main, either descriptive, narrative, or dramatic.'

7   Scholars strongly disagree on which poems should be characterized as epyllia; these might be framed or unframed, or even incorporated into other genres such as hymns (Gutzwiller 1981, 39–48 includes Callimachus' *Hymn to Demeter* into the category of the epyllion) or epics (see e.g. Bartels 2004 who studies narratives from Vergil's *Georgics* and Ovid's *Metamorphoses* as epyllia).

8   Fantuzzi – Hunter 2004, 191 subtly distinguishes between two categories of epyllia, a series of 'ambitious poems of considerable length ... which ran well over a thousand verses' on the one hand, and 'shorter narratives ... between one hundred and three hundred verses' on the other. The first category is exemplified by Callimachus' *Hecale*, the second by Moschus' *Europa*.

9   In this respect, it should be contrasted with the Aristotelian notion of *praxis*, the coherent plot which forms the core of tragedy and 'tragic' epic of the type of the *Iliad* (*Po.* 6.1450a4–5 λέγω γὰρ μῦθον τοῦτον τὴν σύνθεσιν τῶν πραγμάτων, 38–39 ἀρχὴ μὲν οὖν καὶ οἷον ψυχὴ ὁ μῦθος τῆς τραγῳδίας). On Callimacheanism as a literary countercurrent to the Aristotelian conception of plot, see Lowe 2000, 98–9.

Theocritus' *Idyll* 13 presupposes a rapidly developing plot, beginning with Heracles' love for Hylas, their sailing with the Argo, the loss of the young lover and the desperation of the hero who finally abandons the expedition in search of his beloved, it is mainly centered around the static episode of how the Nymphs abduct Hylas. Another example is Bion's (?) *Epithalamion for Achilles and Deidameia*, where the well-known story of Achilles, who, dressed in women's clothing, goes to the court of Lycomedes in Scyros, marries the king's daughter Deidameia and fathers a son by her, provides a vague background to the narrative, while the scene describing how Achilles flirts with the young princess becomes the primary focus of the poem. These episodes scarcely last more than a few hours; from a narratological viewpoint, this brief period of time is ideally suited to the recounting of a moment of crisis, an instant that marks a decisive turn of events in a person's life.[10] The short duration of the epylliac *fabula* in combination with the demand for ὀλιγοστιχία forms a distinctive feature of this modern type of narrative, in contrast with large-scale epic poetry.[11]

If we take a closer look at the transformation of the epylliac *fabula* into a *story*, we can discern the basic strategies involved in the handling of time. The central episode unfolds in linear chronological order, from a moment selected at random within a wider temporal frame to its appointed ending; therefore, on a textual level, openings and closures in the epyllia are extremely important.[12] Although not present in all narratives that, broadly speaking, might be categorized as epyllia, a common opening device is the employment of ποτέ. Indicating an 'unknown point of time' (*LSJ*) in the past, this fairytale-like beginning reflects an indefinite, almost achronical temporal setting, which stands in stark contrast with dating according to mythical events or heroic genealogy; this is how Callimachus' *Hecale*, Theocritus' *Little Heracles* and Moschus'

---

10 I refer here to the distinction introduced by Bal (1985) 1997, 38–40 between two kinds of *fabula*: the type of *crisis*, covering a short span of time into which events have been compressed, and the type of *development*, covering a long period during which characters and events are represented in detail.

11 Bal (1985) 1997, 39 lists the categories of grand literature whose *fabulas* extend over a long time span: autobiographies, Bildungsroman, war novels, frame novels (such as *The Thousand and One Nights*) and travel stories – with the remark that 'the most important topic presented in them is precisely the passing of time.' On 'magnitude' and 'length' referring to extent measured by time in Aristotle's poetical theory, see Belfiore 2002.

12 On epylliac openings and closures, see Fantuzzi – Hunter 2004, 192–3.

Europa begin. Closures, on the other hand, are frequently abrupt, thus rendering the epylliac narratives open to alternative endings. Theocritus' *Idyll* 13 ends with Heracles' desperate quest for his lover which finally brings him to Phasis and Colchis on foot; Callimachus, in his epylliac-like *Hymn to Demeter*, freezes the narration on Erysichthon's misfortunes at the moment when the king's son goes around begging for food at crossroads – thus neglecting to mention his gruesome death from autophagy. Aitia at the end of the epyllia mark a transition from mythical time to historical present, thus adding a diachronic and universalizing dimension to the 'snapshot'. Callimachus' *Hecale*, Eratosthenes' *Erigone* and presumably the majority of Euphorion's mythological epyllia (*Anius, Dionysus, Inachus, Hyacinthus, Philoctetes*) ended with cult or naming aitia, related to the reader's present. Despite the fact that the central event was narrated linearly in the epyllia, distortions of the chronological sequence, at least on a secondary narrative level, must have been the norm. Analeptic and proleptic narratives, falling inside or outside the actual time limits of the *fabula*, embedded stories delivered by the characters, and digressions common in the epyllia, such as dreams, prophecies and descriptions, resulted in a shifting between various temporal levels.[13] I hardly need mention such famous digressions, as the narration of Athens' mythical past by the two birds in Callimachus' *Hecale* or the recounting of Europa's prophetic dream and the description of her basket in Moschus' *Europa*.

Finally, what remains to be outlined is the rhythm of the narration in the epyllion, i.e. the relation between *fabula*-time and *text*-time. Since the epyllion does not really have a plot or a dramatic climax, but centres around a 'snapshot', the time of the *text* matches or even exceeds the time of the *fabula*. In other words, mimetic *scenes*, *retardations* or even descriptive *pauses* highlight the static episode; events from the past or future framing the chief 'snapshot' are summarized or passed over in silence. These narrative choices draw the reader's attention to the dynamic of the 'here and now', functioning as a vantage point from which other events, and hence the past and future, might be observed and interpreted. In fact, through the exploitation of this technique, the neoteric poet throws into relief marginal events of a myth, while, at the same time, devalues major and well-known episodes. An

---

13 I agree on this point with Bartels 2004, 15 who only characterizes as digressions passages where the primary narrative level is interrupted, thus bringing 'time' of the main episode to a standstill.

extreme case is the Ps.-Theocritean *Heracles the Lionslayer*, which consists of three scenes, namely between Heracles and a rustic character (dialogue), the king Augeas (description) and the king's son, Phyleus (narration); these detailed episodes are merely excerpts from 'the full story', whereas the central event, the actual cleaning of the stables, is not even mentioned in the poem.[14]

In order to explore these temporal patterns, I shall examine three much-discussed epyllia of the Hellenistic age as test-cases: Callimachus' *Hecale*, Theocritus' *Little Heracles* and Moschus' *Europa*. It is no coincidence that all three poems suggest their poets' preoccupation with time; in *Hecale* it is youth and old age that are thematized, in *Little Heracles*, the growing up of the baby hero, and in *Europa*, a girl's transition from the age of innocence to adult life through the experience of love making. In the following analysis, I intend to show how time is organized within the narrative and how the temporal strategies employed reflect the ideology regarding time in each poem.

1. The recollections of an old woman (Callimachus' *Hecale*)

We do not remember days,
we remember moments.
Cesare Pavese

Despite the fact that Callimachus' *Hecale* is only preserved in fragments and the accompanying *Diegesis* is a mere summary of the poem, the attempted reconstructions of this epyllion, first by Pfeiffer 1965 and more recently by Hollis 1990, provide valuable insights into its narrative organization.[15] According to the *Diegesis*, the *fabula*-time of Callimachus' *Hecale* covers less than 24 hours: one day Theseus decides to flee secretly from his father's custody to kill the bull of Marathon, a feat that will be accomplished the next morning. Although such a plot would have been quite appropriate to a small-scale *Theseid* recounting one heroic feat in linear sequence,[16] Callimachus went much further than this, by choosing to focus on an episode of an even more limited duration (and practi-

---

14 This approach to *Idyll* 25 in Hunter 2004, 88–9.
15 Ideas on the temporal structure of *Hecale* are also proposed by Barigazzi 1954 and 1958.
16 Cf. Hollis 1990, 5–6.

'Snapshots' of Myth: The Notion of Time in Hellenistic Epyllion 299

cally with no plot).[17] The majority of *Hecale*'s surviving fragments support the hypothesis that the epyllion centered around the encounter between Theseus and Hecale, taking place in the latter's hut from the evening until early in the morning; in fact, this episode functions as a major retardation blocking the normal flow of the epic-like plot, i.e. the killing of the Marathonian bull by Theseus. This 'snapshot', beginning when Theseus finds shelter from the tempest in the old woman's cottage, culminates in the long dinner-scene, during which Hecale has the opportunity to recount the story of her life, and rounds off with the hero's staying overnight at her hut. We cannot exclude the possibility that these scenes contained also narrations on Theseus' life story, and that his perspective was of some importance to the Callimachean narrative; but it should be beyond doubt that the real protagonist was Hecale, a character strongly recalling Eumaeus and Eurycleia from the *Odyssey*, and that the factor of time was primarily perceived through her retrospective viewpoint.[18]

This general impression is confirmed in the first line of the epyllion (fr. 1 H.): Ἀκταίη τις ἔναιεν Ἐρεχθέος ἔν ποτε γουνῶι 'once lived an Attic woman on the hill of Erechtheus'. Scholars agree that this is a 'once upon a time'-opening, typical of fairytale narratives, which is used by Callimachus to introduce the protagonist of his poem, Hecale.[19] But the 'time' referred to is not as vague as it seems, since both the epithet Ἀκταίη and the periphrastic toponym Ἐρεχθέος γουνός project the dim and distant past of Athens into the poem's setting;[20] we might call this

---

17 The limits of the 'snapshot' are not only temporal but also spatial: Barigazzi 1954, 309 rightly observes that the house of Hecale is a panoramic point, from where the poem starts and where it finishes and at which all events aim.
18 This assumption does not contradict the idea expressed by Hollis 1990, 6 that 'one of the most striking features of the work must have been the poignant contrast between the two principal characters ... Theseus at the outset of his heroic career, the old woman once rich but robbed of all those closest to her by a series of disasters and reduced to living alone in a desolate place.' It goes without saying that this dramatic contrast brings to the fore the antithesis between two different angles of experiencing time, that of youth and that of old age. – On the 'twin' character of Molorkos as compared to Hecale, see Ambühl 2004; on the youth of Theseus and his literary prototypes, Jason and Telemachus, see Ambühl 2005, 31–58.
19 Hollis 1990, 137 and Fantuzzi – Hunter 2004, 192.
20 Hollis 1992, 3 regards Ἀκτή as a primitive name of Attica, before the synoecism of Theseus. As for Erechtheus, the mythical king of Athens, he was at least four generations older than Theseus.

the mythical temporal level, recalled again in the famous digression of the crow and the raven (frs. 70 ff. H.). According to the editors, the rest of the introduction was dedicated to praising Hecale's main virtue, her hospitality, recorded over a long period of time (as reflected in the use of the imperfect in fr. 2 H.): τίον δέ ἑ πάντες ὁδῖται/ἧρα φιλοξενίης· ἔχε γὰρ τέγος ἀκλήιστον 'all travellers honoured her for her hospitality because her house was always open'. Moreover, if fr. 2 H. was linked to the paretymology of her name from εἰσκαλεῖν or εἰς καλιὴν πρὸς ἑαυτὴν προτρέπειν (Et. Gen.), and, consequently, to fr. 81 H., we cannot rule out the possibility that the narrator was foreshadowing, at this early stage of the poem, the aitiological finale of the epyllion.[21]

Charting the organization of time in *Hecale* is a daunting task. If we based our reconstructions solely on the *Diegesis*, it would be reasonable to conclude that *Hecale*'s plot developed in a linear and straightforward manner, whereas the 'snapshot' of the *philoxenia* was passed over by the narrator as a technical detail (*Dieg.* X 29–31 οἰκίδιον θεασάμενος [sc. ὁ Θησεύς] Ἑκάλης τινὸς πρεσβύτιδος ἐνταῦθα ἐξενοδοκήθη 'Theseus saw the hut of an old woman, whose name was Hecale, and was received there as a guest'). However, the surviving fragments and testimonies, indicating that narrative analepses and prolepses had a prominent role in the poem, prove this approach to be rather misleading; therefore, the conventional arrangement of the fragments '*ad ordinem narrationis*' is open to doubt.[22] For instance, it is beyond doubt that the events before the Marathonian adventure, namely how Theseus left Troezen and went to Athens where he was recognized first by Medea and then by Aegeus (frs. 3–17 H.), were included in the narrative;[23] according to

---

21 Though Hollis 1990, 139 is reluctant to accept that the aition was slotted in at the beginning rather than near the closing of the poem.
22 On this arrangement, suggested by previous scholarship and especially the summary provided by the *Diegesis*, see Pfeiffer 1949 on fr. 230; cf. Hollis 1990, 46–8 who moves along the same lines as Pfeiffer.
23 These past adventures might have included the following events (in chronological order): Aegeus' confiding of Theseus in Aethra's care and the handing over to her of a sword and sandals (fr. 10 H.), Theseus' childhood in Troezen (frs. 12–15 H.) and the recovery of the tokens left behind by Aegeus (cf. frs. 9–11 H.), Theseus' feats after leaving Troezen up to his arrival in Athens (for these events in the Callimachean narrative we know next to nothing, see Hollis 1990, 150), Medea's attempt to poison Theseus (frs. 3–7 H.), Theseus recognition by his real father, Aegeus, by means of the tokens left to him when he was a child (frs. 8–11 H.), Theseus' decision to fight the bull and his secret escape (frs. 16–17 H.). Editors of the text seem to agree that at

the linear summary of the *Diegesis*, these events were recounted near the opening of the poem. Is it legitimate to assume that the details of Theseus' background were not narrated as early as this, but were actually incorporated into his dialogue with the old woman over dinner?[24] This would challenge the common reconstructions of the epyllion; the hypothesis that the adventures of Theseus up to the point where he set out to kill the Marathonian bull constituted a major analeptic narration within the poem, delivered by the hero himself, is a possibility which can neither be adequately proved nor utterly excluded.[25]

After his brief sojourn in Athens, Theseus sets out on his enterprise in the evening (*Dieg.* X 27–28 περὶ ἑσπέραν ἀπῆρεν, cf. fr. 18.5–6 H. μητέρι δ' ὁππ[ότε ... δειελὸν αἰτίζουσιν); on his way to Marathon the sweltering weather of the Attic countryside gives way to a violent storm (frs. 18–26 H.). It is a *communis opinio* of Callimachean scholarship that the scene of the tempest marks a major turning point within the epyllion.[26] From a dramatic aspect, the storm is the imponderable which brings together the two *dramatis personae*, Theseus and Hecale, the actions of whom might have been happening simultaneously (and probably described as such) up to this critical moment.[27] By portraying life on a summer evening, when a storm is about to break, as experi-

---

least the events of Troezen were part of the analeptic narrations incorporated into the dialogue between Theseus and Aegeus (Hollis 1990, 148).

24 A serious objection might be raised if we take into account fr. 238 Pf., which seems to imply that the narration about Troezen in fact preceded the scene of the storm. Pfeiffer 1949 on fr. 230 notes that '*ante tempestatem in pagina versa descriptam a poeta in pagina recta (nisi graviter erravi) res Troezeniae narrantur.*' In dividing fr. 238 Pf. into two separate pieces, namely fr. 17 and 18, Hollis 1990 is indirectly implying that the two events were not necessarily so closely connected to each other as Pfeiffer had supposed; cf. Hollis 1990, 156 who remarks that 'the lacuna between frs. 17 and 18 ... is of uncertain length.'

25 Hollis 1990, 150 suggests that the killing of Cercyon and Sciron was probably recounted by Theseus during his conversation with Hecale. I am inclined to think that many more stories from Theseus' childhood and youth might have been included in the epyllion's central 'snapshot'; the strong presence of direct speech in these stories (frs. 7, 8, 10, 16?, 17 H.) supports the speculation.

26 On this passage, see Livrea 1992.

27 This is a mere hypothesis, based on the fact that the narrator divided the overture of his poem between his protagonists, by concentrating upon Hecale's style of living in the countryside on the one hand (frs. 1–2 H.) and Theseus' adventures in Athens on the other (frs. 3–17 H.); in this case, Callimachus would be dealing with the problem of presenting simultaneous actions, known from the Homeric epics. Hollis 1990, 136 argues, however, that the introduction which was dedicated to the presentation of Hecale must have been quite brief.

enced by men and beasts and as foreshadowed by distinct weather signs,[28] the narrator slows down the rhythm of his story and generates suspense; in highlighting a common moment in human and natural time, Callimachus manages to individualize it, and thereby stress its narrative function as an anticipation of the encounter that is about to take place in the next lines. It is no coincidence that a similar portrayal, in this case of the early morning, was connected with the end of the 'snapshot', right after the prophetic speech of the birds, thus anticipating the death of the old woman (fr. 74.22 ff. H.).[29] These two 'moments' function as a magnifying glass, through which the actual subject matter of the poem may be perceived.

Thus, we come to the 'snapshot', the entertainment of Theseus in Hecale's hut (frs. 27 ff. H.). The nocturnal setting of the scene is a distinct feature of numerous Hellenistic narratives.[30] If we accept Lobel's supplementations on the *argumentum* of P.Oxy. 2258 in lines 7–9 ὑε]τοῦ κα[τ]αρραγέντος ... νυκτὸς ἐ[πιλαμβανούσης ... ο]ἶκον Ἑκάλης, then it was not only the tempest, but also the late hour – probably illustrated vividly by Callimachus –[31] that forced the hero to seek refuge in the humble cottage. The narrative rhythm is further retarded, as the narration turns into a scene, comprising actions, dialogue, direct speech and descriptions. Fragments 27–39 H. monitor the successive stages of a typical scene of arrival and hosting: Theseus' entrance, his reception by Hecale, his sitting down on the couch, the lighting of the fire, the foot-washing, the preparation and serving of the dinner.[32] Suspense increases, as the narrator recounts the minutiae of the hospitality routine, thus delaying the exchange of speeches between the two protagonists. Finally, Hecale asks Theseus about his mission (fr. 40.3 H. ἃ μ' εἴρεο),

---

28 Livrea 1992, 147–8 succinctly speaks of Callimachus creating a 'Stundenbild'.
29 On the illustration of hours or seasons in terms of human or animal activity in Alexandrian poetry – note esp. how Apollonius depicts the coming of the night in *Arg.* 3.744 ff. – see Hollis 1990, 254. The antithesis of night and day, an antithesis which had a central role in *Hecale*'s setting, is also suggested by the reference to the evening and morning star in fr. 113 H.
30 Other famous Alexandrian 'nocturnes' are Theocritus' *Id.* 2 and 24, and Medea's meditation in the third book of Apollonius' *Argonautica*.
31 Fr. 19 H. καὶ ἠέρος ἀχλύσαντος along with Suida's explanation of the participle *ad loc.* ἀντὶ τοῦ σκοτισθέντος suggest that the darkness of the night was an additional factor for Theseus' seeking refuge; it might also imply that the teenager hero was frightened by the surrounding darkness! Cf. fr. 25 H. and Hollis 1990, 164–5.
32 An analysis of the scene is provided by Ambühl 2005, 72–8.

and the hero responds (fr. 40.1 H. Μαραθῶνα κατέρχομαι); it is now Theseus' turn to enquire about Hecale's peculiar circumstances (fr. 40.4–5 H. ποθὴ σέο τυτθὸν ἀκοῦσαι ... γρηῢς ἐρημαίη ἔνι ναίεις 'I desire to hear something little about you ... an old woman living in an isolated place') and the woman embarks upon her lengthy narration (its size being suggested by fr. 58 H. ἀείπλανα χείλεα γρηός 'the ever-wandering lips of an old woman').[33]

In contrast with Theseus' announcing of plans to be realized in the near future, Hecale with her autobiographical speech takes a walk down memory lane (cf. fr. 42.4 H. μέμνημαι). The analeptic narrative starts from the very beginning, her descent from a wealthy family (fr. 41.1–2 H. οὐ γάρ μοι πενίη πατρώιος, οὐδ' ἀπὸ πάππων/εἰμὶ λιπερνῆτις 'my poverty is not inherited from my father nor did my ancestors make me poor'). The next important stage of her life, alleged to be the acquaintance with her husband-to-be,[34] takes the form of yet another, this time embedded, 'snapshot': if the detailed description of the finely dressed man stood out as a unique moment in the old woman's recollections, then the Hellenistic *topos* of 'love at first sight' would have been exploited here (frs. 42–46 H.).[35] After that, Hecale might have recounted how she had to look after two boys, probably her own children, who, however, perished (frs. 47–49 H.), with the villain Cercyon playing an active role in their untimely death (fr. 49.8 ff. H.). The recollection of the tragic incident probably caused a dramatic change of mood; the memory of how Hecale passed from well-being and happiness to a life of desolation and poverty brings her *apologos* to an end.[36] On hearing about Hecale's cruel fate, and especially the

---

33 Hollis 1990, 177 thinks that the speech was 'not fewer than 100 lines, and perhaps appreciably longer'.
34 At least according to the reconstruction of the plot by Hollis 1990, 176; however, Ovid's testimony in *R.Am.* 747 *cur nemo est Hecalen, nulla est quae ceperit Iron?* conflicts with this hypothesis.
35 Passages which record the viewing of a lover-to-be often bring narrative time to a standstill, see e.g. Theoc. 2.76–86 and the celebrated ecphrasis of Jason's cloak in A.R. 1.721–781.
36 Perhaps it is the recollection of the tragic incidents, and not the description of the sufferings of the inhabitants of Marathon (cf. Hollis 1990, 205), that fills Hecale's eyes with tears (fr. 57 H. ἁλυκὸν δέ οἱ ἔκπεσε δάκρυ, cf. incert. fr. 158 H. τί δάκρυον εὗδον ἐγείρεις;). Whatever the cause of this reaction, the presentation of Hecale bursting into tears further emphasizes the solemn atmosphere of the scene. On Hecale as a lamenting mother figure, see McNelis 2003.

name of Cercyon, it is likely that Theseus responded with an account of his recent deeds, including the punishment of this villain (fr. 62 H.), and probably the killing of another hardened criminal, Sciron (frs. 59–61 H.). This long, atmospheric scene, where the experiences of a hero at the beginning of his career are juxtaposed with those of a woman on the threshold of death, concludes with an anticlimax, the everyday, human action of getting into bed and falling asleep (fr. 63 H. λέξομαι ἐν μυχάτῳ· κλισίη δέ μοί ἐστιν ἑτοίμη 'I will lie in the inmost part of the house; a bed is ready for me there').

The story proceeded as follows: Theseus wakes up early in the morning (fr. 64 H. ὡς ἔμαθεν κἀκεῖνον ἀνιστάμενον); on his departing for Marathon, Hecale bids farewell to the hero and prays to Zeus for his safe return (cf. Plut. *Thes.* 14.3.1–3); then Theseus goes to Marathon to kill the bull; after the celebrations of his triumph, he returns to Brilettus, only to find Hecale dead, whereupon he decides to rename the demos after her and introduce a local cult in her honour (*Dieg.* X.31-XI.7). Textual evidence, however, suggests that the arrangement of these events, with the narrative emphasis being placed on particular levels of time, was more elaborate than this. It remains a philological enigma how the long digression of the crow (frs. 70–74 H.) was slotted into the Callimachean narrative. If we accept the prevailing assumption that it was a paradigm of how the bearers of bad news are punished by the gods, thematically linked to the announcement of Hecale's death to Theseus, then it obviously functioned as a prolepsis, albeit by analogy, of the epyllion's ending.[37] Another problem concerns the nocturnal setting of this digression. One is tempted to think that it refers to the same night which Theseus spent in Hecale's house, although this temporal synchronization is not easily supported by the transmission of the text.[38] Should this assumption be correct, then Callimachus would have achieved a powerful dramatic effect by shifting his focus from the sleeping protagonists to the awakening birds within the same night, thus juxtaposing the narrative present with the mythical past of Athens. The birds at the end of the night were shown to fall asleep (fr. 74.21 H. τὴν μὲν

---

[37] See Hollis 1990, 224–6 for an overview of the issues involved in the digression. For a detailed commentary, see also Barigazzi 1954, 317–30.
[38] The difficulty arises from the fact that the capture of the Marathonian bull (fr. 69 H.) is found in column (i) of the Vienna Tablet and followed (after a lacuna of some 22 lines) by the mythological digression on Erichthonius and the conversation of the two birds (frs. 70, 73 and 74 H.) in columns (ii), (iii) and (iv).

ἄρ' ὡς φαμένην ὕπνος λάβε, τὴν δ' ἀΐουσαν 'the one fell asleep while talking, the other while listening') until daybreak (fr. 74.22–23 H. καδδραθέτην δ' οὐ πολλὸν ἐπὶ χρόν[ο]ν, αἶψα γὰρ ἦλθεν/στιβήεις ἄγχαυρος ... 'they both didn't sleep for a long time, as the chilling dawn came quickly'). At this point, when dawn broke and human activity resumed (fr. 74.24 H. ἤδη γὰρ ἑωθινὰ λύχνα φαείνει, cf. *Dieg.* X.31–32 πρὸς δὲ τὴν ἕω [sc. Θησεὺς] ἀναστάς), the main thread of the story might have been picked up (cf. fr. 64 H. ὡς ἔμαθεν κἀκεῖνον ἀνιστάμενον 'when she saw that he also had risen').[39] It should be noted, though, that this ordering of the events is purely conjectural, and suggested here only due to the dramatic impact it would have had upon the narrative.[40]

To conclude. In *Hecale,* Theseus' lingering on with the old woman might be viewed as a pointless delaying of his mission; in terms of epic ideology, the encounter with Hecale works as a retardation of the poem's major *praxis*. However, within this context, marked out by Theseus' deeds and, secondarily, by the mythical digression on Ericthonius, human measuring of time assumes symbolic dimensions. Illustrations of different times of the day – dawn, afternoon, evening, night – correspond to the stages of human life – childhood, youth, old age. As night falls, Theseus enters into the world of men; as he converses over dinner, his resolution for heroic action weakens; as Hecale's memories unfold, the hero adopts an alternative perspective on life. This experience, occurring unexpectedly on a rainy night, helps Theseus reconsider his own, problematic, family relations, as reflected in the search for his real father and in the death threat represented by his stepmother, Medea; thus, at the end of the poem, his accomplished mission can only

---

39 Plutarch in *Thes.* 14.2.4–3.1 Ἑκαλίνην ὑποκοριζόμενοι διὰ τὸ κἀκείνην νέον ὄντα κομιδῇ τὸν Θησέα ξενίζουσαν ἀσπάσασθαι πρεσβυτικῶς καὶ φιλοφρονεῖσθαι τοιούτοις ὑποκορισμοῖς seems to suggest that the contrast between old age and youth played a key role in Callimachus' narrative.

40 The problem is not new (see Hollis 1990 Appendix IV): already Wilamowitz suggested that, given the distance between Marathon and Athens, it is likely that Theseus returned to Athens after spending one more night somewhere near Marathon. Hollis 1990, 355–7, although hesitant to draw conclusions, is inclined to accept that Theseus returned to Athens at the same day, but waited until the next morning to go back to Hecale's house; nevertheless, he admits (p. 356) that 'a second night's stay near Marathon would be a sad anticlimax after the hospitality of Hecale.'

be dedicated to the memory of Hecale, the emerging mother figure of the poem.[41]

2. The feat of an infant prodigy (Theocritus' *Little Heracles*)

> *There is always one moment in childhood when the door opens and lets the future in.*
> Graham Greene

In the dead of night a baby boy wakes up to find two huge serpents in his cradle; he grapples with them and strangles them, to the astonishment of everyone in the household; his mother, amazed to discover that her son is an infant prodigy, sends for a seer and inquires about her child's future. Although the setting of this miraculous event is domestic and the secondary characters strongly recall ordinary people,[42] the 'snapshot' is mythological and stems from the host of stories relating to Heracles. *Idyll* 24 of Theocritus, modelled upon Pindar's first *Nemean* ode, centres around an early feat of Heracles, covering (again) a *fabula*-time of less than a day – it should be noted, though, that the temporal perspective of the poem is much wider, spanning Heracles' life and afterlife.[43] Thus, as in the case of *Hecale*, the unforeseen event takes place during a single night and its immediate consequences are felt in the next morning – although its long-term effects last for an eternity. Human and heroic time are juxtaposed here as in Callimachus' epyllion; Theocritus thematizes the prospects of an extraordinary childhood, by throwing into relief the different ways in which men and heroes experience time.[44] In order to highlight this contrast, Theocritus chooses to narrate

---

41 Cf. the apostrophe μαῖα in fr. 80.4 H. A new approach to the mother-son relationship of Hecale to Theseus in Ambühl 2005, 41–5; on Hecale treating Theseus more like a son and less like a guest, see Barigazzi 1958, 469; Hutchinson 1988, 57–9 likens Hecale to Hecabe. On Aithra as a prototype of mother, see fr. 78 H. Αἴθρην τὴν εὔτεκνον. On Hecale as a new 'epic' hero whose glory is celebrated both by cult and poetry, see McNelis 2003.
42 As Gow 1952, 2.415 notes, 'Theocritus follows the narrative of Pindar in his first Nemean ode but he is at pains to reduce it from a heroic to a domestic level.'
43 Fantuzzi – Hunter 2004, 201 points out that 'the repeated insistence ... on youth and old age (vv. 1–2, 102–103, 133) foreshadows Heracles' triumph over the natural process of ageing.'
44 For a reading of the idyll from the perspective of the 'lost infancy' of Heracles, see Cusset 1999.

a feat of heroic proportions as seen from the perspective of an everyday maternal figure, Alcmena.[45]

The idyll's first line Ἡρακλέα δεκάμηνον ἐόντα ποχ' ἁ Μιδεᾶτις couples the vague once-upon-a-time opening (known from other epylliac introductions) to a particular point in mythical time: when Heracles was ten months old...[46] Precision, also in terms of mythical chronology, is accomplished by the observation that his twin brother, Iphicles, was just a night younger than him (2 νυκτὶ νεώτερον Ἰφικλῆα). Theocritus emphasizes this curious detail in order to suggest that only a brief span of human time separates Heracles the superhero from his mortal brother.[47] Moreover, the use of νυκτί instead of the common ἡμέρῃ highlights the symbolism this particular time of day acquires throughout the idyll, since it is the events of a single night that bring the miraculous powers of Heracles to the fore. In fact, the reader is invited to watch Heracles' transformation into a god – probably praised as such at the hymnic closure of the poem –[48] on three different temporal levels: the night of crisis (1–63), the next morning (64–102, including a digression on Heracles' future glory, and 73–87) and the years of the hero's youth and education (103–140).

The daily routine of feeding, bathing and lulling the babies to sleep sets the scene of the 'snapshot' (3–10); nevertheless, the accumulation of aorists (3 λούσασα and ἐμπλήσασα, 4 κατέθηκεν, 6 μυθήσατο, 10, δίνησε and ἕλεν) stresses the uniqueness of these activities during this special night. Alcmena's lullaby forms the first direct speech of the idyll (7–9). Its dramatic significance within the narrative is obvious: the idea of a mother praying that her children sleep well during the night (7 εὕδετ', 9 εὐνάζοισθε), but also that they wake up in the morning (7 ἐγέρσιμον ὕπνον, 9 ὄλβιοι ἀῶ ἵκοισθε), ominously anticipates the crisis

---

45 Fundamental to this reading is Davidson 2000.
46 The presentation of Heracles as a baby boy in Theocritus stands in sharp contrast with the account of the same incident in Pindar's *Nemean* 1, where the hero is supposed to kill the snakes immediately after his birth; other ancient sources also disagree on Heracles' age, see Gow 1952, 2.416.
47 Theocritus does not contradict the Pindaric version according to which the twins were born simultaneously (*N.* 1.36 ὠδῖνα φεύγων διδύμῳ), as Gow 1952, 2.416 implies. The night that separates the twins recalls their double conception, namely by Zeus and by Amphitryon; thus, Heracles is properly called ὀψίγονος 'born late' in verse 31, since his birth was delayed by Hera, see White 1979, 35–6.
48 See e.g. Fantuzzi – Hunter 2004, 201.

that is about to befall the family. The narrative rhythm slows down, as the hour of the extraordinary events approaches. Two verses, replete with astronomical lore, mark the exact time: it is midnight (11–12 ἆμος δὲ στρέφεται μεσονύκτιον ἐς δύσιν Ἄρκτος/Ὠρίωνα κατ' αὐτόν, ὃ δ' ἀμφαίνει μέγα ὦμον 'when at midnight the Bear turns westward over against Orion, who shows his big shoulder'). Observing the night sky and recognizing the constellations is a human activity; as is the case with the interpretation of weather signs in *Hecale*, the time of the 'snapshot' is described in terms of everyday experience.[49] Hera sends two huge serpents to devour baby Heracles, and they enter the house through a crack in the doorpost (13–16). Upon their entrance, time is perceived as expanding, as the repeated use of the imperfect seems to imply (18 ἐκύλιον, 19 λάμπεσκε, 19 ἐξέπτυον). Three aorists, ἦνθον in v. 20, ἐξέγροντο in v. 21 and ἐτύχθη in v. 22, mark the transition from the background events (whose expanded duration has created considerable suspense) to the actual moment of crisis. Moreover, the verbs correspond to three actions taking place simultaneously: the snakes approaching the cradle, the babies waking up and a divine light filling the room. In the next 10 verses (23–33), the contrasting reactions of Iphicles and Heracles to the attack of the snakes are narrated in detail; whereas Iphicles is struggling in vain to escape the serpents (his desperate attempt is underlined by φευγέμεν ὁρμαίνων in v. 26), Heracles remains resolute in his decision to act in time against the godsent intruders (26–27 ὁ δ' ἐναντίος ἵετο χερσὶν/Ἡρακλέης, ἄμφω δὲ βαρεῖ ἐνεδήσατο δεσμῷ 'but Heracles made against them with his hands, and tied them with a heavy bond'). By the end of the passage, though, the outcome of the fight between Heracles and the snakes is still undecided.

At the point when Heracles grasps the snakes by the neck while they are struggling to escape his tight grip, the action is left hanging in the air.[50] The perspective shifts from the actual feat to its effects upon the

---

[49] Gow 1952, 2.417–9 attempts a thorough analysis of this pseudo-scientific passage and suggests that Theocritus not only alludes to a midnight setting but also to a particular season of the year, namely February, in order to make some point connected to the birth of Ptolemaeus Philadelphus; Gow, in insisting on the political symbolism of this temporal specification, fails to see its dramatic function within the narrative. Cf. White 1977 on the midnight setting, and the remarks in her commentary (White 1979, 17–9) on the time of the year, which she identifies with the beginning of autumn.

[50] Theocritus exploits the epic device of narrating simultaneous events according to the 'continuity of time' principle (after de Jong's phrasing 2001a, xii-xiii):

'others', i. e. the mortal parents and the household (34–53). Alcmena is the first to be woken by the uproar (34 Ἀλκμήνα δ' ἄκουσε βοᾶς καὶ ἐπέγρετο πρᾶτα). In her address to the sleeping Amphitryon the same command is repeated in a staccato tone; ἄνστα9ι and ἄνστα along with οὐ ἀίεις and οὐ νοέεις reflect her growing anxiety and, at the same time, highlight her husband's idleness. Amphitryon's first reaction is to reach for his weapons, objects which, like Pterelaus' shield in vv. 4–5, evoke his heroic past; the brief description of these weapons in vv. 42–45 further postpones any real activity on his part.[51] The expectations for a saving intervention are once more misdirected, when the divine illumination is suddenly extinguished and the house is plunged into darkness (46). As the narrative grows into a scene, the quest for light becomes the dominant *praxis* – the only one to be performed by Amphitryon in the idyll (47–53). Descriptive pauses, direct speech and the mimesis of trivial incidents add up to a major retardation of the completion of Heracles' feat, which is resumed when Amphitryon enters the babies' bedroom (54–59). The nocturnal scene, divided between the *tableau*-like struggle of Heracles and the hectic (but unheroic) activity of the household, reaches its anticlimax when the babies are put

---

when switching from storyline A to storyline B and back to A' again, time ticks on and B takes over where A stopped, A' where B stopped etc.; on the device, see the thorough analysis by Rengakos 1995. Theocritus adds a new twist to this technique by abruptly 'freezing' Heracles' action to form a stationary *tableau*, which comes to life again at v. 55; obviously an interplay between narration and the conventions of visual arts is intended here, cf. on the illustrations of the episode Davidson 2000, 7 n. 14; according to Fantuzzi – Hunter 2004, 210, 'this is a device of *enargeia*, of allowing the audience to envision what is taking place.' Moreover, we might also recall the famous Iliadic passage, where Achilles considers to use violence against Agamemnon only to be restrained by Athena herself (1.188–222): action freezes at the intervention of Athena while Achilles draws his sword in slow motion; according to the scholiast, Achilles' hesitation explains the narrative device of retardation here (Sch. *Il.* 1.193b ἡ παράτασις τοῦ χρόνου τὴν ἀπὸ τῶν ἐπιλογισμῶν ἔνστασιν δηλοῖ). It should be nevertheless noted that while in the *Iliad* this freezing of action heightens the dramatic tension and offers a profound insight into Achilles' psychology, in the Theocritean epyllion it is the 'unheroic' reactions of Heracles' family that are underlined by this narrative strategy.

51 Fantuzzi – Hunter 2004, 203–4 aptly remarks that the sense of delay is heightened here by the expectation that a fuller ecphrasis will follow, which, as elsewhere in the idyll, remains unfulfilled.

to bed and Amphitryon is at last free to fall into his deep slumber (60–63).[52]

The 'snapshot' rounds off with the meeting of Alcmena with Teiresias during which human and heroic time are once more juxtaposed. Without delay, Alcmena summons Teiresias at dawn, a time of the day signalled in terms of everyday activity, in this case the crowing of the cocks (64 ὄρνιθες τρίτον ἄρτι τὸν ἔσχατον ὄρθρον ἄειδον).[53] Alcmena senses that the feat of her 10-month-old baby marks the beginning of an unusual life, the outcome of which she feels the need to know (67 ὅπως τελέεσθαι ἔμελλεν). The seer responds with a prophecy, in narrative terms an external prolepsis, recounting the events of his future in reverse order: Alcmena will be celebrated among the Argives (76–79), after Heracles' deification and ascension into heaven (79–81), due to the accomplishment of the twelve labours (82–83) and the deliverance from his mortality that will be consumed in the funeral pyre of Trachis (83). Heracles' apotheosis is predicted again in vv. 84–85; in the next two verses (86–87), suspected to be an interpolation, we are transfered to a utopian temporal level, that of the Golden Age.[54] With ἀλλά (88) the present lived by the idyll's characters is restored; the final part of Teiresias' speech is dedicated to a series of instructions, intended as a re-enactment of the crucial events to be performed in symbolic time: 92 νυκτὶ μέσᾳ, ὅκα παῖδα κανεῖν τεὸν ἤθελον αὐτοί 'at midnight, when

---

52 The contrast between Alcmena's preoccupation with action and Amphitryon's inability to act promptly is already present in the Pindaric model (N. 1.50–53): whereas Alcmena rushes from bed to save the baby, Amphitryon urges the Theban leaders to take up arms; cf. Davidson's 2000, 3 observation that 'a most effective contrast is achieved between the lone and unarmed woman for whom the need for immediate action is paramount, and the group of men characterized by martial attitudinising.'
53 Gow's 1952, 2.426 remark that the time implied is the earliest gleam of dawn cannot be supported here. Τρίτον and ἔσχατον clearly point to the last phase of dawn; the earliest point seems to be indicated in Id.18.56–7 νεύμεθα κἄμμες ἐς ὄρθρον, ἐπεί κα πρᾶτος ἀοιδός ... κελαδήσῃ. On the phases of ὄρθρος, cf. the parallels collected by White 1979, 63–4. The dramatic significance of this detail is obvious: after the events of last night, Alcmena is willing to get up with the first crow of the cock – but too tired to do so; the delay once more reflects the 'realistic' sketching of time as experienced by mortals within the idyll.
54 Effe 2000 argues for the authenticity of verses 86–7, which, in his opinion, should be interpreted as an ironic comment upon the illusionary prospect of the return of the Golden Age.

they tried to kill your son' and 93 ἦρι δὲ συλλέξασα κόνιν πυρός 'at dawn you must gather the ashes of the fire'.

Alcmena's changed view of her son's fate is mirrored in the idyll's coda, a detailed account of the princely education and the daily habits of the hero-to-be during the years of his youth (103–140). This section has been criticized for not being organically incorporated into the idyll's main plot,[55] since it seems to bear close relation to the political background of the poem rather than to its mythical subject matter.[56] However, in stressing Alcmena's crucial role in the development of her baby into a mature hero (103–104 Ἡρακλέης δ' ὑπὸ ματρὶ νέον φυτὸν ὣς ἐν ἀλωᾷ/ἐτρέφετ' 'but Heracles was nurtured by his mother like a young plant in an orchard' and 134 ὧδε μὲν Ἡρακλέα φίλα παιδεύσατο μάτηρ 'thus did his loving mother educate him'), Theocritus brings into view the perception of heroic time by an everyday mother; because of the exceptional feat of her child prodigy, as described in the first part of the poem, Alcmena realizes that the duration of her son's lifetime is to be unnaturally prolonged – and thus his teenage years will allow him to be initiated into liberal and martial arts by a host of excellent hero-tutors.[57]

Idyll 24 documents Heracles' life during the stages of infancy, adolescence, maturity and afterlife through a double perspective, a human (focalization through Alcmena's eyes) and a divine (as echoed in Teiresias' prophecy). Within the context of the 'snapshot', heroism emerges from the dynamic of the moment, symbolizing the transition from the everyday and the human, reflected in the mundane setting of the idyll, to the extraordinary and the supernatural. But the main focus of the idyll is upon the psychological perception of time and, in particular, upon the agonizing lengthening of the moment of crisis; the slow approaching of the snakes, Iphicles' laborious but futile attempt to escape, the paralyzing effect of Alcmena's fear, the procrastination of Amphitryon's action and his pressing need for rest and the hurrying of the servants to find light are brought into sharp contrast with Heracles' power to manipulate

---

[55] On the problem, also related to the transmission of Theocritus' text, see e.g. Griffiths 1996, 113–5 who thinks that the idyll must have ended at verse 104.
[56] On the figure of Heracliscus within the context of the Ptolemaic court, see Cusset 1999, 205–7 and Stephens 2003, 123–46.
[57] Stern 1974, 361 thinks that the Pindaric topos according to which human *paideia* is a necessary preparation for immortality underlies this last section of the idyll.

3. The sexual encounter of a young virgin (Moschus' *Europa*)

Be fully in the moment, open yourself
to the powerful energies dancing around you.
Ernest Hemingway

Making love for the first time is undoubtedly an intriguing experience; when this experience involves the father of gods and men, and disguised as a bull too, then it turns out to be unique. Moschus narrates his 'snapshot', namely Europa's erotic encounter with Zeus, in a sequence of three *vignettes* – a dream, a description and a scene –, and unlike Callimachus' *Hecale* and Theocritus' *Little Heracles*, his *Europa* involves neither a hero nor a heroic feat in its plot. However, as in the above-discussed epyllia, the erotic subject matter provides a clear insight into an epic background, as echoed in the last verse of the poem (165–166) ἡ δὲ πάρος κούρη Ζηνὸς γένετ' αὐτίκα νύμφη,/Κρονίδῃ τέκε τέκνα καὶ αὐτίκα γίνετο μήτηρ 'and she that was a virgin before at once became the bride of Zeus and bore children to the son of Cronus, and at once became a mother'.[59] Hesiodic genealogical poetry is evoked here not only by the idea of the union between a god and a woman leading to the birth of divine children, but also by its exact articulation;[60] it is no coincidence, though, that this epic *praxis* is postponed until the end of the poem, i.e. after its mundane preliminaries have been treated in a series of Hellenistic *vignettes*. Once more, the *fabula*-time is quite limited, and, although it is not stated clearly, the epyllion covers a duration of a few hours, be-

---

[58] See e.g. Fantuzzi – Hunter 2004, 201 who stresses that the insistence on youth and old age throughout the entire poem foreshadows Heracles' triumph over the natural process of ageing; cf. Stern 1974, 353–61 who views the idyll as a description of a hero's search for immortality.
[59] In these last verses, Moschus actually compresses the elaborated catalogue of Zeus and Europa's offspring, as preserved in Hesiod fr. 140 M.-W., in order to further undercut the epic quality of the episode.
[60] In effect, the Hesiodic story of Europa, as recounted in the *Catalogue of Women* (frs. 140–145 M.-W.), serves as a principal model for Moschus' narrative; for a comparative reading, see Campbell 1991, 1–3 and Hunter 2005c, 254–6.

ginning just before dawn and coming to an end at some point during the course of the same day.[61]

The opening with ποτέ is typical of the fairytale-like atmosphere of the epylliac genre, an atmosphere reinforced by the statement that Aphrodite is the one who sets the poem's plot in motion (1 Εὐρώπῃ ποτὲ Κύπρις ἐπὶ γλυκὺν ἧκεν ὄνειρον 'once upon a time Aphrodite sent a sweet dream to Europa').[62] The god-sent dream, however, occurs at a fixed point in time, namely on the exact borderline between night and day (2): νυκτὸς ὅτε τρίτατον λάχος ἵσταται, ἐγγύθι δ' ἠώς 'it was the third watch of the night when dawn draws near'.[63] This hour has particular qualities: it is the time when sleep is sweeter than honey and dreams are most likely to come true (3–5). Collective experiences of sleep and dreaming, reflected in the repetition of the present tense (3 ἐφίζων, 4 πεδάᾳ, 5 ποιμαίνεται), lend the passage a tone of universality – a tendency sensed throughout the entire epyllion due to the use of everyday images and the reference to routines or basic truths of human life.[64] Within this universalizing context, Europa is presented as an ordinary teenage girl, entangled in the uncertainties about virginity; but, as with the 10-month-old Heracles of Theocritus, Europa, still a virgin (7 ἔτι παρθένος), marks a particular point in mythical time.

After the double determination of time, both on the level of human experience and on that of myth, the epyllion's story unfolds linearly.[65]

---

61 Cusset 2001, 66 emphasizes the unity of time within Moschus' narrative, by highlighting the fact that the story unfolds between two moments, the first when Europa agitated from her dream gets out of bed and the second when she lies down again under Zeus' soothing influence.

62 For a slightly different interpretation, see Campbell 1991, 26 who notes that ποτέ, recurrent in Hellenistic 'miniature epics', means 'in bygone days': the reader is thus transported back to the legendary past.

63 On the tripartite division of the night, attested in the Homeric epics, see Bühler 1960, 49–50 and Campbell 1991, 28–9.

64 The interpretation of Moschus' narrative in terms of the 'universalization of Europa's experience' is suggested by Fantuzzi – Hunter 2004, 216–20: to achieve this effect, Moschus emphasizes timeless truths, compares his heroine with typical models of previous epic (such as Homer's *Nausicaa* and Apollonius' *Medea*) and exploits stereotype expressions and metaphors (e.g. the image of the young girl as a heifer or filly to be tamed by a man).

65 According to Schmiel 1981, 261–6, who suggests that *Europa's* structure is demarcated by thematically related 'rings', this 'linearity' is only superficial, since Moschus seems to work from the final event (by foreshadowing at the beginning of the poem) back to the initial event (at the middle) and back to the final event (at the end).

The poem's introductory *vignette* comprises Europa's dream of how two continents in the form of women struggle to possess her, and how she has a strong desire to abandon the one who is her mother and nurse, and follow the other, the strange, alluring figure (8–15).[66] Shivering with terror, she jumps out of bed (16–17); under the influence of fear, she gets the feeling that time has 'frozen' (18 ἑζομένη δ' ἐπὶ δηρὸν ἀκὴν ἔχεν 'and sitting down she kept silent for a long time', 20 ὀψὲ δὲ δειμαλέην ἀνενείκατο παρθένος αὐδήν 'at last, after a long time, the girl raised her voice in fear'), she fancies that her vision haunts her waking moments (18–19 ἀμφοτέρας δὲ/εἰσέτι πεπταμένοισιν ἐν ὄμμασιν εἶχε γυναῖκας 'she still had both women before her waking eyes'), and only after a while is she capable of recollecting her dream, as perceived from her own, subjective viewpoint (20–27).[67] Whereas the core of the dream, with its mythological connotations relating to the eponymous heroine of Europe, points to the end result of her union with Zeus, and thus to a future well beyond the limits of the poem's *fabula*-time, its erotic atmosphere and specific anticipations clearly suggest the epyllion's climax. In narratological terms, we might speak of an explicit *announcement* of the poem's end in the declaration that Europa is destined to become Zeus' bride (14–15 μόρσιμον εἶναι/ἐκ Διὸς αἰγιόχου γέρας ἔμμεναι Εὐρώπειαν 'it is destined on the authority of the aegis-bearer Zeus that she, Europa, should be a prize of honour'),[68] but also of an implicit *hint* at the point where Europa expresses her feelings for the unknown woman in terms of erotic desire (25 ὥς μ' ἔλαβε κραδίην κείνης πόθος 'how desire for her takes hold of my heart').[69]

The narrative present comes into view, as Europa resolutely leaves her chamber and sets out for the meadows in search of her beloved friends (28 ὣς εἰποῦσ' ἀνόρουσε, φίλας δ' ἐπεδίζεθ' ἑταίρας 'thus did she speak, and leaping up, she sought for her beloved friends'). A striking feature of the subsequent passage is the emphasis on repeatedness and duration; by joining her companions, Europa seems to enter into

---

66 For a detailed discussion of the dream, see Walde 2001, 202–8.
67 The routine of sitting in silence for a long time and being able to speak again after quite a while is common in epic, see the passages collected by Bühler 1960, 64–5 and Campbell 1991, 40.
68 Μόρσιμον εἶναι (in the manuscripts) instead of μόρσιμον εἶο (suggested by Ahren) is defended by Campbell 1991, 38.
69 On the distinction of the two terms, see Bal (1985) 1997, 65–6. Fantuzzi – Hunter 2004, 217–8 suggest that Europa's sexual arousal is due to her misinterpretation of the dream during the stage of recollection.

an unchanging, everlasting world. The sense of stability in time is reflected in a series of lexical and stylistic choices: the repetition of ἀεί/ αἰέν (30, 35), the use of imperfects (30 συνάθυρεν, 34 ἔβαινον, 35 ἠγερέθοντο), the description of actions taking place on a regular basis (temporal clauses with ὅτε ... ἢ ὅτε ... ἢ ὁπότε... in vv. 30–32). Of the activities in which Europa and her girlfriends are customarily engaged, namely dancing (30 ὅτ' ἐς χορὸν ἐντύνοιτο), bathing (31 ὅτε φαιδρύνοιτο χρόα προχοῇσιν ἀναύρων) and flower-picking (ὁπότ' ἐκ λειμῶνος εὔπνοα λείρι' ἀμέργοι), it is the last of these that constitutes the background of the unfolding episode.[70] Yet, the focusing on the activity of flower-picking comes as a narrative surprise, since it is suggested to the reader in an oblique manner: the girls appear as if of nowhere (33 αἱ δέ οἱ αἶψα φάανθεν), each one of them holding a basket in her hands (33–34 ἔχον δ' ἐν χερσὶν ἑκάστη/ἀνθοδόκον τάλαρον).

As the girls make their way to the idyllic setting of the meadow by the sea (34–36), the focus shifts from their collective activity to a symbolic object, Europa's golden basket. Narrative time comes to a standstill for almost 30 verses, dedicated to the detailed description of the basket (37–62); retrospection and foreshadowing are simultaneously present in this *ecphrasis*.[71] The passage's retrospective viewpoint is suggested by reference to Europa's lineage on the one hand (mirrored in the basket's history in vv. 39–42), and by narration of the myth of Io on the other (in three 'acts' in vv. 44–49, 50–54 and 55–61 respectively). But, although the mythical past is evoked, what Moschus achieves by embedding the myth of Io into a description is to anticipate the epyllion's future events thus creating a proleptic *ecphrasis*.[72] In recounting how Europa's mythical ancestor was raped by Zeus when still a virgin (45 εἰσέτι πόρτις), Moschus ironically stresses the key motifs of his

---

70 It has been rightly pointed out that the scenery of a flowery meadow and the activity of gathering flowers is a conventional scenario for a sexual encounter in Greek myths, see Bühler 1960, 75, 108–9 and Campbell 1991, 50–1. Thus, its presentation here functions as an anticipation of the approaching events.
71 For a thorough discussion of the description, see Manakidou 1993, 174–211.
72 Harrison 2001 gives an overview of proleptic *ecphrases* from Homer up to Virgil, i.e. of descriptions of artefacts replicating in miniature the poem's whole plot and thus closely resembling the device of *mise en abyme*. In his analysis of Moschus' *ecphrasis* (p. 84), Harrison points out the creation of dramatic irony: 'this produces dramatic irony and pathos, for Europa is in effect given a coded warning which she cannot decipher and which only the reader and omniscient divine maker [sc. of the basket] can unscramble.' On the prophetic character of the description, see Manakidou 1993, 192–5.

own narrative: the abnormal sexual union between a man and a cow (50–51 ἐπαφώμενος ἠρέμα χερσί/πόρτιος Ἰναχίης), the theme of bovine metamorphosis (45 εἰσέτι πόρτις ἐοῦσα, φυὴν δ' οὐκ εἶχε γυναίην, cf. 52), the marine setting (46–47), the presence of spectators (49 φῶτες ἀολλήδην θηεῦντο δὲ ποντοπόρον βοῦν), even the symbolic crossing of borders (hinted at by ποντοπόρον βοῦν in v. 49).

After this narrative pause, time is set in motion again, as the girls eventually reach the flowery meadows (63 λειμῶνας ἐς ἀνθεμόεντας ἵκανον).[73] The gathering of flowers as a time-consuming process is stressed by a series of imperfect tenses and iterative forms (64 ἔτερπον, 66 ἀπαίνυτο, 67 θαλέθεσκε, 69 δρέπτον)[74] – but only temporarily, since the narrator proleptically emphasizes that the idyllic situation is very soon to change (72 οὐ μὲν δηρὸν ἔμελλεν...). Zeus is destined to put an end to Europa's hedonistic lingering over flower-picking, and also to her dwelling on the idea of virginity: 72–73 οὐ μὲν δηρὸν ἔμελλεν ἐπ' ἄνθεσι θυμὸν ἰαίνειν,/οὐδ' ἄρα παρθενίην μίτρην ἄχραντον ἔρυσθαι 'but not for long was she destined to delight her heart with the flowers nor keep her maiden girdle undefiled'. The god's response to Aphrodite's blows is immediate, recalling the motif of 'love at first sight' (74–75 Κρονίδης ὥς μιν φράσαθ' ὡς ἐόλητο/θυμόν 'no sooner did the son of Cronus notice her than his heart was in turmoil'); a similar readiness is expressed in his swift decision to appear in the guise of a bull, echoed in the accumulation of aorists in v. 79 κρύψε θεὸν καὶ τρέψε δέμας. With the imperfect γείνετο ταῦρος (v. 79) narrative time freezes once more, as we watch Zeus transform himself into a desirable beast (80–8), and it resumes, as he finally enters the setting (89 ἤλυθε δ' ἐς λειμῶνα).[75]

The subsequent scene, the climax of the poem, starts unexpectedly from what constitutes its natural end: Europa falls in love with the bull,

---

73 Campbell 1991, 51 appositely remarks that ἔβαινον in v. 34 refers to the girls as they make their way to the meadows, while ἵκανον in v. 63 to the point when they reach their destination: the intervening period is taken up by the description of the basket.

74 According to Campbell 1991, 73, the iterative θαλέθεσκε suggests the fact that the supply of flowers for picking was constantly being renewed.

75 Campbell 1991, 82 rightly remarks on the sequence of the tenses in v. 79: 'The aorist expresses the initial shock generated by the series of sudden transformations; with the imperfect the narrator "settles down", dwelling on the end-result rather than on the phenomenon of transformation *per se*; and also on the long-term implications.'

and, moreover, is willing to have intercourse with him without delay (89–100). But, although the sexual preliminaries performed by the bull and Europa in vv. 93–96 strongly suggest lovemaking, the actual act, along with the revelation of the bull's true identity, will only take place at the poem's conclusion. Thus, the anticipated *praxis* is postponed for more than 60 verses, which detail how Europa, seated on the back of the bull, crosses the sea and arrives at Crete (100–161).[76] During this long scene, symbolizing the passage from girlhood to womanhood, the narrative tempo slows down and the dynamic of the moment is brought to the fore. Its first phase (100–112), namely mounting the bull, highlights the contrast between her impulsiveness and the cautiousness of her friends, who, as a result, miss the opportunity to ride upon the bull, i. e. to become Zeus' brides (108–109 ὣς φαμένη νώτοισιν ἐφίζανε μειδιόωσα,/αἱ δ' ἄλλα μέλλεσκον, ἄφαρ δ' ἀνεπήλατο ταῦρος 'thus did she speak, and sat upon his back with a smile; the others were thinking of doing the same, but suddenly the bull sprung up'). In its second phase, clearly suggesting a wedding ceremony, the narrator exploits the ritual dimension of time, by presenting the deities and the creatures of the sea solemnly marching in procession ahead of the young couple (113–130).[77] As Europa and Zeus the Bull eventually reach the open sea, the scene develops into a dramatic dialogue between the two protagonists (131–161). In response to the anxieties expressed by Europa the bull reveals his divine identity; he then prophesies that they will soon arrive at Crete (158 Κρήτη δέ σε δέξεται ἤδη), where they will couple (159–160 ὅπη νυμφήια σεῖο/ἔσσεται) and, as a result, Europa will bear sons (160 ἐξ ἐμέθεν δὲ κλυτοὺς φιτύσεαι υἷας) destined to become great kings (161 οἳ σκηπτοῦχοι ἅπαντες ἐπιχθονίοισιν ἔσονται). When the poem reaches its climax, the narrative tempo suddenly speeds up as Zeus' prophecy is rapidly fulfilled. In a flash he is transformed back into his proper shape and deflowers the maiden (162–164); the fact that she at once becomes a bride and a mother (165 Ζηνὸς γένετ'

---

[76] In attempting to understand the repeated retardations of Moschus' narrative, we should not underestimate the artistic background of the epyllion; it is obvious that Moschus both in the *ecphrasis* of the basket as well as in the narration of Europa's abduction combines literary and artistic techniques, see Fantuzzi – Hunter 2004, 223–4. For an 'artistic' interpretation of the epyllion's central episodes, see Manakidou 1993, 199–211.

[77] For this scene of 'sea cortège', strongly recalling visual arts, and its imitations, see Bühler 1960, 156–73.

αὐτίκα νύμφη ... 166 αὐτίκα γίνετο μήτηρ) is yet another wonder performed by Zeus within the context of the epyllion.[78]

Moschus' *Europa* deals with a crucial stage of human life, the passage into adulthood as seen from the perspective of a young virgin. Its ramifications are explored in three different situations, namely a prophetic dream, an *ecphrasis*, comprising the mirror story of Io, and a scene, evoking at the same time a rite of passage and a wedding procession. The manipulation of the time factor within the narrative highlights the psychological perception of this transition by Europa's teenage friends; inevitable though it is, this passage, the main *praxis* of the epyllion, is constantly delayed by a series of narrative retardations, thus rendering the joy of procrastination – expressed as hedonistic lingering over flower-picking, observing, dreaming, lovemaking or sailing across the sea – a central idea of the poem.[79]

4. As an epilogue

Epyllia focus on 'snapshots' rather than on plots; major mythical events remain in the background, or, to put it more accurately, their narration is postponed until after the unfolding of secondary episodes; in most cases, the main event is summarized, whereas the minor episodes, presented as scenes or decriptions, slow down the narrative pace or even bring it to a standstill; these episodes, while functioning as retardations of the anticipated main event, provide new insights into the different ways in which heroes and humans perceive time; and, although the dominant praxis, a mission of epic proportions, inevitably takes place at the end, the dynamic moment leading the protagonists to enlightenment and self-awareness towers over the entire narrative.

---

[78] On this 'speedy conclusion' in the Callimachean manner, see Campbell 1991, 128–30. For this 'condensation' of narrative as a feature of lyric poetry, see Bühler 1960, 198.

[79] This explains the lack of a teleological orientation of the plot. As Fantuzzi – Hunter 2004, 216 point out 'aetiology, teleology and narrative consequence are replaced by the portrait of a (paradoxically) universal experience. What dominates the poem is Europa's own awakened sexuality and her naive innocence.' Cusset 2001 emphasizes the metaliterary character of the poem, since, in his opinion, Moschus' epyllion should be interpreted as a metaphor for the pleasure of poetic composition in general. On *Europa* as an 'unusually sensual poem', see Schmiel 1981, 270–2.

As I hope to have shown, these temporal patterns correspond to a broader conception of time within the *fabula* of each epyllion. All three epyllia thematize a different aspect of time. In *Hecale*, the encounter of an old woman with the adolescent Theseus promotes his fuller understanding of key issues in human life; in the Callimachean epyllion this idea is explored through constant reference to the mechanism of memory. In his *Little Heracles* Theocritus highlights divergent, subjective perceptions of time as experienced by an infant prodigy, destined to gain control over eternity, and by his mortal parents, in the grips of their ephemeral fears. Moschus' *Europa*, set against the background of genealogical stories concerning the union between a god and a heroine, is dominated by an insatiable desire for the *hic et nunc*, for the delight of the moment lived. Thus, what the above discussed Hellenistic poets bring to the fore is the antithesis between objective and phenomenological time, between time measured and time experienced. In a sense, we might say that the Hellenistic poets attempted to give an unepic response to diachronic 'aporias of time'; by emphasizing the 'snapshot' in their epyllia, they seem to suggest that the perspective of eternity, as mirrored in the traditional notions of *kleos*, heroism or immortalization, has irrevocably become a thing of the past.[80]

---

80 For the use of terms such as 'aporias of time' and 'thematization of time' as well as for my concluding remarks on how literature might reconcile cosmological/objective time with phenomenological time as experienced by individuals, see Paul Ricoeur's analysis of narrative time (e.g. see Ricoeur 1984, 194 ff. on the function of time in Proust; cf. the discussion of Ricoeur's terminology by Goldthorpe 1991).

Aeneid 5.362–484: Time, Epic and the Analeptic Gauntlets

Theodore D. Papanghelis

Broadly described, my project is to evaluate, from a narratologically biased point of view, a significant object featuring on a significant occasion. The occasion is the funeral games for Anchises in the fifth book of Virgil's *Aeneid*, more particularly the boxing event that comes up in the course of the games; the object is the boxing gear, or rather the different sets of boxing gear, referred to in the text. Since, as I will be noting, significant objects surface in epic narrative complete with a history of their own, close attention to their narrativity potential may shed light on those points where the 'biography' of things seems to link up with epic narrative's broader movement in time, especially its analeptic moments, while also becoming a vehicle for epic's important thematic emphases and/or gestures of literary self-consciousness. Thus, the paper's main claim is that as a result of Virgil's special emphasis the significant object in question provides a unique focus for narratological manoeuvre, thematic signalling and generic reflexion.

1. The games: time present, past and future

First, the occasion. Despite some collateral influence from the Phaeacian games of *Odyssey* 8, the principal model for the funeral games of *Aeneid* 5 is the series of athletic contests in honour of dead Patroclus in *Iliad* 23. The Homeric fixture list is more comprehensive (8 competitive events as against 4 in the *Aeneid*), and there is a sense in which Homer's, as one would expect, is overall the more detailed coverage, even to the extent of zooming in on two potential hooligans like Idomeneus and the lesser Ajax on the terraces (23.448–98). However, this is by no means the

---

My thanks to the members of the conference, and to the editors of the present volume, especially Jonas Grethlein who, besides kindly allowing me access to unpublished work of his, offered a number of very helpful comments and suggestions.

most important difference between the two accounts. The Iliadic games mark a relaxation of tension after a series of dramatic confrontations on the battlefield, the climactic fight between Achilles and Hector and the majestic excess of grief displayed at Patroclus' funeral. As has been noted,[1] by comparison with book 2, which within the overall structure of the poem balances book 23, there is here a sense of calm and order restored to the Greek army, with the mourning Achilles making highly visible gestures of reconciliation while most of the major protagonists who will not appear in the closing book bow out after taking part in the games. Thus the whole of book 23 looks strongly retrospective and closural.

By contrast, *Aeneid* 5 recapitulates the Odyssean experience of the preceding books and, coming after the tragic *crescendo* of the events in Carthage, marks a *stasis* just before the all-important revelations of the *katabasis* in the next book; it thus points forward to the second half of the poem and the epic struggles awaiting the Trojans in Italy.[2] This double perspective is embodied by Anchises, in whose memory the games are held: before his death, he represents fixation on an irrecoverable past and is practically in charge of a misguided quest; after his death, an all but divine figure, he authoritatively beckons his son into the Roman future. Thus, we might say, the games organised in his honour, unlike those for Patroclus, are strongly prospective as, besides constituting a memorial event, they also mark the point at which the Trojan leader, after formally laying to rest a past managed by the fatherly figure, assumes full and sole responsibility as 'his own man'. Further, whereas Patroclus' life and death are bound up with, and in a sense serve mainly, the highly visible individualism of Achilles, it is above all as a 'public figure' affecting the Trojans' destiny as a nation in transition that Anchises

---

[1] See Richardson 1993.
[2] Cf. Nelis 2001, 198: '*Aeneid* 5 marks an important stage in Aeneas' casting off of his past and preparation for his future, a transition from tragedy to the hope of brighter things to come'. Nelis also associates the games of book 5 with the death of Dido, viewing them as part of a process of expiation following the queen's suicide (190 ff.). There is though room for wondering how easily this fits together with another remark of his to the effect that 'Aeneas' return to his father's grave underlines his *pietas* and marks a commitment to his duty and the future while accentuating the break with Dido and the past' (197). Had he been alive, Anchises would never have countenanced Aeneas' lingering in Carthage, and indeed as an apparition in dream he works to tear his son away from the queen. Can the games be both *for* Anchises and a *novemdiale sacrum* in memory of Dido?

acts out his role in the *Aeneid*, and on these grounds the games marking the anniversary of his death take on added significance as a collective rite. Virgil took pains to underline the difference: he interposed a year between Anchises' death and the celebrations, pointed to the values of collectivity, public-spiritedness and team work, especially in the boat race, and, uncharacteristically for individual events in epic funeral games, opened up the foot-race to the Trojan rank and file.[3]

Perhaps the most effective way to pin down the difference between the Homeric and Virgilian narratives is to compare their respective patterns of movement in time. The Homeric account's rapid, linear, forward movement seems to be bound to the requirements of a live coverage focused on the foreground and the circumstantial details of an ongoing series of athletic events.[4] This narrative thrust is only modified on a couple of occasions and only when character-text takes over from the primary narrator. This is, for instance, what happens when Nestor, on being given an honorary prize by Achilles after the chariot race, starts strolling down his long memory lane and flashes back to his antediluvian athletic prowess (23.626–50). It is worth noting in this connexion that, although Nestor's tracking backward in time entails a reference to the generational distance between young and old, his point goes no further than emphasizing the natural disqualification of the latter from any competition like the present one[5].

By contrast, in Virgil both narrator- and character-text show a more complex pattern of movement in time and a highly charged concern with the generational issue. This is evident in the non-competitive *lusus Troiae* which rounds off the games with a colourful equestrian show poised between Trojan past and Roman future. Here, to take just one example, young Priam, the leader of one of the formations,

---

3   Cairns 1989, 225–6 and 237–40 has some pertinent comments on these points.
4   The pace and the stylistic features of the Homeric coverage of the games should, of course, be seen in the light of Auerbach's 1953, 3–23 famous analysis of Homer's narrative style which, in Auerbach's formulation, tends to present 'externalized, uniformly illuminated phenomena, at a definite time and in a definite place, connected together without lacunae in a perpetual foreground'. In this respect, Virgil's way often seems to point towards the Bible narrative Auerbach holds as a foil to Homer.
5   The generational issue is also touched upon by young Antilochus, who crosses the finishing-line as a poor third after Odysseus and Ajax. His point in 23.787–92 that gods are partial to old-timers is made in a deferential but light-hearted manner.

rides the wave of a generational celebration as the narrator reaches back to his father Polites and his grandfather Priam before anticipating his prolific Italian issue in a vibrant apostrophe (5.563–5) – the young boy thus becoming the pivot of an analeptic and a proleptic movement, both of which stretch beyond the starting point and the close of the *Aeneid's* primary narrative respectively. To put it another way, the anachronic extensions on either side of the temporal level of the primary narrative make characters like young Priam look like provisional effects, the outcome of a negotiation between generational spaces that either precede or follow the epic's narrated time. The effect is compounded by the conspicuous aetiology informing the account of *the lusus Troiae*, and the same applies to the presentation of the participants in the boat race: *uelocem Mnestheus agit acri remige Pristim/mox Italus Mnestheus, genus a quo nomine Memmi* ('Mnestheus is in command of fast *Pristis* with her eager crew; he was soon to become the Italian Mnestheus from whom the Memmii take their name', 116–17) ... *Sergestusque, domus tenet a quo Sergia nomen/Centauro inuehitur magna, Scyllaque Cloanthus/ caerulea, genus unde tibi, Romane Cluenti* ('Sergestus, after whom the Sergian family is named, is sailing in great *Centaur*, and Cloanthus, the founder of the Roman Cluentii, in sea-green *Scylla*', 121–3)[6].

Although continuity of civic and social structures is a central concern of epic in general,[7] the Virgilian account with its lightning anachronies, especially those encapsulated in dramatic apostrophe, conveys a peculiarly Roman anxiety over generational continuity and thickens the temporal texture of the games narrative. Mnestheus, in the lines I have just quoted, is about to shed his Trojan past, soon (*mox*) to become Italian Mnestheus and, from the perspective of the contemporary reader, the originator of the Memmii family – three time layers, a double movement, backwards and forwards, with the dramatic present as an intersection monumentalized in the transitional ritual of the games. In this connexion, it is worth reminding that the *Aeneid*'s pervasive concern to authenticate the Roman future through the Trojan past is played out over the heads, as it were, of the epic's characters, at a level reserved for the interaction between primary narrator-focalizer and primary narratee-focalizee (and by extension with the external reader of Virgil's

---

6   See Williams's 1960 notes on 5.116 ff. (boat race) and 568 ff. (*lusus Troiae*); also Cairns 1989, 225–6; Nicoll 1985; and Sammartano 1998, 116–17.
7   See Hardie 1993, 88 ff., who also remarks that the theme of generational continuity is privileged by epic's compulsive drive for repetition.

time),[8] and the apostrophe, formally addressed to the character but in fact directed at the primary narratee-focalizee, thus becomes the vehicle of a benign irony at the expense of the former: neither the young Priam of the *lusus Troiae* nor the Cloanthus of the boat race are in a position to know the shape of things to come; thus a narrative ploy which otherwise might expend its force as a more or less rhetorical flash marks an especially intense moment in the advertisement of the epic's main ideological project.

2. These gloves are made for watching

As part of the games for Anchises, the boxing match between Dares and Entellus in *Aen.* 5.362–484 offers a new, and highly interesting, twist to the pattern of temporal movements which structure the relationship between old and new.[9] It should first be noted that the Iliadic model, which has Euryalus take on Epeius, a predictably unbeatable opponent, is a comparatively short affair of 46 lines (23.653–99) with only a slight, two-line retrospective excursion into Euryalus' background as a boxer (679–80) – an external homodiegetic analepsis which hardly interferes with the impression of a matter-of-fact, linear narrative hastening to declare Epeius' victory. By comparison, the 122 line-long Virgilian boxing event constitutes a more leisurely account in the course of which Virgil marshals a number of intertexts and creates a composite portrait for each contestant by mixing features and background information from earlier boxing encounters.[10] It thus calls for closer scrutiny.

After Aeneas has announced the match and set the prizes, forward steps Dares. He was the sole challenger of Paris in Troy's heavyweight league, and, rather impressively, has scored a signal victory over huge Butes at the funeral games for Hector; and Butes hailed from the race of Bebrycian Amycus (368–74), that thug of a boxer-king with whom Polydeuces wipes the floor twice, in Apollonius Rhodius (*Argon.* 2.1–97) and Theocritus 22. Not only is this a fascinating case

---

8 On the interaction between primary narrator-focalizer and primary narratee-focalizee in the case of apostrophe see Block 1982 and cf. de Jong (1987) 2004, 60.
9 For the central place of the boxing match not only within the athletic events but also in book 5 as a whole see Sammartano 1998, 115–16.
10 See Nelis 2001, 13–21.

of boxing pedigree metaphorising a textual lineage,[11] but also the intertextual time scale on which Dares operates as a boxer (from the epic cycle through to Hellenistic modernism) seems to belie his youth. Is it possible for this Dares to be challenged? The Iliadic boxing episode (23.651–99), with Epeius as role model for Dares, might lead the reader to doubt it, but Virgil has designs upon the reader. After a few moments of collective paralysis, which give arrogant Dares the opportunity to claim the prize for lack of a competitor, up rises the veteran boxer Entellus at Acestes' behest (387 ff.). Who is he, what is he? Despite his illustrious record, Dares is a boxing hero on the human scale.[12] Not exactly so Entellus: he is a Sicilian, once an associate of divine Eryx – Eryx, Venus' son and Aeneas' mythical half-brother, who trained Entellus and put him through his boxing paces. As he rises to meet the challenge, Entellus hurls to the ground a pair of gauntlets (400–5).

---

11 See Nelis 2001, 8–21 and cf. Feldherr 2002, 76 with n. 34: 'Dares' defeat of a Bebrycian can thus be correlated with Vergil's recasting of the epic narrative that records an earlier Bebrycian boxing match, Apollonius' *Argonautica*, just as that episode in turn signals its own manipulation of the *Iliad* and the *Odyssey*'.

12 Nelis 2001, 13–21 treats in detail the ways in which Virgil, in describing the boxing match between Dares and Entellus, creates a composite portrait of each of the two contestants by mixing features and background information from earlier boxing encounters. Readers who pick up an initial intertextual allusion may thus find themselves on a false trail, expecting victory for the eventual loser and vice versa, as in the case of the intertextual pair of Dares and Entellus. Whether such manipulation of and play with previous texts (a ubiquitous feature of Virgilian redrafting) supports a meticulously detailed Virgilian programme of revisions and revaluations which brings national identities, cultural orders, readers' and audiences' perspectives, historical perceptions et al. into play is an interesting question with which Feldherr in his above-mentioned article gets to grips, at times, it seems to me, with more determination and thoroughness than cogency. Certainly, the intricate pattern of responses his reading is designed to encourage takes no account of the principal grounds on which, on my reading of the episode, the figure of Entellus and what he stands for are starkly contrasted with Dares (see below). Like other critics, Feldherr seems to assimilate Dares to a general impression of more-than-human boxing scale which, I think, is mainly due to Virgil's portraiture of Entellus (for all his record, Dares is only referred to in lines 368–9 as *uastis cum viribus effert ora* whereas Entellus' description in lines 421–3 is far more impressive). After all, it is this crucial distinction between the opponents that Entellus' background and inherited boxing gear mean to bring home to the reader, and no amount of 'confusion', 'blurring', 'repetition' (or, indeed, special pleading) should make one lose sight of it. Sammartano 1998, 121–5 argues that Dares' career evokes Heracles' victorious adventures in Troad and Bithynia.

Exhibit no 1: seven huge ox-hides armed with lead and iron – our significant object. It will be evident that I am borrowing the terms Jasper Griffin has used to designate objects with a strong symbolic and evocative potential for Homeric narrative.[13] One specimen of this class of objects, commented on by Griffin, is Agamemnon's sceptre at *Il.* 2.100–108, a symbol of power and authority which, in the context of the lying dream sent by Zeus to Agamemnon and the ensuing muddle, passes to the hands of Odysseus who makes of it both a stick and a carrot. Odysseus succeeds where Agamemnon had failed, and the sceptre becomes the focal object-symbol of a situation that leaves the latter discredited at the same time as the former has yet another feather added to his cap – a significant object telling a parable about the guts and alertness true leadership requires[14]. Further, this sceptre is no high-tech, new generation accoutrement, but a thing of venerable antiquity, fashioned by Hephaestus and through a number of illustrious owners going back to Zeus himself – and it triggers a substantial external analepsis, as such significant objects tend to do[15].

When the flashback does not just clarify the origin of the object, as in the case of Agamemnon's sceptre, it may also bring up some event of the past narrated more or less for its own sake, as happens with Odysseus' bow in *Od.* 21.11–33. Significant objects may also be characterised by two aspects which, albeit not ubiquitous, are endowed with a dramatic effect and are important for my purposes. First, they may sustain the laudatory motif 'only he could wield it', as, for instance, in *Il.* 19.387–91 where Achilles is said to be the only hero capable of handling Peleus' spear[16]; and secondly, they may be represented as things of awe and fear unfit for the gaze of lesser men, as in *Il.* 19.12–15, where the Myrmidons cannot bear to look straight upon the armour Thetis

---

13 See Griffin 1980, 1–49.
14 See Griffin 1980, 9–11.
15 Griffin's point of view and his illuminating remarks come close to the insights of the 'archaeology of the past' and its concern with material objects. Especially in the context of epic poetry, such objects, ranging from highly visible monuments to everyday commodities, are important indexes to the past and to the perceived difference between heroic past and performative present. Jonas Grethlein's article (2008b) offers a very perceptive and detailed discussion of the relevant material in the Homeric epics from precisely this angle. Although my approach was formed independently, readers who will have the chance to compare the main lines of my argument with, especially, the third section of Grethlein's paper will not fail to notice strong parallels and convergences.
16 See Edwards 1991, n. on 19. 387–921.

brings her son.[17] Admittedly, in this case the significant object is fresh from the smith's workshop; on the other hand, one may be forgiven for presuming that 'cute' or 'smart' would not have been the first words springing to the mind of someone looking at Achilles' previous, and lost, outfit. Thus, to sum up, significant objects, apart from their symbolic and evocative potential, may either occasion a retrospection or be reserved for special use by unique figures or constitute an awe-inspiring spectacle or all of these together.

Now Eryx's gauntlets partake of all three aspects. 'Manufactured in age-old Homeric epic' is stamped on their seven ox-hides, with every hide layer archeologically, as it were, measuring their distance from the dramatic present. Entellus in his character-speech (410–20) also makes it clear that, far from being the one-size-fits-all type, they have been the exclusive preserve of divine Eryx to be subsequently handed down to their present owner. The primary narrator-focalizer describes them as huge and heavy, but the expression *immani pondere* is even more pointed if it is also taken to represent the implicit embedded focalization of the bystanders, which becomes explicit in their astonished reaction in lines 404–8. And the main secondary focalizer here is Dares (*ante omnis stupet*) who looks as if he has been knocked off his perch. Judging by design, weight and size, he will no doubt be surmising that this gear antedates his own boxing career, previously summed up in narrator text. But what exactly is the analeptic range of these gauntlets? The answer is given by Entellus himself: the thing is stained with ancient gore from the times when Eryx was lord of the ring and Entellus, in his green prime, put up the sequel to his master's performance; nay, these are the very gauntlets Eryx wore when he relinquished both championship and life at the mighty hands of Heracles – and if you haven't seen the latter's gauntlets, you ain't seen nothing yet!

This is a case where character-text both complements and intensifies narrator-text; it is also a case where the significant object becomes the vehicle of a spectacular analeptic escalation which makes Dares' record look like a spot of new-fangled, text-based history beside the expanse of a timeless legend featuring the archetypal figure of Heracles. Eryx's and Heracles' gauntlets put together make for an external analepsis which outsizes the one occasioned by Dares by a wide mythical margin. As I

---

17 On significant objects as evidence of an awsome past and of the superiority of previous generations over present ones, see the third section of Grethlein's paper, mentioned above, n. 16.

have just hinted, character-text competes with narrator-text by capping the latter's retrospective move. We will presently see the sequel to the analeptic escalation triggered by our significant object. But this is bound up with the question of whether and how the more or less formalist aspects of the boxing-match narrative bear on the *Aeneid*'s broader thematic concerns and, at another level, on its perceived generic self-awareness.

Now, it is obvious that the gauntlets make of Entellus a figure of hyperbole.[18] I will come back to this in a moment. First, let it be noted that in the interests of fair play Entellus foregoes his own gauntlets and accepts to confront Dares with matched ones (417–20). I don't know much about boxing champions' average IQ, but I would guess that Entellus understands the implications of significant objects at least as well as Jasper Griffin does. By splashing Eryx's gauntlets over the place and by inviting everyone to visualize those of Heracles, he makes an analeptic leap far beyond the range and class of Dares; then, to make himself a match for Dares, he reverses the process by, precisely, consenting to use ordinary, matched gauntlets. He comes back to the first narrative after shedding, as Philip Hardie would have put it, his chthonic, elemental qualities and after extricating himself from the patterns of Gigantomachic allusion, where Eryx's and Heracles' gauntlets had analeptically taken him – and where we might have looked upon

---

18 See Hardie 1986, 245. Elsewhere (p. 254, n. 38) Hardie singles out the account of the ship race and the boxing match of *Aeneid* 5 as 'notoriously hyperbolical', remarking that '[t]his hyperbole does not seem to cohere with the thematic structures of the poem, unless an attempt is made to see these sporting episodes as in some sense "dummy runs" for the serious contests later on … the mountainous boxers Dares and Entellus are matched by the hyperbolically presented figures of Aeneas and Turnus in the last scene of the poem'. On this cf. also Galinsky 1968, 183. As I have noted earlier on, Dares' unproblematic assimilation to the figure of Entellus is a miscalculation that precludes a crucial distinction on the basis of which Entellus takes on a significance all of his own. If, as I will presently argue, the latter is presented as in some sense another Sicilian 'Cyclops', then something of what, on Hardie's reading (pp. 264–7), applies to the Cyclops (he is a threat to the cosmological order that, much like Mezentius, Cacus and Turnus later on, has to be eliminated before Aeneas can establish the order he stands for) may also apply to Entellus. Cf. Galinsky 1968, 174 who sees the fight between Entellus and Dares, like that between Heracles and Cacus, as foreshadowing the final combat between Aeneas and Turnus. Correspondences between pairs of opponents readily suggest themselves, but pressing them too hard is bound to produce the kind of centrifugal associations that impairs any single interpretative scheme.

him as a Mezentius[19] or Turnus of the boxing ring or, perhaps, as a kind of Cyclops[20] (*haec fatus duplicem ex umeris reiecit amictum/et <u>magnos membrorum artus</u>, <u>magna ossa lacertosque</u>/exuit atque <u>ingens</u> media consistit harena*, 'With these words, he threw the double cloak off his shoulders, baring the great joints of his limbs, the great bones and muscular arms, and stood giant-like in the middle of the arena', 421–3) – one may remember that his abode, just like Cyclops', displays a rich collection of what

---

19 *moles*, an otherwise frequent word in Virgil, is only shared by three individuals, Entellus (5.431), Cacus (8.199) and Mezentius (10.771). See Glenn 1971, 151.
20 Entellus is an admirable patchwork of a boxer. In responding to Dares' challenge and being urged on by Acestes he corresponds with Iliadic Euryalus who rises up against Epeius and is likewise encouraged by Diomedes; in his initial reluctance to fight on account of advanced age he points to *Od.* 18.14–107 where Odysseus 'the old beggar' agrees to engage the younger Irus, egged on, as he cunningly states, by hunger; and he shares with Odysseus the paradoxical quality of robust (and victorious) old bones; finally, Entellus, native to the land where the Trojans are only visitors, possessed of an enormous and uncannily sturdy built and of a long record of ruthless victories over hapless opponents, is strongly and primarily suggestive of Apollonius' and Theocritus' Amycus (although his final victory and Acestes' support also edge him slightly over to the side of Polydeuces whom Apollonius represents as being reassured by Castor and Talaus). If Virgil, through allusion to the figure of Amycus, meant to depict an Entellus on the Gigantomachic scale, it is worth noting that both Theocritus and Apollonius compare Amycus with fearsome gigantic creatures like Tityus and Typhoeus: Τιτυῷ ἐναλίγκιος ἀνήρ, 'a Tityus-like figure' (Theocr. 22.94), ἀλλ' ὁ μὲν ἢ ὀλοοῖο Τυφωέος, ἠὲ καὶ αὐτῆς/Γαίης εἶναι ἔϊκτο πέλωρ τέκος, οἷα πάροιθεν/χωομένη Διὶ τίκτεν, 'The one seemed to be a huge son of evil Typhoeus or of Earth herself, the kind of offspring she brought forth in old days when she was cross with Zeus' (*Argon.* 2.38–40). The difference, emphasized by Apollonius in lines 38–42, between the monstrous heavyweight stature of Amycus and the youthful grace of Polydeuces has been transposed by Virgil onto his boxers, with Entellus being described as a more or less cumbersome mass contrasting with the nimbleness and agility of his opponent, while Theocritus' πᾶς δ' ἐπὶ γαίῃ/κεῖτ' ἀλλοφρονέων, 'out of balance, he stretched the whole length of his body on the ground' (128–9), which refers to Amycus' final fall to the ground, is echoed by *et ultro/ipse grauis grauiterque ad terram pondere uasto/concidit* (446–8), a phrase of the μέγας μεγαλωστί type appropriate, precisely, of a giant's 'displacement'. In respect of the preponderant analogy between Amycus and Entellus, it may not be without significance that the former is explicitly said by Theocritus to be 'Poseidon's over-confident son' (97), an expression one might easily transfer to the Cyclops. On the correspondence Amycus-Entellus see also Poliakoff 1985. Poliakoff argues that Entellus' eruption into violence after his fall signals a descent to the savagery suggested by his alignment with Amycus while the substitution of a bull instead of Dares as victim is proof of reasonable behaviour restored.

must have been equally gory and blood-bespattered spoils (*ubi fama per omnem/Trinacriam et spolia illa tuis pendentia tectis?*, 'where is that fame of yours once spread throughout Sicily, where are the trophies hanging in your house?', 392–3[21]); we should remember, too, that like Polyphemus, he is a Sicilian; above all, we should remember that Sicily and its shoreline are a traditional place of wonders, a kind of Jurassic Park for monsters like the Cyclopes and Charybdis.

So now the match can go ahead on equal terms – in theory, at least, for it is hard for this Entellus to be broken in, not quite yet. In the ensuing fight, and on being helped to his feet after a miscalculated blow that causes him to seismically fall to the ground, Entellus flies into a violent rage and comes back with a torrent of punches that would have deflated poor Dares to yet another of his hanging spoils had not Aeneas rang the referee's bell and talked him out of the ring: 'Come on, son, quit; can't you see this is "strength of a different order"'? *cede deo* ('*infelix, quae tanta animum dementia cepit?/non uiris alias conuersaque numina sentis?/cede deo*, 465–7). You can't possibly explain to a boxer, let alone a punchdrunk one, that there is a generic, metapoetic side to this fatherly advice. But I suppose you can try it with your audience. Entellus comes from an epic world of a different order – a Gigantomachic and Titanic narrative. Dares, for all his distinguished record but also because of it, inhabits an epic discourse (Virgil's epic discourse) that, while recalling the fantastic brutes and monsters of the archaic epic at the level of narrative intertext, steers clear of them at the level of narrated action.

---

21 Cyclops' cave is described as *domus sanie dapibusque cruentis,/intus opaca, ingens*, 'his home was huge and dark, filled with the gory remains of his feasts' (3.618–19) ; the spoils hanging in Entellus' dwelling are not specified (*et spolia illa tuis pendentia tectis*, 393) but the exhibition is uncannily reminiscent of that in Cacus' cave *(foribusque adfixa superbis/ora uirum tristi pendebant pallida tabo*, 'and nailed to his arrogant doors there were hanging heads of men, pale and dripping with gore', 8.196–7), and the visual evidence of bloody violence displayed in the domestic environment of two explicit ogres is hardly suggestive of medals or olive wreaths in the case of Entellus. Besides, 5.413 (*sanguine cernis adhuc sparsoque infecta cerebro*, 'you see it is still befouled with blood and scattered brains') is calculated to bring home to the reader the nature of the latter's spoils.

3. Better to shoot the bull

Dares grows aware of the full significance of the analeptic gauntlets too late and the hard way. Otherwise he would have stood clear of his Sicilian giant, just as Aeneas himself had done with his *(this is not our kind of epic, son!)*. And since Entellus, after the boxing match, still looks like a square peg in a round hole, a more drastic procedure is called for. Thus, after his victory he substitutes the 'beneficial violence' of sacrifice for the uncontrolled violence that would have resulted in Dares' death,[22] and the mortal knock-out is reserved for the bull earmarked as the victor's prize (477–84).[23] If there is a civic and cultural order to which Entellus is presented as something of a misfit, his sacrificial act is intended, if not to integrate, at least to bring him closer to it.[24] Unlike other readers, I see here no story of decline.[25] Virgil reverses what I have termed the analeptic escalation; the archaic, chthonic Sicilian descends of his own will to a status compatible with the values represented by the

---

[22] On sacrificial substitution in the *Aeneid* in general see Hardie 1993, 19–36 and, especially on the boxing match between Entellus and Dares, 52. According to Hardie, confusion between sacrificial frame and sporting event in this as in other events of the games is an ever-present danger.

[23] Not only is the bull a prize for the winner but the boxers themselves are often represented as fighting, or falling, like bulls and vice versa. On this interesting interchangeability see Hunter 1989a. The bovine element informs Virgil's boxing match in more than one ways, as Feldherr 2002, 69–70 remarks: there are gauntlets made of ox-hide, Dares' previous opponent is called Butes and Eryx's boxing sobriquet was 'bull'. This bulls-fight-like-boxers-and-boxers-fight-like-bulls nexus alerts Feldherr to the possibility of a confusion between sacrificant and victim in the sacrificial conclusion to Virgil's boxing match on the grounds that '[t]he bull is killed [by Entellus], not as a sacrificial victim, but as a boxing opponent' (69). Yet Entellus' hands-on technique, as has often been noted, repeats that of Heracles in *Argon.* 1.425–31, although for the latter hero it is the club, naturally, that comes in handy for the occasion. Thus Entellus' gesture aligns him with Heracles whose presence is throughout vibrant in the background of the boxing episode. In my view, there is little point in claiming, as Feldherr 2002, 70–1 does, that there is as much identification, as there is distinction, between bull and Dares as Entellus' victims when the latter takes grammatical pains to underline the definitiveness of the substitution: *hanc tibi, Eryx, m e l i o r e m animam p r o morte Daretis/persoluo*, 'Eryx, this better life I offer to you in place of Dares' death' (483–4). See below.

[24] Sammartano 1998, 128–9 marshals a detailed argument to the effect that Entellus' victory over Dares should be viewed as 'la rivincita dell'elemento locale, amico delle genti troiane, sull'elemento allogeno, di marca filo-ellenica'.

[25] See Feldherr 2002, 66.

new epic, into which he only stepped as a kind of guest-star from a superseded order of things.[26] His final act of laying down the boxing gloves and retiring from the sport reflexively thematises a transitional moment between retrospection and renewal within the boundaries of epic discourse. Virgil plots generic retrospection on to the analeptic movement embodied by the figure of Entellus and his gauntlets and then allows the same Entellus to reverse the process with a view to clearing the epic field for a new kind of regulated heroic action. *Well, says Aeneas to Dares, we can't and we won't take these figures on in their own ring and on their own terms. They either have to be sailed past or made to bow out of their own free will.*

The funeral games of the *Aeneid* are held in honour of a transitional figure that straddles both past and future. Further, they occupy the transitional space between two modes of thematic repetition (repetition as regression *to* and repetition as reversal *of* the past) and two corresponding narrative forms (romance narrative and teleological-epic narrative) brilliantly analysed by David Quint.[27] I have generally claimed that, placed in such a transitional space, the games for Anchises seem to contribute in their own way to this broader transitional process. The boat race allows the presentness of its first narrative to have grafted onto it both an analeptic and a proleptic movement. In their transitional space the ship captains come fraught with Trojan background while their names function as entries in a double sense: foundation entries in the historical Roman Registrar's generation records as well as entries for the athletic event. The boxing match, the main focus of this paper, introduces further complications of temporality through analeptic escalation and its reversal, executed in a reflexive mode that throws up questions of internal generic distinctions, measures the distance between old and new, and in doing so links up with the poem's broader thematic argument.[28]

---

26 As Feldherr 2002, 68 notes, '[t]he substitution for the monstrous and deadly arms of Eryx powerfully defines the separation between past and present'.
27 Quint 1993, 50–96, esp. 50–65.
28 Traill 2001 makes out a strong case for 5.437–42 (where Dares, looking for ways to attack Entellus, is likened to a general engaged in siege warfare) alluding to the siege by Hamilcar of a Roman garrison placed at the summit of Mount Eryx, during the First Punic War. In referring to this siege, Polybius (56.1–57.2) compares the warring generals to boxers, though it is hard to say whether Virgil borrowed directly from Polybius or whether they were both drawing on a common source. Yet Traill's claim that '[c]learly, the aggressive

In the case of this boxing event, Virgil's operation hinges on Entellus' pair of gauntlets, a typically epic significant object, a powerfully evocative thing that both narrator and character text, in their interactive relationship, think with. By the way, 'Evocative Objects. Things we think with' is the title of a collection of essays recently edited by Sherry Turkle, Professor of the Social Studies of Science and Technology at the MIT. And it is from this refreshing and fascinating volume that I have copied the following: 'In doing the biography of a thing, one would ask questions similar to those one asks about people ... Where does the thing come from and who made it? What has been its career so far, and what do people consider to be an ideal career for such things? What are the recognised "ages" or periods in the thing's "life", and what are the cultural markers for them? How does the thing's use change with its age and what happens to it when it reaches the end of its usefulness?...'.[29] Against the background of this anthropological reflection, I might perhaps be forgiven for contending that these gauntlets are, from a narratological point of view, one of the most versatile and resourceful of epic's significant objects.

---

and restless Dares is intended to prefigure Hamilcar, and the wary, unbudging Entellus the besieged Roman general' (411) leaves us with a rather awkward correspondence between Trojan and Carthaginian. The considerations out of which Virgil has to make Entellus slow and heavy by contrast to Dares' agility are quite clear, and if, as is likely, geographical association caused an historiographical passage to contribute to the multiple origin of the boxing episode, one might perhaps take note of the historical allusion without having to accommodate every single detail of the boxing simile. Irrespective of the extent to which the Sicilian events narrated in the *Aeneid* may be specifically linked to events in Roman history, there can be little doubt that, as Galinsky 1968 argues, '[i]n the Aeneid the emphasis on Sicily within Rome's Trojan legend is the poetic reflection of the Roman national experience' (184).

29 Turkle 2007, 152. In fact, Turkle is quoting from the anthropologist Igor Kopytoff's 'The Cultural Biography of Things: Commodization as Process', an essay contained in *The Social Life of Things* (ed. by Arjun Appadurai), Cambridge 1986.

IV. Narratology and the Interpretation of Tragedy

Sophocles and the Narratology of Drama

Francis Dunn

To what extent (if at all) can narratology be applied to the study of drama? This is one of the major questions animating this collection, and to date, there have been two main lines of response. The first, following Gérard Genette's insistence on the presence of a narrator[1] and endorsed by Irene de Jong (see below), is a piecemeal approach which accepts that there can be no narratology *of* drama, since drama is not narrated (it shows rather than tells), and turns instead to narratology *in* drama – that is, the study of smaller parts within a play such as messenger speeches and true or false stories told by the characters. The second approach is comprehensive: it argues that narratology can nevertheless be extended to drama and takes its inspiration from productive narratologies of film. Judging from the attempts made so far, the comprehensive approach has had limited success (Gould and others on tragedy, Richardson on modern drama, discussed below). The first part of this paper considers why this is so and proposes an alternative line of response – a narratology *of* drama that is strategic rather than comprehensive and that is appropriate both to modern drama and to Greek tragedy. The second part of the paper shows how strategic narrative devices are used to full effect in Sophocles' *Electra*.

1. Is there a narratology of drama?

In introducing the collection, *Narrators, Narratees, and Narratives*, Irene de Jong 2004, 6–7 strictly limits the application of narratology to narratives *in* drama, and in the process criticizes briefly – and I would say quite rightly – some classicists who have adopted what I am calling a comprehensive approach. To highlight the issues at stake, I focus on one of those whom she criticizes.

---

[1] Articulated in Genette (1972) 1980, 163–4 and forcefully restated in Genette (1983) 1988, 41, where he speaks of 'the truly insurmountable opposition between dramatic representation and narrative'.

Gould (and others) on Greek tragedy

An early attempt to apply narratology to Greek tragedy occurs in a lecture delivered in 1991 by John Gould, ' "… And Tell Sad Stories of the Deaths of Kings": Greek tragic drama as narrative', later published as Gould 2001, 319–34. Gould identifies several features of Greek tragedy that, in his view, warrant the consideration of tragedy as a form of narrative. The most important of these features is temporal duality, that is, a difference between the 'story time' of the underlying *fabula* and the 'discourse time' of staged events. Gould assumes that such duality is sufficient for him to identify a work as 'narrative', but this is not true: as Genette points out ((1972) 1980, 33–4), the distinction between story time and discourse time is a feature also of cinema, oral tales, and comic strips. It so happens that others have used the temporal ordering of literary works to argue for a wider category of narrative. For example, Seymour Chatman 1990, 114–15 suggests that novels, epics, short stories and so on be labeled 'diegetic narratives' while the likes of plays, movies, and comic strips (sometimes termed narratives without a narrator) be called 'mimetic narratives'. Gould, however, neither argues for widening the category of narrative nor seems aware that such an argument is even necessary. Instead, he compounds the confusion about the significance of temporal duality with a strange idea of what it is. For Gould, the difference between story time and discourse time betrays an implied author, 'a controlling and selecting mind' (2001, 320), who shapes the *fabula* into a narrative. In these terms we are actually dealing, not with the temporal procedures identified by narratologists, but with an implied creator whose role in shaping an artistic product can just as easily be posited for a poem or sculpture or any other work of art. This critical drift, sliding all too easily from the formal role of a narrator to the general subject of an author or creator, is not unique to Gould's essay. Andreas Markantonatos, for instance, addresses the absence of a narrator in drama by observing, 'we can easily obviate the apparent difficulty by simply arguing for the presence of a governing consciousness, which we choose to identify with the playwright or the director, whose omniscience shapes the narrative and brings the story to life' (2002, 5).

Gould's next point is a corollary of the first, namely that a play such as Aeschylus' *Agamemnon*, which handles time in complex ways and meditates at length on the past, should be classed with the narrative fictions of Tolstoy and James which likewise 'control our response as readers to the characters and events' (2001, 324).

Gould's second major argument involves the internal narrators of Greek tragedy (any characters who act as narrators within the drama). He claims that all such narrators, chorus and messengers included, speak with the limited perspective of agents within the action (for which Gould adopts the term 'focalization') rather than the 'privileged' and 'omniscient' perspective of an external narrator (326). For some scholars, the abundance of internal narrators suggests that the distinction between drama and narrative is not a firm one. Classicist Barbara Goward goes much further, concluding from this fluid boundary that 'at a fundamental level, narrative and drama are indistinguishable' (1999, 11). Gould, however, follows the observation in a different direction. Already satisfied that drama is a kind of narrative, he insists on the limitations of tragedy's internal speakers in order to circle back and tease out the difference between drama and narrative. The distinction he wants us to recognize is evident in his emphasis on the 'omniscience' of an external narrator (2001, 324), namely that narrative has one all-powerful narrator and drama many partial or limited narrators, but his argument is strongly judgmental. Proceeding from Plato's famous distinction between *mimesis* and *diegesis* (*Republic* 3, 392c-397b[2]), he argues that the philosopher admits only *diegesis* in his utopia because narrative exercises 'absolute and total control' over its readers (333) whereas mimesis, in giving autonomy to individual speakers, subverts Plato's totalizing fantasy in which the narrator fully 'determines closure and meaning' (333). From insisting that drama is narrative, to describing drama's internal narratives, to marking out a stark opposition between subversive drama and totalitarian narrative, the argument's rhetorical drift leads almost to self-contradiction.

More problematic to my mind than this rhetorical circle are the assumptions on which it rests. The external narrator, according to Gould, is omniscient (324) and univocal (333), controlling the movement of the work (321), determining meaning (333), and guiding the reader toward 'a foreseen and ultimately perfected "closure"' (321–22). These assumptions, however, are not supported by argument, and the resulting generic opposition between 'open' drama and 'closed' narrative runs counter to most narrative criticism which, at least since Bakhtin 1975 (1981), has underscored the openness and polyphony of the novel.

---

2   For a close reading of this passage, see Stephen Halliwell's essay in this volume.

Gould is a thoughtful critic of Greek drama, but in proposing to treat drama as narrative he either confuses or misapplies central narratological concepts. Similar confusions occur, as I have noted, in Markantonatos and Goward; I therefore think it fair to conclude, with de Jong, that among classicists the attempt to offer a comprehensive narratology *of* drama has not succeeded.

Chatman and Richardson on film and drama

The situation is quite different, however, in film studies, where Seymour Chatman's book, *Coming to Terms*, argues in great detail for the 'cinematic narrator' as an analogue to the narrator of the novel. This cinematic narrator makes use of devices such as camera angle, fade-in, and voice-over to determine what Chatman calls 'slant' and 'filter' – the cinematic equivalents of the points of view of the narrator and characters respectively (1990, 143–5). To put this another way, 'telling' in film is mediated by a range of formal devices as is 'telling' in the novel. The same, however, cannot be said of 'showing' in drama. The presentation of events there is shaped and colored in many ways: by the playwright's presentation of the *fabula*, the director's adaptation of the script, the set designer's interpretation of setting, the actors' creation of their roles, and so on. But these are not analogous, either individually or collectively, to the mediation of narrator or camera. Each is analogous instead to the shaping of material by an implied author, and one feature that drama does share with cinema is a plurality of external authors or creators who contribute to the work's overall effect. But unlike cinema, drama presents its many-authored action directly to the audience without mediation.

Chatman himself includes plays, along with movies and cartoons, in the set of 'mimetic narratives,' classing novels, epics, and short stories as 'diegetic narratives' (1990, 115), but makes no attempt to argue for a narrating agent in drama as he does for film. As far as I can see, this remains an obstacle to applying narratology to drama. For example, the narratologist Manfred Jahn (2001) proposes a narrating agent for drama but relies mainly upon two special cases: the prologue speaker in Elizabethan drama who plays the part of internal narrator, and the elaborate stage directions in the works of George Bernard Shaw and other modern playwrights that seem to emanate from the author. Jahn then goes on to create new problems by distinguishing two dramatic modes: the performance mode of live theater and the playscript mode of the printed text, the latter including those unperformable 'stage directions' so common in Shaw or Eugene O'Neill (Jahn, 2001, 674–5). Nevertheless, seeking a comprehensive narratology of drama by introducing a new category of scripted performance is, as Jahn himself acknowledges, awkward at best.³

More productive is an essay by the narrative theorist Brian Richardson (2001) that puts observation before theory: he first describes modern and postmodern plays, from Tennessee Williams to Samuel Beckett and Paula Vogel, that experimentally break down the divide between narrative and drama, before going on to argue that theorizing these hybrid forms can enrich theories of narrative and of drama. These exotic contemporary forms might seem far removed from classical literature or Sophocles – Richardson himself begins by noting that his interest is in dramatic appropriations of narrative that are 'ontologically larger acts' than 'the recounting of an offstage death in Greek tragedy' (2001, 682) – yet several of his examples do have parallels in Sophocles and Euripides, and I would like to mention two in particular.

Under the heading of 'memory plays', Richardson discusses Tennessee Williams' *Glass Menagerie*. This play begins with a single actor onstage who identifies himself as 'the narrator of the play, and also a character in it' ((1945) 1999, 5). After setting the scene he steps into the action as the character Tom Wingfield, then at several points steps out again to comment on the action, and at the end of the play he delivers an extradramatic epilogue. The technique recalls the prologues of Shakespeare. There is a distinct difference, however: whereas in memory plays the prologue speaker is homodiegetic (that is, also a character in the drama), in those of Shakespeare this same *dramatis persona* is heterodiegetic. In Greek tragedy we find a similar technique in the narrative prologues of Euripides. These prologues are actually closer to those of Williams than of Shakespeare, since the Euripidean prologue speaker is homodiegetic, although the gods who sometimes appear in this role (with the exception of Dionysus in *Bacchae*) do not directly participate in the drama as do humans like the Nurse in *Medea* or Amphitryon in *Heracles*.⁴ Richardson goes on to mention Bertolt Brecht's

---

3   'The model seems to multiply categories unnecessarily', Jahn 2001, 675.
4   The human prologue speakers are the Nurse in *Medea*, Andromache in *Andromache*, Aethra in *Suppliant Women*, Iolaus in *Children of Heracles*, Amphitryon in *Heracles*, Iphigenia in *Iphigenia among the Taurians*, Helen in *Helen*, the Farmer

Caucasian Chalk Circle under the heading 'generative narrators.' By this he refers to the Singer who introduces a play called 'The Chalk Circle' and prompts his companions to perform it ((1955) 1988, 8). The Singer's role is thus heterodiegetic, occupying what Richardson (2001, 685) calls 'a distinct ontological level' since he ostensibly creates the enacted fiction. Brecht's technique also has parallels in Euripides whose divine prologue speakers typically generate the action of the play, as when Apollo announces his plan to rescue Alcestis from death, or when Aphrodite inaugurates her plan to punish Hippolytus. The ambivalence in Brecht, whose singer and musicians break the dramatic illusion even as their constant presence and recurrent interventions place them on the same ontological level as the other characters, is paralleled in Euripides, whose gods inhabit the same mythical world as his characters even as their pronouncements from on high elevate them above the others both physically and ontologically.[5]

Internal playwrights in Greek tragedy

It should be clear from these examples that there is indeed room for a narratology *of* Greek tragedy — at least if by this we mean not a comprehensive approach that assimilates drama to narrative, but a strategic approach that recognizes those situations in which drama makes use of a narrating agent. The plays of Euripides, for example, regularly combine 'showing' us events of the play in dramatic mimesis with 'telling' us what precedes and follows in the diegesis of his (sometimes lengthy) prologues and epilogues. It would seem worthwhile to explore and theorize the hybrid narratological status of these plays. However, since Euripides is often considered exceptional in his dramatic techniques, I turn instead to Sophocles, the playwright who for many critics embodies the norms of Greek tragedy.

---

in *Electra*, Electra in *Orestes*, and Jocasta in *Phoenician Women*. The supernatural prologue speakers are, strictly speaking, homodiegetic (they belong to the fictional world, and are not external narrators) but nevertheless stand outside the action: Apollo and Death in *Alcestis*, Aphrodite in *Hippolytus*, Polydorus' ghost in *Hecuba*, Poseidon and Athena in *Trojan Women*, and Hermes in *Ion*. The two exceptions are *Bacchant Women*, where the god Dionysus speaks the prologue and plays a central role in the action, and *Iphigenia at Aulis*, where (if our text is correct) such a narrative prologue is lacking.

5   On the entrance of gods on a level above other characters, see Mastronarde 1990.

A good example of how Sophocles embodies these norms is his avoidance of narrative prologues and epilogues, which Euripides regularly employed and for which he was criticized since antiquity.[6] Aeschylus provides a partial precedent for Euripides in that he begins the *Oresteia* and *Seven against Thebes* with narrative prologues, and ends both the *Oresteia* and the *Danaids* with a god who speaks about the future. Sophocles, by contrast, uses this kind of exposition only in Heracles' prophecy at the conclusion of *Philoctetes*, and the exceptional nature of this hero *ex machina* is often explained by the drama's late date or by the influence of Euripides.[7] Whether normative or not, Sophoclean tragedy provides useful instances of how drama might function as narrative even without narrative prologues or epilogues. I focus here upon two components of his plays, one a technique found in three of his seven surviving tragedies, the other a formal component of all Greek tragedy that lends itself to narratological study.

The technique I refer to falls under the heading of metatheater. Three different plays begin with a character who functions as an internal playwright or author and thus stands in relation to the body of the play as the narrator does to a novel. The prologue of *Ajax*, for instance, features Athena looking down upon Odysseus and offering to bring onstage the maddened hero so that Odysseus may enjoy the spectacle of his misfortune; the roles of Athena as playwright and Odysseus as spectator are underscored by the god's explanation (69–70, 83–86) that Ajax will remain unaware that Odysseus is watching him. This mini-drama has been discussed as metatheater (e.g. Easterling 1993, 81–4, Ringer 1998, 31–7), but also, I would argue, lends itself to narratological analysis. As an internal dramatist, Athena presents for all to see the maddened Ajax ('and I show you this most visible derangement', δείξω

---

6 The criticism of 'detached prologues' is implicit in Aristophanes (*Frogs* 945–7), might be inferred from Aristotle's definition of the 'whole' (*Poetics* 1450 b.26–31), and is explicit in the scholiast (on *Trojan Women* 36): 'This [Hecuba's misery] should have been shown through action, as she laments onstage. That is how tragedy arouses emotion, but instead he coldly addresses the audience', ἄμεινον ἦν ἀπὸ τῶν πραγμάτων παρεισάγεσθαι, ὀδυρομένην τὰ παρόντα. οὕτως γὰρ ἡ τραγῳδία τὸ πάθος εἶχε, νῦν δὲ ψυχρῶς τῷ θεάτρῳ προσδιαλέγεται. On Euripides' detached prologues, see Segal 1992, 104–10; on Aristotle, see Roberts 1992. On his narrative epilogues, see Dunn 1996, 64–83.

7 Bates 1940, 162 considered Sophocles' use of the *deus* in *Philoctetes* an imitation of Euripides catering to popular tastes; Hoppin 1990, 150–1 adds that metrical innovations in the exodos attempt to outdo Euripides; and Jouanna 2001, 375–6 argues that his use of the crane is the same as that of Euripides.

δὲ καὶ σοὶ τήνδε περιφανῆ νόσον, 66[8]), but her role is hardly dispassionate. Just as a novel's narrator is not neutral, but a speaker with a voice and point of view, so too Athena designed the hero's madness as an evil snare (ἕρκη κακά, 60). She wants Odysseus to spread the news, presumably to heighten the other's humiliation (67), and she assumes he will take pleasure in mocking his enemy's plight ('Isn't mocking enemies the sweetest mockery?' οὔκουν γέλως ἥδιστος εἰς ἐχθροὺς γελᾶν; 79). Athena concludes the scene with tendentious observations on divine power and human suffering (118–20, 127–33) that reinforce her role as internal dramatist and endow her with the conventional voice of a tragic author. These and other indications of the internal playwright's point of view[9] I shall term 'slant', following Chatman's use of this word for the point of view of the 'cinematic narrator' in film.

It is to Odysseus as internal spectator that Athena presents the spectacle of the maddened Ajax, saying that she will show (δείξω, 66) him the other's illness, asking afterwards, 'Do you see, Odysseus, how great is the power of the gods?' (118), and reassuring him that although he will see Ajax, Ajax cannot see him (69–70, 83–86). Just as narration in a novel disposes the reader to respond in particular ways, the reactions of Odysseus to what he sees offer cues for the drama's external audience. At first, Odysseus requests not to see this sight at all (74–76, 88), afterwards expressing sympathy ('I pity him in such great misfortune', ἐποικτίρω δέ νιν/δύστηνον ἔμπας, 121–22) and explaining that all humans are subject to the same misfortunes (125–26). This concluding moral, comparing humans to phantoms or shadows (126), casts Odysseus as a conventional viewer of tragedy. These indications of the internal spectator's point of view,[10] which complement slant in important ways, I shall term 'angle'. Odysseus' sympathetic angle is re-established at the end of the play when he asks Agamemnon to respect Ajax (1338–42), not least because death and the need for burial will come to him as well (1365); in this way he again appeals to the universal

---

8 Quotations of Sophocles follow the text of Lloyd-Jones and Wilson (1990), except as noted. Translations are my own.
9 For further instances of focalization in Athena's description of Ajax, see de Jong 2006a.
10 De Jong 2006a, 78 suggests that Odysseus, in applying the honorific epithet σακεσφόρος (19) to Ajax, provides an early instance of his sympathetic angle.

human condition. As we shall see, the angle of an internal spectator is an important aspect of dramatic communication.[11]

Two other plays begin with mini-dramas that continue to frame the action long after the prologue scene is over. *Electra* opens as the Tutor, Orestes, and a silent Pylades rehearse their plans for revenge: the Tutor will pretend to be a messenger from Phocis, and will gain entrance to the house by reporting that Orestes has died at the Pythian Games; Orestes and Pylades will follow disguised as messengers bringing Orestes' ashes; having entered on these pretenses, they hope to destroy the usurpers (1–76). The Tutor as director and Orestes as actor then withdraw into the wings until the key moments when they re-enter to perform their roles, the Tutor delivering an elaborate speech on the death of Orestes (680–763), and Orestes carrying the urn with his supposed ashes (1113–14). As critics have observed (Batchelder 1995, 5–46, Ringer 1998, 127–46), this extended play-within-a-play is a striking example of metatheater, yet it also raises narratological questions about the relation between the script of the conspirators and that of the Athenian playwright.

Even more ambitious in this regard is Sophocles' *Philoctetes*. The play begins with Odysseus as author coaching Neoptolemus on the script they will follow to get the famous bow of Heracles from Philoctetes and bring it to Troy: the younger man will say he has been cheated by Odysseus and is sailing for home; having thus gained Philoctetes' trust, he will try to get the bow; finally, in case of difficulty, Odysseus will send a disguised sailor with instructions (1–134). The older man departs offstage, leaving Neoptolemus to play his role deceiving Philoctetes. The intended victim, however, plays upon the young man's sympathy until the disguised sailor indeed arrives bringing extra prompts from Odysseus (542–627). Finally, as Philoctetes and Neoptolemus, instead of following the scripted course for Troy, are poised to sail for Greece with the bow, Heracles enters *ex machina* to rewrite the story and send them both to join the Greek army as planned (1409–71). What is the audience to make of this unexpected entrance of a new author – a generative narrator, in Richardson's terms – who enters after the fact to write a new version of the plot?

---

11 The point of view of an internal viewer or listener does not figure prominently in the narratology of fiction or film. For a good general discussion of story-telling (and story-listening) in the novel, see Hardy 1975.

Internal spectators in Greek tragedy

These are intriguing examples; nevertheless they are exceptional examples in the sense that an internal playwright, like an internal narrator, is a device that need not be, and in many plays is not, employed. Less striking than these devices, but common to all Greek tragedies, is the chorus. Narratologically it is significant that Greek tragedy includes among its formal constituents a chorus as an internal audience that reacts to and reflects upon the dramatic action.[12] The attitude that the chorus adopts to what it sees I shall again call 'angle.' The angle of the chorus is often expressed in conventional or formalized ways; this was true also of Odysseus as internal spectator in *Ajax*. When Athena promises the spectacle of a deranged Ajax, Odysseus voices his reluctance with a gnomic expression worthy of any chorus: 'for I see that we are nothing but phantoms or empty shadow, all who live', ὁρῶ γὰρ ἡμᾶς οὐδὲν ὄντας ἄλλο πλὴν/εἴδωλ᾽ ὅσοιπερ ζῶμεν ἢ κούφην σκιάν (125–26). Yet however commonplace its wording, the angle of the internal audience in tragedy can provide the external audience with important cues.

Interest in the narratological role of the chorus might seem at odds with recent attempts to situate the chorus as a character within the drama (thus Gardiner 1987) or as an embodiment of civic values (thus Longo (1978) 1990), but this is true only if we insist on the chorus as a full character within the play or as fully embodying Athenian attitudes. The chorus is, in fact, many things at the same time: a *dramatis persona* that sometimes fades into a bystander, a collective body that sometimes speaks as an individual, and a mediating feature of theatrical narration that sometimes falls silent and sometimes takes an active role in the plot. Although the voice of a fictional narrator or the slant of a cinematic narrator directs the viewer more consistently, the chorus' unbroken presence onstage, whether silent or speaking, is an ever-present frame analogous to that of the cinematic camera. The distinction regularly made between the 'fourth wall' of drama, which allows unmediated access to the action onstage, and the camera frame in film, which directs

---

12 Hence the chorus is, for Bertolt Brecht, an 'epic' form of alienation characteristic of Greek tragedy ('Forward' to *Antigone*, in Brecht 1964, 210). For a similar argument, emphasizing emotional response, see Marianne Hopman's essay in this volume.

the spectator in subtle ways,[13] must therefore be corrected to include the outdoor theaters of ancient Greece, where spectators view the action over the heads of an internal audience. A narratological study of tragedy will thus take seriously the rhetorical role of the chorus, as Wayne Booth noted, 'to comment on [the play's] meaning or control our emotional response' ((1961) 1983, 99). Booth himself was endorsing Coleridge's observation that the chorus assumes 'the supposed impressions made by the drama, in order to direct and rule [the spectators]' ((1818) 1902, 192). So I find myself in a round-about way updating Coleridge's obsolete account of the 'ideal spectator.'

To summarize: theatrical communication in Greek tragedy may be mediated by the slant of an internal playwright as well as by the angle of the chorus and any other internal spectators. In the remainder of this essay, I consider in detail a single example from Sophocles.

2. Sophocles' *Electra*

Sophocles' *Electra*, as I noted earlier, begins with an internal dramatist, the Tutor, who rehearses with Orestes the show they are about to stage: the Tutor will gain access to the house by bringing false news of Orestes' death in a chariot race at the Pythian Games (*Electra* 44–50), and Orestes, after making an offering at Agamemnon's tomb, will follow suit, bringing an urn that supposedly holds his own ashes (51–58).

Directing the action

Insofar as the Tutor and Orestes play the part of author or playwright, they communicate to the external audience expectations about the plot, namely that the primary challenge facing the conspirators is gaining entrance to the house. The two murders will presumably follow without difficulty, since nothing is said about this part of the scheme, and the plot apparently has no need of Electra, since she is not mentioned at all. The Tutor and Orestes are also at the same time characters within

---

13 Compare Pfister (1977) 1988, 25: 'The film audience, like the readers of a narrative text, is not confronted directly with the material presented, as is the audience in the theatre, but indirectly, via the selective, accentuating and structuring medium of the camera or narrator'.

the plot they are generating, so each has a participant's more immediate motivations as well as a narrator's larger perspective; in articulating their own motivations as well as in revealing a larger perspective, Orestes and the Tutor provide a slant on events to the external audience. When the Tutor says 'this is no moment to hesitate; it is high time for action' (οὐκέτ' ὀκνεῖν καιρός, ἀλλ' ἔργων ἀκμή, 22), he generates a sense of urgency, and when Orestes rationalizes the false report of his death by saying 'no words that bring gain seem evil to me' (δοκῶ μέν, οὐδὲν ῥῆμα σὺν κέρδει κακόν, 61) he reeks of blunt expediency. The authorial task of entering the house is thus colored and reinforced by the characters' attitudes. The resulting expectations, however, are immediately challenged by the sound of Electra grieving (77). When Orestes asks if they should stay and listen to her, the Tutor is all business: 'Not at all. We can think of nothing but doing what Loxias wants' (ἥκιστα. μηδὲν πρόσθεν ἢ τὰ Λοξίου/πειρώμεθ' ἔρδειν, 82–3). What part can Electra play, the audience must wonder, in a hardnosed scheme that does not involve her? The question only becomes more puzzling as the play proceeds.

After Electra's lamentation song (86–120), the chorus enters imploring her to stop: 'O child, child, daughter of a wretched mother, why do you waste away forever in this endless lament?' (ὦ παῖ παῖ δυστανοτάτας/Ἠλέκτρα ματρός, τίν' ἀεὶ/τάκεις ὧδ' ἀκόρεστον οἰμωγάν...; 121–3[14]). This reaction chimes with that of the Tutor inasmuch as Electra's outbursts are as distracting to the conspirators' plot as they are to the women's sense of decorum; the old man does not want to hear her, and the women of Argos want her to be silent, saying 'resolve to say no more' (φράζου μὴ πόρσω φωνεῖν, 213). Their tone is almost the opposite of his: while the Tutor is all brusque indifference, the chorus tempers its criticism with expressions of sympathy and maternal concern: 'at least I advise with kindness, like a faithful mother, do not add disaster on top of disaster' (ἀλλ' οὖν εὐνοίᾳ γ' αὐδῶ,/μάτηρ ὡσεί τις πιστά,/μὴ τίκτειν σ' ἄταν ἄταις, 233–5). The chorus thus provides an ambivalent angle on Electra's situation, and this ambivalence is deepened by its ignorance of the plot underway. On the one hand, Electra's irrelevance is impressed upon the external audience by the fact that these sympathetic women, unaware of Orestes' return, are just as interested in

---

14 I give here the manuscript reading; Lloyd-Jones and Wilson 1990 print Schwerdt's conjecture λάσκεις for τάκεις.

silencing her. On the other hand, their ignorance of his return frees them to reflect upon Electra's situation and offer their sympathy.

Further complicating this angle is the chorus' first exchange with Electra in dialogue. After asking whether Aegisthus is at home or away (310–11), the chorus uses his absence to speak confidentially with Electra: 'if that is true [that he is in the countryside], then I will have the courage to speak with you' (ἦ δὴ ἂν ἐγὼ θαρσοῦσα μᾶλλον ἐς λόγους/τοὺς σοὺς ἱκοίμην, εἴπερ ὧδε ταῦτ' ἔχει, 314–15). This is a striking reversal of the stage routine in which one character asks another whether it is safe to speak in the presence of the chorus (as Orestes asks Electra later in this play, 1203–4[15]). The standard routine draws attention to, and reaffirms, the passive role of the chorus as a group of internal spectators; the reversal of this routine highlights instead the active engagement of this internal audience and, in particular, its anxious concern about the course of events: 'Here is my question – do you say your brother will return, or is delaying? I want to know' (καὶ δή σ' ἐρωτῶ, τοῦ κασιγνήτου τί φῄς,/ἥξοντος, ἢ μέλλοντος; εἰδέναι θέλω, 317–18). The chorus' urgent need to know whether Orestes will return projects onto the action the external audience's interest in the scheme announced in the prologue. Angle thus helps to define the different levels in the drama that encourage, respectively, discomfort with Electra's outbursts, sympathy with her grief, and a desire to see some connection with the plot of the absent conspirators.

In the next scene, Chrysothemis reports Aegisthus' threat to imprison Electra far from the house, and the latter in turn reveals the extremity of her grief and isolation by hoping he will do so (387–91). The end of this scene replays the prologue of *Libation Bearers*, where the Aeschylean chorus advises Electra on making offerings at her father's tomb (106–23), which pious gesture in that play leads directly to the recognition scene with Orestes. In Sophocles' version, it is Electra who advises Chrysothemis, and the hard-won agreement between the sisters as well as the replay of Aeschylus seem to presage a reunion with their brother. The stasimon that follows adds lyric angle to these expectations. Reflecting on the ominous dream of Clytemnestra, the chorus in the strophe like a prophet foretells (472) the arrival of Justice (476) and sings now of its confidence in revenge: 'just now as I heard these

---

15 Likewise Orestes to Electra at Eur. *Electra* 272–3, and Pylades to Orestes at *Orestes* 1103–4. For the similar routine in which a character asks the chorus to keep silent, see Finglass 2007 on 469.

sweet-whispered dreams, confidence came over me' (ὕπεστί μοι θάρ-σος/ἀδυπνόων κλύουσαν/ἀρτίως ὀνειράτων, 479–81). In the antistrophe the women sing that the spirit of Revenge (Ἐρινύς, 491) will arrive, and they use the same word θάρσος (495) of their confidence that the dream portends punishment of the usurpers. Nevertheless events again frustrate the expectations of this internal audience by first interposing the entrance of Clytemnestra and her debate with Electra and then the arrival of the Tutor in disguise.

As the action proceeds, the internal audience helps to condition our understanding of it. For nearly half the play (up to line 660), the women of the chorus observe Electra alone and in confrontations with her sister and mother and they remain all the time unaware of the scheme announced in the prologue. This spotlight on Electra is, for the external audience, an interruption in the primary thread of the play. As the action continues, the drama of Electra, abetted by the concern of the chorus, starts to gain a life of its own – even though, in a real sense, it does not rise to the level of a 'drama'. By this I mean that what we see of Electra – the staging of her towering grief, stubborn loyalty, and self-destructive passion – does not acquire direction or momentum, does not promise to develop into a story that is going somewhere. She spends her energies stirring up conflict with her sister as well as her mother and concentrates her desires on the impossible goals of being buried alive or single-handedly murdering Aegisthus. Electra's display of emotion thus commands our attention while remaining in narrative terms unproductive.

A new direction

Nevertheless, at one point, Electra's emotions do threaten to acquire this kind of direction. When the Tutor finally re-enters and belatedly sets his scheme in motion, her presence is at first more irrelevant to the plot than ever. He asks the women onstage whether this is the house of Aegisthus (660–61) and whether this woman (referring to Clytemnestra) is Aegisthus' wife (663–64), ignoring the younger woman who is also before him. As far as the internal dramatist is concerned, Electra need not exist. Yet after the Tutor and Clytemnestra go inside, the chorus shares Electra's grief in a *kommos* (823–70). As before, the women combine an attempt to quiet or silence her ('no more loud cries', μηδὲν μέγ' ἀύσῃς, 830) with expressions of sympathy ('in your misery you find more miseries', δειλαία δειλαίων κυρεῖς, 849) and platitudes urging restraint ('death awaits all mortals', πᾶσιν θνατοῖς ἔφυ μόρος, 860). The difference is that now the formal structure of the duet and the emotional register of the lyrics draw the internal audience closer to Electra.

In narrative terms, however, this sympathy seems misdirected. Why arouse interest in a character outside the narrative thread whose own story can go nowhere? This impasse is compounded by the return of Chrysothemis, who ecstatically reports that she has found offerings at her father's tomb and therefore Orestes must have returned. For a moment we seem to be turning back to the Aeschylean model in which the reunion of Orestes and Electra is both necessary to and symbolic of the justice of their cause. Sophocles' Electra, however, immediately shatters this impression by telling Chrysothemis the news of Orestes' death. She then startles her sister (and presumably the play's internal and external audiences as well) by announcing that she will kill Aegisthus herself. With this announcement she portends not a replay of Aeschylus, but a radical revision. With this revision, instead of being irrelevant to the plot of revenge, she comes into direct competition with her brother and the Tutor and threatens to usurp their place in the drama. Her story comes to dramatic and narrative life – it can finally go somewhere – even as the external audience, aware of the designs of Orestes and the Tutor and knowing that Electra's plan lacks mythical precedent, will suspect that it must fail. This suspicion is bolstered by Chrysothemis's forceful rejection of the plan on the grounds that it cannot succeed and will lead to disaster (1026, 1042, 1056–57).

The internal spectators, however, respond differently. To Electra's speech proclaiming her resolve, the chorus answers by urging forethought, προμηθία (990), and when Chrysothemis refuses to help, the chorus renews this call for forethought: 'Take her advice. The greatest advantage for human nature lies in forethought and prudence' (πείθου. προνοίας οὐδὲν ἀνθρώποις ἔφυ/κέρδος λαβεῖν ἄμεινον οὐδὲ νοῦ σοφοῦ, 1015–16). Nevertheless, in the stasimon following Chrysothemis' departure the chorus sings Electra's praises: 'with no forethought for death, she is ready to leave the light after defeating the double Fury. Who could be born so noble?' (οὔτε τι τοῦ θανεῖν προμηθής/τό τε μὴ βλέπειν ἑτοίμα,/διδύμαν ἑλοῦσ' Ἐρινύν./τίς ἂν εὔπατρις ὧδε βλάστοι; 1078–81); 'out-dueling disgrace, she is doubly renowned as a wise child and the finest' (τὸ μὴ καλὸν καθοπλίσα-/σα δύο φέρειν <ἐν> ἑνὶ λόγῳ,/ σοφά τ' ἀρίστα τε παῖς κεκλῆσθαι, 1086–9[16]); and the women conclude by hoping that Electra will prevail over her enemies, 'on account of the greatest laws, winning the prize for devotion to Zeus' (ἃ δὲ μέγιστ' ἔβλα-/στε νόμιμα, τῶνδε φερομέναν/ἄριστα τᾷ Ζηνὸς εὐσεβείᾳ, 1095–7). The chorus, in other words, reacts to Electra's new resolve with a combination of dismay at her recklessness and admiration for her noble principles. Such an angle recalls the typical response to tragic heroes, who inspire admiration while pursuing a deluded or self-destructive course. What is especially interesting here is the difference between external and internal audiences. The former, thanks to its superior knowledge, is likely to consider Electra's plan futile and pointless, whereas the latter sees her torrent of lamentation as belatedly acquiring a focus or narrative direction with her heroic-tragic pursuit of revenge. The angle of the chorus thus enables conflicting responses to Electra in the final scene before Orestes returns.[17]

The marginalized spectators

At last Orestes arrives, and although, formally, his situation is identical to that of the Tutor – helping to generate a plot that has no place for Electra – events in this case unfold differently because only Electra and the chorus are present. Like the Tutor he asks, 'Is this the house of Aegisthus?' (1101). But whereas the Tutor then inquired whether he should address himself to Clytemnestra, here the disguised Orestes suggests that one of the women take his news to those inside ('Which one of you will tell those inside that I am finally here to join [the Tutor]?' τίς οὖν ἂν ὑμῶν τοῖς ἔσω φράσειεν ἂν/ἡμῶν ποθεινὴν κοινόπουν παρουσίαν; 1103–4). Orestes thus lumps together Electra and the women of the chorus, just as the women have consistently associated themselves with her. So it is entirely by happenstance that Electra hears his news and sees the urn that is supposed to carry his ashes. During the develop-

---

16 I give here the manuscript reading; Lloyd-Jones and Wilson 1990 print Lloyd-Jones' conjecture ἄκος for τὸ μή.
17 Failing to recognize the tragic overtones of the chorus's response, some scholars exaggerate the conspiratorial joint purpose of Electra and the chorus (Gardiner 1987) or Electra's submersion into a united community of women (Ierulli 1993).

ments that follow and the huge emotional swings thereby aroused, the internal audience watches almost in silence. They offer but three lines of consolation at the end of Electra's speech in which she embraces the urn (1171–3), and then a single couplet after the recognition scene where, in answer to Electra's question, 'Do you see Orestes saved from death?' (1227–29), they answer, 'Yes we do, my child, with tears of joy' (1230–1). In both the lyric duet between the siblings that follows (1232–87), and the scene where the Tutor returns to silence Electra and call Orestes inside (1288–1383), they utter not a word. Why this silence for 150 lines just as the action approaches its climax?

If the separate threads of the play had been brought together, and if Electra had by now been fully integrated into the scheme of the conspirators, then we might expect the chorus, whose sympathies throughout have been with Electra, to likewise join in and actively encourage the protagonists. As it is, despite the recognition Electra remains irrelevant to the plan for revenge and, rather than assist the conspirators as she does in Aeschylus and Euripides, threatens to derail their scheme with her emotional outcry. Immediately after the recognition, Orestes silences her cries of joy ('better to be silent, so no one inside can hear', σιγᾶν ἄμεινον, μή τις ἔνδοθεν κλύῃ, 1238); her subsequent attempts to speak or celebrate are cut short first by her brother (1257, 1259, 1271–72, 1322) and then by the Tutor. The latter bursts onstage calling them 'utter fools who have lost their minds' (1326) for talking when Orestes should go inside, and tells Electra in particular to be quiet (1335–36, 1364). As the chorus has only been involved in Electra's thread of the drama, her silencing likewise leaves the women wordless.

In the remaining short scenes, the chorus participates only to express a visceral response, with almost none of the reflective commentary on events by which it might provide angle. As the murderers go inside, the chorus sings a brief ode of anticipation: 'Look where Ares advances, breathing blood of evil strife ...' (ἴδεθ' ὅπου προνέμεται/τὸ δυσέριστον αἷμα φυσῶν Ἄρης ..., 1384–97). The women do not have to wait long; Clytemnestra's death-cry rings out (1404–5) and they exclaim, 'The unbearable sound makes me shudder in misery' (ἤκουσ' ἀνήκουστα δύσ-/τανος, ὥστε φρῖξαι, 1407–8). Clytemnestra's unanswered plea for pity (1410–11) then prompts the women's first generalization: 'O city, O wretched clan, now your daily fortunes die and are gone' (ὦ πόλις, ὦ γενεὰ τάλαινα, νῦν σοι/μοῖρα καθημερία φθίνει φθίνει, 1413–14). At her final cry, they observe more straightforwardly that revenge has been accomplished: 'Curses are complete; those under ground are living; long dead they take in return the killers' blood' (τελοῦσ᾽ ἀραί· ζῶσιν οἱ/γᾶς ὑπαὶ κείμενοι./παλίρρυτον γὰρ αἷμ᾽ ὑπεξαιροῦσι τῶν κτανόντων/οἱ πάλαι θανόντες, 1417–20). From here to the end of the play – in the brief report from Orestes, the entrance of Aegisthus, the display of Clytemnestra's body, and the exit of Aegisthus to his death – the chorus says nothing in our received text beyond its announcement of Aegisthus' entrance (1428–9). Even in the few lines editors usually attribute to it, the chorus simply announces Orestes' entrance (1422–23) while cautioning against arousing Aegisthus' suspicions: 'Some gentle words in this man's ear might help, so he will rush to retribution in ignorance' (δι᾽ ὠτὸς ἂν παῦρά γ᾽ ὡς/ἠπίως ἐννέπειν/πρὸς ἄνδρα τόνδε συμφέροι, λαθραῖον ὡς ὀρούσῃ/πρὸς δίκας ἀγῶνα, 1437–41).[18] The closest it comes to the generalizations more typical of the chorus is in the brief closing anapests (1508–10).

This reticence is hardly surprising, if we think of the action. The play ends in the middle of things; Clytemnestra has just been killed and Aegisthus awaits his doom: how could the chorus possibly digest and make sense of events before they are even finished? But of course that is the point: by ending the play before the revenge is complete, Sophocles prevents not only the internal audience from thinking through what has happened, but also the external audience. To articulate this more precisely, the external audience is immersed in the final stages of revenge and has no chance, on its own, of reflection, while the internal audience fails to provide a wider or more synoptic view.

The final scene stands in counterpoint to the prologue. There, the Tutor spurred on Orestes' plan to use deception to enter the house, leaving unsaid the murders that were their goal. In the exodos, Orestes uses deception – the covered body of his mother – to lure Aegisthus toward his death; however, once he recognizes Clytemnestra, Aegisthus does not go easily. Electra has to urge her brother on, who this time forces Aegisthus indoors at the point of a sword. As they exit to a murder unsaid and unstaged, Orestes again leaves his sister alone with the chorus. Electra has briefly adopted the role of internal dramatist, helping to orchestrate the movements of Aegisthus (1455) and Orestes (1483–90). In the latter case she adopts language that recalls the Tutor's impatient words to Orestes: 'By the gods, brother, don't let him say any

---

[18] These lines are spoken by Electra according to the manuscripts. Most editors, including Lloyd-Jones and Wilson 1990, follow Triclinius in assigning them to the chorus instead.

more or drag words out!' (μὴ πέρα λέγειν ἔα,/πρὸς θεῶν, ἀδελφέ, μηδὲ μηκύνειν λόγους, 1483–4). But now the two men once again depart on their urgent mission, and Electra once more stands alone with only the chorus for company.[19] The internal dramatists set their plot in motion, Electra waits, and the chorus as internal audience concludes with a vague anticipation of the outcome: 'Seed of Atreus, after great suffering you barely emerged into freedom, completed in the present effort' (ὦ σπέρμ' Ἀτρέως, ὡς πολλὰ παθὸν/δι' ἐλευθερίας μόλις ἐξῆλθες/τῇ νῦν ὁρμῇ τελεωθέν, 1508–10).

3. Conclusion

Narratology, as a formal practice, does not claim to uncover new meanings in a literary work, but rather describes more clearly how the work produces its effects. In particular, my narratological reading of Sophocles' *Electra* traces in finer detail how the drama so unsettles its audience. The internal authors convey the urgency and necessity of their plot for revenge, and this slant frames revenge as the primary thread and goal of the drama. Yet the internal spectators primarily engage with and respond to the distress of a character who is incidental to that plot, and their angle frames that character's experience as (at best) a noble but quixotic gesture. The ending is troubling not so much because it comes prematurely, before revenge is complete,[20] as because it reasserts and reinforces the contrast between these two frames. An authorial slant emphasizes the action of the drama and heightens narrative movement and suspense, whereas the angle of viewers dwells, more statically, upon a deepening pathos. Those components of Greek tragedy that, I have argued, may allow it to be understood as a kind of narrative, are in fact used to full effect in *Electra*. This entails, as we have seen, not total control by an author, but a performance that leaves the audience with two fully valid though irreconcilable ways to view it.

---

19 On the staging of the exodos, see Calder 1963.
20 The most recent editor, Finglass 2007, replaces the interpretive crux with a textual one by deleting lines 1505–10 and leaving the play incomplete.

Layered Stories in Aeschylus' *Persians*

Marianne Hopman

Our earliest extant Greek tragedy and only preserved Greek historical drama, *Persians,* is one of the Athenian tragedies whose effect on its original audience is most debated. Current scholarship on its original reception falls into two groups. Some – most recently Edith Hall (1996) and Thomas Harrison (2000) – read the play as an Athenian auto-celebration suffused with chauvinist overtones and Orientalizing clichés. Others – notably Desmond Conacher ((1974) 1996) and Nicole Loraux (1993) – view it as a surprising vehicle for identification with the enemy whereby cultural and military polarities are overcome by a shared experience of loss and death.[1] Much is at stake here. Beyond the interpretation of the play itself, the debate impinges on the definition of tragedy as a genre and the relevance of the Aristotelian categories of fear and pity to its first extant example. In addition, the controversy raises psychological issues about the Athenian – and ultimately our own – ability to transcend personal resentment and hatred in order to embrace a larger human perspective on pain and death.

This paper reconsiders the pragmatic question through the lens of narrative structures.[2] Since tragedy is a narrative genre, my methodological premise is that its pragmatics largely depends on its progression as performance time unfolds.[3] To define the narrative structure of the play, I use some of the tools developed by structural narratology, espe-

---

I am most grateful to the organizers for their generous invitation and to the participants for their stimulating comments. I also wish to thank Claude Calame, Vivasvan Soni, and Robert Wallace for their helpful suggestions when I was revising the paper.

1   For a survey of the history of interpretation of the play, see Hall 1989, 69–73.
2   Recent analyses of *Persians* have paid strikingly little attention to its structure. Harrison 2000, whose thesis is largely based on the stichomythia between the chorus and the queen in the first episode, is characteristic of the trend.
3   Here and throughout the article, I use the term narrative in the broad sense of a discourse that – unlike argument or description – presents a story combining a set of characters, events, and a setting. For such a definition (which contrasts with Genette's restrictive use of the term narrative to epic), see Ricoeur 1983, 55–84 and Chatman 1990, 6–21 and 109–23.

cially the actantial model proposed by Algirdas Greimas (1966, 174–85 and 192–212) that breaks down an action around the positions of subject, object, helper, opponent, sender, and receiver.[4] This approach allows me to capture the oft-neglected dynamic progression of the play and to argue that *Persians* is organized around not one but two storylines, one centered around Xerxes' expedition against Greece and the other around the chorus' *pothos* – their desire to be reunited with the army (I).[5] The *pothos* story culminates in the identification of Xerxes as the chorus' opponent. In the second half of the final scene, Xerxes expresses longing for the dead youth and therefore moves from opponent to co-subject position (II). At the level of external communication, the *pothos* story actively engages the emotions of the Athenian audience and creates a complex experience in which anger gives way to pity and compassion (III).

1. War Story and *Pothos* Story

As Louis O. Mink (1970) and Paul Ricoeur (1983, 219–27) have emphasized, the interpretation of a narrative relies on a dialectic understanding of its plot. As we read a novel or watch a play, we develop provisional hypotheses about the nature of the main story that subsequently

---

[4] I do not attempt to use or even to transpose to tragedy the tools of formal narratology developed by Gérard Genette and Mieke Bal. As defined in *Discours du récit*, Genettian narratology focuses on the three parameters of time, voice, and mood that shape the transformation of a story into a narrative told by a narrator (Genette (1972) 1980). The distinction between story and narrative that is valid for epic can be applied to drama, especially with regards to the contrast between action shown and action told. In addition, the treatment of time is a fundamental parameter of dramatic storytelling, as recently demonstrated by Goward 1999 and Markantonatos 2002. Yet it is difficult to find a dramatic equivalent for the categories of voice and mood. Genettian narratology provides an elegant model and a powerful series of tools to describe the narrative semiotics of epic. One hopes that a similarly elegant and powerful model will be developed to discuss the narrative semiotics of drama. Manfred Pfister (1977) 1988 represents an important step in that direction. For a survey of various attempts to formulate a narratology of drama (with attention to the specificities of Greek drama), see Nünning – Sommer 2002. See also Francis Dunn, this volume.

[5] Gagarin 1976, 29–56 and Hall 1996, 16–19 have remarked that *Persians* creates a tension between Greek and Persian, celebratory and mournful viewpoints. My analysis takes their observation from the thematic to the narrative level and discusses the combination of perspectives in terms of intertwined stories.

inform the relative importance we assign to the narrative's characters, actions, and events. According to a long tradition of interpretation, *Persians* tells the story of Xerxes' invasion of Greece, his defeat at Salamis, and his lonely return to Susa. It is summarized in these terms in the ancient hypothesis preserved in the tenth-century manuscript *Laurentianus*:

> καὶ ἔστιν ἡ μὲν σκηνὴ τοῦ δράματος παρὰ τῷ τάφῳ Δαρείου· ἡ δὲ ὑπόθεσις, Ξέρξης στρατευσάμενος κατὰ Ἑλλάδος καὶ πεζῇ μὲν ἐν Πλαταιαῖς νικηθεὶς, ναυτικῇ δὲ ἐν Σαλαμῖνι, διὰ Θεσσαλίας φεύγων διεπεραιώθη εἰς τὴν Ἀσίαν.

> The drama is set beside the tomb of Darius, and its argument is this: Xerxes conducted a campaign against Greece; his infantry was defeated at Plataea and his navy at Salamis, and he fled through Thessaly and crossed over to Asia. (transl. E. Hall)

This interpretation implicitly underlies the work of scholars who view the messenger's narrative as the climax of the play; of those who discuss the pragmatics of the play in the context of the rivalry between Athens and Sparta (the cities who played a prominent role at Salamis and Plataea respectively); and of those who connect it to the political prospects of Themistocles, the Athenian general who engineered the victory at Salamis.[6] According to this model, the play primarily narrates Xerxes' failure to conquer Greece; the reversal at Salamis coincides with the Aristotelian model for the tragic plot;[7] *Persians* follows, albeit in inverted fashion, the quest model identified as a basic narrative pattern by Vladimir Propp ((1928) 1968) and subsequently formalized by Greimas (1966). The defining moments of the war story match the semio-narrative schema of Manipulation (the necessity to carry on Darius' legacy), Competence (the crossing of the Hellespont), Performance (Salamis and, proleptically, Plataea), and Sanction (lonely return). In the vocabulary of Greimas' actantial model, the subject of the action is Xerxes, the object Greece, the sender Darius, the receiver Xerxes, the helper the Persian army, and the opponents – at least at a surface level to be reconsidered in part II below – are the Greeks.

The interpretative emphasis on the war story matches, and is supported by, the importance that stage characters attach to it. *Persians* offers no less than three narratives of Xerxes' crossing of the Hellespont: the first, which is told and sung by the chorus in the parodos (12–60; 65–91; 126–31); the second, which is reiterated in a symbolic mode

---

[6] For such approaches, see especially Podlecki 1966 and more recently Harrison 2000.
[7] On the linguistic and visual aspects of the reversal, see Saïd 1988.

in the queen's narrative of her dream (181–99); and the third, which is revisited in the queen's conversation with Darius (717–58). The events at Salamis, Psyttaleia, and the retreat are the focus of three remarkably detailed reports (353–432, 447–71, 480–514) and the longest messenger scene in extant Athenian tragedy (353–514). Xerxes' return is highlighted by anticipatory references to it by the chorus (νόστῳ τῷ βασιλείῳ, 8), the queen (529–31), and Darius (837–38).[8] The amount of performance time devoted to retelling the expedition makes it an important narrative component in the play.

In addition, the beginning and end of the performance approximately coincide with verbal or visual presentations of the beginning and end of the war story. Although Xerxes' departure from Persia is recounted and not shown, the action performed in the parodos (the Elders' entrance on marching anapests) thematically coincides with the narrated action (the march of Xerxes' army) and symbolically reenacts it (1–64). At the other end, Xerxes' entrance closes off the war story at the beginning of the kommos (907). Xerxes' rags visually confirm the messenger's report that the king had torn off his robes in view of the disaster at Salamis (468). In addition, as William Thalmann (1980) and others have stressed, the torn clothes (στολή, 1017) metaphorically signify the failure of the war expedition (στόλος, 795). With the exception of Xerxes' return and Plataea, all events in the war story have already happened when the play opens. Yet the performance unfolds to present a polyphonic narrative of the war story. In the terminology of Manfred Pfister ((1977) 1988, 283–84), tertiary fictional time (the duration of verbally-related background events) is projected into primary fictional time (the length of time covered by the action presented on stage).

Understood as a narrative of Xerxes' failure to conquer Greece, the 472 B.C.E. *Persians* performance belongs with the many discourses spoken or written in the 470s to commemorate the Greek victory over Persia.[9] It must be contextualized with: the dedicatory epigram inscribed on the most famous Greek celebratory offering – a gold tripod resting on a spiral-twisted column made of three bronze snakes and dedicated

---

8   The anticipatory references to Xerxes' return that construct the plot as a *nostos* story are carefully discussed by Taplin 1977, 123–27.
9   For useful surveys of the different modes of commemoration of the victory in the 470s, see Barron 1988 and Raaflaub 2004, 60–66. On commemoration and memory as themes and performance in *Persians*, see Grethlein 2007.

to Delphic Apollo by the Spartan Pausanias (Thuc. 1.132.2 = Simon. 17 Page); the inscription recorded by Plutarch as the dedication on the altar of Zeus Eleutherios at Plataea (Plut. *Arist.* 19.7); and the funerary epigrams (many attributed to Simonides) for those fallen at Thermopylae (Simon. fr. 6 and fr. 22b Page), Plataea (Simon. fr. 8–9 Page), and Salamis (Meiggs – Lewis (1969) 1988, no. 24 and 26 I). Most importantly, as emphasized by Oliver Taplin (2006), *Persians* must be contextualized with Simonides' elegiac and lyric battle poems. While very little has survived of the *Sea Battle at Artemision* (fr. 1–4 W^2) and the *Sea Battle at Salamis* (fr. 5–9 W^2), the publication in 1992 of POxy 3965, edited by P.J. Parsons, has significantly advanced our understanding of Simonides' *Battle of Plataea* (fr. 10–18 W^2).[10] In Martin West's reconstruction of Simonides 11 (POxy 2327 fr. 5 + 6 + 27 col. i; + 3965 fr. 1+2), after a proemium praising Achilles (1–20) and an invocation to the Muse (20–28), the narrator relates the march of the Spartans from their hometown past Corinth and Megara (29–42). While POxy 3965.2 unfortunately disintegrates as the Spartans reach Eleusis, POxy 2327 fr. 27 col. ii suggests that the poem included a battle narrative (fr. 13 W^2). Simonides' *Battle of Plataea* thus seems to have offered a narrator-based account of the Spartan advance and of the battle of Plataea. Similarly, *Persians* includes narrated accounts of the Persian march into Greece and of the battle of Salamis. The drama's embedded narratives thematize the same war story as the elegy, albeit from the opposite perspective.[11]

The generic comparison between *Persians* and Simonides' *Battle of Plataea* brings yet another point to the fore. Both the drama and the

---

10 On the text and significance of the 'New Simonides,' see the essays collected in Boedeker – Sider 2001. The current orthodoxy that ascribes the 'New Simonides' to three separate poems (on Artemisium, Salamis, and Plataea) has been questioned by Kowerski 2005 who exposes the difficulty of arrangement in the papyrus fragments and proposes that the 'New Simonides' may in fact belong to a single poem that was multi-battle in perspective. If Kowerski is right, my use of the title *Battle of Plataea* to refer to Simonides' composition is incorrect. My more general point, that Simonides's narrator-based account of the Persian Wars is thematically and narratologically comparable to the war story told in Aeschylus' *Persians*, remains valid.

11 The date of Simonides' Plataea poem is unknown. If Simonides died in 468/7 (*Marm. Par.* 73), the poem's composition precedes *Persians* or shortly follows it. My argument does not depend on the relative chronology of *Persians* and the *Battle of Plataea*. Rather, I use the Simonides poem to reconstruct the horizon of expectations that informed the Athenian experience of Aeschylus' drama.

elegy offer narrator-based accounts of the war story. Yet telling stories is not a generic hallmark of drama. Since Plato and Aristotle, drama has been defined as a mode of storytelling that presents an action (πρᾶξις, πράγματα) through enacted imitation while epic presents its story through a narrative mediated by a narrator (Plat. *Rp.* 3.392d-394d; Arist. *Poet.* 1448a19–28). Both genres are in fact mixed; epic includes dialogue, and drama includes rheseis. Yet it seems fair to say that the story presented in an Athenian drama usually coincides with the actions performed on and off stage during the time of the performance. Aeschylus' *Suppliants* focuses on a series of events: the Danaids supplicate the Argives to give them asylum, the Argives agree to do so, the sons of Aigyptos arrive off stage, their herald attempts to seize the girls, and the king of Argos prevents him from doing so. In contrast, as N.J. Lowe (2000, 167) has stressed, with the exception of Xerxes' return, *Persians* presents the war story through embedded narratives. In other words, it confines the distinctively dramatic mode of storytelling – showing rather than telling – to actions and events that lie outside of the war story. Narrated accounts of the war are framed by, and subsumed to, a second action that is specific to *Persians*. *Persians'* generically specific contribution to the commemoration of the war lies in the actions shown rather than the narratives told.

Stripped of the embedded narratives, the actions and events shown on stage may be summarized along the following lines: the Elders and the Queen are waiting for the return of Xerxes and the army; they hear from the messenger that Xerxes has lost a large part of the army at Salamis, Psyttaleia, and in the retreat over Greece; they attempt to thwart further losses by offering libations to the dead and conjuring the ghost of Darius; they learn from Darius that further woes await the remaining troops at Plataea; the chorus confronts Xerxes; they mourn their losses with him. The characters in this story are impersonated by the actors on stage. Its duration – about an hour – coincides with the duration of the performance. Its location – Susa – is the space presented on stage.

At the core of the performed action is the Persian desire to be reunited with the army.[12] The theme is introduced at the opening of

---

[12] The few scholars who have focused on the performed action tend to analyze it in terms of an intellectual and emotional response to the reported events. In the fine analysis offered by Adams 1952, the play is structured in Aristotelian manner around the anagnorisis of the chorus and falls into three parts followed by a

the parodos. Immediately after their self-introduction, the Elders announce their concern for the return of the army (8–11). In the first episode, the chorus' longing is replicated and highlighted by the queen's parallel but more specific concerns about the duration of prosperity (164, 166) and about the return of Xerxes (167, 169). In its most extreme form, that longing takes the form of the erotic pangs of wives deprived of their spouses (ἀνδρῶν πόθῳ, 134; πόθῳ φιλάνορι, 135; ἀνδρῶν/ποθέουσαι ἰδεῖν ἀρτιζυγίαν, 541–42). Yet the use of words on the same ποθέω root in relation to the entire land of Asia (πόθῳ, 62) and the whole city of Susa (ποθοῦσαν, 512) makes it clear that the women's longing epitomizes a general feeling. Accordingly, the Elders proleptically enact the lament which they imagine the women will perform if the army does not return (115–25). The desire to see the army return is shared by the imagined women, the chorus, and the queen.

Although the chorus is limited in its power to act, its desires, hopes, and disappointments still unify the actions and events represented on stage. The messenger's entrance fulfills the longing for news expressed in the parodos (12–15). The libations poured by the queen (624) and the kletic hymn performed by the chorus (634–80) are motivated by the hope that Darius may find a remedy to prevent further losses (219–25, 521–26, 631–32). The Darius scene amounts to an attempt to find a helper able to perform on the chorus' behalf. In the first part of the kommos, as will be discussed in detail below, the chorus reacts to the character whom they have come to consider responsible for the loss of the army. In the second part of the kommos jointly sung with Xerxes (1002–1078), the dirge (μέλος, 1042) and mourning gestures ritually enact the loss and represent the end of the chorus' hopes. The staged actions not only respond to narrated news but constitute a sequence of events centered on the chorus' *pothos*. *Persians* combines two related but distinct storylines. The war story thematized in other

---

'scherzo': Realization of Forebodings (parodos and first episode), Realization of Divine Wrath (messenger scene), and Realization of Hybris (Darius scene). While this structure nicely illustrates the hermeneutic function of the tragic genre, it does not account for the final scene, which it lists as a mere counterpoint. I believe that a fuller understanding of the dynamics of the play can be achieved by recognizing that the performed action is arranged around the chorus' desire to be reunited with the army. The importance of *pothos* in the action of *Persians* is suggested but not developed by Hall 1996, 19 and *ad* 61–2. Dué 2006, 57–90 analyzes it from a thematic but not a narrative viewpoint.

genres is told in embedded speeches. The *pothos* story that is specific to the play is shown on stage. *Persians* is remarkable not simply for its interest in the emotions and losses of the defeated party, but also for its combination of these emotions in a story that unifies the staged action.[13]

2. Elders and King

Viewing the chorus as desiring subjects in the staged action, and not solely – as in later tragedies – passive respondents to embedded speeches, gives us a new point of entry into the play's economy. In particular, it explains and highlights the increasing tension between the chorus and the king, whom they progressively come to identify as their opponent. Polyphony is of course a hallmark of drama. In *Persians,* while the characters agree on the brutal 'facts' of the war – the departure, the defeat, the lonely return – they offer diverging perspectives on the causes of, and responsibilities in, the Persian defeat.[14] Three models stand out. In other commemorations of the war, the valor and courage of the Greeks are singled out as the main cause for their victory. Simonides' *Battle at Plataea* defines itself as a celebration of the Spartans who fought there and accordingly emphasize their 'courage' (ἀρε]τῆς, fr. 11.27 W^2) and 'immortal glory' (κλέος] ... ἀθάνατο‹ν›, fr. 11.28 W^2). *Persians* alludes to that cause, but only indirectly and mostly in the first half of

---

13　Intriguingly, the two stories that I have identified as war story and *pothos* story both are reminiscent of a Homeric epic, the *Iliad* and the *Odyssey* respectively. The Iliadic echoes of the war story have often be noted. Among many examples, the list of departing contingents in the parodos resembles the Catalogue of ships in *Iliad* 2 (Hall 1996 *ad* 21–58) while the inglorious deaths of the young Persian nobles in the messenger speech (δυσκλεεστάτῳ μόρῳ, 444) invert the Iliadic trope of the *kleos*-bringing death. On the other hand, the *pothos* story represented on stage shares many features with the *Odyssey*. The chorus labels it *nostos* in the parodos (8) and the story of a queen and people waiting for the return of their king echoes the plot of the *Odyssey*. Taplin 1977, 124 views the *Odyssey* as the most important archetype behind the dramatic plot of *Persians*. As will become clear below, my analysis suggests that the analogy may go even further than has previously recognized and that the problem of Odysseus' reintegration as king of Ithaca (on which see e.g. Nagler 1990) has a parallel in the Xerxes scene of *Persians*. From an intertextual viewpoint, then, *Persians* combines and reworks the two main poems of the epic tradition.

14　For a comparative analysis of *Persians*, Herodotus' *Histories*, and the Hippocratic corpus as reflections on the causes for the Persian defeat, see Jouanna 1981.

the play. In the first episode, the stichomythia between the queen and the Elders sets up a series of oppositions between Persian gold and Athenian silver (237–38), bow and arrows against spear and shield (239–40), and Persian submission versus Athenian freedom (241–42) that is connected to the Greek victory over Darius at Marathon (244). In the messenger speech, references to the organization and determination of the Greeks fighting for freedom contrast with the unarticulated clamor on the Persian side (384–407). Yet the messenger himself does not highlight Greek valor, but rather the intervention of a jealous *daimōn* as the cause for the Persian defeat. Accordingly, he ties the 'beginning' (ἀρχή, 350) of the disaster with the appearance of a 'vengeful or malignant divinity' (ἀλάστωρ ἢ κακὸς δαίμων, 354) and the queen responds to his account by blaming a 'loathsome deity' (στυγνὲ δαῖμον, 472). Their interpretation of the disaster squares with the chorus' foreboding that a mortal cannot avoid the 'cunning deceit of a god' (δολόμητιν δ' ἀπάταν θεοῦ, 92). Up to and including the messenger speech – that is, throughout the first half of the play – the defeat is attributed implicitly to Greek valor or explicitly to a jealous *daimōn*.

The second half of the play devotes increasing attention to Xerxes' responsibility. In the first stasimon, the Elders tie their grief to Xerxes' actions. They emphasize his responsibility by hammering his name as the subject of destructive verbs in a threefold anaphora:

κἀγὼ δὲ μόρον τῶν οἰχομένων
αἴρω δοκίμως πολυπενθῆ.

νῦν γὰρ δὴ πρόπασα μὲν στένει
γαῖ' Ἀσὶς ἐκκενουμένα·
Ξέρξης μὲν ἄγαγεν, ποποῖ,
Ξέρξης δ' ἀπώλεσεν, τοτοῖ,
Ξέρξης δὲ πάντ' ἐπέσπε δυσφρόνως
βαρίδεσσι ποντίαις.

And I myself genuinely sustain deep grief
For the fate of the departed.

For now the entire land of Asia mourns
emptied out of its men.
Xerxes led them away, *popoi*,
Xerxes destroyed them, *totoi*,
Xerxes wrong-headedly drove everything on in seafaring ships.
(Aeschylus, *Persians* 546–54, transl. E. Hall)

In the second episode, Darius further criticizes Xerxes. Revisiting the crossing of the Hellespont, the father denounces the incomprehension

(744), audacity (744), and mental sickness (750) that led his son to believe he could overcome Poseidon (744–50). In his third and last speech, the Plataea prophecy, the dead king develops a model of hybris and punishment based on a strictly retributive logic (ὕβρεως ἄποινα, 808). The religious exactions performed by the Persians on their way to Greece will result in no fewer tribulations for them (813–14). All Persian disasters, past and future, are now considered to be 'penalties' (τἀπιτίμια, 823) for hybristic behavior. The final admonition that Xerxes 'behave temperately' (σωφρονεῖν, 829) and stop 'offending the gods' (θεοβλαβοῦνθ', 831) ties the defeat to earlier mistakes. Accordingly, in the second stasimon, Darius' praise is emphatically contrasted with the present disaster (νῦν δ', 904) and thus implicitly attaches blame to his son.

The increasing insistence on Xerxes' responsibility bears important consequences for the dynamics of the final scene, when the chorus finally meets the king whom they now view as the agent of their loss. In terms of the actantial model of the *pothos* story, the subject confronts his opponent. I argue that the Xerxes scene is structured around a sequence of tension and resolution that redefines Xerxes' actantial role from opponent to co-subject and therefore brings closure to the *pothos* story.[15]

The first half of the Xerxes scene is characterized by a tension between Xerxes and the chorus. Xerxes's concerns at this stage are mostly self-centered. His lament emphatically connects first-person pronouns or verbal forms with epithets denoting misery (δύστηνος ἐγώ, 909; τί πάθω τλήμων, 912; ὅδ' ἐγών ... αἰακτός, 931; ἰὼ ἰώ μοι, 974). Unaware of his own responsibility, Xerxes puts the burden of the disaster on a hostile *daimōn* (911–12; 942) and asks the Elders to lament his fate (941–43). In turn, the chorus cares for the army (στρατιᾶς, 918; ὄχλος, 956). After an initial reference to the *daimōn* (921), they increas-

---

15 Obvious from the meter, the twofold structure of the Xerxes scene has often been noted (Broadhead 1960 *ad* 1002 ff.; Avery 1964; Gagarin 1976, 41–42; Hall 1996 *ad* 1002–78) but not satisfactorily explained. Avery's idea that new clothes are brought to Xerxes and account for the change is interesting but highly speculative. As Taplin 1977, 122 n. 1 points out, it is unlikely that such a spectacular change would happen without being mentioned verbally. Taplin himself dismisses the change as a formal convention. This explanation is not satisfactory. Form and content should combine if the play is to be successful, as we know it was. My hypothesis – that the change is brought about by Xerxes' new focus on the lost army (988) – relies on and confirms the importance of *pothos* in the dynamics of the staged action.

ingly emphasize that Xerxes is the one who killed the Persian youth
(ἥβαν Ξέρξᾳ κταμέναν, 923) and 'crammed' Hades with Persian corpses
(Ἅιδου/σάκτορι Περσᾶν, 923–24). Accordingly, the Elders angrily list
the names of fallen Persians and ask Xerxes where they are:

οἰοιοῖ <βόα>, ποῦ σοι Φαρνοῦχος
Ἀριόμαρδός τ' ἀγαθός;
ποῦ δὲ Σευάλκης ἄναξ
ἢ Λίλαιος εὐπάτωρ,
Μέμφις, Θάρυβις, καὶ Μασίστρας,
Ἀρτεμβάρης τ' ἠδ' Ὑσταίχμας;
τάδε σ' ἐπανερόμαν.

Oioioi – cry it out; where are your Pharnouchos
And noble Ariomardos?
Where lord Seualkes
Or Lilaios of noble birth?
Memphis, Tharybis and Masistras,
Artembares and Hystaichmas?
I put the question to you again.
(Aeschylus, *Persians* 967–73, transl. E. Hall)

The catalogue is reminiscent of the lists of departing Persians in the parodos (21–58) and of the lists of fallen Persians in the messenger's report (302–30). Yet the form of the catalogue is now embedded in direct interrogative clauses introduced by the interrogative adverb 'where' (ποῦ, 967 and 969; cf. 956 and 957) that give it an angry significance.

The dynamics of the scene suddenly change in the third antistrophe of the kommos. For the first time, Xerxes participates in the chorus' emotions and expresses longing for the young men:

ἴυγγά μοι δῆτ'
ἀγαθῶν ἑτάρων ἀνακινεῖς,
<ἄλαστ'> ἄλαστα στυγνὰ πρόκακα λέγων.
βοᾷ βοᾷ <μοι> μελέων ἔνδοθεν ἦτορ.

You stir up in me longing
For my noble comrades,
Telling of unforgettable – unforgettable – and loathsome evils beyond evils.
My heart cries out – cries out – from within my limbs.
(Aeschylus, *Persians* 987–91, transl. E. Hall)

The erotic connotations of the word ἴυγξ (*LSJ* s.v.) parallel those of the chorus' and the women's *pothos* for the army. By expressing the same longing as the chorus, Xerxes moves from the actantial position of opponent to that of co-subject in the *pothos* story. Logically enough, soon after Xerxes' expression of longing, the chorus mentions unnamed *dai*-

mones – in contrast to its previous accusations on Xerxes – as the cause for the disaster (1005–7). Xerxes' longing for the army reintegrates him in the Persian community and confirms the pivotal role of *pothos* in defining the relation between the characters on stage.[16]

The second half of the kommos (last four strophic pairs) unites king and chorus in a joined lament for the lost army (1002–78). The meter switches from lyric anapests to lyric iambics. The antiphonic division of strophes between the king and the chorus gives way to a sung exchange of individual lines. Xerxes and the chorus now share the same grief and mourn the same losses. The second person verbs angrily used by the chorus to incriminate Xerxes (ἔλιπες ἔλιπες, 985) are replaced by verbal forms in the first person plural that construct Xerxes and the chorus as a single entity (πεπλήγμεθ', 1008 and 1009; ἐσπανίσμεθ', 1024). Instead of referring to the deaths of the recent past, the kommos now self-referentially describes the lament process including the arm gestures (1046), weeping, high-pitched voices, breast beating, plucking of hair and beards (1056), and tearing of robes (1060). From a meta-poetic or musical viewpoint, the king and the chorus now sing the same song. Xerxes sings instructions or introduces lexical items that are in turn taken up by the chorus (1038–78). As commentators have stressed, the antiphony is reminiscent of the Trojan laments in *Iliad* 24 and probably reflects the structure of primitive *thrēnoi*.[17] The lyric dialogue has become a *thrēnos* for the dead that is led by Xerxes. Taken as a whole, the Xerxes scene constitutes both the climax and the resolution of the *pothos* story that structures the staged action. Like the *Odyssey*, *Persians* ends with the return and reintegration of a king responsible for the death of the 'flower' of the land.

---

16 Xerxes' evolution from self-involvement to communal sorrow is noted by Rehm 2002, 249–50. According to Kuhns 1991, 1–34, the plot follows the stages of psychoanalytic development and dramatizes Xerxes' progression through the stages of mourning. Although I do not share Kuhns' focus on character development, I think that he is right to stress the narrative importance of the mourning theme.

17 Broadhead 1960 *ad* 1002 ff.; Alexiou (1974) 2002, 10–14; Hall 1996 *ad* 1002–78.

3. Persian Chorus and Athenian Audience

How can we move from an analysis of the play's narrative structure to a discussion of its pragmatics? In what follows, I rely on two methodological premises. First, since tragedy is a narrative genre – as opposed to argument or description – and therefore constructs a double temporal logic, external (in the experience of the work) and internal (the fictional duration of the sequence of events), I assume that its pragmatics depends primarily on its narrative progression.[18] Second, I take it that the effects of a play (or any text or performance for that matter) on its audience depend on its specificity vis-à-vis contemporary discourses. Intertextuality, in other words, contributes to define the horizon of expectations and therefore the response of the audience.[19] Since the narrative specificity of *Persians* in the 470s – as opposed to the inscriptions or Simonides' elegies – lies in the chorus-centered *pothos* story represented on stage, its specific effects are to be found there rather than in the war narratives. This is of course not to deny that individual references to Athenian freedom (241–42) or to the paean sung by the Greeks at Salamis (402–5) would have caused the audience to beam with pride. I only wish to stress that the overall effect of the play would have arisen from the progression of the staged action.

A specific evaluation of the play's pragmatics requires some sense of – or at least some hypotheses about – the emotional condition of the spectators as they came into the theater of Dionysos to watch Aeschylus' drama. Pride in the Athenian achievements is usually considered the dominant mood (Barron 1988, 616). Yet Athenian emotions may have been more complex than acknowledged in official discourses and celebratory inscriptions. As Christopher Pelling (1997, 12) has

---

18 For the distinction between narrative, argument, and description, see Chatman 1990, 6–21. My emphasis on narrative progression departs significantly from the approach to *Persians* pioneered by Edith Hall 1989. Hall focused on the polar oppositions that organize the characterization of Greeks and Persians throughout the play. Yet as Harrison 2000, 58–91 has argued, the play does not construct these stereotypes. Rather, they come from popular assumptions that also surface in Herodotus' *Histories*. *Persians* is a product of its time and can be used (as Hall does) to document the history of Athenian ideologies, but that project must be distinguished from the attempt to capture the specific pragmatics of the play.
19 About the notion of 'horizon of expectations' as a basic tenet of reception theory, see Jauß 1982a, 22–32.

pointed out, Persia was not a dead issue even after 480. The very foundation of the Delian league in 478/7 B.C.E. assumed that the Greek states still needed to join forces to repel Persia. It may well be that Persian preparations for the Eurymedon campaign were already starting in the late 470s and that Athenians were getting wind of them. As Rachel McMullin (2001) has argued, the charge of medizing that caused the fall of the Spartan Pausanias and the ostracism of the Athenian Themistocles suggests that fear of the Persians still loomed large in the 470s. In addition, the sight of the damaged temples left in ruins on the Acropolis, perhaps in accordance with an oath taken at Plataea, is likely to have incited feelings of resentment and anger toward the agents of the destruction.[20] Subsequently, it is likely that the Athenians who sat down in the theater of Dionysos to witness the performance of Aeschylus' play brought with them the complex emotional baggage of pride in their victory, anger at the thought of the destructions and losses caused by the enemy, and fear of further woes.

Since the staged action of *Persians* is centered on the chorus, our appreciation of the performance pragmatics largely hangs on the question of whether the chorus was, in the terminology of Malcom Heath (1987, 90–98), a 'focus' for the sympathetic attention of the audience.[21] The question is tricky. Edith Hall (1989) has argued that the Persians mentioned and shown in the play are constructed as the polar opposite of the Greeks. The fictional identity of the chorus – stressed by such visible signs as old age (1056) and long ceremonial robes (1060) – surely separated them from the Athenian ideal of youthful activity. On the other hand, since at least A.W. Schlegel, dramatic choruses have often been considered as the 'idealized spectator' and a model for audience response.[22] The chorus replicates the audience's hermeneutic experience of interpreting the often contrasting viewpoints voiced by the actors.

---

20 For a full discussion of the historicity of the Oath of Plataea found on a stele at Acharnai, see Siewert 1972.
21 About the central role of the chorus in *Persians*, see Michelini 1982, 27–40.
22 Schlegel (1809–1811) 1966. Schlegel's idea has been more recently taken up by Vernant – Vidal-Naquet 1986 who viewed the chorus as embodiment of the polis. For a critical discussion of the Vernant – Vidal-Naquet model, see Gould 2001, 378–404. For the suggestion that the chorus of *Persians* replicates the hermeneutic experience of the audience, see Grethlein 2007, 373. Grethlein emphasizes the contrast between the chorus' and the audience's perspectives on the war story. I argue in turn that the progression of the *pothos* story brings them surprisingly close.

In this sense, the genre of Athenian drama constructs a formal analogy between internal and external audiences. The relevance of this argument to *Persians* is not definite. *Persians* is our earliest play and may differ from later tragedies. Yet it is important to note that the chorus is a distinct performative entity whose identity and voice may not be as clearcut as those of the actors.[23]

The structure and diction of *Persians* suggests that the performance constructed an increasing proximity between Persian Elders and Athenian audience. In the parodos, the emphasis on the chorus' ignorance of the army's situation detaches them from the actors of the war story and casts them as victims of a story which unfolds beyond their will and knowledge.[24] The staging of fearful and powerless Elders rather than ambitious soldiers would have placated the fear and anger that the Persian empire may still have instilled in Athens in 472 B.C.E. Unlike the war story told in the speeches, the *pothos* story represented on stage does not include the Greeks in its actantial model. Its subject is the chorus; the object is the army; the opponent is – depending on the viewpoint and moment – the *daimōn* or Xerxes. The *pothos* story leaves the Athenian audience free to respond to the staged action and to focalize on the chorus in a relatively disinterested way.

As the play unfolds, the chorus expresses its *pothos* – in both senses of longing and mourning – in panhellenic or distinctively Athenian language. As shown by Casey Dué (2006, 57–90), the flower metaphor repeatedly used to refer to the Persian youth (59, 252, 925–27) goes back to the Iliadic imagery of plant-like young men who blossom beautifully and die too quickly (*Il.* 18.54–60 [Achilles]; 17.49–60 [Euphorbus]). In addition, Mary Ebbott (2000) has demonstrated that the list of the Persians fallen at Salamis carries some formal resemblances with Athenian casualty lists. In both instances, names are catalogued according to place of origin, function in the army, place of death. The chorus' *pothos* is articulated in terms that align it with panhellenic or Athenian expressions of longing and loss.

---

23 See Calame 1999 for an analysis of the different voices of the chorus and Foley 2003 on the fluid identity of tragic choruses.

24 The ignorance of the chorus is a distinctive feature that differentiates *Persians* from the *Phoenician Women* of Aeschylus' predecessor Phrynichus. We know from the hypothesis to *Persians* that Phrynichus' play opened with a eunuch's report of Xerxes' defeat. In contrast, Aeschylus delays the announcement of the event and devotes almost a fifth of his play to the representation of Persian fear and ignorance.

The confrontation with Xerxes in the kommos takes the connection between chorus and audience one step further. As I have argued above, the chorus at this stage views Xerxes as the prime cause for the Persian defeat. In actantial terms, the chorus now identifies Xerxes as their main opponent. The opposition between Xerxes and the chorus in the *pothos* story parallels and mirrors the antagonism between Xerxes and his Greek opponents in the war story. Common opposition to (or scapegoating of) Xerxes structurally aligns the chorus with the Greeks of both the fiction and the audience.

The actantial 'Hellenization' of the chorus is confirmed by its political stance vis-à-vis Xerxes in the final scene. From a political viewpoint, the questioning to which the chorus submits Xerxes is reminiscent of the practice of frank speech (*parrhēsia*) that defines Athenian democracy.[25] Earlier utterances in the drama construct frank speech as a practice that does *not* belong in the Persian empire and accentuate the traditional contrast between the unaccountability of Persian kings and the accountability of Athenian magistrates (Hdt. 3.80). In the first episode, the queen emphasizes that Xerxes is not accountable to his subjects (οὐχ ὑπεύθυνος πόλει, 213). In the first stasimon, the chorus fearfully evokes the end of tribute payment, the end of proskynesis, and the re-establishment of free speech (ἐλεύθερα βάζειν, 593) as concrete and impending manifestations of Xerxes' defeat (584–96). The limitation of free speech in Persia is forcefully enacted in the Darius scene. After singing the kletic hymn that constitutes the second stasimon, the Elders find themselves incapable to speak to Darius face to face 'on account of [their] old fear of [him]' (694–96). As a result, most of the conversation with Darius is performed by the Queen who informs him of the recent disaster and of the circumstances of Xerxes' expedition (703–58). The chorus' abrupt questioning of Xerxes in the final scene represents a strong departure from the Persian practices described and performed earlier in the play. The evolution reflects the changes brought upon by Xerxes' failed expedition and discussed in Part II. It also brings the chorus closer to the Athenian values of accountability and frank speech.

---

25 About the practice of free speech as one of the parameters of the Athenian self-definition of democracy, see Monoson 2000, 51–63. About the critical attitude of the chorus and its overtones of *parrhēsia*, see Broadhead 1960, xxiv-xxvi.

The chorus' confrontation with Xerxes structurally and ideologically assimilates them to the Athenian audience.[26]

The Hellenization of the chorus in the first three strophic pairs of the lyric dialogue culminates in the final dirge led by Xerxes. As the choreutai depart and tramp the ground of the orchestra, they complain that 'the Persian earth is hard to tread' (Περσὶς αἶα δύσβατος, 1070 and 1074). The collocation of an ethnic adjective, the word for land, and a deictic gesture is reminiscent of the chorus' self-definition as 'the faithful of the Persians who have gone to the land of Greece' (τάδε μὲν Περσῶν τῶν οἰχομένων/Ἑλλάδ' ἐς αἶαν, 1–2) at the opening of the parodos. At the same time, the difference between the two passages captures the changing relation between chorus and audience across the performance. In the parodos, the Elders define themselves in relation to other characters. As foreigners and fictional characters, they are at a double remove from the audience. In the kommos, the Elders mention the Persian land while simultaneously pointing at the ground of the theater of Dionysos. Through the extra-diegetic deixis, the dramatic illusion breaks down. The dramatic space set in Susa merges with the scenic space of the theater – itself grounded in the reflexive space of Athenian landscape (Rehm 2002, 20–25 and 250). Subsequently, the action performed on stage takes on an extra-diegetic dimension. The Persian dirge spills over from the stage into the Athenian polis.

---

26 My interpretation here goes against the idea that the kommos is formally marked as an un-Athenian, effeminizing song that constitutes the climax in the play's Orientalizing strategy (Hall 1996 *ad* 908–1078). Hall's argument rests on the idea that Athenian mourning practices had been effectively restricted by Solon's legislation and that laments were normally sung by women in fifth century Athens. Yet as Margaret Alexiou (1974) 2002, 22 points out, it is unclear that Solon's legislation was fully enforced. Plato's prescriptions in the *Laws* (Pl. *Lg.* 800e and 959e) and the sumptuary laws passed by Demetrius of Phaleron in the late fourth century, suggest the persistence of many forbidden practices. Second, the approach to tragic lament as a female-gendered activity that marked the past two or three decades of research on the topic is now being reconsidered. As Ann Suter 2008 has recently argued, male laments are not unusual in tragedy. Creon laments the death of his son in *Antigone* (1261–1346). Theseus mourns the death of Phaedra in *Hippolytus* (811–73). In Aeschylus' *Choephoroi*, the kommos for the dead Agamemnon is sung by Orestes, Electra, and the chorus. The kommos that ends *Persians* does not fundamentally differ from other expressions of male grief in tragedy. It is an extreme, but not necessarily an alienating expression of loss.

The Hellenization of the chorus carries important implications for the pragmatics of the play. In particular, it raises the possibility of an audience response involving pity for the Persian chorus. Recent scholarship has emphasized the cultural specificity of emotions and highlighted the difference between Greek pity and our contemporary notions of sympathy (Konstan 2006a, 201–18). In the *Rhetoric,* Aristotle defines pity in the following terms:

ἔστω δὴ ἔλεος λύπη τις ἐπὶ φαινομένῳ κακῷ φθαρτικῷ ἢ λυπηρῷ τοῦ ἀναξίου τυγχάνειν, ὃ κἂν αὐτὸς προσδοκήσειεν ἂν παθεῖν ἢ τῶν αὐτοῦ τινα, καὶ τοῦτο ὅταν πλησίον φαίνηται.

Pity may be defined as a feeling of pain caused by the sight of some evil, destructive or painful, which befalls one who does not deserve it, and which we might expect to befall ourselves or some friend of ours, and moreover to befall us soon.
(Aristotle, *Rhetoric* 1385b13–16, transl. W. Rhys Robert)

In terms of the Aristotelian definition, pity includes a moral judgment of whether the other's suffering is deserved or not. In addition, it requires a double condition of proximity and distance between pitier and pitied. The pitier must be close enough to the pitied to fear experiencing the same troubles but also distant enough to not be engulfed in the pitied's pain. The relation between Persian chorus and Athenian audience in the kommos meets these criteria. The Elders suffer undeservedly since they are not responsible for the invasion of Greece. Since they share the Athenian anger at Xerxes and enact the Athenian practice of *parrhēsia,* their behavior makes them enough alike that the audience may remember or think of their own losses, past or future, and feel pain in response to the chorus' grief. At the same time, the ethnicity of the Persian chorus keeps it distant enough that – unlike the spectators of Phrynichus' *Capture of Miletus* (Hdt. 6.21) – the audience does not burst into tears. The chorus' characterization in the kommos offers the exact combination of undeserved pain, proximity, and distance that are the conditions for Aristotelian pity.[27]

The emotional dynamics of the kommos may even take the implied Athenian audience one step further. If the spectators are encouraged to

---

[27] It is debated whether the Aristotelian emphasis on unmerited suffering was or not shared by popular conceptions. Halliwell 1986, 174 stresses that it cannot have been a universal presupposition of Greek pity; Konstan 2006a argues that the criterium was widely shared. For an attempt to check the Aristotelian definition against 'folk psychology,' see Sternberg 2005.

pity the chorus (Part III) while the chorus reintegrates Xerxes in its midst (Part II), it follows that the chorus' mediation in the second part of the kommos encourages the audience to relate to Xerxes. The emotion aroused by Xerxes' grief would have differed from that aroused by the chorus. It does not qualify as pity in the Aristotelian sense since the kommos clearly emphasizes Xerxes' responsibility for his troubles. Yet while Aristotelian pity involves a moral judgment on the pitied, Aristotle mentions in the *Poetics* the possibility that the sight of deserved pain arouses an emotion that he calls *to philanthrōpon* (Arist. Po. 1453a2–6). Although its exact significance is debated, *to philanthrōpon* seems to denote a sentiment analogous to sympathy or human concern and would precisely apply to Xerxes' situation vis-à-vis the Athenian audience.[28] In my interpretation, then, the kommos of *Persians* would have performed remarkable emotional work upon its Athenian audience. Through the chorus' mediation, spectators would have been invited to first relive their anger at Xerxes, then transcend their anger and feel compassion for the enemy king. This trajectory parallels the Iliadic movement that brings Achilles from anger (μῆνιν, *Iliad* 1.1) to an emotion that Homer calls pity (ἔλεος) but which, unlike Aristotelian pity, does not involve a moral judgment and comes closer to the modern notion of compassion.[29] In book 24, the double anger caused in Achilles by Briseis' loss and later Patroklos' death gives way to compassion. Priam's appeal to pity (ἐλέησον, *Il.* 24.503) stirs in Achilles a grief that aligns him with the old king. Priam and Achilles weep together, one for Hector, the other for Peleus and Patroclus (*Il.* 24.507–12). Similarly, *Persians* performed the tour de force of inviting a Greek audience to feel compassion for a Persian king. The dynamics of the *pothos* story and the fluid identity of the chorus offered the Athenian audience the occasion to live an Iliadic experience.

Recent studies of the narrative semiotics of Greek tragedy have focused on its treatment of time (Goward 1999; Markantonatos 2002). I would like to suggest that two additional parameters – the contrast between staged and reported events and the narrative position and voice of the

---

28 About the much debated significance of the Aristotelian concept of *philanthrōpon*, see Halliwell 1986, 219 n. 25 and Konstan 2006a, 215–18, with bibliography.
29 About the relation between anger and pity in the *Iliad*, see especially Most 2003.

chorus – define Athenian drama as a storytelling medium. Applied to *Persians*, these parameters allow us to better appreciate the position and function of Aeschylus' drama in the commemorative atmosphere of the 470s. *Persians* responds to other discourses by framing the war story told in embedded speeches in a *pothos* story enacted on stage. The *pothos* story builds up an increasing tension between the chorus and Xerxes that is released and resolved in the kommos. While the Darius scene and its model of hybris and retribution may be called the hermeneutic climax of the play, the emotions of the characters culminate in the Xerxes scene.

At the pragmatic level, the relegation of the war story to embedded speeches and the fluid identity of the chorus allow the play to engage the audience in a complex manner. We know from Herodotus that staging a historical tragedy in Athens could be a tricky business. In the 490s, Phrynichus' dramatic rendition of the capture of Miletus had caused the audience to burst into tears. Phrynichus had subsequently been fined for 'reminding the audience of their personal woes' (ἀναμνήσαντα οἰκήια κακά, Hdt. 6.21). The structure of Aeschylus' *Persians* – and perhaps that of Phrynichus' own *Phoenician Women* – suggests that the point was well taken. By relegating the war story to embedded speeches, *Persians* stages an action that only indirectly engages the memories of its audience. The entrance of Xerxes, the only character involved in the war story and therefore the most challenging to the Athenians, is carefully and gradually prepared. The increasingly Athenian overtones in the chorus' voice allow the audience to project their emotions onto the Elders and to engage the Xerxes scene through the mediation of the chorus. When the war story and the *pothos* story finally intersect on stage in the last scene, the chorus' evolution from anger to shared grief offers a model for the evolution of the external audience. The combination of two storylines allows *Persians* to deeply engage and rework the emotions of its audience. This surely deserved first prize in the dramatic competition of 472 B.C.E.

Narrative Technique in the *Parodos* of Aeschylus' *Agamemnon*

Seth L. Schein

1. Introduction

Narrative technique in the *parodos* of Aeschylus' *Agamemnon* is best understood in light of the function and practice of Greek choruses generally, especially tragic choruses. A chorus in ancient Greece was, in the words of Helen Bacon, 'a group of people more or less homogeneous in age, sex, and social station witnessing, participating in, responding to an event in which they are deeply involved'. Choral poetry was a normal component of 'almost all significant public and private occasions – funerals, weddings, celebrations of military or athletic victories, prayers for deliverance from siege or plague or drought, the turning points of the agricultural year', so the members of an audience in the theater of Dionysos would have been familiar with how choral language and movement worked in different kinds of ritual performance. They would have considered choral poetry, including tragic choral poetry, 'something quite close to daily reality', even if it was 'treated in a more or less stylized way for dramatic purposes'.[1]

The most salient fact about any Greek chorus is that it dances and sings to musical accompaniment with a collective voice, the voice of a community. Tragic choruses, in particular, understand particular events as 'affect[ing] the community's sense of itself and its relation to the gods'.[2] They 'represent mimetically' through song and dance 'a

---

I would like to thank the editors of this volume, participants in the Narratology and Interpretation Conference in Thessaloniki, and audiences at the University of Lyon, the University of Verona, and the Scuola Normale Superiore di Pisa for helpful responses to earlier versions of this paper. I am also grateful to Luigi Battezzato, Carolyn Dewald, Nancy Felson, Enrico Medda, and Maria Serena Mirto for constructive criticism, advice, and encouragement.
1   Bacon 1982, 99. Cf. Bacon 1994–95, 6, 11.
2   Bacon 1982, 110.

kind of order in the relationships between the natural, divine, and human worlds'.[3] Unfortunately, we know little about the music and song and even less about the dance. Therefore, analysis of what Bernard Knox, speaking of *Agamemnon*, called 'the poetic and intellectual content of the lyric portions of the play' – including the narrative technique by which, in the *parodos*, the chorus represent and address questions of cosmic order – must rely on the close interpretation of language, rhetoric, and verbal style.[4] In the *Oresteia* generally, cosmic order is 'the system of Justice (*Dikē*) enforced and administered by Zeus and the Furies, an order that includes, but is not confined to, the moral order on which human society is based'.[5] Therefore a discussion of narrative technique in the *parodos* of *Agamemnon* will, at least in part, be a discussion of how the chorus' lyric song contributes to the poetic working out of ideas about this system of Justice.

Most tragic choruses, especially in Sophocles and Euripides, do not themselves act, but rather express ideas about the actions and speeches of the characters through their singing and dancing. In Aeschylus, however, the role of choruses is more diverse: the so-called 'protagonist choruses' of the *Supplices* and *Eumenides* act in the manner of a major character, and in the other plays too, including *Agamemnon*, the chorus sometimes intervene, or conspicuously choose not to intervene in the action at critical moments. There is in Aeschylean tragedy a 'double register' of choral expression: one register has to do with the chorus' social and emotional relation to individual characters, who, in Kitzinger's words (though she is speaking of Sophoclean choruses), 'act … to shape their position[s] within the culture of the *polis*'; the other 'involve[s] a communal tradition with a very different relationship to time and history'.[6] There is a kind of 'sliding scale' on which one of these two registers predominates in any given play. In *Agamemnon*, the chorus are at the end of the scale where they do not shape dramatic events by what they say or do, except for the occasional intervention by the Chorus Leader in spoken verse. To be sure, the old men of Argos are characterized to some extent not only by their gender and age, but also by their social attitudes, values, and relation to the characters.

---

3   Kitzinger 2007, 9.
4   Knox 1979, 73.
5   Bacon 1982, 110.
6   Kitzinger 2007, 9. The term 'double register' was suggested by Maria Serena Mirto.

Nevertheless, any psychological or other approach that treats this chorus as, in effect, another character, misses the special tension between its distinctive, 'lyric' point of view and mode of expression – grounded in the linguistic and performative traditions of Greek choral poetry – and what the actors say and do.[7]

No chorus is omniscient in their perspective on the 'cosmic order', but they stand outside the action and are attuned to the divine, so their song demands to be taken at least as seriously as the action itself. We may find this difficult to do, but it would have been easier for an audience whose members, unlike ourselves, were familiar both with the traditions of choral performance and with how choral language and movement work. Such an audience would have had personal experience as performers in the 'choral dancing' that, as Albert Henrichs says, 'in ancient Greek culture always constitutes a form of ritual performance, whether the dance is performed in the context of the dramatic festival or in other cultic and festive settings'.[8]

The tension or dissonance between the choral awareness, perception, and representation of a cosmic order and the decisions and actions of the dramatic characters is as fundamental to the distinctive quality of Attic tragedy as are the civic, social, and historical tensions and ambiguities that have been studied so fruitfully in recent decades.[9] The members of a tragic audience, with experience both as social and political decision-makers and actors and as participants in choruses performing ritual, see these two different aspects of their lives as citizens enacted by the actors and the chorus.[10] They are challenged in the course of a play or trilogy to negotiate the often irreconcilable conflicts between two modes of expression and points of view, which they consider 'their own' but which also, in the course of the play, turn out to be both 'limited and in conflict and cannot be reconciled either by com-

---

7 Kitzinger 2007, 7–9.
8 Henrichs 1994–95, 59, cf. Bacon 1994–95, 15–16. Calame 1999, 149 argues that 'the fact that the spectators in classical Athens had themselves received a musical education based essentially on choral activity' helped them to 'address [themselves] to the actors or to the gods with the thoughts and feelings of the chorus ... to delegate part of their choral competence and authority to the choros which is at the heart of the dramatic representation'.
9 Cf. Kitzinger 2007, 5–6; Vernant 1988.
10 For tragic choruses as consisting exclusively of Athenian citizens, see Wilson 2000, 80.

promise or by hierarchizing their value and eliminating one in deference to the truth of the other'.[11]

Tragic choruses have a kind of authority that derives from their communal wisdom and from the performance traditions of non-dramatic choruses in Greek culture, but they differ in one important respect from performing choruses in other Greek poetic genres. As scholars have established over the past few decades, when a lyric chorus says 'I', they may refer to themselves, to the poet (the composer of the poem), or to both at different times; in other words, in any given poem either the collectivity of performers or the poet or both may be the 'deictic center' of the poetic discourse.[12] This is not true of a tragic chorus, whose first-person language never refers to the poet, but always to the performers themselves in their assumed *personae*; who 'speak not with their own voices but with those of the group they are impersonating'.[13] On the other hand, though a tragic chorus are clearly embodied and in a sense establish themselves simply by using 'I' or 'we' as the subject of a verb, they do not establish themselves in the same way as actors who impersonate characters – actors whose bodies, masks, non-musical speech, names, actions, and sufferings serve to individuate them. The opposition between chorus and characters is basic to the genre of tragedy. It is both constituted and exemplified by contrasts between their respective diction, modes of expression and movement, location in the *orchêstra*, costume, and demeanor, all of which tell an audience to hear the chorus as 'not an actor' and to understand its personal *deixis* differently from that of the characters.[14]

---

11 Kitzinger 2007, 9.
12 Cf. D'Alessio 2009, 114–129: 'From a reading of the texts themselves and from comparative evidence drawn from other song cultures…, it emerges that lyric poems meant for oral performance are not necessarily deictically centered on the performance circumstances … first-person statements may include both the composer of the poem and its performer(s)'.
13 Bacon 1994–95, 17. Calame 1999, 151 argues (unconvincingly, in my view) that 'the I/we of choral odes … carries and assumes, in the performance of the ode here and now, both the voice of the real audience (with its ritual role), and that of the biographical poet (with his educative function)'.
14 For a full list of instances of the first (and second) person 'in or adjacent to … narrative passages' in the choral odes of extant tragedies, see Rutherford 2007, 35–36.

2. Narrative Technique and Interpretation

I turn now to the *parodos* of *Agamemnon*:[15]

ANAPESTS

Chorus
This is the tenth year, since Priam's
great opponent in justice and law,   40
King Menelaos and Agamemnon,
the strong yoke of Atreidai, of double-throned,
double-sceptered honor from Zeus,
put forth from this land   45
a fleet of a thousand Argive ships,
an army in support,
shouting angrily from their hearts a great cry of war
in the manner of vultures
who, in extreme sorrow for their children,   50
high above the nest whirl and turn,
rowing with an oarage of wings,
having lost the bed-watching
toil over their young chicks;
but someone hearing high above, Apollo   55
or Pan or Zeus, the shrill, bird-throated lamentation
of these resident aliens <in the heaven>,
against the transgressors
sends a late-avenging Fury.
In this way Zeus, the mightier one,   60
the god of guests and hosts, sends the sons of Atreus
against Alexandros, about to impose
on Trojans and Greeks alike, for a woman of many
    husbands,
many wrestlings that weigh down the limbs,
as the knee is pressed in the dust   65
and the spear-shaft shattered in the
preliminary offerings. It is now where
it is, and will be fulfilled in what is destined.
Neither secretly burning sacrifices nor pouring libations
nor weeping tears will he charm aside   70
the intense anger at fireless sacrifices.
But we, dishonored by our aged flesh, left behind then,
left out of the supporting expedition,

---

15 I translate basically the text of Fraenkel 1950, but with τῶνδε, the reading of the MSS, instead of Hermann's τῶν δὲ in 57. Some phrases are borrowed from other versions.

remain here, managing on staffs our strength equal to a 75
    child's.
For the young marrow ruling
within the breast
is equal to an old man's, and Ares is not in place;
while the excessively old, its leafage now
withering, walks three-footed ways 80
and wanders no more warlike than a child,
a dream appearing in daylight.
But you, daughter
of Tyndareos, Queen Klutaimestra,
What is it? What news? What have you seen or heard, 85
persuaded by what message,
do you send around to make sacrifices?
Of all the gods acknowledged by the city,
those above, those in the earth,
both those of our house doors and those of the market- 90
    place,
the altars blaze with gifts;
here one torch-fire, there another
rises as high as heaven,
medicated by the soft, guileless
encouragement of pure unguent, 95
by the oil of kings from the inner chambers.
Of these things consent to say whatever can be said
and whatever is right,
and become a healer of this anxiety,
which sometimes ends in evil thoughts, 100
but sometimes, from the sacrifices which you exhibit,
hope wards off from my mind insatiate thought,
the mind-consuming grief.

                                                STROPHE A

I have authority to tell aloud the auspicious power
    along the way,
the power of men in command; for still from the gods
    the life force that has grown old with me 105
breathes down persuasion as my strength of song:
how the Achaians' double-throned power, the joint-
    minded leadership
of Greece's youth in their prime, 110
is sent with avenging spear and hand by a swift bird-
omen
against the Teukrian land,
the king of birds to the kings of the ships, the dark one
    and the one white behind, 115
appearing near the palace on the hand that shakes the
    spear
in a conspicuous spot where the birds settled,

feeding on a mother hare heavy with offspring,
prevented from running her final race. 120
Say sorrow, sorrow, but let the good triumph.

ANTISTROPHE A

The army's trusty seer, observing the two sons of Atreus
    twofold in temper,
recognized the warlike feasters on the hare as
the escort commanders; and thus he spoke, interpreting the
    portent: 125
'In time this expedition seizes Priam's city,
and before the walls Destiny will plunder with violence
the people's many herds; 130
only let not some curse from the gods darken the great
    bridle struck in advance for Troy,
the assembled army. For pure Artemis out of pity 135
    begrudges
the winged hounds of her father,
which sacrifice the wretched hare, offspring and all, before
    the birth;
she hates the eagles' feast'.
Say sorrow, sorrow, but let the good triumph.

EPODE

'Well-intentioned as she is, the fair goddess,
to the helpless dewdrops of ravenous lions, 140
and delighting in the breast-loving
young of all the wild beasts roaming the country,
she seeks to accomplish the portents of these things—
revelations favorable, but also blameworthy. 145
But I call upon the god invoked as healer,
lest she devise for the Danaans lengthy non-sailings
    caused by opposing winds that hold back 150
the ships, eager for some other sacrifice, lawless
    and without music, one that is not eaten,
an inborn builder of conflicts, without fear of a man;
for there abides, rising again in response, a terrible,
treacherous housekeeper, a mindful, child-avenger 155
wrath'.
Such things Kalkhas, along with great benefits,
    clashed forth,
fated for the royal house from the birds of omen along
    the way;
in harmony with which
say sorrow, sorrow, but let the good triumph.

STROPHE B

Zeus, whoever he is, if it pleases him 160
    to be called by this name,

this is how I address him.
I have nothing to compare,
    weighing all things,
except Zeus, if I must truly throw   165
from my mind the vain burden.

ANTISTROPHE B

Not even he who previously was great,
    abounding in boldness for every battle—
he will not even be spoken of, being of the past;   170
and he who was born next is gone, having met
    his conqueror in three falls.
But someone clashing out with good will the triumph
    of Zeus
will hit the bull's eye of understanding totally;   175

STROPHE C

Zeus who put mortals on the road to understanding,
    making learning by suffering valid.
There drips in place of sleep before the heart
pain-remembering toil; sound thinking   180
    comes even to the unwilling.
From divinities, no doubt, grace comes violently,
    divinities sitting on the helmsman's awesome
    bench.

ANTISTROPHE C

And then the older leader
    of the Achaian ships,   185
blaming no seer,
breathing with the winds of fortune that struck against
him,
when the Achaian host was oppressed
with famishing non-sailing,
occupying the shore across from Khalkis in the region   190
of Aulis, where the waves crash to and fro;

STROPHE D

and winds from the Strymon coming
with evil delays, starvation, bad anchorage,
wanderings of men—winds unsparing of ships and cables, 195
making the time last twice as long—
were tearing to shreds the flower of the
Argives; and when for the bitter storm
the seer clashed out to the chiefs another,   200
another remedy, mentioning
Artemis, so that the sons of Atreus
    struck the earth with their staffs
    and could not hold back a tear;

ANTISTROPHE D

the king, the older one, spoke and said: 205
'To disobey is a heavy doom,

but heavy, too, if I tear apart my child,
    the delight of my house,
staining with streams of virgin blood
a father's hands, close to the altar;   210
    Which of these is without evils?
How may I become a deserter of the ships
    and fail the alliance?
For it is right and proper with passion
passionately to desire a sacrifice   215
    of virgin blood that will
    stop the winds. Yes, may it be for the best.'

STROPHE E

When he put on the yoke-strap of necessity,
breathing from his mind an impious change of wind,
impure, unholy—from then   220
he changed his mind to think the all-daring.
For mortals are made bold by the ugly cunning
of wretched derangement, first cause of disaster. He
    dared
to become his daughter's sacrificer,   225
    in support of a war to avenge a woman
and first offering for the ships.

ANTISTROPHE E

Her prayers and calls of 'Father'
and her virgin youth, the commanders
eager for battle counted as nothing.   230
Her father told his servants after a prayer
to take her and urgently lift her up,
above the altar, just like a goat, face down,
wrapped in her robes as she urgently reached forward
    to grasp at his,
and by a guard on her beautiful mouth to hold back   236
a sound that would curse the house,

STROPHE F

by violence and the speechless strength of a bridle.
Pouring toward the ground her saffron-dyed robe,
she struck each of her sacrificers with an arrow
from her eye evoking pity,
conspicuous as in a painting, wishing
to speak to them, for often,
at her father's tables where the men dined,
she had sung and, a virgin, with her pure voice
had lovingly honored her dear father's   245
paean-song at the third libation to good fortune.

ANTISTROPHE F

What happened from that point on I neither saw nor
    speak of;
the crafts of Kalkhas are not unfulfilled.

Justice tips the balance for those who have suffered   250
    to learn. And as for the future,
when it happens, you may hear of it; before then, rejoice!–
but that's the same as groaning in advance;
for it will come clear with the rays at first dawn.
But in what follows, may achievement be successful,   255

(Enter Klutaimestra through the central door of the palace)

as this ever-present sole-guarding bulwark of the land of
    Apia wishes.

This entry-song is 218 lines long, or 144 lines if one counts only the sung portion (104–257) and not the anapests (40–103). It is far and away the longest and most complex passage of choral lyric in extant Attic tragedy, in keeping with the length of *Agamemnon*, which is roughly 600 lines longer than any other extant work by Aeschylus and longer than any surviving Attic tragedy except Sophocles' *Oedipus at Colonus* and Euripides' heavily interpolated *Phoenician Women*. Nearly 50% of *Agamemnon* consists of choral lyric, more than in *Libation Bearers* or *Eumenides*, and in its length as well as its diction, imagery, and ideas, the parodos of *Agamemnon* is an overture not just to the play but to the entire trilogy.

    The *parodos* is characteristically Aeschylean in two important ways: first, its lyric narrative presents past events that the chorus have themselves experienced and that are linked by diction, imagery, and ideas to the main dramatic action. The *parodos* of *Persians* similarly narrates the setting forth of Xerxes and his expedition, the *parodos* and second stasimon of *Suppliants* tell the story of Io, and the second stasimon of *Seven against Thebes* relates the effect of the curse in the house of Laios. Sophocles and Euripides generally avoid this kind of 'internal' lyric narrative. When such narrative does occur, as in the history of the Labdacidae in *Antigone* 582–630, the story of the wooing of Deianeira in *Women of Trachis* 497–530, or the narrative of the sack of Troy in *The Trojan Women* 511–567, it tends to be briefer and less directly related to the main action of the play.

    The second, related way in which the lyric narrative in the *parodos* of *Agamemnon* is typically Aeschylean is that, like almost all Aeschylean choral narrative, its mythical allusions are to figures and events in the family-history of the main characters. The only choral ode in Aeschylus that tells of 'parallel mythical figures' wholly 'external' to such a family history is the central ode of the *Libation Bearers* (585–652), with its brief versions of the stories of Althaea, Skylla, and the Lemnian women. Most Sophoclean and Euripidean choral narrative, by contrast, tells of events that the chorus has not itself experienced, and 'evokes a parallel world outside the story'.[16]

Metrically the *parodos* of *Agamemnon* falls into two parts: the anapestic sequence, during which the Chorus enter and take their place in the *orchestra* (40–103), and the *parodos* proper, consisting of a metrical triad (104–59) plus five additional pairs of corresponding strophes and antistrophes (160–257). Rhetorically the *parodos* proper has three main sections: (1) the metrical triad, which is framed ring-compositionally by ὅδιον κράτος αἴσιον ἀνδρῶν/ἐντελέων ('the auspicious power along the way of men/in command', 104–5) and μόρσιμ' ἀπ' ὀρνίθων ὁδίων οἴκοις βασιλείοις ('things fated for the royal house from the birds of omen along the way', 157), includes the portent of the eagles devouring the mother hare, fetuses and all, as well as Kalkhas' prophecy, and all three stanzas end with the same acknowledgment of sorrow and prayer for the good to prevail, αἴλινον αἴλινον εἰπέ, τὸ δ' εὖ νικάτω; (2) the second section of the *parodos* proper consists of strophe and antistrophe β' and strophe γ' (lines 160–183), comprising the 'Hymn to Zeus'; (3) antistrophe γ' and strophes and antistrophes δ', ε', and ζ' (lines 184–257), contain the resumed choral narrative of Agamemnon's decision to sacrifice Iphigeneia and of the preparations for the sacrifice. The event itself is not told, but the Chorus' conspicuous way of not telling it keeps it in the forefront of the mind of the audience or reader: τὰ δ' ἔνθεν οὔτ' εἶδον οὔτ' ἐννέπω·/τέχναι δὲ Κάλχαντος οὐκ ἄκραντοι ('What happened from that point on I neither saw nor speak of;/the crafts of Kalkhas are not unfulfilled', 247–8). The *parodos* ends with a wish, 'May there be, following on this, successful achievement, as/this nearest, sole-guarding bulwark/of the Apian land wishes' (πέλοιτο δ' οὖν τἀπὶ τούτοισιν εὖ πρᾶξις, ὡς/θέλει τόδ' ἄγχιστον Ἀπίας γαί-/ας μονόφρουρον ἕρκος, 255–57). This wish, however, can only increase the anxiety and foreboding of anyone who has been following the choral narrative up to this point (and the speech of the Watchman before it), especially after the Chorus' fatalistic attempt to reassure themselves: Δίκα δὲ τοῖς μὲν παθοῦσιν μαθεῖν ἐπιρρέπει. τὸ μέλλειν <δ'>/ἐπεὶ γένοιτ' ἂν κλύοις·

---

16 Goward 1999, 22–23. For a conspectus of extended choral narrative passages in extant tragedies, see Rutherford 2007, 33–34. Rutherford omits the choral odes of Aeschylus' *Persians* from consideration, cf. 3. n. 11.

προχαιρέτω·/ἴσον δὲ τῶι προστένειν ('Justice tips the balance for those who have suffered to learn. And as for the future,/when it happens, you may hear of it; before then, rejoice – /but that is equal to lamenting in advance', 250–2).[17]

Yet the clear formal organization of the *parodos* into four main sections is honored as much in the breach as in the observance. For example, the Hymn to Zeus is less self-contained than it might seem, because strophe β', its third and final stanza, responds metrically with antistrophe β', the first stanza of the resumed choral narrative. This responsion means, first, that 'the older leader of the Achaian ships' (184–85) is juxtaposed in music, song, and dance with '[Zeus] who put mortals on the road to understanding' (176–77) and 'made learning by suffering valid' (177–78); second, that Agamemnon's 'breathing with the (winds of) fortune that struck against him, when the Achaian host were oppressed with famishing non-sailing' (187–89) is heard in relation to the 'drip ... before the heart of pain-remembering toil' and the 'sound thinking' (σωφρονεῖν) that 'comes even to the unwilling' (179–81). Similarly the choral declaration in the Hymn that Zeus 'made learning by suffering valid' (177–78) is made relevant toward the end of the *parodos* to the sacrifice of Iphigeneia, especially when they sing, 'Justice tips the balance for those who have suffered to learn' (250–51). The strongest thematic bridge between formally distinct sections of the *parodos* is the recurrent motif of sacrifice, which brings together the omen of the 'winged birds/sacrificing the wretched hare, young and all, before the birth' (136–37), and the 'other sacrifice' that Kalkhas anticipates Artemis may exact, 'lawless and without music, one that is not eaten, an inborn builder of conflicts,/without fear of a man' (151–53). This turns out to be the sacrifice of Iphigeneia (224–46), which recalls 'the first such sacrifice of young within the house of Atreus, the festal banquet served Thyestes'.[18]

Patterns of language and dramatic action also link the anapestic and lyric sections of the *parodos* in thematically significant ways. For example, the vulture simile in 49–59 is picked up by the omen of the eagles that gives rise to Kalkhas' prophecy (109–20). As Anne Lebeck ob-

---

17 Cf. Goward 1999, 48–49. Barrett 2007, 262 comments that despite the Chorus' 'refusal' to narrate the actual sacrifice of Iphigeneia, the sacrifice 'is the center of gravity around which the rest of the narrative turns'. Cf. Goldhill 1984, 31.
18 Lebeck 1971, 34. Cf. Winnington-Ingram 1983, 86.

serves, the 'similarity of content in the two passages is underlined by repetition': just as the simile is framed by the description of the Atreidae as 'the strong yoke of double-throned (διθρόνου), double-sceptered honor from Zeus' (43–44) and the statement that 'just so Zeus, the mightier one, the god of guests and hosts, sends the sons of Atreus against Alexandros' (60–62), so strophe α' of the lyric tells 'how a swift bird-omen sends the Achaeans' double-throned (δίθρονον) power against the Teukrian land' (109–12). Similarly, as 'the simile ends by comparing the Atreidai to a ὑστερόποινος Ἐρινύς ('a late-avenging Fury', 59), come at last to avenge the birds who were stolen when the comparison began', so 'at the close of the omen Kalkhas foretells that a like power lies in wait for Agamemnon, 'a mindful, child-avenging Wrath (155)'.[19]

Still another parallel between the anapestic and lyric sections of the *parodos* works against the formal division into discrete units according to meter and subject matter. This is the similarity between the chorus' address to Klytaimestra at the end of the anapests (83–103), wondering why she is sacrificing throughout the city to both chthonic and heavenly gods and asking her to heal their perplexity and anxiety, and their wish at the end of the lyric section (255–57), 'In what follows, may achievement be successful,/as this ever-present, sole-guardian bulwark of the land of Apia wishes'. Ironically, in both cases, the aim of the sacrifice and the favorable result are quite different for the Chorus and the queen.

One striking difference between the anapestic and lyric portions of the *parodos* lies in their quite different specificity as to the time and location of the events being narrated.[20] The anapests begin with strong temporal deixis: δέκατον μὲν ἔτος τόδ' ἐπεί ... ὀχυρὸν ζεῦγος Ἀτρειδᾶν ... στόλον ... ἦραν ('This is the tenth year since ... the strong yoke of Atreidae put forth ... a fleet', 40–47).[21] Through the end of the anapests, the temporal relations of the verbs are clear and specific, as are the places where the actions they denote take place. The only possible uncertainty is the subject of παραθέλξει in 71, but as Wilamowitz says, '*indefinitum pronomen latet verbo*'.[22]

---

19 Lebeck 1971, 8, with her discussion of how the vulture simile and omen '"go together" poetically' in the context of the trilogy'.
20 On the treatment of time in the *parodos*, cf. Barrett 2007, 260–63.
21 Cf. D'Alessio 2007, 98.
22 Wilamowitz 1914, 185, quoted by Fraenkel 1950, 2.44–45.

In the lyric portion, from the Chorus' initial claim to poetic authority through the end of the metrical triad (103–56), there is much less clarity as to when and where actions and events take place. For example, 116–17 say that the omen appeared ἴκταρ μελάθρων χερὸς ἐκ δοριπάλ-του/παμπρέπτοις ἐν ἕδραισιν ('near the palace on the side of the spear-hand,/in a conspicuous spot where the birds settled', 116–17), but we don't know where that place is: at Aulis, as in *Iliad* 2.300–30, where Odysseus recalls a similar omen interpreted by Kalkhas, or at Argos, as the word μελάθρων ('palace') might suggest. As Fraenkel observes, μέλαθρον and μέλαθρα are used of 'the lodging of the Atridae' in Euripides' *Iphigeneia in Aulis* 612, 678, and 685, so either location is possible.[23] The significant point is that the Chorus themselves do not specify a location. What matters for them is not where, geographically speaking, the omen took place, but that it took place near the royal house and was therefore intended for the kings; that it appeared 'on the hand that shakes the spear' (χερὸς ἐκ δοριπάλτου, 116), and so must have to do with warfare; that the spear hand is the right hand, so the omen must be favorable – a δεξιὸς ὄρνις.

Perhaps the relative spatial and temporal vagueness in the lyric portion of the *parodos* has to do with the Chorus' way of viewing human events in the perspective of a divine or cosmic order, not unlike the perspective of Kalkhas himself, who, as the *Iliad* puts it, 'knew the things that are and the things that will be and the things that were before' (ὃς ᾔδη τά τ' ἐόντα τά τ' ἐσσόμενα πρό τ' ἐόντα, *Il*. 1.69–70). A prophet, by a kind of second sight, sees past, present, and future in a single vision – not in the eternal present of the Judeo-Christian-Muslim God, but in a combination of past, present, and future events linked causally and ethically.

The Chorus begin the lyric portion of the *parodos* by claiming authority to sound out ὅδιον κράτος αἴσιον ἀνδρῶν/ἐντελέων ('the auspicious power along the way of men/in command', 104–105) – to tell of the Achaian expedition, its commanders, and the omen of the two eagles devouring the pregnant hare and her fetuses, in which Kalkhas sees the warlike sons of Atreus sacking Troy. The general location 'along the way' is, as I have said, reiterated near the end of the epode, when the Chorus recur ring-compositionally to Kalkhas having 'clashed out such things .../fated for the royal house from the birds of omen along the way' (τοιάδε Κάλχας ... ἀπέκλαγξεν/μόρσιμ' ἀπ' ὀρνί-

---

23 Fraenkel 1950, 2.70.

θων ὁδίων οἴκοις βασιλείοις, 156–57). This line is conspicuous for the verb ἀποκλάζω, a rare word found only here in classical Greek,[24] used of articulated human speech. Usually κλάζω and its compounds refer to animal sounds, sounds made by artificial objects, or unarticulated human sounds.[25] κλάζω is sometimes associated with especially harsh and horrific suffering, like the tearful lament of the chorus in response to Xerxes' lament in line 948 of Aeschylus' *Persians*, or when Kreousa in Euripides' *Ion*, after angrily reminding Apollo how he raped, impregnated, and abandoned her and how the son she bore was 'snatched away, a meal for winged creatures' (as she thinks), goes on to say with bitter sarcasm, 'but you keep clashing out sounds with your kithara, singing paeans' (σὺ δὲ καὶ κιθάραι κλάζεις/παιᾶνας μέλπων, Eur. *Ion* 905–906).[26] There are just two other occurrences in Aeschylus of κλάζω used of articulated human speech, both in this same *parodos*: first, in the 'Hymn to Zeus', where the Chorus sing that 'someone clashing out with good will the triumph of Zeus/will hit the bull's-eye of understanding totally' (Ζῆνα δέ τις προφρόνως ἐπινίκια κλάζων/ τεύξεται φρενῶν τὸ πᾶν, 174–5); second, when Kalkhas 'clashed out ... another remedy' (ἄλλο μῆχαρ ... μάντις ἔκλαγξεν, 199–201), which turns out to be the sacrifice of Iphigeneia. Given the normal associations of κλάζω, perhaps one should understand both the prophetic speech of Kalkhas and the cry of τις screaming out Zeus' victory as specially marked utterances, well suited to inhuman and savage events. At least in the case of Kalkhas, this would be in keeping with the conspicuously ambivalent nature of the portent he is interpreting. It also would be in keeping with the Chorus' transformation of what one might call their 'source text', Odysseus' speech at *Il.* 2.305–29, describing the omen of a serpent devouring a mother bird and her chicks at Aulis and quoting Kalkhas' interpretation of that omen.

In Odysseus' description, the birds are victims, not, as in the *parodos*, aggressors. The serpent, sent by Zeus, devours the mother and her eight chicks, before Zeus makes it vanish, and Kalkhas sees in this the nine years the Greeks will fight, before they take Troy in the tenth year. Zeus, Kalkhas says, 'revealed the prodigy' (ἔφηνε τέρας, 324) as a 'great sign' (μέγα σῆμα, 308) of something that will be 'accomplished

---

[24] The word recurs in an epigram by the first-century BCE poet Archias, *AP* 7.191.
[25] See *LSJ* s.v. κλάζω.
[26] I owe this reference to Maria Serena Mirto.

late, whose glory will never perish' (ὀψιτέλεστον, ὅου κλέος οὔ ποτ' ὀλεῖται, 325). In the *parodos*, however, there is no mention of glory. The birds are aggressors who devour the pregnant hare and her brood, and when Kalkhas speaks τεράιζων ('interpreting the portent', 125 – another ἅπαξ λεγόμενον), he does so with ambivalence, mentioning δεξιὰ μὲν κατάμομφα δὲ φάσματα ('revelations favorable, but also blameworthy', 145). The hare devoured by the eagles symbolizes the horrible massacre of innocents as the necessary complement to the victorious sack of the city, so that the occasion of triumph is also one of catastrophe.[27]

At the same time, the omen of the hare devoured by the eagles corresponds, as I have pointed out, to the simile of vultures circling their plundered nest in the anapestic part of the *parodos* (47–62), and Aeschylus' audience must have heard it in relation both to this simile and to the two Homeric similes on which, by a process of *contaminatio*, the Chorus' simile is based: *Od.* 16.216–19 and *Il.* 16.428–30. In the former passage, Telemachos and Odysseus weep as they embrace one another like parent birds shrilly bewailing the abduction of their children (τέκνα) by hunters, before they are fully fledged; in *Il.* 16.428–30, Patroklos and Sarpedon charge one another, 'both screaming inhumanly' (κλάζοντε) like eagles or vultures 'screaming inhumanly' (κεκλήγοντες) as they engage in battle. The vultures in the choral anapests simultaneously lament their lost chicks (οἰωνόθροον γόον ὀξυβόαν, 56) and show their warrior-rage (μέγαν ἐκ θυμοῦ κλάζοντες Ἄρη, 48). Despite the savagery of their cries, their feelings are virtually human, since παίδων, the word used in 50 to denote the young for whose loss the vultures cry out, is normally used only of *human* children, and the word γόον also suggests a human ritual lament. This humanizing of the vultures' stolen chicks and their parents' feelings is more appropriate to the loss of children by Thyestes (and the citizens of Argos) than to Menelaos' loss of Helen, and the simile is, in a way, a better basis for Kalkhas' prophecy of violence to the innocent young in the royal family than is the omen of the eagles tearing the hare and her unborn young.[28] Clearly, Kalkhas

---

27 See Bollack – Judet de la Combe 1981–82, vol. I.1, 152–3.
28 Cf. Edwards 1977, 23. There is a similar effect at *Iliad* 24.41–43, where Apollo compares Achilles' savagery toward Hektor to that of 'a lion who, yielding to great violence and his proud spirit, will go after the flocks of mortals to take a meal' (... ἵνα δαῖτα λάβῃσιν). δαίς is normally used only of a human meal; here it both humanizes the lion and, more importantly, assimilates Achilles to this

in antistrophe α' and the epode of the metrical triad (123–55) cannot be said to 'know' the words of the Chorus in their anapests, but the fact that the vultures have 'human' feelings and that Zeus sends a Fury to avenge them, must affect how Aeschylus' audience and we ourselves interpret both the omen and Kalkhas' prophecy as transmitted by the Chorus – words which recall the Chorus' earlier simile. Similarly, though neither Kalkhas nor the Chorus who quote his words can be said to 'know' the portent and prophecy of *Iliad* 2, at the same time they *do* 'know' it, because, like all Greek choruses (and audiences), they are familiar with poetic tradition generally and the *Iliad* in particular.

Kalkhas' embedded direct speech is framed in epic style by εἶπε τεράιζων ('he spoke, interpreting the protent') in 125 and τοιάδε Κάλχας ... ἀπέκλαγξεν ('such things Kalkhas ... clashed forth') in 156. It has four indications of place or directionality, all rather vague in keeping with its quasi-prophetic nature: (1) 'Fate', he prophesies, 'will violently sack the herds *before the walls* [sc. of Troy]', πρόσθε πύργων (127); (2) 'may Artemis', he wishes, 'not devise for the Danaans any lengthy non-sailings *caused by opposing winds*' (τινας ἀντιπνόους ... ἀπλοίας, 149–50); (3–4) 'for there abides, *rising again in response*, a terrible,/ treacherous housekeeper, a mindful, *child-avenger* wrath' (μίμνει γὰρ φοβερὰ παλίνορτος/οἰκονόμος δολία, μνάμων μῆνις τεκνόποινος (154–55); here παλίνορτος, 'rising again in response', suggests indefinite rebounding back and forth, and the verbal force of τεκνόποινος, 'child-avenger', also works in two directions, evoking the parent who will avenge the child (Klutaimestra) and the child who will avenge the parent (Aigisthos, Orestes).[29] The deictic imprecision or ambiguity of Kalkhas' speech is a function of its being a prophetic interpretation of a bird-omen and of his prophet's knowledge of what is happening simultaneously in more than one time and place.

---

figure of utter savagery in a way that puts his treatment of Hektor's corpse at one remove from the horrific cannibalism that Achilles envisages for himself at 22.346–7, when he wishes he could cut off Hektor's flesh and eat it raw. For a reverse effect, cf. *Agamemnon* 718 when the word ἶνις, which properly denotes a human offspring, is used of a 'lion cub reared by a man in his house, which gets no milk from the breast that is dear to it': ἔθρεψεν δὲ λέοντος ἶ-/νιν δόμοις ἀγάλακτον οὕ-/τως ἀνὴρ φιλόμαστον, 717–9).

29 On the multiple senses of τεκνόποινος, see Thomson 1966, 2.19 on 154–55. Cf. Edwards 1977, 35 n. 32: 'The lines deserve the widest possible interpretation ... This is the way Aeschylus works'.

Kalkhas' speech is the only extended, embedded direct discourse in a choral ode in Attic tragedy that is framed by specific attributions to its speaker, like almost all speeches in Homeric epic. It also is one of only three examples of extended, embedded direct discourse in extant tragic choral lyric, all of which occur in *Agamemnon*. The second of the three comes later in the *parodos*, when Agamemnon wrestles with whether or not to sacrifice his daughter (205–17). Here the embedded direct speech has a virtually deictic function, marking Agamemnon's decision more vividly and powerfully than mere narrative could do. The third example of extended, embedded direct discourse comes in the first *stasimon*, when the 'spokesmen of the house' (δόμων προφῆται, 409) cry out in pain at what they see happening there, after the departure of Helen. Unlike Kalkhas' speech, neither of the other two embedded speeches has a closing statement of attribution ('thus he/they spoke' *vel sim.*). Instead, Agamemnon's deliberation on the sacrifice of Iphigeneia ends at 217, the final line of strophe δ', with the words εὖ γὰρ εἴη ('may it be well'), and the conclusion of the speech is marked by the Chorus' proceeding to sing of his subsequent actions in the third person: ἐπεὶ δ' ἀνάγκας ἔδυ λέπαδνον ('When *he* put on the yoke-strap of Necessity...'). The words of the spokesmen of the house in the first *stasimon* begin in line 410 with cries of pain 'for the house, the house and the leaders' (ἰὼ ἰώ, δῶμα δῶμα καὶ πρόμοι), but unlike Agamemnon's words in 205–17, they lack a clearly marked close indicated by change of person or change of context.[30]

Apart from the three extended passages I have been discussing, Aeschylus has only three other, very brief examples of embedded direct discourse in choral lyrics: (1) a short exclamation at *Eum.* 511–12, 'ὦ Δίκα,/ὦ θρόνοι τ' Ἐρινύων' ('O Justice,/O Furies enthroned'), which is attributed first to 'someone' (τις) and then to 'some ... father/or

---

30 Wilamowitz opts for the end of 411; Murray, Thomson, and Lattimore for the end of 415; A.Y. Campbell for the end of 419 at the conclusion of the strophe; and most recent editors, including Fraenkel, Page, and West, place the final quotation marks at the end of line 426. One scholar proposed, implausibly, that the quotation continues through line 455, the end of strophe γ', arguing that the whole passage to that point is prophetic, with verbs mostly in the oracular present tense. προφῆται, however, in 410 means 'spokesmen', not 'prophets', and there is nothing anywhere in the speech or its introductory attribution to indicate that it is a prophecy, such as εἶπε τεράιζων ('he spoke prophesying', 125), or future tense verbs like λαπάξει ('will sack', 130), that might suggest taking nearby present tense verbs as oracular futures. Cf. Fletcher 1999, 35–38.

new-suffering mother' (τις ... πατήρ/ἢ τεκοῦσα νεοπαθής); (2) the exclamatory exchange between Klutaimestra and Orestes anticipated by the Chorus at *Libation Bearers* 828–29, ἐπαύσας θροεούσαι/'τέκνον', 'ἔργωι πατρός' ('when she is crying out 'child,' shout back 'by the father's deed' – though the text is uncertain); (3) the cry of 'the whole Earth', (πᾶσα ... χθών), following the birth of Epaphos at *Suppl.* 584–5, 'This is truly the lineage of life-producing Zeus' ('φυσιζόου γένος τόδε/Ζηνός ἐστιν ἀληθῶς'). There is no such embedded direct speech of any length in Sophoclean choral poetry, and only about fifteen very short examples in Euripides' choral lyrics.[31] Clearly, extended, embedded direct speech suits the distinctive prophetic and epicizing style of choral lyric in *Agamemnon*, even if it is not appropriate in tragic choral lyric generally.

With the prophetic style of the first triad of the parodos in mind, we can better appreciate the Chorus' imprecision in the 'Hymn to Zeus' as to where the actions and events they sing of take place. For example, when they sing τεύξεται φρενῶν ('He will hit the bull's-eye of understanding totally', 175), and τὸν φρονεῖν βροτοὺς ὁδώ-/σαντα ('the one having set mortals on the road to understanding', 176–77), they use spatial metaphors – a 'target' and a 'pathway' – but do not specify any actual location of the target and pathway. The figurative δαιμόνων ... σέλμα σεμνὸν ἡμένων ('from divinities ... sitting on the lofty [helmsman's] bench', 182–83) is similar in its local vagueness, as are the phrases ἀπὸ φροντίδος ('from [my] mind', 165) and πρὸ καρδίας ('before the heart', 179). In these two examples, however, the physicality of the organs and the surrounding language make the expressions of location both literal and metaphorical: εἰ τὸ μάταν ἀπὸ φροντίδος ἄχθος/χρὴ βαλεῖν ἐτητύμως ('if I must truly throw/from my mind the vain burden) and στάζει δ' ἀνθ' ὕπνου πρὸ καρδίας/μνησιπήμων πόνος ('there drips in place of sleep before the heart/pain-remembering toil').

After the Zeus-hymn, when the Chorus resume their narrative, they finally do mention a specific location where the events they are describing take – or took – place: Χαλκίδος πέραν ἔχων παλιρρό-/χθοις ἐν Αὐλίδος τόποις ('occupying the land across from Khalkis in the region of Aulis, where the waves crash to and fro', 191–2); they also sing of 'winds coming from the Strymon' (πνοαὶ δ' ἀπὸ Στρυμόνος μολοῦσαι, 193), that is, from the NE. But when they sing of the sacrifice of Iphigeneia, their references to place and direction again become less specific

---

31 Fletcher 1999, 32 n.11.

and serve mainly to mark changes in focalization from themselves to Agamemnon to Iphigeneia and back to themselves. Agamemnon, 'breathing from his mind an impious change of wind' (φρενὸς πνέων δυσσεβῆ τροπαίαν, 219),[32] tells his 'attendants' (ἀόζοις) 'urgently to lift [Iphigeneia] above the altar just like a goat, wrapped in her robes as she urgently reached forward to grasp at his' (δίκαν χιμαίρας ὕπερθε βωμοῦ/πέπλοισι περιπετῆ παντὶ θυμῶι προνωπῆ/λαβεῖν ἀέρδην, 231–5).[33] Again, the Chorus' point in their vivid song is not the actual location at which the sacrifice takes place but the irreligious perversity of a father sacrificing his desperate daughter like a goat. The double force of περιπετῆ, both active and passive, expresses the double focalization of the same event by the onlookers (including the father) and by the victim herself, just as παντὶ θυμῶι describes both the attendants' 'urgently' lifting Iphigeneia and Iphigeneia herself 'urgently' reaching forward. Similarly, when, in 239–43, Iphigeneia

> pours toward the ground her saffron-dyed robe,
> and strikes each of her sacrificers with an arrow
> from her eye evoking pity,
> conspicuous as in a picture, wishing
> to speak ...
>
> κρόκου βαφὰς δ' ἐς πέδον χέουσα
> ἔβαλλ' ἕκαστον θυτήρων ἀπ' ὄμ-
> ματος βέλει φιλοίκτωι,
> πρέπουσα τὼς ἐν γραφαῖς, προσεννέπειν
> θέλουσ' ...,

the details focus and refocus the Chorus' (and audience's) view of Iphigeneia's urgent efforts to make human contact with her sacrificers, with whom she had a previous social relationship, but for whom, now, 'an arrow evoking pity' is not the kind of arrow they have in mind.[34] Finally the Chorus return to their own viewpoint, 'What happened from that point on I neither saw nor speak of' (τὰ δ' ἔνθεν οὔτ' εἶδον οὔτ' ἐννέπω, 248), using the first person as they modulate from being the implied deictic center of their song and acknowledge deictically the presence of Klutaimestra, 'this ever-present sole-guarding bulwark of the land of Apia' (τόδ' ἄγχιστον Ἀπίας γαί-/ας μονόφρουρον ἕρκος,

---

32   For τροπαίαν meaning a 'change of wind, not a veering or alternating wind', see Edwards 1977, 35 n. 36.
33   On the translation of this passage, see Lebeck 1971, 82–84; Ferrari 1997, 2–4.
34   Cf. Ferrari 1997, 3–4.

255–7). Their modulation is marked as complete, when the Chorus Leader addresses Klutaimestra directly and formally in iambic trimeters in lines 258–63.

Conclusion

The Chorus, as they indicate in 83–103, enter the *orchêstra* to learn why Klutaimestra is sacrificing throughout the city and to relieve the

> ...anxiety
> which sometimes ends in evil thoughts,
> but sometimes, from the sacrifices which you exhibit,
> hope wards off from my mind insatiate thought
> the grief that torments my heart.
>
> ...μερίμνης
> ἣ νῦν τοτὲ μὲν κακόφρων τελέθει,
> τοτὲ δ' ἐκ θυσιῶν ἃς ἀναφαίνεις
> ἐλπὶς ἀμύνει φροντίδ' ἄπληστον
> †τὴν θυμοφθόρον λύπης φρένα†.
>
> (99–103)

The text and precise sense of the last line are uncertain; it becomes clear, however, in the rest of the *parodos* that the old men of Argos collectively share in anxiety and depression triggered by Klutaimestra's sacrifices but arising from the omen of the eagles, the prophecy of Kalkhas, and the sacrifice of Iphigeneia ten years earlier, when the army set off for Troy. At first the Chorus speak of their departure as a mission of just retribution (40–59), but as they imagine the fighting, they describe it catachrestically in misplaced ritual language: διακναιομένης τ' ἐν προτελείοις/κάμακος ('the spear-shaft shattered/in the preliminary offerings', 65–66), anticipating their narrative of the 'corrupted' sacrifices of the 'wretched hare' (137–38) and of Iphigeneia (207–17, 224–37).[35] Their memory of these 'sacrifices', rather than those 'exhibited' by Klutaimestra, is the real source of their 'insatiate thought/and mind-consuming grief' (102–103), and it triggers the Chorus' shift from anapests to lyric narrative in 104, much as, later in the play at 1121, their terror at Kassandra's prophetic visions of past and future bloodshed and corrupted sacrifices in the house of Atreus trigger their jump from iambic trimeters to impassioned dochmiacs.

---

35 Cf. Lebeck 1971, 10, 33–36, 48, 60–63, 70, 81–84; Zeitlin 1965, 464–66, 502–505.

In terms of the 'double register' of choral expression in Attic tragedy (above, p. 378), the Chorus are more like citizens of the *polis* in their anapests, but in 104 they self-consciously take on the traditional communal authority of a singing and dancing chorus: κύριός εἰμι θροεῖν... ('I have authority to tell aloud...'). From this point on their relative vagueness as to time and place increases, and they sing of past, present, and future events with a prophetic perspective resembling that of Kalkhas's, but without his clarity about how these events are related to one another. Their 'choral' concern with the cosmic order of Δίκη, which they themselves cannot articulate rationally, reveals itself in a richly ambiguous lyric narrative that implicitly associates past, present, and future events causally and morally, as they explore the consequences for the Argive community of its leaders' transgressions.

This cosmic order turns out to have internal contradictions, to be shattered by acts of justice that are also acts of injustice, as is clear, for example in lines 135–38, when Kalkhas warns that

> pure Artemis out of pity begrudges
> the winged hounds of her father
> sacrificing the wretched hare, offspring and all, before the birth;
> she hates the eagles feast.
>
> ... οἴκτωι γὰρ ἐπίφθονος Ἄρτεμις ἁγνὰ
> πτανοῖσιν κυσὶ πατρὸς
> αὐτότοκον πρὸ λόχου μογερὰν πτάκα θυομένοισιν·
> στυγεῖ δὲ δεῖπνον αἰετῶν.
>
> (135–38)

Such contradictions, like Kalkhas' vision of a victorious outcome that is also catastrophic for the victors, terrify the Chorus. Unlike the Watchman in the opening scene, who responds to terror with silence, the Chorus struggle to 'throw from [their] mind the vain burden of fear' by turning to Zeus. Their lyric narrative, in prophetic-epic language and style, is an effort to address this fear by trying to understand and articulate the justice of Zeus and the cosmic order. Through their singing and dancing, as Helen Bacon says, the Chorus situate the 'transitory anguish of individuals ... in a larger context', enabling 'the Athenian audience and all subsequent audiences to make the characters' actions and sufferings – and the moral meanings of these actions and sufferings – part of their own experience.[36]

---

36 Bacon 1994–95, 20.

Knowing a Story's End:
Future Reflexive in the Tragic Narrative of the Argive Expedition Against Thebes

Anna A. Lamari

> *Time present and time past*
> *Are both perhaps present in time future*
> *And time future contained in time past*
> T. S. Eliot[1]

1. Introduction

In his narrative of the battle of Arginusae, Diodorus of Sicily stresses the martial preparations preceding the actual engagement: the night before the battle, the Athenian general Thrasyllus[2] dreamed that he and six other Athenian generals were in Athens, participating in a dramatic contest in the crowded theatre of Dionysus. Thrasyllus and the rest of the Athenian generals were playing Euripides' *Phoenician Women*, while their competitors were performing Euripides' *Suppliants*. According to the dream, a 'Cadmean victory' for the competitors led to the defeat of the party of Thrasyllus, who died with the rest of his generals, just like the seven attackers of Thebes (13.97.6). Apart from the shockingly prophetic character of the dream, what is of particular interest is the effective pairing of two chronologically remote Euripidean plays by a first century author. It appears that the decade which separated the performances of the *Phoenician Women* and the *Suppliants* did not prevent Diodorus (via Thrasyllus) to treat the two plays within the framework of a continuous mythological span. The example of the narrative of Diodorus shows that for the readers, myth is seen as a sequence even when narrated in segments that are chronologically separated. Authors

---

[1] 'Four Quartets: Burnt Norton', *The Complete Poems and Plays*, Faber and Faber 1969.
[2] Thrasyllus is in fact mistakenly called Thrasybulus by Diodorus (13.97.6; cf. Oldfather 1950 *ad loc.*).

seem to take advantage of this mythological continuity in order to create complex intertextual games that fuse two different dimensions: the myth and the *story* as reconstituted by the text itself.[3] My aim is to study *future reflexivity*[4] as a specific manifestation of this temporal conflation between mythological time and narrative time and explore an unobserved, at least to my knowledge, use of this technique in Greek drama.

The expedition of the Argives against the city of Thebes has been dealt with by a long series of famous narratives pertaining to the so called Theban mythological corpus. This dense intertextual matrix composed by the overlapping, completing or conflicting versions regarding Oedipus' royal house finds its most sophisticated treatment in the Theban plays of the three classical tragedians. Considering the sheer vastness of possible references that each play could trigger and most importantly the large amount of literary information that is nowadays fragmentary or completely lost, one could hardly hope to fully reconstruct the intertextual 'map' upon which each play expands. However, given that some intertextual correspondences within the framework of the narrative of the Argive expedition are so striking, it may be plausibly argued that they constitute a coherent narrative plan orchestrated by the author, rather than a fuzzy distribution of intertextual hints.

I will focus on a very specific part of the Theban myth, including the attack of Polyneices against Eteocles, the battle between Argives and Thebans, as well as the mythical 'future' of the dead of the battle. Apart from highlighting their parallel – almost identical – stories, I will mainly concentrate on the fact that both Aeschylus' *Seven Against Thebes* and Euripides' *Phoenician Women* narrate an early part of the myth (the battle between Argives and Thebans), whereas a much later one (the burial of the dead Argives) is already a set *narrative text* in each of the

---

3   I will be using the tripartite distinction of *fabula* (i. e. the events of the narration in their 'real', chronological order), *story* (i. e. the events of the narration in the 'pseudo-order' of the text) and *text* (i. e. the verbal or other representation of the *story*) as defined by Bal (1985) 1997, 5 and widely used by classicists (see for example de Jong-Nünlist-Bowie 2004). The term *story* as opposed to *narrative* was coined by Genette (1972) 1980, 27, who made the distinction between the 'narrative content' and the 'narrative text itself' respectively (the French equivalents of the terms are *histoire* –for *story*– and *narration* –for *narrative*–, trans. by J. E. Lewin).

4   A definition and thorough presentation of the concept of *future reflexivity* will follow.

two playwrights' narrative repertoire, namely Aeschylus' *Eleusinians* and Euripides' *Suppliants*. Such a relation between the time of the story and the time in which the narration occurred initially falls under the theoretical category of future reflexive, but therein expands onto an even more complex net of conscious intertextual allusion which I would like to coin as 'double and inter-authorial' future reflexivity. Such a 'second-degree' future reflexive undoubtedly invades the sphere of the *extradiegetic* or *metadiegetic narrative level*,[5] i.e. of the narrative act itself, revealing conscious metatheatricality as one of Euripides' *modi operandi*.

Being well aware of the fact that such an interpretation, crediting Euripides with poetic self-consciousness and specific awareness of previous performances might seem too sophisticated, I would like to start by tracing this line of thought in certain current approaches to Greek drama. Recent studies rightly emphasize that intertextual cross-references between the plays not only exist, but they also represent an integral as well as indispensable part of the process of the making of theatrical meaning. In short, ancient audiences constructed meaning by 'placing' a given play in the context of both previous performances and/or readings of theatrically relevant plays. As debated by Burian, 'intertextuality depends not so much upon recollection of parallel narratives as upon the evocation of prior theatrical experience'.[6] In this light, the concept of intertextual dialogue may be expanded to that of 'intertheatrical' or 'interperformatory' correspondences, pursued by the authors and understood by the audience.

In fact, the construction of theatrical meaning must be seen as a dynamic process transcending the boundaries of a single performance; this is not to say that dramatic performances are deprived of cohesion or totality. On the contrary, their theatrical autonomy is aptly combined with the two principal strategies employed by such a civic-oriented form of art: (i) the use and activation of various religious, political and cultural filters through which the spectators are encouraged to make meaning and be immersed in the presentation of the mythical

---

5   The term *extradiegetic narrative level* was coined by Genette (1972) 1980, 228–229, in order to define the narrating instance of the first narrative, since by definition a narrator is 'above' or 'superior' to the story he narrates. The term *extradiegetic narrative level* corresponds to what is later and more widely referred to as the *metadiegetic narrative level* or simply the *metanarrative*; see for example Bal (1985) 1997, 53–54.
6   Burian 1997, 195.

past; and (ii) the interactive and open-ended process of a kind of 'performative rivalry', that designates a built-in feature of the civic aspect of theatrical performance: public presentation, frequent repetition of mythical material, and massive production cannot help but result in a thick web of associations and interconnections.[7]

Following from that, it is unlikely that Euripides was composing the *Phoenician Women* without being specifically aware of the way Aeschylus treated the myth in the *Seven*.[8] Actually, Euripides' sophistication and careful planning of his plays according to previous performances is generally acknowledged and has led to his portrayal as an 'Alexandrian before his time',[9] an intellectual endowed with a 'proto-Alexandrian literary sophistication'.[10] What is more, Euripides was recognized as a literary figure from as early as the fifth century, with Aristophanes presenting him in the *Frogs* as an erudite.[11]

---

7 Aristophanic comedy is not only replete with traces of this intertextual or intertheatrical dialogue, but it is famously marked by a special part of metatheatrical interaction between author and spectators. It only suffices to bring to mind the 'apologetic' parabasis of the *Clouds* (518–626) with its reference to a previous unsuccessful performance of the play and the poet's anxiety to win the favor of an educated and theatrically informed audience. In particular, the designation of the spectators with such loaded terms as σοφοί and δεξιοί is re-interpreted by Aristophanes in clear theatrical terms (see 520–527). He also declares that he has been 'reared' and educated by his audience (532).

8 This is indicated by the allusion to the Aeschylean shield scene in *Phoenician Women* 751–752. See Craik 1988, 209; Mastronarde 1994, 360, with additional bibliography. Besides, the only surviving group of plays on the same mythical subject by all three tragedians (Aeschylus' *Libation Bearers*, Sophocles' *Electra* and Euripides' *Electra*) amply shows that later writers were not just aware of the previous treatments of the myth, but they also drew their line of difference in order to redirect the audience towards a different interpretation (Burian 1997, 180; Easterling 1997, 168–69).

9 Allan 2000, 4.

10 McDermott 1991, 132; on Euripides' sophistication, see also the seminal article of Winnington-Ingram 2003.

11 *Frogs* 943, [Eur. to Aesch.] χυλὸν διδοὺς στωμυλμάτων ἀπὸ βιβλίων ἀπηθῶν; 1409, [Aesch. to Eur.] ἐμβὰς καθήσθω, ξυλλαβὼν τὰ βιβλία. Also note Latacz 2003, 255, 'Offenbar hat Euripides wenig anderes getan als gedacht, gelesen und geschrieben. ... Wirklich könnte man Euripides als *ersten Literaten* der Antike bezeichnen' [the italics for emphasis are mine]. Similarly, modern scholars refer to Euripides as 'bookish' (Thomas 1989, 19 and n. 16).

2. Future reflexive

Intertextual allusions usually work retrospectively, building on the connection between a current and a previous narrative text. In the vertical axis which links a given text to other texts, the earlier one/s is/are evoked by means of thematic and/or dictional *reflections* or *echoes* attested in the most recent one. Through this process, the audience are invited to activate their literary familiarity, so that all kinds of 'literary luggage' carried by the author or the readers can be conjured up. In this case, the older text intrudes in the newer as a literary tide which is generated *ad hoc*, upon the genesis of the new narration, and moves back and forth according to the narrator's plan. Usually, an intertextually shaped storyline follows a linear/regular temporal sequence where earlier events precede later ones. In this light and if literary tradition is seen holistically, as a coherent narrative text, *Oedipus the King* and the subplot of the revelation of the incest is narrated before *Oedipus at Colonus* and the subplot of the end of the incestuous king's life. From this vantage point, a spectator of the 401 BC performance of *Oedipus at Colonus*[12] would have certainly recalled the story of the disclosure of Oedipus' secret as well as the hero's act of self injury, as narrated in *Oedipus the King*, commonly attributed to the period between 430 and 420 BC.[13]

But what happens when a prior narration has already foretold the 'future' of a mythical figure? In other words, what kind of intertextuality is at work when prior texts invade into later ones not as fossilized *literary memory* but rather as *literary forecast*? In most cases, a sense of dramatic irony is created or the author invites his readers to share a metanarrative comment.[14] Such a narrative technique was first coined as fu-

---

12 For the date of the posthumous staging of the play, see Markantonatos 2007, 30–39.
13 Such an assumption inevitably leads to the discussion about the theatrical knowledge of the Athenian spectators deriving from the original performances, reperformances, or dramatic text books. As also discussed above, the evocation of prior theatrical experience was a kind of cultural competence that the spectators were expected to have (Burian 1997, 194–195). For reperformances during the fifth century, see below, n. 65. For the circulation of books during the fifth century, see below, p. 416 ff.
14 Barchiesi 2001, 106. The use of *future reflexive* could be paralleled to that of mythological paradigms, often found in other literary genres, such as Homeric epic and Hellenistic poetry; the narrative effect of both the *future reflexive* and the mythological *exempla* depends much on the mythological knowledge of the narratees. In Theocritus for example, the *exempla* are used in order to enrich

ture reflexive by Barchiesi, who has observed the systematic tendency of Ovid's *Heroides* to precede with regard to the time of the story the events of well known narratives of the classical period.[15] The knowledge of 'what happens next' in the story on the part of the spectators helps the poet increase the tragic gap between onstage- and offstage-reality, while simultaneously highlighting the poet's self-consciousness. Although covertly indicated, a narrator in the present has been a narratee in the past, and is often aware of previous treatments of the same story; hence, a *narrative continuum* of texts is established with narrators and narratees switching identities as they continuously wander within a narrative labyrinth. Since the most recent text grows through its reading of other previous texts, the external narratees are immersed in a world of texts or even performances.

Therefore, within a wide intertextual nexus, earlier writers paradoxically narrate late parts of the mythological *megatext*[16] whose complete narration is then going to be retrospectively filled in by later writers. For example, Euripides' *Medea* narrates the sequel – in modern cinema terminology – of the story of Apollonius' *Argonautica* and Virgil narrates the sequel of Ovid's *Heroides*, constructing an intertextual relation in which Apollonius fills in the narration of Euripides and Ovid that of Virgil.[17] In the case of drama though, playwrights seem to be contesting their own selves, since the oxymoronic concept of future reflexivity is a common tendency in all three tragedians. In Sophocles, *Antigone*'s performance was a future reflexive narrative with respect to the *Oedipus at Colonus* performance, while Gibbons and Segal are actually naming Sophocles' requiem a 'pre-quel', as opposed to the term 'sequel'. According to Gibbons' and Segal's intertextual viewing of the Sophoclean corpus, the playwright commits a literary 'return' to his previous play,

---

the interpretive possibilities, even leading to 'untraditional' conclusions, as they generally highlight the poet's concern for polyphony (Fantuzzi 1995).

15 Barchiesi 2001.
16 The term is coined by Segal, to refer to the totality of the mythical narratives and the system upon which they are patterned. The mythical *megatext* therefore points to an endless, intertextually constructed, mythical 'plot-bank'. In his words (1986b, 52), 'by megatext I mean not merely the totality of themes or songs that the poets of an oral culture would have had available in their repertoires but also the network of more or less subconscious patterns, or deep structures, or undisplaced forms, which tales of a given type share with one another. The term thus includes the Greeks' own consciousness of the thematic affinities among the privileged narratives that we call myths'.
17 See Barchiesi 2001, esp. 107–119.

proved by the fact that at the end of *Oedipus at Colonus* Antigone returns to Thebes and potentially re-initiates the story of Polyneices' burial, although this has been already narrated in an earlier Sophoclean play.[18]

Likewise, in the case of Aeschylus' *Eleusinians* and *Seven*, future reflexive is not observed in connection to other writers, but within a narrower intertextual nexus, which we may call intra-authorial since it operates within a single playwright's narrative corpus. In Euripides' *Suppliants* and *Phoenician Women*, a similar tendency is also noticed, but in a way that not only reveals an intra-textual dialogue with the rest of the Euripidean narrative, but also drops a hint at Aeschylus' parallel narrative technique, making future reflexivity 'double and inter-authorial'.

3. 'Double and inter-authorial' future reflexive

'Double' future reflexivity concerns the way a pair or dyad of texts – in our case Aeschylus' *Eleusinians* and *Seven* – share the same future reflexivity that links another pair of texts –Euripides' *Suppliants* and *Phoenician Women* – with respect to the theme of the burial of the dead. Future reflexivity, becomes hereby inter-authorial since it involves two playwrights, Aeschylus and Euripides, but also intra-authorial for it pairs plays of the same composer. In this conception, future reflexivity may be seen as a form of complex intertextuality expanding on simple intra-authorial intertextuality, which it eventually exploits at length. Euripides, may be surmised, did not wish to rival or allude to a given text of his famous predecessor but aimed at reproducing a dynamic relation between two texts written by Aeschylus. In this light, future reflexivity becomes the vehicle of a bold manifestation of a metatheatrical comment, since Euripides does not simply refer to an earlier text but re-enacts the entire mechanism of creating textual cross-references. *Ars latet arte sua.*

Euripides' *Suppliants*, which was performed somewhere towards the end of the 420's – possibly in 423–,[19] more than ten years before the *Phoenician Women*, narrates the mythological events that are supposed to have taken place after the story of *Phoenician Women*, i.e. after the war between Argos and Thebes and the mutual fratricide of Polyneices and Eteocles. The *Suppliants* stages the story of the mothers of the fallen

---

18 Gibbons – Segal 2003, 156.
19 Kovacs 1998, 3.

of the attack against Thebes, who, in the company of Adrastus, take refuge to Eleusis and turn to Theseus, begging him to intervene and convince the Thebans to allow the recovery of their sons' dead bodies. Theseus initially rejects their request, however the intervention of his mother Aithra and the appearance of a Theban herald who advises the king not to interfere, convince him to help. He leads the Athenian army to Thebes putting the city for a second time under attack. The Athenian victory[20] comes after a bloody battle and is reported to the spectators through an extensive messenger speech. Five bodies are collected and are brought to Athens,[21] while the burial of Polyneices in Theban soil remains implicit.[22]

Thus if the authorial activity of Euripides is considered as a unified narrative act, one notices that the Theban narrative starts by narrating a late event of the fabula in 423 and moves backwards, with the narration of the earlier events more than ten years later. Somewhere around the 410's, Euripides intertextually 'fills-in' the story of the *Suppliants*, referring to the events that preceded the supplication to Theseus. The *Phoenician Women*, performed between 411–409,[23] recounts the preparation of the battle between Argives and Thebans, the verbal confrontation that deepened the enmity of Polyneices and Eteocles, as well as the battle itself, the final duel of the brothers and the suicide of Jocasta. From this vantage point, it may be argued that the narrative act of *Phoenician Women*, which with hindsight rounds off the narration of the Theban mythological cycle, narrates a much earlier part of the mythological past, although it happens much later in real time, forming an intertextual, albeit intra-authorial future reflexive.

Things start becoming far more interesting though, when one notices that in Aeschylus, just like in Euripides, the exact same narration of the Argive expedition against Thebes is expressed by an identical occurrence of paired intra-authorial future reflexivity. Aeschylus' *Eleusinians*

---

20 For the description of Theseus' victory as fusing contemporary and epic elements and constructing a blurred image of Theseus as both hero and tyrant, see Mendelsohn 2002, 182–184.
21 The play's setting is not Athens in general, but Eleusis in particular, which in Euripides' time had become an Athenian deme. As many 'suppliant' dramas, the *Suppliants* is staged in an area that is close to, but also away from Athens (see Goff 1995). The play's geography is fully discussed in Morwood 2007, 17–23.
22 Kovacs 1998, 6.
23 See Mastronarde 1994, 11–14.

narrates the *story* of the removal of the dead of the battle, while the *Seven Against Thebes* narrates mainly the preparation for the battle, listing the catalogue of Argive and Theban warriors. Although there is no existing evidence regarding the date of the *Eleusinians*, the play is traditionally dated before the *Seven* (467), somewhere around 475 BC, having as *terminus post quem* the return of the bones of Theseus by Cimon from Scyros to Athens.[24]

The desperately fragmentary condition of the *Eleusinians* – only two fragments survive[25] – would have made impossible any secure assumption regarding its plot, if it was not for an indirect comment coming from Plutarch, who in his *Theseus* refers to the stories of both the *Suppliants* and the *Eleusinians*, as part of the narration of the great deeds of the Athenian king. As reported by Plutarch, while Aeschylus presents Theseus taking up the bodies of the Argive dead thanks to his ability to persuade the Thebans,[26] Euripides makes Theseus recover the dead by waging war (Plutarch *Theseus* 29.4–5):

συνέπραξε [Theseus] δὲ καὶ Ἀδράστῳ τὴν ἀναίρεσιν τῶν ὑπὸ τῇ Καδμείᾳ πεσόντων, οὐχ ὡς Εὐριπίδης ἐποίησεν ἐν τραγῳδίᾳ, μάχῃ τῶν Θηβαίων κρατήσας (*Suppl.* 560 sqq.), ἀλλὰ πείσας καὶ σπεισάμενος· οὕτω γὰρ οἱ πλεῖστοι λέγουσι· Φιλόχορος (*FGrH* 328 F112) δὲ καὶ σπονδὰς περὶ νεκρῶν ἀναιρέσεως γενέσθαι πρώτας ἐκείνας. ὅτι δ' Ἡρακλῆς πρῶτος ἀπέδωκε νεκροὺς τοῖς πολεμίοις, ἐν τοῖς περὶ Ἡρακλέους (*mor.* VII 144 Bern.) γέγραπται.[27] ταφαὶ δὲ τῶν μὲν πολλῶν ἐν Ἐλευθεραῖς δείκνυνται, τῶν δ' ἡγεμόνων περὶ Ἐλευσῖνα,[28] καὶ τοῦτο Θησέως Ἀδράστῳ χαρισα-

---

24 Aélion 1983, 233. For the dating of the play to this particular period, see Hauvette 1898, 170–173; Gastaldi 1976, 50–71; Wilamowitz 1891, 226–227, also gives an earlier date to the *Seven Against Thebes*. A date around the 470's could also be indicated by a vase (Athens N.M. 18606), datable just after 470, illustrating three pairs of men standing on three altars. Karusu 1972 has proposed that it could be a representation of a scene of the *Eleusinians*, although the depiction of the supplication scene of the *Heraclidae* is also possible. For Cimon's expedition to Scyros in 476–475 BC and the removal of Theseus' bones, see Walker 1995, 55–61.
25 *TrGF* 3.53a (Radt) and *TrGF* 3.54 (Radt).
26 Given that Theseus' presence in the myth is not attested before Aeschylus' *Eleusinians*, it has been argued (Föllinger 2003, 295) that this piece of information comes either from a local Eleusinian or Attic source, or from the epic *Theseis*.
27 For a discussion of the parallelism between Theseus and Heracles, see Morwood 2007, 11–14.
28 For the certainty or uncertainty of the information referring to the separate burial of the generals, see Jacoby 1954, 1.444.

μένου. καταμαρτυροῦσι δὲ τῶν Εὐριπίδου Ἱκετίδων <καὶ> οἱ Αἰσχύλου Ἐλευσίνιοι (fr. p. 18 N^2), ἐν οἷς [καὶ] ταῦτα λέγων ὁ Θησεὺς πεποίηται.

4. The burial of the dead at Thebes and Greek historical memory

Before exploring further the future reflexive linking the former to the latter plays of both dyads, it is advisable to discuss the common practices of burying the war dead, as well as the position that the burial of the dead at Thebes had in Greek historical memory. During the classical period, a city's obligation towards its war victims was an extremely crucial issue of civic life. Hence, Spartan tradition prescribed that only the names of those men who were killed in battle be inscribed on their gravestone;[29] as for the city of Athens, it either repatriated the ashes of the dead, or even buried the victims in the battlefield.[30] In this social context, the recovering of the bodies of the Argives thanks to the mediation of Theseus was not just a popular historical event, but was also frequently used as a means of sanctifying the Athenian king and glorifying the city's past.[31] In this light, Athenian familiarity with diverse narratives referring to the burial of the Seven can be readily assumed.

The event is first attested in Herodotus (9.25–27), who in his narrative of the battle at Plataea (479 BC), describes the disagreement between the Athenians and the Tegeans upon deciding who will take the left wing of the Greek army, with both sides trying to prove that their own history is more glorious. The Athenian argumentation includes – amongst other great deeds – the Athenian superiority showed in the case of the burial of those who died at Thebes. According to this account of the story, the Argive soldiers remained unburied until the

---

29 Plutarch, *Lycurgus* 27.3, ἐπιγράψαι δὲ τοὔνομα θάψαντας οὐκ ἐξῆν τοῦ νεκροῦ, πλὴν ἀνδρὸς ἐν πολέμῳ καὶ γυναικὸς [τῶν] λεχοῦς ἀποθανόντων.

30 Loraux 1986, 18. The emphasis led on this custom is historically proved by the condemnation and execution of the generals at Arginusae, who although victorious, did not collect the dead bodies of their soldiers. Cf. Diodorus 13.97–103, esp.101.1, Ἀθηναῖοι δὲ πυθόμενοι τὴν ἐν ταῖς Ἀργινούσαις εὐημερίαν ἐπὶ μὲν τῇ νίκῃ τοὺς στρατηγοὺς ἐπῄνουν, ἐπὶ δὲ τῷ περιιδεῖν ἀτάφους τοὺς ὑπὲρ τῆς ἡγεμονίας τετελευτηκότας χαλεπῶς διετέθησαν.

31 As clearly put by Aélion 1983, 232, '[l]es écrivains attiques, chaque fois qu'ils veulent exalter la grandeur d'Athènes, rappellent l'histoire de la sepulture des Sept'.

Athenians sent an army against the Thebans, took the dead and buried them at Eleusis (9.27.3):³²

τοῦτο δὲ Ἀργείους τοὺς μετὰ Πολυνείκεος ἐπὶ Θήβας ἐλάσαντας, τελευτήσαντας τὸν αἰῶνα καὶ ἀτάφους κειμένους, στρατευσάμενοι ἐπὶ τοὺς Καδμείους ἀνελέσθαι τε τοὺς νεκροὺς φαμεν καὶ θάψαι τῆς ἡμετέρης ἐν Ἐλευσῖνι.

The next piece of information comes from the 4th-3rd century historian Philochorus (Plutarch, *Theseus* 29.4–5), adding that Theseus accomplished the first truce ever made for recovering the bodies of those slain in battle. As Plutarch recounts, the simple soldiers were buried at Eleutherai (ταφαὶ τῶν πολλῶν), while the generals (ταφαὶ ... τῶν δ' ἡγεμόνων) at Eleusis.³³ The Athenian propaganda is obvious, since Philochorus is taking advantage of the mythical background in order to consolidate the glory of Athens and praise its mythical king, Theseus.³⁴

As for the geographical differentiation of the burial of the soldiers, it is consonant with the information the messenger gives to Adrastus in the *Suppliants* (754–759):

[ΑΔ.] ὧν δ' οὕνεχ' ἀγών, ἦν νεκροὺς κομίζετε;
[ΑΓ.] ὅσοι γε κλεινοῖς ἕπτ' ἐφέστασαν δόμοις.

---

32 According to Aélion 1983, 232, it is highly probable that Herodotus was not *reproducing* the real argumentation that the Athenians used before the battle at Plataea, but was *inventing* it on the basis of possible arguments concerning Athenian superiority drawn from any kind of relevant narrative texts (paintings, poems, wall representations) he must have been exposed at while he stayed in Athens (probably between 447 and 443). Such an approach agrees with the relevant comment of Fowler – Marincola 2002, 155, who believe that φαμεν is emphatic, signaling the Athenians' innovation in the tradition. For Herodotus' years in Athens, see Moles 2002; Fowler 2003.

33 *FGHist* 3 [= Jacoby 1950, 328. fr. 112 (Philochorus)]. As observed by Mills 1997, 231, 'the Eleusis-Eleutherai distinction itself points to some sort of compromise between two different versions of the story. Eleutherai in Boeotia is likely to have been the original resting place of the seven, and Athenian claims to their burial depend entirely on the physical existence of tombs at Eleusis'. Actually, a group of eight tombs has been excavated in the western section of the cemetery in Eleusis, six of which had been opened and investigated in antiquity (somewhere in the second half of the eighth century BC). Those six tombs have been regarded by Mylonas 1955, 60 as those 'attributed by the ancient Greeks to the legendary heroes who at the instigation of Polyneikes undertook the fateful war against Thebes'. On the contrary, the presence of a cenotaph in Argos commemorating the Argives who died in the expedition and dating to the middle of the sixth century testifies to a local hero-cult (Pariente 1992).

34 Jacoby 1954, 1.442.

[ΑΔ.] πῶς φής; ὁ δ' ἄλλος ποῦ κεκμηκότων ὄχλος;
[ΑΓ.] τάφῳ δέδονται πρὸς Κιθαιρῶνος πτυχαῖς.
[ΑΔ.] τοὐκεῖθεν ἢ τοὐνθένδε; τίς δ' ἔθαψέ νιν;
[ΑΓ.] Θησεύς, σκιώδης ἔνθ' Ἐλευθερὶς πέτρα.

Much later, in the first century BC, the historian Diodorus indicates that Adrastus, the only survivor of the expedition, returned to Argos leaving all his soldiers unburied. Since there was nobody daring to bury the deceased, the Athenians took the initiative to offer burial to the dead proving once more their χρηστότης, surpassing all the rest in terms of nobleness and kindness (4.65.9):

ὁμοίως δὲ καὶ τῶν ἄλλων ἡγεμόνων ἀπολομένων πλὴν Ἀδράστου, καὶ πολλῶν στρατιωτῶν πεσόντων, οἱ μὲν Θηβαῖοι τὴν ἀναίρεσιν τῶν νεκρῶν οὐ συνεχώρησαν, ὁ δ' Ἄδραστος καταλιπὼν ἀτάφους τοὺς τετελευτηκότας ἐπανῆλθεν εἰς Ἄργος. ἀτάφων δὲ μενόντων τῶν ὑπὸ τὴν Καδμείαν πεπτωκότων σωμάτων, καὶ μηδενὸς τολμῶντος θάπτειν, Ἀθηναῖοι διαφέροντες τῶν ἄλλων χρηστότητι πάντας τοὺς ὑπὸ τὴν Καδμείαν πεπτωκότας ἔθαψαν.

Not even a century later, the insistence of the Athenian playwrights to narrate this specific achievement of Theseus is interpreted by Dionysius of Halicarnassus as a sign of Athenian self-flattery (5.17.4):

ἐπαίνους δὲ λεγομένους ἐπ' αὐτοῖς οὐ γράφουσιν ἔξω τῶν Ἀθήνησι τραγῳδοποιῶν, οἳ κολακεύοντες τὴν πόλιν ἐπὶ τοῖς ὑπὸ Θησέως θαπτομένοις καὶ τοῦτ' ἐμύθευσαν.

Finally, Pausanias condemns the Thebans once again, certifying the denial of Creon to bury the seven generals and rejecting all opposing Theban claims (1.39.2):

Κρέων γάρ ... οὐ παρῆκε τοῖς προσήκουσιν ἀνελομένοις θάψαι· ἱκετεύσαντος δὲ Ἀδράστου Θησέα καὶ μάχης Ἀθηναίων γενομένης πρὸς Βοιωτούς, Θησεὺς ὡς ἐκράτησε τῇ μάχῃ κομίσας ἐς τὴν Ἐλευσινίαν τοὺς νεκροὺς ἐνταῦθα ἔθαψε. Θηβαῖοι δὲ τὴν ἀναίρεσιν τῶν νεκρῶν λέγουσιν ἐθελονταὶ δοῦναι καὶ συνάψαι μάχην οὔ φασι.

Moreover, he glances at the Theban political propaganda, for which the burial of the Seven was an important issue as well. In his discussion of the topography of Thebes, he refers to a mound, which the Thebans say to have been the burial place of Tydeus and even quote a verse of Homer[35] in support of their claim (9.18.2):

Θηβαίων δὲ οἱ τὰ ἀρχαῖα μνημονεύοντες Τυδέα φασὶν εἶναι τὸν ἐνταῦθα κείμενον, ταφῆναι δὲ αὐτὸν ὑπὸ Μαίονος, καὶ ἐς μαρτυρίαν τοῦ λόγου παρέχον-

---

35 *Il.*14.114.

ται τῶν ἐν Ἰλιάδι ἔπος:
Τυδέος, ὃν Θήβῃσι χυτὴ κατὰ γαῖα καλύπτει.

To sum up, pre-tragic tradition provides Aeschylus and Euripides with an extremely fertile field, which generates a large variety of possible choices, allowing both playwrights to come up with a 'personal' viewing of the story. From as early as the lost epic *Thebais,* the aftermath of the defeat of the Seven appears to have been a very popular theme whose starting point was set by Adrastus' departure from Thebes.[36] Herodotus offers a more detailed account of the events, trying to solemnize the ensuing tradition that Adrastus asked for the help of Theseus, who then managed to make the removal of the dead possible. After the tragedians, Plutarch's version added more to the story by highlighting the fact that the point of differentiation between Aeschylus and Euripides concerns *the means* Theseus employed in order to effectuate the removal. According to Aeschylus, Theseus peacefully persuaded the Thebans to give back the bodies, while the Euripidean Theseus had to issue war against them.[37]

It seems almost certain that two traditions were in circulation at the same time and that each tragedian was free to choose the one that fitted best to the literary or even socio-political context. In this light, Isocrates, who in the *Panathenaicus* (168–174) followed the version of Aeschylus, while in the *Panegyricus* (54–56) that of Euripides, audaciously admitted that he had used both the war- and the peace-versions of the story according to what each time suited him better (*Panathenaicus* 172):

Καὶ μηδεὶς οἰέσθω μ' ἀγνοεῖν, ὅτι τἀναντία τυγχάνω λέγων, οἷς ἐν τῷ Πανηγυρικῷ λόγῳ φανείην ἂν περὶ τῶν αὐτῶν τούτων γεγραφώς· ἀλλὰ γὰρ οὐδένα νομίζω τῶν ταῦτα συνιδεῖν ἂν δυνηθέντων τοσαύτης ἀμαθίας εἶναι καὶ φθόνου μεστόν, ὅστις οὐκ ἂν ἐπαινέσειέ με καὶ σωφρονεῖν ἡγήσαιο τότε μὲν ἐκείνως, νῦν δ' οὕτω διαλεχθέντα περὶ αὐτῶν.

---

36 As stated by Pausanias (8.25.8), the *Thebais* specifically refers to the horse Arion, son of Poseidon, with whose help Adrastus managed to leave the city: ἐν δὲ τῇ Θηβαΐδι ὡς Ἄδραστος ἔφευγεν ἐκ Θηβῶν *εἵματα λυγρὰ φέρων σὺν Ἀρίονι κυανοχαίτῃ* αἰνίσσεσθαι οὖν ἐθέλουσι τὰ ἔπη Ποσειδῶνα Ἀρίονι εἶναι πατέρα (=*Thebais*, fr. 6a Davies). However, there is no specific reference to Adrastus' subsequent refuge in Athens.

37 It has been proposed that the aforementioned Theban defeat after the attack of Theseus, or even the Theban defeat after the attack of the Epigonoi, could be connected to the Theban denial to participate in the Trojan War (Higbie 2002, 183 n. 15, 187 n. 18).

No matter what version of the story is followed, the dead of the battle are not buried at Thebes,[38] and the Thebans are blamed because of their refusal to hand over the bodies of the fallen. According to Athenian warfare-rules, the return of the dead both symbolizes and expresses the admission of defeat on the part of the suppliant and shall thus be satisfied.[39] In such a context, both the *Eleusinians* and the *Suppliants* condemn the Theban impious behaviour.[40]

By fostering an even more harsh presentation of the myth on the dramatic stage, the *Suppliants*, is inevitably connected to the historical reality and in specific to the battle at Delion. In the spring of 431 BC, Thebes provoked the war by attacking Plataea, and mercilessly slaughtered the city's inhabitants in the summer of 427. The *Suppliants* was possibly performed just a little bit after the campaign of Delion in November 424, where the Athenians suffered a heavy defeat and the

---

38 Cf. also sch. ex. *Il.* 14.114, Τυδέος, ὃν Θήβῃσι <χυτὴ κατὰ γαῖα κάλυψεν>: ὅτι οὐ κατὰ τοὺς τραγικοὺς ἐν Ἐλευσῖνι μετηνέχθησαν οἱ περὶ τὸν Καπανέα. For an extensive discussion of the line and its literary criticism by ancient scholars, see Higbie 2002.

39 *FGHist* 3, Comm. II (= Jacoby 1954, 2.354, n. 39). Epic poetry treated the respect towards the enemies' dead bodies as a value that should be kept (Segal 1971; Mills 1997, 232). Cf. also *Republic* 469 d-e, where Plato parallels refusal concerning the return of the dead to the behavior of dogs: when they are stoned, they do not attack the people who stoned them, but the stones that have fallen next to them. He also condemns such a behavior as 'illiberal', 'greedy', and of 'womanish and petty spirit': ἀνελεύθερον δὲ οὐ δοκεῖ καὶ φιλοχρήματον νεκρὸν συλᾶν, καὶ γυναικείας τε καὶ σμικρᾶς διανοίας τὸ πολέμιον νομίζειν τὸ σῶμα τοῦ τεθνεῶτος ἀποπταμένου τοῦ ἐχθροῦ, λελοιπότος δὲ ᾧ ἐπολέμει; ἢ οἴει τι διάφορον δρᾶν τοὺς τοῦτο ποιοῦντας τῶν κυνῶν, αἳ τοῖς λίθοις οἷς ἂν βληθῶσι χαλεπαίνουσι, τοῦ βάλλοντος οὐχ ἁπτόμεναι; οὐδὲ σμικρόν, ἔφη. Ἐατέον ἄρα τὰς νεκροσυλίας καὶ τὰς τῶν ἀναιρέσεων διακωλύσεις; Ἐατέον μέντοι, ἔφη, νὴ Δία.

40 Under the influence of the strong anti-Theban sentiment created by Theban medism during the Persian wars and the impact of the version endorsed by Aeschylus' *Eleusinians* concerning the refusal to bury the Seven in Theban territory, Jacoby (1954, 1.445) has argued that Pindar's *Olympian* 6.15–16 (ἑπτὰ δ' ἔπειτα πυρᾶν νεκροῖς τελεσθέντων Ταλαϊονίδας / εἶπεν ἐν Θήβαισι τοιοῦτόν τι ἔπος), which was dedicated to the victory of Hagesias in 472 or 468 BC (see Hutchinson 2001, 371–374), may be seen as a pro-Theban reaction against the recently prevailing Aeschylean version. Conversely, Hutchinson 2001, 383 maintains that the '[t]he placing of ἐν Θήβαισι in this clause makes it less likely that Pindar is polemicizing against the Athenian tale that the Seven were buried at Eleusis'.

Boeotians refused to return the dead.[41] Such an imposing historical context is regarded as the *terminus post quem* for the performance of the *Suppliants*.[42] In the words of Bowie, 'the similarities between the events at Delium and the plot of the play are striking, and in addition there is an unusually prominent series of references to contemporary aspects of Athenian society and culture; both of these focus the play onto the fifth century. The differences, such as that between the fifth-century Thebans' willingness to hand over the bodies if the Athenians left the temple, and the mythical ones' refusal to hand them over at all, mean the play is not a simple parable based on the recent events, but do not disqualify it as a consideration of the issues raised by those events'.[43] Similarly, Pelling admits that 'real life still matters; but it must be seen through a blurring filter, appropriate to the timeless nature of the reflections it inspires'.[44]

I hope it has by now become evident that the part of the Theban myth concerning the burial of the Seven and the historical atmosphere that hosted it enjoyed great popularity. It seems that the issue of the burial of the Seven was constantly debated throughout Greek history because it also incorporated other important political, religious or social issues.[45] Having discussed the historical context, it is now time we dwell upon the ways later narratives make use of future reflexive references contained in previous narratives and investigate how the playwrights treated the parts of the myth that have already been narrated in earlier plays. In drama, future reflexivity seems to work as a fertile field for the development of narrative *ellipses*.[46]

---

41 Cf. Thucydides 4.97–99. For the importance of the battle at Delion in connection to the defeat at Amphipolis, as both influencing the will of the Athenians to negotiate, see Thucydides 5.14.1.
42 Collard 1975, 10; Bowie 1997, 45; See also Mills 1997, 91, who also uses the *Suppliants* as the starting point of a thorough discussion on the relationship between history and tragedy in Athenian society (91–97). For a reading of the play as a commentary on the role of pity in Athens, especially after the debate over the fate of Mytilene in 427, see Konstan 2006b, 54–60. Athenian pity towards any suppliants has also been connected to the growth of Athenian power (Tzanetou 2006).
43 Bowie 1997, 45.
44 Pelling 2000, 165.
45 Higbie 2002, 187–188.
46 Genette (1972) 1980, 95 schematically defines *ellipsis* as a part of the story that corresponds to no narration at all ($NT=0$, $ST=n$). For a fuller discussion, see Genette (1972) 1980, 106–109.

5. The narrative use of future reflexive

In the case of Aeschylus and the dyad of the *Eleusinians* and the *Seven*, much of our knowledge is either assumed or sparingly provided, thus the narrative result detected in the latter is a cautious – though highly possible – assumption. The early treatment of a posterior part of the myth in the *Eleusinians* can explain a substantial narrative ellipsis widely noticed in the *Seven*. In particular, the lack of narration of the actual battle between Argives and Thebans in the *Seven*[47] has been justified by its supposed narration in the *Eleusinians* or at least the *Argives*, one of the accompanying plays of the trilogy.[48] Apart from the *Argives* and the *Eleusinians*, two other plays could have been part of the trilogy, the *Nemea* (in the first position)[49] or the *Epigonoi* (in the third position).[50] Nemea was supposed to be the mother of Archemoros, the baby who died from a snake-bite while the Argives were marching against Thebes. The play could have presented Adrastus founding the Nemean games in honor of Archemoros and Amphiaraus predicting the impending deaths of the Seven, while the *Epigonoi* must have dealt with the second attack against Thebes, performed by the sons of the Seven.[51] In the *Argives*, the central theme must have been the defeat of the Argives, the negation of their burial rights,[52] as well as the lament of the chorus, possibly consisting of their mothers or widows.[53] The *Eleusinians* on the other hand may have included Adrastus' plea to Theseus and the burial at Eleusis.[54] In both plays, Adrastus must have been one of the prevailing characters, having (in the *Argives*) a climactic ap-

---

47 For a discussion of the limited description of the battle in the *Seven*, see Hutchinson 1985, 173–178.
48 Aélion 1983, 233; *TrGF* 3 16, 17, 18 (Radt).
49 Wilamowitz 1891, 227; Zielinski 1931, 17; Mette 1959, fr. 260, 261.
50 Wecklein 1896, 587–589; also endorsed by Aélion 1983, 231–243.
51 See Gantz 2007, 65–66, who also notes that according to another possible scenario, *Nemea* could have also been the satyr play, featuring the foundation of the Nemean games as a compensation for the lack of any reference to Archemoros' death.
52 Hubbard 1992, 302.
53 Aélion 1983, 233; See also Mette 1963, 40. The proposals of both Aélion and Mette presuppose the existence of a female chorus and thus dictate the Greek title Ἀργεῖαι. See below, n. 56.
54 Aélion 1983, 233.

pearance next to the lamenting chorus, similar to that of Xerxes in the *Persians*.[55]

By fully exploiting the mythical storage of the audience, who were already familiar with the 'future' of the characters, Aeschylus builds elliptical narratives insisting less or at all on the part of the *fabula* he has already referred to in previous plays. What mostly strikes us is that Aeschylus does reveal his intra-authorial self-consciousness, since the lamenting chorus of women surrounding king Eteocles in the *Seven*, must have been composed in parallel to the female chorus of the lamenting Argive women confronting king Adrastus in the *Argives*.[56]

Similarly, the loose end of the burial of Polyneices in the *Phoenician Women* seems not to worry Euripides, since his spectators could use their performatory knowledge coming from the earlier staging of the *Suppliants* and infer that Polyneices was finally buried. Additionally, some arcane sayings of Polyneices, who, again in the *Phoenician Women*, had paralleled Tydeus and himself to a boar and to a lion[57] become all the more obvious when read in the light of Adrastus' account of the same story in the *Suppliants*. The Argive king therein explains the Apollonian oracle that he had once received, according to which he should marry his daughters to a boar and to a lion (135–146):

[ΘΗ.] ἀλλὰ ξένοις ἔδωκας Ἀργείας κόρας;
[ΑΔ.] Τυδεῖ <γε> Πολυνείκει τε τῷ Θηβαιγενεῖ.
[ΘΗ.] τίν' εἰς ἔρωτα τῆσδε κηδείας μολών;
[ΑΔ.] Φοίβου μ' ὑπῆλθε δυστόπαστ' αἰνίγματα.
[ΘΗ.] τί δ' εἶπ' Ἀπόλλων παρθένοις κραίνων γάμον;
[ΑΔ.] κάπρῳ με δοῦναι καὶ λέοντι παῖδ' ἐμώ.
[ΘΗ.] σὺ δ' ἐξελίσσεις πῶς θεοῦ θεσπίσματα;
[ΑΔ.] ἐλθόντε φυγάδε νυκτὸς εἰς ἐμὰς πύλας—
[ΘΗ.] τίς καὶ τίς; εἰπέ· δύο γὰρ ἐξαυδᾷς ἅμα.
[ΑΔ.] Τυδεὺς μάχην συνῆψε Πολυνείκης θ' ἅμα.

---

55 Hubbard 1992, 302–303.
56 The Greek title is recorded as Ἀργεῖοι or Ἀργεῖαι, according to the male or female chorus attributed to the play. Radt opts for the masculine title (*TrGF* 3.16, 17, 18), which is attested in *Etymologicon Magnum* 341.5 (Gaisford); the feminine one is found in Harpocration 306.4 (Dindorf) and Hesychius α 6627 (Latte) and is recently preferred by Gantz 2007, 65 n. 94. Regardless the sex of the chorus, the figure of Adrastus must have kept a central position, reflecting dramatically his change of state from holding the royal power to being defeated (Hubbard 1992, 302).
57 *Phoenician Women* 409–413, esp. 411, [ΠΟΛ.] κάπρῳ λέοντί θ' ἁρμόσαι παίδων γάμους.

[ΘΗ.] ἦ τοῖσδ' ἔδωκας θηρσὶν ὡς κόρας σέθεν;
[ΑΔ.] μάχην γε δισσοῖν κνωδάλοιν ἀπεικάσας.

In this light, future reflexivity points to deep intertextual awareness not just on the part of the playwrights, but most prominently on the part of the audience. There is no need to question Euripides' knowledge of his predecessor's treatment of the same parts of the myth. In fact, despite the limited evidence, it has been proposed that the references that Theseus and Adrastus make to the Theban battle in the *Suppliants* (846–917) perhaps allude to a similar description that must have been part of the narration either in the *Eleusinians* or, at least the *Argives*.[58] Seen from this angle, it can be additionally argued that the appearance of the mothers of the fallen in the *Suppliants* is to be interpreted as part of a conscious opposition to Aeschylus, who did not include such a chorus in his *Eleusinians*.[59]

I therefore see no reason to doubt that playwrights aimed at fully exploiting specific knowledge of former performances by their spectators. Although strong familiarity with earlier plays cannot be proved, one cannot easily discard the fact that the Athenian spectators were expected to 'sense' the playwrights' intertextual games.[60] It is widely accepted that towards the end of the fifth century dramatic texts were circulating and that literacy was an important aspect of Athenian lifestyle.[61] Textual evidence coming from the *Frogs* points not just to a culture of silent reading[62] but also to the existence of small copies of short tragic passages like choral odes or monologues,[63] possibly as *aide mémoire*. As put by Kovacs,

---

58 Aélion 1983, 233 n. 16. The possible Euripidean allusion to a messenger speech of a lost Aeschylean play was first noticed by Wilamowitz 1923, 202, though no proposal of a specific play was made. Cf. also Fraenkel 1963, 56 n. 1; Winnington-Ingram 2003, 51.

59 Zuntz 1955, 24–25. With reference to the connection between the *Suppliants* and the *Eleusinians*, cf. the illuminative comment of Aélion 1983, 242, 'cette pièce [the *Suppliants*], dont l'ésprit est peu eschyléen, est pleine de souvenirs eschyléens et reste, en plusieurs endroits, très eschyléenne dans le ton'.

60 For a general discussion of this Euripidean dramatic intention, see Winnington-Ingram 2003.

61 Thomas 1989, esp. 19–24; 1992, 13, 123; Hutchinson 1985, xl n. 16; Kovacs 2005, 379.

62 *Frogs* 52–54, καὶ δῆτ' ἐπὶ τῆς νεὼς ἀναγιγνώσκοντί μοι/τὴν Ἀνδρομέδαν πρὸς ἐμαυτὸν ἐξαίφνης πόθος/τὴν καρδίαν ἐπάταξε πῶς οἴει σφόδρα. See also Denniston 1927, who believes that Aristophanes in the *Frogs* might be making jokes about book-jargon and other technical lingo.

63 *Frogs* 151, ἢ Μορσίμου τις ῥῆσιν ἐξεγράψατο.

'[t]hough reading plays was not a common activity and papyrus rolls containing an entire tragedy did not enjoy wide circulation, it would seem that it was not difficult to get access to a copy of a play one admired'.[64]

Aeschylus in specific was undoubtedly one of the most popular authors: the Athenians voted for the reperformances of his plays right after his death in 456[65] and students were supposed to memorize entire passages of the tragic corpus (*Clouds* 1364–1372). Following from that, it is very likely that the *Seven* were in high demand given their triumphant welcome by the Athenian audience in the performance of 467,[66] and that Euripides himself or the Athenian spectators of the *Phoenician Women* were easily able to bring the Aeschylean play in mind.[67]

Aristophanes for instance, is especially instructive in regard to the popularity of the *Seven Against Thebes*, since in the 411 performance of *Lysistrata*, he takes for granted that the audience specifically know the Aeschylean text. In lines 189–190, Lysistrata is urged to take an oath, but not *à la manière* of Aeschylus and the seven generals who swore by their shields:[68]

[ΚΑ.] μὴ σύ γ', ὦ Λυσιστράτη,
εἰς ἀσπίδ' ὀμόσῃς μηδὲν εἰρήνης πέρι.

Aristophanes' point seems to be that such a ceremony would be old fashioned. However, what *we* get of it is that the poet is clearly counting on the textual knowledge of the narratees. Such knowledge would be

---

64 Kovacs 2005, 380.
65 *Vita Aeschyli* 12 (*TrGF* 1, Radt). See also Wilson 2000, 192 ('we are starting to see more clearly just how much reperformances there in fact was in and outside Athens, and from how early a date. We can be fairly sure, for instance, that after Aeschylus died in 456 "anyone who wished to" could "ask the archon for a chorus" to produce his work ... This seems to reflect a political decision of the Athenian people as a whole, and demonstrates the cultural and political importance of Aeschylus to the city'). For fifth century reperformances outside Athens, see Easterling 1994; Taplin 1999, 33–43; Allan 2001. For reperformances during the Hellenistic and Roman periods as documented in papyri of dramatic texts, see Gammacurta 2006.
66 Aeschylus won the first prize, Aristias the second and Polyphrasmon the third, cf. DID. a. 467 in *TrGF* 1, Snell.
67 It has even been proposed that Euripides composed the *Phoenician Women* under the influence of a recent, interpolated (by the addition of the theme of the burial of Polyneices) fifth century revival of the *Seven* (Webster 1967, 218–219).
68 See Henderson 1987, 92.

impossible to be based on memories of the first production, but could have been acquainted through books or even reperformances.[69]

6. Conclusions

I have argued that Euripides' *Phoenician Women* is intertextually linked to his *Suppliants,* just as Aeschylus' *Seven Against Thebes* is to his *Eleusinians,* since in both cases the myth has been proleptically narrated in the earlier plays of the aforementioned dyads and analeptically in the later ones. Euripidean differentiation from the Aeschylean experiment lies in the way Athenian power is imposed: Euripides, once more, finds himself involved in a metatheatrical dialogue with his predecessor.

Along these lines, I would like to suggest that Euripides consciously reproduces the Aeschylean future reflexive technique in the context of poetic rivalry. By inaugurating double inter-authorial self reflexivity, he makes a profound gesture to his audience: not only does he engage them in recalling his own *Suppliants*,[70] but also the fact that Aeschylus had equally engaged his own audience to an analogous narrative game. In such a 'reception-oriented' context, it seems difficult to resist the scholarly temptation pointing to the existence of a 'theatrical-performatory' megatext, which in the case of drama works as drastically as the mythical one.[71] Both narrators and narratees are expected to be able to recall both their mythical knowledge and their theatrical experience of previous performances. Future reflexivity thus becomes a convenient way either to draw a line of difference, or to fill the gaps of previous narratives and construct new narrative ellipses.

---

69 In fact, it has been argued that there was a continuous written transmission of the Aeschylean texts soon after their first production, even under the supervision of the poet himself (Hutchinson 1985, xli).

70 It is worth observing that even within the narrow limits of the *Suppliants'* narrative micro-structure one also detects a type of complex intertextuality, which expands both to the past and future. With respect to the narrative structure of the play, the *Suppliants* belongs to the 'supplication pattern' plays, but by developing the burial motif it retrospectively uses the model of the Sophoclean *Antigone*. At the same time, the play involves proleptic allusions to the story of the Sophoclean *Oedipus at Colonus*, since it sets the theme of the burial in a foreign land that proves to be more hospitable than the homeland (Zeitlin 1986, 106).

71 The performatory conscience of the Athenian spectators must have been so strong, that the 'dialogue' between the dramatic texts should be called 'intertheatrical' rather than 'intertextual'. See above, p. 401.

Euripides' aberration and stark differentiation from the standard version of the myth, namely the burial of the dead, would have strongly struck his audience, just as the Athenians of the post-Delion period would have been appalled by the refusal of the Boeotians to allow them to bury their war dead. This annoying coda could have reminded the Athenian spectators of the distance between the political reality during Aeschylus' time and the grimness of the present situation. And all that, through the means of a narrative technique that lingers on the spiral movement of 'time present and time past [that]/Are both perhaps present in time future/And time future contained in time past'.[72]

---

[72] T. S. Eliot, see n. 1.

Ignorant Narrators in Greek Tragedy

Ruth Scodel

This paper will examine narratives in tragedy that either explicitly stress that a homodiegetic narrator does not have all the information he/she considers relevant, or that present narrative information that I think almost any member of an audience would perceive as deficient even without such marking. I shall suggest a loose typology of such inadequate narratives in tragedy based on frames and on Martin/Phelan's adaptation of Booth's categories for narrative unreliability.[1] By 'frames' I mean *schemata*, the information about the world that a given person, or fictional character, treats as relevant to a situation in attempting to understand it. The most common cause of deficient narrative is divine intervention, and narrators who are recounting episodes of supernatural action within a purely naturalistic frame are often deeply perplexed. Narrator-focalizers in tragedy, though, also have difficulties that result from failures of 'Theory of Mind,' the ability to understand other people as having intentions, thoughts, and desires. They are unwilling or disinclined to think about the motives of other people. Homer already shows an interest in the gap between omniscient and limited narrative when the gods are involved – this is Jörgenson's Rule, that the characters speak only of 'a god' or 'Zeus' where the external narrator offers precise information (Jörgenson 1904). However, when only mortal actions are in question, Homer represents narrators who are deceived about what others are thinking, but not narrators who refuse to make inferences. Cognitive literary studies have become a subfield of their own, emphasizing particularly Theory of Mind – how people form inferences about what other people are thinking and feeling. One recent book argues, in a contemporary twist on Aristotle, that the pleasure and value of reading fiction lies in the exercise it gives in Theory of Mind (Zunshine 2006). Such a view of fiction takes the novel as the defining form of fiction. Tragedy, as a strictly dramatic form, makes rich demands on the spectator's Theory of Mind. Having no direct access to characters' intentions, the audience must constantly attempt to judge

---

1   Phelan – Martin 1999, reworking Booth (1961) 1983.

what they think by what they say. It also frequently represents the difficulties its characters have in figuring out what other characters mean and intend.

I. F. de Jong has shown that Euripidean messengers are subjective narrators, who include their own inferences and judgments in their accounts. She notes how often messengers include inferences about characters' thoughts as focalizations (de Jong 1991, 24–9). However, I would suggest that it is a characteristic of messengers that, because they are relatively self-effacing narrators, their inferences about what other people are thinking are usually obvious and therefore unobtrusive – unlike, for example, narrators within an *agon*, who are ready to impute far from transparent motives to the past actions of their opponents (so, for example, Hecuba describes Helen's psychological response to the sight of Paris at E. *Tr.* 988–97).

1. Simple Limitations

Sometimes the narrator's problem is entirely a matter of information. Narratives typically need to be properly contextualized before they make sense. In Sophocles' *Electra*, Chrysothemis interprets the facts of her narrative correctly (that the offerings at Agamemnon's tomb indicate Orestes' return), but Electra misinterprets, because she has heard another, false narrative that is irreconcilable with the correct interpretation of Chrysothemis'. She hypothesizes a false narrative that would cohere with the lie of Orestes' death, that someone performed offerings at Agamemnon's tomb in memory of Orestes (*El.* 932–3). Often, though, the problems are more complicated. Theseus does not just believe Phaedra's false narrative in *Hippolytus*; he implicitly but obviously interprets everything he knows about Hippolytus through it. We often think of the quintessentially tragic event as the moment of recognition, in which a character receives new information that forces him or her to reconfigure a previous narrative. Theseus' reception of Phaedra's letter is a pseudo-recognition. He uses it as the *telos* to which the narrative of Hippolytus' life has been directed. Although Theseus does not offer a specific story for Hippolytus, Hippolytus' attempt at self-defense is mostly a catalogue of narratives that he argues are unbelievable.

That is, the tragedians are often interested in how difficult it is for people to understand events around them when they lack the right interpretive frame. If they had more information, they would be able to interpret events more clearly. Often, though, characters' difficulty in constructing the right narrative goes beyond a lack of information. For example, the audience may infer that Theseus was already prejudiced against Hippolytus before Phaedra's accusation. Characters in a tragedy do not know that they are characters in a tragedy, while the spectators do, and the spectators therefore have a very different frame for understanding, because they automatically apply typical tragic story-patterns to what they see. Even with a completely invented plot, the spectator is likely to be able to frame the action more effectively than the characters, because the genre offers likely frames.

Some of the inadequate narratives are messenger-speeches, while some are not. But some in which the narrator is not a messenger share affinities with messenger-speeches, and I hope that a study of the limited narrator generally can contribute to our understanding of how messenger-speeches function. Yet Barrett (2002) has convincingly shown how Aeschylean messengers especially can tend to omniscience, and how authoritative the messenger tends to be. So a theoretical distinction may be helpful. Booth defines two axes of reliability, the axis of fact and the ethical axis (Booth (1961) 1983). A narrator can be unreliable by distorting what happened, or by judging it wrongly and misdirecting sympathy. The Euripidean messenger is subjective, but not unreliable, on the axis of fact, and his judgments and inferences are generally reliable on the ethical axis—his sympathies are properly shared by the external audience. Phelan and Martin add a third axis, knowledge and perception (Phelan–Martin 1999). Here the narrator is reliable as far as his or her narrative goes, but misses essential information. Messengers, like other tragic narrators, are sometimes inadequate on the axis of perception. Either they fail to see things (I think of the chorus of *Agamemnon*, who suddenly announce that they did not witness Iphigenia's sacrifice), or they cannot make sense of what they see, especially when gods are involved.

Sometimes, of course, they understand completely. One group I would call *Wise Narrators*. The first messenger in *Bacchae* advises Pentheus to receive Dionysus (769–7), the second guesses that the voice from the sky is that of Dionysus (1079–80). The messenger in *Heraclidae* says that οἱ σοφώτεροι ('the wise') say that the stars who appear in response to Iolaus' prayer were Heracles and Hebe (856–7). In these cases, the messenger is prepared to expect divine intervention, and so has the right frame. Sometimes, the matter is slightly more complicated and the narrator is *Almost Wise*. The messenger in *Ion* interprets the failure of Creusa's attempt to murder Ion as an intervention by the god to save himself from pollution (1118); the audience assumes that Apollo is concerned about his son. The messenger's interpretation is framed by his knowledge of the sacred location of the action, while the audience has a more precise basis of understanding.[2]

In Sophocles, some messengers (quite apart from those who tell outright lies) are self-interested. Although *Self-interested Narrators* are not unreliable, their self-concern gives their focalization a particular effect, since they are not self-effacing, as messengers typically are. The guard in *Antigone* is the clearest case. I have argued elsewhere that both burials invite the audience to suspect that the gods have helped *Antigone*, and I shall assume that here (Scodel 1984). In his first report to Creon, the messenger is concerned mostly to demonstrate his own innocence—as Creon's response shows, not without cause. The messenger thus describes what he observed in a way that makes it mysterious, but that does not invite a narratee to assume divine involvement. His decisions about what he will report are sharply marked and do not seem self-evident, since he includes the emotional response of the guards to their discovery of the burial, and a simile that suggests an inference about the motive of the person who performed it:

ὅπως δ' ὁ πρῶτος ἡμὶν ἡμεροσκόπος
δείκνυσι, πᾶσι θαῦμα δυσχερὲς παρῆν.
ὁ μὲν γὰρ ἠφάνιστο, τυμβήρης μὲν οὔ,
λεπτὴ δ' ἄγος φεύγοντος ὡς ἐπῆν κόνις.

But when the first day-watchman showed us, all experienced an unpleasant surprise. For he had vanished, not laid in a tomb, but a fine dust lay above him, as if from someone avoiding pollution.

(*Ant.* 253–6)

The chorus-leader then suggests divine intervention, but without specifying whether he means that the gods have assisted a mortal or have acted themselves (278–9). When Creon rejects this possibility, their following song (the 'Ode on Man') implies that they have re-interpreted the event as an example of human ingenuity and daring. Creon has a false frame already, so that he incorporates the burial into an (incorrect)

---

2   de Jong 1991, 17, thinks that the Messenger of *IT* 328–9 implies that Artemis has saved the two strangers so that they can be sacrificed; I would stress instead that the Messenger's vagueness about the cause of the wondrous event allows him to be right even though he does not realize that the gods are helping the strangers.

narrative of political opposition and bribery; the chorus suggests that the gods may provide a better explanation, but do not pursue it. Again, when the guard narrates Antigone's capture, his self-interested focalization blurs the question of how Antigone reached the body. Since both Creon and the messenger have their own interests in the story, neither has any reason to complicate it beyond 'Antigone.' The messenger in *Antigone* is not quite unreliable on the ethical axis, but it is the ethical axis rather than fact or perception that complicates response to his report.

Most messengers are not focal characters and, one might say, know that they are not focal characters: even as the messenger describes his own responses to events, he does so in order to convey the event, not himself. Such a messenger, if he has a valid frame, may not know or entirely understand what has happened, but he can precisely delimit what he knows and does not know. These are *Limited Narrators*. In *Oedipus Coloneus*, for example, the messenger stresses that he does not know exactly how Oedipus died. He does, however, realize that the gods are directly involved in what happened. So he is not unreliable, although he feels he must insist that he is in his right mind, because his narrative breaks the usual limits of what is credible (1665–6). The limits of his information are unproblematic (see Markantonatos 2002, 145–7). Even the Phrygian in *Orestes* is precise about the limits of his knowledge (1495–99): Helen disappeared, and he knows nothing more because he ran away. This, then, is my first category of inadequate narrative: the unproblematically incomplete, where the narrator is aware of his or her own perceptual limits and explicitly clarifies them. Such messengers are reliable on fact and ethically normative, but their perception is qualified.

2. Severe Limitations: *Rhesus* and *Ajax*

Sometimes, though, characters fail to perceive divine intervention, without which they have no frame for making sense of events. These are *Desperate Narrators*. The most confused narrator in tragedy is probably the charioteer in *Rhesus*. After the army went to sleep in disorder, he woke up and fed the horses, preparing for the morning, and noticed two men moving through the darkness. Assuming they were Trojan or other allied thieves, he shouted at them and they left. He then went back to sleep, but had a nightmare that he was driving Rhesus' horses as they were ridden by wolves. Waking in terror, he found himself surrounded by dying men, including Rhesus; as he looked for his sword in the dark, somebody stabbed him. He does not know how this came about, but he guesses it was friends (802–3). When Hector enters, he insists that Hector must be responsible; he assumes that Hector had Rhesus murdered for his horses (839). He engages in an extended argument from probability: Greeks would have had to come through the Trojan army unseen; they would surely have killed or wounded Trojans, none of whom are injured. Finally, he says, Greeks did not know that Rhesus was there, let alone know where to look for him:

τίς δ' ἂν χαμεύνας πολεμίων κατ' εὐφρόνην
Ῥήσου μολὼν ἐξηῦρεν, εἰ μή τις θεῶν
ἔφραζε τοῖς κτανοῦσιν; οὐδ' ἀφιγμένον
τὸ πάμπαν ᾖσαν· ἀλλὰ μηχαναὶ τάδε.

For who, going at night among the bivouacs of the enemy, would have found that of Rhesus, unless some god showed it to those who were going to kill him? They didn't even know that he had arrived. No, this is all contrived.

(*Rh.* 852–5)

This example is extraordinarily explicit, since the charioteer realizes that the enemy could have killed Rhesus with a god's help, but does not consider the god's help possible. The charioteer has presumably witnessed the tense meeting between Hector and Rhesus, so he is primed to misinterpret the action. Earlier in the play, Alexander, who has heard a rumor among the sentries that Greek spies have entered the camp, is deflected by Athena, who pretends to be Aphrodite (642–54). The narrator's inability to imagine divine intervention is itself the result of divine intervention. The messenger is unreliable on the ethical axis – his judgment is completely wrong – but not because his ethical orientation is wrong. He is in the characteristically tragic situation of having a frame that almost forces him to misconstrue what he (accurately) perceives.

Tecmessa in *Ajax* is another narrator who simply has no adequate frame through which to interpret what she has witnessed.[3] She overtly signals the limits of her ability to tell the whole story. She tells the chorus that Ajax, after recovering from his madness, demanded that she tell him what happened:

---

3   De Jong 2006a meticulously compares her account to the other narratives of Ajax's madness.

κἀγώ, φίλοι, δείσασα τοὐξειργασμένον
ἔλεξα πᾶν ὅσονπερ ἐξηπιστάμην.

And I, friends, in fear told him what had been done, everything as far as I knew it.

(*Aj.* 315–6)

Tecmessa's narrative is especially remarkable because it includes both events the audience has actually witnessed for itself and events outside the drama for which she is the only witness:

κεῖνος γὰρ ἄκρας νυκτός, ἡνίχ' ἕσπεροι
λαμπτῆρες οὐκέτ' ᾖθον, ἄμφηκες λαβὼν
ἐμαίετ' ἔγχος ἐξόδους ἕρπειν κενάς.
κἀγὼ 'πιπλήσσω καὶ λέγω, 'τί χρῆμα δρᾷς,
Αἴας; τί τήνδ' ἄκλητος οὔθ' ὑπ' ἀγγέλων
κληθεὶς ἀφορμᾷς πεῖραν οὔτε του κλυὼν
σάλπιγγος; ἀλλὰ νῦν γε πᾶς εὕδει στρατός.'
ὁ δ' εἶπε πρός με βαί', ἀεὶ δ' ὑμνούμενα·
'γύναι, γυναιξὶ κόσμον ἡ σιγὴ φέρει.'
κἀγὼ μαθοῦσ' ἔληξ', ὁ δ' ἐσσύθη μόνος.
καὶ τὰς ἐκεῖ μὲν οὐκ ἔχω λέγειν πάθας·
εἴσω δ' ἐσῆλθε συνδέτους ἄγων ὁμοῦ
ταύρους, κύνας βοτῆρας, εὔερόν τ' ἄγραν.
καὶ τοὺς μὲν ηὐχένιζε, τοὺς δ' ἄνω τρέπων
ἔσφαζε κἀρράχιζε, τοὺς δὲ δεσμίους
ἠκίζεθ' ὥστε φῶτας ἐν ποίμναις πίτνων.
τέλος δ' ἀπᾴξας διὰ θυρῶν σκιᾷ τινι
λόγους ἀνέσπα, τοὺς μὲν Ἀτρειδῶν κάτα,
τοὺς δ' ἀμφ' Ὀδυσσεῖ, συντιθεὶς γέλων πολύν,
ὅσην κατ' αὐτῶν ὕβριν ἐκτείσαιτ' ἰών.

For that man, in the depth of night, when the evening torches were no longer burning, taking a sharp spear set off on pointless ways. And I rebuke him and say, 'What on earth are you doing, Ajax? Why with no call or summons from a messenger are you setting off on this venture, without hearing a trumpet? Really, the entire army is asleep now!' And he said to me a few words that are endlessly sung over: 'My wife, silence is an ornament to women.' And I stopped trying to understand, and he rushed out alone. I cannot say what he experienced there. But he came in again leading bulls bound together, herding dogs, and woolly prey. He cut the throats of some, others he turned over and slaughtered and broke their backs, and some he bound and mutilated as if they were men, though he was attacking herds. But finally, he rushed through the door and threw words around to some shadow, some against the Atridae, some about Odysseus, adding lots of laughter, what insult he had gone and paid them back.

(S. *Aj.* 285–304)

Tecmessa realizes that Ajax's actions indicate insanity — but lacks the other crucial piece of information, Athena's intervention. Without that knowledge, she has no way of deciding when Ajax's madness began, and she interprets the prologue, in which he talks to Athena, as further evidence of his madness. This is especially remarkable because it violates epic norms for divine interventions. In *Iliad* 1, nobody thinks Achilles is crazy when he has a conversation with an Athena nobody else can see. The entire action takes place in a bubble in which no time passes and nothing is visible on the outside. During Athena's extended conversation with Diomedes at *Il.* 5.793–834, Sthenelus seems to be a silent witness, and nobody else notices. Those around people who are talking to gods do not perceive that they are acting oddly.

Strikingly, the scene being narrated has already foregrounded the audience's exceptional position. In the scene as it takes place, Ajax can apparently see Athena but not Odysseus, while Odysseus can see Ajax and hears Athena but does not see her.[4] Interpreters disagree about where Athena stood, and those who locate her on the same level as the mortal characters often assume that the audience forgets that Athena is supposed to be invisible (Garvie 1998, 124). I suspect, though, that the spectator should be reminded that Odysseus does not see Athena when she promises Odysseus that Ajax will not see him (83–5), and when it seems that Ajax does see her (91). Athena displays Ajax for Odysseus' benefit; he is like the theatrical spectator, able to watch from safety. So the audience has been primed: they alone actually see everybody. Tecmessa's narrative adds yet another point of view — and I use this term rather than focalization because, in this case, actual seeing is so important. If Odysseus told this story, he would include Athena's presence, but he could not specify what she looked like. Odysseus consciously does what Ajax appears to Tecmessa to be doing: he talks to a void. So when we hear this episode, we are getting a view from the far side of the stage: Tecmessa was watching from one side while we watched from the other, and Athena and Odysseus were invisible to her almost as the audience is invisible to the actors. There are two realms of action: from the theater, we see the divine realm, but from inside the *skene*, only the human world is visible, and Ajax is in both at the same time. Ajax himself interprets events correctly, re-

---

4 There has been much dispute about how this scene was played; see Calder 1965, Ziobro 1972, Calder 1974. I think that Athena simply followed Odysseus and stood behind him.

ferring to Athena's role at 401–3 and 450–4. It is not, however, clear how much of Ajax's account is memory, and how much inference.

Tecmessa's account is inadequate in other ways, too. She does not know what Ajax plans when he leaves the tent, so she has no idea what, in his madness, the massacre and abuse of the cattle mean for him. Yet she hears, in his conversation with the 'shadow,' that he talks about the Atridae and Odysseus and how he has avenged their *hybris*. Yet she does not hypothesize that he may have confused the animals with his enemies. For Tecmessa, apparently, the realization that Ajax is mad blocks any further Theory of Mind work. Although she describes the killing of the cattle in sacrificial language, she does not explicitly say that she thinks Ajax was trying to sacrifice, and she nowhere even approaches a guess at his initial motive for leaving the tent or the basis of his actions later. This may be in part because she functions as an ἄγγελος.

Tecmessa and the charioteer in *Rhesus* both realize that they have difficulties. They constitute my second category, in which the narrator recognizes limits on the axis of perception but nonetheless attempts to interpret events. The charioteer explicitly rejects the hypothesis of divine intervention, while Tecmessa apparently does not consider it. A *Limited Narrator* sees limits on what can be told, but still has a story that makes sense; a *Desperate Narrator* cannot understand what has happened.

3. Evasive Narratives: *Prometheus Vinctus* and *Oedipus*

The third and most problematic and interesting category, in my view, is the narrative that demands explanation that the narrator does not provide. These are in one sense minimalist narratives, but of a peculiar kind. They do not report just the facts. In the narratives of this category, the narrator is not simply ignorant of some important information, but avoids framing the events any more than is required to present a story at all: these are *Evasive Narrators*. That is, these are narratives where the limits of the narrator's information are important within a narrative strategy. Two examples of such narratives are Io's story in *Prometheus Vinctus* and the report of the *exangelos* of *Oedipus*.

Io in *Prometheus* does not present herself as ignorant, although her narrative will actually be severely limited:

οὐκ οἶδ' ὅπως ὑμῖν ἀπιστῆσαί με χρή,
σαφεῖ δὲ μύθῳ πᾶν ὅπερ προσχρῄζετε
πεύσεσθε· καίτοι καὶ λέγουσ' αἰσχύνομαι
θεόσσυτον χειμῶνα καὶ διαφθορὰν
μορφῆς, ὅθεν μοι σχετλίᾳ προσέπτατο.

I do not see how it would be right for me not to accede to your request, and you will learn all you seek in a true account. Still, I am embarrassed even at telling the storm brought on me by the gods and the destruction of my shape, from what source it swooped down on me and made me miserable. (640–44)

Io apparently sees no problems with her knowledge or perception; any difficulty in her narrative lies in her embarrassment. Yet the narrative itself is remarkably puzzling.

αἰεὶ γὰρ ὄψεις ἔννυχοι πωλεύμεναι
ἐς παρθενῶνας τοὺς ἐμοὺς παρηγόρουν
λείοισι μύθοις· ὦ μέγ' εὔδαιμον κόρη,
τί παρθενεύῃ δαρόν, ἐξόν σοι γάμου
τυχεῖν μεγίστου; Ζεὺς γὰρ ἱμέρου βέλει
πρὸς σοῦ τέθαλπται καὶ συναίρεσθαι Κύπριν
θέλει· σὺ δ', ὦ παῖ, μὴ 'πολακτίσῃς λέχος
τὸ Ζηνός, ἀλλ' ἔξελθε πρὸς Λέρνης βαθὺν
λειμῶνα, ποίμνας βουστάσεις τε πρὸς πατρός,
ὡς ἂν τὸ Δῖον ὄμμα λωφήσῃ πόθου.
τοιοῖσδε πάσας εὐφρόνας ὀνείρασι
ξυνειχόμην δύστηνος, ἔστε δὴ πατρὶ
ἔτλην γεγωνεῖν νυκτίφοιτ' ὀνείρατα·
ὁ δ' ἔς τε Πυθὼ κἀπὶ Δωδώνην πυκνοὺς
θεοπρόπους ἴαλλεν, ὡς μάθοι τί χρὴ
δρῶντ' ἢ λέγοντα δαίμοσιν πράσσειν φίλα.
ἧκον δ' ἀναγγέλλοντες αἰολοστόμους
χρησμούς, ἀσήμους δυσκρίτως τ' εἰρημένους.
τέλος δ' ἐναργὴς βάξις ἦλθεν Ἰνάχῳ
σαφῶς ἐπισκήπτουσα καὶ μυθουμένη
ἔξω δόμων τε καὶ πάτρας ὠθεῖν ἐμὲ
ἄφετον ἀλᾶσθαι γῆς ἐπ' ἐσχάτοις ὅροις·
κεἰ μὴ θέλοι, πυρωπὸν ἐκ Διὸς μολεῖν
κεραυνὸν ὃς πᾶν ἐξαϊστώσοι γένος.
τοιοῖσδε πεισθεὶς Λοξίου μαντεύμασιν
ἐξήλασέν με κἀπέκλῃσε δωμάτων
ἄκουσαν ἄκων· ἀλλ' ἐπηνάγκαζέ νιν
Διὸς χαλινὸς πρὸς βίαν πράσσειν τάδε.
εὐθὺς δὲ μορφὴ καὶ φρένες διάστροφοι
ἦσαν, κεραστὶς δ', ὡς ὁρᾶτ', ὀξυστόμῳ
μύωπι χρισθεῖσ' ἐμμανεῖ σκιρτήματι
ᾖσσον πρὸς εὔποτόν τε Κερχνείας ῥέος

Λέρνης τε κρήνην· βουκόλος δὲ γηγενὴς
ἄκρατος ὀργὴν Ἄργος ὡμάρτει πυκνοῖς
ὅσσοις δεδορκὼς τοὺς ἐμοὺς κατὰ στίβους.
ἀπροσδόκητος δ' αὐτὸν †αἰφνίδιος† μόρος
τοῦ ζῆν ἀπεστέρησεν, οἰστροπλὴξ δ' ἐγὼ
μάστιγι θείᾳ γῆν πρὸ γῆς ἐλαύνομαι.
κλύεις τὰ πραχθέντ'·

> For visions by night constantly wandered into my maiden's rooms and addressed me in smooth words: 'Most fortunate young woman, why do you remain so long a virgin, when you could make the greatest of marriages? For Zeus is hot with a bolt of desire from you, and he wishes to join in Cypris. Do not, child, kick away the bed of Zeus, but go out to the deep meadow of Lerna, your father's pastures and cattle-corrals, so that the eye of Zeus may get rest from its longing.' I was trapped in such dreams every night, until I brought myself to declare to my father these dreams that came by night. And he sent one messenger after another to Pytho and Dodona, to learn what he needed to do or say to please the gods. But they came reporting tricky-mouthed oracles, without signification, uttered so that they were hard to evaluate. But finally, a clear enunciation came to Inachus explictly ordering and declaring that he had to drive me out of my house and native country, to wander unsupervised over the farthest boundaries of the earth. And if he refused, a fiery thunderbolt would come from Zeus and obliterate the entire race. Persuaded by such prophecies of Loxias, he drove me out and shut me out of his house, though he and I were unwilling. But the bridle of Zeus compelled him by force to do this. Immediately my form and mind were twisted around, and as a horned animal, as you see, stung by a sharp-mouthed gadfly I raced with insane leaps to the stream of Cerchnea, good to drink from, and the spring of Lerna. The earthborn herdsman Argus, unmixed in his fierceness, went with him, looking along my steps with his many close-set eyes. Unexpectedly, a sudden fate deprived him of life. But I, driven by the gadfly, wander from land to land under a scourge of divine origin. (645–683)

Now we, the external audience, mostly understand this narrative, and the internal audience also finds it comprehensible. Prometheus has explicitly referred to Hera at 592, and Io herself has almost certainly ascribed her mad wandering to Hera at 600.[5] We know that Hermes killed Argus.[6] The oracles, however, are mysterious even to the external audience. Why should Inachus have received a series of incomprehensible replies? Why does the last oracle, which finally tells him what to do,

---

5   Griffith 1983, 200 on *Pr.* 599–601. Ἥρας is a supplement of Hermann, but two syllables are needed for responsion and it is the obvious choice.
6   Podlecki 2005, 182 on *Pr.* 680 suggests that Hermes' name is suppressed because he is so unsympathetic later in the play.

come from Delphi instead of Dodona? Even the external audience cannot know at exactly what moment in the story Hera has intervened, and without this knowledge the exact sequence is difficult. The dreams tell her to go to the meadow of Lerna and her father's 'pastures,' the oracle tells her father to drive her away to wander at the boundaries. Once she leaves her father's house, her transformation is immediate and the gadfly apparently attacks her at once, yet she goes to the spring of Lerna and the river Cerchneia, apparently the same place the dreams told her to go. Since the dreams address Io as ὦ μέγ' εὔδαιμον κόρη and promise marriage with Zeus, the spectator must assume that the dreams come from Zeus and reflect an intention of having sexual relations with Io in Argos – but then do the oracles indicate that Zeus' plans have changed in response of Hera's knowledge; or does Zeus' plan change only when Io is expelled; or were the dreams deceptive from the start? Prometheus can predict the fate of Io in detail, but we do not know whether Zeus knows this, too.

Io's narrative ends as summary: γῆν πρὸ γῆς ἐλαύνομαι. The audience realizes how much has been omitted here when Prometheus proves his foreknowledge of what will happen to Io by recounting earlier events. He, too, is a very selective narrator, though he is explicit about his selectivity:

ὄχλον μὲν οὖν τὸν πλεῖστον ἐκλείψω λόγων,
πρὸς αὐτὸ δ' εἶμι τέρμα σῶν πλανημάτων.

I shall leave out the greatest crowd of tales, but go right to the very limit of your wanderings.

(827–8)

He narrates, in fact, two moments in Io's wanderings. First, when she arrived at Dodona, προσηγορεύθης ἡ Διὸς κλεινὴ δάμαρ/μέλλουσ' ἔσεσθαι· τῶνδε προσσαίνει σέ τι; ('You were addressed as "you who will be the glorious wife of Zeus"; does any of this please you?', 834–5). Then, she reached the 'great gulf of Rhea', to be known in the future as the 'Ionian Sea' (839–41). Prometheus has a clear principle of selection: he takes the two moments in Io's past that point directly to the future, the prophecy at Dodona and the aetiology of the Ionian Sea. His ability to select what he tells on the basis of an easily-grasped principle stands in contrast to her difficulty.

But what is most remarkable here is the gap between what Io apparently knows and the narrative as she tells it. She says that her father was unwilling to drive her out, so she is capable of considering the motivations of others, and she offers a further comment that the 'bridle of Zeus' forced him to expel her. She also recognizes that the gadfly is sent by a god. She organizes the section of the narrative in which her father appears so that there can be no doubt of his blamelessness, but elsewhere the narrative seems to have no point and no plot. If she is deliberately suppressing the role of Hera in her sufferings, a role she has mentioned in her preceding lyric, it is hard to see why.[7]

It is not just that she confines herself to experiencing focalization, for she avoids saying much about her own reactions to any of these events. She uses the verb ἔτλην of finally bringing herself to tell her father her dreams, and calls herself ἄκουσαν when she must leave her home, and she calls herself δύστηνος in referring to the recurring dreams. We cannot know whether this word belongs to her experience at the time, and, if so, why, or whether it is reflective. We do not know whether she was frightened or attracted by the dream's assertion that Zeus desired her, whether Argus' death made her feel hopeful or simply increased her confusion and terror, or how she felt at the moment of her metamorphosis. We do not know whether she narrates Argus' death as she does because her experience was like Tecmessa's in *Ajax*, and she really has no idea what actually happened, or whether she chooses not to say what she knows. There is a vast gap between the vocatives that are addressed to Io in the dreams and at Dodona and her experience, but she does not point to this gap.

Although the narrative is about her, she seems disconnected from herself. The narrative is odd not just for what Io does not know, but also for what she chooses not to tell. Io avoids clarity about the causes of her misfortunes where she knows them, does not guess about causes she does not know, and does not reveal her inner life – although her preceding lyric is more direct. Io should have complete access to her own feelings, but she reports almost as little of what she does know about herself as she does about the divine forces that drive her. It is, of course, not uncommon in tragedy for a woman to sing and then speak about the same matters, using the song to express her feelings and trimeters to speak rationally about her situation, but the gap in ap-

---

7   Conacher 1980, 59–60 suggests that the role of Zeus is exaggerated to prepare for a later, contrasting perception of events. Griffith 1983, 209 *ad* 669–82 notes but does not try to explain the suppression of Hera's role, and he comments 'the story is told as if the main details are already well known.'

parent information between Io's lyrics and her trimeters is not paralleled by Aeschylus' Cassandra or Euripides' Alcestis.[8]

Io's bare narrative is especially striking because she is not just a narrator-focalizer but also a focal character within her episode. Although the play does not prepare for her entrance and nobody refers to her after she leaves, while she is present, both Prometheus and the chorus direct their sympathy to her, and the audience must as well.[9] Io's account works almost as if Ajax gave Tecmessa's version of his actions. Io mirrors the passivity of her experience in her narrative passivity. She concludes κλύεις τὰ πραχθέντ', which sounds as if she has deliberately confined her account to τὰ πραχθέντ'. Whether or not we find this technique successful in engaging the audience, it certainly defines Io's peculiar situation.

Also, the narrative says that from the moment she became a cow and was tormented by the gadfly, her mind as well as her body was changed. Her few references to her own mental state and her father's come in the early part of the story; as a cow, she seems to have lost the ability to fashion a meaningful narrative for herself, as long as she is speaking. Yet since she mentions Hera when she sings, I am inclined to see the peculiarities of her narrative as a product of her rational control over it. Either, as a cow, she can no longer integrate feeling and understanding, so that she loses access to her past emotions when she tells events chronologically, or she is so frightened of the gods that she cannot bring herself to say what she knows except in the heightened realm of song. Io's limits, then, either belong to the ethical axis – she avoids saying as much as she knows, or revealing what she feels, because she is afraid – or they are mimetic of her condition, or they would have to be understood as meaningless for the character herself and simply imposed by the author. Prometheus, in contrast, is ready to tell Io her future in considerable detail, and is completely forthcoming about his own feelings and about the past, but has an essential secret that he will not reveal. So although the play's thematic concerns with speech and reticence determine Io's ignorant narrative, the audience can construct inferences about why she is so restricted as a storyteller.

The messenger in *Antigone* is a *self-interested narrator*. His only real concern is that he not be blamed for the burial. Yet we do not believe that he is unreliable on the axes of fact or perception. Instead the audi-

---

8   Dale 1954 on *Alc.* 280 (p. 74).
9   On the peculiar self-containment of the episode, see Taplin 1977, 265–67.

ence blames Creon for threatening him, while accepting his report as authoritative within its limits. The narrator makes no real attempt to explain how what he reports could be possible, because he is afraid to say more than he needs to say. The messenger in *OT* is also self-interested, but in a more complex way. A central event in his report is Jocasta's suicide. In both the other reports in the Sophoclean corpus of the suicides of women, the messenger explains why the suicide could not be prevented. Deianeira's death is narrated by the Nurse (O. *Tr.* 899–946), whom the audience has already assigned to a 'loyal slave' stereotype. The Nurse describes how she hid to watch Deianeira. Although she does not explicitly give a motive, we use our own Theory of Mind to infer that she was worried about how Deianeira would react to her son's denunciation of her. When the Nurse sees Deianeira preparing to kill herself, she runs to fetch Hyllus, but she is too slow and Deianeira is already dead. She then describes Hyllus' response: Hyllus laments, since the servants have told him how she came to send the peplus to Heracles: the Nurse is presumably making a coherent story from what Hyllus says in his laments, or adding information that other servants have given her. Although the Nurse is performing considerable narrative work in 932–5 in reducing Hyllus' enlightenment about his mother's action to summary, she is making only an obvious inference about his state of mind, and her narrative work does not draw attention to itself.

In *Antigone*, the messenger goes into the house to observe Eurydice because the chorus is worried that her silence portends trouble (*Ant.* 1255–6). As she laments and curses Creon, she strikes herself beneath the liver (1315–6), presumably with a knife she has hidden in her robes. Since there is no messenger-speech, and the narrative is given entirely in dialogue, the messenger does not try to give a fuller account, but the audience has the impression that the messenger simply could not react quickly enough to prevent the suicide. Since the messenger entered the house precisely in order to prevent such an event, the audience has no reason to be suspicious of the messenger on the ethical axis. The messenger in *OT*, in contrast, who also does not prevent a suicide, is open to suspicion because he has a motive to distort his account.

The *exangelos* of *OT* stresses his own lack of knowledge: he does not know exactly how Jocasta died. Barrett's *Staged Narrative* includes an extensive discussion of the speech (Barrett 2002, 194–222). He considers its emphasis on the difficulty of knowledge in relation to this theme in the rest of the play, and notes that the messenger offers an account not of what happened, but of his experience of what happened. My approach, with its emphasis on Theory of Mind, is slightly different. In an unpublished paper, David Kovacs comments in passing that the messenger insists that the gods must have helped Oedipus find where Jocasta is (*OT* 1258), even though you would think that her own rooms would be the first place Oedipus would look for her anyway. So the messenger prefers an explanation through supernatural intervention to using ordinary Theory of Mind, which would infer that Oedipus inferred where Jocasta must be.

So let us first look closely at what precedes the messenger's narrative, and then at the speech itself. Jocasta recognizes the situation at 1053 at the latest. She then tries to persuade Oedipus to abandon the search for his identity. This attempt occupies 1056–72. In this exchange, Jocasta is clearly desperate, while Oedipus evidently becomes annoyed:

> Οι. θάρσει· σὺ μὲν γὰρ οὐδ' ἐὰν τρίτης ἐγὼ
> μητρὸς φανῶ τρίδουλος, ἐκφανῇ κακή.
> Ιο. ὅμως πιθοῦ μοι, λίσσομαι· μὴ δρᾶ τάδε.
> Οι. οὐκ ἂν πιθοίμην μὴ οὐ τάδ' ἐκμαθεῖν σαφῶς.
> Ιο. καὶ μὴν φρονοῦσά γ' εὖ τὰ λῷστά σοι λέγω.
> Οι. τὰ λῷστα τοίνυν ταῦτά μ' ἀλγύνει πάλαι.
> Ιο. ὦ δύσποτμ', εἴθε μήποτε γνοίης ὃς εἶ.
> Οι. ἄξει τις ἐλθὼν δεῦρο τὸν βοτῆρά μοι;
> ταύτην δ' ἐᾶτε πλουσίῳ χαίρειν γένει.
> Ιο. ἰοὺ ἰού, δύστηνε· τοῦτο γάρ σ' ἔχω
> μόνον προσειπεῖν, ἄλλο δ' οὔποθ' ὕστερον.

> Oed. Cheer up. Not even if I am shown to be triply enslaved from a mother three generations in slavery will you be shown to be base.
> Jo. Still, obey me, I beg you. Don't do this.
> Oed. I could not obey so as not to learn this truly.
> Jo. But I know what I am doing[10] and telling you what is best for you.
> Oed. Well, that 'best' has been annoying me for some time.
> Jo. Unfortunate man, may you never learn who you are.
> Oed. Will someone go and bring the herdsman to me
> And leave her to rejoice in her wealthy ancestry?
> Jo. Woe, woe, miserable man. For this is the only word I can speak to you, but none other, ever again.
>
> (1062–72)

---

10 Jebb 1914 translates εὖ φρονοῦσα as 'I wish thee well' and does not comment. Kamerbeek 1967 points to the ambiguity of the expression

She then exits in a condition that disturbs the chorus: Oedipus, however, assumes that she is ashamed of his origins, and dismisses their worries·

Χο. τί ποτε βέβηκεν, Οἰδίπους, ὑπ' ἀγρίας
ᾄξασα λύπης ἡ γυνή; δέδοιχ' ὅπως
μὴ 'κ τῆς σιωπῆς τῆσδ' ἀναρρήξει κακά.
Οι. ὁποῖα χρῄζει ῥηγνύτω· τοὐμὸν δ' ἐγώ,
κεἰ σμικρόν ἐστι, σπέρμ' ἰδεῖν βουλήσομαι.
αὕτη δ' ἴσως, φρονεῖ γὰρ ὡς γυνὴ μέγα,
τὴν δυσγένειαν τὴν ἐμὴν αἰσχύνεται.

Wherever has your wife gone, Oedipus, rushing under the impulse of wild grief? I am worried that troubles will break out from this silence.
Oed. Let break what will. I will want to see my own origin, even if it is small. She perhaps – for she is proud, in a woman's way – is ashamed of my bad birth.

(1073–9)

After a short choral song, Oedipus realizes the truth in the next episode, when he interrogates the herdsman (who is very unwilling to say what he knows). Oedipus then exits with a farewell to the light:

ἰοὺ ἰού· τὰ πάντ' ἂν ἐξήκοι σαφῆ.
ὦ φῶς, τελευταῖόν σε προσβλέψαιμι νῦν,
ὅστις πέφασμαι φύς τ' ἀφ' ὧν οὐ χρῆν, ξὺν οἷς τ'
οὐ χρῆν ὁμιλῶν, οὕς τέ μ' οὐκ ἔδει κτανών.

Woe, woe! Everything would come out clearly. Light, may I see you now for the last time, who am shown to have been born from parents from whom I should not have been born, living with those with whom I should not have lived, killing those I should not have killed.

(1182–5)

After the stasimon, the *exangelos* enters.

What does the audience expect at this point? Because, for us, this play is the canonical form of the story, we too easily forget that Sophocles had other possibilities. Oedipus' farewell to the light sounds like a declaration of suicidal intent, and the chorus suggests to him later that suicide would have been a better choice (1368). Tiresias, though, has already predicted that Oedipus will be blind. Jocasta/Epikaste hangs herself in the *Nekyia* in the *Odyssey* (*Od.* 11.271–80). The Lille Stesichorus presents a woman whose doubts of the prophet seem to be a model for Sophocles' Jocasta, and who may be the mother-wife of Oedipus, surviving after the revelation as she does in Euripides' *Phoenissae*. So audience expectations may not have been as sharply defined as we imagine. On the other hand, a rule of economy tells us that if the chorus suggests a dire possibility that the character rejects, the worst will indeed happen.

Finally, the speech itself. The messenger begins by describing Jocasta as angry:

ὅπως γὰρ ὀργῇ χρωμένη παρῆλθ' ἔσω
θυρῶνος, ἵετ' εὐθὺ πρὸς τὰ νυμφικὰ
λέχη, κόμην σπῶσ' ἀμφιδεξίοις ἀκμαῖς.

> When, in anger, she went through the doorway inside, she rushed straight to her marriage bed, pulling her hair with the fingertips of both hands.
> (1241–3)

Is Jocasta angry?[11] The hair-pulling is surely a gesture of grief, and from inside her chamber she laments. Nothing immediately suggests that she is angry, and the commentators agree that ὀργῇ χρωμένη means something else – 'frantic,' in Jebb's translation.[12] Yet the Sophoclean parallels strongly support the sense 'angry.' At her exit she has just been quarreling with Oedipus. And in the *Odyssey*, the suicide of Oedipus' mother apparently causes suffering to him from her Erinyes:

ἡ δ' ἔβη εἰς Ἀΐδαο πυλάρταο κραταιοῖο,
ἁψαμένη βρόχον αἰπὺν ἀφ' ὑψηλοῖο μελάθρου
ᾧ ἄχεϊ σχομένη· τῷ δ' ἄλγεα κάλλιπ' ὀπίσσω
πολλὰ μάλ', ὅσσα τε μητρὸς ἐρινύες ἐκτελέουσι.

> She went to the house of mighty Hades whose gates are strong, by attaching a steep noose from the high house, possessed by her grief. To him she left behind miseries, many, all that the Furies of a mother fulfill.
> (*Od.* 11.277–80)

This implies that she curses him, and her suicide confirms and strengthens the curse.[13] Why she curses him we do not learn. Eurydice's suicide in *Antigone* is closely comparable: she blames and curses Creon just before she dies (*Ant.* 1304–5, 1311–12).

---

11 Singular forms of ὀργή appear 23 times in the extant plays and fragments of Sophocles; in all instances but one it clearly denotes the response to a perceived offense. In the one exception, *Aj.* 1153, it is dispositional rather than occurent, but the disposition is to anger.

12 Jebb 1914 *ad loc.*, Kamberbeek 1967 *ad loc.* translates 'passion of grief,' basing the translation on the chorus' description of Jocasta at 1073–4. Dawe 1982 *ad loc.* says '"anger" is not in point.' Bollack 1990, 3.836 argues that 'anger' is better because it 'is closer to the hate that divides Jocasta from herself.'

13 Heubeck 1989, 2.94 on *Od.* 11.279–80.

So the messenger sees her as angry, and the audience has no reason immediately to assume that he has misunderstood her – indeed, if I am right that messengers rarely go beyond the obvious in considering others' motives, the audience will assume that the messenger is right. Her attempt to halt Oedipus' search is a moment – there is another such moment in the messenger's speech, Oedipus' attempt to get a sword – at which the characters' motives are not fully intelligible, even though the action is entirely credible dramatically. If they were real people, we would probably guess that their intentions are not entirely present to consciousness, or at least not available for self-scrutiny. Suppose Jocasta somehow convinced Oedipus to halt the investigation. What would she do, when she knows the truth and he does not? Is she already intending to kill herself, and does she imagine that her death would somehow protect him? If he halted his search now, but she killed herself, he would of course restart his investigation, since she would have added a further, evidently linked mystery. Does she intend to continue living with him? The scene moves so quickly that we do not question what she is thinking, or automatically assume that she is not really thinking, but is only trying to delay the crisis so that she will be able to think. At her exit, the chorus calls her emotion ἀγρία λύπη ('wild grief,' 1073–4). That is surely right, but it does not mean that she is not also angry at Oedipus.

The messenger does not say where he is when Jocasta leaves the stage. There are two possibilities: either he is an attendant who follows her from the stage and then remains outside her locked door, or he was already inside, perhaps in the courtyard, and observed her as she entered. It is odd that he does not clarify his vantage point, since messengers usually explain this if there is any space for confusion. The messenger in *Ajax*, for example, says that he happened to be present when Calchas spoke to Teucer (748); the messenger in *Antigone* explains that he followed Creon to the place Polynices had been exposed (1196); Hyllus says that he met his father at the shrine of Zeus at Cenaeum (*Tr.* 753–5). This messenger simply narrates what Jocasta did. He is, however, present outside Jocasta's door, and listening to her, from the time she exits the stage until Oedipus arrives. That means that he does not hear the actual revelation, and indeed does not hear the chorus' expression of concern about Jocasta.

He, therefore, does not know why Jocasta is so angry and grieved. Her laments, however, should make the basis of her distress clear, if not the exact mixture of emotions she feels:

> καλεῖ τὸν ἤδη Λάιον πάλαι νεκρόν,
> μνήμην παλαιῶν σπερμάτων ἔχουσ', ὑφ' ὧν
> θάνοι μὲν αὐτός, τὴν δὲ τίκτουσαν λίποι
> τοῖς οἷσιν αὐτοῦ δύστεκνον παιδουργίαν.
> γοᾶτο δ' εὐνάς, ἔνθα δύστηνος διπλῆ
> ἐξ ἀνδρὸς ἄνδρα καὶ τέκν' ἐκ τέκνων τέκοι.

> She calls on Laius, already long dead, remembering the old offspring, by whom he was killed, and left the mother as a creator of bad children with his own. She lamented the bed, where doubly unfortunate she bore a husband from her husband and children from her children.
>
> (1245–50)

The messenger, however, does not report his own understanding of Jocasta's cries (or that of the other attendants who turn out to be there also). He simply summarizes without comment.

Then Oedipus enters:

> χὤπως μὲν ἐκ τῶνδ' οὐκέτ' οἶδ' ἀπόλλυται·
> βοῶν γὰρ εἰσέπαισεν Οἰδίπους, ὑφ' οὗ
> οὐκ ἦν τὸ κείνης ἐκθεάσασθαι κακόν,
> ἀλλ' εἰς ἐκεῖνον περιπολοῦντ' ἐλεύσσομεν.

> And how she died I do not know from here on anymore. For Oedipus broke in shouting, and because of him it was not possible to be a spectator of her trouble, but we looked toward him and he went from one to another.
>
> (1251–4)

This is the point at which the messenger declares himself an ignorant narrator. Commentators have been unhappy about the word ἐκθεάσασθαι, since the attendants have not been watching Jocasta, but only listening to her cries through the closed doors. Some have assumed that there must be a chink in the door.[14] I would suggest, however, that we consider how theatrical this narrative has suddenly become. The setting is now very much like a stage, and the messenger and the other slaves are in a situation familiar to dramatic spectators, perhaps even metatheatrical: the focal character is behind the locked door/inside the *skene*, and the messenger/spectator, deprived of visual access to the critical action, can only hear cries. The messenger introduces his account by stressing that he is the messenger, who has had actual visual experience, while the members of the chorus will experience only a narrative filtered through his memory:

---

14 Bollack 1990, 843 catalogues views. Kamerbeek 1967, 234 on *OT* 1253 suggests that a verb like εἰσπεσόντας is implied (Jebb 1914 does not comment).

τῶν δὲ πραχθέντων τὰ μὲν
ἄλγιστ' ἄπεστιν· ἡ γὰρ ὄψις οὐ πάρα.
ὅμως δ', ὅσον γε κἀν ἐμοὶ μνήμης ἔνι,
πεύσῃ τὰ κείνης ἀθλίας παθήματα.

The most painful part of what has been done is absent. For there is no vision. All the same, as much as I have of memory, you will learn the sufferings of that poor woman.

(1237–40)

Actually, he himself does not see Jocasta's suffering.[15] This group is also not unlike a chorus, generically doomed to be ineffectual. But as long as she is lamenting, it is, in a sense, all right. When Oedipus enters, however, they stop listening to her, because Oedipus absorbs all their attention.

One of Sophocles' crucial decisions in this scene is to follow the Homeric tradition that Oedipus' mother hangs herself (*Od.* 11. 277–9). It completely controls the dynamics of the event, because a hanging requires unmistakable preparation. Loraux 1987 assumes that hanging is the 'normal' method of suicide for women in tragedy and that a woman who dies by the sword is somehow masculinized, and this opinion seems widespread. I am not sure. Both Eurydice and Deianeira use swords, and while Deianeira's death has erotic overtones that could explain the choice, Eurydice's use of a sword is practical as well as symbolic; it prevents the messenger from stopping her, and it reiterates the deaths of her sons. Similarly, Jocasta in *Phoenissae* uses a sword not because she is mother rather than wife, as Loraux argues, but because she is on the battlefield, the sword is available, and there is no beam handy. Women always have the necessary tool for self-strangulation available, so this is the default method they use if they do not fear outside intervention (Phaedra, Antigone). Jocasta does not have a sword in her bedroom, but she could not easily be interrupted–she has locked the doors.

Oedipus asks the attendants for a sword, as he also looks for Jocasta:

φοιτᾷ γὰρ ἡμᾶς ἔγχος ἐξαιτῶν πορεῖν,
γυναῖκά τ' οὐ γυναῖκα, μητρῴαν δ' ὅπου
κίχοι διπλῆν ἄρουραν οὗ τε καὶ τέκνων.
λυσσῶντι δ' αὐτῷ...

---

15 The sequence thus plays with the dynamic of seeing/not seeing through the play; Seale 1982, 246–47.

> He wanders, demanding that we provide him with a sword, and tell him where to find his wife-no wife, the double maternal field of himself and his children. And to him as he raved...
>
> (1255–8)

This is the messenger's second venture into Theory of Mind: he concludes from Oedipus' shouting and general demeanor that he is crazed.

He does not, however, go any further in reporting any views about what Oedipus was trying to do. If a man comes chasing a woman who has locked herself in a room and demands a sword, the obvious inference is that he intends to kill her. Neither Jebb nor Kamerbeek says anything on the subject. Dawe does:

> In this rapid recital we have no time to ask ourselves what Oedipus intended to do with the sword. If we do ask ourselves, we cannot avoid the answer that he intended to kill his wife/mother.[16]

Dawe is surely right. If he is asking for a sword, he is not planning to blind himself with it. A sword is not the best tool for attacking one's own eyes, and I think the spectator assumes that the self-blinding is prompted by the sight of the dead Jocasta and her brooches. Certainly the messenger's version of Oedipus' reaction invites us to see a spontaneous reaction of horror.

The messenger presumably guesses what Oedipus intends, but since giving a sword to a crazy person is almost proverbial for a stupid action, the servants do not need to consider Oedipus' intentions in refusing to help him. I think we can fairly call this a paralipsis, since the narrator's explanation of what Oedipus is doing would be actually necessary for the audience (both the chorus as internal audience and for us) to make sense of the actions of both Oedipus and the narrator. And it is an interesting one, as if the potential matricide is the point at which we reach the genuinely unspeakable.

If the messenger had told us what Oedipus intended, the tendency to treat messengers as authoritative would doubtless have meant that we would assume that we knew. Because he does not say, although we know more than the messenger tells us—we know, for example, what god is likely to be involved – we do not know what Oedipus is thinking. And because the action he seems likely to be considering is counterfactual – it is not what happens in this play, and it is not what happens in any other version – both we and Oedipus forget about it. This is eas-

---

16 Dawe 1982, 225 on *OT* 1255.

ier because the messenger describes him as out of his mind. Yet once I focused for a moment on the implications of this scene, I found myself rethinking the character of Oedipus. It is not that his tendencies to violence and to reckless action are not clear enough elsewhere in the play, but this moment makes them more salient. And if we take seriously the messenger's description of Jocasta as angry, we have a peculiarly horrible symmetry: she is angry at him, whether for refusing to stop his search or for killing Laius or for both reasons, and probably intends to kill herself while cursing him; he is seeking to murder her. In this scene, these two people who combine the closest of all relationships want to destroy each other. Oedipus' intention is not fulfilled, and since nothing points to a further curse on Oedipus, Jocasta's presumably is not fulfilled either.

Once we consider these changes of mind, the contrast between the actual improvisation of the self-blinding and Oedipus' extended defense of it later becomes more striking. In an earlier discussion of 1369–90, I treated it as a bravura piece of clever argument (Scodel 1999, 106–7). I am now inclined to psychologize it more, to see it as Sophocles' intuitive recognition of the procedures people use to explain their own actions. Nowhere in this speech does Oedipus actually claim that the considerations he catalogues motivated the self-blinding, only that they prove that it was the best choice available; yet it seems to imply that he chose rationally (and he uses imperfects when he sings about the logic of the self-blinding at 1334 and 1337). We may well imagine, if we choose to think this way, that if Jocasta had killed herself with a sword, Oedipus would have pulled it out and used it on himself, and that if he had a sword and entered the room in time, he would have killed her and himself. For Oedipus, however, it would apparently not be tolerable to acknowledge that he blinded himself because Jocasta's brooches were there in front of him at the moment his earlier intention had to be redirected and, because a sword was not available, that the outcome is utterly contingent. He displays an extraordinary choice-supportive bias, a form of attributional bias. That is, he exaggerates the rationality of his choice.[17] What is remarkable, though, is that because the messenger's narrative allows the spectator so easily to gloss over Oedipus' earlier intention, the spectator can easily be drawn into Oedipus' later version of the events, especially since his account coheres so well with Tiresias' prophecy.

---

17 For this bias, see Mather–Shafir–Johnson 2000.

The messenger, after his quick mention of the sword, insists on the divine intervention that was the entry-point for this paper:

λυσσῶντι δ' αὐτῷ δαιμόνων δείκνυσί τις·
οὐδεὶς γὰρ ἀνδρῶν, οἳ παρῆμεν ἐγγύθεν.
δεινὸν δ' ἀύσας ὡς ὑφ' ἡγητοῦ τινος
πύλαις διπλαῖς ἐνήλατ'...

As he raves, some one of the gods shows him. For none of the men who were there and present did. With a terrible cry, as if directed by some leader, he drove into the double doors...

(1258–161)

In general, narrators in tragedy miss divine involvement rather than overstating it. So an audience must be inclined to believe a messenger who sees divine involvement in an action. The narrator generates credibility by following Jörgenson's Rule and keeping his references to divine interference vague (Jörgenson 1904). Yet there is a real issue about the narrator here. The messenger says that Oedipus was obviously raving. Madness would perhaps explain why Oedipus could not draw the obvious inference that his wife was in the room whose door was locked from the inside, her bedroom. If Oedipus was so obviously out of his mind, however, why do the attendants not attempt to restrain him? There are several of them, apparently.

What about Jocasta? If Jocasta actually left with the firm intention of committing suicide immediately, she has had abundant time to carry out that intention. She has presumably locked the door because she has guessed that Oedipus will come looking for her, or because she wants to prevent the servants from interfering with her suicide. We do not know to what extent her suicide is a form of vengeance against Oedipus, as that of Epikaste in the *Odyssey* apparently is. The cries the servant reports do not constitute a curse, but also indicate no pity for Oedipus; she is concerned with Laius and with herself. And she does not mention her children by Oedipus either, except as their birth is a misfortune to her.

In any case, since she does not act immediately, there is a possibility that she will change her mind. There is also the possibility that the servants will realize the situation and will themselves break down the door. We can assume, however, that just as the slaves can hear Jocasta's laments through the closed doors, Jocasta hears the arrival of Oedipus and his pleas for a weapon. So she kills herself at this particular moment, between his arrival in the space in front of the bedroom and his breaking in the room, either in order not to see him again, or to avoid being murdered. We do not know which. We have no way of being absolutely certain that the obvious inference that he planned to kill her is correct, or what he would have done afterwards — probably killed himself, too, as Haemon kills himself after failing to murder his father.

So it is essential to the narrative logic that Jocasta hang herself. If Jocasta has used a sword, Oedipus will use it on himself. However, it is not possible to hang yourself in the presence of others without their being able to interfere. Hence Sophocles has Jocasta lock herself in from the start. So the messenger has to stress his lack of access to what Jocasta was doing. If he had been watching, he would be expected to try to stop her, and he would have been able to stop her. Here the narrator's various peculiarities all come together. He identifies her distress as anger. He must assume that she is angry at Oedipus for not yielding to her entreaties and for insisting on finding out what she thinks will be a base origin. I have argued that the messenger is not unreliable here, although he does not know what the real motives for her anger would be. The audience would not be surprised to find anger among her emotions. The messenger's version is self-serving, however, for there would be nothing wrong with allowing a woman who is angry with her husband to lock herself in her room. He does not say how he understood Jocasta's cries, since if he understood what had happened, he would surely have to worry about her intentions and with the other servants break down the door before Oedipus arrives.

There is another considerable peculiarity in the messenger's report. He enters with general comments about how terrible is the news he brings, how polluted the house. He adds that the evils that will soon be revealed are deliberate, and so sets them in contrast to the earlier troubles. The chorus asks for specifics:

Χο. λείπει μὲν οὐδ' ἃ πρόσθεν ᾔδεμεν τὸ μὴ οὐ
βαρύστον' εἶναι· πρὸς δ' ἐκείνοισιν τί φής;
Εξ. ὁ μὲν τάχιστος τῶν λόγων εἰπεῖν τε καὶ
μαθεῖν, τέθνηκε θεῖον Ἰοκάστης κάρα.

Ch. Even what we knew already is not inadequate for heavy lament—what do you say besides that?
Ex. The quickest of speech to say and understand: the godlike head of Jocasta is dead.

(1232–5)

The messenger does not refer to the self-blinding until he actually narrates it. There is a partial parallel for this in *Antigone*, where the messenger explicitly mentions only Haemon's death: Αἵμων ὄλωλεν· αὐτόχειρ δ' αἱμάσσεται ('Haemon has perished: he is drenched in blood by his own hand,' 1175), although he has used the plural just above, τεθνᾶσιν· οἱ δὲ ζῶντες αἴτιοι θανεῖν ('They are dead, and the living are to blame for the death,' 1173). In *Antigone*, though, the messenger begins by moralizing about Creon's fall, and Eurydice is the audience of the full narrative. The play treats her suicide primarily as a further source of grief for Creon. So there is a certain sense in the suppression of Antigone's death, which is in this context a subordinate event. In *OT*, however, Oedipus is the more important figure. This is a genuine misdirection, since the audience might take it to mean that whatever is going to happen to Oedipus has not yet happened. The audience may assume that the *exangelos* is a household slave whose primary loyalty is to the queen, and this loyalty would motivate the emphasis on her death.

So the messenger is not quite unreliable. At no point do we think his facts are wrong. If we want to describe his story generously, we would say that because he, unlike the external audience, has no idea where the play has been leading, he does not realize Jocasta's situation until too late, and Oedipus' actions overwhelm him. His account is thin because he is traumatized. If we are less generous, his account is self-interested. And this complicates his claim that a god must have been inspiring Oedipus' actions. Nothing Oedipus does really requires that we assume divine intervention. Simply the fact that several slaves seem to be standing in this spot is a strong clue that Jocasta is there. The messenger could have attributed the strength that enables Oedipus to break down the door unassisted to a god, but he does not; instead he sees the god as leading Oedipus to Jocasta. Yet precisely because he is a messenger, and messengers are normally reliable, most members of any audience will asssume that the god is, indeed, directing events to this particular outcome.

There is actually very little that the messenger does not know.[18] Although he must infer that Jocasta hanged herself, this is not a difficult inference. What he does not know is exactly how Jocasta performed the various preparations. Yet is this important? What is really striking is not his ignorance of these details, but his failure to infer anything about the intentions of either Jocasta or Oedipus, to report anything of what he and the other servants thought was happening. That is, he seems to exaggerate the messenger's usual reluctance to move too far

---

18 So Kamerbeek 1967 on *OT* 1257.

beyond what he could reasonably know or guess, because he does not want to make obvious inferences. The messenger is extraordinary because his limits, although he presents them as if they belonged on the axis of knowledge, operate on the ethical axis, and messengers are usually reliable on the ethical axis. Barrett interprets the messenger's ignorance thematically, and compares the gaps in his narrative to the absence of a messenger-speech about the killing of Laius (Barrett 2002, 204–21). Although I do not agree with every point in his discussion, he is surely right that in this play, it is thematically essential that all the accounts the audience hears are overtly biased, filtered, and limited. Oedipus is the very opposite of this messenger: he has an overactive Theory of Mind, and attributes motives to others with insufficient evidence.

So the differences among the kinds of ignorance matter. An ordinary *limited narrator* knows that the gods are active in events, and so can mark the limits of human knowledge without difficulty. *A desperate narrator* does not know that the gods are active, and so narrates in extreme perplexity. Tecmessa in *Ajax* and the messenger in *Rhesus* do their best to say exactly what they experienced, but their frame is so ill-fitted to the story that their narratives are deeply confused. However, the messenger in *Oedipus Tyrannus* and Io in *Prometheus* are *evasive narrators*. They restrict themselves. Io does not try to make sense of her narrative, and the messenger speaks of divine intervention not because only such intervention could clarify what happened, but because the inference allows him to avoid responsibility. Neither is quite unreliable. But they show the complexity of the tragedian's engagement with the problems of how people convert events into narratives.

V. Narratology and the Interpretation of Historiography

Names and Narrative Techniques in Xenophon's *Anabasis*

Christos C. Tsagalis

It is no novelty to argue that scrupulous etymologizing has been the interpretive lens through which Greek personal names were studied in the past. The seminal chapter by Simon Hornblower on 'Narratology and Thucydides' published in a volume on *Greek Historiography* thirteen years ago has broken new ground regarding the exploration of narrative techniques in the most dense and arcane Greek historian. A significant part of Hornblower's chapter was devoted to the study of names in Thucydides from a narratological point of view, i.e. as mechanisms that produce semantic nuances that go beyond the mere manifestation of identity. Such a methodological approach has never before, at least to my knowledge, been applied to Xenophon, whose narrative abilities have only to a small extent been studied, despite the fact that we now possess, thanks to V. Gray, a good, though brief, overview in the respective chapter of *Narrators, Narratees, and Narratives in Ancient Greek Literature*.[1] I have decided to map out the broad range of the use of names in the *Anabasis* and explore the multiple functions they have within the unfolding of Xenophon's narrative. Before setting out, I would like to draw attention to the following 'questions' related to authors and authorship in Xenophontean historiography: the first concerns the plot of the *Anabasis* and the second the famous and enigmatic reference in *Hellenica* 3.1.2, where Xenophon refers to the author of the *Anabasis* by the name Themistogenes of Syracuse.[2]

With respect to the plot of the *Anabasis*, it must be taken into account that Xenophon has reserved for himself a rather magisterial 'entrance' in the beginning of the third Book. It is no exaggeration to say that he has, in all probability, taken great pains at keeping himself in the background – if at all – during the first two Books where he

---

1 2004, 129–146.
2 *Hell.* 3.1.2; Plut. *Mor.* 345E. See MacLaren 1934. Krentz 1995, 157 argues that the name Themistogenes (born of Themis) implies a narrator who tells the truth. I owe this observation to Gray 2004, 130 n. 7.

creeps up in the plot just three times (1.8.15; 2.5.37, 2.5.40–41) and even then he is nothing more than a mere name. Viewed from the vantage point of the continuous upheavals and turmoils that the Greek mercenary army is going through in the first two Books as a result of both the conception and effective carrying out of a master-plan of deception by the treacherous Tissaphernes and the rivalry between various Greek generals (Clearchus and Menon being the most outcrying example), it is plausible to argue that Xenophon has deliberately erased his presence during this tormented first phase of the plot. It is, for example, quite surprising that he does not report any of the conversations he no doubt had with his close friend Proxenos from Boeotia, the man who lured him to the expedition and one of the five Greek generals who feature as key figures in the first two Books.

As far as the attribution of the *Anabasis* to this – otherwise unknown – Themistogenes of Syracuse (*Hell.* 3.1.2) is concerned, what is of particular interest to my investigation is Xenophon's preoccupation with authorship and names. First, a closer look at this passage is needed:

ὡς μὲν οὖν Κῦρος στράτευμά τε συνέλεξε καὶ τοῦτ' ἔχων ἀνέβη ἐπὶ τὸν ἀδελφόν, καὶ ὡς ἡ μάχη ἐγένετο, καὶ ὡς ἀπέθανε, καὶ ὡς ἐκ τούτου ἀπεσώθησαν οἱ Ἕλληνες ἐπὶ θάλατταν, Θεμιστογένει τῷ Συρακοσίῳ γέγραπται.

As to how then Cyrus collected an army and with it went up against his brother, and how the battle was fought and how he died, and how in the sequel the Hellenes escaped to the sea (all this), is written by Themistogenes the Syracusan.[3]

This summary of *Anabasis* Books 1–4 is replete with diction that is typical of interpolations and may well have been the work of a later copyist[4] if it was not for the mention of Themistogenes; for it is plausible that an interpolator would have been interested in adding an exegetical comment, not in inventing a fictional author.[5] That this passage is not the work of a copyist but of Xenophon himself gains considerable support by Plutarch's following observation (*Mor.* 345E):

---

3 Translation by Dakyns 1890–1897.
4 Prentice 1947, 73–77.
5 Cf. the interpolated summaries in the beginning of Books 2–5 and 7 of the *Anabasis*, e.g. 2.1: ὡς μὲν οὖν ἠθροίσθη Κύρῳ τὸ Ἑλληνικὸν ὅτε ἐπὶ τὸν ἀδελφὸν Ἀρταξέρξην ἐστρατεύετο, καὶ ὅσα ἐν τῇ ἀνόδῳ ἐπράχθη καὶ ὡς ἡ μάχη ἐγένετο καὶ ὡς ὁ Κῦρος ἐτελεύτησε καὶ ὡς ἐπὶ τὸ στρατόπεδον ἐλθόντες οἱ Ἕλληνες ἐκοιμήθησαν οἰόμενοι τὰ πάντα νικᾶν καὶ Κῦρον ζῆν, ἐν τῷ πρόσθεν λόγῳ δεδήλωται.

As for Xenophon, he was his own historian, relating the exploits of the army under his command, but saying that Themistogenes the Syracusan had written the history of them; dedicating the honor of his writing to another, that writing of himself as of another, he might gain the more credit.

Lucian made a comment along the same lines, when he called Xenophon 'a stranger in his text, a man without a city'.[6] Although Xenophon's self-distancing from his text bestows reliability and objectivity on his narrative, the reference to Themistogenes is still very puzzling. The case of Isocrates who 'addressed one work to Nicocles of Cyprus [*ad Nicoclem*] in his own voice [and] another to the subjects of Nicocles, calling this work *Nicocles* ... [and introducing] Nicocles as narrator [who says] that the king will instruct his own subjects more persuasively than the author could' is indeed instructive, but it fails to explain why Xenophon referred to Themistogenes as the author of *only* the first four Books of the *Anabasis*.

This is hardly the place to deal with such a thorny issue but one further point may be useful with respect to the topic of this paper, i.e. Xenophon's fascination with and narrative exploitation of names. Themistogenes is not the only person who has been ascribed an *Anabasis*. There is also a certain Sophaenetus who has been identified by some scholars[7] with his namesake from Stymphalos in Arcadia, a minor character with a trivial role in Xenophon's *Anabasis*. So, three different pictures concerning a work or works entitled *Anabasis* have been painted: (a) there existed at least 3 *Anabaseis*, one by Themistogenes containing only a portion of the adventures of the Ten Thousand, one by Sophaenetus, and one by Xenophon; (b) there existed two *Anabaseis*, one by Sophaenetus and one by Xenophon who used the *alias* Themistogenes in *Hell.* 3.1.2;[8] (c) there was only one *Anabasis* by Xenophon who used the *alias* Themistogenes in *Hell.* 3.1.2.[9]

The first scenario seems to me implausible, since it is unlikely that Xenophon would have referred *en passant* to an *Anabasis* by Themisto-

---

6   *Hist. Conscr.* 38–41.
7   See e.g. Cawkwell 2004, 61.
8   See Gwynn 1929, 38–39.
9   The situation is complicated even more by the fact that there is no general consensus concerning the sources of Ephorus on whom the account of Diodorus Siculus (14.19–31 and 37) on the expedition of Cyrus is based. Both Sophaenetus and Xenophon have been suggested as the possible sources of the Ephoran narrative; on the former, cf. Cawkwell 2004, 50–55, 61; on the latter, cf. Stylianou 2004, 68–69.

genes in the *Hellenica* but never in his own *Anabasis*. The other two scenaria are equally plausible and arguments can be adduced in favor either of the one or the other: Xenophontean secrecy, highlighted by Cawkwell, may explain the absence of any reference in Xenophon's *Anabasis* to an *Anabasis* by Sophaenetus but fails to catter for the mention of other sources Xenophon used, like the *Persica* by Ctesias (1.8.26–28); on the other hand, the existence of an *Anabasis* by Sophaenetus, which rests on the four entries offered by Stephanus of Byzantium,[10] would offer the most plausible scenario, at least in my view: Xenophon started writing a work on the expedition of Cyrus after this great adventure was over; at this stage he covered only the events down to the arrival of the Ten Thousand at the Black Sea, i.e. the end of Book 4; in the *Hellenica* he wanted to 'hide' behind a false name, for the reasons Plutarch successfully explained. But then another event, the publication of a rival *Anabasis* by one of his comrades-in-arms, Sophaenetus the Stymphalian,[11] was completed and Xenophon felt the need to rival him. Sophaenetus was much older than Xenophon, so the latter knew well that time was on his side and that if he waited his competitor would have no chance of replying. When in Scyllus, the time was ripe for Xenophon to expand and improve his older work; if this was indeed his plan, then he must be applauded, for history has clearly proved him more than right.

This digression shows that given Xenophon's special attention on names with respect to both narrative and authorship, it is only too natural to investigate their function in a work like the *Anabasis* where names of persons and places are abundantly attested.

1. Proper Names and Toponymics

In this section, I will attempt to survey various uses of personal names and toponymics and investigate their role as narrative mechanisms which allow the historian to shed light on a specific person or topic, make an evaluative comment, dislocate a character, produce dramatic effect, bridge scattered passages, and (re)direct the readers' attention.

---

10 On the fragments of Sophaenetus, see *FGrHist* 109; see also Bux, *RE* s.v.
11 See Westlake 1989, 267–270.

1.1 Narrative Emphasis

What Hornblower has rightly observed regarding the use of patronymics in Thucydides, i. e. that some characters like Pericles and Melesippus 'are given full patronymics not on the occasions of their first appearance but on their most *solemn* first appearance'[12] is applicable to Xenophon's use of a person's special toponymic right after his name.

Xenias is the first Greek introduced in the *Anabasis* as the leader of 300 hoplites who accompanied Cyrus together with Tissaphernes to the palace of his mother Parysatis at the event of Darius' death. This is the only case in the entire work where Xenias is not designated as an Arcadian but as a Parrasian, i. e. by means not of his area of origin but of the specific city of Arcadia he came from, named after the mountain Parrasion. This is an *implicit* indication that Xenias was a close friend of Cyrus, a person of great loyalty and trust, the only Greek leader whom Cyrus deemed worthy to accompany him at one of the most critical moments of his life.

In *Anabasis* 1.4.7 two of the Greek leaders, Xenias the Arcadian and Pasion the Megarian, mount a ship and after taking with them their most valuable belongings sail out, since they were insulted by Cyrus' decision to put under the command of Clearchus almost half of their men (1.3.7: παρὰ δὲ Ξενίου καὶ Πασίωνος πλείους ἢ δισχίλιοι λαβόντες τὰ ὅπλα καὶ τὰ σκευοφόρα ἐστρατοπεδεύσαντο παρὰ Κλεάρχῳ), who had gone to Clearchus in hope of returning to Greece instead of continuing their march against Artaxerxes. The Greek text reads as follows:

> καὶ Ξενίας ὁ Ἀρκὰς [στρατηγὸς] καὶ Πασίων ὁ Μεγαρεὺς ἐμβάντες εἰς πλοῖον καὶ τὰ πλείστου ἄξια ἐνθέμενοι ἀπέπλευσαν, ὡς μὲν τοῖς πλείστοις ἐδόκουν φιλοτιμηθέντες ὅτι τοὺς στρατιώτας αὐτῶν τοὺς παρὰ Κλέαρχον ἀπελθόντας ὡς ἀπιόντας εἰς τὴν Ἑλλάδα πάλιν καὶ οὐ πρὸς βασιλέα εἴα Κῦρος τὸν Κλέαρχον ἔχειν.

> Xenias the Arcadian general, and Pasion the Megarian got on board a trader, and having stowed away their most valuable effects, set sail for home; most people explained the act as the outcome of a fit of jealousy, because Cyrus had allowed Clearchus to retain their men, who had deserted to him, in hopes of returning to Hellas instead of marching against the king.

Although manuscript tradition unanimously offers the reading στρατηγός with respect to Xenias the Arcadian, E. C. Marchant, the editor of volume III of Xenophon's OCT, following the suggestion of Cobet,

---

12 Hornblower 1994, 161.

has put it into square brackets. Conversely, the reading στρατηγός, when viewed from the vantage point of narratology, may have indeed been the original reading. This may well be a case where the external narrator makes a covert statement concerning the decision of Xenias to withdraw from the expedition. Let us recall that Xenias was a key-figure among the Greeks who supported Cyrus. He had gathered no less than 4000 hoplites (1.2.3), almost 1/3 of the total number of Greek mercenaries who fought at Cunaxa in 401 BCE. Given that assembling such a significant amount of heavily armed soldiers was not an easy task, Xenophon makes sure to highlight the fact that these hoplites – and most notably Xenias himself – trusted Cyrus, who had promised to help them return home, once they accomplished the goal of the expedition (1.2.2):

> ... ὑποσχόμενος αὐτοῖς, εἰ καλῶς καταπράξειεν ἐφ' ἃ ἐστρατεύετο, μὴ πρόσθεν παύσεσθαι πρὶν αὐτοὺς καταγάγοι οἴκαδε.
>
> promising them that if he were successful in his object, he would not pause until he had reinstated them in their native city.

In the light of this initial underscoring of the role of Xenias in the preparation of the expedition, I would like to argue that the term στρατηγός juxtaposed to his name + toponymic is not an interpolation but a sophisticated method of implicitly pointing at the importance of Xenias' withdrawal. Being Cyrus' right hand in gathering a large hoplite army, which he had brought to Sardis (1.2.3), Xenias appears on the top of the *second catalogue* of the Greek forces (1.2.3–5), with Proxenus the Boeotian, one of Cyrus' best friends occupying only the second rank. To make a long story short, the term στρατηγός may be a means of emphasizing the discrepancy between the close link between Xenias and Cyrus and the former's withdrawal from the expedition, since – of all people – Xenias was the least expected to abandon his friend Cyrus. Taking into account the fact that the theme of πίστις (trust) and its continuous and consistent violations by both Greeks and Persians permeates the entire *Anabasis*, the dry reference to Xenias acquires a deeper significance.

This line of argumentation is further supported by the fact that Pasion the Megarian is deprived of any reference to his rank in the army. Of course, Pasion is not a general, since he had arrived in Sardis being in charge of only 300 hoplites and 300 light-shielded soldiers (1.2.3). Conversely, if some copyist had felt the need to insert the word στρατηγός after Xenias' name he could have very well have added something like λοχαγός after Pasion's name. The lack of any reference to Pasion's military status is, I maintain, due to Xenophon's narrative technique of downplaying his role. It is as if the historian aimed at indicating the different status of the two Greek leaders who had withdrawn in secret from Cyrus' army, Xenias the Arcadian, a general and close friend of Cyrus, and Pasion the Megarian, a third-rate figure in the *Anabasis*.

1.2 Absence of Toponymics

Aberration from common practice, which is to mention one's toponymic the first time he is introduced in the *diegesis*, may also be narratively significant. A characteristic example is offered in 3.1.26, when some Apollonides who speaks in the Boeotian dialect (Ἀπολλωνίδης τις ἦν βοιωτιάζων τῇ φωνῇ) and is deprived of a toponymic suggests that the only way to salvation in view of all the troubles the Greeks have to deal with is to convince the Persian king to let them return home. The way this Apollonides is introduced markedly diverges from Xenophontean name-typology in the *Anabasis*, as it can be easily seen from numerous other cases but most importantly from the narrator's first reference to Proxenus the Boeotian, a friend (ξένος) of Cyrus (1.1.11) and a positively portrayed character. Contrary to Proxenus, Apollonides will be negatively described not only with respect to his proposal but also, and most importantly, on the basis of *his falsifying his origin* (3.1.30–31).[13]

> '... οὗτος γὰρ καὶ τὴν πατρίδα καταισχύνει καὶ πᾶσαν τὴν Ἑλλάδα, ὅτι Ἕλλην ὢν τοιοῦτός ἐστιν.' (end of Xenophon's speech) ἐντεῦθεν ὑπολαβὼν Ἀγασίας ὁ Στυμφάλιος εἶπεν· 'ἀλλὰ τούτῳ γε οὔτε τῆς Βοιωτίας προσήκει οὐδὲν οὔτε τῆς Ἑλλάδος παντάπασιν, ἐπεὶ ἐγὼ αὐτὸν εἶδον ὥσπερ Λυδὸν ἀμφότερα τὰ ὦτα τετρυπημένον.'

> 'The man is a disgrace to his own fatherland and the whole of Hellas, that, being a Hellene, he is what he is.' Here Agasias the Stymphalian broke in, exclaiming: 'Nay, this fellow has no connection either with Boeotia or with Hellas, none whatever. I have noted both his ears bored like a Lydian's.'

The fact that the narrator introduces Apollonides *by emphasizing his use of the Boeotian dialect although nobody knows where he comes from* (hence his lack of a toponymic) 'foreshadows' his role in the plot, namely his at-

---

13 See Rinner 1978, 146 who suggests that Apollonides functions as an anti-hero ('Anti-Held').

tempt to fake his origin. Xenophon is coy about giving more information regarding this incident but in light of the abovementioned observations, I would like to suggest that the τις following Apollonides in the text may be *disparaging*, contrary to other passages in the *Anabasis* where it is not (3.1.4).

1.3 Dramatic Effect

Instead of the Thucydidean practice of giving patronymics on the occasion of one's first appearance, Xenophon employs toponymics in the same way. Having done this systematically from the very beginning of the *Anabasis*, Xenophon can assume the readers' familiarity with this technique in order to make other, more revealing from a narrative point of view, statements. A noteworthy example creeps up in 3.1.46–47, when the new Greek leaders are introduced:

> '... παρέστω δ' ἡμῖν, ἔφη, καὶ Τολμίδης ὁ κῆρυξ. καὶ ἅμα ταῦτ' εἰπὼν ἀνέστη, ὡς μὴ μέλλοιτο ἀλλὰ περαίνοιτο τὰ δέοντα. ἐκ τούτου ἡρέθησαν ἄρχοντες ἀντὶ μὲν Κλεάρχου Τιμασίων Δαρδανεύς, ἀντὶ δὲ Σωκράτους Ξανθικλῆς Ἀχαιός, ἀντὶ δὲ Ἀγίου Κλεάνωρ Ἀρκάς, ἀντὶ δὲ Μένωνος Φιλήσιος Ἀχαιός, ἀντὶ δὲ Προξένου Ξενοφῶν Ἀθηναῖος.'

> 'Let Tolmides, the herald,' he added, 'be in attendance.' With these words on his lips he got up, in order that what was needful might be done at once without delay. After this the generals were chosen. These were Timasion the Dardanian, in place of Clearchus; Xanthicles, an Achaean, in place of Socrates; Cleanor, an Arcadian, in place of Agias; Philesius, an Achaean, in place of Menon; and in place of Proxenus, Xenophon the Athenian.

This small *third catalogue* acquires its full semantic potential only when knowledge of the previous two, longer catalogues in Book 1 is taken for granted. By assuming that his readers would bring to mind the extended catalogues placed in the beginning of the *Anabasis*, Xenophon aims at creating a dramatic effect. Both the brevity of the catalogue and the use of the ἀντί-formula allude to the tragic events that have taken place in the recent past and the perils that will follow in the future. In particular, the terse meaning of the ἀντί-formula ('instead of')[14] func-

---

14 The use of the ἀντί-formula consitutes a covert reminiscence of the 'funerary' list in 2.5.31. See Hornblower 1994, 157–158, who argues that the ἀντί-formula is a form of implied negation and refers to its early use in *Od.* 20.307. This same formula with its funerary overtones is abundantly attested in fourth-century Attic inscribed epitaphs, see Tsagalis 2008, 201–204, 278–280.

tions as a covert cross-reference and creates a pathetic effect, since the absence of a toponymic points back to their commemorative, almost 'funerary', list in 2.5.31 and stands for a bitter reminder of the fact that the five Greek leaders (Clearchus, Socrates, Agias, Menon, Proxenus) have been killed by Tissaphernes and that their replacements are taking the lead *under extremely difficult circumstances*. The juxtaposition of the personal names of the five dead Greek leaders and the personal names + toponymics of the five new leaders epitomizes in a *solemn* way the gravity of the present situation. As an aside, I would also like to draw attention to five more features of this *third catalogue:* (a) Cheirisophus is clearly singled out by not being included in this catalogue. Interestingly enough, he will be the only of these new leaders who will die in the *Anabasis* (6.4.11); (b) Xenophon leaves his readers to understand that one of the main aims of the Greek army was to keep its cohesion, and so it would have been better if each dead leader was replaced by one of his countrymen. This was not an absolute rule but seems to have been followed to a certain extent (Socrates is replaced by Xanthicles, both Achaeans – Agias by Cleanor, both Arcadians, but Clearchus the Lacedaemonian by Timasion the Dardanian, Menon the Thessalian by Philesios the Achaean, Proxenus the Boeotian by Xenophon the Athenian); (c) by occupying the last place, Xenophon aims at highlighting his personal contribution and role to the salvation of the Greek army, and so his placement at the end of the list may not be accidental; (d) in both catalogues toponymics are not preceded by the article ὁ, as it is common practice;[15] (e) the almost complete reversal in the order of names in comparison to the scene before their death in Book 2 is dramatically effective (see 2.5.31):

> Ἐπεὶ δὲ ἦσαν ἐπὶ θύραις ταῖς Τισσαφέρνους, οἱ μὲν στρατηγοὶ παρεκλήθησαν εἴσω, Πρόξενος Βοιώτιος, Μένων Θετταλός, Ἀγίας Ἀρκάς, Κλέαρχος Λάκων, Σωκράτης Ἀχαιός.
>
> On arrival at the doors of Tissaphernes's quarters the generals were summoned inside. They were Proxenus the Boeotian, Menon the Thessalian, Agias the Arcadian, Clearchus the Laconian, and Socrates the Achaean.

Xenophon aims at dropping a hint for his audience that what happened to the first Greek leaders *will not happen* to those who replaced them. In this respect it is implied that, despite the grimness of the present situation for the Greeks, things will finally turn out well. Viewed from this

---

15 On this topic, see section 2.

vantage point, this catalogue stands in stark contrast to the first two catalogues in Book 1, which had been narrated within the framework of a rather positive and ambitious undertaking but were followed by deceit and death at the hands of Tissaphernes.

1.4 Narrative Dislocation

Sometimes new characters are narratively dislocated by being *properly* introduced not at the point of their entrance in the plot but later on. The most prominent example of this technique is the pronounced introduction of Xenophon in the plot at the beginning of Book 3 (3.1.4: ἦν δέ τις ἐν τῇ στρατιᾷ Ξενοφῶν Ἀθηναῖος, ὅς…), despite the fact that he had been incidentally mentioned in 1.8.15, 2.5.37 and 2.5.41. In cases like this, Xenophon feels the need to offer a kind of explanation for this late entrance.[16] The following example belongs to what I would call the 'default mode' or 'innocuous'[17] (as opposed to profound) dislocation, where a detail is not given in its proper place but later on with no apparent other reason for suppressing its previous presentation.

A typical example is offered by the *second catalogue* of Greek forces gathered at Sardis (*Anabasis* 1.2.3):

> Ξενίας μὲν δὴ τοὺς ἐκ τῶν πόλεων λαβὼν παρεγένετο εἰς Σάρδεις ὁπλίτας εἰς τετρακισχιλίους, Πρόξενος δὲ παρῆν ἔχων ὁπλίτας μὲν εἰς πεντακοσίους καὶ χιλίους, γυμνῆτας δὲ πεντακοσίους, Σοφαίνετος δὲ ὁ Στυμφάλιος ὁπλίτας ἔχων χιλίους, Σωκράτης δὲ ὁ Ἀχαιὸς ὁπλίτας ἔχων ὡς πεντακοσίους, Πασίων δὲ ὁ Μεγαρεὺς τριακοσίους μὲν ὁπλίτας, τριακοσίους δὲ πελταστὰς ἔχων παρεγένετο· ἦν δὲ καὶ οὗτος καὶ ὁ Σωκράτης τῶν ἀμφὶ Μίλητον στρατευομένων. οὗτοι μὲν εἰς Σάρδεις αὐτῷ ἀφίκοντο.

> So, too, Xenias arrived at Sardis with the contingent from the cities, four thousand hoplites; Proxenus, also, with fifteen hundred hoplites and five hundred light-armed troops; Sophaenetus the Stymphalian, with one thousand hoplites; Socrates the Achaean, with five hundred hoplites; while the Megarian Pasion came with three hundred hoplites and three hundred peltasts. This latter officer, as well as Socrates, belonged to the force engaged against Miletus. These all joined him at Sardis.

Since the very last entry (Pasion the Megarian) in the catalogue of Greek troops summoned at Sardis has not been mentioned before (all the other leaders appear in the *first catalogue* or, in the case of Xenias, immediately

---

16 On narrative dislocation in Thucydides, see Hornblower 1994, 141–143.
17 See Hornblower 1994, 143 n. 35.

after it), Xenophon feels the need to add a piece of *explanatory* information that allows him to 'anticipate' potential complaints by his readers who unexpectedly come across a new name in this list. By disrupting the formal order of the list at its very end, Xenophon flags for his readers the *prima facie* casual observation ἦν δὲ καὶ οὗτος καὶ ὁ Σωκράτης τῶν ἀμφὶ Μίλητον στρατευομένων. This is not, I hope, philological trivia, the more so since Xenophon had systematically explained in the first catalogue the reason that made each leader join the expedition on Cyrus' side. Under this scope, Xenophon informs his audience *who* Pasion was *in terms of* his involvement in the siege of Miletus, even at the expense of reiterating the same piece of information about Socrates the Achaean, who had been already introduced – partly within the same framework – in the *first catalogue* (1.1.11).

1.5 Names as Cross-References

Personal names can be also used as cross-references that allow the narrator to create internal links between close or distant parts of his work. By facilitating the making of these links, the narrator is then able to produce stronger effects and comment on the development of the plot. In 3.3.5, we suddenly hear the name of Nicarchus the Arcadian, who was deceived by Mithradates' words and followed him together with twenty more soldiers:

> διέφθειρον γὰρ προσιόντες τοὺς στρατιώτας, καὶ ἕνα γε λοχαγὸν διέφθειραν Νίκαρχον Ἀρκάδα, καὶ ᾤχετο ἀπιὼν νυκτὸς σὺν ἀνθρώποις ὡς εἴκοσι.
>
> For they used to come and corrupt the soldiers, and they were even successful with one officer, Nicarchus, an Arcadian, who went off in the night with about twenty men.

Is this just an isolated piece of information or is Xenophon aiming deeper? Who is this Nicarchus the Arcadian, who is here designated as a captain (λοχαγός)? Before we discuss this question and focus our attention on the specific verbalization of the abovementioned passage, let us recall that in his thorough description of Herodotus' oral strategies, Slings[18] refers to the technique of *chunking* and *addition of information units*. One subcategory of this technique concerns the introduction of a new element, which conjures up the technique of *chunking*. The new

---

18 Slings 2002, 64–71.

element is of course the captain but this does not necessarily entail the repetition of the verb, the more so since we are not dealing, as Slings has rightly observed, with dense information that results in the reiteration of the verbal form as a recapitulation device. In fact, the repetition of the verb is accompanied by the particle γε and a change of tense, the aorist taking the place of the imperfect.

Given that the aorist often expresses a present-oriented point of view within a narrative describing a past event and that the sequence καί ... γε 'serves to focus the attention upon a single idea, and place it, as it were, in the limelight',[19] it may be plausibly argued that Xenophon aims at zooming his narrative lens on the fact that *even* a captain was seduced by Mithradates' offer. *Chunking* mechanisms are not independent from narrative strategies; on the contrary they occasionally stand for sophisticated techniques of producing literary effects. In the words of Slings:[20]

> There is an important lesson to be drawn from this instance: chunking devices may be used as literary devices. In Slings (1997) 175 I formulated the general rule for detecting such phenomena, and formulated it within the framework of reader-response stylistics: 'As a general rule it may be stated that the more complex the information supplied in a clause or sentence is, the higher the chances are for one of these distribution phenomena (i.e., chunking) to occur. In reader-response stylistics it follows automatically that the simpler the information supplied in a clause or sentence is, the higher the chances are that the distribution phenomena were experienced as being "literary". Put differently: A figure of speech is a fixed strategy used for arranging information, borrowed from everyday language but employed in such a way that the competent native reader/listener will recognize it as untypical of everyday language and interpret it as literary.'

The purpose of this digression was to indicate how the technique of *chunking* is used as a literary device in order to emphasize the awkwardness of the situation described in 3.3.5, where Nicarchus is singled out and flagged for the readers.

In this conception, I would like to suggest that by giving the captain's name, Xenophon aims at creating an implicit cross-reference bridging this passage with the famous 2.5.33, where an otherwise unknown Nicarchus the Arcadian escaped from the camp of Tissaphernes wounded in his belly and holding his entrails in his hands and informed the stunned Greeks about the treachery of the Persian satrap.

---

19 Denniston ²1950, 114.
20 Slings 2002, 62–63 quoting Slings 1997, 175.

... πρὶν Νίκαρχος Ἀρκὰς ἧκε φεύγων τετρωμένος εἰς τὴν γαστέρα καὶ τὰ ἔντερα ἐν ταῖς χερσὶν ἔχων, καὶ εἶπε πάντα τὰ γεγενημένα.

Until Nicarchus the Arcadian came tearing along for bare life with a wound in the belly, and clutching his protruding entrails in his hands. He told them all that had happened.

By using the name of Nicarchus as a link between the two passages, Xenophon aims at making a comment concerning human nature: the very person who had witnessed with his own eyes the slaughter of the Greeks at the hands of Tissaphernes and had escaped death at the last moment was now seduced by Mithradates. Contrary to E. C. Marchant, the editor of the *Anabasis* for OCT who in the index nominum designates the Nicarchus of 2.5.33 as a different person from Nicarchus in 3.3.5, I would like to suggest that Nicarchus may be one and the same person, since Xenophon has used other personal names as a mechanism that would link the two passages together. Interestingly enough, in 2.5.35, i.e. right after the wounded Nicarchus tells the Greeks about the slaughter in the camp of Tissaphernes and while the Greeks are expecting a large-scale attack by the Persians, it is only Ariaios, Artaozos and Mithradates, the three Persian leaders who were most loyal to Cyrus and had now joined forces with Artaxerxes, that approached (accompanied by 300 soldiers) the Greek army and asked them to lay down their weapons. These three names comprise the full list of Persian leaders, who narratively bridge the first false offer by the Persians to the Greeks in 2.4.16 (where the anonymous messenger said that he was sent by Ariaios and Artaozos, who were loyal to Cyrus) with the second in 3.3.2 (where Mithradates without success attempted to deceive the Ten Thousand).

In this light, I would like to argue that the names of the three Persian leaders (Ariaios, Artaozos, Mithradates) allow the narrator to present continuous false offers by the Persians to the Greeks as parts of an extended narrative chain. Nicarchus the Arcadian is, I suggest, intrinsically linked to this narrative sequence, thus connecting widely dispersed passages and also engaging readers in the process of *evaluating* the ways of human nature.

2. Article and Proper Name

The standard view concerning the use of the article in Ancient Greek was, according to authoritative grammarians like Gildersleeve[21] and Humbert,[22] that there are only general tendencies (lack of the article before a proper name in epic and lyric, rare use in drama etc.) and that more precise rules and, by extension, interpretive trends cannot be established, the more so in prose authors like Plato and Xenophon.[23] In a recent study, Rijksbaron[24] after 'resurrecting' the pathbreaking but virtually inaccessible work of Zucker,[25] made the following suggestions concerning the use of the article before a proper name with respect to Xenophon's *Anabasis*: (a) the majority of the cases where the article is used before a proper name belong to 'turn-takings' (alternance des prises de parole, Wechselgespräch);[26] (b) in the rest, the occurence of the article before a proper name aims at *highlighting* the role of a given figure in a specific episode; (c) the use of the article before a proper name is restricted to the narrative of the *Anabasis* and never features in the speeches; (d) Xenophon's role as a main figure of the plot can be amply seen by investigating the frequent use of the article before his name in the narrative parts of the work: in 154 attestations of his name (Ξενοφῶν) in the nominative, 73 (47.4%) are preceded by the article, whereas the relevant numbers for Cyrus, who is also a key figure in Books 1–2, are 21 with the article (30.88%) out of a total of 68 in the nominative.

In this light, it becomes clear that Xenophon adopted a sophisticated use of the article that allowed him to shed light on characters according to their importance for the plot and also to create a system of differentiation between the narrative and the speeches. In the former the article before a proper name points to identity and is therefore *une anaphore forte*,[27] while in the latter its use would have been redundant, since the presence of any speaker in a speech is guaranteed by the communicative situation itself.[28]

---

21 1900–1911, 215.
22 1960, 46–47.
23 Rijksbaron 2006, 245.
24 Rijksbaron 2006, 243–257.
25 1899. See also the even earlier study of Schmidt 1890.
26 Cf. e.g. the interrogation of Orontas by Cyrus in 1.6.7–8.
27 Grimes 1975, 92; Rijksbaron 2006, 248.
28 Rijksbaron 2006, 247.

3. Anonymity vs Eponymity

Anonymity may sometimes reflect narrative intentions rather than lack of information, especially when similar situations are narrated. A case worth studying concerns 2.4.15–2.4.22 and 3.3.1–3.3.4:

μετὰ δὲ τὸ δεῖπνον ἔτυχον ἐν περιπάτῳ ὄντες πρὸ τῶν ὅπλων Πρόξενος καὶ Ξενοφῶν· καὶ προσελθὼν ἄνθρωπός τις ἠρώτησε τοὺς προφύλακας ποῦ ἂν ἴδοι Πρόξενον ἢ Κλέαρχον· Μένωνα δὲ οὐκ ἐζήτει, καὶ ταῦτα παρ' Ἀριαίου ὢν τοῦ Μένωνος ξένου. ἐπεὶ ὁ Πρόξενος εἶπεν ὅτι αὐτός εἰμι ὃν ζητεῖς, εἶπεν ὁ ἄνθρωπος τάδε. 'ἔπεμψέ με Ἀριαῖος καὶ Ἀρτάοζος, πιστοὶ ὄντες Κύρῳ καὶ ὑμῖν εὖνοι, καὶ κελεύουσι φυλάττεσθαι μὴ ὑμῖν ἐπιθῶνται τῆς νυκτὸς οἱ βάρβαροι· ἔστι δὲ στράτευμα πολὺ ἐν τῷ πλησίον παραδείσῳ. καὶ παρὰ τὴν γέφυραν τοῦ Τίγρητος ποταμοῦ πέμψαι κελεύουσι φυλακήν, ὡς διανοεῖται αὐτὴν λῦσαι Τισσαφέρνης τῆς νυκτός, ἐὰν δύνηται, ὡς μὴ διαβῆτε ἀλλ' ἐν μέσῳ ἀποληφθῆτε τοῦ ποταμοῦ καὶ τῆς διώρυχος.' ἀκούσαντες ταῦτα ἄγουσιν αὐτὸν παρὰ τὸν Κλέαρχον καὶ φράζουσιν ἃ λέγει. ὁ δὲ Κλέαρχος ἀκούσας ἐταράχθη σφόδρα καὶ ἐφοβεῖτο. νεανίσκος δέ τις τῶν παρόντων ἐννοήσας εἶπεν ὡς οὐκ ἀκόλουθα εἴη τό τε ἐπιθήσεσθαι καὶ λύσειν τὴν γέφυραν. δῆλον γὰρ ὅτι ἐπιτιθεμένους ἢ νικᾶν δεήσει ἢ ἡττᾶσθαι. ἐὰν μὲν οὖν νικῶσι, τί δεῖ λύειν αὐτοὺς τὴν γέφυραν; οὐδὲ γὰρ ἂν πολλαὶ γέφυραι ὦσιν ἔχοιμεν ἂν ὅποι φυγόντες ἡμεῖς σωθῶμεν. ἐὰν δὲ ἡμεῖς νικῶμεν, λελυμένης τῆς γέφυρας οὐχ ἕξουσιν ἐκεῖνοι ὅποι φύγωσιν· οὐδὲ μὴν βοηθῆσαι πολλῶν ὄντων πέραν οὐδεὶς αὐτοῖς δυνήσεται λελυμένης τῆς γεφύρας. ἀκούσας δὲ ὁ Κλέαρχος ταῦτα ἤρετο τὸν ἄγγελον πόση τις εἴη χώρα ἡ ἐν μέσῳ τοῦ Τίγρητος καὶ τῆς διώρυχος. ὁ δὲ εἶπεν ὅτι πολλὴ καὶ κῶμαι ἔνεισι καὶ πόλεις πολλαὶ καὶ μεγάλαι. τότε δὴ καὶ ἐγνώσθη ὅτι οἱ βάρβαροι τὸν ἄνθρωπον ὑπέπεμψαν, ὀκνοῦντες μὴ οἱ Ἕλληνες διελόντες τὴν γέφυραν μείναιεν ἐν τῇ νήσῳ ἐρύματα ἔχοντες ἔνθεν μὲν τὸν Τίγρητα, ἔνθεν δὲ τὴν διώρυχα.

After supper, Proxenus and Xenophon were walking in front of the place d'armes, when a man came up and demanded of the advanced guard where he could find Proxenus or Clearchus. He did not ask for Menon, and that too though he came from Ariaeus, who was Menon's friend. As soon as Proxenus had said: 'I am he, whom you seek,' the man replied: 'I have been sent by Ariaeus and Artaozus, who have been trusty friends to Cyrus in past days, and are your well-wishers. They warn you to be on your guard, in case the barbarians attack you in the night. There is a large body of troops in the neighbouring park. They also warn you to send and occupy the bridge over the Tigris, since Tissaphernes is minded to break it down in the night, if he can, so that you may not cross, but be caught between the river and the canal.' On hearing this they took the man to Clearchus and acquainted him with his statement. Clearchus, on his side, was much disturbed, and indeed alarmed at the news. But a young fellow who was present, struck with an idea, suggested that the two statements were inconsistent as to the contemplated attack and the proposed destruction of the bridge. Clearly, the attacking party must either conquer or be worsted: if they conquer, what need of their breaking down the bridge? 'Why! if there were half a dozen bridges,' said he, 'we should not be any the more able to save ourselves by flight – there would be no place to flee to; but, in the opposite case, suppose we win, with the bridge broken down, it is they who will not be able to save themselves by flight; and, what is worse for them, not a single soul will be able to bring them succour from the other side, for all their numbers, since the bridge will be broken down.' Clearchus listened to the reasoning, and then he asked the messenger, 'How large the country between the Tigris and the canal might be?' 'A large district,' he replied, 'and in it are villages and cities numerous and large.' Then it dawned upon them: the barbarians had sent the man with subtlety, in fear lest the Hellenes should cut the bridge and occupy the island territory, with the strong defences of the Tigris on the one side and of the canal on the other.

ἀριστοποιουμένων δὲ αὐτῶν ἔρχεται Μιθραδάτης σὺν ἱππεῦσιν ὡς τριάκοντα, καὶ καλεσάμενος τοὺς στρατηγοὺς εἰς ἐπήκοον λέγει ὧδε. 'ἐγώ, ὦ ἄνδρες Ἕλληνες, καὶ Κύρῳ πιστὸς ἦν, ὡς ὑμεῖς ἐπίστασθε, καὶ νῦν ὑμῖν εὔνους· καὶ ἐνθάδε δ' εἰμὶ σὺν πολλῷ φόβῳ διάγων. εἰ οὖν ὁρῴην ὑμᾶς σωτήριόν τι βουλευομένους, ἔλθοιμι ἂν πρὸς ὑμᾶς καὶ τοὺς θεράποντας πάντας ἔχων. λέξατε οὖν πρός με τί ἐν νῷ ἔχετε ὡς φίλον τε καὶ εὔνουν καὶ βουλόμενον κοινῇ σὺν ὑμῖν τὸν στόλον ποιεῖσθαι.' βουλευομένοις τοῖς στρατηγοῖς ἔδοξεν ἀποκρίνασθαι τάδε· καὶ ἔλεγε Χειρίσοφος· 'ἡμῖν δοκεῖ, εἰ μέν τις ἐᾷ ἡμᾶς ἀπιέναι οἴκαδε, διαπορεύεσθαι τὴν χώραν ὡς ἂν δυνώμεθα ἀσινέστατα· ἢν δέ τις ἡμᾶς τῆς ὁδοῦ ἀποκωλύῃ, διαπολεμεῖν τούτῳ ὡς ἂν δυνώμεθα κράτιστα.' ἐκ τούτου ἐπειρᾶτο Μιθραδάτης διδάσκειν ὡς ἄπορον εἴη βασιλέως ἄκοντος σωθῆναι. ἔνθα δὴ ἐγιγνώσκετο ὅτι ὑπόπεμπτος εἴη· καὶ γὰρ τῶν Τισσαφέρνους τις οἰκείων παρηκολουθήκει πίστεως ἕνεκα.

While they were breakfasting, Mithridates came with about thirty horsemen, and summoning the generals within earshot, he thus addressed them: 'Men of Hellas, I have been faithful to Cyrus, as you know well, and to-day I am your well-wisher; indeed, I am here spending my days in great fear: if then I could see any salutory course in prospect, I should be disposed to join you with all my retainers. Please inform me, then, as to what you propose, regarding me as your friend and well-wisher, anxious only to pursue his march in your company.' The generals held council, and resolved to give the following answer, Cheirisophus acting as spokesman: 'We have resolved to make our way through the country, inflicting the least possible damage, provided we are allowed a free passage homewards; but if any one tries to hinder us, he will have to fight it out with us, and we shall bring all the force in our power to bear.' Thereat Mithridates set himself to prove to them that their deliverance, except with the king's good pleasure, was hopeless. Then the meaning of his mission was plain. He was an agent in disguise; in fact, a relation of Tissaphernes was in attendance to keep a check on his loyalty.

Given that these two passages develop similar themes and share a number of common features, the difference between the anonymity of both the Persian messenger and the young Greek in the former, and Mithradates and Cheirisophus in the latter becomes all the more intriguing. I am not inclined to interpret the anonymous characters of the first incident as a by-product of a fictitious story, especially since Proxenus and Xenophon are directly involved in it. On the contrary, I think that by comparing the two stories we can better understand Xenophon's narrative exploitation of the use of personal names. In the first story, there is one internal feature that is not attested in the second one, namely the explanation of the way the Greeks suspected the Persian messenger. As soon as Xenophon the narrator informs us that some anonymous Persian messenger approached the Greek camp asking where he could find Proxenus or Clearchus, he inserts a negative clause ('He was not looking for Menon, although he was sent by Ariaios, who was a friend of Menon'). This insertion is an *authorial comment* made by Xenophon the historian that something is going wrong. But what exactly is going wrong? Is it simply that Proxenus and Xenophon who met with the Persian messenger in the first place suspected that this was a set up because the one person whom the messenger sent by Ariaios should be looking for would be his friend, Menon, or is this an *authorial hint* that they did not realize from the beginning what the Persians were planning to do and, even more, that Menon might have been collaborating in secret with the enemy? In fact, it would make perfect sense, if the messenger did not look for Menon because (a) Menon already knew the plan and (b) because Ariaios did not want to raise suspicions against him among the Greeks, since they knew that the Thessalian general was in close terms with him. Surprisingly enough, the jigsaw puzzle of the Persian suggestion is solved not by Clearchus, Proxenus or even Xenophon but by an anonymous young man (2.4.19: νεανίσκος τις) who explained the *non sequitur* of the Persian army launching an attack and destroying the bridge at the same time. The Greeks finally realize that this is a trap but it is clear that Clearchus is afraid of Tissaphernes and as soon as they arrive at Zapatas river (2.5.1) he tries to reach an agreement with the powerful and treacherous Persian satrap. Xenophon paves the way for the execution of Tissaphernes' master plan. The speeches of both Clearchus and Tissaphernes show that the Lacedaemonian will soon be snared, together with other Greek leaders, in the Persian camp.

In the incident with Mithradates in 3.3.1–5, the *authorial comment* concerning the revelation of the Persian plan comes only after the almost formulaic expression ἔνθα δὴ ἐγιγνώσκετο ὅτι ὑπόπεμπτος εἴη by means of an implicit embedded focalization introduced by γάρ: καὶ γὰρ τῶν Τισσαφέρνους τις οἰκείων παρηκολουθήκει πίστεως ἕνεκα (an alternative of which in the form of τότε δὴ καὶ ἐγνώσθη ὅτι οἱ βάρβαροι τὸν ἄνθρωπον ὑποπέμψειαν, ὀκνοῦντες μὴ οἱ Ἕλληνες διελόντες τὴν γέφυραν μείναιεν ἐν τῇ νήσῳ ἐρύματα ἔχοντες ἔνθεν μὲν τὸν Τίγρητα, ἔνθεν δὲ τὴν διώρυχα was also used in 2.4.22). Moreover, and in direct contrast to the aforementioned incident in Book 2 where Clearchus was terrified,[29] here it is Cheirisophus, the Lacedaemonian general who plainly declares his intentions to Mithradates. In a nutshell, whereas in the first case the core of the incident is based on the speeches of two anonymous speakers, in the second it is orchestrated by two eponymous, key-figures of the plot, Mithradates and Cheirisophus. The difference is more than clear. While in the first case the Greeks will be soon after deceived by Tissaphernes, in the second they will not be taken in by Persian deception.

In this light, the use of personal names draws a line between the two incidents. The external narrator aims at actively engaging his audience in the very process of *evaluating* the two incidents and realizing that the Greeks have learned their lesson after being deceived by Tissaphernes in the first case. Additionally, he lets his readers entertain the possibility that he too, like Clearchus, suspected Menon the Thessalian. To this end, he has gradually alluded to Menon's suspicious actions in the *Anabasis*. Menon's friendship to Ariaios has been already highlighted in *Anabasis* 2.1.6, when Clearchus sent Cheirisophus and Menon to Ariaios. The choice of Cheirisophus was in all probability done by Clearchus himself, who trusted his fellow citizen. Menon, on the other hand, insisted himself, for he was a friend of Ariaios:

> ταῦτα εἰπὼν ἀποστέλλει τοὺς ἀγγέλους καὶ σὺν αὐτοῖς Χειρίσοφον τὸν Λάκωνα καὶ Μένωνα τὸν Θετταλόν· καὶ γὰρ αὐτὸς Μένων ἐβούλετο· ἦν γὰρ φίλος καὶ ξένος Ἀριαίου.

> With these words he sent back the messengers and with them he sent Cheirisophus the Laconian, and Menon the Thessalian. That was what Menon himself wished, being, as he was, a friend and intimate of Ariaeus, and bound by mutual ties of hospitality.

Interestingly enough, in 2.2.1 Menon does not return together with Cheirisophus from Ariaios' camp:

---

29 See 2.4.18–19: ὁ δὲ Κλέαρχος ἀκούσας ἐταράχθη σφόδρα καὶ ἐφοβεῖτο.

οἱ δὲ παρὰ Ἀριαίου ἧκον Προκλῆς καὶ Χειρίσοφος· Μένων δὲ αὐτοῦ ἔμενε παρὰ Ἀριαίῳ.

But the messengers from Ariaeus, Procles and Cheirisophus came back. As to Menon, he stayed behind with Ariaeus.

This, like the previous, example seems to be another *authorial comment* pointing at Menon's dubious role. Finally, there is one more occasion (2.5.28) where a third *authorial comment* will bring this sequence of *authorial interventions* to an end,[30] a comment placed just before the climactic point of the arrival of the Greek generals and captains at Tissaphernes' camp where they will be killed:

ὑπώπτευε δὲ [sc. Κλέαρχος] εἶναι τὸν διαβάλλοντα Μένωνα, εἰδὼς αὐτὸν καὶ συγγεγενημένον Τισσαφέρνει μετ' Ἀριαίου καὶ στασιάζοντα αὐτῷ καὶ ἐπιβουλεύοντα, ὅπως τὸ στράτευμα ἅπαν πρὸς αὐτὸν λαβὼν φίλος ᾖ Τισσαφέρνει.

The slanderer and traducer was Menon; so, at any rate, he [sc. Clearchus] suspected, because he knew that he had had meetings with Tissaphernes whilst he was with Ariaeus, and was factiously opposed to himself, plotting how to win over the whole army to him, as a means of winning the good graces of Tissaphernes.

Menon's distrustful role has been also clear by the fact that he advised his men to cross the river Euphrates before all the other Greeks decide what they should do, so that Cyrus may reward them for being so eager to follow him (1.4.14–15). Personal gain had always been a high priority in Menon's agenda. His obituary (2.6.21–29), which testifies to that in the most emphatic manner, comes to a closure with a hint to his betrayal of the Greeks:

Μένων δὲ ὁ Θετταλὸς δῆλος ἦν ἐπιθυμῶν μὲν πλουτεῖν ἰσχυρῶς, ἐπιθυμῶν δὲ ἄρχειν, ὅπως πλείω λαμβάνειν, ἐπιθυμῶν δὲ τιμᾶσθαι, ἵνα πλείω κερδαίνοι· φίλος τε ἐβούλετο εἶναι τοῖς μέγιστα δυναμένοις, ἵνα ἀδικῶν μὴ διδοίη δίκην.

As to Menon the Thessalian, the mainspring of his action was obvious; what he sought after insatiably was wealth. Rule he sought after only as a stepping-stone to larger spoils. Honours and high estate he craved for simply that he might extend the area of his gains; and if he studied to be on friendly terms with the powerful, it was in order that he might commit wrong with impunity.

ἀποθνῃσκόντων δὲ τῶν συστρατήγων ὅτι ἐστράτευσαν ἐπὶ βασιλέα ξὺν Κύρῳ, ταὐτὰ πεποιηκὼς οὐκ ἀπέθανε, μετὰ δὲ τὸν τῶν ἄλλων θάνατον

---

30 On interventions and citations in Xenophon, see Gray 2003; on narrator-ambiguity, see Dorati 2007, 105–116.

στρατηγῶν τιμωρηθεὶς ὑπὸ βασιλέως ἀπέθανεν, οὐχ ὥσπερ Κλέαρχος καὶ οἱ ἄλλοι στρατηγοὶ ἀποτμηθέντες τὰς κεφαλάς, ὅσπερ τάχιστος θάνατος δοκεῖ εἶναι, ἀλλὰ ζῶν αἰκισθεὶς ἐνιαυτὸν ὡς πονηρὸς λέγεται τῆς τελευτῆς τυχεῖν.

When his fellow-generals were put to death on the plea that they had marched with Cyrus against the king, he alone, although he had shared their conduct, was exempted from their fate. But after their deaths the vengeance of the king fell upon him, and he was put to death, not like Clearchus and the others by what would appear to be the speediest of deaths – decapitation – but, as report says, he lived for a year in pain and disgrace and died the death of a felon.

This may well be a covert indication to the historian's endorsing or, at least, entertaining, the view that Menon had been the one who, through his friendship with Ariaios, was in secret contact with Tissaphernes (2.5.25–26):

'καὶ ἐγὼ μέν γε, ἔφη ὁ Τισσαφέρνης, εἰ βούλεσθέ μοι οἵ τε στρατηγοὶ καὶ οἱ λοχαγοὶ ἐλθεῖν, ἐν τῷ ἐμφανεῖ λέξω τοὺς πρὸς ἐμὲ λέγοντας ὡς σὺ ἐμοὶ ἐπιβουλεύεις καὶ τῇ σὺν ἐμοὶ στρατιᾷ.'

'Even so,' replied Tissaphernes, 'and if your generals and captains care to come in some open and public way, I will name to you those who tell me that you are plotting against me and the army under me.'

It would have been consonant with the practice of Tissaphernes and Artaxerxes to have used Menon, as long as he was useful to their plan of deceiving Clearchus and the Greeks, and then punish him, since they knew very well that he was completely untrustworthy and disloyal. After all, the expression ἀλλὰ ζῶν αἰκισθεὶς ἐνιαυτὸν ὡς πονηρὸς λέγεται τῆς τελευτῆς τυχεῖν (2.6.29) may cause enormous head-scratching as to what exactly Xenophon is alluding to but may also suggest that Xenophon regarded Menon's punishment as just or, at least, as becoming. A last *authorial comment* in 2.6.28 may be also a covert indication of Xenophon suspecting Menon.

καὶ τὰ μὲν δὴ ἀφανῆ ἔξεστι περὶ αὐτοῦ ψεύδεσθαι, ἃ δὲ πάντες ἴσασι τάδ' ἐστί.

As to certain obscure charges brought against his character, these may certainly be fabrications. I confine myself to the following facts, which are known to all.

Xenophon has decided to avail himself only of information that had become common knowledge among the army. The rest will not be reported, since it may be doubted, but at least it can be hinted at.

4. Patronymics

It has been rightly observed that in the *Hellenika* Xenophon's use of patronymics is arbitrary.[31] Does the same hold for the *Anabasis*, where patronymics are extremely rare? In 3.3.20, Xenophon uses both a patronymic and a toponymic at the same time, when he introduces Lycius, son of Polystratus, an Athenian. Given that this is indeed a *rara avis* regarding regular Xenophontean practice in the *Anabasis*, I think that we should dwell more on this exceptional occasion:

> καὶ ταύτης τῆς νυκτὸς σφενδονῆται μὲν εἰς διακοσίους ἐγένοντο, ἵπποι δὲ καὶ ἱππεῖς ἐδοκιμάσθησαν τῇ ὑστεραίᾳ εἰς πεντήκοντα, καὶ σπολάδες καὶ θώρακες αὐτοῖς ἐπορίσθησαν, καὶ ἵππαρχος ἐπεστάθη Λύκιος ὁ Πολυστράτου Ἀθηναῖος.

> These proposals were carried, and that night two hundred slingers were enrolled, and next day as many as fifty horse and horsemen passed muster as duly qualified; buff jackets and cuirasses were provided for them, and a commandant of cavalry appointed to command – Lycius, the son of Polystratus, by name, an Athenian.

Why does Xenophon mention Lycius *in such a formal way* (name, father's name, city of origin)? The use of his toponymic should not strike the wrong note, for it is consonant with Xenophon's standard usage in the *Anabasis*, where he regularly gives a person's toponymic on his first appearance. Lycius is also mentioned in 4.3.22, 4.3.25 and 4.7.24 where he is deprived of both patronymic and toponymic. This Athenian leads the cavalry in pursuit of the fleeing Carduchi, steals clothing and cups from these dangerous people, and last but certainly not least, it was he and Xenophon who drove their horses forward to see what was taking place when the Greek soldiers saw the sea and shouted 'Thalatta, Thalatta'. Is it completely accidental that Xenophon mentions only in this case a person's patronymic, especially since Lycius is a rather third-rate figure in the *Anabasis*?

The reference to Lycius follows a speech delivered by Xenophon (3.3.16) who had stressed the fact that the army immediately needed slingers (σφενδονῆται) and horsemen (ἱππεῖς):

> ἡμεῖς οὖν εἰ μέλλοιμεν τούτοις εἴργειν ὥστε μὴ δύνασθαι βλάπτειν ἡμᾶς πορευομένους, σφενδονητῶν τὴν ταχίστην δεῖ καὶ ἱππέων.

---

31   Hornblower 1994, 162.

If, then, we are to exclude them from all possibility of injuring us as we march, we must get slingers as soon as possible and cavalry.

Xenophon's proposal is welcomed by the army and so the next day the Greeks are equipped with 200 slingers and 50 horsemen who, as Xenophon had probably suggested, were furnished with leather garments (σπολάδες) and breastplates (θώρακες). Xenophon was particularly well informed with respect to horses. This can also be seen in various passages of the *Anabasis*[32] but pre-eminently in his two treatises Ἱππαρχικός and *De re equestri* (περὶ ἱππικῆς), where he discusses in detail various matters pertaining to the leader of the cavalry in the former, and the purchase, feeding, training etc. of horses according to their use by their owners in the latter. In the very last chapter of his work *De re equestri* (περὶ ἱππικῆς), Xenophon explains the way a horseman should be equipped and lays emphasis on the use of a breastplate. A similar interest on exactly the same topic can be found in Xenophon's *Memorabilia* (Ἀπομνημονεύματα) in the discussion between Socrates and Pistias. Given the special interest and knowledge of Xenophon in equestrian matters, it may be assumed that the appointment of Lycius as commander of the cavalry was his own suggestion and that Lycius was, in all likelihood, also experienced in equestrian matters. In this conception, the mention of Lycius' patronymic may imply that Xenophon knew his fellow-citizen Lycius on a personal level and that there was some sort of connection between himself and the family of Lycius. In the words of Robert Lane Fox:[33]

> Lycius was one of three brothers, all of whom were horsemen in the later fifth century; two of them are known to us from funerary inscriptions in Attica. Their father Polystratus was the infamous oligarch who was twice tried in court during the political upheavals of 411 and was defended by one of his sons in Lysias' Speech 20.[34] This son, a horseman, was in my view Lycius himself; he was no natural democrat; he had served in Sicily and survived, he said, to fight and plunder there after 413; he returned home, but he presumably had had to leave Athens in 404/3 for participating too keenly in the months of rule by the Thirty Tyrants. Xenophon, his

---

32 Like the description of the way the Persian horses were equipped in 1.8.7–8 or the incident with Soteridas the Sicyonian in 3.4.47–48 or 3.2.18–20 in contrast to Thucydides, where Nikias argues that Sicily will have two big advantages against the Athenians, cavalry and supplies. See Rood 1998, 165–166. On horses in the *Anabasis*, see Fox 2004, 10–11.
33 Fox 2004, 11–12.
34 *IG* II² 12499, 12658, 12969. See also Davies 1971, 467–468.

fellow horseman, had had to leave too: the two of them, mounted warriors, had many an undemocratic memory which they could have shared, two partners in prejudice on the winter march north to the sea.

Xenophon feels coy about revealing such a connection, in the same way Thucydides (as Hornblower has suggested) feels coy about showing off his special knowledge concerning place names, thus finding recourse to the expression 'the so-called'. The historian's reserve regarding the revelation of his exact liaison with Lycius may be due to his ultimate political aspirations concerning his future return to Athens[35] but it is also consonant with Xenophon's constant aim to 'give his audiences an impression of unmediated historical objectivity.'[36]

Xenophon's utmost care in the narrative exploitation of this Lycius may be also seen in his choosing two different ways to introduce him in the plot. Fox[37] has argued that, if the identification between the speaker in Lysias 20.11 ff. and Lycius is correct and if Lysias' information regarding Lycius' military service for Catana, a city opposed to Syracuse, in and after 413 is dishonest, then '[Lycius] the "Syracusan"[38] [may well be] Xenophon's allusion (witty, perhaps, or actually true) to one and the same Lycius and his wicked western escapades.' If this holds true, then his reintroduction in a positive light in 3.3.20 accompanied by his patronymic becomes all the more narratively functional.

5. Periphrastic Denomination (ἀντωνομασία)[39]

The term periphrastic denomination or *antonomasia* designates 'a reference to a character not by proper name but by a form of indirect description.'[40] A typical case is Artaxerxes, who is constantly designated as 'king' (βασιλεύς). This is, of course, the usual Greek practice for referring to the king of Persia, but given that the *Anabasis* begins as the struggle between Artaxerxes and his younger brother Cyrus about who should be king of Persia, royal denomination may be hinting at

---

35 This attitude is fully compatible with Xenophon's systematic use of his autobiography in the last two Books of the *Anabasis* as 'a vehicle for personal apologetic.' See Hornblower 1994, 31.
36 Gray 2003, 111 n. 2.
37 Fox 2004, 11–12 n. 34.
38 Lycius from Syracuse is mentioned in 1.10.14 as a prominent horseman.
39 See scholia *ad Il.* 13.154 and de Jong 1993, 289–306.
40 See de Jong 2001a, xvi.

the unsuccessful outcome of Cyrus' undertaking. This line of interpretation is further supported by another form of periphrastic denomination employed for Artaxerxes. Just before the fatal battle at Cunaxa, Clearchus asks Cyrus whether he thinks that his brother will fight against him. Cyrus' answer is revealing (1.7.9–10):

> Νὴ Δί', ἔφη ὁ Κῦρος, εἴπερ γε Δαρείου καὶ Παρυσάτιδός ἐστι παῖς, ἐμὸς δὲ ἀδελφός, οὐκ ἀμαχεὶ ταῦτ' ἐγὼ λήψομαι.

> Cyrus answered: 'Not without a battle, be assured, shall the prize be won; if he be the son of Darius and Parysatis, and a brother of mine.'

By designating Artaxerxes as the son of Darius and Parysatis, Xenophon allows Cyrus, as a speaker, to give his own point of view and cue the readers to the beginning of the plot.

When periphrastic denomination is juxtaposed to a personal name, it seems pleonastic but is narratively exploited in order to link scattered passages and redirect the readers to a key-point in the plot. In 2.4.27, the mention of the name Parysatis is followed by the periphrastic denomination 'the mother of Cyrus and the king', which also contains the periphrastic denomination 'king':

> ἐντεῦθεν δ' ἐπορεύθησαν διὰ τῆς Μηδίας σταθμοὺς ἐρήμους ἓξ παρασάγγας τριάκοντα εἰς τὰς Παρυσάτιδος κώμας τῆς Κύρου καὶ βασιλέως μητρός. ταύτας Τισσαφέρνης Κύρῳ ἐπεγγελῶν διαρπάσαι τοῖς Ἕλλησιν ἐπέτρεψε πλὴν ἀνδραπόδων. ἐνῆν δὲ σῖτος πολὺς καὶ πρόβατα καὶ ἄλλα χρήματα.

> From this place they marched through Media six desert stages – thirty parasangs – to the villages of Parysatis, Cyrus's and the king's mother. These Tissaphernes, in mockery of Cyrus, delivered over to the Hellenes to plunder, except that the folk in them were not to be made slaves. They contained much corn, cattle, and other property.

This double *antonomasia* is narratively effective for it invites readers to recall the very beginning of the *Anabasis*, where Parysatis was designated as the mother of the two princes (1.1.1) and, more importantly, as a supporter of the younger Cyrus against his brother Artaxerxes (1.1.4):

> Δαρείου καὶ Παρυσάτιδος γίγνονται παῖδες δύο, πρεσβύτερος μὲν Ἀρταξέρξης, νεώτερος δὲ Κῦρος. [...] Παρύσατις μὲν δὴ ἡ μήτηρ ὑπῆρχε τῷ Κύρῳ, φιλοῦσα αὐτὸν μᾶλλον ἢ τὸν βασιλεύοντα Ἀρταξέρξην.

> Darius and Parysatis had two sons: the elder was named Artaxerxes, and the younger Cyrus. [...] Parysatis, his mother, was his first resource; for she had more love for Cyrus than for Artaxerxes upon his throne.

In this light, readers do not need to cudgel their brains about the function of this piece of information. The reference to Tissaphernes' allowing the Greeks to loot the small towns belonging to Parysatis, in his attempt to show his utmost content against the dead Cyrus, invites the readers to make a narrative leap to the very beginning of the *Anabasis*, where all these *players* had initially appeared, at the very first instance of the narrative shuffling of the cards. In this way, Tissaphernes' vicious slander against Cyrus and Parysatis' intervention to save her younger son are easily conjured on the narrative surface giving cohesion to the deployment of the plot.

6. Floating Kindreds: τις and εἷς

Hornblower has rightly drawn attention to the use of τις in Thucydides, which he calls a 'buttonholing device', i. e. a mechanism employed to buttonhole the reader. Contrary to Fornara, Hornblower argues or at least leaves to understand that sometimes τις may be *disparaging*, as is the case with Dolon in *Iliad* 10.314 and Hyperbolus in Thucydides 8.73. In a famous passage of the *Anabasis* (3.1.4) where Xenophon is also designated by τις, its *disparaging* function is absent but still the use of this indefinite pronoun covertly indicates that Xenophon is a special character, one who 'followed [Cyrus] neither as a general nor as a captain nor as a soldier but because Proxenus summoned him from home since he was an old friend of his.' Not being *disparaging*, we can securely classify τις as a device accompanying the introduction of a character or his first important appearance or his undertaking of a more active role than before, and this is certainly the case with Xenophon in this passage. But, apart from τις, which is used 137 times in the *Anabasis*, Xenophon avails himself of εἷς, which is attested 12 times. When εἷς is not employed as a numeral, does it have any specific narrative function?

εἷς is employed 5 times in speeches uttered by Xenophon and 7 in plain narrative (once with respect to Xenophon, Clearchus and Phalinos, twice for anonymous Greeks and twice for anonymous barbarians). Of all these cases, only those where εἷς accompanies a name or has the same meaning with the indefinite pronoun τις are worth studying further.

In all the cases where εἷς goes with a name, there is no toponymic. This use is emphatically different from the use of τις with a personal name followed by its toponymic. Given that toponymics are used only for Greeks in order to highlight their specific origin, its absence shows that εἷς is a *special* term *marking* someone as Greek, not as Thessalian or Lacedaemonian or Athenian. When a character is designated by εἷς, then Xenophon buttonholes him as Greek either in positive or negative manner but always as Greek par excellence. This narrative technique is particularly apt in the case of Phalinus (2.1.7), where Xenophon aims at alerting his readers to the fact that the ensuing dialogue will take place between two Greeks, one in the service of Artaxerxes and the other being one of the Ten Thousand. Phalinus is not a simple messenger sent by the king but a Greek in the service of Artaxerxes and the way he is going to converse with the Greeks will be a special one.

In the single case where εἷς is used for an anonymous speaker, the first person intrudes, so to speak, in the indirect discourse that is blurred with direct speech (1.3.13–14):

> ἐκ δὲ τούτου ἀνίσταντο οἱ μὲν ἐκ τοῦ αὐτομάτου, λέξοντες ἃ ἐγίγνωσκον, οἱ δὲ καὶ ὑπ' ἐκείνου ἐγκέλευστοι, ἐπιδεικνύντες οἵα εἴη ἡ ἀπορία ἄνευ τῆς Κύρου γνώμης καὶ μένειν καὶ ἀπιέναι. εἷς δὲ εἶπε προσποιούμενος σπεύδειν ὡς τάχιστα πορεύεσθαι εἰς τὴν Ἑλλάδα στρατηγοὺς μὲν ἑλέσθαι ἄλλους ὡς τάχιστα, εἰ μὴ βούλεται Κλέαρχος ἀπάγειν· ... ἐλθόντας δὲ Κῦρον αἰτεῖν πλοῖα ὡς ἀποπλέοιεν· ἐὰν δὲ μὴ διδῷ ταῦτα, ἡγεμόνα αἰτεῖν Κῦρον ὅστις διὰ φιλίας τῆς χώρας ἀπάξει. ἐὰν δὲ μηδὲ ἡγεμόνα διδῷ, συντάττεσθαι τὴν ταχίστην, πέμψαι δὲ καὶ προκαταληψομένους τὰ ἄκρα, ὅπως μὴ φθάσωσι μήτε Κῦρος μήτε οἱ Κίλικες καταλαβόντες, ὧν πολλοὺς καὶ πολλὰ χρήματα ἔχομεν ἀνηρπακότες.

> Then various speakers stood up; some of their own motion to propound their views; others inspired by Clearchus to dilate on the hopeless difficulty of either staying, or going back without the goodwill of Cyrus. One of these, in particular, with a make-believe of anxiety to commence the homeward march without further pause, called upon them instantly to choose other generals, if Clearchus were not himself prepared to lead them back ... he added, 'go to Cyrus and ask for some ships in order to return by sea: if he refused to give them ships, let them demand of him a guide to lead them back through a friendly district; and if he would not so much as give them a guide, they could but put themselves, without more ado, in marching order, and send on a detachment to occupy the pass–before Cyrus and the Cilicians, whose property,' the speaker added, 'we have so plentifully pillaged, can anticipate us.'

The same is the case with a speech delivered immediately afterwards by another anonymous Greek designated as ἄλλος. Since εἷς is used as indefinite in *contrapposizione*, this is a covert indication that another speech will follow against this one. In fact, Xenophon may well be projecting his own point of view at a point of the plot where he wishes to remain in the background. In this conception, the εἷς employed for an anonymous speaker may be a slighting device, but a slighting device alluding to the fact that the speaker will present a Greek, though negatively colored, point of view.

In this light, τις and εἷς may be called *floating kindreds* since they are both buttonholing devices but with a different emphasis and scope.

7. Mythical Names and Intertextuality

In the *Anabasis*, there are at least two cases, where recourse to mythical names fulfills a specific narrative goal, i. e. it engages the readers into a future-oriented intertextuality. Instead of the well-known Barchesian *reflessivo futuro*,[41] which designates an intratextually future but intertextually past event, Xenophon introduces mythical names to exploit his readers' mythical storage and foreshadow the way the plot will unravel. One of the most prominent areas of intertextual exploitation is the *Odyssey*, since Xenophon systematically draws analogies between the return and perils of the Ten Thousand on their way from Kunaxa to Trapezous and then to the Aegean and the adventures of Odysseus.[42] In particular, Lossau has convincingly argued, on the basis of numerous relevant examples, that the analogy between the *Anabasis* and the *Odyssey* is profound. He has also offered a possible scenario for Xenophon's intertextual play with Homeric poetry, claiming that Xenophon was not content with the plain 'memoir-style' and the pattern of περίοδος-literature but dallied with the idea of exploiting a famous work of undeniable excellence such as the *Odyssey*.[43]

In *Anabasis* 3.2.25–26, Xenophon in his long speech to the Greek army expresses his only fear about the future not only in terms of a famous Odyssean episode but also in Odyssean diction (9.97 & 102) par excellence:[44]

---

41 Barchiesi 2001, 105–127.
42 On this topic, see Lossau 1990, 47–52 with further bibliography. Apart from the *Odyssey*, Xenophon has also exploited, though to a smaller extent, the *Iliad*; on possible Iliadic echoes in the *Anabasis*, see Rinner 1978, 144–149; Tsagalis 2002, 101–121.
43 1990, 52.
44 See Lossau 1990, 47.

ἀλλὰ γὰρ δέδοικα μή, ἂν ἅπαξ μάθωμεν ἀργοὶ ζῆν καὶ ἐν ἀφθόνοις βιοτεύειν, καὶ Μήδων δὲ καὶ Περσῶν καλαῖς καὶ μεγάλαις γυναιξὶ καὶ παρθένοις ὁμιλεῖν, μὴ ὥσπερ οἱ λωτοφάγοι ἐπιλαθώμεθα τῆς οἴκαδε ὁδοῦ.

For I fear, if once we learn to live in idleness and to batten in luxury and dalliance with these tall and handsome Median and Persian women and maidens, we shall be like the Lotus-Eaters, and forget the road home altogether.

λωτὸν ἐρεπτόμενοι μενέμεν νόστου τε λαθέσθαι (9.97)

to browse on the lotus and to forget all thoughts of return

μή πώς τις λωτοῖο φαγὼν νόστοιο λάθηται (9.102)

[for fear] that others of them might eat the lotus and think no more of home

Xenophon's fear will not materialize but the reference to the Lotus-Eaters aims mainly at his external audience. Readers are invited to use the mythical name Lotus-Eaters as a specific hint to the *Odyssey*, which will soon begin for the Ten Thousand. Xenophon thus makes a profound narrative gesture to his audience, a gesture that makes the most of an intertextual reference of undisputed authority and widespread diffusion, in order not only to allude to the perils the Greeks are about to face but also to the *way Xenophon wants his readers to interpret these perils*.

In *Anabasis* 5.1.2, Leon from Thourioi emphatically declares that he is tired of these long adventurous wanderings, and desires, Odysseus-like, to stretch himself out and arrive at Greece:

Ἐγὼ μὲν τοίνυν, ἔφη, ὦ ἄνδρες, ἀπείρηκα ἤδη ξυσκευαζόμενος καὶ βαδίζων καὶ τρέχων καὶ τὰ ὅπλα φέρων καὶ ἐν τάξει ὢν καὶ φυλακὰς φυλάττων καὶ μαχόμενος, ἐπιθυμῶ δὲ ἤδη παυσάμενος τούτων τῶν πόνων, ἐπεὶ θάλατταν ἔχομεν, πλεῖν τὸ λοιπὸν καὶ ἐκταθεὶς ὥσπερ Ὀδυσσεὺς ἀφικέσθαι εἰς τὴν Ἑλλάδα.

He said: 'For my part, sirs, I am weary by this time of getting kit together and packing up for a start, of walking and running and carrying heavy arms, and of tramping along in line, or mounting guard, and doing battle. The sole desire I now have is to cease from all these pains, and for the future, since here we have the sea before us, to sail on and on, stretched out in sleep, like Odysseus, and so to find myself in Hellas.'

The reference to Odysseus is basically intended for the external audience. Xenophon invites his readers to interpret the adventures and dangers the Ten Thousand will face in the light of the Odyssean tradition. After all, his narrative abilities owe much to his famous epic predecessor, whose *Iliad* and *Odyssey* he has struggled to fuse into the two distinct parts of his *Anabasis*, the first one with its Iliadic warlike tone, and the second one with its colorful Odyssean character.

8. Conclusion

To sum up, Xenophon, like his predecessor Thucydides, often uses proper names as narrative mechanisms that allow him to illuminate the function of a person within the plot in terms of either highlighting or downplaying his importance. Patronymics and toponymics that may accompany the proper names of Greeks are occasionally employed as a sophisticated means of inviting the readers to explore a whole web of interwoven intratextual threads: distant passages are thus bridged revealing unnoticed aspects of events, evaluative comments are shored up disclosing the historian's own point of view, dramatic effect is produced, and last, but certainly not least, the readers' attention is directed to views that are implied and not explicitly stated. The use of proper names is so systematically and vigorously pursued by Xenophon that their absence can be also narratively significant, 'foreshadowing' a character's negative role in the plot or implying a disparaging and unfavorable comment on the part of the historian. Finally, mythical names are employed, at times, as narrative devices that allow Xenophon not only to make full use of his readers' mythical storage and foreshadow the way the plot will unravel but also to enrich the generic apparatus on which the *Anabasis* relies, thus encompassing a wide range of genres such as *memoir*, περίπλους-literature and even Homeric epic. In light of the fact that the *Anabasis* is a mosaic of peoples and places, Xenophon's exploitation of their names must be interpreted within his larger aim to create a sense of narrative cohesion in an ever-changing medley of men, space and events.

The Perils of Expectations: Perceptions, Suspense and Surprise in Polybius' *Histories*

Nikos Miltsios

All historians, whether they consciously strive to produce a work of literary merit or not, are keen on rendering their narratives attractive to their readers. Even when like Polybius they do not rate style very highly, nevertheless we should expect them to be concerned with structure and organization of material, if only to secure their readers' attention and thus ensure the realization of their other aims as well. Polybius, to be sure, had not regarded literary virtuosity as an essential part of his task.[1] Betraying his pragmatic approach, he clearly articulated what skills were required in order to be a worthwhile historian – inquiry, effort and experience.[2] This fact has seriously affected the way critics both ancient and modern approached him. Dionysius of Halicarnassus did not appreciate his artistic qualities, and in a famous passage (*de comp.* 4.30), which throws some light on the stylistic choices made by later historians, remarked that Polybius was one of those whom no

---

1 For Polybius' conscious disregard of stylistic elegance see Polyb. 29.12.9–10; in 16.17.10, however, he grants it some importance, and in 12.28.10 he praises Ephorus as 'admirable in his phraseology.' Still, he is deeply critical of Zeno of Rhodes 'because he is not for the most part so much concerned with inquiry into facts and proper treatment of his material, as with elegance of style, a quality on which he, like several other famous authors, often shows that he prides himself' (16.17.9). On this see the discussion of Meister 1975, 177–8 and Walbank 1990, 256 n. 19.

2 Polybius constantly emphasized his autopsy and travels; cf., for instance, 9.25.2–4, 12.3.6, 12.4.2–3, 12.25d.1–7, 12.25h.1–6. That actual participation in politics and warfare constitutes the most valuable exercise for the would-be historian comes across most clearly in Polybius' harsh attack on Timaeus, esp. in 12.26e.2–28.5, where he argues that the Sicilian historian, for all his learning, failed to accomplish something worthwhile because of his lack of personal experience (αὐτοπάθεια), and concludes by claiming that then 'it will be well with history either when men of action undertake to write history … or again when would-be authors regard a training in actual affairs as necessary for writing history.'

one could endure reading through to the end. His modern colleagues have not always displayed much more sensitivity to the subtlety of Polybius' work. Early scholarly interest centered on the ways in which it could be exploited as a 'veritable mine' of solid information.[3] Polybius' truthfulness and reliability have been repeatedly stressed,[4] but there have been few attempts to approach him in an essentially literary way, that is, to investigate his careful structuring of events and understand his history as a finely constructed work of literature and as a narrative with its own interests.[5] So an essential aspect of his work, not to say crucial for the understanding of his purposes in writing it, has been consistently neglected.

Yet from the very outset Polybius' narrative illustrates a high degree of concern with structural problems. How was he to describe events which occurred in several different parts of the world, and at the same time produce a work of history with a unifying subject and pattern, as if it were 'an organic whole'?[6] From Book 7 onwards the difficulty is resolved by a system of synchronisms and the regular switching from theatre to theatre, perhaps a complex method of presentation, but one which enables the narrator to create some major thematic patterns and render his account both more historically interesting and artistically arresting.[7] Of course, the issue of Polybian narrative is very broad and cannot be treated in full here. In what follows I will concentrate on a number of features of Polybius' narrative technique, in particular from the perspective of their ability to stimulate the reader's interest.

---

3 Marsden 1974, 294–5: 'As he wanted to be, Polybius is a veritable mine of information for the military man. It may be positive advantage that he did not include more interpretative sections, which might have contaminated the evidence rather than clarified it.'

4 Lehmann 1967, *passim*, esp. 349–359, has provided the most comprehensive and sustained defense of Polybius' impartiality and reliability. Walbank 1979, 24 also discussed the issue of Polybius' objectivity and admitted that in general Polybius meets a strict criterion of honesty and truthfulness. For further references see Davidson 1991, 11 and Champion 2004, 23.

5 Two important exceptions establishing Polybius as an author of greater depth and complexity than he had been given credit for in early scholarship are now Eckstein 1995, who afforded fresh insights into the moral dimension of *The Histories*, and most recently Champion 2004, who investigated Polybius' methods of constructing Roman culture and ethnicity.

6 1.3.4; cf. 14.12.5. On this concept see the valid remarks of Walbank 1972, 67–8.

7 For an analysis of this structural system see Walbank 1975, 197–212.

I will first discuss the account of Achaeus' capture in Book 8 and attempt to demonstrate how subtly the narrator exploits the cognitive gap between the narratee and the participants to develop a pattern emphasizing the characters' non-realistic or illusory expectations (I). Then I will suggest that this pattern functions as an author's weapon which works on more than one level simultaneously. In addition to providing a non-explicit interpretation of the various episodes, it serves as a suspense-heightening device, both because it foreshadows the future action so as to arouse curiosity as to what may happen in the later stages of the narrative, and also because it reinforces the sense of dramatic irony created by the clash between perceptions and actuality.[8] In the same section I will also explore the ways in which the characters' (non-realistic) expectations are thematized throughout Polybius' narrative (II). Next, I will offer an analysis of the account of the Hannibalic War in Book 3 that will help us get a better grip on the narrator's shaping of his material (III). Finally, I will conclude with Polybius' own comments on the mechanism of identification with negative or peripheral heroes (IV). In the course of this investigation, I hope to show that it is through the *dynamics of expectation* that Polybius impels the narrative forward and compels us *to read his work through to its end.*

The use of the tools of narratology, especially its categories of time and focalization, can help shed light on the process of communicating suspense to the readers and will provide the framework of my approach. Focalization as a cognitive term is not only heuristically valuable for my purposes but rather analytically essential in affording insights into the perceptions of both readers and characters. Suspense is based upon expectations about the future, but the expectations of the readers may or may not coincide with those of the characters. It is the handling of narrative time that shapes them. A piece of information can be imparted to the readers in advance, so that they are accorded a privileged position, or it can be temporarily concealed, so that they discover it at the same time as the characters. Or it may be known only at the level of the action, so that the readers know less than the characters. In any case, focalizing techniques are linked with temporal ones: together they offer a powerful tool for analyzing the process of reception through suspense.

---

8   Grethlein 2006a, 193–310 demonstrates that the same interplay between expectations and experiences, both at the level of reception and the action, is at work in Homer. For the tension between anticipation and realization in Herodotus and Thucydides see Grethlein, this volume.

My use of the term 'suspense' perhaps requires some justification. On the one hand, theorists assume that suspense involves a combination of hope and fear and 'derives mainly from the unpredictable but well motivated turn of events' (Kintsch 1980, 89). Then, what does suspense stand for in a work of ancient narrative literature, especially a historical one, where the end result is not just predictable, but actually known? Polybius himself at the preface draws his reader's attention to the outcome, claiming to be recording 'how and why' the Romans in so short a time made themselves masters of the *oecumene*. We must of course beware of exaggerating the difficulty. Precisely because the end result of *the Histories* is foretold, Polybius' chances of securing his audience's interest from the very start by the merits of his account are considerably improved. After all, he claims to be describing a process unique in kind, namely the unification of the *oecumene* under Rome's aegis. Moreover, even if the readers' uncertainty concerning the main events of a story is removed when the outcome is well known or after it has been foreshadowed or foretold to them or all of the above, it is the anxiety the readers feel about the smaller and separate episodes that arises and can be intensified. Polybius' audience and readers must have been well informed of Perseus' revolt, of the destruction of Macedon, as well as of the disastrous Achaean War with Rome, for it is clear that he is writing primarily for Greeks,[9] and these events constituted their recent past. They must have also been well informed of the Roman defeat at Cannae and their success at Zama; the influence of the Carthaginian Wars has been very powerful on the Hellenistic Mediterranean. But what could they have possibly known about the secret talk and action in conspiracy narratives, such as in the account of Achaeus' capture, or about the role played by Polybius himself in organizing Demetrius' of Syria successful escape from Rome?

On the other hand, beyond the suspense of uncertainty that arises in response to unknown outcomes, those familiar with the theory of suspense would argue that ancient narrators make use of what may be termed 'suspense of anticipation'.[10] As is well known, the foreshadowing of future events does not destroy suspense, and where it occurs it usually adds to the anticipation an element of uncertainty concerning not the

---

9 So Walbank 1972, 3–6 and nn. 16–19; for recent discussion see Champion 2004, 4 and n. 5 with earlier bibliography; see also Rood 2004, 159–160.
10 On anticipatory suspense see Duckworth 1933, *passim*, esp. 37–79; cf. Rengakos 1999, *passim* and 2005, 81–2 on the Homeric 'Spannung auf das Wie'.

outcome, but the manner of fulfillment. In this way, various possible future courses of action are opened up for us as readers, who are left free to wait and watch what we either wish or dread to see happen. As we are led to share the emotions of the characters and hope or fear with them, our expectancy is all the more intensified. Hence the foreshadowing of the future action lessens by no means our interest in the story; on the contrary, it leaves us in a state of emotional tension as to the way in which the action will unfold. Besides, the idea that suspense can persevere in the face of *complete knowledge* of the outcome has received much authoritative support in recent years. Many theorists observe that people returning to suspenseful texts re-experience the emotion of suspense they felt on their first encounter with these texts almost no matter how familiar they are with them.[11] The study of ancient writers', including historians', handling of narrative suspense is, therefore, not only a perfectly legitimate, but also a promising avenue of inquiry.[12]

1. Achaeus and Bolis

A good beginning for this investigation in Polybius is provided by the account of Achaeus' capture in Book 8 (15–21). Achaeus was a relative of Antiochus III, presumably his maternal uncle (cf. Walbank 1957, 501–2), a Seleucid prince praised by Polybius for his initial devotion toward his young kinsman (4.48.9–10). But the situation soon changed, and Achaeus, elated by his military successes in Asia Minor, and favored by Ptolemy,[13] decided to declare himself king. His prosperity, though, was not lasting and, since he indulged in desires greater than his powers would allow, he eventually met with defeat; Antiochus' seizure of Sardes in spring 214 marked the culminating point in the crushing of his revolt. The events described probably take place in 213, one year after the fall of Sardes, which left Achaeus besieged in the citadel and Sosibius, the main figure at the court of Ptolemy, eager to rescue him. As he was engaged in such a hazardous task, Sosibius appealed

---

11 See for instance Gerrig 1989a, 1989b, 1993, 1996, with the comments of Carroll 1996, esp. 89–90; for a review of theories of rereading in regard to their implications for the topic of narrative suspense see Brewer 1996, 119–123.
12 As de Jong 1999, 242–251 (on Herodotus) and Rengakos 2005, 81–99 (on Herodotus) and 2006a, 292–95 (on Thucydides) have demonstrated.
13 On Ptolemy's support to Achaeus see Walbank 1957, 502 with further bibliography.

for help to Bolis, a Cretan 'being regarded as a man possessed of superior intelligence, exceptional courage, and much military experience' (15.1). The language of the passage reminds us how strongly perceptions contribute to the people's response to the choices before them.[14] Thus although deprived of authoritative information related to Bolis' virtues, yet relying on the mention of how Bolis seemed to others, we, too, are inclined to believe that this man has the potential to play a significant role in rescuing Achaeus. Our presentiment is further reinforced by what follows:

> Sosibius, who had by continued intercourse with this man secured his confidence and rendered him favourably disposed to himself and ready to oblige him, put the matter in his hands, telling him that under present circumstances *there was no more acceptable service he could render the king than to contrive a plan to save Achaeus* (15.2).[15]

Bolis, indeed, agreed to undertake action, emphasizing to Sosibius that he had been in Sardes and knew its topography, and that Cambylus, the commander of the Cretans in Antiochus' army, who was in charge of one of the outposts behind the citadel, was his fellow-citizen, relative and friend (15.4–5). Inspired by this most welcome news, Sosibius had no doubt about the appropriateness of his choice:

> Sosibius received his suggestion warmly, and since he was firmly convinced either that it was impossible to rescue Achaeus from his dangerous situation, *or that once one regarded it as possible, no one could do it better than Bolis* … the project rapidly began to move (15.6).

Similarly, our confidence in Bolis' ability to accomplish his perilous enterprise owing to these reassuring remarks is firmly established and our hopes concerning Achaeus' chances are strongly raised. Bolis himself in his urge to carry out the plan sent one of his officers named Arianus to Cambylus in order to fix a date and place where they could meet (16.2–3). And shortly before their encounter is reported to us, the Polybian narrator decides to speak in his own person and declare, explicitly and definitely, Bolis' real intentions. Naturally shrewd and calculating person that he was, we are told, Bolis had been doing what he could to preserve his own interests (16.4). And when he finally

---

[14] On the role of the 'gaze' in Polybius see Davidson 1991, 10–24; see also Rood 1998, *passim*, esp. 61–108, offering a highly sophisticated approach to the way perceptions of the participants influence the unfolding of events in Thucydides.

[15] All translations are by Paton, W.R. (1922) 1992. Polybius, *The Histories*, 6 vol., Loeb Classical Library, Cambridge, MA.

met Cambylus, both of them took into account neither the rescue of Achaeus nor their loyalty to those who had charged them with the task, but only their personal security and advantage (16.6). No wonder, then, that their decision was to reveal the plan to Antiochus and undertake to deliver Achaeus into his hands on receiving a sum of money (16.8).

It is particularly interesting to note how subtly the Polybian narrator takes pains to conceal the cunning and treacherous character of Bolis at the early stages of the narrative. His focus on perceptions, on the mistaken opinions of others, contrasts with his silence about Bolis' true intentions and planning. The misdirection of the reader, which derives precisely from the withholding of authoritative and factual information, and results in this unanticipated turn of events, is something consciously aimed at by the Polybian narrator who makes use of formal devices such as focalization and temporal displacement to manipulate narrative interest. For the delayed exposition of Bolis' repulsive character traits and unscrupulous motives is apparently part and parcel of Polybius' overall strategy of surprise. This is the primacy effect, we now realize, the narrator wished to generate up to this point and that is why he was at pains to induce the reader to form hypotheses which retrospectively turned out to be wholly invalid. Moreover, in the light of this unpredictable disclosure the reader is now able to fully appreciate the dramatic irony of the words used by Sosibius to assign the mission to Bolis: 'there was no more suitable service he could render the king (scil. Ptolemy)' (15.2). The dramatic irony can also be seen, conspicuously strengthened, in Sosibius' considerations after he had sought Bolis' aid: 'once one regarded Achaeus' rescue as possible, *no one could do it better than Bolis*' (15.6). All these subtleties would have been eliminated were the disclosure made earlier – say at the beginning of the account, where Bolis' negotiations with Sosibius were first mentioned.[16]

---

16 A potential objection, as Jonas Grethlein remarked to me, would urge that it is strange indeed to detect at the same time surprise and dramatic irony. Since the latter presupposes that the reader knows more than the participants, the two notions are hardly compatible with each other. But I would still maintain that there is a case of dramatic irony here. It is certainly true that in the beginning the reader, not unlike the participants, ignores Bolis' real intentions (8.15). But he/she becomes aware of them soon (8.16); in any case, sooner than the participants (8.21). The clash, then, of differing insights and levels of understanding of reader and participants presupposed in dramatic irony, in the final analysis, exists, even if the proper (ironic) meaning of Sosibius' words becomes evident

Besides, the newly revealed conspiracy puts the immediate danger into perspective and has a direct bearing on the reader's expectations about the final outcome of the adventure. Having previously established a careful balance of fear and hope by conveying conflicting clues and hypotheses in regard to the fate of Achaeus, Polybius now tilts it toward the side of fear. For the time being the possibility of Achaeus' rescue is thrown into doubt; in fact, not even a shred of hope is left that he may emerge safe and unscathed from the harsh situation.

The rest of the story is told in detail and deals with the execution of the plan. First, Bolis contacted Nicomachus at Rhodes and Melancomas at Ephesus, who at that time remained devoted to Achaeus, and tried to persuade them to assist him. The two men, being convinced that 'the attempt was being made in all good faith', drew up letters to Achaeus in the code they used to employ and sent them, begging him to show confidence in Bolis and Cambylus (17.4–5). The importance of perceptions is also clear in what follows. Arianus, who had no knowledge of the crucial part of the agreement between Cambylus and Bolis, handed the letters to Achaeus and, precisely because of his ignorance, managed to answer his questions in a frank and forthright manner (17.6–8). Thus, after some exchange of letters Achaeus finally decided to entrust himself to Nicomachus and Bolis, *'there being now no other hope of safety left to him'* (17.9). Achaeus fails to see the light, but for the narratee the dramatic irony is manifest. Polybius can be seen here writing through the eyes of his character, who unaware of the ambush in store for him bases his last hope on Bolis' plan and proceeds to his destiny.

Polybius constantly provides us with reports of what was going on in Achaeus' mind:

> It should be known that the notion of Achaeus was, when once he had escaped from his present perilous position, to hasten without any escort to Syria, for he had the greatest hope, that by suddenly and unexpectedly appearing to the people in Syria while Antiochus was still occupied in the siege of Sardis, he would create a great movement in his favor and meet with a good reception at Antioch and throughout Coele-Syria and Phoenicia. Achaeus, then, his minds full of such hopes and calculations, was waiting for the appearance of Bolis (17.10–18.1).

Time and again portraying Achaeus as being not only oblivious to the impending doom, but at times even confident of success, Polybius exploits the clash between the perspectives of reader and character to cre-

---

retrospectively. Polybius' reader and characters share the same cognitive limitations, but only initially.

ate a cognitive dissonance, which is considerably effective as a suspense-heightening device. The unawareness of the participants and their mistaken hopes and trust in the future maximize the readers' anticipation of the final resolution of the events and divert their focus from the present moment to some distant point in the narrative. In this state of mind, we, as readers, cannot help asking how Achaeus will cope with the dangers that await him. Moreover, as we sympathize with him and share his emotions of fear and hope, we become less conscious of our own foreknowledge of the conspiracy that lies ahead and more anxious to see *what* will occur. After all, the possibility that Achaeus may against overwhelming odds flee and stay alive cannot be entirely precluded. Theoretically, then, a modicum of optimism still exists that he will overcome the jeopardy. Hence the suspense the reader feels is further intensified, since it involves a combination of anticipation *and* uncertainty.

Next, Polybius has Bolis and Cambylus carefully arranging the ambush in its details. They agreed that Arianus, 'in conducting Achaeus out of the citadel, should lead the way, whereas Bolis would have to be last of all, in order that, on arriving at the place where Cambylus was to have the attack launched, he could catch hold of Achaeus and hold him fast, so that he would neither escape in the confusion of the night across the wooded country, nor in his despair cast himself from some precipice' (18.7–8). Of course, suspense builds up from moment to moment as Polybius, instead of reporting actions, embeds in his narrative the 'scenic' representation of the plans Bolis and Cambylus were setting up against Achaeus. His emphasis on their planning provides a structuring device, which has the effect of slowing down the speed of the narrative and thus serves to delay the long anticipated climax. Equally retardatory is the very next scene too (18.9–11); Bolis' negotiations with Antiochus do little to promote the development of the action.

Later on, the encounter of Achaeus and Bolis is invested with essentially dramatic value. Achaeus questioned Bolis at length about the enterprise and, 'judging both from his appearance and his manner of talking that he was a man *equal to the gravity of the occasion*', was at first *overjoyed* (περιχαρής) at the hope of rescue (19.2). Aside from the patent dramatic irony emphasizing Achaeus' limited perspective, it is also interesting to note the conscious patterning that links high optimistic expectation with approaching disaster. Premature and excessive joy often goes hand in hand in the Greek historiographical tradition with lack of self-awareness and eventually emerges as an emotional condition rich in ominous connotations, signalling failure or worse.[17]

Nevertheless, Achaeus had not lost all sense of his vulnerability. Rather, since he was aware of the seriousness of the consequences, and since *he was a person of high intelligence and great experience in managing affairs* (19.3), he tried to take every possible precaution to protect himself:

> He therefore informed Bolis that it was impossible for him to come out of the citadel at the present moment, but that he would send three or four of his friends, and after they had joined Melancomas, he would himself get ready to leave (19.4).

The main function this crucial passage fulfills is to counteract the sinister foreshadowing implications projected so far. It particularly counterbalances the distressing effect of Bolis' astuteness by buttressing the reader's confidence in Achaeus' abilities to prevail upon his foes. The outcome of the conflict is made to look all the more ambiguous through an elaborate ring composition juxtaposing Achaeus' portrayal with that of Bolis. The two rivals are presented as sharing identical qualities – as Polybius' terminology emphasizes: Achaeus' intelligence combined with experience of affairs (τριβήν) echoes Bolis' depiction at 15.1. Furthermore, Achaeus' unwillingness to follow Bolis at once encourages us to hope that he may have an alternative plan in mind, which may ultimately enable him to escape the trap. Yet, in order not to neutralize totally our suspense, Polybius states that, although Achaeus was doing his best, 'he did not consider that he was trying to play the Cretan with a Cretan' (19.5).[18] The tempo of the narrative here is strikingly slow, because it seems that the two opponents are on the point of engagement.

However, before letting the account draw toward its climax, the narrator frustrates our expectations again by inserting a new retardation. He abruptly breaks off the action at the most exciting moment and very cleverly shifts the scene to concentrate on Achaeus' encounter with his

---

17 Cf. Eckstein 1995, 276. For a similar use of conventional narrative structures see Lateiner 1977, 1982, who notices that thoughtless laughter in Herodotus acts as a sign of impending doom and discusses the sinister implications of explicitly mentioned prosperity.

18 For the proverb see Walbank 1967 *ad loc.* Polybius regards the Cretans as naturally cunning and deceitful (cf. 6.46.3, 24.3, 28.14.1–2, 33.16.5), a characteristic stressed throughout the account of Achaeus' capture (cf. 16.4–7, 20.2). On Polybius' hostility towards the Cretans see Walbank 1957, 508 with further bibliography.

wife Laodice. The episode is neither long nor very elaborate, but the pathos of their last meeting is sure to receive proper attention. In the face of the hazards awaiting her husband, Laodice 'almost lost her wits, so that he had to spend some time in beseeching her to be calm and in soothing her *by dwelling on the brightness of the prospect before him*' (19.7). Based more upon wishing than upon reckoning, and fostered by Bolis' lies, Achaeus' enthusiasm is easily recognized as fallacious; we know that there is a vast discrepancy between what Achaeus fancies and what actually occurs. But we, as readers, are not placed in a position of omniscience, and this time it is *our* perspective that proves limited. In fact, Polybius now reveals what we may have inferred from the narrative so far: Achaeus entrusted himself to Nicomachus' benevolence, yet certainly he had a counter-plan in mind. Soon we learn the measures he was going to take to enhance his chances for survival. Quite consistently with his craftiness, he intended to adopt a plain appearance and to come out of the citadel in disguise taking four companions with him. One of them was going to make the necessary enquiries, as the others would pretend not to know Greek (19.8–9). His optimism, then, in due course is presented not as foolish hopes, but as founded on some rational calculation, while we gradually appreciate that his position is by no means as desperate as had at first been thought.

Indeed, when Achaeus' stratagem was put into effect, all seemed at first perfectly arranged. Despite his resourcefulness Bolis could not make out whether Achaeus was present or not, or – even if he assumed that he was nearby – which one he might be (20.2). As long as the camouflaged hero is covered by the darkness of the night, the reader's anxiety intensifies and reaches its pinnacle, the whole situation being on a razor's edge. There then occurs, suddenly, but perhaps not unexpectedly, the last reversal. Bolis very soon realized that Achaeus was among them, since the others were unable 'to put aside for the time their habitual attitude of respect to him', still he did not undertake action until he met his comrades (20.4–5). The scenic treatment of Achaeus' capture provides a vivid account that places the reader with the hero as he is being encircled, and then led to Antiochus (20.5–7).

The last scene is detailed too, although we would expect that the narrative pace, in view of the approaching resolution of suspense, would accelerate. But now it is the depiction of pathos rather than the upholding of suspense that far outweighs other concerns. Watching a leading opponent, 'the sovereign of all Asia on this side of the Taurus', lying down on the ground bound hand and foot, Antiochus, taken by surprise as he was, could not refrain from bursting into tears (20.9). This emotional reaction, which arises precisely from the melancholy thought of the meaninglessness of human effort, appears only here and in a more famous passage in Book 38 (22.1) with Scipio Aemilianus weeping over the ruins of Carthage.[19] Emotion, however, has little effect on war or politics, and somewhat later the royal Friends, who flocked to the king's tent, must decide what punishment to impose on Achaeus (21.1–2). After many proposals the final decision was to amputate his extremities, to cut off his head, and to impale the body on a stake (21.3). Polybius once again emphasizes the mistaken assessments made by the characters:

> Achaeus was supposed by his own forces and those of the enemy to be dwelling secure in the strongest fortress in the world … not a soul being aware of what had happened except the actual perpetrators of the deed (20.12).

It was not until Achaeus had been killed, and the rival army was filled with enthusiasm and wild excitement that Laodice, who alone was informed of her husband's departure from the citadel, divined the truth. A half page later, the narratorial comment crowns the account and makes explicit the lessons to be extracted. It is dangerous to trust anybody, and wise to expect a reversal of fortune in time of success, because being but men we must bear in mind the transience of prosperity (21.10–11).

2. Illusory expectations

It goes without saying that the importance of the preceding episode lies not in the military significance of the event but in what it tells about the perspectives of its participants and human fragility. The account of Achaeus' fall is a dramatic development of the theme of illusory expectations, so prominent in the *Histories*. Polybius many times depicts people as founding their optimism on an expectation that they will eventually meet with success in their ventures, only to have their hopes harshly crushed. We have seen that Sosibius seriously misjudged Bolis' inten-

---

19 In fact, it occurs once again at 10.18.13, but in a totally different context. Here it is the dignity of the captive women (successfully) supplicating for their honor that impresses Scipio Africanus and moves him to tears. Jonas Grethlein drew my attention to a similar scene in Herodotus (7.46): Xerxes weeps when, gazing at his vast army, he reflects on the brevity of human life.

tions and found himself betrayed by the man he considered most appropriate to handle the project. Similarly, Nicomachus and Melancomas were convinced that the enterprise was being made in all good faith. More strikingly, Achaeus, despite his desperate position, did not abandon his enthusiasm. Such ill-founded optimism is in itself ominous and portentous, and it is mentioned explicitly when some great calamity is to follow. Indeed, excessive joy, since it generally indicates a lack of awareness of one's own mortal limits, seems to guarantee an imminent catastrophe.

But how does this pattern affect the dynamics of expectation? To what extent does it help the ancient historian to hold his audience in suspense? These questions and related ones point to two salient features of Polybius' suspense strategy. The first of these features is the foreshadowing of the later action in a more or less vague manner. In particular, the narrator establishes through this conscious patterning some internal canons of probability that are meant to function as hints and premonitions of future events. The more we, as readers, familiarize ourselves with this pattern, the more alert we become to its sinister implications. Yet, that is not to say that in Polybius' suspense strategy anticipatory suspense is the be-all and end-all. However paradoxical it may sound, *suspense of uncertainty* endures *despite certainty* about the outcome. One may be excited as intensely about Demetrius of Syria while rereading the account of his escape from Rome, as would a person reading it for the first time. Or one may find oneself hoping, despite one's certain knowledge, that – this time – Achaeus will not fall into Bolis' ambush. Still, there is no need to reach that far. For to foreshadow signifies not to foretell, definitely and authoritatively, events to come, but to prefigure and reveal only enough to awaken the reader's expectation as to what *may occur in the future.*

The second feature is the artistic use of dramatic irony. It has been shown above that the Polybian narrator reinforces the cognitive gap between reader and participants by stating or implying that certain events will have a diametrically opposite outcome from the one the participants expect. The dramatic irony, which arises precisely from the shortsightedness of some characters, is reminiscent of their impending doom and thus intensifies all the more the suspense the reader feels as to the way they will cope with the dangers awaiting them.[20] The emphasis on the

---

20 On dramatic irony as a means of generating suspense cf. Duckworth 1933, 70–79.

knowledge the reader has and the characters lack enables, therefore, the narrator to build up an atmosphere of foreboding and anticipation that elevates the reader's anxiety to still greater heights.

The issue of illusory expectations, under its various manifestations, matters a lot to our historian. This is evident if we recollect the great prominence given to it in the narrative. To begin with, it is explored and developed in the relationship between project and reality, particularly in the contrast between plan and execution.[21] In fact, scattered through the *Histories* are plans which seemed feasible or promising to their inventors, while they were actually quite impossible and disastrous. Hermeias' treacherous plan against Antiochus swiftly led to his own fall, when it was perceived and conveyed by one of his foes (5.55.4–56). In a similar vein, Apelles and Leontius unscrupulously struggled to intimidate and isolate Aratus in the hope of enhancing their influence upon Philip only to find the tables turned on them afterwards (5.16.9–10). In both cases Polybius attempts to justify for the reader the participants' destruction by calling attention to the fact that they engaged in deceitful and self-aggrandizing behaviors.

The narrator invites the narratee to view these stories from a moralizing perspective. But of course, there are also those who, without having violated or overstepped moral boundaries, yet meet with failure. Antiochus, ever worried about Prusias' willingness to take the side of the Romans, 'and calculating that the only way to prevent the enemy's army from crossing and generally avert the war from Asia was to obtain definite command of the sea' (21.11.13), decided to provoke a naval battle, but his hopes did not materialize; instead he brought defeat upon himself.

Certainly, the dissonance between intentions and actuality conforms to our pattern and provides further illustrations of human limitations. But expectations are most commonly thwarted when the participants endeavor to predict the actions and reactions of their opponents. Philip's plan to besiege Psophis came as a complete surprise to its defenders, because, Polybius says, 'all in the town had been convinced that the enemy would neither venture to attempt to assault by storm such a strong city, nor would open a lengthy siege at this disadvantageous season of the year' (4.71.5).

---

21 In Thucydides, too, the events often seem to have their own existence, irrespective of the wishes or expectations of the participants; on this see Stahl 2003, *passim*.

Surprise has an important role in the account of Hannibal's march to Italy. Through their unfolding, the events of the first few years of the Second Punic War decisively belie Roman expectations about the Carthaginians. When P. Scipio reached the first mouth of Rhone, he was convinced that Hannibal 'was still at a distance of many days' march owing to the difficulty of the country and the numbers of Celtic tribes between them' (3.41.6). Later, he did not expect that Hannibal would be daring enough to cross the Alps, 'and if he ventured on it he thought that certain destruction awaited him' (3.61.5). But Scipio underestimated his rival. Hannibal, to the great surprise of the Romans, 'was in Italy with his army and already laying siege to some cities' (3.61.9). Despite all hindrances, moral and physical, he held his panic-stricken men together and compelled them to do more than their powers allowed. Indeed, when action was undertaken, it resulted in some astounding accomplishments, such as the raft of elephants across the Rhone (3.46) and the crossing of the impassable marshes that cost Hannibal himself the loss of one eye (3.79). Nevertheless, although surprise and paradox prevail throughout the narrative of this portion of the work, the military achievements of the Carthaginians do not remain inexplicable. Rather, the account moves beyond the idea of 'Fortune' and traces the Carthaginian success to Hannibal's leadership qualities – his restless energy, his resourcefulness, his willingness to take risks, his swiftness to act and, above all, his *unpredictable* ability to come out of every setback with his fighting spirits still higher than before.

However, a prediction entails the risk of proving catastrophic even without being mistaken. Sometimes people, although perceiving the danger lurking nearby, yet resort to the wrong countermeasures and precipitate their catastrophe by trying to avert it. There is a tragic resonance in the way in which people are depicted in their grappling with the inevitable hardships of life. Mossman rightly pointed out that this issue fits comfortably within the traditions of Greek ethical thinking: 'this kind of story-pattern ... was one embedded deeply in the Greek mind, and which could be used in their different ways either by Herodotus in prose or by Sophocles in a tragedy' (Mossman 1992, 91).

In the *Histories*, perhaps the clearest demonstration of this pattern appears in the account of Agathocles' downfall in Book 15 (25–34). The initial mourning following the news of Arsinoe's murder gradually gave way to a determination to revolt against the oppressive conduct of the Ptolemaic prime minister Agathocles. 'But since the Alexandrians had no leader of any weight, through whom to vent their anger on Agathocles and Agathoclea, they kept quiet, their only remaining hope, to which they eagerly clung, being in Tlepolemus' (25.25). Popular, vigorous, over-confident and impulsive in his youth, Tlepolemus eventually became the *bête noir* of Alexandria's most powerful politician. Agathocles, in his turn, did not lose any chance to obscure his rival's reputation, accusing him of showing disaffection toward the king and of treacherously inviting Antiochus to assume the government (25.34). Polybius comments: 'All this he did with the object of working up the populace against Tlepolemus, but it had the contrary result' (25.36).

The narrative of Agathocles' downfall receives a full and dramatic development. In summary, when rumors circulated that a member of the king's personal staff had been conveying information to Tlepolemus, Agathocles became all the more suspicious and ordered Nicostratus to investigate the case and arrest the man who was implicated (27.6–7). Moeragenes, when directly questioned, denied all charges and caused the anger of his torturers, but he enjoyed ample good fortune, since at the last moment he managed to flee and stay alive. The emphasis on the narrowness of his escape reinforces the sense of surprise and especially recalls the technique of the epic *Beinahe-Episoden*.[22] Moeragenes would have had no chance, had not a servant turned up unexpectedly just as the torturers were about to begin and asked them to follow him without delay (27.10–11). A bit later, Moeragenes, much to his surprise, was left by himself (28.4). A chain of events links his escape with Agathocles' downfall. Moeragenes, naked as he was, rushed toward the Macedonians, begging them to 'avail themselves of the present opportunity, when the hatred of the populace was at its height ... and it only wanted someone to begin' (28.8–9). Thus, he set in motion a series of violent acts that eventually led to scenes of horror as the domination of Agathocles was bloodily overthrown. Still, whatever Moeragenes may have done to encourage the revolt, however determinedly, however efficiently, it was Agathocles himself who paradoxically paved the way for his own destruction. He had tried to get rid of Tlepolemus, but he did not succeed. Instead he inflamed the enmity of the Alexandrians and prompted what he feared by his attempt to avert it.

The terms employed to encapsulate the perils of expectations are most carefully chosen and especially reserved for this function. We have already seen that explicitly mentioned joy alerts the reader to the

---

22 See de Jong (1987) 2004, 68–81 on the Homeric '*if not*-situations', and Nesselrath 1992 on 'Beinahe-Episoden' in epic in general.

possibility of approaching disaster. When we encounter the adjective περιχαρής (joyful), then, it is fraught with sinister implications.[23] Εὐελπ- as a stem appears six times in the *Histories* – the adjective four times, the noun twice – on four occasions to foreshadow future frustration and distress.[24] But the word most often used to signal false perceptions is the participle πεπεισμένος (convinced). Forty-four times we find it employed when participants fail in their calculations.[25] Stronger than mere expectation, and hence richer in ironic potentialities, conviction of success, particularly when conveyed by key words, is meant to prefigure that the pendulum is likely to swing in the opposite direction from the one anticipated.

A few men, indeed, enjoy the privilege of predicting and thereby exercising control over events. Hannibal was engaged in the siege of Saguntum because of his conviction that many advantages would emerge from the city's capture (3.17.5). And it proved to be so: 'The result did not deceive his expectations, nor did he fail to accomplish his original purpose' (οὐ διεψεύσθη τοῖς λογισμοῖς οὐδ' ἀπέτυχε τῆς ἀρχικῆς προθέσεως: 17.11). Later on, in the battle that had immediately followed the preparations for crossing the Rhone, he defeated the Celts, 'all falling out favourable as he had purposed' (3.43.11). Of course, Hannibal does not stand alone. Edeco, the prince of Edetani, on learning that New Carthage has fallen to the Romans, thought it in his immediate interests to encourage the Iberians to side with Scipio Africanus, 'chiefly owing to his conviction that by this reason he would recover his wife and children and would appear to have taken the part of the Romans not under compulsion but deliberately' (10.34.3). His hopes eventually came true and his success became all the sweeter when he achieved the goal he so earnestly desired (10.35.2). In a similar way An-

---

23 For references see Eckstein 1995, 276 n. 14. In Herodotus, too, the adjective carries ominous connotations; see Chiasson 1983, 115–6.
24 Cf. Polyb. 2.27.4 (Gaius Atilius in 225, shortly before his death at Telamon); 18.22.10 (Philip V in 197, at Cynoscephalae); 21.4.11 (the Aetolians in 190, during their negotiations with the Romans); 33.3.2 (the Achaeans in 155, when elated by the news concerning the return home of the surviving exiles).
25 See, e.g., 1.82.1 (Hamilcar during the Carthaginian Mercenary War); 3.101.1 (Minucius in Apulia); 4.64.5 (the Aetolians during the Social War); 5.35.1 (Cleomenes at Alexandria); 10.39.5 (Hasdrubal during the battle of Baecula); 16.2.4 (Philip V before the battle of Chios); 23.5.14 (Deinocrates of Messenia returning to Greece). Examples can easily be multiplied; cf. also 1.43.1 and 68.7; 2.27.5; 3.43.5; 4.76.6; 5.17.5; 10.41.5; 15.25.11; 29.8.3.

tiochus, after he had executed Achaeus, continued to besiege the citadel, 'feeling convinced that some means of taking the place would be furnished him by the garrison itself and more especially by the rank and file' (8.21.8). The siege developed just as he expected, since the remaining defenders, divided into two competing factions, one under Aribazos and the other under Laodice, very soon surrendered themselves and the citadel (8.21.9). In each case, the initial adherence to, and then the divergence from, the familiar narrative pattern serve an artistic purpose and produce considerable effects. Paradox and surprise abound, as the readers' expectations are being constantly arranged and rearranged.

So Polybius communicates his belief about the way in which plans are tested against outcomes. Despite exceptions, then, it may be stated as a general truth that overconfidence, in life and literature, places one in a precarious position, not because it is wicked in itself, but because it is frequently coupled with a lack of self-awareness. It takes a relatively small step to cross from ignorant optimism to mistaken assessments and illusions, especially when successes have been attained and when the proper bounds of human expectations have been transgressed. The lesson is taught explicitly already in Book 1: in the reported events there will be found 'much to contribute to the better conduct of human life', particularly 'the precept to display Fortune, and especially when we are enjoying success' (35.1–2). Nevertheless, to recognize the moral aspect of the pattern discussed above is not to exhaust it. For it is also the pivot about which Polybius' suspense strategy revolves. Indeed, as we have seen, it is through this conscious patterning that the combination of the two, suspense of anticipation and suspense of uncertainty, is so skilfully achieved.

3. The third book

In the preceding sections, I have focused on the thematic pattern of illusory expectations, but also discussed the function of other suspense-heightening devices such as narrative retardation, misdirection of the reader, and the so-called *Beinahe-Episoden*. To be sure, however, Polybius stimulates his readers' interest in many other ways. Indeed, a glance through the pages of the third book of the *Histories*, and a cursory one, should suffice to further confirm Polybius' strengths as a narrator. In it he portrays events linked to the Hannibalic War from the siege of Saguntum in 219 to the crushing Roman defeat at Cannae in 216. For several reasons the narrative of these operations generates the impression that the elaborate and vivid account Polybius has given of them is indeed an artful creation, constructed in an awareness of what disposition or arrangement of material can be made to do.

In the first place, the narrator builds up for his narratee in the prefatory section an atmosphere of foreboding (3.1–32). In autumn 220 the Romans responded to the constant appeals for help made by the Saguntines against the growing Carthaginian pressure by sending an embassy to warn Hannibal off Saguntum. Yet Hannibal, as he was filled with hatred of the Romans engendered by his father, and as he had enjoyed unbroken success in his previous campaigns, reacted imprudently or undiplomatically and rejected all their complaints. Then, the Roman legates, seeing clearly that the road to war had been opened, proceeded to Carthage to repeat their complaints there. The interview at Carthage is not reported, perhaps because it produced no practical result, but the confident calculations of the Roman envoys are lavishly described: they hoped that, once the war became inevitable, at least they would have to fight not in Italy but 'in Spain with Saguntum for a base' (3.15.13). And this, together with the emphasis laid on the folly of their confidence, creates the necessary atmosphere for stimulating the readers' imagination.[26] The Roman expectations that the war would be kept away from Italy were overturned, however reasonable they may have seemed at first: 'For Hannibal forestalled them by taking Saguntum, and, as a consequence, the war was not waged in Spain but *at the very gates of Rome* and through the whole of Italy' (3.16.6). At this point, the narrator's chief concern is to ensure our emotional involvement in the coming war and its serious consequences for Rome.

As we soon realize, one reason for this manipulation of the readers' attention is that unless their interest is stimulated, they may consider that the effort required to absorb the mass of information that lies ahead is

---

26 Walbank 1957, 324 argues that 'the dilatory Roman policy after Hannibal's attack on Saguntum is hardly reconcilable with a firm decision to fight, still less with a decision to fight in Spain from Saguntum. *The real purpose of Polybius' remark is to bridge the gap to the second Illyrian War,* which is here introduced as an operation to "close the back door" before a long struggle.' The narrator, though, probably had more than connectedness in mind when he laid such emphasis upon the unfounded optimism of the Romans. In any case, I will suggest that the narrative of the Hannibalic War works in a rather more subtle way than has generally been allowed.

not worth making. On a rough count, rather over two-thirds of the prefatory section of the Hannibalic War does not contain action, one third being devoted to an examination of the causes and preliminaries of the war (3.6–15), one-third to a systematic survey of the treaties between Rome and Carthage (3.22–30), and about 5 percent to criticism of earlier and contemporary historians. In the remaining quarter (3.16–21), some 7 pages out of 31, the static state of the preliminary exposition is destabilized, particularly in ch. 17 with the account of the fall of Saguntum, an event invested with essentially propulsive value. But even here the tempo of the narrative is quite slow, as the narrator switches between the successful operations of Hannibal in 219 and the unsuccessful ones of Demetrius during the Second Illyrian War in an instance of small-scale interlace technique.

The account of the Second Illyrian War begins with ch. 16, where we hear in passing that Demetrius of Pharos is challenging Rome by seizing and destroying a number of Illyrian towns placed under her protectorate. Demetrius' expedition does not leave the Romans unconcerned; rather, it provokes an immediate response, one rapidly turning into alarm and involving the senatorial decision to dispatch forces to Illyria under the command of L. Aemilius Paullus. In ch. 17 we return to Hannibal's operations in Spain and accompany him on his march against Saguntum. Unlike the activity they display in Illyria, the Romans do nothing in response to Carthaginian attacks; on the contrary, they allow the blockade and conquest of Saguntum to run its course, endowing Hannibal with enough wealth and energy to keep fighting on the most favorable conditions –a foreboding reminder, albeit an indirect one, that the fall of Saguntum may be merely a prelude to the future awaiting Rome during the ensuing war. In chs. 18–19 Polybius resumes the thread of the narrative interrupted at 3.17, and describes the Roman expedition in Illyria, which ends in a heavy defeat for the Illyrians at Pharos. Rome joyfully receives the news of victory, and Aemilius enters the city in triumph (3.19.12–13). After ch. 20 the focus of the narrative shifts back to Saguntum and the repercussions of its capture at Rome.

This constant switching of the narrative between the operations of the Carthaginians in Spain and Aemilius' campaign in Illyria is an ideal technique enabling the narrator to deal with the problem of presenting simultaneous events, yet interestingly there is every reason to suspect that it is employed for purposes beyond conveying the impression of synchronicity.[27] Indeed, what is most remarkable about this portion of the work is the way in which the events derive their meaning from being juxtaposed to other ones. The Romans' reluctance to take strong action against Hannibal at Saguntum contrasts with the feverish activity with which they responded to Demetrius' challenge in Illyria. Looked at in parallel, the two accounts draw attention to the Romans' miscalculation and indirectly allow the reader to form an opinion about the narrated events: had they devoted their energy to Saguntum, they could have stopped Hannibal's march through Spain, and they would have been able to inflict damage on the Carthaginians rather than suffer it themselves.

An ironic perspective, however, also emerges out of the placement of the celebration of Aemilius' Illyrian triumph immediately before the reception of the news of the fall of Saguntum in Rome. The reader is alerted to this irony by his knowledge of what is to come, even if he has not yet been told precisely how grave the danger menacing Rome will be. In many ways the direct juxtaposition of the two accounts is powerful, and cannot be accidental: 'Aemilius, the Roman Consul, took Pharos at once by assault and … returned to Rome late in summer and entered the city in triumph, acclaimed by all, for he seemed to have managed matters not only with ability, but with very high courage. The Romans, when the news of the fall of Saguntum reached them …' (3.19.12–20.1). The abrupt transition serves to replicate some of the emotions experienced at the time of the events, namely the mingled sense of surprise and anxiety evoked by the distressing reports that arrived from Spain. Obviously, there was no room for delay: 'The Romans, on hearing of the calamity that had befallen Saguntum, at once appointed ambassadors and sent them post-haste to Carthage, giving the Carthaginians the options of two alternatives, the one of which, if they accepted it, entailed disgrace and damage, while the other would give rise to extreme trouble and peril' (3.20.6). All parts of this sentence converge to underscore the irony of the situation. The disgraceful disaster to which the envoys allude will prove to be a sinister omen of what is to befall the Romans themselves (at Trebia, at Trasimene, at Cannae) during Hannibal's march to Italy. The scene shifts back to Rome many

---

27 On the same technique in Thucydides see Rengakos 2006a, 289–90 and nn. 36–38, who discusses the constant switching of the narrative in Book 4 between the Athenian expedition against Boeotia and Brasidas' campaign in Northern Greece, with earlier bibliography.

times after Aemilius' return, not, however, to represent victorious celebrations and triumphs, but to describe the radical change which is brought about in the atmosphere prevailing in the city due to the continuous defeats.[28] In retrospect the misassessment of Carthaginian power that has been repeatedly made earlier in the war is recognized as particularly costly.

To extend the analysis to the second, and main, section of the book (3.33–118), one could summarize by saying that its techniques do not differ significantly from the ones already encountered. Once again we have a persistent interest in portraying events from both sides. The two threads of the narrative, the operations of the Carthaginian army and the response of the Romans to these, become interwoven with, and then disentangled from, one another again and again, thus establishing thematic and structural links between them.[29] Surely it is mainly the Carthaginians who receive the most extensive treatment, for Polybius wants the reader to adopt their perspective, at least up to their arrival in Italy (3.57.1).[30] Through this strategy the reader is invited to share along with the Carthaginians their sense of discovery, their puzzlement, and their wonderment as they accomplish their almost impossible journey across the Alps. In 3.54.1–3, for example, where Hannibal is said to revive the spirits of his troops encamped on the summit by pointing out to them the rich and beautiful plains of Italy below, the images evoked by the description of the view are so vivid and attractive that they convert the reader into a spectator gazing out upon Italy from the Alps. This is a delightful scene, all the more effective because of the fertility of the Po valley we have already heard about several times before,[31] and thereby one which enhances the sense of expectancy and anticipation about the pleasures the foreign place promises and the dangers that these pleasures may bring in their wake.

---

28 See, e.g., 3.61.7–9 (alarm caused by the news of Hannibal's arrival in Italy); 85.7–10 (dismay following the reports of the losses at Trasimene); 112.6–9 (anxiety and fear before the battle of Cannae); 118.5–6 (despair after the defeat at Cannae).

29 See for instance 3.61.1–6, where both Hannibal and Scipio are represented as being struck with amazement at one another's accomplishments. Walbank 1957, 395–6 discusses the parallelism, and rightly stresses that it forms part of the rhetorical elaboration.

30 Note the phrasing: 'Now that I have brought my narrative and the war and the two generals in Italy …'.

31 Cf. (all from Book 3) 34.2; 34.8; 44.8; 48.11.

As the narrative progresses, however, and the two sides get nearer and nearer to each other, Polybius gradually decreases the size of the passages focalized around the Carthaginians,[32] for this portion of the book concentrates more on the close interdependence between the actions of the adversaries than on the reactions of each group separately. The perceptibly accelerated tempo of the narrative also serves to impress upon the reader the rapidity of Hannibal's advance through northern Italy. The Roman armies, almost isolated from allies and humiliated on the field, prove incapable of defending Italian territory from destruction and pillage. So the eyes of all, Polybius tells us, 'were now turned to the Carthaginians, who *had great hopes of even taking Rome itself* at the first assault' (3.118.3–4). The reader may by now be aware that great expectations leave little room for reason or prediction, still less for the control over future events, yet the narrator prefers to make the message more transparent by foretelling the final outcome of the war:

> For though the Romans were now incontestably beaten and their military reputation shattered, yet by the peculiar virtues of their constitution and by wise counsel they not only recovered their supremacy in Italy and afterwards defeated the Carthaginians, but in a few years made themselves masters of the whole world (3.118.8–9).

Thus the concluding chapter explicitly establishes that the disaster at Cannae, despite seeming insurmountable, is not the end of the war, but only a hindrance on the road to Rome's ultimate victory. Its optimistic tone, however, is already implicitly present, I believe, in the earlier portions of this book, where the account of the successful activities of the Romans under Gn. Scipio in Spain (chs. 76 and 95–99) figures as a thematic counterpoint to the main narrative of their sufferings in Italy. We are now a long way removed from Polybius' supposedly poor artistry. In fact, we have come full circle: the narrative that began by being focused on Roman illusory expectations ends by being focused on Carthaginian ones – perhaps an anti-climax, but one which reminds us that we are dealing with a carefully developed structure.

---

32 When he turns to narrating preparations and battles, Polybius alternates between the Carthaginians and Romans more quickly: contrast, e.g., 66.9-68-72 (events leading up to the battle of the Trebia) and 101–2 (events around Gerunium) with 49.5–56.4, where the treatment of Hannibal's crossing of the Alps consists of six full chapters. See Marincola (1997) 2001, 126 n. 60 for examples of the same technique from Book 1.

Now these scene changes, so frequent in the third book, far from being limited to the relatively short narratives in which they most often appear, are skillfully transferred to the larger architecture of the work as well. This is most evident in the narrative of the later books, where Polybius follows what he calls his normal procedure, that is, a strict scheme of arrangement: for each Olympiad the narration commences with events in Italy, then continues with Sicily, Spain, Africa, Greece and Macedonia, and concludes with Asia and Egypt.[33] We immediately recognize, then, another example of a familiar technique now operating on the macrostructural level, without any concomitant disruption in the development of the main theme, since the fact that Polybius moves from one field to another within each Olympiad year in order to narrate in parallel events occurring in the same time but in different spaces automatically and regularly lends to his vast work the variety and tension required to compensate for the reader's tremendous effort of reading it through to its end.

4. Empathy

The analysis in the preceding pages has, I hope, shown that this approach to Polybius, while being motivated by contemporary literary theory, is nevertheless one deeply grounded in the text. It broadens our understanding of the complexity and nuances of Polybius' presentation and accounts for features that are likely to be overlooked or underestimated by scholars. One last point deserves attention, for it constitutes a necessary component of any suspenseful narrative. Indeed, independently of the means by which it is aroused, suspense almost universally entails the reader's identification or empathy with one or more of the characters of the story. It need not be the protagonist, since we know that suspense can be experienced 'in reaction to whole narratives, or in response to discrete scenes or sequences within a larger narrative whose overall structure may or may not be suspenseful' (Carroll 1996, 74). The reader can be concerned about characters whose peripeties are tangential to the main narrative. Nor need the characters be positive in order to win the reader's empathy. It has been brought out that stories involving a potential negative outcome for negative characters develop in a crescendo of suspense too, but that the suspense is not 'as

---

33 On these synchronisms see Walbank 1975, 197–212.

strong as for a positive character in the same circumstances' (Brewer 1996, 115). Interestingly, we can observe Polybius analyzing this mechanism of identification with a negative or peripheral hero. The crucial passage is 27.9–10 and particularly 27.9.2–6, where he explains metaphorically the popular reaction to Perseus' victory against the Romans at Callicinus, and it is worth quoting in full:

> The phenomenon was very like what happens in boxing contests at the games. For there, when a humble and much inferior combatant is matched against a celebrated and seemingly invincible athlete, the sympathy of the crowd is at once given to the inferior man. They cheer him on, and back him up enthusiastically; and if he manages to touch his opponent's face, and gets in a blow that leaves any mark, there is at once again the greatest excitement among them all. They sometimes even try to make fun of the other man, not out of any dislike for him or disapproval but from a curious sort of sympathy and a natural instinct to favour the weaker. If, however, one calls their attention at the right time to their error, they very soon change their minds and correct it (27.9.2–6).

From the general, Polybius moves to the specific. He furnishes a further illustration of the emotional response elicited during a fight by appending to this 'preface' the story of Aristonicus, a boxer from Egypt who ventured to challenge the invincible Cleitomachus at Olympia. Indeed, once the fight started, Aristonicus managed to strike one or two quite hard blows against his rival. The viewers, on seeing that someone at last appeared to be a capable adversary of their champion, cheered on Aristonicus and in a delirium of excitement backed him up all they could. But then Cleitomachus turned to the crowd and reminded them that he himself was fighting for the glory of Greece, whereas Aristonicus for that of King Ptolemy (9.7–12). This was enough to convince them to change their minds, and such was the revulsion of feeling they had undergone that, as they say, 'Aristonicus was beaten rather by the crowd than by Cleitomachus' (9.13). The metaphor is especially suggestive, with Perseus being compared to the weaker athlete who gains a temporary advantage over his opponent.

Mirroring the main narrative of the war between Perseus and Romans, the story of the two boxers invites interpretation as a thematic *mise en abyme*. Perseus, too, will soon be defeated, this time permanently. Once again we acknowledge Polybius' subtlety in foreshadowing the future action; once again, indeed, we have something of the same effect as in the account of Achaeus' capture, for we can see how the narrator creates an expectation in us that Perseus' success augurs him no good, how his foreboding becomes all the more tragic as it is provided at a time of great elevation, and how this story too leaves us in a state of suspense in which fear and hope are intricately intertwined. Perhaps this sophisticated interplay of sentiments pervading his work is what, more than anything, secures Polybius' place as a master of suspense.

Seeing through Caesar's Eyes: Focalisation and Interpretation

Christopher Pelling

1. One-man literature and one-man rule

Julius Caesar does things to a narrator: he 'grabs the writer, and forces one to linger, however eager one may be to press on' (Vell. 2.41.1). And Julius Caesar tends to do interesting things to a narrative too, especially if one thinks generically. If it is legitimate by the time of Caesar-narratives – and it surely is[1] – to think of some generic difference between history and biography, that difference is precisely what Caesar blurs. If one is writing biography, it becomes something close to history, as the single individual comes to dominate everything; if one is writing history, it is the other way round, and Rome's story becomes Caesar's story. The path towards one-man rule is mapped by Caesar's lifespan: not always simply, for the great insight conveyed by Eduard Meyer's title is intermittently intimated by ancient authors, that it was Pompey's *Principat* as much as Caesar's *Monarchie* that was the true precursor of the Augustan style;[2] but, one way or another, Caesar's experience can be-

---

1 It is hard to think that Nepos and Plutarch could draw the distinction so snappily unless it were familiar: cf. Nepos *Pel.* 1.1, *Pelopidas Thebanus, magis historicis quam uulgo notus, cuius de uirtutibus dubito quem ad modum exponam, quod uereor, si res explicare incipiam, ne non uitam eius enarrare, sed historiam uidear scribere* ('Pelopidas of Thebes, better known to historical experts than to the general public. I am not sure of the best way to set out his merits, because I am afraid that if I begin to set out the facts in detail I may seem not to be telling his life but to be writing history'); Nepos, *praef.* 1, on *hoc genus scripturae*, 'this kind of writing'; and among various Plutarch passages esp. *Alex.* 1.2 ('it is not history we are writing, but lives'), *Nic.* 1.5, *Galba* 2.5. To say this is not to imply that generic boundaries were firmly established or non-negotiable (this paper will itself be arguing the contrary); nor to deny that biography could also be thought of as *a variety* of historical inquiry. See Duff 1999, 15–30.

2 Meyer 1922: that title – *Caesars Monarchie und das Principat des Pompejus* – brilliantly captures the way that Pompey's position in the late fifties, ruling provinces through legates while remaining near Rome, operating with a measure of

come the vehicle for seeing and conveying the most crucial transition of Rome's history. These generic aspects I have discussed elsewhere in the cases of particular Greek narratives, those of Cassius Dio, Appian, and Plutarch.[3] I suggested that Dio maps out the way that Caesar comes to control the narrative and very nearly turns Rome's story into his own – very nearly, but not quite, as the time for one-man rule has not yet come, and the last stages of Dio's Caesar-narrative subtly tracks Caesar's mistakes as preparation for the way that Augustus will do things differently. With Appian and Plutarch it is more a question of that generic tension between biography and history. Appian's narrative in *BC* 2 begins as multi-textured, with many principal actors, both individuals and collectives: but it veers closer and closer to biography, as Caesar comes to call the tune. With Plutarch it is the other way round: *Alexander–Caesar* is the pair where he draws the clearest distinction between the genres of history and biography (*Alex.* 1.2),[4] as it is indeed this pair where the risk of writing full-scale history is at its greatest; and, even more in *Caesar* than in *Alexander*, it is a risk Plutarch willingly takes, and that *Life* becomes perhaps the most 'historical' of all his production in its interpretative and thematic texture. It is no coincidence (or so I argued) that this is one of those Plutarchan pairs which dispenses with the final synkritic epilogue, as by now the story has encompassed more than just the two principals; and it is no coincidence either that Appian's narrative *does* end with an Alexander-Caesar comparison, as if Appian were filling the gap which Plutarch has left. Appian has almost become a Plutarchan biographer, and Plutarch has almost become an Appianic historian: almost, but not quite.

---

constitutional propriety (even if the constitutional position was unprecedented as in 52) but more importantly through a less formal authority, was closer than Caesar's cruder dictatorship to Augustus' 'principate'. Plutarch in particular has various hints of Pompey as the precursor of one-man rule, especially the jingle at Plut. *C.min.* 45.7, where in 54 Cato attacks Pompey for 'using anarchy to create his own monarchy'. For the moment, people may be talking about Pompey as the 'doctor' to cure the anarchy (Plut. *Caes.* 28.6, *Pomp.* 55.4, App. *BC* 2.20.72); then the apparent doctor will be Caesar (*Comparison of Dion and Brutus* 2.2); but in fact fortune is carrying Rome to a different one-man rule, and the answer will be Augustus (*Antony* 56.6).

3   Pelling 2006a.
4   Cf. n. 1 above.

Here I shall try to trace the way in which narrative focalisation[5] interacts with those generic suggestions, and reinforces them as a tool of historical interpretation: for, in history as in life, perceptions do not merely reflect reality (more or less well), they also drive it, and both his own perceptions and those of others can be vital in explaining a great man's failure or success. I have already used the word 'control', and that can be a matter of the principal figures' intellectual as well as physical control over events: do their perceptions in fact see everything as it is, and do they drive matters in the way that the actors aspire to do, and often assume they can? And how do those questions go with that issue of narrative 'control' that I have phrased in generic terms, the degree to which the author controls the story by ordering it around the actions and perceptions of the principal character?

If we start with that generic question, we might make some pretty clear guesses about what we will find. We might expect the biographers – Suetonius as well as Plutarch, for let us bring Latin authors too into the analysis[6] – to focalise more through their principals than the historians; Velleius might be expected to be an interesting test-case, a historian, but one who has experienced that daunting feeling of Caesar's grasping hand on his shoulder, and whose history can be separated by his great modern commentator into the 'Caesarian and Augustan' as well as the 'Tiberian' narrative,[7] assimilating the late Republican Big Man to the domination, at least the narrative domination, exercised by his imperial successors. We might also expect those questions of intellectual and

---

[5] Davidson 1991, 10–11, followed by Rood 1998, 296, is reluctant to apply the term 'focalisation' to characters in historical narratives, on the grounds that a term coined for the analysis of fictional texts should not be applied to 'a discourse of the real' (Hayden White's term). He prefers 'gaze'. If I stay with 'focalisation', this is partly for reasons which are the converse of Davidson's, reminding us that the 'Caesar' or 'Cato' in point is a construct of Dio or Appian or Plutarch, not the historical character; and partly because 'gaze' makes the perceptual register too distinctively visual, when other forms of cognition and response are also important. See further n. 11 below.

[6] The one Latin author who most clearly invites inclusion is Caesar himself; but his narrative raises such interesting and distinctive narratological issues, especially the relation between the narrator Caesar and the character Caesar, that it requires separate treatment.

[7] This is again a reference to titles: Woodman 1977 and 1983, entitling his two volumes of commentary *The Tiberian Narrative* and *The Caesarian and Augustan Narrative*. In Pelling forthcoming I discuss how close to 'biography' Velleius' narrative really comes.

physical control to be reflected in the focalisation: we might find something similar to Tim Rood's analysis of Thucydides 6–7, where Nicias' ineffectual leadership is marked by a lack of consistent Nicias-focalisation, contrasting with the strong focalisation we find earlier and later when other generals are guiding events.[8] In these texts we might expect Caesar's physical control of events to be similarly strongly marked – though, if there is anything in the 'almost-but-not-quite' argument about generic drift, we might not be surprised if that viewpoint is never totally dominant in a work that remains history rather than biography. And within the biographies themselves we might expect the same matters to be focalised differently in different *Lives*, through Pompey's and Caesar's and Brutus' perceptions respectively.

Sometimes those expectations are more or less met. In Suetonius, for instance, the dominance of the Caesar viewpoint is more or less total. In Velleius the picture is a little more complex, with the strong Caesar-centre of the introductory panel 2.41–3 giving way to a notable absence of Caesar-focalisation through the narrative itself. In Plutarch the narrative of the assassination is told differently in *Brutus* and in *Caesar* itself, with *Brutus* seeing things much more from the conspirators' side, while *Caesar* starts from the dictator himself and the actions and mindset that caused such offence: in that *Life* the conspirators come into the narrative only at a point when Caesar's own behaviour seems already to have made his downfall inevitable.

Still, even in these cases there are some lessons to learn, as we shall see.

2. Velleius

In Velleius one reason for the lack of Caesar-focalisation even within a 'Caesarian' narrative may be his desire to keep it generically 'history' rather than 'biography'; but there are other features too of Velleius' style that may be playing a part, his tendency for example to favour impersonal or supra-personal subjects – *fortuna, fatorum uis, ducis causa* – or to construct his sentences with passive verbs.[9] Neither feature precludes secondary focalisation, but neither promotes it, and where we do get

---

8   Rood 1998, ch. 8.
9   At 2.46, for instance, more of the narrative of the fifties is focalised through Crassus than through Caesar. Caesar-focalisation is sparse even in the treatment of the Gallic wars, 2.47.

Caesar-focalisation it can be interestingly problematic. Take for instance 2.50.1–2:

> *At Caesar Domitio legionibusque Corfini quae una cum eo fuerant, potitus, duce aliisque, qui uoluerant abire ad Pompeium, sine dilatione dimissis, persecutus Brundusium <u>ita ut appareret</u> malle integris rebus et condicionibus finire bellum quam opprimere fugientes, cum transgressos reperisset consules, in urbem reuertit redditaque ratione consiliorum suorum in senatu et in contione ac <u>miserrimae necessitudinis</u>, cum alienis armis ad arma compulsus esset, Hispanias petere decreuit.*

> Once Caesar had gained control of Domitius and the legions which had been with him at Corfinium, he immediately released the leader and the others who had wanted to go over to Pompey, and he gave pursuit to Brundisium *in such a way as to convey* that he preferred to complete the war when all was still intact and by negotiation rather than to catch those who were fleeing; when he discovered the consuls had crossed, he returned to Rome and gave an explanation, both in the senate and before the people, of his thinking and of *the terrible compulsion* whereby other people's arms had driven him to arms himself; then he decided to depart for Spain.

Ita ut appareret: is that a consecutive ('with the result that....') or a final clause ('in order to')? At first sight the *ita* might suggest that the construction is consecutive (*OLD* s.v. *ita* 18), but that is not decisive: *OLD* also correctly classifies one use of *ita* as 'in such a way as to make sure that' (16a). But, if it is final, should we then take it as 'to give an appearance that...' or 'to make it clear that...', alternative renderings which give a very different impression of Caesar's degree of disingenuousness? And how exactly is that *miserrimae necessitudinis* focalised? Is this talk of a 'terrible compulsion' simply Caesar's presentation in his speech, or is Velleius adding his own authority to it? The earlier narrative has left pointers in both directions, with indications both of Caesar's clear-sighted unscrupulousness and of the moderate line that he had been taking in his negotiations.[10] So, even when Caesar's actions and motives are central to Velleius' narrative, it is surprisingly difficult to be sure exactly how he is thinking, as difficult doubtless as observers and participants found it at the time.

There may be several ways of interpreting such elusive focalisation. It surely goes closely with Velleius' taste for *primary* focalisation, with a strong moral commentary injected by the narrator's own engaged, often disapproving texturing of his story: it may even be that this distinctive style of focalisation helps to focus that commentary on the deficiencies *of*

---

10 I discuss these syntactic problems in more detail in Pelling forthcoming.

the situation, while leaving it tactfully unclear how far the moralising extends to Caesar himself. It may also, though, reflect the way that by this stage we do not *need* any strong Caesar-focalisation, for that initial panel at 2.41–3 has already made it clear what we are to expect from a phenomenon like Caesar, strong-minded and resolute and ambitious, ruthlessly driving towards a self-interested end. We may not know quite what he is thinking or quite how disingenuous he is being, but that matters less than where he is driving; and we are clear enough about that. This is not the only time that we will see how, once an author has made a determined character clear, focalisation is a relatively crude form of using that character's mindset to make events intelligible. The mindset can be taken for granted. And that taste for impersonal subjects tells a story too, for the narrative can be presented as driven equally by Caesar's personality and by those forces of fate and fortune. The one may even collapse into the other, as the momentum injected by Caesar can seem itself to have something preternatural about it. Caesar is, indeed, a phenomenon, a force of nature itself. Focalisation and interpretation go very closely together indeed.

3. Plutarch (i)

The contrast between Plutarch's *Brutus* and *Caesar* can teach a lesson too, for in *Caesar*, particularly, it may enable us to disaggregate several of the aspects that it normally makes sense to take together under focalisation[11] – cognition (seeing through Caesar's eyes), motivation (seeing

---

11 Or so I assume, given that one's emotional perspective not merely builds on one's perceptions, it also conditions what one notices and how one notices it. Hence emotional perspectives (what Chatman 1986, 197–8 included within narratorial 'slant', which may or may not be 'filtered' through a character) are thoroughly relevant to 'how one sees'. On the normal inextricability of emotion, ideology and focalisation see Rimmon-Kenan (1983) 2002, 80–2, and in a classical context especially Fowler 1990, though he is treating much more intricate issues (and I find it hard to agree with him that 'deviant' is the right word for the phenomenon he describes: in many of his cases of embedded focalisation 'complex', 'polyvalent', or 'blurred' would be better). Davidson 1991, 18–20 also emphasises the emotional corollaries of cognition in discussing the 'gaze' in Polybius (see above, n. 5). In this broad use I am closer to Bal, who talks e.g. of 'interpretative focalization' ((1985) 1997, 108), than to Genette (1972) 1980, despite the other difficulties in Bal's terminology (cf. e.g. Nelles 1990, Rood 1998, 294–6). I therefore put the point here in terms of disaggregating different aspects of focalisation. Those who prefer to define fo-

what Caesar is up to), emotion (seeing how Caesar reacts). Here the focalisation rests very much on cognition: Caesar can see the forces at play. These forces are initially the ones that give Caesar his strength, but now they are turning against him: that suits the way that this *Life* starts from the dictator's side. In 47 BCE Caesar returns to Rome:

> Καὶ κακῶς ἤκουσεν, ὅτι τῶν στρατιωτῶν στασιασάντων καὶ δύο στρατηγικοὺς ἄνδρας ἀνελόντων, Κοσκώνιον καὶ Γάλβαν, ἐπετίμησε μὲν αὐτοῖς τοσοῦτον ὅσον ἀντὶ στρατιωτῶν πολίτας προσαγορεῦσαι, χιλίας δὲ διένειμεν ἑκάστῳ δραχμὰς καὶ χώραν τῆς Ἰταλίας ἀπεκλήρωσε πολλήν. ἦν δ' αὐτοῦ διαβολὴ καὶ ἡ Δολοβέλλα μανία, καὶ ἡ Ματίου φιλαργυρία, καὶ μεθύων Ἀντώνιος καὶ Κορφίνιος τὴν Πομπηΐου σκευωρούμενος οἰκίαν καὶ μετοικοδομῶν, ὡς ἱκανὴν οὐκ οὖσαν. ἐπὶ τούτοις γὰρ ἐδυσφόρουν Ῥωμαῖοι· Καῖσαρ δὲ διὰ τὴν ὑπόθεσιν τῆς πολιτείας οὐκ ἀγνοῶν οὐδὲ βουλόμενος ἠναγκάζετο χρῆσθαι τοῖς ὑπουργοῦσι.

> He was met by popular disapproval. That was partly because some of his soldiers had mutinied and killed two former praetors, Cosconius and Galba, but Caesar had ventured no harsher punishment than to call the men 'citizens' instead of 'soldiers': he had then given each of them a thousand drachmas, as well as parcelling out a large part of the Italian countryside in land-grants. Dolabella's madness also started tongues wagging against Caesar, and so did Matius' avarice; so too did Antony's drunken excesses, and Corfinius' ransacking and rebuilding of Pompey's private house, as if it was not big enough already. The Romans did not like all this. Caesar himself knew what was going on, and it was against his will. But he had no choice. His political strategy forced him to make use of the men who were willing to be his agents.

> (Plut. *Caes.* 51)

Note the double focalisation, and both aspects matter. This is the reaction of 'the Romans' – it is 'popular disapproval', and there were 'tongues wagging against Caesar'. But Caesar is no fool: he notices that reaction, *and yet* he still has to continue making use of these men, because of 'his political strategy'. That διὰ τὴν ὑπόθεσιν τῆς πολιτείας is a most interesting phrase. This ὑπόθεσις is here created by an underlying set of political conditions, so it does relate to the external situation: but it is also an 'underlying supposition', something that requires

---

calisation in strictly cognitive terms can readily rephrase it to say that focalisation does not here go as closely as we would normally expect with other forms of entering others' minds. I have also preferred to keep talk of 'primary' and 'secondary' focalisers, largely because of the clarity which I hope it will give when I go on to discuss 'tertiary' focalisation (below, pp. 515–6, 523). Those who wish may also rephrase the primary–secondary distinction in terms of external and internal focalisers.

somebody to be performing the mental process of premiss-and-inference, someone to be ὁ ὑποτιθείς.[12] That word πολιτεία too embraces both the nature of the state and the 'political line' that Caesar is taking.[13] Political realities are portrayed through Caesar's alertness to them.

In *Caesar* it is some time later that the conspirators themselves become important players (62), but then too the focus rests on the central figure's cognition, what Caesar sees and understands of their motives and ambitions, including what he gets wrong (his over-readiness to trust Brutus, 62.6). The main point, though, is that Caesar is alert to the conspiracy, and still does not take many pains to protect himself, refusing a bodyguard (57.7), willingly going to the senate-house despite all those warning dreams of Calpurnia (though that decision too is implicitly a point of cognition, as Caesar is brought to realise how politically disastrous it would be if he were to refuse to come, 64.2–6). What does that tell us, not merely of the cognition, but also of the mindset? Is Caesar so arrogant by now that he thinks he is somehow invulnerable, despite all the signs of danger? Does he overrate his capacity to win popularity by the same old tricks that once served him so well, colonies and banquets and corn-doles (57.8)? Is he creditably philosophical, a model to us all of the insight that it is better to suffer death once than to spend one's whole life nervously anticipating it (57.7)? Or is he simply tired, willingly or half-willingly baring his neck to those who want to kill him (a gesture that at 60.6 he actually performs, theatrically enacting his readiness to die)? We are not told; just as so often in that *Life* we are

---

12 Compare for instance *Brut.* 4.2, where Brutus thinks τὴν Πομπηίου ὑπόθεσιν better than that of Caesar: that is, the sets of assumptions that Pompey and Caesar are bringing to the war, pretty well each man's 'cause' (Scott-Kilvert): cf. *Cic.* 37.3. The Gracchi have the fairest possible ὑπόθεσις for their political programme (πολιτεία, *Ag.–Cl.* 2.7 and *Comp. Ag. Cl. Gracch.* 5.6), i.e. the principles on which that programme is based: cf. *Dem.* 12.7, *Arat.* 43.2. At *Lyc.* 31.2 Plato takes as τῆς πολιτείας ὑπόθεσιν the assumption that the well-being of a state or individual depends on virtue and internal harmony, and is followed in this by Diogenes and Zeno: that blurs between 'axioms for his polity' or 'political thinking' and 'axioms for his *Republic*', but again implies the particular thinker to posit those axioms. But such a 'principle' can carry an emphasis on the external element too: at *Arist.* 25.2 the ὑπόθεσις of the state, the principle generated by Athens' needs, requires Aristides to lay aside his high standards.

13 There are plenty of examples of both uses in Plutarch. For 'political line' cf. *Ag –Cl.* 2.7, *Dem.* 12.7, and *Arat.* 43.2, all cited in last note; for 'the state' or 'the constitution', e.g. *Lyc.* 5.11, 29.4, *Cic.* 10.2, *Praec. reip. ger.* 802c.

told little about motives or emotions, but in the earlier narrative the inference is usually more straightforward and Velleius-like, as the reader *knows* that so ambitious a man has his eyes on final dominant power. Here too there is a little on motives – his 'lust for kingship' in the context of the Lupercalia, 60.1 – but not very much. So the cognitive focalisation raises as many questions about Caesar's mentality as it answers, and the reader is left wondering exactly what is going on, finding Caesar as fascinating and as impenetrable as people found him at the time.

Still, at the end the mindset does not matter. It is the power and the position that matters, just once again as was the case at the time; and the reader is left wondering if our emotional response to that position is or should be the same as the conspirators' response, especially as a different, more supernatural sort of 'force' is already beginning to make its presence felt, guiding both the assassination – 'some *daimon*' seems to be directing the location of Caesar's fall, at the foot of Pompey's statue (66.1) – and then the vengeance for it that the conspirators will suffer. That is the note on which the *Life* ends, in that marvellous chapter on the *daimon* that appears to Brutus at Philippi (69).

4. Cassius Dio

If Plutarch, at least Plutarch's *Caesar*, is parsimonious with motive-statements, Dio teems with them. He will speculate about anyone's mindset, Pompey, Crassus, Caesar, Cicero, plebs, soldiers – even, on one wonderful occasion, not merely the emotions of those who pitied the elephants in the arena, but also those that the onlookers sense in the elephants themselves, so the animals are at least tertiary focalisers (39.38). Motivation is indeed Dio's prime technique for interpretation: and interpretation, often highly intelligent interpretation, is what Dio does – sometimes, as we will see, perhaps too highly intelligent for Dio's own good. That penchant is particularly clear in Dio's adaptation of the Gallic war-narrative, where it is possible to trace an extremely close dependence on Caesar's *Bellum Gallicum*, but with two pervasive types of expansion, first the injection of stereotypes of battle-behaviour (how the Gauls or the Germans do things), and secondly a confident reading of the military mind: such readings normally cover Caesar's own intentions but sometimes those of his lieutenants or antagonists.[14]

---

14 On these expansions see Pelling 1981.

The first campaign against the Helvetii and Ariovistus is a good example (Dio 38.31–5): among Dio's additions are the notes that (apparently, though there is a textual difficulty) 'war and success' were what Caesar 'particularly desired' in 58, that his motive in striking quickly was to exploit Gallic hostility to the Helvetii rather than wait for the Helvetii to force the Gauls into an understanding, that the German threat offered him an opportunity to fulfil his own ambitions as well as do the allies a favour, that he wanted to avoid the impression of being an aggressor, and that he made his demands in order to get a plausible pretext for fighting the Germans; then, if we turn to agents other than Caesar himself, that the Helvetii were reluctant to split their forces because they feared becoming more vulnerable to those they might offend, and that his own men were annoyed because Caesar was inflaming an unnecessary war simply for the sake of his own ambition. That last piece of mind-reading (38.35.2), picked up in the extensive speech which Dio makes Caesar deliver to these disaffected troops (38.37.1, 41.1), is particularly interesting, as it makes the double step: Dio finds his own key to events in his reconstruction of what one group is feeling (the soldiers), and makes those feelings themselves depend on that group's mental picture of what a second figure (Caesar himself) is thinking – so primary, secondary, and tertiary focalisers are all relevant.

But it is not just the soldierly mind that Dio reads. Politics too are dowsed in analyses of the principals' motives for this or that Machiavellian move, most strikingly in the extensive exploration of the reasons why Pompey, Caesar, and Crassus should each have thought it a good idea to enter into the triple alliance of 60 BCE at the end of Book 37. These motive analyses are very thoughtful, even if they do tend to make all the big players think in the same ways, all playing for their own advantage, all carefully weighing the likelihoods and working out how to manipulate one another, all carefully reading *each other*'s minds (so once again it is not just Dio himself and not just the readers that the author expects, but also Dio's characters, who like this particular game). This can have interesting effects: if everyone understands one another's mindset so well, then matters can easily develop into stalemate, with everyone discounting everybody else's actions as not really amounting to very much. Take the case of the relations between Caesar, Crassus, and Cicero at 39.10. Caesar and Crassus have no time for Cicero, *but* they support his return from exile because they think it is going to happen anyway and they might as well get some goodwill from it; *but* Cicero sees through this, and so is not grateful at all; *but* he also knows from experience that it is dangerous to speak out, and so he limits his venom to a work – presumably the notorious *de consiliis suis* – that was not published until after the principals were dead. So everyone cleverly reading everyone else's mind means that no-one does anything that has any effect at the time. The quest for intelligibility means that all these motives do not explain anything, for they produce nothing that would not have happened anyway.

It may be that one of Dio's most striking narrative peculiarities can be explained in similar ways, his omission of the agreement of Luca in 56 BCE. By that point he has so set up his narrative that his usual exploration of the principals' motives would leave him (and were he to have included Luca, his reader) baffled. In particular, he has reconstructed Pompey's mindset in such a way as to have him deeply annoyed and worried at Caesar's growing power (39.24–7). Once he has got that far, it would genuinely be hard to see why Pompey could think a further alliance a good idea: instead Dio infers that whatever happened in 56–5 BCE must have been an alliance of Pompey and Crassus *against* Caesar – something that left no room for the usual way of treating Luca as a triple alliance.[15] He must have been familiar with that tradition,[16] but must also have thought it mistaken: and motives, imaginative focalisations, are why he would be so suspicious. The focalisation may help us to understand, not merely what the narrative does say, but what it does not.

To state a motive is almost always to invite a reader to read on, to see how far an aspiration is realised and how far a character gets his or her way: questions of mindset, intellectual control, easily become questions of physical control over what is to happen. In Caesar's case, at least at first, the answer is that Caesar gets his way very regularly indeed. It is he that sets up the original triple alliance in 60 BCE (37.54.3); his perceptions of the political realities are spot-on, and it is symptomatic that in that passage some reflections of Caesar on human nature are, both syn-

---

15 As usual, Dio's interpretation is not at all stupid: it was not unintelligent to think that Crassus and Pompey got more out of Luca than Caesar did, and to find that odd in view of the strength of Caesar's position (which he doubtless overestimated, 39.26.3). But the awkwardness is clear: see next note.

16 Thus Dio knows of the troops Caesar sent to Rome to aid the election of Pompey and Crassus (39.31.2); he has to explain Caesar's Gallic extension in terms of 'Pompey and Crassus winning over Caesar's *friends*' (33.4), and he then leaves it obscure why they neglected a golden opportunity to double-cross (36.2). None of this suggests an author ignorant of the usual way of taking Luca: its suppression and rewriting must be a matter of deliberate reinterpretation.

tactically and in content, similar to the reflections that Dio himself tends to produce – hatred is more powerful a bond than friendship, hindering a man's career wins more friends than promoting it, and so on. It is not unnatural for the events of the 59 BCE consulship to be told in terms of Caesar's own actions and intentions, but this is more consistently true of Dio's account than of the parallel versions; similarly there is more of an eye on Caesar's long-range influence from Gaul in his account of the 50s than we find in Appian or Plutarch. That is not always done through straightforward Caesar-focalisation: indeed, one of the most striking passages bringing out Caesar's power is that reconstruction of Pompey's mentality which we have already seen, with Pompey deeply nervous of that growing power and pervasive influence that Caesar is exercising (39.24–6).

That has a further aspect, for there is a sense here in which Pompey's response is proleptic of something bigger. For the moment, it is just Pompey who is alienated by the way that Caesar is growing too powerful for others' own good; by the mid-forties, it is everyone who is thinking that way. That affects the way that Dio traces the path from Caesar's initial strong control – the historical Caesar's control over the events, the character Caesar's control over the way the narrative is told – to the less sure-footed and mistake-ridden actions of Caesar as dictator. Mind-reading continues to be central; but by then Caesar reads minds much less well. He misreads Antony, thinking that his delay in crossing the Adriatic is a piece of deliberate temporising (41.46.1): this is one time when Caesar, the great self-seeker, is too ready to assume that others are like himself. He misreads the Roman people too, failing to see how they will react to the way he treats the death of Pompey or how willing they will be to trust his conciliatory rhetoric on his return (42.8, 43.18.6); there are other misreadings too (43.19–20.1, 24, 47.6, 49.3). Caesar is by now less astute a reader of the popular temper than Pompey had been, partly because he does not care (41.54.1), partly because he simply gets things wrong.[17]

But everyone has to be a mind-reader now, and just as important is the way the people are reading Caesar's mind. They have been doing it for some time, and that is why the participants at Pharsalus are so depressed about the prospects: whichever man wins, and whatever their differences of motive (and this time there are differences, but they are slight ones), both Caesar and Pompey will turn the citizens into their

---

17 I expand on some of these points in Pelling 2006a, 261–2.

slaves (41.53–7); both have that desire for domination, τῆς δυναστείας ἐπιθυμία (41.57.4); the city can only be the loser. The people at Rome have to be mind-readers too, and it is not easy. Dio brings that out in a fine passage stressing how carefully everyone has to tread while it is still uncertain who will be the victor (42.17–18). But by the end Caesar's mind has become rather easy to read – much easier to read than it is in Plutarch. His delight in the honours he is offered is very clear (e.g. 44.6.1, 7.2): his enemies see that, and know how to exploit it, rendering him so vulnerable to envy (44.7.3–4). As Caesar has got so much worse at gauging the popular mindset, others have got so much better at gauging his own: and it is these failures of perception, particularly his failures in reading and predicting the perceptions of others, that explain so much of his fall. We see little in Dio from the conspirators' own mindset because we do not need to. It is the interplay of the two other mindsets and capacities for perception, Caesar's and the people's, that explains the downfall, not any quirks of Brutus or Cassius themselves. No wonder focalisation is so central to interpretation here. Perceptions, and perceptions of perceptions – perceptions lazy or thoughtful, perceptions right or wrong – are indeed the drivers of reality.

What Dio's Caesar gets wrong is what Dio's Augustus will later get right. A capacity not merely to build power, but to manage its public presentation in a way that is as effective as it is disingenuously traditional, is to be the key to Augustus' success: Book 52, and the way Augustus listens not merely to Maecenas but to Agrippa too, will make that clear. The time for one-man rule is not too far away, but the manner as well as the time will need to be right. Central to that manner will be Augustus' gift for anticipating the perceptions of others, of focalising others' focalisations even before they happen.

5. Appian

Dio's Caesar bullies his way through the fifties. Appian's Caesar is subtler. He is much less interventionist, and the key to this Caesar is his gift for setting things up so that others get his own way. The triumvirate itself is now Pompey's initiative, not Caesar's (2.9.33): we can take it as read that Caesar is ambitious (the beginning of *Civil Wars* 2 has made that clear), but those ambitions are what Pompey is taking into account and trying to exploit, they are not the driving force itself. Then it is in the mid- and later-fifties that Caesar's presentation becomes particularly interesting. Take the conference of Luca. When Plutarch describes it in *Pompey* (51) and in *Caesar* (21),[18] he does so in terms of Caesar's ambitions and policies. Appian starts from that angle of Caesar's concern with Rome, but swiftly moves to seeing it from the viewpoint of those who go to Luca to pay court, and what *they* intend to get out of this:

> ὅθεν αὐτῷ περιπέμποντι ἐς Ῥώμην πολλὰ πολλοῖς χρήματα αἵ τε ἐτήσιοι ἀρχαὶ παρὰ μέρος ἀπήντων καὶ οἱ ἄλλως ἐπιφανεῖς ὅσοι τε ἐς ἡγεμονίας ἐθνῶν ἢ στρατοπέδων ἐξῄεσαν, ὡς ἑκατὸν μέν ποτε καὶ εἴκοσι ῥάβδους ἀμφ' αὐτὸν γενέσθαι, βουλευτὰς δὲ πλείους διακοσίων, τοὺς μὲν ἀμειβομένους ὑπὲρ τῶν ἤδη γεγονότων, τοὺς δὲ χρηματιουμένους, τοὺς δ' ἄλλο τι τοιουτότροπον ἐξεργασομένους. πάντα γὰρ ἤδη <u>διὰ τούτου</u> ἐπράσσετο στρατιᾶς τε πολλῆς οὕνεκα καὶ δυνάμεως χρημάτων καὶ σπουδῆς ἐς ἅπαντας φιλανθρώπου. ἀφίκοντο δ' αὐτῷ καὶ Πομπήιος καὶ Κράσσος, οἱ κοινωνοὶ τῆς δυναστείας. καὶ αὐτοῖς βουλευομένοις ἔδοξε Πομπήιον μὲν καὶ Κράσσον αὖθις ὑπατεῦσαι, Καίσαρι δ' ἐς τὴν ἡγεμονίαν ὧν εἶχεν ἐθνῶν, ἄλλην ἐπιψηφισθῆναι πενταετίαν.

> Caesar had sent a lot of money to many people in Rome. The magistrates of the year came there to meet him, and so did the other men of note, including those who were on their way to provincial and military commands: the result was that at one point there were one hundred and twenty lictors there and more than two hundred senators. Some were repaying him for past services, some were looking to make money, others had something similar in mind. For already everything was being done <u>through him</u>: this was because of the size of his army and the power of his wealth and the generous enthusiasm with which he treated everyone. Pompey and Crassus came too, his partners in power, and they consulted and decided that Pompey and Crassus should be consuls again and that Caesar should be given an extra five years of command over the peoples he governed.
> (App. *BC* 2.17.61–3)

That διὰ τούτου is an interesting phrase: not 'by him', which would be ὑπό, nor 'for his sake', which would be διὰ τοῦτον, and certainly not 'all things were now possible for Caesar' (which is what White's Loeb has), but 'through him'. He *filters* everything: his hand is there, but not so clearly initiating or directing as in our other accounts.

As the war approaches, Caesar's hand in political matters is much less clear in Appian than it is in Dio. The exception is *BC* 2.25.96–7, which makes it clear that he is setting up tribunes to act on his behalf.[19] But

---

18 Though the account in *C. min.* (41) is here rather different: see below, p. 522–3. The one in *Crassus* (14.6–15.1) is very brief.

19 At that point alone Appian's Caesar is made more directly active than Plutarch's, for in Appian it is Caesar himself who, when told he will not be allowed an extension of his command, says that 'this sword will give it to me' (2.25.97):

thereafter all the activity springs from others, from Pompey or Curio or the legionaries, and it is only in flashback that we are reminded that Caesar has made sure that both tribunes and soldiers were lavishly treated (2.28.111, 30.116). We are not told how far the particular initiatives are Caesar's own or those of his supporters, following their own ideas and instincts: contrast Plutarch, who each time makes it clearer that instructions are coming from Caesar. So, as with that διὰ τούτου, Appian leaves it uncertain exactly how Caesar's ideas and intentions come into the causal chain.[20] All we know is that he is there somewhere, and what is happening is just as he would have wished.

The same rhythm is found in the tense final days before the war. Caesar has told Antony to negotiate on his behalf (2.32.145), but thereafter Antony, and to a lesser extent Cassius, play large roles of their own: notice especially Antony's dramatic prophecies and imprecations, almost Shakespeare-like, at 2.33.131–2. It is when the fighting starts that Caesar becomes more directly active, and now the talking is over the actions are Caesar's own, 'with that delight of his in stunning speed and in intimidating courage rather than strong preparation' (2.34.136). It is when he is absent or relying on lieutenants – including Curio once more, but this time on the battlefield rather than in the forum – that things begin to drift. Warfare is like that: the time to be indirect, to stay discreetly behind the scenes, has gone. A director, not a filter, is needed.

And he wins. Back at Rome, in power, he revives some of the previous techniques, and the narrative regains some of that earlier texture. As in our other accounts, the honours he receives are crucial in making him unpopular, but this time it is left unclear whether he wants them himself: here too, as at the outbreak of the war, the friends are active, and we do not know what is their initiative and what is not. When the question is raging about the title of king, he turns his mind to the Parthian expedition, 'either giving up [ἀπογνούς, which makes it sound as if he wanted the title] or in weariness and attempting already to get away from the attempt [τὴν πεῖραν, suggesting without quite say-

---

at Plut. *Caes.* 29.7 it is a centurion. The same story is told of an officer of the young Octavian in 43 BCE (Dio 46.43.4), and, by a similar variation, of Octavian himself (Suet. *Aug.* 26.1); also of Niger in 193 CE (Dio 75 [74].6.2a). All of them may be true: male posturing has a limited range.

20 Rather as elsewhere in this volume Ruth Scodel analyses the Hera of *Prometheus*: Hera figures somewhere in the causal chain that explains Io's suffering, but it is hard to pinpoint where.

ing that the attempt came from him] or the slander [τὴν διαβολήν, suggesting that it did not]': or perhaps he is leaving the city to avoid his enemies, or for the sake of his health… (2.110.459). As with Plutarch's *Caesar*, we are left uncertain how to mind-read Caesar, and that riddlingness itself recreates some of the atmosphere of the time; yet also, as with Dio's Caesar, we may sense the change from the earlier style of control, and notice how the same narrative techniques are here tracing the way Caesar is losing the capacity to dominate events, not exercising it. His inscrutability is not what it was, or at least is not as effective as it was. The world has moved on, and at the end history does not become biography after all – not quite.

6. Plutarch (ii)

Let us go back to Plutarch at the end. In that initial comparison of *Brutus* and *Caesar* our expectations were right in one respect, for *Caesar* concentrated on Caesar's side of things and *Brutus* on the conspirators'. Yet matters are not always so predictable, and that is particularly true in the case of focalisation. *Pompey* is here particularly interesting. With Caesar's arrival centre-stage, Pompey's life changes. Up to that point he had been the strong, Alexander-like figure (*Pomp.* 46); now his domination wavers, and he becomes a much more passive phenomenon, the man to whom things happen.[21] It is unsurprising that this affects the presentation. Both in 60–59 and in 56 BCE, events are told in such a way that Pompey comes at the end of sequences rather than the beginning: there is more interest in what Caesar hopes to get out of the triumvirate than in Pompey (in fact, Caesar's part is treated in rather more coloured language in *Pompey* than it is in *Caesar* itself, *Pomp.* 47.2–4 ~ *Caes.* 13.3–6), and Pompey's role is largely in providing the soldiers to allow Caesar to get what he wants. True, Pompey gets his *acta* ratified, but by now that seems yesterday's issue. The same is true with the Luca conference: *Pompey* makes it even more Caesar's show than *Caesar* does (*Pomp.* 51 ~ *Caes.* 21).

It is another *Life* again, *Cato minor*, that focalises Luca most through Pompey, along with Crassus (*C.min.* 41.1–2). The emphasis there falls on *their* meeting Caesar and deciding on *their* second consulship: Caesar gets his extra time in Gaul, but *they* get the especially attractive provin-

---

21 I have again discussed this elsewhere, esp. in Pelling 2002, 96–102.

ces. There are good reasons for that, as the account of the consulship of 55 itself will polarise things around the consuls on the one side and Cato on the other. Particularly interesting there is a passage stressing Cato's insight into the way things are tending. Cato is often the lone voice predicting what will come (*C. min.* 31.7, 42.6, 43.3): his insight gradually deepens, and by now it has deepened a great deal. But 43.9–10 is particularly interesting, for here there is some sort, though an odd sort, of tertiary Pompey focalisation, with Cato making an attempt to see it from Pompey's point of view. Perhaps we might call it a *potential* focalisation,[22] the sort of view that Pompey might take or should have taken of his own predicament, but that in fact the different, more perceptive character Cato takes instead:

τῷ δὲ Καίσαρι πάλιν νόμου γραφομένου περὶ τῶν ἐπαρχιῶν καὶ τῶν στρατοπέδων, οὐκέτι πρὸς τὸν δῆμον ὁ Κάτων, ἀλλὰ πρὸς αὐτὸν τραπόμενος Πομπήϊον, ἐμαρτύρατο καὶ προὔλεγεν, ὡς ἐπὶ τὸν αὑτοῦ τράχηλον ἀναλαμβάνων Καίσαρα νῦν μὲν οὐκ οἶδεν, ὅταν δ' ἄρχηται βαρύνεσθαι καὶ κρατεῖσθαι, μήτ' ἀποθέσθαι δυνάμενος, μήτε φέρειν ὑπομένων, εἰς τὴν πόλιν ἐμπεσεῖται σὺν αὐτῷ, καὶ μεμνήσεται τότε τῶν Κάτωνος παραινέσεων, ὡς οὐδὲν ἧττον ἐν αὐταῖς τὸ Πομπηΐου συμφέρον ἐνῆν ἢ τὸ καλὸν καὶ δίκαιον. ταῦτα πολλάκις ἀκούων ὁ Πομπήϊος ἠμέλει καὶ παρέπεμπεν, ἀπιστίᾳ τῆς Καίσαρος μεταβολῆς διὰ πίστιν εὐτυχίας τῆς ἑαυτοῦ καὶ δυνάμεως.

Then a law was proposed giving Caesar his provinces and legions. At this point Cato no longer turned to the people but to Pompey himself. He solemnly called on him to witness what was happening, and prophesied that Pompey was lifting Caesar as a burden on to his own shoulders: he did not

---

22 A phrase also used by Elsner 2007, 31 in discussion of Campanian wall-painting, though the difference between the cases points the distinctiveness and complexity of this one. Elsner's point is the different ways in which Theseus and Ariadne might potentially regard the same event (his desertion): that is similar, then, to the way that (say) Aeneas and Dido provide alternative secondary focalisers of one event. Here one secondary focaliser (Cato) addresses the perspective of another (Pompey) – a perspective that is both genuinely Pompey's own (making Pompey another secondary focaliser) and seen by Cato to be so (making Pompey a tertiary focaliser). Cato then provides an alternative tertiary focalisation of his own. In each case the focalisation embraces (a) the way things are (cognitive), (b) the way it would be wise to feel about them (emotional), and (c) the way things are likely to turn out (a different sort of cognition). As the narrative has left little doubt as to Cato's insight, his tertiary focalisation also approximates to the narrator's primary focalisation. The analysis is cumbersome, but none of this feels at all strained within the narrative itself; and – the crucial point for the present argument – Plutarch is not simply playing narratorial games for their own sake, but exploiting the variety of perspectives to encourage interpretative reflection on historical responsibility and causation.

realise it yet, but there would come a time when he would begin to feel it too much for him, and then he would not be able either to carry it or to put it down: he would fall upon the city, burden and all – and that was when he would remember Cato's advice, and see that it contained not just what was good and right, but also what was in Pompey's own interest. Pompey heard this many times, but paid no attention and let things slide. He was so convinced of his own good fortune and power that he could not believe Caesar would change.

(*C. min.* 43.9–10)

Two points about this 'insight'. First, the contrast with *Pompey*, for Pompey's own policy is treated rather differently in the two *Lives*. In *Cato* Pompey is simply wrong: he does not notice what is going on, he underrates the danger, and that makes him a much more straightforward foil for Cato's own insight. In his own *Life* Pompey's policy is different: Pompey *is* alert to the danger, and sees the threat coming distinctly earlier than he does in *Cato* (or, it seems, than in *Caesar*), but he thinks his best political line is to give the impression that he is unconcerned while 'seeking to protect himself with the city magistracies' (*Pomp.* 54.2). Inactivity is here policy, not blindness.[23]

That affects the earlier point about the focalisation within *Pompey*, as it is now no longer true that Pompey's lack of control over events is mirrored by an absence of Pompey-focalisation: on the contrary, *Pomp.* 54 gives a clear and intricate analysis of his own view of affairs. If we move to emotion as well as cognition, other parts of the narrative too generate a particularly empathetic picture of Pompey's mindset, especially his love for his wives, Julia and then Cornelia, and his taste for getting away from all those urban nastinesses to spend time with them (*Pomp.* 53, 55); then, a little differently, the way that the Italian joy at his recovery from illness generates his false confidence at 57.1–6. We are seeing and feeling with Pompey all too much at this point; but we are also noticing his lack of action, how understandable emotions and reactions can issue in catastrophic mistakes. It is the disjunction of focalisation and physical control over reality, with lots of Pompey-focalisation and minimal Pompey-control, that here makes the interpretative point.

Lastly, a point about that passage of *Cato* which I have just quoted. It shows a concerned Cato mapping out an alternative future for Pompey, a world of what-might-have-been. That is a speciality of that *Life*, as so

---

23 Pelling 2002, 97.

often it is others who map out alternative futures for Cato: his womenfolk, who would initially love him to have accepted a marriage-alliance with Pompey (30); his friends, who like his women are recurrently so concerned for his safety when he is particularly bull-headed in the face of physical danger (27.3, 32.7); Cicero, who advises him to grit his teeth, take the oath of allegiance to Caesar's legislation, and live to fight another day (32.8–11). Cato can repay that in kind, giving Cicero some mirroring advice a little later (35.1), and so we have an alternative future once again. And the narrator can do the same, speculating on how much damage might have been avoided if only Cato had bent with the wind and had avoided alienating Pompey over the marriage-affair (30.9–10). These what-might-have-been focalisations, reflecting the insights and perspectives of narrator and characters on unrealised potentialities, matter just as much in this *Life* as the what-really-is focalisations, highlighting as they do these moments of choice and decision, encouraging us to dwell on the other lines characters might have taken and how much difference they would have made. We hear a lot these days of virtual history, the history-that-never-was; there is of course a sense in which any causal historical statement is a statement of virtual history, exploring whether it would have made a difference if X had not happened. Here these elaborate focalisations generate virtual biography, hypothetically constructing the *Life* that Cato might have chosen to live if only he had been a different person. But he was not; nor was Caesar, who also made a choice of life (*Caes.* 3), but a very different one. And these alternative futures are both *personal* futures, keeping these individual works firmly within the biography section of the bookshop, and an interlocking concatenation that explains something of the history too.

'Something' of the history – but how much? Were this a different paper, we might further explore how that interest in alternative choices and alternative history goes with Plutarch's view that, from a larger perspective, there was no alternative at all, that monarchy was bound to come. We might even find that this empathetic interest in Cato's choices, as also in those of Brutus, helps Plutarch to pull off one of the most spectacular ideological balancing acts of all, projecting the attachment to liberty and the resoluteness of these champions of tradition as utterly admirable if we think from their own principled starting-points – and yet utterly wrong if we think of the interlocking picture, of where their politics are heading rather than where they are coming from. Focalise through them, and sympathy pulls one way; adopt the narrator's broader perspective, and matters look different. We might find something similar in Velleius and Dio and (especially) Appian too. We might be able to mount an even bigger argument, that this combination of empathy, seeing things through the focalising eyes of participants at the time, and hindsight, sensing as those participants could not the consequences that their perceptions and actions are generating, is central to the ways that ancient narrative conveys historical explanation. But that would indeed be a different paper, not this one.[24]

---

24 I explored some of these issues of historical explanation in the 2008 Fordyce Mitchel lectures at the University of Missouri at Columbia, and I hope that they will be published in book form by the University of Texas Press. Deep thanks for their help with the present paper, and for organising a conference that was quite remarkably stimulating, are due to Antonios Rengakos and Jonas Grethlein.

History beyond Literature: Interpreting the 'Internally Focalized' Narrative in Livy's *Ab urbe condita*

Chrysanthe Tsitsiou-Chelidoni

1. Prologue

The thoughts presented in this article arise, as its title suggests, from a narratological question. What different forms does the 'internally focalized' narrative take in Livy's history? What is the literary function of these forms and how can we explain their technique as a method of exposition? Such questions can be used as an heuristic tool to understand better Livy's art of writing.[1]

If one of the most important functions of literature is the imitation of the world,[2] and the 'internally focalized' narrative is a highly imitative nar-

---

I would like to offer special thanks to Madeleine Whelpdale for helping me to achieve a more natural style of English in the writing of this text and to five colleagues, Dr. James Cowey, Dr. Demokritos Kaltsas, Dr. Helga Köhler, Prof. Wassileios Fyntikoglou and Prof. Poulcheria Kyriakou, who also helped eliminate many mistakes. I owe special thanks also to Prof. Dr. Jürgen Paul Schwindt, who gave me the opportunity to present a new draft of this paper in the 'Seminar für Klassische Philologie' at the University of Heidelberg. Last but not least, I am grateful to Prof. Dr. Jonas Grethlein and Prof. Dr. Antonios Rengakos, and to all who participated in the discussion following the presentation of my thesis, both in Thessaloniki and in Heidelberg. With their comments they have helped me to reconsider important aspects of my essay. Any remaining weaknesses are of course my own.

1   Interesting narratological questions, relevant to that posed here, like 'in what textual situations does the "internally focalized" narrative appear' or 'who is given a point of view and who is not' (cf. Conte 1986, 156–157 n. 12), are for now beyond the scope of my treatment.
2   The term 'imitation' is here to be understood in its Platonic-Aristotelian sense, according to which 'to imitate' means 'to represent a through the senses perceptible reality'. See Lausberg (1960) 1990, §1159, 4. On the mimetic character of history itself see Lausberg, *ibid.*, §1168. I do not discuss here the complicated meaning with which the term μίμησις often appears in ancient critical texts on historiography. On this topic see Gray 1987.

rative,[3] it is reasonable to think that the degree to which this narrative technique appears in a text and the forms it takes could be a sign of the literary character of this text.[4] The interpretation of Livy's 'internally focalized' narrative could therefore be a way to comprehend, more fully, aspects of the literary nature of his work and to further the debate on its position within the framework of ancient Roman historiography as a literary genre.

2. Theory

Two methodological questions should be discussed at this point. Can we apply a narratological model, originally developed for the interpretation of fiction, to a historical narrative?[5] And how are we to define the 'internally focalized' narrative?

Nobody would dispute that fictional narrative differs in nature from a historical one. However, as has often been pointed out, there are also clear analogies between these two narrative forms.[6] A historian uses fictional elements, imagination and a variety of narrative patterns in the same way that a poet (or a romancier) does – which of course does not necessarily mean that the events narrated by a historian did not happen at all.[7] On the other hand, a poet (or a romancier) places his story in a context which always has something in common with a historical real-

---

[3] On the imitative character of this art of narrative and its use in fictional texts see Martinez–Scheffel (1999) 2003, 48–52, 60.

[4] On the relationship between historiography and poetry in general see Arist. Poet. 9.1451a1–1451b7; Cic. Leg. 1.1.5; Dion. Hal. Thuk. 23; 51; ep. ad Pomp. 3.21; Quint. Inst. 2.4.2; 10.1.31; 10.2.21–22. See also Norden (1898) 1958, 91–126; Wiseman 1979, 143–153; id., 2002; Rengakos 2006b. Especially on Livy see Kroll (1924) 1973, 291, 351, 358, 363, 369; Seeck 1983; Moles 1993, 157–158, 162–163 n. 3.

[5] Cf. Hornblower 1994, 132.

[6] See Booth (1961) 1983, 408; White (1978) 2003, 53–63; id., 1987, X: 'Recent theories of discourse ... dissolve the distinction between realistic and fictional discourses based on the presumption of an ontological difference between their respective referents, real and imaginary, in favor of stressing their common aspect as semiological apparatuses that produce meanings by the systematic substitution of signifieds (conceptual contents) for the extra-discursive entities that serve as their referents.' For a bibliography on the relation between historical and fictional narration see Feichtinger 1992, 3 nn. 1, 2, 3. See also Hornblower 1994, 133 n. 5; Laird 1999, 116–117, 119–120.

[7] See Hornblower 1994, 133.

ity.[8] The use of narratological models in the interpretation of historiographical texts, as currently practised,[9] should therefore be of no surprise.

The second question would be irrelevant, if only we had a commonly accepted definition of the term, which it seems we do not. For this reason a short discussion, in which the banal and obvious cannot always be avoided, is necessary at this point.

Genette introduced ((1972) 1980) the term 'focalization', in order to replace the older, and, in his view, ambiguous terms 'point of view' or 'perspective'.[10] As a result of their confused usage these terms do not allow one to distinguish adequately between the narrator, the person who narrates in a text, and the person whose vision or perception is narrated in the same text.[11] Genette also distinguished between three types of focalization: 'nonfocalization', where the focus of narration is not situated at a particular point in the story – we have in this case a narrator whose information is complete –,[12] 'external focalization', where the narrative focus is situated at a point in the diegetic universe, outside every character of the story,[13] and 'internal focalization', where the focus of narration is situated inside a figure of the story.[14]

---

8 See Genette (1983) 1988, 81: '… pure fiction is a narrative devoid of all reference to a historical framework. Few novels … fit that description, and perhaps no epic narrative does.' Generally Genette seems to have an alert eye for the analogies and the differences between fictional and historical narration; see id., (1972) 1980, 225–226. He refers also to Livius (Liv. 2.32) in order to give an example of a 'metadiegetic' narration (id., (1972) 1980, 243). See also id., (1991) 1992, 65–94.

9 See e.g. Fuhrmann 1983; Hornblower 1994; Jaeger 1997; Rood 1998; de Jong 2001b; Dewald 2005; Grethlein 2006b; Rengakos 2006a; id., 2006b.

10 See Genette (1972) 1980, 203–206. It is basically for the same reason that we also find the use of the term 'focalization' in Mieke Bal ((1985) 1997, 101–102), who developed a very elaborate system where 'focalization' [as 'the relation between the vision and that which is "seen", perceived' (ibid., 100)] and 'focalizors' [as the 'subject of focalization', 'the point from which the elements are viewed' (ibid., 104)] play a very important part. But see the critique of Genette ((1983) 1988, 76 and passim) on Bal's narratological theory. In Genette's view ((1983) 1988, 76–77) the narrative focus cannot be at two different points simultaneously. Above all, he does not use the term 'focalizor'. According to him (1988, 73): '… *focalized* can be applied only to the narrative itself.' For a further polemic against Bal's concept of focalization, see Rood 1998, 294–296. For the term 'focalization' see the bibliography cited by Fowler 1990, 58 nn. 1, 3.

11 See Genette (1983) 1988, 64–65.

12 Genette (1983) 1988, 73–74.

13 Genette (1983) 1988, 75.

The content of an internally focalized narrative can therefore be what a figure sees, what a figure visualizes or what a character perceives with his senses. In an internally focalized narrative different aspects of a person's consciousness can also be presented.[15] In Genette's view, 'consciousness' consists of inner speech and of 'nonverbal forms' too.[16] He recognizes three basic techniques of the presentation of consciousness: 'narratized speech' – the analysis of a character's thoughts taken on directly by the narrator –, 'transposed speech' – a monologue relayed by the narrator in the form of indirect discourse, governed or free –, and 'reported speech' – a literal citation of a character's thoughts as they are verbalized in inner speech.[17]

---

14 Genette (1983) 1988, 74. Mieke Bal also used the term 'internal focalization'. According to her the narrative is 'internally focalized', when the view of a character of the 'fabula' is presented. This character (and not the narrator) is understood as an 'internal focalizor' (Bal (1985) 1997, 105–106). For Rimmon-Kenan ((1983) 2002, 76), who takes an approach similar to Bal, 'the locus of internal focalization is inside the represented events. This type generally takes the form of a character-focalizer'. For Rimmon-Kenan (ibid., 77) 'an external focalizer may perceive an object either from without or from within'; 'the external focalizer (narrator-focalizer) presents the focalized from within', when he penetrates the focalized character's feelings and thoughts.

15 According to Genette, however, the internally focalized narrative does not have very clear limits as a type of focalization. See Genette (1972) 1980, 208 ('... la focalisation interne ..., formule déjà fort souple, ...'). In its strictest sense it implies seeing through the eyes of a character (in proprial and in figurative sense) of the story who is not named, who is never seen from without, and whose thoughts and feelings are not analysed by the narrator; in this form it is rarely ever practised (ibid., 209). Genette thinks that an example of pure internally focalized narrative could be the 'internal monologue' 'où le personnage central se réduit absolument à – et se déduit rigoureusement de – sa seule position focale' (ibid., 210). He also accepts the criterion proposed by Barthes: to distinguish the internally focalized segments of the narrative, we should attempt to 'rewrite' the given segment in the first person. If this is feasible, the segment is internally focalized (see Rimmon-Kenan (1983) 2002, 76–77) – in fact Barthes speaks about 'a personal narrative modus' ('le mode personnel du récit') (see Genette, ibid., 210). But as Rimmon-Kenan points out (ibid., 77) 'it is not clear whether this feasibility can be defined in strictly grammatical terms or in the much more elusive terms of verisimilitude'.

16 Genette (1983) 1988, 58, 60.

17 See Genette (1983) 1988, 58–59. As Genette points out (ibid., 58–61), his categories and the categories of Dorrit Cohn 1978 'are completely interchangeable', but the interchange reveals differences too. Cohn recognizes a 'psycho-narration' (corresponding to the 'narratized speech' of Genette), a 'quoted

In the following paragraphs I am going to concentrate only on a few cases of internally focalized narrative in Livy's work, which would seem to be representative of his overall narrative style.

3. Perspicuity

In Livy's history the narrative focus is very often not concentrated at first on a certain and concrete point or on an object and thereby following a particular contour. However, this narrative 'modus' may be quickly relieved by another where the narration is focused on a more restricted and clear field.[18]

The following textpassage offers an example of this:

Prima deinde luce castra mota et agmen reliquum incedere coepit. Iam montani signo dato ex castellis ad stationem solitam conveniebant, cum repente conspiciunt alios arce occupata sua super caput imminentes, alios via transire hostes. Utraque simul obiecta res oculis animisque immobiles parumper eos defixit; deinde, ut trepidationem in angustiis suoque ipsum tumultu misceri agmen videre, equis maxime consternatis, quidquid adiecissent ipsi terroris satis ad perniciem fore rati, diversis rupibus[19] iuxta per vias ac devia[20] adsueti decurrunt. Tum vero simul ab hostibus simul ab iniquitate locorum Poeni oppugnabantur, plusque inter ipsos, sibi quoque tendente ut periculo prius evaderet, quam cum hostibus certaminis erat. Equi[21] maxime infestum agmen faciebant, qui et clamoribus dissonis, quos nemora etiam repercussaeque valles augebant, territi trepidabant et icti forte aut volnerati adeo consternabantur ut stragem ingentem simul hominum ac sarcinarum omnis generis facerent.

(Liv. 21.33.1−6)[22]

---

monologue' (it corresponds to Genette's 'reported speech') and a 'narrated monologue' (this is the 'transposed speech' of Genette).

18 In his model Genette associates the narrator whose information is complete with the 'nonfocalized' narration ((1983) 1988, 73−74), which he however defines as an *ad libitum* 'variously focalized' narration ((1972) 1980, 208−209; (1983) 1988, 74). This definition makes clear that the category of the 'nonfocalized' narration, which Bal does not recognize, raises some problems. But actually what constitutes the narrator's omniscience is indeed his ability to know what a normal human being or the participants in the narrated events cannot know, to restrict his view (to focalize) and to enlarge it (to not focalize) at will.
19 Walters and Conway prefer *perversis (rupibus)* with the meaning of 'overturn, throw down' (Walters − Conway 1954, ad loc.)
20 *iuxta, invia ac devia* (Walters − Conway 1954, ad loc.).
21 *Et equi* (Walters − Conway 1954, ad loc.).
22 'With the ensuing dawn the Carthaginians broke camp and the remainder of their army began to move. The natives, on a signal being given, were already coming in from their fastnesses to occupy their customary post, when they suddenly perceived that some of their enemies were in possession of the heights

In the lines quoted, actions of the inhabitants of the mountains are described in alternation with those of the Carthaginians. The narrative focus becomes gradually sharper. After the announcement of a situation (*Prima deinde luce castra mota*) the narrator's external view becomes more concrete (*agmen reliquum incedere coepit... montani ... conveniebant*). The narrator sees next through the eyes of the mountaineers: *conspiciunt alios ... alios ...* After a passage in which he describes their outwardly perceived behaviour, behaviour arising from the impressions of their senses (*Utraque simul obiecta res oculis animisque immobiles parumper eos defixit*), the narration again becomes internally focalized, as the narrator relates what the mountaineers see (narrated gaze) and think (transposed speech): *... ut trepidationem in angustiis suoque ipsum tumultu misceri agmen videre, equis maxime consternatis, quidquid adiecissent ipsi terroris satis ad perniciem fore rati ...* At the end we see the *montani* from without: *diversis rupibus iuxta per vias ac devia adsueti decurrunt*.

It is now the Carthaginians's turn to become objects of interwoven external and internal focalization: *... oppugnabantur, plusque inter ipsos, sibi quoque tendente ut periculo prius evaderet, quam cum hostibus certaminis erat*. In the next paragraph the narrative is again variously focalized. We become spectators upon the situation of the Carthaginians (*Equi maxime infestum agmen faciebant*), which is illustrated through the reactions of the animals to the noises that they hear (*qui et clamoribus dissonis territi trepidabant*), and the cause of these noises is also explained (*quos nemora etiam repercussaeque valles augebant*). We actually hear and see what an ordinary participant in this expedition would also perceive: *et icti*

---

and threatened them from above, and that others were marching through the pass. Both facts presenting themselves at the same time to their eyes and minds kept them for a moment rooted to the spot. Then, when they saw the helter-skelter in the pass and the column becoming embarrassed by its own confusion, the horses especially being frightened and unmanageable, they thought that whatever they could add themselves to the consternation of the troops would be sufficient to destroy them, and rushed down from the cliffs on either side, over trails and trackless ground alike, with all the ease of habit. Then indeed the Phoenicians had to contend at one and the same time against their foes and the difficulties of the ground, and the struggle amongst themselves, as each endeavoured to outstrip the rest in escaping from the danger, was greater than the struggle with the enemy. The horses occasioned the greatest peril to the column. Terrified by the discordant yells, which the woods and ravines redoubled with their echoes, they quaked with fear; and if they happened to be hit or wounded, were so maddened that they made enormous havoc not only of men but of every sort of baggage.' (Transl. by B. O. Foster.)

forte aut volnerati adeo consternabantur ut stragem ingentem simul hominum ac sarcinarum omnis generis facerent.[23]

This passage can be seen as representative of many similar ones in Livy's work.[24] What we observe here is a quick (but in no way abrupt) change of the narrative's focus position. This variation obviously heightens the perspicuity of the narration: through the varied focalization the narrated events become elucidated from all sides.[25] At the same time the reader feels the suspense and the tension of the described events, then he experiences the changeovers of the action and the swings in people's moods.[26] The unveiling of the thoughts and feelings of the figures who participate in the events, the discovery of the causes of their actions,[27] testify therefore here to the difficulty of Hannibal's undertaking – the conflict remains for a while indecisive – and at the

---

23 Cf. Walsh 1973, 184: 'The actual engagement is recounted with the regular technique of alternation of standpoint; Livy begins with Hannibal (33.1), then turns to the *montani* (§§ 2–3), then returns to the Carthaginians (§§ 4 ff.).'
24 Cf. e.g. Liv. 1.59; 3.35.3–7; 3.38.1–3; 9.2; 21.8; 21.39; 23.15.
25 Cf. Schneider's remarks (1974, 52) on the narrative art of Thucydides: 'Im Bericht greifen, wie sich anhand weiterer Beispiele leicht zeigen ließe, mimetische Erzählung und narrative Aussagen ständig ineinander, und es läßt sich oft schwer entscheiden, welcher Kategorie eine Aussage zuzurechnen wäre. Tatsachen erscheinen bald durch das Bewußtsein der Handelnden vermittelt, bald vom Erzähler im eigenen Namen berichtet. Dem Leser fällt der Unterschied selten auf, und auch die Analyse kann ihn nur mit Hilfe schematischer Begriffe aufdecken, die der Erzählung selbst fremd sind. Denn dem Erzähler geht es darum, dem Leser Handlungen verständlich zu machen, der Analyse: zu zeigen, wie er dabei verfährt.'
26 See Oakley 1997, 120: 'Important precedents were set by Thucydides and Polybius, who recorded the plans of statesmen and generals in order to make their own work more useful to future practitioners of those arts. L(ivy)'s own technique is marked out not so much by the regularity with which he reports the thoughts of the participants in his history, as by the subtlety with which he does this.'
27 Causes already matter greatly to Herodot, as the proem to his *Historiae* proves. Thucydides too considers that discovering causes was the duty of a historian. According to Polybius (3.31.12–13) '... if one subtracts from history the why, the how, the purpose for which a deed was done, and also whether the end was predictable, what is left is a prize composition [*agonisma*] but not a lesson, and though it gives momentary pleasure, it provides no utility at all for the future.' (Transl. by Fornara 1983, 113.) See also Plb. 2.38.5; 3.7.5–6; 6.2.8; 11.19a.1–3 and Walbank 1957, *ad* Plb. 3.6.3; 3.7.4–7; Cic. *De orat.* 2.15.63; Gärtner 1975, passim and esp. 2–3; Leeman (1963) 1986, 172–173: '*Consilia* and *causae*, not only *acta*, are judged indispensable by Polybius (2.56.16), Dionysius (*Ant. Rom.* 5.56.1), and ... Asellio.'

end to his strategical genius, his skill at making his army, which at first had no prospect of passing through the place, which the mountaineers guarded (Liv. 21.32.8), finally prevail (Liv. 21.33.8–11).[28]

Moreover the quick change of the narrative's focus position makes clear the dominion of the narrator in the narrative. As we do not have different narrators with different focuses, but only one and the same, the surrogate of the author in his work, who transforms the art of his view at will, his authoritarian power in the narration becomes evident.[29] The perspective of the historical figures is of course sometimes – at least for a short while – recognizable, though not always in the same form. It is however the voice of the one and the same narrator which remains constantly strong throughout. With this voice the narrator filters from the perspective of his own time (after the narrated events) incidents (as beheld by the historical figures), their thoughts and their feelings, as if he were the omniscient eye-witness messenger of all the occurences he narrates.[30]

A narrative of the discussed form is indeed more vivid than a narrative where the narrator restrains himself in a short and/or a critical description of the historical events without a detailed depiction of the recorded action or without a penetrating illumination of the psychological background of the historical figures. However, this type of narration is at the same time less 'real' and less 'mimetic' than a narration where the viewpoint of a single intradiegetic figure – despite being filtered through the voice of the narrator – dominates, let alone a narrative where the figures participating in the narrated events have the opportunity to record with observable details, from their own perspective and through their own voice, what they perceive with their senses, what they think or what they feel.[31]

---

[28] Livy acknowledged the admirable qualities of Hannibal. See e.g. Liv. 28.12.2–5. On Livy's portrait of Hannibal see Walsh 1961, 103–105.

[29] Cf. the remarks of Connor 1985 on Thucydides.

[30] Irene de Jong (1991, 25 with n. 64) leaves the possibility open to compare a messenger, who 'has the ability to look into other characters' hearts' with an omniscient narrator. It is an interesting feature of Livy's narrative that Livy often inserts into his narration messenger speeches. On this topic see Lambert 1946, 52.

[31] Cf. here n. 15 on the 'internally focalized narrative' in its strictest sense.

4. Imitation

There are, to be sure, passages in the Livian narrative, in which the narration becomes far more mimetic in character than in the passage discussed above: speeches displaying excellent rhetorical refinement,[32] duels and dialogues are spread throughout all the preserved books.

One such instance of pure internal focalization, of pure *mimesis* in Platonic-Aristotelian sense therefore, is Liv. 21.44.1–2:

> 'Quocumque circumtuli oculos, plena omnia video animorum ac roboris, veteranum peditem, generosissimarum gentium equites frenatos infrenatosque, vos socios fidelissimos fortissimosque, vos, Carthaginienses, cum pro patria[33] tum ob iram iustissimam pugnaturos.'[34]

In the lines quoted Hannibal, who is speaking before his soldiers, describes the exact impression they are making on him while he is looking at them. With gushing phrases he commends qualities which are thought to be reflected in the faces of his men, their 'eagerness' and 'strength', their 'nobility', and also the 'trust' and the 'valour' of the Carthaginians' allies. Other passages convince us that he is fully aware of the positive influence such optimistic, confident images can have upon his army.[35] But if his soldiers take courage thanks to the words of their general, the Roman readers of Livy become filled with fear and awe in the face of them. For Hannibal's reported gaze evokes in the reader's mind the image of warlike fighters as if such an army stood before his own eyes. The threat which hangs over Rome and the Romans thus becomes vivid, almost a reality.[36]

---

32 See Oakley 1997, 117–118.
33 *ob patriam* (Walters – Conway 1954, *ad loc.*).
34 'Wherever I turn my eyes I see nothing but eagerness and strength, a veteran infantry, cavalry from the noblest tribes, riding with bridles or without, here the trustiest and most valiant of allies, there Carthaginians, prepared to fight not only in defence of their native land, but in satisfaction of a most righteous indignation.' (Transl. by B. O. Foster.)
35 Cf. e.g. Liv. 21.35.7–9; 21.42.
36 Cf. *Rhet. Her.* 4.55.68: *Demonstratio est cum ita verbis res exprimitur ut geri negotium et res ante oculos esse videatur.* ('It is Ocular Demonstration when an event is so described in words that the business seems to be enacted and the subject to pass vividly before our eyes.' Transl. by H. Caplan); Quint. *Inst.* 6.2.32: *insequitur ἐνάργεια, quae a Cicerone illustratio et evidentia nominatur, quae non tam dicere videtur quam ostendere; et adfectus non aliter, quam si rebus ipsis intersimus, sequentur.* ['From such impressions arises that ἐνάργεια which Cicero calls *illumination* and *actuality*, which makes us seem not so much to narrate as to exhibit the actual

The following passage also evokes the impression of a tangible reality. We are in 391 B.C.: the Roman army has been defeated in Caudium by the Samnites; moreover, the Romans are disgraced by having made peace (Liv. 9.7.6). The only way to extricate themselves from this calamity is to act in accordance with the proposal of Postumius. This involves giving up Postumius himself together with other military officials to the enemies and declaring a new war against the Samnites (Liv. 9.8.5–7). In the following passage Livy speaks about the reaction of the Roman people to Postumius' proposal:

> *Postumius in ore erat; eum laudibus ad caelum ferebant, devotioni P. Deci consulis, aliis claris facinoribus aequabant: emersisse civitatem ex obnoxia pace illius consilio et opera; ipsum se cruciatibus et hostium irae offerre piaculaque pro populo Romano dare. Arma cuncti spectant et bellum: en unquam futurum ut congredi armatis cum Samnite liceat?*
>
> (Liv. 9.10.3–5)[37]

A narratized external speech (... *in ore erat ... ferebant ... aequabant*) is followed here by a transposed external speech (*emersisse ... offerre ... dare*) and then by a short psycho-narration (*Arma cuncti spectant et bellum.*). The passage closes with a question in indirect speech – although not introduced by a verb –[38] which the Romans are thought to pose to themselves.

As the phrase *ut congredi armatis cum Samnite liceat* does not undergo any changes in the frame of *oratio obliqua*, the text evokes almost the impression of a free indirect speech ('style indirecte libre', 'erlebte Rede'), through which the narrator seems to imitate a group of persons: his voice almost becomes confused with that of the Romans who want war.[39] Clearly this dramatic narrative pattern is used here to express

---

scene, while our emotions will be no less actively stirred than if we were present at the actual occurrence.' (Transl. by H. E. Butler)]. See also Lausberg (1960) 1990, §810: 'Die Versetzung in die Augenzeugenschaft ... ist der Effekt einer Mimesis.'

37 'Postumius was on all men's lips; they extolled him to the skies, and compared his conduct to the devotion of Publius Decius, the consul, and to other glorious deeds. The state, they said, had emerged – thanks to his wisdom and his services – from a slavish peace; he was freely giving himself up to the tortures of a resentful foe, that he might make expiation for the Roman People. Men thought of nothing but war and arms. Would ever the hour come, they asked, when they might encounter the Samnites, sword in hand?' (Transl. by B. O. Foster.)

38 Cf. also e.g. Liv. 2.32.6; 5.45.6.

39 Cf. also e.g. Liv. 5.24.5; 27.44.4. For an example of pure free indirect speech see Liv. 21.11.12 (..., *unica spes*, ...). See also Lambert 1946, 49 n. 1; Genette

strong emotion.[40] Epic poets use free indirect speech with a similar effect.[41] However, the following two examples show that the Livian narrative can also differ greatly from a poetical one.

At the beginning of 218 B.C. the centre of Hannibal's military operation is in Spain. The main purpose of the Carthaginian commander-in-chief, however, is to fight the Romans in their own country. As Livy narrates, Hannibal led his troops across the river Hiberus rejoicing about a dream, which he had had:

> *Ibi fama est in quiete visum ab eo iuvenem divina specie, qui se ab Iove diceret ducem in Italiam Hannibali missum: proinde sequeretur neque usquam a se deflecteret oculos. Pavidum primo nusquam circumspicientem aut respicientem secutum; deinde cura ingenii humani, cum quidnam id esset quod respicere vetitus esset agitaret animo, temperare oculis nequivisse; tum vidisse post sese serpentem mira magnitudine cum ingenti arborum ac virgultorum strage ferri ac post insequi cum fragore caeli nimbum. Tum quae moles ea quidve prodigii esset quaerentem audisse vastitatem Italiae esse: pergeret porro ire nec ultra inquireret sineretque fata in occulto esse.*
> (Liv. 21.22.6–9)[42]

Livy does not dramatize Hannibal's dream in the form of a scene such as those we are familiar with from the *Iliad* (23.62–101) or the *Aeneid* (2.270–297; 5.722–742). This prophetic vision, being a strange, rare

---

(1972) 1980, 192. The mimetic character of this passage becomes clearer in the light of Oakley's remarks on the use of the *en umquam* (2005, *ad* Liv. 9.10.5): 'its distribution suggests that, although common enough in spoken Latin in the second century, it was archaic for Livy and Virgil. It may however be placed amongst those vigorous expressions which L(ivy) avoided in his narrative but occasionally admitted into his speeches.'

40 Cf. the remark of Oakley 2005, *ad* Liv. 9.10.5: '*en umquam futurum*: "will it ever come about …?" … When used with the future it tends to convey strong emotion … here it reflects the yearning of the Roman populace.'

41 See e.g. Verg. *Aen.* 4.281–284 or Ov. *met.* 8.38. See also Rosati 1979; Tsitsiou-Chelidoni 2003, 57–58.

42 'It was there, as they tell, that he saw in his sleep a youth of godlike aspect, who declared that he was sent by Jupiter to lead him into Italy: let him follow, therefore, nor anywhere turn his eyes away from his guide. At first he was afraid and followed, neither looking to the right nor to the left, nor yet behind him; but presently wondering, with that curiosity to which all of us are prone, what it could be that he had been forbidden to look back upon, he was unable to command his eyes; then he saw behind him a serpent of monstrous size, that moved along with vast destruction of trees and underbrush, and a storm-cloud coming after, with loud claps of thunder; and, on his asking what this prodigious portent was, he was told that it was the devastation of Italy: he was therefore to go on, nor enquire further, but suffer destiny to be wrapped in darkness.' (Transl. by B. O. Foster.)

538   Chrysanthe Tsitsiou-Chelidoni

and almost miraculous phenomenon, appears to him rather as an appropriate object for narration by *fama*.[43] The historian therefore introduces here the 'rumour', the 'tradition' (*fama*) as an actual intradiegetic (and probably homodiegetic) narrator, who relates what Hannibal saw in his sleep.[44]

The reader must be on the alert to recognize and understand the different narrative levels, especially those of the indirect speech in the internally focalized narration by *fama* through Hannibal.[45] The authorial narrator chooses to maintain an apparently objective distance from the narrated story and to function as a medium, through which the narration's content is presented. This technique probably reinforces the confidence of the readers in his historical narrative, even if history in the text cited only comes up as a narration of a *fama*'s narration.

The following passage shows also a clear difference from relevant poetical narratives.

> *Haec non hostili modo odio, sed amoris etiam stimulis, amatam apud aemulum cernens, cum dixisset, non mediocri cura Scipionis animum pepulit. Et fidem criminibus raptae prope inter arma nuptiae neque consulto neque exspectato Laelio faciebant tamque praeceps festinatio ut quo die captam hostem vidisset, eodem matrimonio iunctam acciperet et ad penates hostis sui nuptiale sacrum conficeret; et eo foediora haec videbantur Scipioni, quod ipsum in Hispania iuvenem nullius forma pepulerat captivae. Haec secum volutanti Laelius ac Masinissa supervenerunt.*
>
> (Liv. 30.14.1–3)[46]

---

43 Cf. the remark of Oakley 1997, 95: 'L(ivy) was sceptical about reporting the miraculous even in his first two books ...'; Wiseman 2002, 333–334, 353, 361–362. See also e.g. Liv. 7.6.1–6; 9.29.10–11; 25.16.3.

44 Cf. Ph. Hardie, this volume.

45 Cf. the remarks of Jaeger 1997, 28: 'From a succession of changing points of view, Livy constructs a model reader, who does not play a passive role. ... this reader participates in contructing the meaning of the text and decodes its various rhetorical gestures ...' See also here n. 51; Grethlein 2006b, 315 on the function of additional voices in the narrative of Sallust: 'At the same time, the insertion of additional voices has the same functions as the expressions of uncertainty ... The ambiguity expresses the confusion at the level of the action and engages the reader who must weigh the different versions himself.'

   Dr. Dennis Pausch (University of Giessen, Germany) is currently writing a book on this topic. He will present a cross-section of his conclusions in a forthcoming article titled 'Der Feldherr als Redner und der Appell an den Leser. Wiederholung und Antizipation in den Reden des Livius'.

46 'By speaking thus, not only out of hatred as an enemy but also under the goad of jealousy, as he saw his beloved in the possession of his rival, he aroused no slight anxiety in the mind of Scipio. The charges against her were substantiated

If the main theme of the quoted lines – Scipio's estimation of the marriage of Masinissa to Sophoniba – had been the object of a poetical epic narration, it would probably have been presented in the form of reported (internal direct) speech. It is the participle used here, *volutanti*, which triggers this awareness and which calls for comparison to relevant passages in the *Aeneid* (Verg. *Aen.* 1.36–52; 4.533–553). However, the text above begins with a psycho-narration – at first with an internal focalization through Syphax (... *non hostili modo odio, sed amoris etiam stimulis, amatam apud aemulum cernens*) and then through Scipio (... *non mediocri cura Scipionis animum pepulit*) – which does not seem free from the critical comment of the narrator (*hostili odio, mediocri cura*), to continue with a good mix of narratized and transposed speech (*Et fidem criminibus raptae ... nuptiae neque consulto neque exspectato Laelio faciebant tamque praeceps festinatio ut quo die captam hostem vidisset, eodem matrimonio iunctam acciperet et ad penates hostis sui nuptiale sacrum conficeret.*). At the end and after the narratized speech of Scipio (*et eo foediora haec videbantur Scipioni*) the simultaneous prevalence of two perspectives, that of the separate narrator's perspective and that of Scipio's, becomes very clear as the indicative is used in the subordinate clause (*quod ipsum in Hispania iuvenem nullius forma pepulerat captivae*) instead of the expected subjunctive, which would express Scipio's personal view.[47] The whole passage above therefore testifies once again to the dominant presence of the authorial narrator in the narrative.

But even when this presence is clear and the thoughts and sentiments of a figure or a group or a crowd are given in indirect speech,[48] the narrative can achieve a special mimetic effect through concrete techniques.

---

both by the marriage hastily celebrated, almost on the battlefield, without either seeking the advice of Laelius or waiting for his arrival, and by such precipitate haste that on the very day on which he saw her as a captured enemy he took her to wife and performed the nuptial rites before the household gods of his foe. Again, all this seemed the more repulsive to Scipio because in Spain, in spite of his youth, he had himself never been smitten by the beauty of any captive. Such thoughts were in his mind when Laelius and Masinissa arrived.' (Transl. by F. G. Moore.)

47 Cf. also e.g. Liv. 3.20.6. Under this aspect the thesis of Genette ((1983) 1988, 76–77) that the narrative focus cannot be in two different positions simultaneously must be revised.

48 Lambert (1946, 19, 46–49, 50–52) has already pointed out that the indirect speech has been often used by Livy to express thoughts.

Let us consider the following passage:

Ceterum nemini omnium maior ea iustiorque quam ipsi consuli videri; gaudio efferri, qua parte copiarum alter consul victus foret, ea se vicisse, restitutos ac refectos militibus animos, nec quemquam esse praeter collegam qui dilatam dimicationem vellet; eum animo magis quam corpore aegrum memoria volneris aciem ac tela horrere. Sed non esse cum aegro senescendum. Quid enim ultra differri aut teri tempus? Quem tertium consulem, quem alium exercitum exspectari? Castra Carthaginiensium in Italia ac prope in conspectu urbis esse. Non Siciliam ac Sardiniam victis ademptas nec cis Hiberum Hispaniam peti, sed solo patrio terraque in qua geniti forent pelli Romanos. 'Quantum ingemescant' inquit 'patres nostri circa moenia Carthaginis bellare soliti, si videant nos, progeniem suam, duos consules consularesque exercitus, in media Italia paventes intra castra, Poenum quod inter Alpes Appenninumque agri sit suae dicionis fecisse.' Haec adsidens aegro collegae, haec in praetorio prope contionabundus agere. Stimulabat et tempus propinquum comitiorum, ne in novos consules bellum differretur, et occasio in se unum vertendae gloriae, dum aeger collega erat. Itaque nequiquam dissentiente Cornelio parari ad propinquum certamen milites iubet.

(Liv. 21.53.1–7)[49]

There is a noticeable use of infinitives here, although not all of them are used in the same way. *Videri, efferri* (53.1) and *agere* (53.6) are *infinitivi*

---

49 'But to no one did the victory seem greater or more unequivocal than to Sempronius the consul; he was beside himself with joy that with that arm of the service with which the other consul had been beaten, he himself had been successful, that the spirits of the men were restored and renewed, and that no one but his colleague desired to put off the struggle; Cornelius (he thought) was sick in spirit rather than in body, and the recollection of his wound made him dread a battle and its missiles. But they must not droop and languish alongside a sick man. Why indeed should they further postpone the conflict, or waste time? What third consul, what other army were they waiting for? The Carthaginians were encamped in Italy and almost within sight of Rome. Their object was, not to get back Sicily and Sardinia, taken from them after their defeat, nor to cross the Ebro and occupy northern Spain, but to expel the Romans from the land of their fathers and from their native soil. "How would our fathers groan," he cried, "that were wont to wage war about the walls of Carthage, could they see us, their offspring, two consuls and two consular armies, cowering within our camp in the heart of Italy; and the Phoenician in full sway over all the territory between the Alps and the Apennines!" Thus he ran on, as he sat by the bed of his sick colleague; thus he argued in the praetorium, almost as if haranguing the troops. His impatience was increased, too, by the fast approaching elections, lest the war carry over into the term of the new consuls and he lose the opportunity of gaining all the glory for himself, while his colleague was laid up. Accordingly, despite the unavailing protests of Cornelius, he commanded the soldiers to make ready for an early battle.' (Based on the B. O. Foster's translation.)

historici (infinitives of narration); the rest are infinitives of indirect speech.[50] The reader has to take note of the different structures into which these verb forms are woven in order fully to understand the text's meaning.[51]

Although it cannot be ruled out that Sempronius is speaking – at least in the paragraphs 3–4 – not to himself but to other persons,[52] it is possible to think that throughout almost the whole passage the narrative is internally focalized. However, the degree of this focalization is not always the same.

At the beginning, where Sempronius' impression of the Roman victory is given, the critical approach of the narrator is very clear (*Ceterum nemini omnium maior ea iustiorque quam ipsi consuli videri.*). The internal focalization becomes purer, as we move towards transposed speech (*qua ... foret, ea se vicisse, restitutos ac refectos militibus animos, nec quemquam esse ... qui ... vellet.*) through a psycho-narration (*gaudio efferri*). The following transposed speech, without an introductory verb and in the form of infinitives, could, as pointed out, present the thoughts of the Roman consul (*sed non esse ... senescendum, quid enim ultra differri aut teri ..., quem ... exspectari?, castra ... esse, non Siciliam ac Sardiniam ... ademptas nec ... peti, sed ... pelli Romanos*). Yet what he said to Scipio appears in a small segment of direct speech. Then an internally focalized narrative in the mixed form of psycho-narration and transposed speech explains the motives of his behaviour (*stimulabat et tempus propinquum comitiorum, ne in novos consules bellum differretur, et occasio in se unum vertendae gloriae, dum*

---

50 On the use of infinitive of narration by Livy, see Viljamaa 1983, 11–15, 76–77.
51 Cf. the remark of Burck (1933) 1964, 191: 'Dabei hat er (sc. Livy) diese Bindungen niemals besonders betont oder umständlich hergestellt, sondern der Leser soll sie auf Grund feiner innerer Beziehungen aus der besonderen Art der Darstellung der Ereignisse oder auf Grund unauffälliger formaler Verknüpfungen von sich aus erfühlen und herstellen.' See also here n. 45.
52 In B. O. Foster's view we have here (Liv. 21.53.1–4) what Sempronius said (Foster 1996, *ad loc.*). See Foster's translation of Liv. 21.53.2: 'He declared that the spirits of the men were restored and renewed, and that no one but his colleague desired to put off the struggle; Cornelius, he said, was sick in spirit rather than in body ...' But it is difficult to imagine to whom Sempronius could speak to like this without evoking his disgrace against himself and his sympathy for Scipio. In any case the narrative perspective – especially in the paragraphs 3–4 – cannot be conclusively defined. See also Gärtner 1975, 40–41.

aeger collega erat). In the last paragraph of the passage the narrative becomes externally focalized (*Itaque ... iubet.*).[53]

In the quoted lines we therefore obtain our information through the narrator, who functions once again as a medium for all the narrative material, allowing us to see what Sempronius is doing, what he feels and what he thinks. However, by avoiding an introductory verb or phrase when using indirect speech, Livy not only conveys the impression of a fluent narrative style, avoiding the risk of fragmenting his writing, but he also disguises the dominant role of his narrator as a medium of the historical narrative content.[54] The transposed (inner?) speech of Sempronius becomes almost as vivid as his direct external speech.

Moreover, the use of the infinitive not only as the main verb of the sentence (*videri, efferri, agere*) but also as a dependent verb form to register the thoughts of the Roman consul (*vicisse, nec quemquam esse, horrere, non esse senescendum, differri, teri, exspectari, castra ... esse, non ... ademptas (esse), nec ... peti, pelli*) brings the historical figure nearer to the narrator thus creating a mimetic effect.[55] The narrative style is therefore not only characterized by the smooth transition from one sort of internally focalized narrative (psycho-narration) to another (transposed speech). The unified narrative form – infinitives are used to reproduce both the narrator's speech as well as Sempronius' speech – explains too how the paradoxical effect is brought about, that in a passage where the narrator obviously dominates as a medium of the narrative material – even if his presence is not always equally strong –, the distance between him and the historical figure seems, on the surface, very short.[56]

---

53 This art of focalization is perhaps prepared for by the *dum*-phrase, the verb of which appears in the indicative. Although the indicative is the normal mood for a *dum*-phrase, the possibility that Livy uses it instead of the subjunctive in order to express his own opinion remains open. On the use of the subjunctive with *dum* see Kühner–Stegmann (1914) 1992, §182, 3, pp. 199–200; §310, 5, p. 317.

54 Cf. Shuttleworth–Kraus 1994, 13: 'L(ivy) typically omits the verb of speaking to introduce short passages of indirect speech: the reported thoughts surface directly from the narrative, without authorial intervention, as it were.'

55 Cf. the remark of Viljamaa 1983, 14–15: 'In the *narratio obliqua* there is a direct connection to the past but an indirect connection to the experience of the event.'

56 Cf. the remarks of Lambert 1946, 48: 'Ganz besonders erleichtert wird dieser unmittelbare Übergang allerdings durch den häufigen Gebrauch des *infinitivus historicus*, der vor oder nach einer indirekten Rede stehend, diese auch formal gar nicht besonders in die Augen springen lässt.'

A mimetic effect is also created when the question of whose vision is presented in the narration seems open to more than one answer. Whose vision do we have, for example, in the following passage?

> *Erigentibus in primos agmen clivos apparuerunt imminentes tumulos insidentes montani, qui si valles occultiores insedissent, coorti ad pugnam repente ingentem fugam stragemque dedissent. Hannibal consistere signa iussit.*
> (Liv. 21.32.8–9)[57]

Obviously the passage begins with what Hannibal's soldiers saw, when their column began to mount the slopes. But to whom is the following reasoning (*qui si valles insedissent,... dedissent*) to be ascribed? Should it be ascribed to the Carthaginian soldiers, to Hannibal, to the narrator or to all of them? In any case and thanks to the text's openness towards all these suggestions, the narrator may appear here at the same time as an eye-witness of the described event, as a Carthaginian soldier or as Hannibal.[58]

Thus the reader has the impression that the narration is unbiased[59] though at the same time quite mimetic.

---

[57] 'As their column began to mount the first slopes, mountaineers were discovered posted on the heights above, who, had they lain concealed in hidden valleys, might have sprung out suddenly and attacked them with great rout and slaughter. Hannibal gave the command to halt.' (Transl. by B. O. Foster.)

[58] This 'ambiguous focalization' is to be differentiated from the case of a 'double or multiple focalization', in which the coexistence of different focalizations in the same segment is obvious and clear. Cf. on the term 'ambiguous focalization' Bal (1985) 1997, 114; Hornblower 1994, 134–135; Rood 1998, 20 n. 59. Don Fowler (1990, 43) speaks in regard to Virgil's *Aeneid* and to cases, where 'the question of whose point of view language embodies' is difficult to be answered, of the 'deviant focalisation' 'to stress that there is a sense in which these instances "break the rules"'. Fowler points out (1990, 44): 'Because it is *not* explicitly signalled, whether we choose to suppose its presence in a particular instance will be a matter of interpretative choice.' De Jong ((1987) 2004, 118–122) uses the term 'implicit embedded focalization'.

[59] On impartiality as a postulated feature of the historical narrative style, see Fornara 1983, 99–101; Marincola 2004, 158–174, 182–205; ibid., 160: 'For the Romans, at least, bias is presented as the great obstacle to truth, yet even among the Greeks, prejudice is high on the list of undesirable qualities, and its rejection is an essential element in establishing the historian's authority.' Especially on Livy see Marincola, ibid., 170: 'His (sc. Livy's) impartiality was ... of a different type from that expressed by Polybius, for Livy was impartial within an overall favourable treatment.' Cf. also the remark of Leeman (1963) 1986, 172: 'A profession of truth is to be found in nearly all historians from Hecataeus, Herodotus and Thucydides onwards.'

5. Persuasion

In the paragraphs above I have referred to passages where Livy used indirect speech to describe a dream or to present the thoughts of a participant in the narrated events.[60] Our historian in fact uses indirect speech on a large scale[61] and the question is how this wide use is to be explained.[62]

According to Justin, Pompeius Trogus (late C1 B.C.) censured Sallust and Livy for 'transgressing the bounds of history' with the introduction of *contio directa* (Just. 38.3.11 = Pomp. Trog. *Hist. Phil.* fr. 11 Seel). This evidence induces us to think about the conventions of the genre; as Walsh has pointed out, it 'suggests that the normal procedure in the annalists had been to reproduce speeches in *oratio obliqua*'.[63] The use of indirect speech could therefore be seen as a sign of Livy's conformity with the main features of traditional Roman historical narration.[64]

This suggestion is of no surprise as Livy's affinity to the old annalistic tradition has already been underlined many times by several classical scholars.[65] Equally well known is that Livy may have carried out the programme which Cicero drafted for writing history contrary to that tradition.[66] According to this programme history does not only have

---

60 Cf. the remark of Walsh 1961, 244: 'Above all, Livy artistically uses *oratio obliqua* to convey to the reader a psychological impression of the thought processes of groups of people witnessing an event or pondering a course of action.' See also here n. 48.
61 On the very bright use of indirect speech in Livy's history see Lambert 1946, 17.
62 According to Lambert the indirect speech has 'etwas Unbestimmtes, Fliessendes, Unpersönliches' (1946, 46). Lambert seems therefore to suppose that the direct speech is more reliable than the indirect speech. But his thesis needs in any case to be examined in the light of a more systematic comparison between Livy's style of *oratio recta* ('direct speech') and *oratio obliqua* ('indirect speech'). He points also out (1946, 59) that 'Durch diesen Kunstgriff (sc. the *oratio obliqua*) bleibt die Erzählung im Fluss, die Rede fällt nicht aus dem Rahmen, die Handlung steht im Vordergrund, nicht das Wort'.
63 So Walsh 1961, 243.
64 Cf. Petzold 1993, 154 on the annalistic 'Chronikstil, der gewissermaßen für das literarische Genos der *historia* in lateinischer Sprache maßgebend war'.
65 Cf. e.g. Petzold 1993, 160, 178; Oakley 1997, 122–125 and see Liv. 43.13.2.
66 About the influence of Cicero, to whom we owe important statements about 'how history is to be written', upon Livy see McDonald 1957, 160: 'Cicero defined the programme, Livy carried it out'; Ogilvie 1965, 19; Canfora 1993, 171–172; Moles 1993, 146–147, 166 n. 61; Mineo 2006, 20. On Cicero

to communicate the truth, as the older annalists were supposed to have done, but at the same time to do so in a cultured and polished form.[67] Livy was indeed not indifferent to the embellishment of his narrative style as many ancient evidences show.[68] It seems probable therefore that our historian consciously combined two different traditions of historical composition.[69]

Hellenistic historiography, sometimes termed 'tragic history',[70] is another tradition with which Livy has been connected by some of his modern commentators.[71] According to Walsh, Livy 'exploits that facility for psychological observation which is always so prominent in his writing, and ... demonstrates his affinities with the "tragic" approach so popular in Hellenistic historiography ...'[72] A vivid, sensational and emotional representation of events has been seen as a typical mark of such a historiographical tradition.[73] It is probably this art of writing history which Polybius attacks in his own work.[74] In this respect Livy could be seen as a historian who has worked to a large extent contrary to some of the Polybian principles. But this thesis is in fact open to some doubt.[75]

---

and on the relationship of historiography to rhetoric see also Woodman 1988, 86–91; Fornara 1983, 109; Hornblower 1994, 133 n. 5; Fox 2007.

67 See e.g. Leeman (1963) 1986, 171, 173.
68 See e.g. Sen. *epist.* 46.1; 100.9; *Dial.* 3.20.6; Tac. *Ann.* 4.34.3; *Agr.* 10; Quint. *Inst.* 2.5.19; 10.1.32; 10.1.101.
69 See Rambaud 1953, 9; Viljamaa 1983, 70; Levene 1993, 22–24, 115–116; Feldherr 1998, 52, 68–69 with n. 51; Mineo 2006, 62.
70 On this term see Brink 1960, 14.
71 See Walsh 1961, 191; id., 1982, 1072–1073; Burck 1967, 141–142; Pauw 1991; Feldherr 1998, 166; Chaplin 2000, 121. We do not have any reason to suppose that the annalists were not influenced by the manners of Hellenistic historiography. For an example of such an influence see Norden (1915) 1966, 154. But see also Burck 1992, 50–51: 'Ein Vergleich zwischen ihnen (sc. the annalists) und Livius, ..., zeigt die dramatische Straffung und die seelische Differenzierungskunst des Livius gegenüber seinen Vorgängern.'
72 So Walsh 1961, 191.
73 See Walbank 1972, 34–37, who argues against the connection of this historiographical tradition with a Peripatetic school. According to Brink 1960, 19 'It (sc. the 'tragic history') appears to have been a post-Aristotelian form of historical writing in which some of the principles of tragedy as Aristotle saw them were deliberately applied to history, although there must have been many earlier examples of "emotive" historical narrative'.
74 See Walbank 1972, 34, 39.
75 See e.g. the remarks of Lambert 1946, 15: 'Darum verzichtet er (sc. Livy) auf die Wiedergabe übermäßiger Leidenschaftlichkeit, deren Darstellung noch in der

Nobody would dispute that the use of indirect speech by a historical author to represent what happens in the mind or in the soul of a figure is more 'mimetic' (in the Platonic sense of the word) than a narration of the same subject without any details and from a critical and considered distance. But if the 'internal world' of a person is given in indirect discourse, the mediating presence of the narrator is too clear to be ignored.[76]

On the other hand, direct speech used as a vehicle of what has to be seen as a part of the (sub)consciousness of a person, a pure imitation therefore of a situation which no one else except the person involved, i.e. the speaker himself, could attest to, would strongly give the impression that it is the fruit of the author's imagination. In such a case the vividness of the narration would evoke in the readers the illusion that a more or less intensive psychological 'drama' is happening before their eyes, but at the same time this illusion could in fact unsettle the reliability of the representation[77] as a well-known passage by Polybius lets us suggest

---

hellenistischen Geschichtsschreibung zu höchster Blüte entwickelt worden war ...'; Dangel 1982, 2: 'Tite-Live a peut-être été amené à accuser encore les traits essentiels de l'écriture oratoire en raison de la faible dimension donnée dans son oeuvre aux discours, comparativement à la partie narrative ...'; Burck (1933) 1964, 181, 196–197, 228; id., 1992, 58: 'Indes beläßt es Livius nicht bei den Sympathien, in denen die Vertreter der tragischen Geschichtsschreibung eines ihrer wichtigsten Ziele gesehen haben ...' Cf. also Tränkle 1977, 100: 'Auch der Erzählweise des Polybios fehlt neben der immer wieder durchbrechenden Neigung zum abstrakten Ausdruck die ἐνάργεια oder, wie er es genannt haben würde, die ἔμφασις nicht. Der Unterschied zwischen beiden Schriftstellern ist ein gradueller.' Besides Livy has certainly used the work of Polybius as one of his most important authorities; on this topic see particularly Tränkle 1977, passim.

76 Cf. Quint. Inst. 9.2.37: Vertitur interim προσωποποιΐα in speciem narrandi. Unde apud historicos reperiuntur obliquae adlocutiones, ut in T. Livii primo statim: 'urbes quoque ut cetera ex infimo nasci ...' ['At times impersonation takes the form of narrative. Thus we find indirect speeches in the historians, as at the opening of Livy's first book: "That cities, like other things, spring from the humblest origins ..."' (transl. by H. E. Butler)]; Genette (1972) 1980, 192: '... la présence du narrateur y est encore trop sensible dans le syntaxe même de la phrase pour que le discours s'impose avec l'autonomie documentaire d'une citation.'; Laird 1999, 133: 'If the utterances of characters like these are given in indirect discourse, we feel that the narrator's presence is mediating, interfering with what was "actually said".'

77 Cf. the remarks of Sternberg 1982, 120 on the modern novel: '... sometimes the very interests of realism dictate the recourse to the nondirect modes, precisely because their inset openly manifests the presence of a quoter, who regulates and assumes part of the responsibility for its composition. This often happens where, according to the implied mimetic norms of speech or thought, a direct version might appear too stilted, witty, low, smooth, discontinuous, ar-

(Plb. 2.56.10–13). The Greek historian contrasts here the historical method of putting into the mouths of the characters – like a tragic poet would do – invented speeches with what he recognizes as the real task of a historian, to instruct and convince serious students by the truth of the facts and the speeches he narrates.[78]

When Livy prefers to use indirect speech for reproducing the 'internal world' of a person (or persons) instead of introducing into his narrative, for example, an internal monologue as an epic or a tragic poet in such a case would probably do, he lets the narrator appear as a mediator between the historical material and the audience. The narrator is, in effect, a guarantor of the historical truth and takes upon himself the task of informing the readers about events of the past as seen from all viewpoints. As an ancient reader himself Livy might acknowledge in this narrator, the historical-authorial narrator, as in the epic-authorial narrator too, an 'objectifying role as repository of the truth and formulator of that truth'.[79] On the other hand, if the narrator does not undertake the role of a historical character to reproduce what might not be seen as an external historical action witnessed by others, his narration evokes the impression of impartiality.[80] Under both aspects it is the reliability of the historical narrative which is supported.

The following 'metanarrative' comment allows us to conclude that Livy was in fact interested in the opinion of his readers on the reliability of his historiography.

> *Quem decreto sermonem praetenderit, forsan aliquem verum auctores antiqui tradiderint: quia nusquam ullum in tanta foeditate decreti veri similem invenio, id quod constat nudum videtur proponendum, decresse vindicias secundum servitutem.*
> (Liv. 3.47.5)[81]

---

ticulate, self-conscious, minutely recalled, or otherwise far-fetched to be true ... (121) Whether the threat of probability arises from the side of quotee, quoter, original or audience ... it indicates an avoidance of directness ...'

78 Cf. Paton (1922) 1992, *ad* Plb. 2.56.11 and see Walbank 1957, *ad* Plb. 2.56.11–12; 2.56.13. On the Polybius passage see also Burck (1933) 1964, 195–196; Pédech 1964, 394; Fornara 1983, 125–128.
79 So Conte 1986, 169–170 n. 21 with regard to the epic-narrator.
80 On impartiality as a postulated feature of the historical narrative style see here n. 59.
81 'The discourse with which he led up to his decree may perhaps be truthfully represented in some one of the old accounts, but since I can nowhere discover one that is plausible, in view of the enormity of the decision, it seems my duty to set forth the naked fact, upon which all agree, that he adjudged Verginia to him who claimed her as his slave.' (Transl. by B. O. Foster.) On this textpassage see Lambert 1946, 14. On relevant passages see ibid., 8 n. 7.

According to the text we have to imagine that our historian was searching through his sources for genuine material, in order to inform the readers about what had actually been said and what had actually happened. To be sure, this could be more a claim than a truth but what we can certainly conclude from such a statement is that Livy must at least have excluded from his report that which was not in his view probable.[82] The reasons for this are obvious: In the *Praefatio* to his first book (Liv. 1 *praef.* 10) in fact the historian speaks of his purpose to instruct his readers and he encourages them to profit by this instruction. It goes without saying that Livy needs to write a persuasive history to meet this end and therefore it seems reasonable that some features of his narrative style are to be explained in the light of this plan.[83]

We recognize the purpose of the author – to construct a closely woven and persuasive narration – when we find passages of different focalization which correspond to each other in content and form.[84]

---

[82] About Livy's accuracy in the reproduction of the speeches see Sen. *Suas.* 6.22; Tac. *Ann.* 4.34.3. But see also Quint. *Inst.* 10.1.32 and cf. Liv. 1 *praef.* 5–7; 5.21.9; 8.40.4–5. Livy occasionally mentions the sources followed (see e.g. Liv. 10.2.3; 10.3.4; 10.3.7–8; Walsh 1961, 110–137 and esp. 127–128). In this way he supports the credibility of his narration. See also Lambert 1946, 10–11: 'Dass Livius bereits sein Quellenmaterial in bezug auf Authentizität der Reden richtig einschätzte und daraus für sich selbst die richtige Folgerung zog, wird wohl aus Wendungen, wie: ... *dicitur* ... *locutus in hanc fere sententiam esse* (VI 20, 2), oder: ... *in hunc maxime modum respondisse accepi* (XXXVIII 47, 1), hervorgehoben.' But see the general statement of Walsh, ibid., 110: 'The most serious objection to any consideration of Livy as a scientific historian is in part an indictment of Roman historiography generally. It is the failure to search out and evaluate the original documentary evidence.' Livy is therefore still seen as a representative author for the 'pleasure-oriented, highly artificial "rhetorical" historiography' (so Marincola 2004, 2–3).

[83] Cf. the remark of Woodman 1988, 91: '... the Romans required the hard core of history to be true and its elaboration to be plausible ...' A probable narration (*narratio probabilis, narratio veri similis*) is seen as an indispensable part of a forensic speech in ancient rhetoric. Cf. Lausberg (1960) 1990, §322. It is a narration which is clear and evident and therefore can persuade; see Cic. *De orat.* 2.19.80. Livy knew probably that narration can be plausible and credible not only if it simply offers information based on true events, but also if it does this in an immediate, vivid and convincing way; see Quint. *Inst.* 4.2.123. To the topic 'forms and conventions of persuasion employed by the historians' see Marincola 2004, 128–174; especially on Livy, see ibid., 140–141, 153–154, 170–172; see also Shuttleworth-Kraus 1994, 12.

[84] Cf. Conte's remark on the use of different points of view by Virgil (1986, 154): 'To reveal this hidden point of view and reduce the bias of its perspective, Vir-

In Liv. 3.35.3 for example, Livy's narrator reveals in the form of psycho-narration the motives of Appius Claudius, one of the Decemviri:

> *Demissa iam in discrimen dignitas ea aetate iisque honoribus actis stimulabat Ap. Claudium.*[85]

The authorial narrator next makes a statement about the behaviour of Appius Claudius as if he were an eyewitness:

> *Nescires utrum inter decemviros an inter candidatos numerares. Propior interdum petendo quam gerendo magistratui erat.*[86]
>
> (Liv. 3.35.3–4)

He explains this with a more detailed account of what Appius Claudius was doing:

> *Criminari optimates, extollere candidatorum levissimum quemque humillimumque, ipse medius inter tribunicios, Duillios Iciliosque, in foro volitare, per illos se plebi venditare ...*
>
> (Liv. 3.35.4–5)[87]

In the next sentences the narrative gradually becomes internally focalized through Appius Claudius' colleagues:

> *... donec collegae quoque, qui unice illi dediti fuerant ad id tempus, coniecere in eum oculos, mirantes quid sibi vellet: apparere nihil sinceri esse; profecto haud gratuitam in tanta superbia comitatem fore: nimium in ordinem se ipsum cogere et volgari cum privatis non tam properantis abire magistratu quam viam ad continuandum magistratum quaerentis esse.*
>
> (Liv. 3.35.5–6)[88]

---

gil introduces multiple points of views as a more powerful interpretative apparatus.'

85 'The risk of losing his position, at his time of life, and after holding the offices he had held, acted as a spur to Appius Claudius.' (Transl. by B. O. Foster.)
86 'One would not have known whether to reckon him among the decemvirs or the candidates. He was at times more like one who sought a magistracy than like one who exercised it.' (Transl. by B. O. Foster.)
87 'He vilified the nobles; praised all the most insignificant and low-born candidates; and surrounding himself with former tribunes, like Duillius and Icilius, bustled about the Forum, and through them recommended himself to the plebs.' (Transl. by B. O. Foster.)
88 'Till even his colleagues, who had been singularly devoted to him until then, looked askance at him and wondered what this could mean. It was evident there could be nothing genuine about it; so proud a man would certainly not be affable for nothing; excessive self-abasement and mingling with private citizens were not so much the marks of one who was in haste to retire from office as of one who sought the means of re-election.' (Transl. by B. O. Foster.)

The last semicolon (*nimium in ordinem se ipsum cogere ... quaerentis esse*) corresponds to the passage cited above (Liv. 3.35.3–4), where the narrator's point of view dominates. The two perspectives, that of the narrator and that of Appius Claudius' colleagues reinforce each other. It is thus made more and more clear to the reader, through two seemingly different testimonies, that Appius Claudius will not willingly give up his office.

In a similar way Liv. 3.38.7 corresponds to Liv. 3.41.2. In the first passage the thoughts of the worried Decemviri are given in the form of transposed speech:

> *omnes vastati agri periculorumque imminentium causas in se congesturos, temptationemque eam fore abolendi sibi magistratus, ni consensu resisterent imperioque inhibendo acriter in paucos praeferocis animi conatus aliorum comprimerent.*
>
> (Liv. 3.38.7)[89]

In the second, where the narrative is also internally focalized (again in the form of transposed speech), we learn why Appius decided to order the arrest of Valerius:

> *Tum Appius, iam prope esse ratus ut ni violentiae eorum pari resisteretur audacia victum imperium esset ...*
>
> (Liv. 3.41.2–3)[90]

Verbal echoes stress here the correspondence between the two passages (*ni ... resisterent* – *ni ... resisteretur*). The narration's consistency proves or reflects the consistent behaviour of Appius. Liv. 3.38.7 prepares the reader for the reaction of the Decemviri to people who are *praeferocis animi* (bold and impetuous) with respect to them. As Valerius and Horatius themselves behave *ferociter* (Liv. 3.39.3: *Nec minus ferociter M. Horatium Barbatum isse in certamen, decem Tarquinios appellantem admonentemque Valeriis et Horatiis ducibus pulsos reges.*[91]), the reaction of Appius to the first seems only natural.[92]

---

89 'The devastation of the land and the dangers which impended would be laid by everybody at their doors; and this would lead to an attempt being made to abolish their magistracy, unless they presented a united resistance, and by sharply exercising their power upon the few really daring spirits, put a stop to the efforts of the rest.' (Transl. by B. O. Foster.)

90 'Thereupon Appius, thinking the moment was at hand when, unless he opposed their violence with equal boldness, his authority was doomed ...' (Transl. by B. O. Foster.)

91 'With equal spirit, it is said, did Marcus Horatius Barbatus enter the dispute, calling them ten Tarquinii, and warning them that the Valerii and the Horatii had been leaders in the expulsion of the kings.' (Transl. by B. O. Foster.)

It is difficult for a historical report to be plausible as a vehicle of truth, especially with regard to the matter of thoughts or moods. Such cross references in the narration point to the consistency in the contemplations, judgements and feelings which the historian ascribes to historical figures based essentially on (his own?) historical imagination.[93] However, it is exactly this inner congruity which could make a more sceptical mind suspicious about the reliability of the narration. But it is true to say that such a technique seems to appeal rather to the subconsciousness than to the consciousness of the perceiver and it is precisely because of this that it can be thought as so effective.[94]

6. Epilogue

Narratological studies as practised in Classics for the last thirty years[95] are embraced today by some classical scholars as a useful modern approach, but are met with suspicion by others.[96] One reason why the narratolog-

---

92 Cf. Walsh 1961, 233 (about Livy's technique 'of speech construction'): 'Another interesting technique of speech construction is the method by which the historian draws together a number of separate speeches to form a single, coherent, non-redundant statement.' Cf. also Walsh, ibid., 83: 'The advantages of this "indirect" method to the historian are obvious. ... This allows him to pose as an impartial narrator whilst he is enabled to praise particular persons or measures by these indirect methods ...' Cf. also the remarks of Romilly 1956, 33–34 and Rood 1998, 20 on Thucydides.
93 Cf. Woodman 1988, 91; Feichtinger 1992, 11–12, 13 n. 26, 21. But see also Walsh 1961, 231: 'So far as content is concerned, comparison with extant source-material suggests that Livy does not personally introduce many fictitious topics.'
94 See Lausberg (1960) 1990, §§ 325, 326.
95 On the history of narratological studies see Vogt in Genette 1994, 300: 'Sie (sc. the essay "Frontières du récit") stand 1966 neben ihrerseits innovativen (und heute "klassischen") Aufsätzen von Barthes, Greimas, Brémond, Eco, Todorov, Metz, im achten Heft der Zeitschrift *Communications* (Reprint 1981), das heute als Gründungsdokument einer "französischen Schule" der strukturalen Erzählanalyse oder *Narratologie* gilt.' We find the earliest studies in Classics concentrating on narratological questions in the end of the 70s. See the reference of Fowler 1990, 54 to the study of Rosati 1979 and also the bibliography on the application of narratology in classical texts in de Jong–Sullivan 1993, 282–283; see also Schmitz 2002, 74–75.
96 Cf. Schmitz 2002, 15 according to whom classical philology, especially in Germany, has been tardy in reacting to the new challenges of literary theory. Schmitz however seems to consider narratology no part of literary theory, al-

ical approach to Greek and Roman literature had in the past and to some extent still has to compete with much older interpretative models and trends may be that its contribution to the new and better understanding of our texts does not always seem commensurate with the extensive armoury of technical terms and categories it presupposes.[97] Certainly the aim of the employment of narratological models in Greek and Latin texts cannot be simply to select a series of narrative characteristics. Beyond such a selection we have also most importantly to understand constructively and to show persuasively why a literary text is woven in a certain way.[98]

The examination of some representative cases of internally focalized narrative in Livy's historiography developed in the paragraphs above lead here to a reconsideration of an important facet of his work, i. e. the dominant presence and the role of its authorial narrator. The fact that in the light of the thoughts expressed new perspectives open up in the search for a better appreciation of the text is to be seen as a profit of the narratological treatment. It is now clearer, for example, why the question about visuality (ἐνάργεια) and its forms in *Ab urbe condita* deserves to be explored from a more differentiating and critical viewpoint, which will recognize the role and the function of the authorial narrator in the work.[99] Also of importance is the question of how the systematic

---

though in his book he dedicates a chapter to narratological studies in Classics (2002, 55 ff.). But see also e. g. the praise bestowed on Irene de Jong's narratological studies of Homer and Euripides by Hornblower 1994, 135.

[97] Cf. Schmitz 2002, 16, 19–20. For a critique of structuralism in general see Eagleton (1983) 1996, 94–109.

[98] Cf. Bal (1985) 1997, 9: 'Because the theory to which these concepts pertain is a systematic one, it is in principle possible to give a complete description of a text, that is an account of all of the *narrative* characteristics of the text in question. However, such a description would consume a great amount of time and paper, and would, in the end, be rather uninteresting. The researcher, therefore, will always make a choice. Intuitively, on the basis of a careful reading of the text, s/he selects those elements of the theory which s/he thinks particularly relevant to the text that s/he wishes to describe. ... The textual description that results provides the basis for an eventual interpretation. In other words, it is possible on the basis of a description ("the text is so constructed") to (10) attach a meaning to the text ("the text means this").' It should be also stressed that grammar, especially the function of the *modi*, has an important role to play in this kind of literary criticism; on this topic see Bakker 1997c.

[99] On *evidentia* as a feature of Livy's narration see Tränkle 1977, 99 (on a description of a place in Liv. 45.28.2): 'Anschauung wird an den Leser herangebracht; dieser soll den innerhalb der Stadt hochaufragenden Burgfelsen mit seinen reichen Quellen und den schmalen Landeinschnitt zwischen den beiden Mee-

intervention of the narrator within the structure of the work coexists with Livy's treatment of his own authority.[100] Equally provoking are the questions too about how Livy's text in view of its particular narrative features does implement the historiographical 'code'[101] and what its relationship to other normative historiographical texts is.

Questions like these can therefore arise from a narratological reading, but obviously they cannot be regarded as simply restricted to the limits of narratology. In the end, paradoxical though it might sound, I risk claiming that it is precisely the value of narratology as a method of analyzing and, thereby, understanding literary texts which makes us suspicious of its interpretative dynamics. First of all, the concentration upon the form, which narratology demands, evokes almost as a reflex, interest in the text's content and ideology.[102] But also the deciphering of the text's meaning, which we achieve through a narratological reading, makes other aspects (and therefore other meanings too) of the text appear, which were not visible before; for example, its relation to other texts or the transformation which its meaning is subject to, when looked

---

ren gleichsam vor dem inneren Auge sehen.' See also Burck (1933) 1964, 200. On the figure of *evidentia* as 'a distinctly poetic means of expression' see Lausberg (1960) 1990, §810 (transl. by M. T. Bliss, A. Jansen, D. E. Orton). Thought-provoking recent publications stress the importance ascribed by Livy to the spectacle (see e.g. Feldherr 1998, Chaplin 2000). Some of these conclusions, as interesting as they might be, would, I believe, benefit from a re-examination from a narratological aspect.

100 Cf. the remark of Marincola 2004, 11: 'Indeed ... the Roman historians use far fewer explicit methods to create an authoritative persona than do the Greeks. Livy, however, is a significant exception, since he presents himself in a Herodotean manner, sifting through the tradition, comparing accounts and sources, marvelling, or addressing the reader. His use of the first person is more pronounced than in (12) any of the other Roman historians.' On Livy's authority see also ibid., 140–141, 248–249. On the other hand Shuttleworth-Kraus (1994, 13) claims that Livy unsettles 'the authority both of the presentation and of the historian's own voice' in order to engage the reader in the historiographical project. Shuttleworth-Kraus evidently means that such a rhetorical treatment of the historical events could shatter the narrative illusion and therefore undermine the persuasive power of the narration. However, see also Quint. *Inst.* 9.2.19 (*adfert aliquam fidem veritatis et dubitatio* – 'hesitation may lend an impression of truth'. Transl. by H. E. Butler), to which Shuttleworth-Kraus herself refers (ibid., *ad Liv.* 6.12.2, p. 158).

101 See for this term Conte 1986, 142–144 with n. 2.

102 See the excellent remarks of Fowler 1990, 55 on the contribution of the Italian scholarship in understanding the ideological importance of the narrative focalization.

at from the point of view of different audiences. Narratology appears then as an effective albeit partial method of literary criticism. At a certain point it becomes obvious that other interpretative models need to be used, at least for supplementary purposes.

Theoretically therefore, a reader could be moved by an interesting literary narrative text to realize the historical sequence of different interpretative models and trends, which have appeared in the history of ancient and modern literary criticim before and after structuralism. In this historical, i. e. dialectical, process narratology takes the place of 'thesis' as well as that of 'anti-thesis'. In both cases it always leads – though at any given time in a different way – to a much better understanding of literary narrative texts.

Fame's Narratives. Epic and Historiography[1]
Philip Hardie

That fame and narratives are inseparable in ancient epic and historiography goes without saying: narratives of the deeds of heroes or great men of the past are the vehicles of, and indeed constitutive of, the fame of their subjects. My focus in this paper will however not be so much on fame as the product of narratives, as on fame as the process of narrating, and to do this I need to widen the usual meanings of the modern English word fame to cover the meanings of the Latin *fama*, which includes 'report', 'rumour', 'tradition', as well as 'renown' or 'glory'. One of the standard ways of introducing a narrative in Latin poetry is with the formula *ut fertur*, or *ferunt*, 'as they say', or, in an equivalent phrase, *(ut) fama est* 'as the traditional story has it'. If we understand '*fama*' in this sense of 'narrative', my title becomes virtually a tautology: 'narrative's narratives'. And even taking fame in its more restricted modern English sense, some of the other ancient lexical equivalents can also refer both to the famous deeds of great men, and to the narratives that celebrate those deeds. Etymologically *kleos* is an 'oral report', and then more specifically the enduring report of outstanding deeds.[2] κλέα ἀνδρῶν can mean both 'epic songs on heroes' and 'famous deeds of heroes'. In Latin *laudes*, originally words that praise, is also extended to denote the deeds that are so celebrated.

There is for my purposes another important ambiguity in the phrase 'fame's narratives', that between the subjective and objective genitive: stories narrated by *fama*, and stories narrated about *fama*. In this duality of meaning, between *fama* as the narrating subject and *fama* as the object of narrating, is to be located one of the most tricksy qualities of *fama*, its ability to move between narrative levels. *Fama* tells stories about persons and events within the text, and at times emerges to the status of a character within the text (an intradiegetic narrator). The narrator outside the text, the extradiegetic narrator, tells stories about *fama* telling stories. In

---

1 The reflections contained in this paper arise from a larger project on the history of *fama*.
2 See Olson 1995, ch. 1; Greindl 1938, 29.

that shared function lies the possibility for an easy shift between the roles of narrator and his character *fama*. *Fama* flits between the inside and the outside of the text.

It is not the abstract or personified *fama* alone which enjoys this privilege of crossing boundaries. In recent decades it has become fashionable to identify a number of such boundary-crossers: bards in epic narratives become figures of the poet-narrator, as do also some of the gods in epic: Zeus or Jupiter in the Homeric and Virgilian epics, Juno in the *Aeneid*. Conversely extradiegetic narrators have been pitched into their own narratives: Herodotus and Livy have become doubles or rivals of the major characters within their historical narratives; metapoetically Virgil follows in the steps of Aeneas. *Fama* as a figure able to play the parts of both narrator and character is at once more universal and more limited than the individuals, divine and human, just mentioned. More universal in that as an abstract noun of saying, *fari*, *fama* can cover everything that the narrator does. More limited, because there is not just one *fama*, but an indefinite multiplicity of *famae* (despite that fact the plural *famae* is actually very rare).[3] Narratives often narrow this multiplicity down to a duality, or it might be better to say a duplicity, of *famae*. Livy's *History* begins with a generally agreed 'fact', *iam primum omnium satis constat* …, that Aeneas and Antenor were spared by the Greeks at the sack of Troy. A few lines later we come across the first example of the word *fama* in the narrative (I omit the occurrence of *fama* in the *Praefatio*, where, significantly, it refers to what is said about the historian, his reputation or renown), and it is *duplex*, two competing versions of the story of how Aeneas and Latinus met, Livy 1.1 *Duplex inde fama est. Alii … tradunt: alii …* Here the historian expresses no preference of his own as between these two versions, and if we want to see a homology between what *fama* does and what the historian does, then we will have to admit that on its own each of these two *famae* can be no more than a *historicus dimidiatus*.

If *fama* often comes close to being synonymous with narrative, how might we think further about *fama* in relation to the traditional topics of narratology? One perhaps unexpected area relates to the temporal ordering of narrative. One of *fama*'s functions is to preserve a record of things that have happened in the past, and when *fama*'s record-keeping becomes itself an object of narrating, then *fama* may be used to intro-

---

3 *TLL* VI. i. 206.69 ff.

duce an analepsis, as for example within the larger analepsis that is Aeneas' narrative in *Aeneid* 3.121–3:[4]

> *Fama uolat pulsum regnis cessisse paternis*
> *Idomenea ducem, desertaque litora Cretae,*
> *hoste uacare domum sedesque astare relictas.*
>
> Rumour as she flew told the tale of the great Idomeneus, how he had been forced to leave his father's kingdom and how the shores of Crete were now deserted. Here was a place empty of our enemies, their homes abandoned, waiting for us.

A lightly personified *Fama* is introduced to tell the Trojans a story, very short, but still recognizably a narrative of something that happened in the past: Idomeneus has been forced to leave his ancestral kingdom, and as a result the shores of Crete are abandoned. This is also an example of *fama* flitting between the inside and outside of the fictional narrative. Nicholas Horsfall *ad loc.* in his recent commentary on *Aeneid* 3 makes the point that *fama uolat* can also function as what is often labelled an 'Alexandrian footnote' for Virgil's reader, outside the text, a signal to us that the poet is saying something about his own relation to tradition.

Fama as tradition, or as fame, can only introduce an analepsis, but *fama* as report or rumour can also introduce a prolepsis, of a kind. For example report can run ahead of an event: in the historians *fama* of an approaching army may arrive before the army itself. Or *fama* may point to the successful candidate for an office, as in the case of Agricola's appointment to the governorship of Britain, according to Tacitus, *Agricola* 9.7 *haud semper errat fama; aliquando et eligit*. At *Histories* 1.22 rumour reinforces divination in foretelling imperial appointment (of Otho), and in this case credence in the rumour may have played an active part in bringing about that of which it spoke.[5] Rumour, that is, can function as a self-fulfilling prophecy, and in the historians rumour is frequently connected with omens and prodigies, other forms of communication which have a proleptic power. One may reflect on the use of prophecy in literary narrative to introduce a prolepsis.

---

[4] For another example see 3.294–7: *Hic incredibilis rerum fama occupat auris, Priamiden Helenum Graias regnare per urbis coniugio Aeacidae Pyrrhi sceptrisque potitum, et patrio Andromachen iterum cessisse marito.*

[5] Cf. also 2.78 (Basilides' extispicy for Vespasian): *has ambages et statim exceperat fama et tunc aperiebat; nec quicquam magis in ore vulgi. crebriores apud ipsum sermones, quanto sperantibus plura dicuntur.*

The uses of *fama* for the historian, in terms of the construction and manipulation of narrative, are various. In the rest of this paper I want to concentrate on two areas: firstly *fama* as point of view or focalization (*fama* as narrator); and secondly narratives about *fama*, with particular reference to beginnings and endings, overture and closure.

1. Point of view, focalization. *Fama* and *facta*.

Fama etymologically is 'what is said', 'report', as also is κλέος (cognate with κλέ(ι)ω 'tell of', 'celebrate'). In itself the word is neutral as to the point of view of the subject of speaking. Some epic observations, before I turn to historiography. κλέα ἀνδρῶν as the matter of the bard, or hero posing as bard (Achilles), might be thought of as the 'nonfocalized' (Genette's term) narrative of the omniscient poet, a standard way of thinking about the Homeric epic narrator until Irene de Jong showed us how very far the Homeric narrator is from maintaining a scrupulous impartiality. A sense of the partiality of Virgilian epic narrative has a far longer history in twentieth-century criticism, but one may point to uses of the word *fama* in the poem where a claim (and perhaps only a claim) to an omniscient and unbiased narrative is implied, through the inscription within the text of surrogates for the epic poem or epic poet. One such is the summary of the scenes of the Trojan War in the Carthaginian Temple of Juno as (*Aen.* 1.457) *bellaque iam fama totum uulgata per orbem*, a good example of *fama*'s tendency to move between inside and outside of the text: the verse refers both to the worldwide dissemination of reports of the Trojan War in the legendary time of Aeneas, and to the wide readership for the epic poems on the Trojan War, more specifically the Epic Cycle, *orbis* (a pun pointed out by Alessandro Barchiesi).[6] At the same time it is notorious that modern critics have debated fiercely whether a point of view is to be identified in images of the destruction of Troy set up in the temple of Troy's implacable enemy, Juno, and whether Aeneas' own point of view on those events makes him a bad reader of the *fama* contained in these ecphrastic scenes from epic.

The contents of another Virgilian ecphrasis, the Shield of Aeneas, are summed up as (*Aen.* 8.731) *famamque et fata nepotum*, forcing an equivalence between *fama*, human reports of the great deeds of the Ro-

---

6   Barchiesi 1999, 334.

mans, and the unerring word of Jupiter, the speaker of fate. Jupiter's own first-person version of that fixed and fated history (1.257–8 *manent immota tuorum | fata tibi*) in book one of the *Aeneid* works towards a climax in a closural *fama*, 1.287 [Caesar] *imperium Oceano, famam qui terminet astris*. Fixing a *terminus* in the stars has especial point when the speaker of this prophecy is himself seated in the stars, (225–6 *uertice caeli | constitit*) – and we might also think of the particular resonance for the Roman reader of a *terminus* fixed in a high place. Another Jovian formulation suggests a programme for a future tradition of epic narrative in which event and report are not separable by the partiality of competing focalizations, Jupiter's definition of the heroic code for the benefit of his son Hercules, *Aen.* 10.468–9 *sed famam extendere factis, | hoc uirtutis opus*. *Fama* will be increased, extended by deeds, *facta*, with which *fama* will be coextensive. But the suspicious critical mind has seen reason to detect partiality in the words of Jupiter in the *Aeneid*, and if the god is indeed all-seeing and omniscient, he does not necessarily reveal his omniscience in his utterances in the poem.

Another Virgilian character whose multiple organs of seeing and hearing might be thought to give her something like the omniscience of Jupiter – or of the Homeric Helios, 'who sees all things and hears all things' (*Iliad* 3.277; *Odyssey* 11.109, 12.323) – is the *Fama* of *Aeneid* 4, who in her multiplicity of tongues realises the human poet's dream of vocal resources adequate for his task. The epic poet would need ten or a hundred tongues in order to come close to telling of the size and complexity of his subject, but were he up to the job, his would presumably be a univocal and true account of things 'wie es eigentlich gewesen'. *Fama* on the other hand uses her multiplicity of tongues to fill the *populi* with a *multiplex sermo* (*Aen*. 4.189), the various and mutable voices and points of view of the many-headed beast. What *Fama* says about Dido and Aeneas has a very obvious focalization, through a malicious and disapproving – and of course unattributable – view of the couple's behaviour. The indirect relationship of what *Fama* says to the truth (whatever that might be) is given formal expression in the indirect speech in which her words are reported: the primary narrator gives a report of the words of his secondary narrator.[7]

Tacitus is perhaps the most skilful of all ancient historians in exploiting the resources of *fama*, what is said, whether by the historian or by others, and especially by characters within his own historical narrative,

---

7   So Laird 1999, 272.

to shape the reader's response to his subject-matter. This has been extensively explored in his use of rumours and of the 'loaded alternative', that is to say, the provision by the historian of an alternative explanation or account, apparently impartially but in practice guiding the reader to a particular conclusion.[8] In the case of the loaded alternative we are dealing often not with differing focalizations of the same event, but with different versions of the event itself, although I am aware that the distinction that I have just made runs the risk of positing an absolute and in theory knowable set of events, the 'story', the unchanging substrate of the multiple perspectives, embellishments, distortions through which those events may be narrated. Livy, we have seen, introduces *fama* in the context of what are clearly two different 'stories', in the narratological sense, of the meeting of Aeneas and Latinus, presented without any 'loading': by this means Livy perhaps asserts a claim to be an impartial and responsible historian. Very near the beginning of the *Annals* Tacitus offers what might be called a *duplex fama*, in the form of the two versions of the career of Augustus that take the place of the single death notice in the voice of the historian himself, *Ann.* 1.9–10, *multus hinc ipso de Augusto sermo*. Unlike the Livian *duplex fama*, the two groups of speakers are not in dispute over dates and places, but through two very different points of view, and through a differing selection from the totality of incidents in Augustus' life and career, they offer what turn out to be very different narratives. The partiality of the two versions is signalled explicitly in the verbs used to introduce them, *uarie extollebatur arguebaturque*, praise and blame, *fama* and *infamia*. These are not however formal orations delivered by single orators, but the summary of unattributed talk of the chattering classes, a specimen of the *uarius rumor, uaria fama* that will proliferate within Tacitus' further narratings of imperial history. At the same time each of the two accounts is presented not as a miscellaneous set of commendations or criticisms of Augustus, but ordered chronologically: what we have are two sharply focalized narratives. It is often supposed that they are also an example of 'loaded alternatives': the critical obituary comes second and is longer than the laudatory one. Some loading may indeed be felt, but it should be noted that both versions are attributed to *prudentes* (as opposed to *plerique*, whose minds focus only on trivia).[9] Tacitus pointedly does not in-

---

8 Whitehead 1979.
9 For this contrast Goodyear 1972 *ad loc.* compares 1.47.3 (*prudentis/uulgum*), 16.2.1 *nec aliud per illos dies populus credulitate, prudentes diuersa fama tulere.*

terpose himself as an omniscient narrator; he does not present his own account of *facta*, one that might claim to be immune to the distorting effects of *fama*.

One historian who does attempt to force together *facta* and *fama* is the emperor Tiberius.

> '*Ego me, patres conscripti, mortalem esse et hominum officia fungi satisque habere si locum principem impleam et uos testor et meminisse posteros uolo; qui satis superque memoriae meae tribuent, ut maioribus meis dignum, rerum uestrarum prouidum, constantem in periculis, offensionum pro utilitate publica non pauidum credant. haec mihi in animis uestris templa, hae pulcherrimae effigies et mansurae. nam quae saxo struuntur, si iudicium posterorum in odium uertit, pro sepulchris spernuntur. proinde socios ciuis et deos ipsos precor, hos ut mihi ad finem usque uitae quietam et intellegentem humani diuinique iuris mentem duint, illos ut, quandoque concessero, cum laude et bonis recordationibus facta atque famam nominis mei prosequantur.*' *perstititque posthac secretis etiam sermonibus aspernari talem sui cultum. quod alii modestiam, multi, quia diffideret, quidam ut degeneris animi interpretabantur. optumos quippe mortalium altissima cupere: sic Herculem et Liberum apud Graecos, Quirinum apud nos deum numero additos: melius Augustum, qui sperauerit. cetera principibus statim adesse: unum insatiabiliter parandum, prosperam sui memoriam; nam contemptu famae contemni uirtutes.*
>
> <div align="right">Tacitus <i>Annals</i> 4.38</div>

'For myself, Senators, I am mortal and limited to the functions of humanity, content if I can adequately fill the highest place; of this I solemnly assure you, and would have posterity remember it. They will more than sufficiently honour my memory by believing me to have been worthy of my ancestry, watchful over your interests, courageous in danger, fearless of enmity, when the State required it. These sentiments of your hearts are my temples, these my most glorious and abiding monuments. Those built of stone are despised as mere tombs, if the judgment of posterity passes into hatred. And therefore this is my prayer to our allies, our citizens, and to heaven itself; to the last, that, to my life's close, it grant me a tranquil mind, which can discern alike human and divine claims; to the first, that, when I die, they honour my career and the reputation of my name with praise and kindly remembrance.' Henceforth Tiberius even in private conversations persisted in showing contempt for such homage to himself. Some attributed this to modesty; many to self-distrust; a few to a mean spirit. 'The noblest men,' it was said, 'have the loftiest aspirations, and so Hercules and Bacchus among the Greeks and Quirinus among us were enrolled in the number of the gods. Augustus, did better, seeing that he had aspired. All other things princes have as a matter of course; one thing they ought insatiably to pursue, that their memory may be glorious. For to despise fame is to despise merit.'

At *Annals* 4.37–8 Tacitus reports a speech to the Senate in which Tiberius justifies his rejection of the offer on the part of Hispania Ulterior of a temple to himself and Livia, and gives a statement of his own views on fame and memory, ending with a prayer to citizens and provincials 4.38.3 *ut ... cum laude et bonis recordationibus facta atque famam nominis mei prosequantur*. This episode is the culmination of a sequence of episodes 'in which', in the words of T. J. Luce in his insightful discussion of the passage, 'from the latter part of Book Three ... the theme of fame and memory has been building to a climax.'[10] More particularly the speech is the climax of a closely-knit section that begins with the historian's surprised comment on the not impercipient Tiberius' neglect of his *fama* in his encouragement of *maiestas* trials in 4.31, followed by the historian's famous digression on the contrast between republican and imperial history in chs 32–3, followed in turn by the trial and last speech of a famous historian of the end of the Republic, Cremutius Cordus in chs. 34–5. Then, after a short chapter retailing other trials, comes the episode of Tiberius and the rejection of the temple. This shorter sequence is a good example of what I call a '*fama* episode' of a kind frequent in both Livy and Tacitus (and perhaps more common in Roman than in Greek historiography), in which *fama* and related words and concepts are densely and locally thematized, or in which *fama* motivates and punctuates a self-contained stretch of narrative. The episodic nature of this sequence, including the historian's turn away from narrative to comment on his own art, means that this example is not exactly a 'narrative of *fama*', although the framing passages, which relate to Tiberius, taken together form a kind of narrative, in which Tiberius himself, in the speech to the Senate, attempts to assert his own control over the *fama* of which in ch. 31 he had appeared to be negligent:

> *quo magis mirum habebatur gnarum meliorum et quae fama clementiam sequeretur tristiora malle. neque enim socordia peccabat; nec occultum est, quando ex ueritate, quando adumbrata laetitia facta imperatorum celebrentur.*

> Hence it seemed the more amazing that one who knew better things and the glory which waits on mercy, should prefer harsher courses. He did not indeed err from dulness, and it is easy to see when the acts of a sovereign meet with genuine, and when with fictitious popularity.

The last sentence is in effect a comment on the relationship between *fama* and *facta*: praise, *fama*, of the emperor sometimes corresponds to *facta* and sometimes does not. Tiberius' failure – deliberate, Tacitus sug-

---

10 Luce 1991, 2924–5.

gests — to seek for an accurate calibration of *fama* and *facta* foredooms his prayer in chapter 38 to be remembered in a manner both truthful and laudatory.[11]

The immediate sequel to Tiberius' speech in *Annals* 4.38 also undermines his prayer. When Tiberius contrasts temples in the mind with those built of stone, we expect him to go on to say that the latter are subject to physical decay.[12] Instead he says that 'if the judgement of posterity turns into hatred, stone temples are spurned as tombs.' The monument, memory, is threatened not with oblivion, but with transformation into something unintended by its maker. The Tacitean text immediately exemplifies the vulnerability of Tiberius' attempt to control *fama* to its reception, as we leave the senatorial stage of public oratory for the shadow world of rumour, points of view that escape the control of the emperor. The fact that Tiberius himself continues to reject worship of his person in private conversation (*secretis sermonibus*), so far from lending credence to his public statement on the matter of *fama*, is the occasion for a return to the rumours that had prompted his speech in the Senate in the first place (4.37.1 *quorum rumore arguebatur* ...): 4.38.4 *quod alii modestiam, multi, quia diffideret, quidam ut degeneris animi interpretabantur.* This last group, who appear now sincerely to believe what might otherwise seem *adulatio* (namely, encouragement of the emperor to set his sights on godhead), criticizes the emperor for not aspiring to divinity: their gloss on his behaviour ends up as a complete reversal of Tiberius' closing attempt to link *fama* and *facta*: (4.38.5) *nam contemptu famae contemni uirtutes*: Tiberius prayed for a glorious reputation based on his solid achievements; these critics argue from a disregard for a glorious reputation to a disregard for the virtues of which those deeds would be the expression.

What is at stake in Tiberius' speech on memory and fame, and in the reactions to it, is a judgement as to the *fama* of Tiberius' performance as emperor, and, furthermore, a judgement on Tiberius' own attitude to his own *fama*, the *fama* of his *fama* so to speak. We have something like a reworking of the double report on Augustus at the beginning of the *Annals*, with the difference that one side of the debate is here represented by the *princeps* himself, while the other side, once again unnamed speakers, comment not on the reputation of the *princeps* in the

---

11 *fama* appears twice in the passage, at the beginning, 31.2, and end, 38.3. *glori-* appears twice, 32.2 *inglorius* and 33.4 *gloria*.
12 See Nisbet and Rudd on Hor. *C.* 3.30.

light of his *acta* (*facta*), but on the *princeps*' own attitude to his own reputation. And perhaps a third point of view on the emperor emerges from this sequence taken as a whole, that of the historian, critical of Tiberius but better informed than the anonymous bar-pundits in Rome. Tacitus is hardly one to be impressed by emperors who aspire to divinity, but he has a clear view of a ruler who fails in his, in itself not unpraiseworthy, desire for praise.

2. Narratives about *fama*

The sequence in *Annals* 4 that I have just examined, as well as throwing up divergent ways of talking about the emperor, narratives by fame, is also an example of a narrative about fame. I conclude with some thoughts on the part played by *fama* in the structuring of narrative, with particular attention to beginnings and endings. One of *fama*'s roles is to convey a report from A to B, instigating a new narrative, or new stage in a narrative, through the reactions of the new audience to what they hear. Fame is to blame for the oldest narrative in Greco-Roman literature, the story of the Trojan War, which would never have taken place had not reports of Helen's beauty traveled from Sparta. According to the Hesiodic *Catalogue of Women* one of Helen's suitors 'longs to wed Helen of the lovely hair, never having seen her, but hearing the story from others' (fr. 199.2–3 M-W ἱμείρων Ἑλένης πόσις ἔμμεναι ἠυκόμοιο, εἶδος οὔ τι ἰδών, ἀλλ'ἄλλων μῦθον ἀκούων); and later in the same fragment we hear of the μέγα κλέος of Helen.[13] Beauty's fame inaugurates other erotic narratives, for example Apuleius' Cupid and Psyche, *Metam.* 4.28.1–3:

> Erant in quadam ciuitate rex et regina. hi tres numero filias forma conspicuas habuere, sed maiores quidem natu, quamuis gratissima specie, idonee tamen **celebrari** posse **laudibus** humanis **credebantur**, at uero puellae iunioris tam praecipua tam praeclara pulchritudo nec exprimi ac ne sufficienter quidem **laudari** sermonis humani penuria poterat. multi denique ciuium et aduenae copiosi, quos eximii **spectaculi rumor** studiosa celebritate congregabat, inaccessae formonsitatis admiratione stupidi et admouentes oribus suis dexteram primore digito in erectum pollicem residente ut ipsam prorsus deam Venerem uenerabantur religiosis adorationibus.

---

13 In the late-antique *Rape of Helen* by Collouthos (193) Paris 'yearns for love in quest of a woman he had never seen'.

There were in a certain city a king and queen, who had three beautiful daughters. The two eldest were very fair to see, but their beauty was such that it was thought human praise could do it justice. The loveliness of the youngest, however, was so perfect that human speech was too poor to describe or even praise it satisfactorily. Indeed huge numbers of both citizens and foreigners, drawn together in eager crowds by the fame of such an extraordinary sight, were struck dumb with admiration of her unequalled beauty; and raising the right thumb and forefinger to their lips they would offer outright religious worship to her as the goddess Venus.

For another kind of inaugural *fama* we may turn to Ovid, who places his House of Fame on the threshold of the 'little Iliad' at the beginning of book 12 of the *Metamorphoses*. Fame marks the end as well as the beginning of narratives: a successfully achieved narrative constitutes its own fame, through its claim on the repeated listenings and readings of audiences into an indefinite future. The end of a narrative is also the point at which its writer asserts his own undying fame in a sphragis, sealing the finished work. Ovid prophesies his own undying life in *fama* at the end of the *Metamorphoses*; at the end of the *Agricola*, very possibly looking to the Ovidian discourse of *fama*, Tacitus pairs the undying fame of his father-in-law Agricola and the undying fame of his book, the *Agricola*, in an indissoluble symbiosis.[14] The self-allusion to the ending of the *Agricola* in Tiberius' speech on fame at *Annals* 4.38 points by contrast the inability of the would-be historian, the *princeps*, to write a *finis* to his own narratives.

In one instance Tiberius is successful in bringing a narrative of *fama* to a conclusion favourable to himself. Tacitus has a fascination for the theme of the imperial impostor, partly because it allows him to explore the gap that always exists for him between appearance and reality in the person of the *princeps*. The successful impostor would be one whom *fama*, rumour and report, really did elevate to the imperial throne. Tacitus uses the paired verbs *fingere et credere* in his accounts of the false Drusus (*Ann*. 5.10) and false Nero (*Hist*. 2.8–9), the actions respectively of the producers and consumers of rumour, *fama*, all the more potent when producer and consumer are one and the same: the fabricators of rumour slip easily into believing their own lies. The longest (surviving) Tacitean account of an impostor is the earliest, in historical time, the slave Clemens' imposture of his master Agrippa Postumus, at *Annals* 2.39–40:

---

14 See Harrison 2007.

Eodem anno mancipii unius audacia, ni mature subuentum foret, discordiis armisque ciuilibus rem publicam perculisset. Postumi Agrippae seruus, nomine Clemens, comperto fine Augusti pergere in insulam Planasiam et fraude aut ui raptum Agrippam ferre ad exercitus Germanicos non seruili animo concepit. ausa eius inpediuit tarditas onerariae nauis: atque interim patrata caede ad maiora et magis praecipitia conuersus furatur cineres uectusque Cosam Etruriae promunturium ignotis locis sese abdit, donec crinem barbamque promitteret: nam aetate et forma haud dissimili in dominum erat. tum per idoneos et **secreti** *eius socios* **crebrescit** *uiuere Agrippam,* **occultis** *primum* **sermonibus**, *ut uetita solent, mox* **uago rumore** *apud inperitissimi cuiusque promptas auris aut rursum apud turbidos eoque noua cupientis. atque ipse adire municipia obscuro diei, neque propalam aspici neque diutius isdem locis, sed quia* **ueritas** *visu et mora,* **falsa** *festinatione et incertis ualescunt, relinquebat* **famam** *aut praeueniebat. [40]* **Vulgabatur** *interim per Italiam seruatum munere deum Agrippam,* **credebatur** *Romae; iamque Ostiam inuectum multitudo ingens, iam in urbe clandestini coetus celebrabant, cum Tiberium anceps cura distrahere, uine militum seruum suum coerceret an* **inanem credulitatem** *tempore ipso* **uanescere** *sineret: modo nihil spernendum, modo non omnia metuenda ambiguus pudoris ac metus reputabat. postremo dat negotium Sallustio Crispo. ille e clientibus duos (quidam milites fuisse tradunt) deligit atque hortatur,* **simulata** *conscientia adeant, offerant pecuniam, fidem atque pericula polliceantur. exequuntur ut iussum erat. dein speculati noctem incustoditam, accepta idonea manu, uinctum clauso ore in Palatium traxere. percontanti Tiberio quo modo Agrippa factus esset respondisse fertur 'quo modo tu Caesar.' ut ederet socios subigi non potuit. nec Tiberius poenam eius palam ausus, in* **secreta** *Palatii parte interfici iussit corpusque* **clam** *auferri. et quamquam multi e domo principis equitesque ac senatores sustentasse opibus, iuuisse consiliis dicerentur, haud quaesitum.*

That same year the daring of a single slave, had it not been promptly checked, would have ruined the State by discord and civil war. A servant of Postumus Agrippa, Clemens by name, having ascertained that Augustus was dead, formed a design beyond a slave's conception, of going to the island of Planasia and seizing Agrippa by craft or force and bringing him to the armies of Germany. The slowness of a merchant vessel thwarted his bold venture. Meanwhile the murder of Agrippa had been perpetrated, and then turning his thoughts to a greater and more hazardous enterprise, he stole the ashes of the deceased, sailed to Cosa, a promontory of Etruria, and there hid himself in obscure places till his hair and beard were long. In age and figure he was not unlike his master. Then through suitable emissaries who shared his secret, it was rumoured that Agrippa was alive, first in whispered gossip, soon, as is usual with forbidden topics, in vague talk which found its way to the credulous ears of the most ignorant people or of restless and revolutionary schemers. He himself went to the towns, as the day grew dark, without letting himself be seen publicly or remaining long in the same places, but, as he knew that truth gains strength by notoriety and time, falsehood by precipitancy and vagueness, he would either withdraw himself from publicity or else forestall it. It was rumoured meanwhile throughout Italy, and was believed at Rome, that Agrippa had been saved by the blessing of Heaven. Already at Ostia, where he had arrived, he was the centre of interest to a vast concourse as well as to secret gatherings in the capital, while Tiberius was distracted by the doubt whether he should crush this slave of his by military force or allow time to dissipate a silly credulity. Sometimes he thought that he must overlook nothing, sometimes that he need not be afraid of everything, his mind fluctuating between shame and terror. At last he entrusted the affair to Sallustius Crispus, who chose two of his dependants (some say they were soldiers) and urged them to go to him as pretended accomplices, offering money and promising faithful companionship in danger. They did as they were bidden; then, waiting for an unguarded hour of night, they took with them a sufficient force, and having bound and gagged him, dragged him to the palace. When Tiberius asked him how he had become Agrippa, he is said to have replied, 'As you became Caesar.' He could not be forced to divulge his accomplices. Tiberius did not venture on a public execution, but ordered him to be slain in a private part of the palace and his body to be secretly removed. And although many of the emperor's household and knights and senators were said to have supported him with their wealth and helped him with their counsels, no inquiry was made.

This is a good example of a self-contained 'episode of *fama*': Tacitus carefully anatomizes the birth and growth of the rumour, which here, unusually, has a single, identifiable, father, Clemens the skilful manipulator of what people say and believe. A typical shape for a '*fama* episode' is that of a movement from equilibrium to disorder, followed by the restoration of order. In this case the threatened disorder, according to Tacitus, is nothing less than *discordiae* and *arma ciuilia*. Disruptive *fama* may be dealt with through varying mixtures of persuasion and force: it is rare that an initial growth *crebrescere* is answered simply by a closing *uanescere*, as the rumour just runs out of steam (and in any case that would not make for a good narrative). Here Tiberius makes his opening move by adopting the arts of pretence at which Clemens himself has proved so successful (*simulata conscientia*), before violently cutting off the source of *fama*, wrapping up the act in the secrecy (*in secreta Palatii parte*) from which Clemens had first emerged (cf. *secreti sui socios*).

I said that Tiberius was 'successful in bringing a narrative of *fama* to a conclusion favourable to himself.' Things are a little more complicated. W. Ries in his analysis of the episode fittingly describes Clemens and Tiberius as 'Gegenspieler';[15] Clemens himself says that he and Tiberius are doubles in the only direct speech put into his mouth: 'when Tiberius asked him how he had become Agrippa, he is said to have answered 'As you became Caesar'.' Goodyear (1972) comments *ad loc.*: 'Clemens

---

15 Ries 1969, 162.

does not mean he too had been adopted, but that they had both usurped places to which they had no right.' There is rather more to it, for in his own narrative of the accession of Tiberius at the beginning of the *Annals* Tacitus had highlighted the role of *fama*, in particular in the form of Livia's news management. That *fama* about the shady means by which Tiberius came to power cannot be smuggled out of the palace as easily as the body of Clemens. Note finally how *fama* as it were leaks out of the main story about Clemens into other details of the closing sentences of Tacitus' narrative. Clemens' retort is introduced with *fertur*: it too is the subject of *fama*, appropriately enough since the historian can have at best indirect access to what is said in Tiberius' secret places on the Palatine. By contrast, in the parallel account in Dio (57.16.4) the words of the characters are framed in the narrator's own direct speech.[16] In Tacitus the whole episode ends with another report of something said and left unverified: many were said to have supported Clemens' plans, but no inquiry was made. Ries is of the view that Tacitus adds this detail in order to reinforce the notion that the imposture really was a serious threat to Roman stability, and that in omitting to make further inquiries, Tiberius was avoiding the possibility of stirring up further trouble.[17] Shatzman dissents: 'This was a rumour ..., as Ries admits ...; hence the danger may not have existed at all. It might be that Tiberius did not make investigations because he was sure the rumour was false, and not because he felt the situation was dangerous.' It might be: but the point is also made that the historian makes the last move in this episode of *fama*: Tiberius has successfully dealt with the immediate threat, but he cannot control the subsequent adventures of this narrative about a plot against his person – as the disagreement between modern scholars bears witness.

Here the historian himself has an interest in leaving open the closure to the story, at the same time as the reader is left to admire the narrative skill with which Tacitus has given shape to the story. In general there is an obvious point to be made about the tension between the desire of writers and readers to construct self-contained narratives with beginnings and ends, and the messy and amorphous quality of words, spoken and written, as they circulate in the 'real world'. I end with a couple of

---

16 ἐπύθετο αὐτοῦ "πῶς Ἀγρίππας ἐγένου;" καὶ ὃς ἀπεκρίνατο ὅτι "οὕτως ὡς καὶ σὺ Καῖσαρ." He asked him 'How did you come to be Agrippa?' And he answered, 'In the same way that you came to be Caesar.'
17 Ries 1969, 16.

examples where historians exploit, or lament, this fact. First, Tacitus again, the final comment on the death of Germanicus and its aftermath, *Ann.* 3.19.2:

> is finis fuit ulciscenda Germanici morte, non modo apud illos homines qui tum agebant, etiam secutis temporibus uario rumore iactata. adeo maxima quaeque ambigua sunt, dum alii quoquo modo audita pro compertis habent, alii uera in contrarium uertunt, et gliscit utrumque posteritate.

> This was the end of avenging the death of Germanicus, a subject of conflicting rumours not only among the people then living but also in after times. So obscure are the greatest events, as some take for granted any hearsay, whatever its source, others turn truth into falsehood, and both errors find encouragement with posterity.

Here there is an end, marked by the closural formula *is finis*, which very often marks a death, but here signals the end to the story of the vengeance of Germanicus' death, which 'is mentioned separately, in terms which confuse the closural signals', as Woodman and Martin note. Germanicus' death itself is final, but not so the rumours about it that continue to swirl and grow. The allusions here to Thucydides' programmatic statement of the difficulty of the historian's task[18] seem to privilege rumour as something peculiarly important for Tacitus' own practice of the historian's art, and it is Tacitus himself who appears to have made of the return and trial of Piso a tale of proliferating rumours and innuendos, as emerges sharply from the intertextuality with the monumental certainties inscribed on the bronze of the *Senatus Consultum de Pisone Patre*.[19] If the rumours continue, that is in large part owing to Tacitus' own version of events. The language used of the continued expansiveness of *fama*-as-rumour coincides with that used of the poet's fame: with *gliscit utrumque posteritate* Woodman and Martin compare Propertius 3.1.33–4 *Homerus | posteritate suum crescere sensit opus*; Propertius alludes to Horace's boast of fame, *Odes* 3.30.7–8 *usque ego postera | crescam laude recens*. It is only through the chances of archaeology, and the discovery

---

18 With *alii quoquo modo audita pro compertis habent* cf. Thuc. 1.20.1 οἱ γὰρ ἄνθρωποι τὰς ἀκοὰς τῶν προγεγενημένων ... ὁμοίως ἀβασανίστως παρ' ἀλλήλων δέχονται 'People accept from each other all reports of what happened in the past in an uncritical way; with *alii uera in contrarium uertunt* cf. (formally, if not in sense) Thuc. 1.20.3 οὕτως ἀταλαίπωρος τοῖς πολλοῖς ἡ ζήτησις τῆς ἀληθείας, καὶ ἐπὶ τὰ ἑτοῖμα μᾶλλον τρέπονται 'Most people will not take trouble to find out the truth, but are inclined to accept the first story they hear.'
19 See the fine discussion in Woodman – Martin 1996, 114–18.

of the *Senatus Consultum de Pisone Patre*, that it turned out that Tacitus' narrative of the episode could not claim to be *aere perennius*.[20]

Secondly, an example from Livy, who on a number of occasions places 'episodes of *fama*' at the ends of books, with closural force, for example 30.45 the bestowal of the cognomen 'Africanus' on Scipio; 38.54–60 the death of Africanus, with an extended account of the *gloria* and *inuidia* of the Scipiones. The end of book 8 (40) is marked by a historiographical reflection on the difficulties of *fama*:

> *Hoc bellum a consulibus bellatum quidam auctores sunt eosque de Samnitibus triumphasse; Fabium etiam in Apuliam processisse atque inde magnas praedas egisse. nec discrepat quin dictator eo anno A. Cornelius fuerit; id ambigitur belline gerendi causa creatus sit an ut esset qui ludis Romanis, quia L. Plautius praetor graui morbo forte implicitus erat, signum mittendis quadrigis daret functusque eo haud sane memorandi imperii ministerio se dictatura abdicaret. nec facile est aut rem rei aut auctorem auctori praeferre. uitiatam memoriam funebribus laudibus reor falsisque imaginum titulis, dum familiae ad se quaeque famam rerum gestarum honorumque fallente mendacio trahunt; inde certe et singulorum gesta et publica monumenta rerum confusa. nec quisquam aequalis temporibus illis scriptor exstat quo satis certo auctore stetur.*

> Some authorities state that this war was managed by the consuls and it was they who celebrated the triumph over the Samnites, and further that Fabius invaded Apulia and brought away great quantities of spoil. There is no discrepancy as to A. Cornelius having been Dictator that year, the only doubt is whether he was appointed to conduct the war, or whether, owing to the serious illness of L. Plautius, the praetor, he was appointed to give the signal for starting the chariot races, and after discharging this not very noteworthy function resigned office. It is difficult to decide which account or which authority to prefer. I believe that the true history has been falsified by funeral orations and lying inscriptions on the family busts, since each family appropriates to itself an imaginary record of noble deeds and official distinctions. It is at all events owing to this cause that so much confusion has been introduced into the records of private careers and public events. There is no writer of those times now extant who was contemporary with the events he relates and whose authority, therefore, can be depended upon.

The desire for fame on the part of individual Roman noble families, expressed in the standard vehicles for stamping *fama* on the end of a life, the *laudes funebres* and the *imagines*, the expression of the Republican *certamen gloriae*, impedes the historian's desire to write a true account of

---

20 The *SCPP* announces that it is set up *quo facilius totius actae rei ordo posterorum memoriae tradi posset*. The instructions for the erection of the inscription, *in urbis ipsius celeberrimo loco in aere incisum figeretur*, suggest that this will be the official, fixed, version of events.

what actually happened, who did what. The families' best efforts to secure the maximum of fame for their ancestors, to write their own version of history in funeral oratory and wax images, leads only to a perpetually open-ended account of the past, of which there can never be a final and fixed *fama*. The book ends with the lexicon of certainty and stability, but cancelled by the negative *nec*.

List of Contributors

LUCIA ATHANASSAKI is Associate Professor of Classical Philology at the University of Crete. She is the author of numerous articles on archaic and early classical poetry. Her recent publications include *Apolline Politics and Poetics* (a volume she has co-edited with R. P. Martin and J. F. Miller, 2009) and ἀείδετο πᾶν τέμενος: Οι χορικές παραστάσεις και το κοινό τους στην αρχαϊκή και πρώϊμη κλασική περίοδο (2009).

EGBERT J. BAKKER is Professor of Classics at Yale University. He works on Greek epic and historiographical narrative and is interested in the linguistic and cultural aspects of narratological analysis. Among his main publications are *Poetry in Speech: Orality and Homeric Discourse* (1997) and *Pointing at the Past: From Formula to Performance in Homeric Poetics* (2005).

DEBORAH BECK's research focuses on various aspects of Homeric speech and storytelling. She is the author of *Homeric Conversation* (Harvard, 2005) and is currently at work on a book about the range of ways that speech is represented in Homeric poetry. She has taught at Swarthmore College as well as Rice, Colgate, and the Pennsylvania State Universities.

GEORG DANEK is Associate Professor at the University of Vienna. He has published widely on Greek Literature, especially on Homer and South Slavic Epics, including *Studien zur Dolonie* (1988), *Epos und Zitat. Studien zu den Quellen der Odyssee* (1998), and *Bosnische Heldenepen* (2002).

IRENE J.F. DE JONG studied classics at the University of Amsterdam. Since 2000 she holds the chair of Ancient Greek at that same university. She has published extensively on Homer, Herodotus, and Euripides, and at present is editing a multi-volume history of ancient Greek narrative, of which two volumes have appeared (with R. Nünlist and A. Bowie, *Narrators, narratees, and narratives in Ancient Greek literature*: 2004; with R. Nünlist *Time in Ancient Greek Literature*: 2007).

FRANCIS DUNN is the author of *Present Shock in late fifth-century Greece* (University of Michigan Press 2007) and has published on Greek tragedy, Latin poetry, and aspects of narrative such as time and closure. He teaches at the University of California, Santa Barbara.

JONAS GRETHLEIN is Professor of Classics at the University of Heidelberg. He has published articles on archaic and classical Greek literature and Roman historiography and is the author of *Asyl und Athen* (2003) and *Das Geschichtsbild der Ilias* (2006). His new book *The Greeks and their Past* is forthcoming from Cambridge University Press.

STEPHEN HALLIWELL is Professor of Greek at the University of St Andrews. His books include *Aristotle's Poetics* (1986), *Plato Republic 10* (1988), *Aristophanes:*

Birds and Other Plays (1998), *The Aesthetics of Mimesis: Ancient Texts and Modern Problems* (2002) and *Greek Laughter: a Study of Cultural Psychology from Homer to Early Christianity* (2008). He is currently completing a work entitled *Between Ecstasy and Truth: Problems of Poetics from Homer to Longinus*.

PHILIP HARDIE is a Senior Research Fellow at Trinity College, Cambridge, and Honorary Professor of Latin Literature in the University of Cambridge. His *Lucretian Receptions. History, The Sublime, Knowledge* is forthcoming with Cambridge University Press, and he is currently completing a study of rumour and renown in the classical tradition.

MARIANNE HOPMAN's research focuses on the modalities and pragmatics of storytelling in ancient Greece, especially in epic and tragedy. She has published articles on Euripides' *Medea*, the Niobe figure in Sophocles, the *Orphic Hymns*, and Juvenal's *Fifth Satire*. Her current book project, entitled *Scylla: Myth, Gender, and Monstrosity from Greece to Rome*, investigates the trope of the *Mischwesen* as a cultural symbol. She is Assistant Professor of Classics at Northwestern University.

RICHARD HUNTER is Regius Professor of Greek at the University of Cambridge and a Fellow of Trinity College. His research interests include ancient comedy, the novel, Hellenistic poetry and its reception in Rome, and ancient literary criticism. His most recent books are *The Shadow of Callimachus* (Cambridge 2006) and *Critical Moments in Classical Literature* (Cambridge 2009). Many of his essays have been collected in *On Coming After: Studies in Post-Classical Greek Literature and its Reception* (Berlin 2008).

ANNA A. LAMARI received her PhD in Classics from the Aristotle University of Thessaloniki in 2008. She is currently revising her thesis, a narratological study of Euripides' *Phoenissae*, for publication. She has published articles on Greek drama, Theocritus and Thucydides.

NIKOS MILTSIOS is a graduate student at the Aristotle University of Thessaloniki. He is currently working on his PhD thesis concerning the study of Polybius' *Histories* from a narratological perspective.

RENÉ NÜNLIST is Associate Professor of Classics at Brown University (Rhode Island, USA). His research interests include: Homer and other early Greek poetry, literary criticism (ancient and modern) and papyrology (esp. Menander).

THEODORE D. PAPANGHELIS is Professor of Latin in Aristotle University, Thessaloniki. His published work includes *Propertius: A Hellenistic Poet on Love and Death*, Cambridge 1987, *A Companion to Apollonius Rhodius* (co-edited with Antonios Rengakos), 2nd edition Brill 2008, and *A Companion to Greek and Latin Pastoral* (co-edited with Marco Fantuzzi), Brill 2006.

CHRISTOPHER PELLING is Regius Professor of Greek at Oxford University. His books include *Plutarch: Life of Antony* (Cambridge, 1988), *Literary Texts and the Greek Historian* (Routledge, 2000), and *Plutarch and History* (Classical Press of Wales, 2002). He is currently completing a commentary on Plutarch's *Life of Caesar* for the Clarendon Ancient History series.

SETH L. SCHEIN is Professor of Comparative Literature at the University of California at Davis. He works mainly on Homeric epic, Attic tragedy, receptions of classical literature, and the history, politics, theory and practice of translation. He has written the *The Mortal Hero: an Introduction to Homer's Iliad* and *Sophokles' Philoktetes: Translation with Introduction, Notes, and Interpretive Essay*, and his current projects include a commentary on *Philoctetes* and a translation of Aeschylus' *Oresteia*.

RUTH SCODEL (AB Berkeley 1973, PhD Harvard 1978) is D. R. Shackleton Bailey Collegiate Professor of Greek and Latin at the University of Michigan, Ann Arbor. Her publications include *Credible Impossiblities: Strategies of Verisimilitude in Homer and Greek Tragedy* (Teubner 1999); *Listening to Homer* (University of Michigan Press 2002); (with Anja Bettenworth) *Whither Quo Vadis* (Blackwell 2008) and *Epic Facework: Self-presentation and social interaction in Homer* (Classical Press of Wales 2008). She was editor of *TAPA* from 1986 to 1991 and President of the American Philological Association in 2007.

EVINA SISTAKOU is Assistant Professor of Greek Literature at the Aristotle University of Thessaloniki. Her publications include a monograph on the reception of the Trojan myth in Hellenistic poetry (*Reconstructing the Epic. Cross-Readings of the Trojan Myth in Hellenistic Poetry*, Hellenistica Groningana vol. 14, Leuven 2008) and on the use of geography in the poetry of Callimachus (Athens 2005). Her recent contributions concern the study of Greek epigram, Lycophron, Apollonius and Callimachus from the perspective of Hellenistic poetics.

MARIOS SKEMPIS is an 'Assistent' at the Classics Department of the University of Basel, Switzerland. He obtained his PhD from the University of Göttingen, Germany in 2008 with a dissertation on the intertextual relations of Callimachus' *Hecale* to Homer's *Odyssey*. He has published papers mainly on Hellenistic poetry and is currently working on the association of Hermes with Aphrodite and Eros in myth, literature and cult.

CHRISTOS C. TSAGALIS is Associate Professor in Classics at the Aristotle University of Thessaloniki. He is the author of *Epic Grief: Personal Laments in Homer's Iliad* (Walter de Gruyter 2004), *The Oral Palimpsest: Exploring Intertextuality in the Homeric Epics* (Harvard University Press 2008), *Inscribing Sorrow: Fourth-Century Attic Funerary Epigrams* (Walter de Gruyter 2008). He is co-editor (together with F. Montanari and A. Rengakos) of *Brill's Companion to Hesiod* (Brill 2009).

EVANTHIA TSITSIBAKOU-VASALOS is Associate Professor of Classical Studies at the Aristotle University of Thessaloniki. Her areas of interest include Greek Lyric Poetry, Homeric Epic, Myth and Ritual. She has published a number of articles on Lyric Poetry, Homer and his Scholiasts. She is the author of *Ancient Poetic Etymology. The Pelopids: Fathers and Sons* (2007).

CHRYSANTHE TSITSIOU-CHELIDONI is a lecturer in Latin Literature at the University of Thrace (Department of Philology). Her book *Ovid, 'Metamorphosen' Buch VIII. Narrative Technik und literarischer Kontext* (2003) is based on her PhD (University of Heidelberg). Her interests and publications are in the field of poetry and historiography of the Augustan Age.

IOANNIS ZIOGAS completed an MA on etymology in Ovid's *Fasti* at the Aristotle University of Thessaloniki, and is currently at Cornell University, writing a PhD thesis entitled *Hesiod in Ovid: The Metamorphosis of the Catalogue of Women*.

Bibliography

Adams, S.M. 1952. "Salamis Symphony: the *Persae* of Aeschylus", in: M.E. White (ed.), *Studies in Honour of Gilbert Norwood*, Toronto, 46–54.
Adkins, A.W.H. 1960. *Merit and Responsibility. A Study in Greek Values*, Oxford.
Aélion, R. 1983. *Euripide héritier d'Eschyle*, vol. 1, Paris.
Ahl, F. – Roisman, H. 1996. *The Odyssey Reformed*, Ithaca – London.
Alden, M. 2000. *Homer Beside Himself. Para-Narratives in the Iliad*, Oxford.
Alexiou, M. (1974) 2002. *The Ritual Lament in Greek Tradition*, Lanham, MD.
Allan, W. 2000. *The Andromache and Euripidean Tragedy*, Oxford.
– 2001. "Euripides in Megale Hellas: Some Aspects of the Early Reception of Tragedy", *G&R* 48, 67–86.
Allen, W. 1940. "The Epyllion: A Chapter in the History of Literary Criticism", *TAPhA* 71, 1–26.
Aly, W. 1913. "Hesiodos von Askra und der Verfasser der Theogonie", *RhM* 68, 22–67.
Ambühl, A. 2004. "Entertaining Theseus and Heracles: The *Hecale* and the *Victoria Berenices* as a Diptych", in: M.A. Harder – R.F. Regtuit – G.C. Wakker (eds.), *Callimachus II*, Leuven, 23–48.
– 2005. *Kinder und junge Helden. Innovative Aspekte des Umgangs mit der literarischen Tradition bei Kallimachos*, Leuven.
Anderson, M.J. 1997. *The Fall of Troy in Early Greek Poetry and Art*, Oxford.
Annas, J. 1981. *An Introduction to Plato's Republic*, Oxford.
Arnim, H. von. 1898. *Leben und Werke des Dio von Prusa*, Berlin.
Aronen, J. 2002. "Genealogy as a Form of Mythic Discourse: The Case of the Phaeacians", in: S. des Bouvrie (ed.), *Myth and Symbol I. Symbolic Phenomena in Ancient Greek Culture. Papers from the First International Symposium on Symbolism at the University of Tromso, June 4–7, 1998*, Bergen, 89–111.
Arrighetti, G. 2008. "Il *Catalogo* esiodeo: un genere letterario?", in: G. Bastianini – A. Casanova (eds.), *Esiodo: Cent'anni di papiri. Atti del convegno internazionale di studi. Firenze, 7–8 giugno 2007*, Florence, 11–27.
Arthur, M.B. 1984. "Early Greece: The Origin of the Western Attitude toward Women", in: J. Peradotto – J.P. Sullivan (eds.), *Women in the Ancient World: The Arethusa Papers*, Albany, 7–58.
Athanassaki, L. 1990. *Mantic Vision and Diction in Pindar's Victory Odes*. PhD thesis, Brown University.
– 2003. "Transformations of Colonial Disruption into Narrative Continuity in Pindar's Epinician Odes", *HSPh* 101, 93–128.
– 2004. "Deixis, Performance, and Poetics in Pindar's *First Olympian Ode*", in: N. Felson (ed.), *The Poetics of Deixis in Alcman, Pindar, and Other Lyric*, *Arethusa* 37, 317–41.
– 2009. *ἀείδετο πᾶν τέμενος. Οι χορικές παραστάσεις και το κοινό τους στην αρχαϊκή και πρώιμη κλασική περίοδο*, Herakleion.

- forthcoming a "Giving Wings to the Aeginetan Sculptures. The Panhellenic Aspirations of Pindar's *Eighth Olympian*", in: D. Fearn (ed.), *Aegina: Contexts for Choral Lyric Poetry*, Oxford.
- forthcoming b "Performance and Reperformance: The Siphnian Treasury Evoked (Pindar's *Pythian 6*, *Olympian 2*, and *Isthmian 2*)", in: P. Agócs – C. Carey – R. Rawles (eds.), *Proceedings of the 2006 UCL Conference on the Epinician Ode*.

Auerbach, E. 1953. *Mimesis. The Representation of Reality in Western Literature*, Princeton.

Austin, N. 1994. *Helen of Troy and her Shameless Phantom*, Ithaca – London.

Avery, H.C. 1964. "Dramatic Devices in Aeschylus' *Persians*", *AJPh* 85, 173–84.

Bach, M. 1997. *Erzählperspektive im Film: eine erzähltheoretische Untersuchung mithilfe exemplarischer Filmanalysen*, Essen.

Bacon, H. 1982. "Aeschylus", in: T.J. Luce (ed.), *Ancient Writers: Greece and Rome*, vol. I, New York, 99–155.

- 1994–95. "The Chorus in Greek Life and Drama", *Arion* 3, 6–24.

Bakhtin, M.M. (1975) 1981. "Epic and Novel: Toward a methodology for the study of the novel", in: *The Dialogic Imagination: Four essays*, tr. C. Emerson and M. Holquist, Austin, 3–40.

Bakker, E.J. 1993. "Discourse and Performance: Involvement, Visualization, and 'Presence' in Homeric Poetry", *ClAnt* 12, 1–29.

- 1997a. *Poetry in Speech: Orality and Homeric Discourse,* Ithaca – London.
- 1997b. "Verbal Aspect and Mimetic Description in Thucydides", in: E.J. Bakker (ed.), *Grammar as Interpretation: Greek Literature in its Linguistic Contexts*, Leiden, 7–54.
- 1997c. *Grammar as Interpretation. Greek Literature in its Linguistic Contexts*, (*Mnemosyne Supplementum* vol. 171), Leiden.
- 1999. "Homeric ΟΥΤΟΣ and the Poetics of Deixis", *CPh* 94, 1–19.
- 2002. "Remembering the God's Arrival", *Arethusa* 35, 63–81.
- 2005. *Pointing at the Past: From Formula to Performance in Homeric Poetics*, Washington.
- 2006a. "Contract and Design: Thucydides' Writing", in: A. Rengakos – A. Tsakmakis (eds.), *Brill's Companion to Thucydides*, Leiden, 109–29.
- 2006b. "Homeric Epic between Feasting and Fasting", in: F. Montanari – A. Rengakos (eds.), *La poésie épique grecque: Métamorphoses d'un genre littéraire* (*Entretiens Hardt* vol. 52), Vandoeuvres-Geneva, 1–39.
- (in prep.) *Food for Song: Meat and Meaning in the Odyssey*.

Bal, M. (1985) 1997. *Narratology: Introduction to the Theory of Narrative,* Toronto (Original Title: *Narratologie,* Paris 1977).

- 1990. "The Point of Narratology", *Poetics Today* 11, 727–53.

Banfield, A. 1982. *Unspeakable Sentences: Narration and Representation in the Language of Fiction*, Boston.

Barchiesi, A. 1999. "Representations of Suffering and Interpretation in the *Aeneid*", in: P. Hardie (ed.), *Virgil. Critical Assessments of Classical Authors*, vol.

III, London – New York, 324–44 (transl. of "Rappresentazioni del dolore e interpretazione nell'*Eneide*", *A&A* 40 (1994) 109–24).
- 2001. "Future Reflexive: Two Modes of Allusion and the *Heroides*", in: A. Barchiesi (ed.), *Speaking Volumes. Narrative and Intertext in Ovid and other Latin Poets*, London, 105–27.

Barigazzi, A. 1954. "Sull'*Ecale* di Callimaco", *Hermes* 82, 308–30.
- 1958. "Il dolore materno di Ecale (P.Oxy. 2376 e 2377)", *Hermes* 86, 453–71.

Barrett, J. 2002. *Staged Narrative: Poetics and the Messenger in Greek Tragedy*, Berkeley etc.
- 2007. "Aeschylus", in: I.J.F. de Jong – R. Nünlist (eds.), *Time in Ancient Greek Literature*, Leiden.

Barron, J.P. 1988. "The Liberation of Greece", in: J. Boardman – N.G.L. Hammond – D.M. Lewis – M. Ostwald (eds.), *Cambridge Ancient History*, vol. 4: *Persia, Greece and the Eastern Mediterranean c. 525–479 BC*, Cambridge, 592–622.

Bartels, A. 2004. *Vergleichende Studien zur Erzählkunst des römischen Epyllion*, Göttingen.

Barthes, R. 1977. *Image, Music, Text*, London.

Bassett, S. 1918. "The Second Nekyia", *CJ* 13, 521–6.
- 1938. *The Poetry of Homer*, Berkeley etc.

Batchelder, A.G. 1995. *The Seal of Orestes: Self-reference and authority in Sophocles' Electra*, Lanham, MD.

Bates, W.N. 1940. *Sophocles: Poet and dramatist*, New York.

Bechtel, F. – Fick, A. 1894. *Die Griechischen Personennamen*, Göttingen.

Beck, D. 2008. "An Interdisciplinary Perspective on Homeric Speech Representation", *TAPhA* 138, 351–78.

Belfiore, E. 2002. "Dramatic and Epic Time: 'Magnitude' and 'Length' in Aristotle's *Poetics*", in: Ø. Andersen – J. Haarberg (eds.), *Making Sense of Aristotle. Essays in Poetics*, London, 25–49.

Bender, J. 1987. *Imagining the Penitentiary. Fiction and the Architecture of Mind in Eighteenth-Century England*, Chicago.

Benveniste, E. 1971. *Problems in General Linguistics*, Coral Gables.

Bergren, A. 1979. "Helen's web: Time and Tableau in the *Iliad*", *Helios* 7, 19–34.
- 1983. "Language and the Female in Early Greek Thought", *Arethusa* 16, 69–95.
- 2008. *Weaving Truth. Essays on Language and the Female in Greek Thought*, Cambridge, MA

Bers, V. 1997. *Speech in Speech: Studies in Incorporated Oratio Recta in Attic Drama and Oratory*, Lanham, MD.

Besslich, S. (1966) 1990. *Schweigen, Verschweigen, Übergehen. Die Darstellung des Unausgesprochenen in der Odyssee*, Heidelberg.

Bethe, E. 1921. "Klytaimestra", *RE* XI.1, cols. 890–93.

Beye, C.R. 1966. *The Iliad, the Odyssey, and the Epic Tradition*, New York.
- 1974. "Male and Female in the Homeric Poems", *Ramus* 3, 87–101.

Bhaba, H. 1994. *The Location of Culture*, London.

Bierl, A. 1994. "Apollo in Greek Tragedy: Orestes and the God of Initiation", in: J. Solomon (ed.), *Apollo. Origins and Influences*, Tucson – London, 81–96.
– 2001. *Der Chor in der alten Komödie. Ritual und Performativität*, Munich – Leipzig.
– 2007. "Die Abenteuer des Odysseus", in: J. Latacz – T. Greub – P. Blome – A. Wieczorek (eds.), *Homer: Der Mythos von Troia in Dichtung und Kunst*, Munich, 171–79.
Bischoff, H. 1932. *Der Warner bei Herodot*, Marburg.
Bing, P. 1990. "A Pun on Aratus' Name in Verse 2 of the *Phainomena?*", *HSPh* 93, 281–85.
Block, E. 1982. "The Narrator Speaks: Apostrophe in Homer and Vergil", *TAPhA* 112, 7–22.
Blondell, R. 2002. *The Play of Character in Plato's Dialogues*, Cambridge.
Boeckh, A. 1821. (repr. 1963) *Pindari epiniciorum interpretatio latina cum commentario perpetuo*, Leipzig (Hildesheim).
Boedeker, D. – Sider, D. (eds.) 2001. *The New Simonides. Contexts of Praise and Desire*, Oxford.
Boegehold, A.L. 1999. *When a Gesture Was Expected*, Princeton.
Bollack, J. 1990. *L'Oedipe roi de Sophocle: Le texte et ses interpretations*, Lille.
Bollack, J. – Judet de la Combe, P. 1981–2. *L'Agamemnon d'Eschyle: Le texte et ses interpretations*, Lille.
Bonifazi, A. 2004. "Communication in Pindar's Deictic Acts", in: N. Felson (ed.), *The Poetics of Deixis in Alcman, Pindar, and Other Lyric*, Arethusa 37, 391–414.
Booth, W. (1961) 1983. *The Rhetoric of Fiction*, Chicago.
Bowie, A.M. 1997. "Tragic Filters for History: Euripides' *Supplices* and Sophocles' *Philoctetes*", in: C. Pelling (ed.), *Greek Tragedy and the Historian*, Oxford, 39–62.
Braswell, B.K. 1982. "The Song of Ares and Aphrodite: Theme and Relevance to *Odyssey* 8", *Hermes* 110, 129–37.
Brecht, B. (1955) 1988. *The Caucasian Chalk Circle*, tr. J. and T. Stern with W. H. Auden, London.
– 1964. *Brecht on Theatre: The development of an aesthetic*, tr. J. Willett, London.
Bremer, J.M. – Furley, W.D. 2001. *Greek Hymns. Selected Cult Songs from the Archaic to the Hellenistic Period*, vols. I-II, Tübingen.
Brewer, W.F. 1996. "The Nature of Narrative Suspense and the Problem of Rereading", in: P. Vorderer – H.J. Wulff – M. Friedrichsen (eds.), *Suspense: Conceptualizations, Theoretical Analyses, and Empirical Explorations*, Mahwah, New Jersey, 107–27.
Brillante, C. 1992. "La musica e il canto nella *Pitica I* di Pindaro", *QUCC* 41, 7–21.
Brink, C.O. 1960. "Tragic History and Aristotle's School", *PCPhS* 186, 6, 14–9.
Brisson, L. 1998. *Plato the Myth Maker*, Chicago.
Broadhead, H.D. 1960. *The Persae of Aeschylus. Edited with introduction, critical notes and commentary*, Cambridge.

Brodersen, K. (1995) 2003. *Terra cognita. Studien zur römischen Raumerfassung*, Hildesheim.
Bruner, J. 1986. *Actual Minds, Possible Worlds*, Cambridge.
Buchan, M. 2004. *The Limits of Heroism. Homer and the Ethics of Reading*, Ann Arbor.
Büchner, K. 1968. "Das Proömium der Theogonie des Hesiod", in: id., *Studien zur römischen Literatur*, vol. vii, Wiesbaden, 9–42.
Bühler, W. 1960. *Die Europa des Moschos*, Wiesbaden (*Hermes Einzelschriften* vol. 13).
Burck, E. (1933) 1964. *Die Erzählkunst des T. Livius. Zweite, um einen Forschungsbericht vermehrte, photomechanische Auflage*, Berlin.
– 1967. "Livius als augusteischer Historiker", in: E. Burck (ed.), *Wege zu Livius*, Darmstadt (*Wege der Forschung* vol. 132), 96–143.
– 1992. *Das Geschichtswerk des Titus Livius*, Heidelberg (*Bibliothek der Klassischen Altertumswissenschaften*, 2. R., vol. 87).
Burian, P. 1997. "Myth into *muthos*: the shaping of tragic plot", in: P. Easterling (ed.), *The Cambridge Companion to Greek Tragedy*, Cambridge, 178–208.
Burkert, W. 1985. *Greek Religion*, Cambridge, Mass.
– 1987. "The Making of Homer in the Sixth Century B.C.: Rhapsodes versus Stesichoros", in: A.P.A. Belloli (ed.), *Papers on the Amasis Painter and his World*, Malibu, 43–62.
Burnett, A.P. 1989. "Performing Pindar's Odes", *CPh* 84, 283–93.
Burnyeat, M. 1999. "Culture and Society in Plato's *Republic*", *The Tanner Lectures on Human Values* 20, 217–324.
Burton, R.W.B. 1962. *Pindar's Pythian Odes*, Oxford.
Bury, J.B. 1892. *The Isthmian Odes of Pindar*, London.
Bux, E. 1927. "Sophaenetus", *RE* III A1, cols. 1008–13.

Cairns, D.L. 1993. *AIDŌS. The Psychology and Ethics of Honour and Shame in Ancient Greek Literature*, Oxford.
Cairns, F. 1989. *Virgil's Augustan Epic*, Cambridge.
Calame, C. 1995. *The Craft of Poetic Speech in Ancient Greece*, Ithaca – London.
– 1996. *Mythe et histoire dans l'Antiquité grecque: la création symbolique d'une colonie*, Lausanne.
– 1997. *Choruses of Young Women in Ancient Greece*, Lanham, MD.
– 1999. "Performative Aspects of the Choral Voice in Greek Tragedy: Civic Identity in Performance", in: S. Goldhill – R. Osborne (eds.), *Performance Culture and Athenian Democracy*, Cambridge, 125–53.
– 2004. "Deictic Ambiguity and Auto-Referentiality. Some Examples", in: N. Felson (ed.), *The Poetics of Deixis in Alcman, Pindar, and Other Lyric*, *Arethusa* 37, 415–43.
Calder, W.M. 1963. "The End of Sophocles' *Electra*", *GRBS* 4, 213–16.
– 1965. "The Entrance of Athena in *Ajax*", *CPh* 60, 114–16.
– 1974. "Once more: the Entrance and Exit of Athena in *Ajax*", *Classical Folia* 28, 59–61.
Cameron, A. 1995. *Callimachus and his Critics*, Princeton.
– 2004. *Greek Mythography in the Roman World*, Oxford.

Campbell, M. 1991. *Moschus'* Europa, Hildesheim.
Canfora, L. 1993. *Studi di storia della storiografia romana*, Bari (*Documenti e studi* vol. 15).
Cantarella, E. 1987. *Pandora's Daughters*, Baltimore – London.
Carey, C. 1989. "The performance of the Victory Ode", *AJPh* 110, 545–65.
– 2001. "Poesia pubblica in *performance*", in: M. Cannatà-Fera – G. B. D'Alessio (eds.), *I lirici greci: forme della comunicazione e storia del testo*, Messina, 11–26.
– 2007. "Pindar, Place, and Performance", in: S. Hornblower – C. Morgan (eds.), *Pindar's Poetry, Patrons, and Festivals. From Archaic Greece to the Roman Empire*, Oxford, 199–210.
Carne-Ross, D.S. 1985. *Pindar*, New Haven.
Carr, D. 1986. *Time, Narrative, and History. Studies in Phenomenology and Existential Philosophy*, Bloomington.
Carroll, N. 1996. "The Paradox of Suspense", in: P. Vorderer – H.J. Wulff – M. Friedrichsen (eds.), *Suspense: Conceptualizations, Theoretical Analyses, and Empirical Explorations*, Mahwah, New Jersey, 71–91.
Cauer, P. 1921. *Grundfragen der Homerkritik*, Leipzig.
Cawkwell, G. 2004. "When, How and Why did Xenophon Write the *Anabasis?*", in: R.L. Fox (ed.), *The Long March: Xenophon and the Ten Thousand*, New Haven – London, 47–67.
Chafe, W. 1994. *Discourse, Consciousness, and Time: The Flow and Displacement of Conscious Experience in Speaking and Writing*, Chicago.
Chaplin, J.D. 2000. *Livy's Exemplary History*, Oxford.
Champion, C.B. 2004. *Cultural Politics in Polybius's Histories*, Berkeley etc.
Chantraine, P. 1946–1947. "Les noms du mari et de la femme, du père et de la mère en Grec", *REG* 59–60, 219–50.
– (1968–1980) 1999. *Dictionnaire étymologique de la langue grecque: histoire des mots*, Paris.
Chatman, S. 1974–5. "Towards A Theory of Narrative", *New Literary History* 6, 295–318.
– 1978. *Story and Discourse. Narrative Structure in Fiction and Film*, Ithaca.
– 1986. "Characters and narrators: filter, center, slant and interest-focus", *Poetics Today* 7, 189–204.
– 1990. *Coming to Terms: The Rhetoric of Narrative in Fiction and Film*, Ithaca.
Chiasson, C.C. 1983. "An Ominous Word in Herodotus", *Hermes* 110, 115–16.
Cingano, E. 1995. "Pitica prima", in: P. Angeli Bernardini – E. Cingano – B. Gentili – P. Giannini (eds.), *Pindaro. Le Pitiche*, Rome, 9–41, 327–64.
– 2005. "A catalogue within a catalogue: Helen's suitors in the Hesiodic *Catalogue of Women* (frr. 196–204)", in: Hunter 2005a, *The Hesiodic Catalogue of Women. Constructions and Reconstructions*, Cambridge, 118–52.
Clader, L.L. 1976. *Helen: The Evolution from Divine to Heroic in Greek Epic Tradition*, Leiden.
Clarke, H.W. 1967. *The Art of the* Odyssey, Englewood Cliffs, New Jersey.
Clarke, M. 1999. *Flesh and Spirit in the Songs of Homer. A Study of Words and Myths*, Oxford.

Classen, C.J. 1994. "Rhetorik und Literarkritik", in: F. Montanari (ed.), *La Philologie grecque à l'époque hellénistique et romaine*, (*Entretiens Fondation Hardt* vol. XL), Vandoeuvres-Geneva, 307–60.
Clauss, J.J. 1993. *The Best of the Argonauts*, Berkeley etc.
Clay, J.S. 1989. *The Politics of Olympus. Form and Meaning in the Major Homeric Hymns*, Princeton.
– 1999. "Pindar's Sympotic Epinicia", *QUCC* n.s. 62, 25–34.
– 2003. *Hesiod's Cosmos*, Cambridge.
Clayton, B. 2004. *A Penelopean Poetics. Reweaving the Feminine in Homer's Odyssey*, Lanham, MD.
Cobet, J. 1971. *Herodots Exkurse und die Frage der Einheit seines Werkes*, Wiesbaden.
Cohen, I.M. 1989–1990. "Traditional Language and the Women in the Hesiodic *Catalogue of Women*", *Scripta Classica Israelica* 10, 12–27.
Cohn, D.C. 1978. *Transparent Minds. Narrative Modes for Presenting Consciousness in Fiction*, Princeton.
Coleridge, S.T. (1818) 1902 "Greek Drama", in: T. Ashe (ed.), *Lectures and Notes on Shakespere and other English Poets*, London, 187–95.
Collard, C. 1975. *Euripides* Supplices. *Edited with introduction and commentary*, vol. II: Commentary, Groningen.
Collins, D. 2001. *Reanimated Voices: Speech Reporting in a Historical-Pragmatic Perspective*, Amsterdam.
Combellack, F.M. 1974. "Odysseus and Anticleia", *CPh* 69, 121–23.
– 1982. "Two Blameless Homeric Characters", *AJPh* 103, 361–72.
Conacher, D.J. 1980. *Aeschylus' Prometheus Bound: a literary commentary*, Toronto.
– (1974) 1996. *Aeschylus: The Earlier Plays and Related Studies*, Toronto.
Connor, R.W. 1985. "Narrative Discourse in Thucydides", in: M.H. Jameson (ed.), *The Greek Historians. Literature and History. Papers Presented to Antony E. Raubitschek*, Saratoga, California, 1–17.
Conte, G.B. 1986. *The Rhetoric of Imitation. Genre and Poetic Memory in Virgil and Other Latin Poets*. Translated from the Italian. Edited and with a Foreword by Ch. Segal, Ithaca.
Corcella, A. 1984. *Erodoto e l'analogia*, Palermo.
Cornford, F.M. 1907. *Thucydides Mythistoricus*, London.
Craik, E. 1988. *Euripides* Phoenician Women. *Edited with translation and commentary*, Warminster.
Crotty, K. 1994. *The Poetics of Supplication. Homer's* Iliad *and* Odyssey, Ithaca – London.
Crump, M. 1931. *The Epyllion from Theocritus to Ovid*, Oxford.
Cuddon, J.A. (1976) ³1991. *Dictionary of Literary Terms and Literary Theory*, Oxford.
Culler, J. 1980. "Fabula and Sjuzhet in the Analysis of Narrative. Some American Discussion", *Poetics Today* 1, 27–37.
Currie, B. 2004. "Reperformance Scenarios for Pindar's *Odes*", in: C.J. Mackie (ed.), *Oral Performance and Its Context*, Leiden, 49–69.
– 2005. *Pindar and the Cult of Heroes*, Oxford.

- forthcoming. "Epinician choregia. Funding a Pindaric chorus", in: L. Athanassaki – E. Bowie (eds.), *Archaic and Classical Choral Song*, Berlin.
Cusset, C. 1999. "L'enfance perdue d'Héraclès: l'image du héros au service de l'autre", *BAGB*, 191–210.
– 2001. "Le jeu poétique dans l'*Europé* de Moschos", *BAGB*, 62–82.

Dakyns, H.G. 1890–1897. *The Works of Xenophon*, London.
Dale, A.M. 1954. *Euripides:* Alcestis, Oxford.
D'Alessio, G.B. 2004. "Temporal Deixis in Greek Archaic Lyric", in: N. Felson (ed.), *The Poetics of Deixis in Alcman, Pindar, and Other Lyric*, Arethusa 37, 267–94.
– 2007. "Ἦν ἰδού: *Ecce Satyri* (Pratina *PMG* 708 = *TrGF* 4 F3): alcune considerazioni sull'uso della deissi nei testi lirici e teatrali", in: F. Perusino – M. Colantonio (eds.), *Dalla lirica corale alla poesia drammatica*, Pisa, 95–128.
– 2009. "Language and Pragmatics", in: F. Budelmann (ed.), *The Cambridge Companion to Greek Lyric*, Cambridge, 114–29.
Danek, G. 1998a. *Epos und Zitat. Studien zu den Quellen der* Odyssee, Vienna.
– 1998b. "Darstellung verdeckter Handlung bei Homer und in der südslawischen Heldenlied-Tradition", *WS* 111, 67–88.
– 1999. "Synchronisation von Handlungssträngen in *Ilias* 14, 1–40", in: J.N. Kazazis – A. Rengakos (eds.), *Euphrosyne. Studies in Ancient Epic and its Legacy in Honor of D.N. Maronitis*, Stuttgart, 76–88.
– 2004. "Der Schiffskatalog der *Ilias*. Form und Funktion", in: H. Heftner – K. Tomaschitz (eds.), *Ad Fontes! Festschrift G. Dobesch*, Vienna, 59–72.
Dangel, J. 1982. *La phrase oratoire chez Tite-Live*, Paris.
D'Arms, E.F. – Hulley, K.K. 1946. "The *Oresteia* Story in the *Odyssey*", *TAPhA* 77, 207–13.
Davidson, J. 1991. "The Gaze in Polybius' *Histories*", *JRS* 81, 10–24.
– 2000. "Alkmene: Mother of a Child Prodigy", *Scholia* 9, 2–11.
Davies, J.K. 1971. *Athenian Propertied Families*, Oxford.
Davies, M.I. 1969. "Thoughts on the *Oresteia* before Aischylos", *BCH* 93, 214–60.
Dawe, R. 1982. *Sophocles:* Oedipus Rex, Cambridge.
Denniston, J.D. 1927. "Technical Terms in Aristophanes", *CQ* 21, 113–21.
– [2]1950. *The Greek Particles*, Oxford.
Desideri, P. 1978. *Dione di Prusa. Un intellettuale greco nell'imperio romano*, Messina – Florence.
Detienne, M. 1996. *The Masters of Truth in Archaic Greece*, New York.
Dewald, C. 1987. "Narrative Surface and Authorial Voice in Herodotus' *Histories*", *Arethusa* 20, 147–70.
– 2005. *Thucydides' War Narrative. A Structural Study*, Berkeley etc.
Dickey, E. 2007. *Ancient Greek Scholarship: A Guide to Finding, Reading, and Understanding Scholia, Commentaries, Lexica, and Grammatical Treatises, from their Beginnings to the Byzantine Period*, Oxford – New York.
Dieterle, B. 1988. *Erzählte Bilder. Zum narrativen Umgang mit Gemälden*, Marburg.
Dodds, E.R. 1951. *The Greeks and the Irrational*, Berkeley etc.

Doherty, L.I. 1991. "The Internal and Implied Audiences of *Odyssey* 11", *Arethusa* 24, 145–76.
– 1992. "Gender and Internal Audiences in the *Odyssey*", *AJPh* 113, 161–77.
– 1993. "Tyro in *Odyssey* 11: Closed and Open Readings", *Helios* 20, 3–15.
– 1995. *Siren Songs. Gender, Audiences, and Narrators in the* Odyssey, Ann Arbor.
– 2006. "Putting the Women Back into the Hesiodic *Catalogue of Women*", in: V. Zajko – M. Leonard (eds.), *Laughing with Medusa. Classical Myth and Feminist Thought*, Oxford, 297–325.
Dorati, M. 2007. "Alcune ambiguità del narratore dell'*Anabasi*", *QUCC* 85, 105–16.
Dornseiff, F. 1933. *Die archaische Mythenerzählung. Folgerungen aus dem homerischen Apollonhymnos*, Leipzig.
Dougherty, C. 1993. *The Poetics of Colonization. From City to Text in Archaic Greece*, Oxford.
Dover, K.J. 1988. "Thucydides' Historical Judgement. Athens and Siciliy", in: *The Greeks and their Legacy*, Oxford, 74–82.
Dräger, P. 1997. *Untersuchungen zu den Frauenkatalogen Hesiods*, Stuttgart.
Dreher, M. 2006. "Die Hikesie-Szenen der *Odyssee* und der Ursprung des Asylgedankens", in: A. Luther (ed.), *Geschichte und Fiktion in der homerischen Odyssee*, Munich, 47–60.
Duckworth, G.E. 1931. "ΠΡΟΑΝΑΦΩΝΗΣΙΣ in the scholia to Homer", *AJPh* 52, 320–38.
– 1933. *Foreshadowing and Suspense in the Epics of Homer, Apollonius and Vergil*, Princeton.
Dué, C. 2006. *The Captive Woman's Lament in Greek Tragedy*, Austin.
Düring, I. 1945. "Klutaimestra – νηλὴς γυνά. A Study of the Development of a Literary Motif", *Eranos* 41, 91–123.
Duff, T. 1999. *Plutarch's Lives: Exploring Virtue and Vice*, Oxford.
Dunn, F. 1996. *Tragedy's End: Closure and Innovation in Euripidean Drama*, Oxford.
– 2007. *Present Shock in Late Fifth-Century Greece*, Ann Arbor.
Dyck, A.R. 1975. *Epimerismoi on Iliad A 1–129*, Diss. Chicago, Illinois.
– 1983. *Epimerismi Homerici*, Berlin – New York.
– 1995. *Epimerismi Homerici. Lexicon ΑΙΜΩΔΕΙΝ*, Berlin – New York.

Eagleton, T. (1983) 1996. *Literary Theory. An Introduction. Second Edition*, Oxford.
Easterling, P.E. 1993. "Gods on Stage in Greek Tragedy", in: J. Dalfen – G. Petersmann – F.G. Schwarz (eds.), *Religio Graeco-Romana*, Graz, 77–86.
– 1994. "Euripides Outside Athens: A Speculative Note", *ICS* 19, 73–80.
– 1997. "Form and Performance", in: P.E. Easterling (ed.), *The Cambridge Companion to Greek Tragedy*, Cambridge, 151–77.
Ebbott, M. 2000. "The List of the War Dead in Aeschylus' *Persians*", *HSPh* 100, 83–96.
Eckstein, A.M. 1995. *Moral Vision in the "Histories" of Polybius*, Berkeley etc.
Edmonds, R.G. 2004. *Myths of the Underworld Journey: Plato, Aristophanes, and the 'Orphic' Gold Tablets*, Cambridge.

Edmondson, W. 1981. *Spoken Discourse: A Model for Analysis*, London – New York.
Edwards, M.W. 1977. "Agamemnon's Decision: Freedom and Folly in Aeschylus", *ClAnt* 10, 17–38.
– 1991. *The Iliad. A Commentary. Volume 5, books 17–20*, Cambridge.
Effe, B. 2000. "Die Apotheose des Herakles und die Wiederkehr der Goldenen Zeit. Theokrit, *Id.* 24, 82–87", *WJA* 24, 89–95.
Ehrlich, S. 1990. *Point of View: A Linguistic Analysis of Literary Style,* London – New York.
Elsner, J. 2007. "Viewing Ariadne: from Ekphrasis to Wall Painting in the Roman World", *CPh* 102, 20–44.
Erbse, H. 1989. *Thukydides-Interpretationen,* Berlin.

Fantuzzi, M. 1995. "Mythological Paradigms in the Bucolic Poetry of Theocritus", *PCPhS* 41, 16–35.
– "Epyllion", *DNP* 4, 31–3.
Fantuzzi, M. – Hunter, R. 2004. *Tradition and Innovation in Hellenistic Poetry,* Cambridge.
Farnell, L. 1921. *Greek Hero Cults and Ideas of Immortality,* Oxford.
– 1932. *The Works of Pindar. Critical Commentary,* London.
Feichtinger, B. 1992. "*Ad maiorem gloriam Romae.* Ideologie und Fiktion in der Historiographie des Livius", *Latomus* 51, 3–33.
Feldherr, A. 1998. *Spectacle and Society in Livy's* 'History', Berkeley.
– 2002. "Stepping out of the ring: repetition and sacrifice in the boxing match in *Aeneid* 5", in: D.S. Levene – D.P. Nelis (eds.), *Clio and the Poets. Augustan Poetry and the Tradition of Ancient Historiography,* Leiden, 61–79.
Felson, N. 1978. "Narrative Structure in Pindar's *Ninth Pythian*", *CW* 71, 353–67.
– 1984. "The Epinician Speaker in Pindar's *First Olympian:* Toward a Model for Analyzing Character in Ancient Choral Lyric", *Poetics Today* 5, 377–97.
– 1994. *Regarding Penelope: From Courtship to Poetics,* Princeton.
– 1995. "Penelope's Perspective: Character from Plot", in: S.L. Schein (ed.), *Reading the* Odyssey. *Selected Interpretive Essays,* Princeton, 163–83.
– 2004. "Introduction", in: N. Felson (ed.), *The Poetics of Deixis in Alcman, Pindar, and Other Lyric, Arethusa* 37, 253–66.
Felson, N. – Slatkin, L. 2004. "Gender and Homeric Epic", in: R. Fowler (ed.), *The Cambridge Companion to Homer,* Cambridge, 91–114.
Fenik, B. 1974. *Studies in the* Odyssey, Wiesbaden.
Ferrari, G.R.F. 1989. "Plato and Poetry", in: G. Kennedy (ed.), *The Cambridge History of Literary Criticism. Volume 1: Classical Criticism,* Cambridge, 92–148.
– 1997. "Figures in the Text: Metaphors and Riddles in the *Agamemnon*", *CPh* 92, 1–45.
Ferrero, L. 1946. "La voce pubblica nel proemio degli Annali di Tacito", *RFIC* 74, 50–86.
Fiesel, E. 1928. *Namen des griechischen Mythos im Etruskischen,* Göttingen.

Finglass, P.J. 2007. *Sophocles, "Electra"*, Cambridge.
Finkelberg, M. 1991. "Royal Succession in Heroic Greece", *CQ* 41, 303–16.
Fletcher, J. 1999. "Choral Voice and Narrative in the First Stasimon of Aeschylus' *Agamemnon*", *Phoenix* 53, 29–49.
Flory, S. 1978. "Laughter, Tears and Wisdom in Herodotus", *AJPh* 99, 145–53.
– 1988. "Thucydides' Hypotheses About the Peloponnesian War", *TAPhA* 118, 43–56.
Fludernik, M. 1993. *The Fictions of Language and the Languages of Fiction*, London – New York.
– 1996. *Towards a 'Natural' Narratology*, London – New York.
– 2003a. "Scene Shift, Metalepsis, and the Metaleptic Mode", *Style* 37, 382–400.
– 2003b. "The Diachronization of Narratology", *Narrative* 11, 331–48.
– 2005. "Histories of Narrative Theory (II). From Structuralism to the Present", in: J. Phelan – P.J. Rabinowitz (eds.), *A Companion to Narrative Theory*, Malden, 48–51.
Föllinger, S. 2003. *Genosdependenzen. Studien zur Arbeit am Mythos bei Aischylos*, Göttingen.
Förstel, K. 1979. *Untersuchungen zum Homerischen Apollonhymnus*, Bochum.
Foley, H.P. 1995. "Penelope as Moral Agent", in: B. Cohen (ed.), *The Distaff Side. Representing the Female in Homer's Odyssey*, Oxford, 93–115.
– 2003. "Choral Identity in Greek Tragedy", *CPh* 98, 1–30.
– 2005. "Women in Ancient Epic", in: J.M. Foley (ed.), *A Companion to Ancient Epic*, Malden, 105–18.
Ford, A. 1992. *Homer. The Poetry of the Past*, Ithaca – New York.
– 2002. *The Origins of Criticism: Literary Culture and Poetic Theory in Classical Greece*, Princeton.
Fornara, Ch.W. 1983. *The Nature of History in Ancient Greece and Rome*, Berkeley etc.
Foster, B.O. (1929) 1996. *Livy, History of Rome V, Books XXI-XXII. With an English Translation*, Cambridge, MA. (*The Loeb Classical Library* vol. 233).
Fowler, D.P. 1990. "Deviant focalization in Vergil's *Aeneid*", *PCPhS* 216, 42–63 (repr. in: id., *Roman Constructions*, Oxford, 2000, 40–63).
Fowler, M.A. – Marincola, J. (eds.) 2002. *Herodotus. Histories, Book IX*, Cambridge.
Fowler, R. 2003. "Herodotus and Athens", in: P. Derow – R. Parker (eds.), *Herodotus and his World. Essays from a Conference in Memory of George Forrest*, Oxford, 305–18.
Fox, M. 2007. *Cicero's Philosophy of History*, Oxford.
Fox, R.L. (ed.) 2004. *The Long March: Xenophon and the Ten Thousand*, New Haven – London.
Fraenkel, E. 1950. *Aeschylus' "Agamemnon"*, 3 vols., Oxford.
– 1963. "Zu den *Phoenissen* des Euripides", *Sitzungsberichte der Bayerischen Akademie der Wissenschaften, Philosophisch-Historische Klasse*, vol. 1, Munich.
Fränkel, H. 1968. *Noten zu den Argonautika des Apollonios Rhodios*, Munich.
Frame, D. 1978. *The Myth of Return in Early Greek Epic*, New Haven – London.

Franchet-d'Espèrey, S. 2006. "Rhétorique et poétique chez Quintilien: à propos de l'apostrophe", *Rhetorica* 25, 163–85.
Frazer, J.G. 1898. *Pausanias's Description of Greece*, vol. 2, London.
Friedrich, R. 1975. *Stilwandel im Homerischen Epos. Studien zur Poetik und Theorie der epischen Gattung*, Heidelberg.
– 2002. "Flaubertian Homer: The *Phrase Juste* in Homeric Diction", *Arion* 10, 1–13.
Frisk, H. 1954–72. *Griechisches etymologisches Wörterbuch* (*GrEW*), 3 vols., Heidelberg.
Führer, R. 1967. *Formproblem-Untersuchungen zu den Reden in der frühgriechischen Lyrik*, Munich.
Fuhrmann, M. 1983. "Narrative Techniken im Dienste der Geschichtsschreibung (Livius, Buch 21–22). Eine Skizze", in: E. Lefèvre – E. Olshausen, *Livius. Werk und Rezeption. Festschrift für E. Burck zum 80. Geburtstag*, Munich, 19–29.
Fusillo, M. 1985. *Il tempo delle Argonautiche. Un'analisi del racconto in Apollonio Rodio*, Rome.
– 1989. *Il romanzo greco. Polifonia ed Eros*, Venice.

Gärtner, H.A. 1975. *Beobachtungen zu Bauelementen in der antiken Historiographie besonders bei Livius und Caesar*, Wiesbaden (*Historia Einzelschriften* vol. 25).
Gagarin, M. 1976. *Aeschylean Drama*, Berkeley.
Galinsky, G.K. 1968. "*Aeneid* V and the *Aeneid*", *AJPh* 89, 157–85.
Gammacurta, T. 2006. *Papyrologica Scaenica*, Alessandria.
Gantz, T.N. 1993. *Early Greek Myth: a guide to literary and artistic sources*, Baltimore.
– 2007. "The Aischylean Tetralogy", in: M. Lloyd (ed.), *Aeschylus*, Oxford, 40–70.
Gardiner, C.P. 1987. *The Sophoclean Chorus: A study of character and function*, Iowa City.
Garner, S.B. 1989. *The Absent Voice. Narrative Comprehension in the Theater*, Urbana.
Garvie, A.F. 1994. *Homer: Odyssey, Books VI-VIII*, Cambridge.
– 1998. *Sophocles: Ajax*, Warminster.
Gastaldi, E.C. 1976. "Propaganda e politicà negli 'Eleusini' di Eschilo", in: M. Sordi (ed.), *I canali della propaganda nel mondo antico* (*Contributi dell'Instituto di storia antica dell'Università cattolica del Sacro Cuore*, vol. 4), Milan, 50–71.
– 1998. "*Paideia/mythologia*", in: M. Vegetti (ed.), *Platone: la Repubblica*, vol. 2, Naples, 333–92.
Gehrke, H.-J. 1998. "Die Geburt der Erdkunde aus dem Geiste der Geometrie. Überlegungen zur Entstehung und zur Frühgeschichte der wissenschaftlichen Geographie bei den Griechen", in: W. Kullmann – J. Althoff – M. Asper (eds.), *Gattungen wissenschaftlicher Literatur in der Antike*, Tübingen, 163–92.
Genette, G. (1972) 1980. *Narrative Discourse: An Essay in Method*, Ithaca, N.Y. (Original Title: "Discours du récit", in: *Figures III*, Paris, 67–267).
– 1982. *Palimpsestes: la littérature au second degré*, Paris.

- (1983) 1988. *Narrative Discourse Revisited*, Ithaca, N.Y. (Original Title: *Nouveau discours du récit*, Paris).
- (1991) 1992. *Fiktion und Diktion*, Munich (Original Title: *Fiction et diction*, Paris).
- 1994. *Die Erzählung*, Munich.
- 2004. *Métalepse. De la figure à la fiction*, Paris.

Gera, D. 1997. *Warrior Women. The Anonymous Tractatus de Mulieribus*, Leiden.

Gerrig, R.J. 1989a. "Reexperiencing fiction and non-fiction", *The Journal of Aesthetics and Art Criticism* 47, 277–80.
- 1989b. "Suspense in the Absence of Uncertainty", *Journal of Memory and Language* 28, 633–48.
- 1993. *Experiencing narrative worlds: On the psychological activities of reading*, New Haven, CT.
- 1996. "The Resiliency of Suspense", in: P. Vorderer – H.J. Wulff – M. Friedrichsen (eds.), *Suspense: Conceptualizations, Theoretical Analyses, and Empirical Explorations*, Mahwah, New Jersey, 93–105.

Gibbons, R. – Segal, C. 2003. *Sophocles. Antigone*, Oxford.

Gibson, B.J. 1998. "Rumours as Causes of Events in Tacitus", *MD* 40, 111–29.

Gildersleeve, B.L. 1900–1911. *Syntax of Classical Greek*, New York.

Giuliano, M. 2005. *Platone e la poesia: teoria della composizione e prassi della ricezione*, Sankt Augustin.

Glenn, J. 1971. "Mezentius and Polyphemus", *AJPh* 92, 129–55.

Goff, B. 1995. "Aithra at Eleusis", *Helios* 22, 65–78.

Goldhill, S. 1984. *Language, Sexuality, Narrative: The Oresteia*, Cambridge.

Goldthorpe, R. 1991. "Ricoeur, Proust and the Aporias of Time", in: D. Wood (ed.), *On Paul Ricoeur. Narrative and Interpretation*, London – New York, 84–101.

Goodyear, F.R.D. 1972. *The Annals of Tacitus. Volume I (Annals I.1–54)*, Cambridge.

Gould, J. 2001. *Myth, Ritual, Memory, and Exchange: Essays in Greek literature and culture*, Oxford.

Gow, A.S.F. 1952. *Theocritus*, vols. I-II, Cambridge.

Goward, B. 1999. *Telling Tragedy: Narrative Technique in Aeschylus, Sophocles and Euripides*, London.

Gray, V.J. 1986. "Xenophon's *Hiero* and the Meeting of the Wise Man and Tyrant in Greek Literature", *CQ* 36, 115–23.
- 1987. "*Mimesis* in Greek Historical Theory", *AJPh* 108, 467–86.
- 2003. "Interventions and Citations in Xenophon", *CQ* 53, 111–23.
- 2004. "Xenophon", in: I.J.F. de Jong – R. Nünlist – A. Bowie, *Narrators, Narratees and Narratives in Ancient Greek Literature (Studies in Ancient Greek Narrative*, vol. 1), Leiden, 129–46.

Graziosi, B. – Haubold, J. 2005. *Homer: The Resonance of Epic*, London.

Greenwood, E. 2006. *Thucydides and the Shaping of History*, London.

Greimas, A.J. 1966. *Sémantique Structurale*, Paris.

Greindl, M. 1938. Κλέος Κῦδος Εὖχος Τιμή Φάτις Δόξα. *Eine bedeutungsgeschichtliche Untersuchung des epischen und lyrischen Sprachgebrauches*, Diss. Munich.
Grethlein, J. 2006a. *Das Geschichtsbild der Ilias. Eine Untersuchung aus phänomenologischer und narratologischer Perspektive*, Göttingen.
– 2006b. "The Unthucydidean Voice of Sallust", *TAPhA* 136, 299–327.
– 2007. "The Hermeneutics and Poetics of Memory in Aeschylus' *Persae*", *Arethusa* 40, 363–96.
– 2008a. "Eine herodoteische Deutung der Sizilischen Expedition (Thuc. 7.87.5 f.)?", *Hermes* 136, 129–42.
– 2008b. "Memory and Material Objects in the *Iliad* and the *Odyssey*", *JHS* 128, 27–51.
– (forthcoming a). *The Greeks and their Past. Poetry, Oratory, and History in the Fifth Century BCE*, Cambridge.
– (forthcoming b). "How Not to Do History. Xerxes in Herodotus' *Histories*", *AJPh* 130.
Gribble, D. 1998. "Narrator Interventions in Thucydides", *JHS* 118, 41–67.
Griffin, J. 1980. *Homer on Life and Death*, Oxford.
– 1986. "Homeric Words and Speakers", *JHS* 106, 36–57.
Griffith, M. 1983. *Prometheus Bound*, Cambridge.
Griffiths, A. 1996. "Customising Theocritus: Poems 13 and 24", in: M.A. Harder – R.F. Regtuit – G.C. Wakker (eds.), *Theocritus*, Groningen, 101–17.
Grimes, J.E. 1975. *The Thread of Discourse*, The Hague.
Gummert, P. 1992. *Die Erzählstruktur in den* Argonautika *des Apollonios Rhodios*, Frankfurt.
Gutzwiller, K. 1981. *Studies in the Hellenistic Epyllion*, Königstein.
Gwynn, A. 1929. "Xenophon and Sophaenetus", *CQ* 23, 38–9.

Hack, R. 1929. "Homer and the Cult of Heroes", *TAPhA* 60, 57–74.
Hadzisteliou-Price, Th. 1973. "Hero-Cult and Homer", *Historia* 22, 129–44.
– 1979. "Hero Cult in the 'Age of Homer' and Earlier", in: G.W. Bowersock – W. Burkert – M.C.J. Putnam (eds.), *Arktouros: Hellenic Studies Presented to Bernard M.W. Knox on the occasion of his 65th birthday*, Berlin – New York, 219–28.
Hall, E. 1989. *Inventing the Barbarian: Greek Self-Definition through Tragedy*, Oxford.
– 1996. *Aeschylus. Persians*, Warminster.
Halliwell, S. 1986. *Aristotle's Poetics*, London.
– 2000. "The subjection of muthos to logos: Plato's citations of the poets", *CQ* 50, 94–112.
– 2002. *The Aesthetics of Mimesis: Ancient Texts and Modern Problems*, Princeton.
– 2007. "The Life-and-Death Journey of the Soul: Interpreting the Myth of Er", in: G.R.F. Ferrari (ed.), *The Cambridge Companion to Plato's Republic*, Cambridge, 445–73.
Hamburger, K. 1957. *Die Logik der Dichtung*, Stuttgart.
Harder, R. 1999. "Klytaimestra", *DNP* 6, 611–12.
– 2003. "Clytaemnestra", *Brill's New Pauly* 3, 487–8.

Hardie, P. 1986. *Virgil's* Aeneid. *Cosmos and Imperium*, Oxford.
– 1993. *The epic successors of Virgil: a study in the dynamics of tradition*, Cambridge.
Hardy, B. 1975. *Tellers and Listeners: The narrative imagination*, London.
Harrell, S.E. 2002. "King or Private Citizen: Fifth-Century Sicilian Tyrants at Olympia and Delphi", *Mnemosyne* 55, 439–64.
– 2006. "Synchronicity: The Local and the Panhellenic within Sicilian Tyranny", in: S. Lewis (ed.), *Ancient Tyranny*, Edinburgh, 119–34.
Harrison, S.J. 2001. "Picturing the Future: The Proleptic Ekphrasis from Homer to Vergil", in: S.J. Harrison (ed.), *Texts, Ideas, and the Classics. Scholarship, Theory, and Classical Literature*, Oxford, 70–92.
– 2007. "From Man to Book: the Close of Tacitus' *Agricola*", in: S.J. Heyworth (ed.), *Classical Constructions. Papers in Memory of Don Fowler, Classicist and Epicurean*, Oxford, 310–19.
Harrison, T. 2000. *The Emptiness of Asia: Aeschylus'* Persians *and the History of the Fifth Century*, London.
Haslam, M. 1972. "Plato, Sophron, and the Dramatic Dialogue", *BICS* 19, 17–38.
Hauvette, A. 1898. "Les *Éleusiniens* d'Eschyle et l'institution du discours funèbre à Athènes", in: A. Fontemoing (ed.), *Mélanges Henri Weil*, Paris, 165–73.
Haynes, H. 2003. *Tacitus on Imperial Rome. The History of Make-Believe*, Berkeley etc.
Heath, M. 1987. *The Poetics of Greek Tragedy*, Stanford.
Heath, M. – Lefkowitz, M. 1991. "Epinician Performance", *CPh* 86, 173–91.
Heilinger, K. 1983. "Der Freierkatalog der Helena im hesiodeischen Frauenkatalog I", *MH* 40, 19–34.
Heinze, R. (1915) 1965. *Virgils epische Technik*, Stuttgart.
Henderson, J. 1987. *Aristophanes* Lysistrata. *Edited with Introduction and Commentary*, Oxford.
Henrichs, A. 1994–95. "'Why Should I Dance?': Choral Self-Referentiality in Greek Tragedy", *Arion* 3, 56–111.
Herington, J. 1985. *Poetry into Drama. Early Tragedy and the Greek Poetic Tradition*, Berkeley.
Herman, D. 1997. "Toward a formal description of narrative metalepsis", *Journal of Literary Semantics* 26, 132–52.
– 1999. *Narratologies: New Perspectives on Narrative Analysis*, Columbus, Oh.
– (ed.) 2003. *Narrative Theory and the Cognitive Sciences*, Stanford.
– 2004. "Towards a Transmedial Narratology", in: M.-L. Ryan (ed.), *Narrative Across Media. The Languages of Story-Telling*, Lincoln, 47–75.
Herzhoff, B. 2008. "Der Flußkatalog der *Ilias* (M 20–23) – ältestes literarisches Beispiel geometrischer Raumerfassung?", in: J. Althoff – S. Föllinger – G. Wöhrle (eds.), *Antike Naturwissenschaft und ihre Rezeption*, vol. 18, Trier, 101–38.
Heubeck, A. 1989. "Books IX–XII", in: Heubeck, A. – Hoekstra, A. (eds.) *A Commentary on Homer's* Odyssey, vol. 2, Oxford, 3–143.
– 1992. J. Russo – M. Fernández-Galiano – A. Heubeck (eds.), *A Commentary on Homer's* Odyssey, vol. 3, Oxford.

Higbie, C. 1995. *Heroes' Names, Homeric Identities* (A.B. Lord Studies in Oral Tradition, vol. 10), New York.
– 2002. "Diomedes' Genealogy and Ancient Criticism", *Arethusa* 35, 173–88.
Hirschberger, M. 2004. *Gynaikōn Katalogos und Megalai Ēhoiai. Ein Kommentar zu den Fragmenten zweier hesiodeischer Epen*, Munich – Leipzig.
– 2008. "Il tema della metamorfosi del *Catalogo* esiodeo delle donne", in: G. Bastianini – A. Casanova (eds.), *Esiodo: Cent'anni di papiri. Atti del convegno internazionale di studi. Firenze, 7–8 giugno 2007*, Florence, 113–27.
Hobbs, A. 2000. *Plato and the Hero*, Cambridge.
Höfer, O. 1890–1894. "Klytaim(n)estra", in: Roscher's *Ausführliches Lexikon der griechischen und römischen Mythologie*, Leipzig, 1230–45.
Hölscher, U. 1960. "Das Schweigen der Arete", *Hermes* 88, 257–65 (also in: J. Latacz – M. Kraus (eds.), *Das nächste Fremde. Von Texten der griechischen Frühzeit und ihrem Reflex in der Moderne*, Munich 1994, 37–44).
– 1967. "Die Atridensage in der *Odyssee*", in: H. Singer – B. von Wiese (eds.), *Festschrift für Richard Alewyn*, Köln, 1–16.
– (1989) ³1990. *Die* Odyssee: *Epos zwischen Märchen und Roman*, Munich.
Hollis, A.S. 1990. *Callimachus' Hecale*, Oxford.
– 1992. "Attica in Hellenistic Poetry", *ZPE* 93, 1–15.
Hommel, H. 1955. "Aigisthos und die Freier. Zum poetischen Plan and zum geschichtlichen Ort der *Odyssee*", *Studium Generale* 8, 237–45.
Hoppin, M.C. 1990. "Metrical Effects, Dramatic Illusion, and the Two Endings of Sophocles' *Philoctetes*", *Arethusa* 23, 141–82.
Hordern, J.H. 2002. *The Fragments of Timotheus of Miletus*, Oxford.
Hornblower, S. 1994. "Narratology and Narrative Techniques in Thucydides", in: S. Hornblower (ed.), *Greek Historiography*, Oxford, 131–66.
– 2004. *Thucydides and Pindar. Historical Narrative and the World of Epinikian Poetry*, Oxford.
– 2006. "Pindar and Kingship Theory", in: S. Lewis (ed.), *Ancient Tyranny*, Edinburgh, 151–63.
Horsfall, N. 2006. *Virgil, Aeneid III. A Commentary*, Leiden.
Hubbard, T.K. 1992. "Tragic Preludes: Aeschylus *Seven Against Thebes* 4–8", *Phoenix* 46, 299–308.
– 2004. "The Dissemination of Epinician Lyric: Pan-Hellenism, Reperformance, Written Texts", in: C.J. Mackie (ed.), *Oral Performance and Its Context*, Leiden, 71–93.
Humbert, J. 1960. *Syntaxe grecque*, Paris.
Hunter, R. 1989a. "Bulls and Boxers in Apollonius and Virgil", *CQ* 39, 557–61 (= Hunter 2008a, 89–94).
– 1989b. *Apollonius of Rhodes. Argonautica III*, Cambridge.
– 1993. *The* Argonautica *of Apollonius. Literary Studies*, Cambridge.
– 1999. *Theocritus. A Selection*, Cambridge.
– 2001. "The Poetics of narrative in the *Argonautica*", in: T.D. Papanghelis – A. Rengakos (eds.), *A Companion to Apollonius Rhodius*, Leiden, 93–125 (= Hunter 2008a, 343–77).

- 2004. "Theocritus and Moschus", in: I.J.F. de Jong – R. Nünlist – A. Bowie, *Narrators, Narratees and Narratives in Ancient Greek Literature* (*Studies in Ancient Greek Narrative*, vol. 1), Leiden, 83–97.
- 2005a. *The Hesiodic Catalogue of Women. Constructions and Reconstructions*, Cambridge.
- 2005b. "Showing and telling: notes from the boundary", *Eikasmos* 16, 179–91 (= Hunter 2008a, 663–77).
- 2005c. "The Hesiodic *Catalogue* and Hellenistic Poetry", in: id. (ed.), *The Hesiodic Catalogue of Women. Constructions and Reconstructions*, Cambridge, 239–65 (= Hunter 2008a, 470–502).
- 2006. "Plato's *Symposium* and the traditions of ancient fiction", in: J.H. Lesher – D. Nails – F.C.C. Sheffield (eds.), *Plato's Symposium. Issues in Interpretation and Reception*, Washington, 295–312 (= Hunter 2008a, 845–66).
- 2008a. *On Coming After. Studies in Post-Classical Greek Literature and its Reception* (*Trends in Classics Supplementary Volumes* 3), Berlin.
- 2008b. "*Polypragmosyne* and the ancient novel", in: Hunter 2008a, 884–96.

Hurst, A. 1983. "Temps du récit chez Pindare (*Pyth.* 4) et Bacchylide (11)", *MH* 40, 154–68.
- 1984. "Aspects du temps chez Pindare", in: A. Hurst (ed.), *Pindare* (*Entretiens sur l'antiquité classique vol. 31*), Vandoeuvres – Geneva, 155–97.

Hutchinson, G.O. 1985. *Aeschylus' Septem Contra Thebas. Edited with Introduction and Commentary*, Oxford.
- 1988. *Hellenistic Poetry*, Oxford.
- 2001. *Greek Lyric Poetry. A Commentary on Selected Larger Pieces*, Oxford.

Ierulli, M. 1993. "A Community of Women? The protagonist and the chorus in Sophocles' *Electra*", *Metis* 8, 217–29.

Immerwahr, H.R. 1954. "Historical Action in Herodotus", *TAPhA* 85, 16–45.
- 1966. *Form and Thought in Herodotus*, Cleveland.

Irigoin, J. 1952. *Histoire du texte de Pindare*, Paris.

Irwin, E. 2005. "Gods among Men? The Social and Political Dynamics of the Hesiodic *Catalogue of Women*", in: R. Hunter (ed.), *The Hesiodic Catalogue of Women. Constructions and Reconstructions*, Cambridge, 35–98.

Iser, W. 1991. *Das Fiktive und das Imaginäre. Perspektiven literarischer Anthropologie*, Frankfurt.

Jacoby, F. (1933) 1961. "Der homerische Apollonhymnus", in: id., *Kleine philologische Schriften*, Berlin, 139–218.
- (ed.) 1950. *Die Fragmente der Griechischen Historiker III. Geschichte von Staedten und Voelkern (Horographie und Ethnographie), B. Autoren ueber Einzelne Staedte (Laender), Nr. 297–607*, Leiden.
- (ed.) 1954. *Die Fragmente der Griechischen Historiker III. Geschichte von Staedten und Voelkern (Horographie und Ethnographie), b. (Supplement). A Commentary on the Ancient Historians of Athens, Nos 323a-334*, vol. I-II. Text, Notes, Addenda, Corrigenda, Index, Leiden.

Jaeger, M. 1997. *Livy's Written Rome*, Ann Arbor.

Jahn, M. 1997. "Frames, Preferences, and the Reading of Third-Person Narrative. Towards a Cognitive Narratology", *Poetics Today* 18, 441–68.
– 1999. "Speak, Friend, and Enter: Garden Paths, Artificial Intelligence, and Cognitive Narratology", in: D. Herman, *Narratologies: New Perspectives on Narrative Analysis*, Columbus, Oh., 167–94.
– 2001. "Narrative Voice and Agency in Drama: Aspects of a narratology of drama", *New Literary History* 32, 659–79.
Jakob, D. – Oikonomidis, Y. 1994. Πινδάρου Πυθιόνικοι, Herakleion.
Janaway, C. 1995. *Images of Excellence: Plato's Critique of the Arts*, Oxford.
Janko, R. 1981. "The Structure of the Homeric Hymns: a Study in Genre", *Hermes* 109, 9–25.
– 1984. *Aristotle on Comedy: Towards a Reconstruction of* Poetics II, London.
Janni, P. 1984. *La mappa e il periplo. Cartografia e spazio odologico*, Rome.
Jauß, H.R. 1982a. *Toward an Aesthetic of Reception*, Minneapolis.
– 1982b. *Ästhetische Erfahrung und literarische Hermeneutik*, Frankfurt.
Jebb, R.C. 1914. *Sophocles: The Plays and Fragments. Part One: The Oedipus Tyrannus*, Cambridge (repr. Amsterdam 1966).
Jörgensen, O. 1904. "Das Auftreten der Götter in den Büchern ι-μ der *Odyssee*", *Hermes* 39, 357–82.
Jong, I.J.F. de (1987) 2004. *Narrators and Focalizers: The Presentation of the Story in the* Iliad, London.
– 1988. "Homeric Words and Speakers: an Addendum", *JHS* 108, 188–9.
– 1991. *Narrative in Drama: The Art of the Euripidean Messenger Speech* (*Mnemosyne Supplementum* vol. 116), Leiden.
– 1993. "Studies on Homeric Denomination", *Mnemosyne* 46, 289–306.
– 1997a. "Homer and Narratology", in: I. Morris – B. Powell (eds.), *A New Companion to Homer*, Leiden, 305–25.
– 1997b. "Narrator Language Versus Character Language: Some Further Explorations", in: F. Létoublon (ed.), *Hommage à Milman Parry. Le style formulaire de l'épopée homérique et la théorie de l'oralité poétique*, Amsterdam, 293–302.
– 1999. "Aspects narratologiques des *Histoires* d'Hérodote", *Lalies* 19, 217–74.
– 2001a. *A Narratological Commentary on the* Odyssey, Cambridge.
– 2001b. "The Anachronical Structure of Herodotus' *Histories*", in: S.J. Harrison (ed.), *Texts, Ideas, and the Classics: Scholarship, Theory and Classical Literature*, Oxford, 93–116.
– 2004a. "Introduction: Narratological theory on narrators, narratees, and narrative", in: I.J.F.de Jong – R. Nünlist – A. Bowie, *Narrators, Narratees and Narratives in Ancient Greek Literature* (*Studies in Ancient Greek Narrative*, vol. 1), Leiden, 1–10.
– 2004b. "Herodotus", in: I.J.F.de Jong – R. Nünlist – A. Bowie, *Narrators, Narratees and Narratives in Ancient Greek Literature* (*Studies in Ancient Greek Narrative*, vol. 1), Leiden, 13–24.
– 2006a. "Where Narratology Meets Stylistics: The Seven Versions of Ajax' Madness", in: I.J.F. de Jong – A. Rijksbaron (eds.), *Sophocles and the Greek Language*, Leiden, 73–93.
– 2006b. "The Homeric Narrator and his own *kleos*", *Mnemosyne* 59, 188–207.

– 2007. "Homer", in: I.J.F. de Jong – R. Nünlist, *Time in Ancient Greek Literature* (*Studies in Ancient Greek Narrative* vol. 2), Leiden, 17–37.
Jong, I.J.F. de – Nünlist, R. 2004. "Epilogue. Narrators, Narratees, and Narratives in Ancient Greek Literature", in: I.J.F.de Jong – R. Nünlist – A. Bowie, *Narrators, Narratees and Narratives in Ancient Greek Literature* (*Studies in Ancient Greek Narrative*, vol. 1), Leiden, 545–53.
– (eds.). 2007. *Time in Ancient Greek Literature* (*Studies in Ancient Greek Narrative* vol. 2), Leiden.
Jong, I.J.F. de – Nünlist, R. – Bowie, A. (eds.). 2004. *Narrators, Narratees and Narratives in Ancient Greek Literature* (*Studies in Ancient Greek Narrative*, vol. 1), Leiden.
Jong, I.J.F. de – Sullivan, J.P. (eds.). 1993. *Modern Critical Theory and Classical Literature* (Mnemosyne Supplementum vol. 130), Leiden.
Jordan, B. 2000. "The Sicilian Expedition was a Potemkin Fleet", *CQ* 50, 63–79.
Jouan, F. 1966, *Euripide et les légendes des Chants cyprien. Des origines de la guerre de Troie à l'Iliade*, Paris
Jouanna, J. 1981. "Les causes de la défaite des Barbares chez Eschyle, Hérodote et Hippocrate", *Ktèma* 6, 3–15.
– 2001. "La double fin du *Philoctète* de Sophocle: Rythme et spectacle", *REG* 114, 359–82.

Käppel, L. 1992. *Paian. Studien zur Geschichte einer Gattung*, Berlin.
Kahane, A. 1994. *The Interpretation of Order. A Study in the Poetics of Homeric Repetition*, Oxford.
– 1997. "Hexameter Progression and the Homeric Hero's Solitary State", in: E. Bakker – A. Kahane (eds.), *Written Voices, Spoken Signs. Tradition, Performance, and the Epic Text*, Cambridge, MA – London, 110–37.
– 2005. *Diachronic Dialogues. Authority and Continuity in Homer and the Homeric Tradition*, Lanham, MD.
Kallet, L. 2001. *Money and the Corrosion of Power in Thucydides. The Sicilian Expedition and its Aftermath*, Berkeley etc.
Kamerbeek, J.C. 1967. *The Plays of Sophocles. Part IV: The* Oedipus Tyrannus, Leiden.
Kamptz, H. von. 1982. *Homerische Personennamen. Sprachwissenschaftliche und historische Klassifikation*, Göttingen.
Karusu, S. 1972. "Choeur de tragédie sur un lécythe à figures noires", *RA*, 195–204.
Katz, M.A. 1991. *Penelope's Renown. Meaning and Indeterminacy in the* Odyssey, Princeton.
Kermode, F. 1967. *The Sense of an Ending. Studies in the Theory of Fiction*, Oxford.
Kim, L. 2008. "Dio of Prusa, *Or.* 61, *Chryseis*, or reading Homeric Silence", *CQ* 58, 601–21.
Kindt, T. – Müller, H.-H. 2003a. "Narrative Theory and/or/as Theory of Interpretation", in: T. Kindt – H.-H. Müller (eds.), *What is Narratology? Questions and Answers Regarding the Status of a Theory*, Berlin, 205–19.

– (eds.) 2003b. *What is Narratology? Questions and Answers Regarding the Status of a Theory*, Berlin.
Kindstrand, J.F. 1973. *Homer in der Zweiten Sophistik*, Uppsala.
Kintsch, W. 1980. "Learning from text, levels of comprehension, or: why anyone would read a story anyway", *Poetics* 9, 87–98.
Kirby, J.T. 1991. "Mimesis and Diegesis: Foundations of Aesthetic Theory in Plato and Aristotle", *Helios* 18, 113–28.
Kitzinger, R. 2007. *The Choruses of Sophokles'* Antigone *and* Philoktetes: *A Dance of Words*, Leiden.
Klooster, J.J.H. 2007. "Apollonius of Rhodes", in: I.J.F. de Jong – R. Nünlist, *Time in Ancient Greek Literature (Studies in Ancient Greek Narrative* vol. 2), Leiden, 63–80.
Knox, B.R.W. 1979. *Word and Action: Essays on the Ancient Theater*, Baltimore – London.
Köhnken, A. 1970. "Hieron und Deinomenes in Pindars erstem Pythischen Gedicht", *Hermes* 98, 1–13.
– 1983. "Mythical Chronology and Thematic Coherence in Pindar's *Third Olympian Ode*", *HSPh* 87, 49–63.
Konstan, D. 2006a. *The Emotions of the Ancient Greeks. Studies in Aristotle and Classical Literature*, Toronto.
– 2006b. "Pity and Politics", in: R. Sternberg (ed.), *Pity and Power in Ancient Athens*, Cambridge, 48–66.
Koselleck, R. 1985. "'Space of Experience' and 'Horizon of Expectation'. Two Historical Categories", in: id., *Futures Past. On the Semantics of Historical Time*, Cambridge, MA, 267–88.
Kovacs, D. 1998. *Euripides*. Suppliant Women, Electra, Heracles, Cambridge, MA.
– 2005. "Text and Transmission", in: J. Gregory (ed.), *A Companion to Greek Tragedy*, Oxford, 379–93.
Kowerski, L.M. 2005. *Simonides on the Persian Wars: A Study of the Elegiac Verses of the "New Simonides"*, New York – London.
Kramer, L. 1991. "Musical Narratology. A Theoretical Outline", *Indiana Theory Review* 12, 141–62.
Kranz, W. 1967. *Studien zur antiken Literatur und ihrem Fortwirken. Kleine Schriften*, Heidelberg.
Kraut, C. 1863. *Die epische Prolepsis, nachgewiesen in der Ilias*, Tübingen.
Krentz, P. 1995. *Xenophon* Hellenika *II.3.11-IV.2.8*, Warminster.
Kretschmer, P. (1894) 1969. *Die griechischen Vaseninschriften, ihrer Sprache nach untersucht*, Gütersloh (repr. Hildesheim – New York).
– 1912. "Literaturbericht für das Jahr 1909", *Glotta* 3, 330.
Krischer, T. 1971. *Formale Konventionen der homerischen Epik*, Munich.
– 1985. "Pindars erste *Pythische Ode* und ihre Vorlage", *Hermes* 113, 491–4.
Kroll, W. (ed.) 1899–1901. *Procli Diadochi in Platonis Rem Publicam Commentarii*, 2 vols., Leipzig.
– (1924) 1973. *Studien zum Verständnis der römischen Literatur*, Darmstadt.
Kroon, C. 1995. *Discourse Particles in Latin: A Study of* nam, enim, autem, vero *and* at, Amsterdam.

Krummen, E. 1990. *Pyrsos Hymnon. Festliche Gegenwart und mythisch-rituelle Tradition als Voraussetzung einer Pindarinterpretation (Isthmie 4, Pythie 5, Olympie 1 und 3)*, Berlin.
Kühner, R. – Stegmann, C. (1914) 1992. *Ausführliche Grammatik der lateinischen Sprache*, Zweiter Teil: Satzlehre, vol. II, Darmstadt.
Kuhns, R. 1991. *Tragedy: Contradiction and Repression*, Chicago.
Kullmann, W. 1992. *Homerische Motive*, Stuttgart.
Kunst, K. 1924–1925. "Die Schuld der Klytaimestra", *WS* 44, 18–32, 143–54.
Kurke, L. 1990. "Pindar's Sixth *Pythian* and the Tradition of Advice Poetry", *TAPhA* 120, 85–107.
– 1999. *Coins, Bodies, Games, and Gold. The Politics of Meaning in Archaic Greece*, Princeton.
Kyriakou, P. 2006. *A Commentary on Euripides'* Iphigenia in Tauris, Berlin – New York.

LaCapra, D. 1982. *'Madame Bovary' on Trial*, Ithaca – London.
Laird, A. 1999. *Powers of Expression, Expressions of Power: Speech Presentation and Latin Literature*, Oxford.
Lambert, A. 1946. *Die indirekte Rede als künstlerisches Stilmittel des Livius*, Zurich.
Lanser, S.S. 1986. "Toward a Feminist Narratology", *Style* 20, 341–63.
Latacz, J. 1994. "Frauengestalten Homers", in: F. Graf – J. von Ungern-Sternberg – A. Schmitt (eds.), *Erschließung der Antike. Kleine Schriften zur Literatur der Griechen und Römer*, Stuttgart – Leipzig, 95–124.
– 2003. *Einführung in die griechische Tragödie*, 2nd ed., Göttingen.
Lateiner, D. 1977. "No Laughing Matter: A Literary Tactic in Herodotus", *TAPhA* 107, 173–82.
– 1982. "A Note on the Perils of Good Fortune in Herodotus", *RhM* 125, 97–101.
– 1989. *The Historical Method of Herodotus*, Toronto.
– 1997. "Homeric Prayer", *Arethusa* 30, 241–72.
Lattimore, R. 1939. "The Wise Advisor in Herodotus", *CPh* 34, 24–35.
– 1951. *The Iliad of Homer: Translated with an Introduction*, Chicago.
– (1967) 1999. *The Odyssey of Homer: Translated with an Introduction*, New York.
Lattimore, S. 1998. *Thucydides. The* Peloponnesian War, Indianapolis.
Lattmann, C. 2005. "Die Dichtungsklassifikation des Aristoteles: eine neue Interpretation von Aristot. poet. 1448a19–24", *Philologus* 149, 28–51.
Lausberg, H. (1960) 1990. *Handbuch der Literarischen Rhetorik. Eine Grundlegung der Literaturwissenschaft*, 3rd ed., Stuttgart.
Lebeck, A. 1971. *The* Oresteia: *a Study in Language and Structure*, Washington, D.C.
Ledbetter, G.M. 2003. *Poetics Before Plato: Interpretation and Authority in Early Greek Theories of Poetry*, Princeton.
Leech, G.N. – Short, M.H. 1981. *Style in Fiction: A Linguistic Introduction to English Fictional Prose*, London – New York.

Leeman, A.D. (1963) 1986. *Orationis Ratio. The Stylistic Theories and Practice of the Roman Orators, Historians and Philosophers,* Vols. I, II, Amsterdam.
Lefèvre, E. – Olshausen, E. 1983. *Livius. Werk und Rezeption. Festschrift für E. Burck zum 80. Geburtstag,* Munich.
Lefkowitz, M. 1976. *The Victory Ode,* Park Ridge.
– 1991. *First-Person Fictions. Pindar's Poetic 'I',* Oxford.
Lehmann, G.A. 1967. *Untersuchungen zur historischen Glaubwürdigkeit des Polybios,* Münster.
Lemarchand, L. 1926. *Dion de Pruse. Les oeuvres d'avant l'exil,* Paris.
Lenz, A. 1980. *Das Proöm des frühen griechischen Epos,* Bonn.
Lesky, A. 1967. "Die Schuld der Klytaimestra", *WS* 80, 5–21.
Lethcoe, J. 1965. "The structure of Robbe-Grillet's Labyrinth", *The French Review* 38, 497–507.
Levaniouk, O. 1999. "Penelope and the Pênelops", in: M. Carlisle – O. Levaniouk (eds.), *Nine Essays on Homer,* Lanham etc., 95–136.
Levene, D.S. 1993. *Religion in Livy (Mnemosyne Supplementum* vol. 127), Leiden.
Levinson, S.C. 1983. *Pragmatics,* Cambridge.
Lieberg, G. 1982. *Poeta Creator. Studien zu einer Figur der antiken Dichtung,* Amsterdam.
Livrea, E. 1992. "The Tempest in Callimachus' *Hecale*", *CQ* 42, 147–51.
Lloyd-Jones, H. – Wilson, N.G. (eds.). 1990. *Sophoclis Fabulae,* Oxford.
Lomas, K. 2006. "Tyrants and the Polis: Migration, Identity and Urban Development in Sicily", in: S. Lewis (ed.), *Ancient Tyranny,* Edinburgh, 95–118.
Longo, O. (1978) 1990. "The Theater of the *Polis*", in: J.J. Winkler – F.I. Zeitlin (eds.), *Nothing to do with Dionysos? Athenian drama in its social context,* Princeton, 12–19.
Loraux, N. 1986. *The Invention of Athens. The Funeral Oration in the Classical City,* Cambridge, MA.
– 1987. *Tragic Ways of Killing a Woman,* Cambridge, MA.
– 1993. "Ce que *Les Perses* ont peut-être appris aux Athéniens", *Epokhè* 3, 147–64.
Lord, A.B. 1960. *The Singer of Tales,* Cambridge, MA.
Loscalzo, D. 2003. *La parola inestinguibile. Studi sull'epinicio pindarico,* Rome.
Lossau, M. 1990. "Xenophon's *Odyssee*", *A&A* 36, 47–52.
Louden, B. 1993. "An Extended Narrative Pattern in the *Odyssey*", *GRBS* 34, 5–33.
– 1995. "Categories of Homeric Wordplay", *TAPhA* 125, 27–46.
– 1999. *The* Odyssey: *Structure, Narration, and Meaning,* Baltimore.
Lowe, N.J. 2000. *The Classical Plot and the Invention of Western Narrative,* Cambridge.
Luce, T.J. 1991. "Tacitus on 'History's Highest Function': *praecipuum munus annalium (Ann.* 3.65)", *ANRW* ii. 33.4, 2904–27.
Lundon, J. 2002. "Aristotle, Aristarchus and Zielinski on the Narration of Simultaneous Events in Homeric Epos", in: *Praktika. Actes of the 11. International Congress of Classical Studies (Kavala 24–30 Aug. 1999),* vol. 2, Athens, 581–91.

Lyons, D. 1997. *Gender and Immortality: Heroines in Ancient Greek Myth and Cult,* Princeton.

Mackay, E.A. 2001. "The Frontal Face and "You": Narrative Disjunction in Early Greek Poetry and Painting", *AC* 44, 5–34.
MacLaren, M. 1934. "Xenophon and Themistogenes", *TAPhA* 65, 240–7.
Mader, B. 1991. "Κλυταιμνήστρη/μήστρη", in: *LfgrE,* 1460–1.
– 1993. "Μέντης", "Μέντωρ", in: *LfgrE,* 143–4.
Maehler, H. 1989. *Pindari carmina cum fragmentis. Pars II. Fragmenta. Indices,* Leipzig.
– 1997. *Die Lieder des Bakchylides II,* Leiden.
Malkin, I. 1987. *Religion and Colonization in Ancient Greece,* Leiden.
Manakidou, F. 1993. *Beschreibung von Kunstwerken in der hellenistischen Dichtung,* Stuttgart.
March, J.R. 1987. *The Creative Poet. Studies on the Treatment of Myths in Greek Poetry,* (*BICS Supplement* vol. 49), London.
Marchant, E.C. 1925. *Xenophon. Scripta minora.* (LCL), Cambridge, MA.
Marinatos-Kopff, N. – Rawlings, H. 1978. "Panolethria and the Divine Punishment", *PP* 182, 331–7.
Marincola, J. (1997) 2001. *Greek Historians (Greece & Rome, New Surveys in the Classics,* vol. 31), Oxford.
– 2004. *Authority and Tradition in Ancient Historiography,* Cambridge.
Markantonatos, A. 2002. *Tragic Narrative: A Narratological Study of Sophocles' Oedipus at Colonus,* Berlin – New York.
– 2007. *Oedipus at Colonus. Sophocles, Athens, and the World,* Berlin – New York.
Markwald, G. 1993. "μνηστήρ", in: *LfgrE,* 235–40.
Marsden, E.W. 1974. "Polybius as a Military Historian", in: E. Gabba (ed.), *Polybe* (*Entretiens sur l'Antichité Classique* vol. 20), Geneva, 269–95.
Martin, R.H. – Woodman, A.J. 1989. *Tacitus: Annals Book IV,* Cambridge.
Martin, R.P. 1989. *The Language of Heroes: Speech and Performance in the Iliad,* Ithaca – London.
– 2005. "Epic as Genre", in: J.M. Foley (ed.), *A Companion to Ancient Epic,* Malden, 9–19.
Martinez, M. – Scheffel, M. (1999) 2003. *Einführung in die Erzähltheorie,* Munich.
Mastronarde, D.J. 1990. "Actors on High: The skene roof, the crane, and the gods in Attic drama", *ClAnt* 9, 247–94.
– 1994. *Euripides Phoenissae. Edited with Introduction and Commentary,* Cambridge.
Mather, M. – Shafir, E. – Johnson, M.K. 2000. "Misrememberance of options past: Source monitoring and choice", *Psychological Science* 11, 132–8.
Matthews, V.J. 1980. "Metrical Reasons for Apostrophe in Homer", *LCM* 5, 93–9.
McClure, L. 1999. *Spoken like a Woman. Speech and Gender in Athenian Drama,* Princeton.

McDermott, E.A. 1991. "Double Meaning and Mythic Novelty in Euripides' Plays", *TAPhA* 121, 123–32.
McDonald, A.H. 1957. "The Style of Livy", *JRS* 47, 155–72.
McHale, B. 1978. "Free Indirect Discourse: A Survey of Recent Accounts", *Poetics and Theory of Literature* 3, 249–87.
– 1987. *Postmodernist Fiction*, London.
McLeod, G.K. 1991. *Virtue and Venom: Catalogs of Women from Antiquity to the Renaissance*, Ann Arbor.
McMullin, R. 2001. "Aspects of Medizing: Themistocles, Simonides, and Timocreon of Rhodes", *CJ* 97, 55–67.
McNeil, L. 2005. "Bridal Cloths, Cover-ups, and *kharis*: The 'Carpet Scene' in Aeschylus' *Agamemnon*", *G&R* 52, 1–17.
McNelis, Ch. 2003. "Mourning Glory: Callimachus' *Hecale* and Heroic Honors", *MD* 50, 155–61.
Méautis, G. 1939. "Le prologue à la Théogonie d'Hésiode", *REG* 52, 573–83.
Mehmel, F. 1940. *Virgil und Apollonius Rhodius. Untersuchungen zu den Zeitvorstellungen in der antiken epischen Erzählung*, Hamburg.
Meier, W.D. 1976. *Die epische Formel im pseudohesiodeischen Frauenkatalog. Eine Untersuchung zum nachhomerischen Formelgebrauch*, Diss. Zurich.
Meiggs, R. – Lewis, D. (1969) 1988. *A Selection of Greek Historical Inscriptions to the End of the Fifth Century BC*, Oxford.
Meijering, R. 1987. *Literary and Rhetorical Theories in Greek Scholia*, Groningen.
Meister, J.C. 2003. "Narratology as Discipline. A Case for Conceptual Fundamentalism", in: T. Kindt – H.-H. Müller (eds.), *What is Narratology? Questions and Answers Regarding the Status of a Theory*, Berlin, 55–71.
– (ed.) 2005. *Narratology beyond Literary Criticism. Mediality, Disciplinarity*, Berlin.
Meister, K. 1975. *Historische Kritik bei Polybios*, Wiesbaden.
Mendelsohn, D. 2002. *Gender and the City in Euripides' Political Plays*, Oxford.
Mesk, J. 1920–1921. "Zur elften Rede des Dio von Prusa", *WS* 42, 115–24.
Mette, H.J. 1959. *Die Fragmente der Tragödien des Aischylos*, Berlin.
– 1963. *Der Verlorene Aischylos*, Berlin.
Meyer, E. 1922. *Caesars Monarchie und das Principat des Pompejus*, 3rd ed., Stuttgart – Berlin.
Michelini, A. 1982. *Tradition and Dramatic Form in the* Persians *of Aeschylus*, Leiden.
Mikalson, J.O. 2003. *Herodotus and Religion in the* Persian Wars, Chapel Hill.
Miller, A.M. 1979. "The Address to the Delian Maidens in the Homeric Hymn to Apollo: Epilogue or Transition", *TAPhA* 109, 173–86.
– 1986. *From Delos to Delphi. A Literary Study of the Homeric Hymn to Apollo*, Leiden.
Mills, S. 1997. *Theseus, Tragedy and the Athenian Empire*, Oxford.
Minchin, E. 1996. "The Performance of Lists and Catalogues in the Homeric Epics", in: I. Worthington (ed.), *Voice into Text. Orality and Literacy in Ancient Greece*, Leiden, 3–20.
– 2007a. "The Language of Heroes and the Language of Heroines: Storytelling in Oral Traditional Epic", in: C. Cooper (ed.), *Politics of Orality (Orality and Literacy in Ancient Greece*, vol. 6), Leiden, 3–38.

– 2007b. *Homeric Voices. Discourse, Memory, Gender*, Oxford.
Mineo, B. 2006. *Tite-Live et l'histoire de Rome*. (Études et commentaires vol. 107), Paris.
Mink, L.O. 1970. "History and Fiction as Modes of Comprehension", *New Literary History* 1, 541–58.
Minton, W.W. 1970. "The Proem Hymn of Hesiod's Theogony", *TAPhA* 101, 357–77.
Moles, J.L. 1993. "Livy's Preface", *PCPhS* 39, 141–68.
– 2002. "Herodotus and Athens", in: E.J. Bakker – I.J.F. de Jong – H. van Wees (eds.), *Brill's Companion to Herodotus*, Leiden, 33–52.
Monoson, S.S. 2000. *Plato's Democratic Entanglements: Athenian Politics and the Practice of Philosophy*, Princeton.
Montgomery, W.A. 1902. "Oration XI of Dio Chrysostomus. A study in sources", in: *Studies in Honor of Basil L. Gildersleeve*, Baltimore, 405–12.
Morales, H. 2005. *Vision and Narrative in Achilles Tatius' Leucippe and Clitophon*, Cambridge.
Morgan, J. (ed.). 2004. *Longus: Daphnis and Chloe*, Oxford.
Morgan, K. 1993. "Pindar the Professional and the Rhetoric of the ΚѠΜΟΣ", *CPh* 88, 1–15.
– 2003. "Plato's Dream: Philosophy and Fiction in the *Theaetetus*", in: S. Panayotakis *et al.* (eds.), *The Ancient Novel and Beyond*, Leiden, 101–13.
– 2004. "Plato", in: I.J.F.de Jong – R. Nünlist – A. Bowie, *Narrators, Narratees and Narratives in Ancient Greek Literature* (*Studies in Ancient Greek Narrative*, vol. 1), Leiden, 357–76.
Mori, A. 2001. "Personal Favor and Public Influence: Arete, Arsinoë II, and the *Argonautica*", *Oral Tradition* 16, 85–106.
Morrison, A.D. 2007. *Performances and Audiences in Pindar's Sicilian Victory Odes*, (*BICS Supplement* vol. 95), London.
Morrison, J.V. 1991. "The Function and Context of Homeric Prayers: A Narrative Perspective", *Hermes* 119, 145–57.
– 1992. *Homeric Misdirections: False Predictions in the Iliad*, Ann Arbor.
– 1999. "Preface to Thucydides. Rereading the Corcyrean Conflict (1.24–55)", *ClAnt* 18, 94–131.
Morson, G.S. 1994. *Narrative and Freedom. The Shadows of Time*, New Haven.
Morwood, J. 2007. *Euripides Suppliant Women. With Introduction, Translation and Commentary*, Oxford.
Mossman, J.M. 1992. "Plutarch, Pyrrhus and Alexander", in: P.A. Stadter (ed.), *Plutarch and the Historical tradition*, London, 90–108.
Most, G.W. 1989. "The Structure and Function of Odysseus' *Apologoi*", *TAPhA* 119, 15–30.
– 2003. "Anger and Pity in Homer's *Iliad*", *YClS* 32, 50–75.
– 2007. *Hesiod: The Shield, Catalogue of Women, Other Fragments*, Cambridge, MA.
Mühlestein, H. 1987. *Homerische Namenstudien*, Frankfurt.
Müller, E. 1968. *Morphologische Poetik*, Tübingen.
Mueller-Goldingen, C. 2000. "Tradition und Innovation. Zu Stesichoros' Umgang mit dem Mythos", *AC* 69, 1–19.

Mullen, W. 1982. *Choreia: Pindar and Dance*, Princeton.
Munson, R.V. 2003. *Telling Wonders. Ethnographic and Political Discourse in the Work of Herodotus,* Ann Arbor.
Mureddu, P. 1983. *Formula e tradizione nella poesia di Esiodo*, Rome.
Murnaghan, S. 1987. *Disguise and Recognition in the* Odyssey, Princeton.
– 1995. "The Plan of Athena", in: B. Cohen (ed.), *The Distaff Side. Representing the Female in Homer's* Odyssey, New York, 61–80.
– 2002. "The Trials of Telemachus: Who was the *Odyssey* meant for?", *Arethusa* 35, 133–53.
Murray, O. 1990. "Sympotic History", in: O. Murray (ed.), *Sympotica. A symposium on the Symposion*, Oxford, 3–13.
Murray, P. 1996. *Plato on Poetry*, Cambridge.
Mylonas, G.E. 1955. "The Cemeteries of Eleusis and Mycenae", *PAPhS* 99, 57–67.

Nagler, M. 1977. "Dread Goddess Endowed with Speech", *Archaeological News*, 77–85.
– 1990. "Odysseus: The Proem and the Problem", *ClAnt* 9, 335–56.
– 1996. "Dread Goddess Revisited", in: S.L. Schein (ed.), *Reading the* Odyssey: *Selected Interpretive Essays*, Berkeley etc., 141–61.
Nagy, G. 1974. *Comparative Studies in Greek and Indic Meter*, Cambridge, MA.
– (1979) 1999. *The Best of the Achaeans. Concepts of the Hero in Archaic Greek Poetry*, Baltimore – London.
– 1990a. *Pindar's Homer. The Lyric Possession of an Epic Past*, Baltimore.
– 1990b. *Greek Mythology and Poetics*, Ithaca – London.
– 1994. "Genre and Occasion", *Metis* 9, 11–25.
– 1996. *Poetry as Performance: Homer and Beyond*, Cambridge.
– 1997. "Ellipsis in Homer", in: E.J. Bakker – A. Kahane (eds.), *Written Voices, Spoken Signs: Tradition, Performance, and the Epic Text*, Cambridge, MA, 167–89.
– 2003. *Homeric Responses*, Austin.
Naiden, F.S. 2006. *Ancient Supplication*, Oxford.
Nails, D. 2002. *The People of Plato: a Prosopography of Plato and other Socratics*, Indianapolis.
Nasta, M. 2006. "La typologie des catalogues d'*Éhées*: un réseau généalogique thématisé", *Kernos* 19, 59–78.
Neitzel, H. 1975. *Homer-Rezeption bei Hesiod. Interpretation ausgewählter Passagen*, Bonn.
Nelis, D. 2001. *Virgil's* Aeneid *and the* Argonautica *of Apollonius Rhodius*, Leeds.
Nelles, W. 1990. "Getting focalization into focus", *Poetics Today* 11, 365–82.
Neschke, A. 1986. "L'*Orestie* de Stésichore et la tradition littéraire du mythe des Atrides avant *Eschyle*", *AC* 55, 283–301.
Nesselrath, H.-G. 1992. *Ungeschehenes Geschehen: 'Beinahe-Episoden' im griechischen und römischen Epos von Homer bis zur Spätantike*, Stuttgart.
Neubauer, J. 1997. "Tales of Hoffmann and Others on Narrativization of Instrumental Music", in: U.-B. Lagerroth *et al.* (eds.), *Interart Poetics. Essays on the Interrelations of Arts and Media*, Amsterdam, 117–36.

Neumann, M. 2000. "Erzählen. Einige anthropologische Überlegungen", in: M. Neumann (ed.), *Erzählte Identitäten. Ein interdisziplinäres Symposion*, Munich, 280–94.
Newton, R.M. 1984. "The Rebirth of Odysseus", *GRBS* 25, 5–20.
Nisbet, R.G.M. – Rudd, N. 2004. *A Commentary on Horace: Odes*. Book 3, Oxford.
Nicoll, W.S.M. 1985. "Chasing Chimaeras", *CQ* 35, 134–39.
Nitzsch, G. 1826–1840. *Erklärende Anmerkungen zu Homers Odyssee*, vols. 1–3, Hannover.
Norden, E. (1913) 1996. *Agnostos Theos. Untersuchungen zur Formengeschichte religiöser Rede*, Leipzig.
– (1898) 1958. *Die antike Kunstprosa vom VI. Jahrhundert v. Chr. bis in die Zeit der Renaissance*, vol. 1, Stuttgart.
– (1915) 1966. *Ennius und Vergilius. Kriegsbilder aus Roms grosser Zeit*, Darmstadt.
Nünlist, R. 1998. "Der Homerische Erzähler und das sogenannte Sukzessionsgesetz", *MH* 55, 2–8.
– 2003. "The Homeric Scholia on Focalization", *Mnemosyne* 56, 61–71.
– 2004. "Hesiod", in: I.J.F.de Jong – R. Nünlist – A. Bowie, *Narrators, Narratees and Narratives in Ancient Greek Literature* (Studies in Ancient Greek Narrative, vol. 1), Leiden, 25–34.
– 2007. "Pindar and Bacchylides", in: I.J.F.de Jong – R. Nünlist, *Time in Ancient Greek Literature* (Studies in Ancient Greek Narrative vol. 2), Leiden, 233–51.
– 2009. *The Ancient Critic at Work: Terms and Concepts of Literary Criticism in Greek Scholia*, Cambridge.
Nünning, A. 1994. "Gender and Narratology: Kategorien und Perspektiven einer feministischen Narrativik", *Zeitschrift für Anglistik und Amerikanistik* 42, 101–21.
Nünning, A. 2000. "Towards a Cultural and Historical Narratology. A Survey of Diachronic Approaches, Concepts, and Research Projects", in: B. Reitz – S. Rieuwerts (eds.), *Anglistentag 1999 Mainz. Proceeddings*, Trier, 345–373.
Nünning, A. 2003. "Narratology or Narratologies? Taking Stock of Recent Developments, Critique and Modest Proposals for Future Usages of the Term", in: T. Kindt – H.-H. Müller (eds.), *What is Narratology? Questions and Answers Regarding the Status of a Theory*, Berlin, 239–275.
Nünning, A. – Sommer, R. 2002. "Drama und Narratologie. Die Entwicklung erzähltheoretischer Modelle und Kategorien für die Dramenanalyse", in: V. Nünning – A. Nünning (eds.), *Erzähltheorie transgenerisch, intermedial, interdisziplinär*, Trier, 105–28.

Oakley, S.P. 1997. *A Commentary on Livy, Books VI-X. Vol. I. Introduction and Book VI*, Oxford.
– 2005. *A Commentary on Livy, Books VI-X. Vol. III. Book IX*, Oxford.
Ogilvie, R.M. 1965. *A Commentary on Livy, Books 1–5*, Oxford.
Oldfather, C.H. 1950. *Diodorus of Sicily*, vol. V, London (*The Loeb Classical Library* vol. 384).

Olson, D.S. 1990. "The Stories of Agamemnon in Homer's *Odyssey*", *TAPhA* 120, 57–71.
– 1992. "Women's Names and the Reception of Odysseus on Scheria", *Classical Views – Echos du Monde Classique* 36, 1–6.
– 1995. *Blood and Iron. Stories and Storytelling in Homer's* Odyssey, Leiden.
Osborne, R. 2005. "Ordering Women in Hesiod's *Catalogue*", in: R. Hunter (ed.), *The Hesiodic Catalogue of Women. Constructions and Reconstructions*, Cambridge, 5–24.

Papageorgiou, P. 1910. Κλυταιμέστρα-Κλυταιμήστρα, Athens.
Pariente, A. 1992. "Le Monument Argien des '*Sept Contre Thèbes*'", in: M. Piérart (ed.), *Polydipsion Argos. Argos de la Fin des Palais Mycéniens à la Constitution de l'État Classique*, Fribourg 7–9 Mai 1987, (*BCH Supplément* vol. XXII), Athens, 195–229.
Parry, A. 1972. "Language and Characterization in Homer", *HSPh* 76, 1–22.
Parry, A. A. 1973. *Blameless Aegisthus. A Study of AMYMΩN and Other Homeric Epithets*, Leiden.
Paton, W.R. (1922) 1992. *Polybius, The Histories. With an English Translation. In Six Volumes*, vol. I, Cambridge, MA (*The Loeb Classical Library* vol. 128).
Patzer, H. 1990. "Gleichzeitige Ereignisse im homerischen Epos", in: H. Eisenberger (ed.), *EPMHNEYMATA. Festschrift H. Hörner*, Heidelberg, 153–72.
Pauw, D.A. 1991. "The Dramatic Elements in Livy's History", *AC* 34, 33–49.
Pédech, P. 1964. *La méthode historique de Polybe*, Paris.
Pedrick, V. 1982. "Supplication in the *Iliad* and the *Odyssey*", *TAPhA* 112, 125–40.
– 1988. "The Hospitality of Noble Women in the *Odyssey*", *Helios* 15, 85–101.
Pelling, C.B.R. 1981. Review of G. Zecchini, *Cassio Dione e la guerra gallica di Cesare* (Milan, 1978), *CR* 32, 146–8.
– 1991. "Thucyides' Archidamus and Herodotus' Artabanus", in: M. Flower – M. Toher (eds.), *Georgica. Greek Studies in Honour of George Cawkell*, London, 120–42.
– 1997. "Aeschylus' *Persae* and History", in: C. Pelling (ed.), *Greek Tragedy and the Historian*, Oxford, 1–19.
– 2000. *Literary Texts and the Greek Historian*, London – New York.
– 2002. *Plutarch and History: Eighteen Studies*, Swansea.
– 2006a. "Breaking the bounds: writing about Julius Caesar", in: B. McGing – J. Mossman (eds.), *The Limits of Ancient Biography*, Swansea, 255–79.
– 2006b. "Herodotus and Homer", in: B. Currie – M. Clarke – R.O.A.M. Lyne (eds.), *Epic Interactions*, Oxford, 75–104.
– forthcoming. "Velleius and biography: the case of Julius Caesar", in: E.R. Cowan (ed.), *Velleius Paterculus: Making History*, Swansea.
Peradotto, J. 1990. *Man in the Middle Voice: Name and Narration in the* Odyssey, Princeton.
Pernot, L. 1993. *La rhétorique de l'éloge dans le monde Gréco-romain. Tome II. Les valeurs*, Paris.

Petzold, K.E. 1993. "Zur Geschichte der römischen Annalistik", in: W. Schuller (ed.), *Livius. Aspekte seines Werkes*, Konstanz (*Xenia* vol. 31), 151–87.
Pfeiffer, R. 1949. *Callimachus I: Fragmenta*, Oxford.
Pfeijffer, I.L. 1999a. *Three Aeginetan Odes of Pindar. A Commentary on Nemean V, Nemean III, and Pythian VIII*, Leiden.
– 1999b. *First-Person Futures in Pindar*, Stuttgart.
– 2004. "Pindar and Bacchylides", in: I.J.F.de Jong – R. Nünlist – A. Bowie, *Narrators, Narratees and Narratives in Ancient Greek Literature* (*Studies in Ancient Greek Narrative*, vol. 1), Leiden, 213–34.
Pfister, M. (1977) 1988. *The Theory and Analysis of Drama*, Cambridge.
Phelan, J. 1989. *Reading People, Reading Plots. Character, Progression, and the Interpretation of Narrative*, Chicago – London.
Phelan, J. – Martin, M.P. 1999. "The Lessons of 'Weymouth': Homodiegesis, Unreliability, and *The Remains of the Day*", in: D. Herman, *Narratologies: New Perspectives on Narrative Analysis*, Columbus, Oh., 88–109.
Phelan, J. – Rabinowitz, P.J. 2005. *A Companion to Narrative Theory*, Malden.
Piaget, J. – Inhelder, B. 1948. *La représentation de l'espace chez l'enfant*, Paris.
Pier, J. (ed.). 2004. *The Dynamics of Narrative Form: Studies in Anglo-American Narratology*, Berlin – New York.
Pier, J. – Schaeffer, J.-M. (eds.). 2005. *Métalepses. Entorses au pacte de la représentation*, Paris.
Podlecki, A.J. 1966. *The Political Background of Aeschylean Tragedy*, Ann Arbor.
– 2005. *Aeschylus: Prometheus Bound*, Oxford.
Poliakoff, M.B. 1985. "Entellus and Amycus: Vergil, *Aen*. 5.362–484", *ICS* 10, 227–31.
Polti, A. 1997. "Zur Rezeption und Kritik von 'Zeit und Erzählung'", in: J. Stückrath – J. Zbinden (eds.), *Metageschichte, Hayden White und Paul Ricoeur. Dargestellte Wirklichkeit in der europäischen Kultur im Kontext von Husserl, Weber, Auerbach und Gombrich*, Baden-Baden, 230–53.
Pomeroy, S.B. 1994. *Goddesses, Whores, Wives, and Slaves. Women in Classical Antiquity*, New York.
Prentice, W.K. 1947. "Themistogenes of Syracuse: an Error of a Copyist", *AJPh* 68, 73–7.
Prince, G. 1988. *A Dictionary of Narratology*, Aldershot.
– 1996. "Narratology, Narratological Criticism, and Gender", in: C.-A. Mihailescu – W. Hamarneh (eds.), *Fiction Updated: Theories of Fictionality, Narratology, and Poetics*, Toronto, 159–64.
Propp, V. (1928) 1968. *Morphology of the Folktale*, Austin, Texas.
Pucci, P. 1995. *Odysseus Polutropos. Intertextual Readings in the* Odyssey *and the* Iliad, Ithaca – London.
Pulleyn, S. 1997. *Prayer in Greek Religion*, Oxford.

Quint, D. 1993. *Epic and Empire. Politics and Generic Form from Virgil to Milton*, Princeton.

Raaflaub, K. 2004. *The Discovery of Freedom in Ancient Greece*, Chicago – London.

Rabau, S. 2005. "Ulysse à côté d'Homère: Interprétation et transgression des frontières énonciatives", in: Pier, J. – Schaeffer, J.-M. (eds.), *Métalepses. Entorses au pacte de la représentation*, Paris, 59–72.
Rabel, R.J. 1997. *Plot and Point of View in the* Iliad, Ann Arbor.
– 2002. "Interruption in the *Odyssey*", *ColbyQ* 38, 77–93.
Race, W.H. 1986. *Pindar*, Boston.
– 1990. *Style and Rhetoric in Pindar's Odes*, Atlanta.
– 1997a. *Pindar:* Olympian Odes – Pythian Odes (*Loeb Classical Library* vol. 56), Cambridge, MA.
– 1997b. *Pindar:* Nemean Odes – Isthmian Odes – Fragments (*Loeb Classical Library,* vol. 485), Cambridge, MA.
Radke, G. 2007. "Die poetische Souveränität des homerischen Erzählers", *RhM* 150, 8–66.
Rambaud, M. 1953. *Cicéron et l'histoire romaine* (*Collection d'études latines* vol. 28), Paris.
Rank, L.Ph. 1951. *Etymologiseering en verwante Verschijnselen bij Homerus*, Diss. Utrecht.
Regenbogen, O. 1930. "Herodot und sein Werk. Ein Versuch", *Die Antike* 6, 202–48.
Rehm, R. 2002. *The Play of Space: Spatial Transformation in Greek Tragedy*, Princeton.
Reinhardt, K. 1960. *Tradition und Geist. Gesammelte Essays zur Dichtung*, Göttingen.
Rengakos, A. 1984. *Form und Wandel des Machtdenkens der Athener bei Thukydides*, Stuttgart.
– 1992. "Homerische Wörter bei Kallimachos", *ZPE* 94, 21–47.
– 1994. *Apollonios Rhodios und die antike Homererklärung*, Munich.
– 1995. "Zeit und Gleichzeitigkeit in den homerischen Epen", *A&A* 41, 1–33.
– 1998. "Zur Zeitstruktur der *Odyssee*", *WS* 111, 45–66.
– 1999. "Spannungsstrategien in den homerischen Epen", in: J.N. Kazazis – A. Rengakos (eds.), *Euphrosyne. Studies in the Ancient Epic and its Legacy in Honor of Dimitris N. Maronitis*, Stuttgart, 308–38.
– 2002. "Zur narrativen Funktion der Telemachie", in: A. Hurst – F. Létoublon (eds.), *La Mythologie et l'Odyssée. Hommage à Gabriel Germain*, Geneva, 87–98.
– 2004. "Die *Argonautika* und das 'kyklische Gedicht'. Bemerkungen zur Erzähltechnik des griechischen Epos", in: A. Bierl – A. Schmitt – A. Willi (eds.), *Antike Literatur in neuer Deutung. Festschrift J. Latacz*, Munich – Leipzig, 277–304.
– 2005. "Strategien der Geschichtsdarstellung bei Herodotus und Thucydides – oder: Vom Ursprung der Historiographie aus dem Geist des Epos", in: V. Borsò – Chr. Kann (eds.), *Geschichtsdarstellung: Medien-Methoden-Strategien*, Köln etc., 73–99.
– 2006a. "Thucydides' Narrative: The Epic and Herodotean Heritage", in: A. Rengakos – A. Tsakmakis (eds.), *Brill's Companion to Thucydides*, Leiden, 279–300.

- 2006b. "Homer and the Historians. The Influence of Epic Narrative Techniques on Herodotus and Thucydides", in: F. Montanari – A. Rengakos (eds.), *La poésie épique grecque. Métamorphoses d'un genre littéraire (Entretiens sur l'antiquité classique* vol. 52), Vandoeuvres-Geneva, 183–209.
Richardson, B. 2001. "Voice and Narration in Postmodern Drama", *New Literary History* 32, 681–94.
Richardson, N.J. 1980. "Literary criticism in the exegetical scholia to the *Iliad*: a sketch", *CQ* 30, 265–87.
– 1993. "Introduction to the commentary on Book 23", in: G. S. Kirk (ed.), *The* Iliad: *A Commentary, Vol. vi: Books 21–4*, Cambridge, 164–66.
Richardson, S. 1990. *The Homeric Narrator*, Nashville, Tennessee.
Ricoeur, P. 1980. "Narrative Time", *Critical Inquiry* 7, 169–90.
– 1983. *Temps et récit*, vol. 1, Paris.
– 1984. *Temps et récit*. vol. 2, Paris.
– 1984–1988. *Time and Narrative*, vols. I–III, Chicago.
Ries, W. 1969. *Gerücht, Gerede, öffentliche Meinung. Interpretationen zur Psychologie und Darstellungskunst des Tacitus*, Diss. Heidelberg.
Rieu, E.V. 1991. Homer. *The Odyssey*, London.
Rijksbaron, A. (1984) ³2002. *The Syntax and the Semantics of the Verb in Classical Greek*, Amsterdam.
– 2006. "Sur l'article avec nom propre", in: J.L. Breuil – Ch. Cusset – Fl. Garambois – N. Palmieri – E. Perrin-Saminadayar (eds.), *En koinônia pasa filia. Mélanges offerts à Bernard Jacquinod*, Saint-Etienne, 243–57.
Rimmon-Kenan, S. (1983) 2002. *Narrative Fiction. Contemporary Poetics*, London.
Rinner, W. 1978. "Zur Darstellungsweise bei Xenophon, *Anabasis* III 1–2", *Philologus* 122, 144–9.
Ringer, M. 1998. Electra *and the Empty Urn: Metatheater and role playing in Sophocles*, Chapel Hill.
Risselada, R. 1993. *Imperatives and Other Directive Expressions in Latin: A Study in the Pragmatics of a Dead Language*, Amsterdam.
Ritoók, Z. 1995. "Some aesthetic views of Dio Chrysostom and their sources", in: J.G.J. Abbenes – S.R. Slings – I. Sluiter (eds.), *Greek Literary Theory after Aristotle*, Amsterdam, 125–34.
Roberts, D.H. 1992. "Outside the Drama: The limits of tragedy in Aristotle's *Poetics*", in: A.O. Rorty (ed.), *Essays in Aristotle's* Poetics, Princeton, 133–53.
Rösler, W. 1975. "Ein Gedicht und sein Publikum. Überlegungen zu Sappho Fr. 44 L-P", *Hermes* 103, 275–85.
Rogkotis, Z. 2006. "Thucydides and Herodotus. Aspects of their Intertextual Relationship", in: A. Rengakos – A. Tsakmakis (eds.), *Brill's Companion to Thucydides*, Leiden, 57–86.
Rohde, E. 1950. *Psyche: The Cult of Souls and Belief in Immortality among the Greeks*, London.
Romilly, J. de 1956. *Histoire et raison chez Thucydide*, Paris.
Rood, T. 1998. *Thucydides: Narrative and Explanation*, Oxford.

– 1999. "Thucydides' *Persian Wars*", in: C.S. Kraus (ed.), *The Limits of Historiography. Genre and Narrative in Ancient Historical Texts*, Leiden, 141–68.
– 2004. "Polybius", in: I.J.F. de Jong – R. Nünlist – A. Bowie, *Narrators, Narratees and Narratives in Ancient Greek Literature* (Studies in Ancient Greek Narrative, vol. 1), Leiden, 147–64.
– 2006. "Objectivity and Authority. Thucydides' Historical Method", in: A. Rengakos – A. Tsakmakis (eds.), *Brill's Companion to Thucydides*, Leiden, 225–50.
– 2007. "Thucydides", in: I.J.F. de Jong – R. Nünlist (eds.), *Time in Ancient Greek Literature*, Leiden, 131–46.
Room, A. 1990. *NTC's Classical Dictionary. The Origins of the Names of Characters in Classical Mythology*, Chicago.
Rosati, G. 1979. "Punto di vista narrativo e antichi esegeti di Virgilio", *Annali della Scuola Normale Superiore di Pisa, Classe di Lettere e Filosofia*, 539–62.
Rose, G.P. 1969. "The Unfriendly Phaeacians", *TAPhA* 100, 387–406.
Ruijgh, C.J. 1967. *Études sur la grammaire et le vocabulaire du grec mycénien*, Amsterdam.
Russell, D.A. 1964. *'Longinus': On the Sublime*, Oxford.
Rutherford, I. 2000. "Formulas, Voice, and Death in *Ehoie*-Poetry, the Hesiodic *Gunaikon Katalogos* and the Odysseian *Nekuia*", in: M. Depew – D. Obbink (eds.), *Matrices of Genre. Authors, Canons, and Society*, Cambridge, MA, 81–96.
Rutherford, R.B. 1991–93. "From the *Iliad* to the *Odyssey*", *BICS* 38, 37–54.
– 1992. *Homer Odyssey. Books XIX and XX*, Cambridge.
– 2007. "'Why should I mention Io?' Aspects of choral narration in Greek tragedy", *CCJ* 53, 1–39.
Ryan, M.-L. (ed.) 2004. *Narrative Across Media. The Languages of Story-Telling*, Lincoln.
Ryberg, I.S. 1942. "Tacitus' art of innuendo", *TAPhA* 73, 383–404.

Saïd, S. 1988. "Tragédie et renversement: l'exemple des *Perses*", *Mètis* 3, 321–41.
– 2000. "Dio's use of mythology", in: S. Swain, *Dio Chrysostom. Politics, Letters, and Philosophy*, Oxford, 161–86.
Sammartano, R. 1998. "Per una rilettura della gara del pugilato nel v libro dell' *Eneide*", *La Parola del Passato* 53, 115–30.
Saussure, F. de 1983. *Course in General Linguistics*, London.
Schapp, W. (1953) 1976. *In Geschichten verstrickt. Zum Sein von Mensch und Ding*, Wiesbaden.
Scheffel, M. 2004. "Erzählen als anthropologische Universalie. Funktionen des Erzählens im Alltag und in der Literatur", in: R. Zymner – M. Engel (eds.), *Anthropologie der Literatur. Poetogene Strukturen und ästhetisch-soziale Handlungsfelder*, Paderborn, 121–38.
Scheid, J. – Svenbro, J. 1996. *The Craft of Zeus*, transl. C. Volk, Cambridge, MA.

Schein, S.L. 1995. "Female Representations and Interpreting the *Odyssey*", in: B. Cohen (ed.), *The Distaff Side. Representing the Female in Homer's Odyssey*, New York, 17–27.

Schinkel, A. 2005. "Imagination as a Category of History. An Essay Concerning Koselleck's Concepts of Erfahrungsraum and Erwartungshorizont", *H&T* 44, 42–54.

Schlegel, A. (1809–11) 1966. *Vorlesungen über dramatische Kunst und Literatur*, vol. 1, Stuttgart.

Schmidt, C. 1890. *De articulo in nominibus propriis apud Atticos scriptores pedestres*, Kiel.

Schmidt, J.U. 2001. "Die Gestaltungen des Atridenmythos und die Intentionen des Odysseedichters", *Hermes* 129, 158–72.

Schmidt, M. 1993 a. "μνάομαι", in: *LfgrE*, 232–4.

– 1993 b. "μνῆμα", in: *LfgrE*, 234.

Schmiel, R. 1981. "Moschus' *Europa*", *CPh* 76, 261–71.

Schmitt Pantel, P. 1990. "Sacrificial Meal and the Symposion: Two Models of Civic Institutions in the Archaic City?", in: O. Murray (ed.), *Sympotica. A symposium on the Symposion*, Oxford, 14–33.

Schmitz, Th.A. 2002. *Moderne Literaturtheorie und antike Texte. Eine Einführung*, Darmstadt.

Schneider, Chr. 1974. *Information und Absicht bei Thukydides. Untersuchung zur Motivation des Handelns*, Göttingen (*Hypomnemata* vol. 41).

Schwyzer, E. 1939. *Griechische Grammatik*, vol. 1, Munich.

Scodel, R. 1984. "Epic Doublets and Polynices' Two Burials", *TAPhA* 114, 49–58.

– 1999. *Credible Impossibilities: Conventions and Strategies of Verisimilitude in Homer and Greek Tragedy*, Leipzig.

– 2008. "Zielinski's Law Reconsidered", *TAPhA* 138, 107–25.

Seale, D. 1982. *Vision and Stagecraft in Sophocles*, Chicago.

Searle, J.R. 1976. "A Classification of Illocutionary Acts", *Language in Society* 5, 1–23.

Seeck, G.A. 1983. "Livius: Schriftsteller oder Historiker? Zum Problem der literarischen Darstellung historischer Vorgänge (Livius, Buch 21)", in: E. Lefèvre – E. Olshausen, *Livius. Werk und Rezeption. Festschrift für E. Burck zum 80. Geburtstag*, Munich, 81–95.

– 1990. "Dion Chrysostomos als Homerkritiker (Or. 11)", *RhM* 133, 97–107.

Segal, C. 1971. *The Theme of the Mutilation of the Corpse in the* Iliad, Leiden.

– 1985. "Messages to the Underworld. An Aspect of Poetic Immortalization in Pindar", *AJPh* 106, 199–212.

– 1986a. *Pindar's Mythmaking. The* Fourth Pythian Ode, Princeton.

– 1986b. "Greek Myth as a Semiotic and Structural System and the Problem of Tragedy", in: C. Segal, *Interpreting Greek Tragedy. Myth, Poetry, Text*, Ithaca, 48–74.

– 1989. "Song, Ritual, and Commemoration in Early Greek Poetry and Tragedy", *Oral Tradition* 4, 330–59.

– 1992. "Tragic Beginnings: Narration, voice, and authority in the prologues of Greek drama", *YClS* 29, 85–112.

- 1994. *Singers, Heroes, and Gods in the* Odyssey, Ithaca – London.
- 1995. "Kleos and its Ironies in the *Odyssey*", in: S.L. Schein (ed.), *Reading the* Odyssey. *Selected Interpretive Essays*, Princeton, 201–21.
- 1998. *Aglaia. The Poetry of Alcman, Sappho, Pindar, Bacchylides, and Corinna*, Lanham, MD.

Segvic, H. 2006. "Homer in Plato's *Protagoras*", *CPh* 101, 247–62.

Shapiro, K. 1988. "Hymnon thesauros: Pindar's *Sixth Pythian Ode* and the Treasury of the Siphnians at Delphi", *MH* 45, 1–5.

Shatzman, I. 1974. "Tacitean rumours", *Latomus* 33, 549–78.

Shorey, P. 1937. *Plato Republic Books 1–5*, Cambridge, MA.

Shuttleworth-Kraus, Chr. 1994. *Livy, Ab urbe condita, Book VI*, Cambridge.

Siewert, P. 1972. *Der Eid von Plataiai*, Munich.

Skempis, M. (forthcoming). *Von Eumaios zu Hekale: Epische "kleine Leute" bei Homer und Kallimachos*, Berlin – New York.

Skulsky, S.D. 1975. "ΠΟΛΛΩΝ ΠΕΙΡΑΤΑ ΣΥΝΤΑΝΥΣΑΙΣ: Language and Meaning in Pythian 1", *CPh* 70, 8–31.

Slater, W.J. 1969. *Lexicon to Pindar*, Berlin.
- 1989. "Pelops at Olympia", *GRBS* 30, 485–501.

Slatkin, L.M. 2005. "Homer's *Odyssey*", in: J.M. Foley (ed.), *A Companion to Ancient Epic*, Malden, 315–29.

Slings, S.R. 1997. "Figures of Speech and their Lookalikes: Two Further Exercises in the Pragmatics of the Greek Sentence", in: E.J. Bakker (ed.), *Grammar as Interpretation: Greek Literature in its Linguistic Contexts*, Leiden, 169–214.
- 2002. "Oral Strategies in the Language of Herodotus", in: E.J. Bakker – I.J.F. de Jong – H. van Wees (eds.), *Brill's Companion to Herodotus*, Leiden, 53–77.
- 2005. *Critical Notes on Plato's* Politeia, Leiden.

Smith, B.H. 1981. "Narrative Versions, Narrative Theories", in: W.J.T. Mitchell (ed.), *On Narrative*, Chicago – London, 209–32.

Snell, B. 1932. "Das Bruchstück eines Paians von Bakchylides", *Hermes* 67, 1–13.

Snell, B. – Maehler, H. 1987. *Pindari carmina cum fragmentis. Pars I. Epinicia*, Leipzig.

Spengel, L. 1856, *Rhetores Graeci*, vol. III, Leipzig.

Spitzer, L. (1928) 1961. "Zum Stil Marcel Prousts", in: id., *Stilstudien II*, Munich, 448–9.

Stahl, H.P. 1975. "Learning through Suffering? Croesus' Conversations in the *History* of Herodotus", *YClS* 24, 1–36.
- 2003. *Thucydides: Man's Place in History*, Swansea.

Stanford, W.B. (1939) 1972. *Ambiguity in Greek Literature. Studies in Theory and Practice*, New York.
- (1947) 1996. *The* Odyssey *of Homer: Edited with General and Grammatical Introduction, Commentary, and Indexes*, vol. 1 (Books 1-XII), New York.

Stanford, W.B. – Luce, J.V. 1974. *The Quest for Ulysses*, London.

Stanzel, F.K. 1955. *Die typischen Erzählsituationen im Roman. Dargestellt an "Tom Jones", "Moby Dick", "The Ambassadors", "Ulysses" u. a.*, Vienna – Stuttgart.
Stehle, E. 1997. *Performance and Gender in Ancient Greece*, Princeton.
Steiner, W. 1988. *Pictures of Romance. Form Against Context in Painting and Literature*, Chicago.
Steinrück, M. 1992. *Rede und Kontext. Zum Verhältnis von Person und Erzähler in frühgriechischen Texten*, Bonn.
– 1999. "Wie entsteht bei Homer der epische Schein? (eine Alternative)", *Poetica* 31, 324–38.
Stephens, S.A. 2003. *Seeing Double. Intercultural Poetics in Ptolemaic Alexandria*, Berkeley.
Stern, J. 1971. "The Structure of Pindar's *Nemean* 5", *CPh* 66, 169–73.
– 1974. "Theocritus' *Idyll* 24", *AJPh* 95, 348–61.
Sternberg, M. 1978. *Expositional Modes and Temporal Ordering in Fiction*, Baltimore – London.
– 1982. "Proteus in Quotation-Land: Mimesis and the Forms of Reported Discourse", *Poetics Today* 3, 107–56.
– 1990. "Telling in Time (I). Chronology and Narrative Time", *Poetics Today* 11, 901–48.
– 1992. "Telling in Time (II). Chronology, Teleology, Narrativity", *Poetics Today* 13, 463–541.
Sternberg, R.H. 2005. "The Nature of Pity", in: R.H. Sternberg (ed.), *Pity and Power in Ancient Athens*, Cambridge, 15–47.
Stoneman, R. 1984. "The Ideal Courtier: Pindar and Hieron in *Pythian* 2", *CQ* 34, 43–9.
Straub, J. (ed.). 1998. *Erzählung, Identität und Historisches Bewußtsein. Die psychologische Konstruktion von Zeit und Geschichte*, Frankfurt.
Struever, N. 1983. "Fables of Power", *Representations* 4, 108–27.
Stylianou, P.J. 2004. "One *Anabasis* or Two?", in: R.L. Fox (ed.), *The Long March: Xenophon and the Ten Thousand*, New Haven – London, 68–96.
Suter, A. 2008. "Male Lament in Greek Tragedy", in: A. Suter (ed.), *Lament: Studies in the Ancient Mediterranean and Beyond*, New York, 156–80.
Suttrop, M. 2000. *Fiction and Imagination. The Anthropological Function of Literature*, Paderborn.
Swain, S. (ed.). 2000. *Dio Chrysostom. Politics, Letters, and Philosophy*, Oxford.
Szarmach, M. 1978. "Le 'Discours Troyen' de Dion de Pruse", *Eos* 66, 195–202.

Tannen, D. 1989. *Talking Voices: Repetition, Dialogue, and Imagery in Conversational Discourse*, Cambridge.
Taplin, O. 1977. *The Stagecraft of Aeschylus*, Oxford.
– 1999. "Spreading the Word through Performance", in: S. Goldhill – R. Osborne (eds.), *Performance Culture and Athenian Democracy*, Cambridge, 33–57.
– 2006. "Aeschylus' *Persai* – The Entry of Tragedy into the Celebration Culture of the 470s?", in: D.L. Cairns – V. Liapis (eds.), *Dionysalexandros: Es-*

says on Aeschylus and his Fellow Tragedians in Honour of Alexander F. Garvie, Swansea, 1–10.

Tarrant, D. 1955. "Plato's Use of Extended *Oratio Obliqua*", *CQ* 5, 222–4.

Thalmann, W.G. 1980. "Xerxes' Rags: Some Problems in Aeschylus' *Persians*", *AJPh* 101, 260–82.

– 1984. *Conventions of Form and Thought in Early Greek Epic Poetry*, Baltimore – London.

– 1998. *The Swineherd and the Bow. Representations of Class in the* Odyssey, Ithaca – London.

Theodoridis, C. 1979. "Die Abfassungszeit der Epimerismen zu Homer", *ByzZ* 72, 1–5.

Thomas, R. 1989. *Oral Tradition and Written Record in Classical Athens*, Cambridge.

– 1992. *Literacy and Orality in Ancient Greece*, Cambridge.

Thomson, G. 1949. *Studies in Ancient Greek Society: The Prehistoric Aegean*, London.

– 1966. *The* Oresteia, 2 vols., 2nd ed., Prague.

Thornton, A. 1984. *Homer's* Iliad: *its Composition and the Motif of Supplication*, Göttingen.

Tracy, S.V. 1997. "The Structures of the *Odyssey*", in: I. Morris – B. Powell (eds.), *A New Companion to Homer*, Leiden, 360–79.

Traill, D.A. 2001. "Boxers and generals at Mount Eryx", *AJPh* 122, 405–13.

Tränkle, H. 1977. *Livius und Polybios*, Basel.

Trumbull, D. – McNamara, P. 2005. *Xenophon's* Anabasis. *A Translation*, Boston (electronic edition).

Tsagalis, C. 2002. "Xenophon Homericus: An Unnoticed Loan from the *Iliad* in Xenophon's *Anabasis*", *Cl&M* 53, 101–21.

– 2003. "Odyssey 24,191–202: a Reconsideration", *WS* 116, 43–56.

– 2008. *Inscribing Sorrow: Fourth-Century Attic Funerary Epigrams*, Berlin – New York.

Tsitsibakou-Vasalos, E. 1993. "Stesichorus: Poet and Thinker", *ΕΕΦΣΠΘ* 3, 27–45.

– 1997–1998. "Gradations of science. Modern Etymology versus ancient. Nestor: Comparisons and Contrasts", *Glotta* 74, 117–32.

– 2000. "Πηλεγών-Σκάμανδρος (*Il.* 21.139–383). Etymological Patterns in Homer", *BICS* 44, 1–17.

– 2001. "Alcman: Poetic Etymology. Tradition and Innovation", *RCCM* 43, 15–38.

– 2003. "Aphrodite in Homer and the Homeric Hymns. Poetic Etymology", in: Chr. Nifadopoulos (ed.), *Etymologia: Studies in Ancient Etymology. Proceedings of the Cambridge Conference on Ancient Etymology, 25–27 September 2000*, Münster, 119–29.

– 2004. "*Ἰλιάς* Ζ: Ραψωδία της νοητικής ταλάντευσης Θεματική και γλωσσική ενότητα", in: Α. Βασιλειάδης – Π. Κοτζιά – Α. Δ. Μαυρουδής – Δ.Α. Χρηστίδης (eds.), *Δημητρίῳ στέφανος. Τιμητικός τόμος για τον καθηγητή Δημήτρη Λυπουρλή*, Thessaloniki, 21–58.

– 2007. *Ancient Poetic Etymology. The Pelopids: Fathers and Sons*, Stuttgart.

Tsitsiou-Chelidoni, Chr. 2003. *Ovid, 'Metamorphosen' Buch VIII. Narrative Technik und literarischer Kontext* (Studien zur Klassischen Philologie vol. 138), Frankfurt.
Turkle, S. (ed.) 2007. *Evocative Objects. Things We Think With*, Cambridge, MA – London.
Tzanetou, A. 2006. "A Generous City: Pity in Athenian Oratory and Tragedy", in: R. Sternberg (ed.), *Pity and Power in Ancient Athens*, Cambridge, 98–122.

Vagnone, G. 2003. *Dione di Prusa. Troiano, Or. XI*, Rome.
Valk, M. van der 1955. "Ἀγαμέμνων", in: *LfgrE*, 34–42.
Vegetti, M. 2007. *Platone la Repubblica*, Milan.
Verdenius, W.J. 1972. "Notes on the Proem of Hesiod's *Theogony*", *Mnemosyne* 25, 225–60.
Vernant, J.-P. 1988. "Tensions and Ambiguities in Greek Tragedy", in: J.-P. Vernant – P. Vidal-Naquet, *Myth and Tragedy in Ancient Greece*, New York, 29–48; 417–22.
Vernant, J.-P. – Vidal-Naquet, P. 1986. *Mythe et tragédie en Grèce ancienne*, vol. 2, Paris.
Vernant, J.-P. – Vidal-Naquet, P. 1988. *Myth and Tragedy in Ancient Greece*, New York.
Vetta, M. 1983. *Poesia e simposio nella Grecia antica*, Rome.
– 1996. "Convivialita pubblica e poesia per simposio in Grecia", *QUCC* 54, 197–208.
Vian, F. 1980: *Apollonios de Rhodes. Argonautiques. Chant III*, Paris.
Viljamaa, T. 1983. *Infinitive of Narration on Livy. A Study in Narrative Technique* (Annales Universitatis Turkuensis vol. 162), Turku.
Vivante, P. 1982. *The Epithets in Homer. A Study in Poetic Values*, New Haven – London.

Wagner, F. 2002. "Glissements et déphasages. Note sur la métalepse narrative", *Poétique* 130, 235–53.
Wagner-Hasel, B. 2000a. "Das Diktum der Philosophen: Der Ausschluss der Frauen aus der Politik und die Sorge vor der Frauenherrschaft", in: T. Späth – B. Wagner-Hasel (eds.), *Frauenwelten in der Antike. Geschlechterordnung und weibliche Lebenspraxis*, Stuttgart – Weimar, 198–217.
– 2000b. *Der Stoff der Gaben. Kultur und Politik des Schenkens und Tauschens im archaischen Griechenland*, Frankfurt – New York.
– 2007. "Der Stoff der Macht – Kleideraufwand, elitärer Konsum und homerisches Königtum", in: E. Alram-Stern – G. Nightingale (eds.), *KEIMELION. Elitenbildung und elitärer Konsum von der mykenischen Palastzeit bis zur homerischen Epoche. The Formation of Elites and Elitist Lifestyles from Mycenaean Palatial Times to the Homeric Period. Akten des internationalen Kongresses vom 3. bis 5. Februar 2005 in Salzburg*, Vienna, 325–37.
Walbank, F.W. 1957. *A Historical Commentary on Polybius I, Books 1–6*, Oxford.
– 1960. "History and tragedy", *Historia* 9, 216–34.
– 1967. *A Historical Commentary on Polybius II, Books 7–18*, Oxford.

- 1972. *Polybius*, Berkeley etc. (*Sather Classical Lectures* vol. 42).
- 1975. "*Symploké*: Its Role in Polybius' *Histories*", *YClS* 24, 197–212.
- 1979. "Introduction", in: *Polybius: The Rise of the Roman Empire*, transl. I. Scott-Kilvert, Harmondsworth, 9–40.
- 1990. "Profit or Amusement: Some thoughts on the Motives of Hellenistic Historians", in: H. Verdin – G. Schepens – E. de Keyser (eds.), *Purposes of History: Studies in Greek Historiography from 4th to the 2nd Centuries B.C.*, Louvain, 253–66.

Walde, C. 2001. *Die Traumdarstellungen in der griechisch-römischen Dichtung*, Leipzig.

Walker, A. 1993. "Enargeia and the Spectator in Greek Historiography", *TAPhA* 123, 353–77.

Walker, H.J. 1995. *Theseus and Athens*, Oxford.

Walsh, P.G. 1961. *Livy. His Historical Aims and Methods*, Cambridge.
- 1973. *T. Livi Ab urbe condita. Liber XXI*, London.
- 1982. "Livy and the Aims of Historia. An Analysis of the Third Decade", in: *ANRW* II, 30.2, 1058–74.

Walters, C.F. – Conway, R.S. (eds.). (1929) 1954. *Titi Livi Ab urbe condita. Tomus III. Libri XXI-XXV*, Oxford.

Waterfield, R. 1998. *Herodotus. The Histories*, Oxford.

Webster, T.B.L. 1967. *The Tragedies of Euripides*, London.

Wecklein, N. 1896. Αἰσχύλου δράματα σωζόμενα, 2 vols., Athens.

Węcowski, M. 2002. "Towards a Definition of the Symposium", in: T. Derda – J. Urbanki – M. Węcowski (eds.), *ΕΥΕΡΓΕΣΙΑΣ ΧΑΡΙΝ. Studies Presented to Benedetto Bravo and Ewa Wipszycka by Their Disciples*, Warsaw, 337–61.

Wees, H. van. 2006. "From Kings to Demigods: Epic Heroes and Social Change c. 750–600 BC", in: S. Deger-Jalkotzy – I.S. Lemos (eds.), *Ancient Greece: From the Mycenaean Palaces to the Age of Homer*, Edinburgh, 365–79.

Wenger, R. 2008a: *Strategie, Taktik und Gefechtstechnik in der Ilias. Analyse der Kampfbeschreibungen der Ilias*, Hamburg.
- 2008b. "Strategie, Taktik und Gefechtstechnik in der *Ilias*", *WS* 121, 29–52.

West, M.L. 1966. *Hesiod: Theogony. Edited with Prolegomena and Commentary*, Oxford.
- 1971. *Iambi et elegi graeci ante Alexandrum cantati*, vol. I, Oxford.
- 1975. "Cynaethus' Hymn to Apollo", *CQ* 25, 161–70.
- 1985. *The Hesiodic Catalogue of Women. Its Nature, Structure, and Origins*, Oxford.
- 1994. *Greek Lyric Poetry. The poems and fragments of the Greek iambic, elegiac, and melic poets (excluding Pindar and Bacchylides) down to 450 BC*, Oxford.
- 1999. "The Invention of Homer", *CQ* 49, 364–82.

West, S. 1988. "Books I-IV", in: A. Heubeck – S. West – J.B. Hainsworth (eds.), *A Commentary on Homer's Odyssey*, vol.1, Oxford, 51–245.
- 1989. "Laertes Revisited", *PCPhS* 35, 113–43.

Westlake, H.D. 1989. *Studies in Thucydides and Greek History*, Bristol.

White, Hayden. 1973. *Metahistory. The Historical Imagination in Nineteenth Century Europe*, Baltimore.

- 1987. *The Content of the Form: Narrative Discourse and Historical Representation*, Baltimore.
- (1978) 2003. *Tropics of Discourse. Essays in Cultural Criticism*, Baltimore.

White, Heather. 1977. "Doors and Stars in Theocritus, *Idyll* XXIV", *Mnemosyne* 30, 135–40.
- 1979. *Theocritus' Idyll XXIV*, Amsterdam.

Whitehead, D. 1979. "Tacitus and the loaded alternative", *Latomus* 38, 474–95.

Whitman, C.H. 1958. *Homer and the Homeric Tradition*, New York.

Whittaker, H. 1999. "The Status of Arete in the Phaeacian Episode of the *Odyssey*", *Symbolae Osloenses* 74, 140–50.

Wilamowitz, U. von 1884. *Homerische Untersuchungen*, Berlin.
- 1891. "Die Sieben Thore Thebens", *Hermes* 26, 191–242.
- 1914. *Aeschyli tragoediae*, Berlin.
- 1916. *Die Ilias und Homer*, Berlin.
- 1922. *Pindaros*, Berlin.
- 1923. *Griechische Tragödien*, vol. 1, Berlin.

Williams, R.D. 1960. *Aeneidos Liber Quintus*, Oxford.

Williams, T. (1945) 1999. *The Glass Menagerie*, New York.

Wilson, P. 2000. *The Athenian Institution of the Khoregia: The Chorus, the City and the Stage*, Cambridge.
- 2005. "Music", in: J. Gregory (ed.), *A Companion to Greek Tragedy*, Oxford, 183–93.

Winkler, J.J. 1985. *Auctor and Actor. A Narratological Reading of Apuleius'* The Golden Ass, Berkeley.

Winnington-Ingram, R.P. 1983. *Studies in Aeschylus*, Cambridge.
- 2003. "Euripides: Poiētēs Sophos", in: J. Mossman (ed.), *Oxford Readings in Classical Studies: Euripides*, Oxford, 47–63.

Wiseman, T.P. 1979. *Clio's Cosmetics. Three Studies in Greco-Roman Literature*, Leicester.
- 2002. "History, Poetry, and *Annales*", in: D.S. Levene – D.P. Nelis (eds.), *Clio and the Poets. Augustan Poetry and the Traditions of Ancient Historiography*, Leiden (*Mnemosyne Supplementum* vol. 224), 331–62.

Wohl, V. 1993. "Standing by the Stathmos: The Creation of Sexual Ideology in the *Odyssey*", *Arethusa* 26, 19–50.

Wolf, W. 1993. *Ästhetische Illusion und Illusionsdurchbrechung in der Erzählkunst. Theorie und Geschichte mit Schwerpunkt auf englischem illusionsstörenden Erzählen*, Tübingen.
- 2002. "Das Problem der Narrativität in Literatur, bildender Kunst und Musik. Ein Beitrag zu einer intermedialen Erzähltheorie", in: V. Nünning – A. Nünning (eds.), *Erzähltheorie transgenerisch, intermedial, interdisziplinär*, Trier, 23–104.

Woodman, A.J. 1977. *Velleius Paterculus: the Tiberian Narrative (2.94–131)*, Cambridge.
- 1983. *Velleius Paterculus: the Caesarian and Augustan Narrative (2.41–93)*, Cambridge.
- 1988. *Rhetoric in Classical Historiography. Four Studies*, London.

Woodman, A.J. – Martin, R.H. (eds.) 1996. *The Annals of Tacitus: Book 3*, Cambridge.

Yamagata, N. 1989. "The Apostrophe in Homer as Part of the Oral Technique", *BICS* 36, 91–103.
– 1994. *Homeric Morality*, Leiden.
Young, D. 1968. *Three Odes of Pindar*, Leiden.

Zeitlin, F. 1965. "The Motif of the Corrupted Sacrifice in Aeschylus' *Oresteia*", *TAPhA* 96, 463–505.
– 1966. "Postscript to Sacrificial Imagery in the *Oresteia*", *TAPhA* 97, 645–653.
– 1978. "The Dynamics of Misogyny: Myth and Mythmaking in the *Oresteia*", *Arethusa* 11, 149–81.
– 1986. "Thebes: Theater of Self and Society in Athenian Drama", in: J.P. Euben (ed.), *Greek Tragedy and Political Theory*, Berkeley, 101–41.
– 1995. "Figuring Fidelity in Homer's *Odyssey*", in: B. Cohen (ed.), *The Distaff Side. Representing the Female in Homer's* Odyssey, New York, 117–52.
Zielinski, Th. 1899–1901. "Die Behandlung gleichzeitiger Ereignisse im antiken Epos", *Philologus Suppl.* 8, 405–49.
– 1931. *Iresione*, vol. 1, Leopoli.
Zimmermann, B. 1992. *Dithyrambos. Geschichte einer Gattung*, Göttingen.
Ziobro, W.J. 1972. "The Entrance and Exit of Athena in the *Ajax*", *Classical Folia* 26, 122–28.
Zucker, A. 1899. *Beobachtungen über den Gebrauch des Artikels bei Personennamen in Xenophons* Anabasis, Nürnberg.
Zunshine, L. 2006. *Why We Read Fiction*, Columbus, Oh.
Zuntz, G. 1955. *The Political Plays of Euripides*, Manchester.

General Index

Achilles: 25 n. 20; 37 f.; 43 f.; 60; 67 f.; 71 f.; 92; 94; 114; 126 f.; 129 f.; 142; 145 ff.; 192 f.; 205; 210; 227 n. 38; 267; 280 n. 15; 296; 309; 322 f.; 327 f.; 361; 371; 375; 392 n. 2; 428; 558
actantial model: 358 f.; 366 f.; 371 f.
Aelius Theon, *Progymnasmata*:   53 ff.
Aeolus: 149 f.
Aeschylus: 37; 273 n. 68; 338; 343; 349; 351; 353; 357 ff.; 377 ff.; 399 ff.; 434
- - *Agamemnon*:   338 f.; 377 ff.; 423
- - *Choephoroi*:   373 n. 26; 386 f.; 402 n. 8
- - *Eleusinians*:   401; 405 ff.
- - *Eumenides*:   378; 386
- - *Persians*:   357 ff.; 386 f.; 391; 415; 422
- - *Seven*:   343; 386; 405 ff.
- - *Suppliants* 362; 378; 400
Agamemnon: 31 f.; 46 ff.; 56 f.; 65; 67 n. 13; 69 f.; 97; 120; 142 n. 18; 177 ff.; 289 n. 31; 309 n. 50; 327; 344; 347; 373 n. 26; 377 ff.; 422
Agrippa Postumus: 565 ff.
Agrippa, M. Vipsanius: 519
Aigisthos: 179; 182 ff.; 195 ff.; 200 ff.; 393
Alcmena: 307 ff.
Amphitryon: 307 ff.; 341
analepsis: 65 ff.; 87; 131; 161 ff.; 166; 203; 278 n. 7; 325; 327 ff.; 557
anastrophic narrative: 53
angle (in drama):   344 ff.

announcement: 102; 314
anonymous witness device: 110; 112
Antikleia: 187 f.; 207; 230 f. n. 47; 239
apostrophe: 93 ff.; 324 f.
Appian: 508; 519 ff.
Arete: 143 f.; 213 ff.
Aristarchus: 44; 67; 70 f.; 81; 114
Aristotle:
- - *Poetics*:   22; 43 f.; 53 f.; 57; 63; 69 f.; 82; 296 n. 11; 343 n. 6; 362; 375; 421; 545 n. 73
- - *Rhetoric*:   76 n. 29; 256 n. 33; 374
assertives: 141 ff.
Athena: 44; 69; 106; 178; 188; 192; 196 f.; 204 ff.; 308 f.; 343 f.; 346; 426; 428 f.
audience, internal: *see* spectator, internal
Augustus: 508; 519; 560; 563
authorial comment: 467, 469, 470
authorial voice: 19; 21 f.; 24 f.; 37 f.; 41; 167; 181 n.10; 469 f.; 538 f.; 549; 552;

Bakhtin, M.:   169 ff.; 339 f.
Barrett, J.:   1; 423; 435 f.; 447
Bassett, S.:   143
'Beinahe'-episodes: 170 f.; 496; 498 f.
biography: 322 ff.; 507 ff.
Bion, *Epithalamion for Achilles and Deidameia*:   296
blending of narrative voices: 99 ff.
Booth, W.:   347; 421; 423
Brecht, B.:   342
Brontë, Ch.:   89

Caesar, C. Iulius: 507 ff.
Callimachus: 222 n. 26;
– – *Hecale*:   296 ff.; 312
– – *Hymn to Demeter*:   295 n. 7; 297 f.
Carthaginians: 495; 500 ff.; 532 f.
Cassius Dio: 515 ff.
Cassius Longinus, C.:   519; 521
Cato, M. Porcius: 508 f.; 523 ff.
character language: 80
character-narrators: 151
character speech: 24 f.; 37; 126; 129 f.; 148 ff.; 328
Chatman, S.:   338; 340 ff.; 344
chorus: 95 n. 23; 99; 104; 107; 110 f.; 265 f.; 273 n. 67; 339; 346 ff.; 358 ff.; 377 ff.; 415 f.; 423 ff.; 434 f.; 437 ff.
Cicero, M. Tullius: 515 f.; 525; 544
cinematic narrator: 340
closure: 257; 259; 262 ff.; 294; 296 f.; 307; 339; 558; 568
Coleridge, S.T.:   347
conversation: 15 f.; 22 n. 13; 23 n. 14; 26 ff.; 137 ff.; 143 ff.; 290; 301 n. 25; 360; 372; 428 f.; 452; 563
Cortazar, J.:   90
Crassus, M. Licinius: 515 ff.
cross-references: 461–463
Curio, C. Scribonius: 521
cyclic epic: 53 f.; 58 f.

deixis: 111 n. 58; 119; 124; 241 ff.; 373; 380; 389
description: 295; 297; 302 f.; 309; 315; 473
diêgêsis: 18 f.
Diktys of Crete: 45
Dio Chrysostom, *Trojan Oration*:   43 ff.
Dionysius of Halicarnassus, *Thucydides*:   55
direct speech: 26 f.; 76; 99; 106; 122; 125 ff.; 137 ff.; 236; 285 f.; 301 f.; 309; 393 ff.; 476; 539; 541 f.

directives: 141 ff.
discourse time: 338
disparaging τις: 458, 475, 479
downslip: 100; 105;
dramatic effect: 454, 458–460, 479
dramatic irony: 315 n. 72; 403 f.; 483; 487 f.; 493
dramatist, internal: *see* playwright, internal
Duris of Samos: 60
Du-Stil: 95

ecphrasis: 303 n. 35; 315; 317 n. 76; 318; 558 f.
Egypt: 48 ff.; 504; 505
ellipsis: 413, 413 n. 46; 414
emotions: 58; 142 f.; 364; 374; 434; 485; 489; 501; 515; 524
emotives: 141
empathy: 128 f.; 504 ff.; 526
enargeia: 58; 95; 127 ff.; 169; 308 f. n. 50
epyllion: 293 ff.
Eratosthenes *Erigone*:   297
Etymology/narratology, interaction: 177 ff.; 213 ff.
Euclides: 15 ff.
Eumaeus: 94 f.; 143; 289 f.; 299
Euphorion: 297
Euripides: 341 ff.; 386; 395; 399 ff.
– – *Alcestis*:   99
– – *Andromache*:   341 n. 4
– – *Bacchae*:   341
– – *Electra*:   341 f. n. 4; 402 n. 8
– – *Hecuba*:   341 f. n. 4
– – *Helen*:   341 n. 4
– – *Heracles*:   341
– – *Hippolytus*:   341 f. n. 4; 373 n. 26
– – *Ion*:   341 f. n. 4; 391
– – *Iphigeneia in Aulis*:   341 f. n. 4; 390
– – *Iphigeneia in Tauris*:   193; 341 n. 4
– – *Medea*:   341; 404
– – *Orestes*:   341 f. n. 4; 425

General Index

– – *Phoenician Women:* 341 f. n. 4; 386; 399 ff.; 402; 405 ff.; 437; 441
– – *Suppliants:* 401; 405 ff.
– – *Trojan Women:* 58; 386
[Euripides] *Rhesus:* 425 ff.
Euryclea (Eurykleia): 143 f.; 197; 204 n. 71; 207; 225 n. 34; 230 f.; 237 n. 67
Eustathius: 53 f.
exhortation: 144 f.
expectations: 68; 92; 155 ff.; 223 n. 27; 309; 347 ff.; 369; 437; 482 ff.; 510; 522
expressive, expressivity: 22; 31; 141 n. 15; 142 ff.
extradiegetic/metadiegetic narrative level: 401; 556

fabula: 36 n. 38; 88 ff.; 131 f.; 157 f.; 294; 296 f.; 319; 338; 340; 415
fabula-time: 293 n. 1; 298; 306; 312; 314
fade out: 104 n. 43; 106 f.; 113
Flaubert, G.: 119 ff.
Fludernik, M.: 2; 92; 115; 138 f.; 142
focalisation 1; 79 ff.; 109 f.; 119 f.; 142; 158; 162; 164 f.; 168 f.; 172; 212; 287; 311; 328; 339; 396; 422; 424 f.; 428; 433; 468; 483; 487; 507 ff.; 529 ff.; 533; 535; 539; 541; 558 ff.
focaliser: 94 n. 17; 110; 161; 324; 328; 421; 434; 512 f. n. 11; 514 f.; 516; 523 n. 22; 530 n. 14
foreshadowing: 65; 162 f.; 170; 214 n. 3; 313 n. 65; 315; 479; 484 f.; 490; 493
free indirect speech: 121 f.; 139 f.; 150; 536 f.
future reflexive/future reflexivity: 399, 400, 401, 403–408, 413, 414, 416, 418

Genette, G.: 31 n. 31; 34 n. 36; 56; 65 ff.; 87 f.; 89; 91 f.; 138; 153 ff.; 241 f.; 275; 337 f.; 358 n. 4; 512 n. 11; 529 ff.
genre: 29; 35; 117; 129; 228 f.; 233; 236; 238 ff.; 271; 294 f.; 313; 357; 362 ff.; 369; 479; 508; 528
Gorgias: 32 n. 33; 57
Gould, J.: 38 n. 41; 337 ff.
Goward, B.: 339 f.; 375
Greimas, A.J.: 358 f.

Hannibal: 495 ff.; 535 ff.
Hector: 43 f.; 46; 58; 69 ff.; 98; 114; 120 f.; 144 f.; 147 n. 31; 148 n. 32; 279 n. 12; 283 n. 22; 285; 288; 322; 325; 375; 426
Heidegger, M.: 154; 156
Helen: 43; 46 f.; 67; 98 f.; 147 n. 30; 188 ff.; 199; 204; 221 f.; 392; 394; 422; 425; 564
Helvetii: 516
Heracles: 105; 280; 296 ff.; 306 ff.; 313; 319; 326 n. 12; 328 ff.; 343; 345; 407 n. 27; 423; 435
heralds: 143
Herodotus: 46; 48 ff.; 55; 159 ff.; 168 ff.; 271 n. 63; 364 n. 14; 369 n. 18; 376; 408 f.; 411; 461 f.; 490 n. 17; 497 n. 23; 556
Hesiod: 101 ff.; 229; 231; 233 ff.; 312; 564
hint: 236; 314; 400; 467; 493
Homer: 22 ff.; 37 ff.; 43 ff.; 65 ff.; 93 ff.; 98 ff.; 117 ff.; 137 ff.; 177 ff.; 213 ff.; 275 ff.; 321; 327 f.; 364 n. 13; 421; 477 f.
– – *Iliad:* 21 f.; 31; 44; 52; 56 ff.; 65 ff.; 76 f.; 88; 92 ff.; 110; 114; 123 f.; 132; 135; 141 f.; 144 f.; 149 ff.; 158; 188 ff.; 238; 277; 287; 293 n. 1; 321 f.; 325 f.; 364 n. 13; 375 f.; 537
– – *Odyssey:* 25; 28; 52 f.; 59; 79; 94; 96 f.; 99 f.; 102; 124; 128 ff.; 143 f.; 149; 177 ff.; 213 ff.; 287; 289; 293 n. 11; 299; 321; 364 n. 13; 438; 477 ff.

Homeric criticism, ancient: 43 ff.; 65 ff.; 71
Horace, *Ars Poetica*:   43 f.; 53 f.; 59 f.; 67 n. 14
horizon of expectations: 155 f.; 361 n. 11; 369
Hornblower, S.:   451; 455; 473

identification: 357 f.; 483; 504 f.
indirect speech: 27 n. 25; 99 ff.; 121 f.; 137 ff.
interrogatives: 141; 143
intertextuality: 275; 369; 401; 403 ff.; 416; 418; 477 ff.
intertheatrical/intertheatricality: 401, 402 n. 7, 418 n. 71

Jahn, M.:   340 f.
Jauss, H.R.:   369
Jong, I.J.F. de: 1; 87 ff.; 117; 120 f.; 126; 138; 140; 162 f.; 223; 337; 340; 422; 558
Julia: 524

Klytaimnestra: 177 ff.
Koselleck, R.:   155 f.; 172
Kroon, C.:   146 f.

Lesches: 58
lexis: 17 f.; 19; 21; 27 f.; 30; 36 f.; 40
linearity: 313 n. 65
Livius: 527 ff.
logos ('discourse'):   17
Luca: 517; 520; 522
Lucian/[Lucian]:   54; 73 ff.; 93; 453
Lupercalia: 515

Maecenas, Cn.:   519
Markantonatos, A.:   1; 338; 340; 358 n. 4; 375; 425
McHale, B.:   91 f.; 138
megatext: 404; 418
memory play: 341
messenger: 337 f.; 345; 359 f.; 362 ff.; 406; 409; 422 ff.
metalepsis: 87 ff.

metatheater: 343; 345
Meyer, Ed.:   507
Milligan, S.:   90
mimesis (vs. diegesis):   30 f. and n. 31; 32; 39; 118; 339; 342; 535
mimesis, as diegetic mode: 19 n. 7; 24
Morson, G.S.:   169 f.
Moschus, *Europa*:   297 f.; 312 ff.
move: 138; 141; 146 ff.
– – initiating move: 147 ff.
– – non-preferred move: 147
– – reactive move: 147 ff.
Muses: 23 n. 16; 27; 101 ff.; 124; 128; 132; 134 f.; 181; 246 ff.
myth, in Plato: 27 ff.
myth, poetic: 45; 47; 50

narratee: 87 ff.; 93; 95; 98; 115; 117 n. 12; 118; 178; 181; 214 f.; 228; 280; 286; 324 f.; 403 f.; 417 f.; 424; 483 f.; 488; 494; 499
narrative, 'plain'/'single-voiced' (ἁπλῆ διήγησις):   18 f.; 21 f.; 24; 30 f.
narrative dislocation: 460 f.
narrative emphasis: 455 ff.
narrator: 19; 22 f.; 24 ff.; 36 f.; 65; 67 ff; 73 ff.; 79 ff.; 88 ff.; 119 ff.; 143; 148 ff.; 158 f.; 161 ff. ; 213 ff.; 275 ff.; 300 ff.; 324 f.; 328 f.; 337 ff.; 403 f.; 421 ff.; 461; 468; 482 f.; 486 f.; 492 ff.; 500 ff; 507 ff.; 529 ff; 555 ff.
narrator cinematic: 340; 344; 346
narrator generative: 342; 345
narrator internal (vs. external):   26; 39; 88; ; 89 n. 9
narrator, omniscient: 25 ff.; 44; 78; 558 f.; 561
narrator language: 80
neo-analysis: 44
Nicias: 167 f.; 510
non-direct speech: 140 ff.

Odysseus: 25 f.; 28; 68; 70; 78 f.; 93; 97; 99; 101; 114; 117 ff.; 143 f.; 147 n. 30; 149 f.; 178 ff.;

216 ff.; 289 f.; 327; 330 n. 20; 343 ff.; 391 f.; 427 ff.; 477 f.
opening: 15 f.; 54; 247; 250; 259 f.; 296; 299; 307; 313
oratio obliqua: 27; 105; 536; 544;
orders: 140; 144
Oresteia: 177 ff.; 345; 347 ff.; 378
Orestes: 44 f.; 178 f.; 182 ff.; 345; 347 ff.; 393; 395; 422
Ovid: 404

Patroclus: 44; 59; 71 f.; 94; 96 f.; 145 ff.; 321 f.; 375
patronymics: 471 ff.
Penelope: 144; 151; 178 f.; 186 ff.; 233 ff.; 290
perceptions: 481 ff.; 509 f.; 512; 517; 519
performance: 23 n. 16; 29; 33; 111; 113 n. 63; 117 ff.; 241 ff.; 294; 341; 355; 357; 360; 362; 370 f.; 377; 379 f.; 400 ff.; 416 f.
periphrastic denomination (ἀντωνομασία): 473 ff.
Phrynichus *Capture of Miletus*: 374; 376
– – *Phoenician Women*: 371 n. 24; 376
Phylarchus: 58
Pindar: 23 n. 16; 76 f.; 103 ff.; 209; 241 ff.; 306; 412 n. 40
pity: 57 f.; 357 f.; 374 f.
Plato: 15 ff.; 73 ff.; 339; 362; 373 n. 26; 412 n. 39; 464; 514 n. 12
playwright, internal: 342 ff.
plot: 156 ff.; 177 ff.; 215; 219; 294 ff.; 318; 345 ff.; 359 f.
Plutarch: 55; 361; 407 ff.; 452 f.; 508 ff.
point of view: 27; 31; 36; 119; 121; 282 n. 20; 344; 428; 462; 528 n. 1; 529; 543 n. 58; 548 n. 84; 558 ff.
Polybius: 58 f.; 481 ff.; 545 ff.
pragmatics: 117 f.; 150
praxis: 295 n. 9; 305; 309; 312; 317 f.
projected indexicality: 123 ff.; 134

prolepsis: 65 ff.; 131; 161 ff.; 187; 196 n. 52; 203; 304; 310; 557

questions: *see* interrogatives

resignified etymology: 180
retardation: 69; 162 f.; 177 f. n. 1; 215; 224; 297; 299; 305; 309; 317 n. 76; 318; 490; 498
retrospection: 156 f.; 315; 328; 333
reversal of etymology: 185; 198; 201
Richardson, Br.: 341 f.; 345
Ricoeur, P.: 154 ff.; 319 n. 80; 358 f.
Rimmon-Kenan, S.: 138
Robbe-Grillet, A.: 90 f.
Rood, T.: 510

Sarpedon: 145; 392
scene: 71; 143; 145; 242 f.; 248 f.; 268; 271; 285 f.; 297; 318; 504
scholia, Homeric: 50; 52 f.; 56 ff.; 63 ff.; 183 f.
seed: 68
sequel:
servants: 143; 150; 442; 445 f.
'showing': 340; 342; 362
similes: 80; 392
Simonides: 209 n. 90; 270; 361; 364; 369
simultaneous events: 69 ff.; 169; 276 f.; 279 f.; 284 f.; 287; 301 n. 27; 308 f. n. 50; 500 f.; 529 n. 10
slant in drama: 340 ff.
slant in film: 340 ff.; 512 n.11
'snapshot': 293 ff.
Socrates: 15 ff.; 52
Sophocles: 337 ff.; 378; 386; 424; 437; 443; 445
– – *Ajax*: 343 ff.; 425 ff.
– – *Antigone*: 386; 404 f.; 418 n. 70; 424 f.; 434 f.; 438 f.; 445 f.
– – *Electra*: 347 ff.; 402 n. 8; 422
– – *Oedipus at Colonus*: 386
– – *Oedipus Tyrannos*: 435 ff.
– – *Philoctetes*: 343; 345

– – *Trachiniae*: 386
spectator, internal: 343 ff.
speech act: 29; 125; 137 ff.
speech act type (*see also* assertives, directives, emotives, interrogatives):   137 ff.
speech mention: 137 f.; 140; 145 f.; 149 ff.
speech mode: 143; 150
speech representation (*see also* direct speech, indirect speech, speech mention, speech mode):   137 ff.; 148 ff.
speech representational spectrum: 137 ff.
Sternberg, M.:   156; 158
Sterne, L.:   89
story: 27; 88 f.; 119 ff.; 131 ff.; 157 f.; 170; 177 ff.; 214; 294; 358 n. 4; 528 ff.; 560
story time: 72 f.; 338; 401
Strabo: 45
style indirect libre: 119 f.
Suetonius: 509 f.
surprise: 156; 169; 171; 315; 487; 496; 498
suspense: 68; 156; 160; 162 ff.; 188; 189; 215; 302; 355; 483 ff.; 533
suspense of anticipation: 484; 498
suspense of uncertainty: 484; 493; 498
symposium: 243 ff.; 257 ff.; 268 f.; 271

Teiresias: 310 f.
Telemachos: 178 ff.; 188; 190; 196 f.; 200; 392
'telling':   340; 342; 362
text-time: 294; 297

Theaetetus: 15 ff.
Theocritus, *Hylas*:   296
– – *Little Heracles*:   306 ff.
[Theocritus] *Heracles the Lionslayer*:   298
Theseus: 106 f.; 298 ff.; 406 ff.; 422 f.
Thucydides: 48 ff.; 121 ff.; 159 ff.; 455; 473; 475; 479; 486 n. 14; 494 n. 21; 501 n. 27; 510; 533 n. 25, 26, 27; 569
Thyestes: 200 f.; 388; 392
time: 69 ff.; 119 f.; 153 ff.; 244 f.; 275 ff.; 293 ff.; 357 f.; 360; 375; 378; 400 ff.; 483 f.
transference of etymology: 196; 219 f.

Velleius: 509 ff.
Virgil, *Aeneid*:   226 f.; 321 ff.; 537; 539; 556 f.
vocatives: 94; 142 ff.; 433

weaving: 179; 190; 199; 205; 211 f.
Wilamowitz, U. von: 260; 264 f.; 389
Williams, Tenessee: 341

Xenophon: 22; 99; 263; 269; 451 ff.
– – *Anabasis*:   451 ff.

Zeus: 26; 28; 38; 44; 65; 97 f.; 102 n. 39; 103; 134; 145; 181 ff.; 205; 217; 224; 245; 247 ff.; 260 f.; 304; 307 n. 47; 312 ff.; 352; 361; 378; 387 ff.; 421; 432 f.; 439; 556

Passages Index*

Aeschylus
Agamemnon
39–256: 381 ff.
99–103: 397
135–38: 398
239–43: 396
681–749: 190 n. 32
1404–05: 208
Choephoroi
106–23: 349
828–9: 395
Eumenides
511–2: 394
Persians
546–54: 365
967–73: 367
987–91: 367
Suppliants
584–5: 395
754–59: 409 f.
fragmenta (*TrGF*)
fr. 154a.15–16: 37
fr. 305: 37

[Aeschylus]
Prometheus
640–44: 429 f.
645–83: 430 f.
827–8: 432

Apollonius of Rhodes
Argonautica
1–2: 277; 279 f.; 282
1.425–31: 332 n. 23
1.496–512: 105
1.1015 ff.: 280
1.1187 ff.: 280
2.1–97: 325 f.

2.38–40: 330 n. 20
2.674 ff.: 281
2.705–13: 105
3: 283 ff.
3.159 ff.: 287 f.
3.253–70: 286
3.572–616: 285 f.
3.673–740: 286
4.1143: 99
4.1223–1781: 291

Appian
Bellum Civile
2.17.61–3: 520 f.

Apuleius
Metamorphoses
4.28.1–3: 564 f.

Aristophanes
Clouds
1364–72: 417
Frogs
52–4: 416 n. 62
151: 416 n. 63
943: 402 n. 11
945–7: 343 n. 6
1409: 402 n. 11
Lysistrata
189–90: 417

Aristoteles
Poetics
3.1448a21–3: 22 n. 11
3.1450b26–31: 343 n. 6
13.1453a2–6: 375
13.1453a37–9: 45
15.1454a29–31: 24 n. 16

---

* See also General Index under author names.

23.1459a31–3:   54
24.1459b22–7:   69
23.1460a5–11:   22 n. 11
23.1460a18–19:   43
Rhetoric
1385b13–16:   374

Athenaeus
4.29.13–14:   120

Bacchylides
3.10–4:   106
3.76 ff.:   106
17.128–32:   106 f.
20.1–3:   106

Callimachus
Hecale (Hollis)
fr. 1:   299
fr. 2:   300
fr. 3–17:   300 f.
fr. 18–26:   301 f.
fr. 18.5–6:   301
fr. 27 ff.:   302
fr. 70–74:   304

Cassius Dio
38.31–5:   516

Dio Chrysostom
Orationes
11.24:   53 f.
11.26:   60
11.28:   56
11.29:   57
11.29–30:   58
11.38:   49
11.49–50:   46
11.62 f.:   47
11.64:   48
11.92:   45 f.
18.10:   49 n. 16
20.19–23:   47

Diodorus
4.65.9:   410
13.84.4 ff.:   169 n. 53

13.97–103:   408 n. 30
13.97.6:   399

Diogenes Laertius
3.50:   20 n. 8

Dionysius of Halicarnassus
Antiquitates Romanae
5.17.4:   410
De Thucydide
9:   55
11:   55

Euripides
Alcestis
445–54:   99
Bacchae
769 ff.:   423
1079–80:   423
Electra
932–3:   422
Heraclidae
856–7:   423
Ion
1118:   424
Iphigeneia in Tauris
208:   193 f.
Suppliants
135–146:   415 f.
846–917:   416
Trojan Women
988–97:   422
1242–5:   99
1260–1332:   58 n. 40
sch. Eur. Tr. 36:   343 n. 6

[Euripides]
Rhesus
852–55:   426

Eustathius
Commentarii in Homeri Iliadem
7.9–10:   53 n. 26
7.42–4:   53
Commentarii in Homeri Odysseam
2.94.23–25:   189 n. 27

Gorgias

Helen (Diels-Kranz)
B 11.9: 57
B 11.13, 15: 32 n. 33

Herodotus
1.5.4: 160
1.13: 162
1.32.1–9: 160
1.34.1: 161 f.
1.43.3: 161
1.45.2: 162
1.54.1: 160
1.55.2: 160
1.71.1: 160; 162
2.116: 48
2.118: 48
2.119: 50
2.120.4: 46
3.123–4: 169 n. 53
6.21: 376
7.220: 98 f.
9.25–7: 408 f.
9.27.3: 409

Hesiod
Theogony
1–115: 102 f.
68–75: 101 f.
fragmenta (Merkelbach-West)
fr. 1.1–4: 234
fr. 1.1–3: 229
fr. 23a.22–6: 221
fr. 25a.10–2: 221
fr. 91: 221
fr. 176.5–6: 192 n. 41
fr. 195.16–7: 231
fr. 197.4–5: 46
fr. 222: 225; 236
fr. dub. 361: 23 n. 15

Homer
Iliad
1.12–42: 31
1.12–16: 21
1.22–3:31 n. 32
2.100–08: 327
2.305–29: 391
2.484: 124; 132; 135

2.760: 128
3.125–28: 189 f.
3.361–8: 50
4.539–44: 110 f.
5.793–834: 428
6.118–237: 71
6.245–46: 192
6.357–8: 98
7.17–43: 69
7.311–12: 120 f.
9.142, 146: 192
9.270–90: 192
10.180–298: 70
10.299–399: 70
11–16: 71 f.
11.242–43: 191 f.
11.285–91: 144 f.
11.363–76: 238
11.602–06: 145 f.
11.611–5: 71
11.648–54: 71
11.656–803: 71
11.769–90: 68
12.23: 96
14.342–5: 44
15.365–6: 95
16.692–3: 93 f.
18.246–8: 81 n. 39
19.12–5: 327
19.387–91: 327
21.218: 80
21.257–62: 60
22.60–71: 58
22.199–201: 44
22.226–47: 44
22.304–5: 98
22.326–9: 114 f.
23.619: 189
23.651–99: 326
24.29–30: 67
24.41–3: 392 f. n. 28
24.102: 142 n. 20
24.720–2: 142 n. 20
24.527 ff.: 37
Odyssey
1.1–28: 181
1.1–9: 130 f.
1.1: 124; 130 f.

1.10:	134	14.196–98:	135
1.29–43:	181 ff.; 187	15.10–23:	188
1.298–300:	196	15.125–28:	189
1.428–33:	230	15.160–78:	190
2.117–20:	234	15.503 ff.:	289 f.
3.301–10:	199 f.	16.130–34:	290
4.219–89:	190	16.328–32:	290
4.524–35:	200 f.	16.337–9:	151 n. 35
4.770–1:	188	16.351–3:	290
5.333–5:	221	16.407 f.:	290
5.491–3:	219 f.	16.450 f.:	290
6.48–53:	223	16.470–75:	290
6.312:	216	16.337–39:	151 n. 35
6.323–7.2:	217	17.518–21:	133
7.67–8:	230 f.; 234	18.14–107:	330 n. 20
7.71:	216	19.12–15:	328
7.75–77:	216	19.387–91:	327
7.139–52:	217	21.11–33:	327
7.237–9:	225	21.107–8:	233 f.
7.241–3:	226	21.320–29:	186
7.334–38:	144	23:	321 f.
8.266–366:	198	23.130–51:	188
8.266–70:	100	23.626–50:	323
8.423–4:	229	23.653–99:	325
8.433–34:	144	24.93–94:	205
9–12:	25; 99 f.; 129 f.; 149	24.96–7:	183; 205
9.39–46:	131	24.191–3:	96 f.
9.97:	478	24.192–202:	206 f.
9.102:	478	sch. Ariston. *Iliad*	
9.154–5:	114	9.19b:	66
10.14–18:	149 f.	10.299a:	70 f.
11.181–83:	187 f.	17.588a:	79
11.198–203:	188 n. 23	sch. bT *Iliad*	
11.225–7:	229	1.1:	60 f.
11.248–52:	25	1.8–9:	52
11.277–80:	438	1.44a:	59
11.328–30:	132	2.39b:	65
11.336–7:	231	2.485–6:	56
11.367–68:	133	2.494–877:	52 f.; 67 f.
11.387–91:	204	3.126–7:	189 n. 29
11.397–403:	202	4.303b:	77
11.406–8:	202	5.408:	60
11.409–12:	202	6.58–9:	56 f.
11.421–53:	203	6.237a:	71
11.429–30:	198	6.377:	80
12.377–88:	26	7.29:	69
12.427–8:	114	11.671–761:	52 n. 24
13.88–92:	130	11.769:	68

12.1–2a: 72
13.665:   52 n. 24
15.390:   72
16.395–8:   60
17.205a: 56
22.375b: 60
23.855b: 77 f.
24.776:   57
sch. D *Iliad*
1.1:   56
14.1:   71 f.
sch. Nic. *Iliad*
18.247–8:   81 n. 39
sch. pap. *Iliad*
2.788:   70 f.
21.218:   80
sch. HQT *Odyssey*
9.229:   79

Homeric Hymns
to Aphrodite
291:          113
to Apollo
119–21:   95
146–76:   107 ff.
299:          98
544–6:   113
to Pan
27–47:   105

Horace
Ars poetica
136–47:   53
136:          54
149–50:   59
151–2:   43

Isocrates
Panathenaicus
18:           52
172:          411 f.

Livy
3.35.3–6:   549 f.
3.38.7:   550
3.41.2–3:   550
3.47.5:   547
8.40:   570 f.

9.10.3–5:   536 f.
21.22.6–9:   537 f.
21.32.8–9:   543
21.33.1–6:   531 f.
21.44.1–2:   535
21.53.1–7:   540 ff.
30.14.1–3:   538 f.

Longus
Daphne and Chloe
2.27:   99

Lucian
Verae Historiae
2.15:   93
2.20:   54

[Lucian]
Encomium of Demosthenes
sch. 58.2:   73 ff.

Moschus
Europa
1 ff.:   313 ff.
165–66:   312

Pausanias
1.38.5:   16 n. 1
1.39.2:   410
8.25.8:   411 n. 36
9.18.2:   410 f.

Philostratus
Heroicus
25.45:   93 n. 15
43.15:   93 n. 15
Vita Apollonii
8.1:   115

Phylarchus (*FGrHist* 81)
F 53:   58

Pindar
Isthmian
2.30–34:   269 f.
2.43–48:   270 f.
Nemean
1.19–20:   262

5.25–39:   103 f.
5.40–54:   104 n. 42
6.29–30:   256
9.1 ff.:   262
sch. 7.106a: 76 f.
Olympian
1.13–17:   268 f.
6.15–6:   142 n. 40
7.34 ff.:   106
13.61–92:   105
Pythian
1.1–4:   246 f.
1.5–12:   248 f.
1.13–16:   249
1.31–40:   251
1.35–40:   247
1.75–80:   252 f.
1.81–84:   253 f.
1.85–100:   254 ff.
6.1–18:   266 f.
6.43–54:   267 f.
11.17–26:   209
sch. 11 inscr. B: 77

Plato
Apologia
28b-d: 37 n. 40
34a: 22 n. 12
38b: 22 n. 12
Critias
116b: 34 n. 35
Laws
834d: 34 n. 35
Hippias Minor
369e-71e: 52
Phaedo
61b: 28 n. 27
Phaedrus
229b-c: 16 n.1
267d: 34 n. 35
Republic
329b-c: 26
359c-60b: 27
365b-6b: 26
366d-7a: 26 f.
376e-98b: 20
376d: 36
376e-392c: 20; 22; 37; 39; 41
376e-7a: 20
377c-d: 29
378c-d: 21 n. 9; 29
378d: 30; 40
379c-d: 38
380c: 32
386c-7b: 37
387b: 32
390a1–2:   21 n. 10
392c-8b: 17 ff.; 24; 30 n. 29; 36; 39; 41
392c-4c: 21; 29; 35 f.; 41
392b-c: 26
392d: 18; 21; 23; 25
393a-d: 21
393d-4d: 31; 74 ff.
393c: 26; 31 f.
394d-8b: 19; 30; 36
394e-5b: 30
394b-c: 25
394c1:   19; 23
394c: 30
394d: 30
395a: 30
395d: 32
395e: 30
396b: 32 f.
396b-7d: 35
396c-e: 33 ff.; 40
396c1:   35 n. 37
396c6:   17 f. n. 4
397b2:   17 n.5
397c: 21 n. 10
397e: 24 n. 17
398a: 50
415a-c: 27
469d-e: 412 n. 39
476e: 27 n. 23
545d-7b: 27
602b: 34
614b: 26 n. 22
614d: 27 f. 25
615d-16a: 27 f. n. 25
617d-e: 27 f. n. 25
619b: 27 f. n. 25
620d: 27 f. n. 25
621b8:   28
Theaetetus

142b:	17	fr. 5–9:	361 f.
142c:	16 f. n. 1	fr. 11:	361 f.; 364 f.
143b1:	16	fr. 13:	361 f.

Plutarch
Moralia
345e: 452
347a–c: 169 n. 53
711b–c: 20 n. 8; 75 n. 28
854 f.:   55 n. 32
855e: 52 n. 22
Caesar
51:       513 f.
Cato minor
43.9–19: 523 f.
Theseus
29.4–5:   407 f.

Polybius
2.56.10:   58
3.1–32:   499 ff.
3.19.12–20.1: 501
3.20.6:   501
3.33–118:   502 ff.
8.15.2:   486
8.15.6:   486
8.17.10–18.1: 488 f.
8.19.4:   490
8.20.12:   492
27.9.2–6:   505

Pompeius Trogus
Historiae Philippicae (Seel)
Fr. 11:   544

Proclus
in rem publicam (Kroll)
1.14.15–15.19:   20 n. 8

Quintilian
Institutio oratoria
4.1.69:   93 n. 16
9.2.37:   546 n. 76
9.2.38–9: 93 n. 16

Simonides
fragmenta (W.²)
fr. 1–4:   361 f.

Sophocles
Ajax
1–126:   343 f.
315–16:   426 f.
285–304:   427 f.
1338 f.:   344 f.
Antigone
253–6:   424 f.
1255–6:   435
1304–5:   438
1311–2:   438
1315–6:   435
Electra
1–76:   345; 347 ff.
44–50:   347
51–58:   347
680–763:   345
932–33:   422
1113–4:   345
Oedipus Tyrannus
1062–72:   436
1073–79:   437
1182–85:   437
1232–35:   445 f.
1237–40:   440 f.
1241–43:   438
1245–50:   440
1251–54:   440
1255–58:   442
1258–61:   444
Philoctetes
1–134:   345
542–627:   345
1409–71:   345

Strabo
1.2.9:   45
1.2.10:   45
1.2.17:   45
1.2.36:   45
1.2.40:   45

Tacitus
Annals

2.39–40:   565 ff.
3.19.2:   569 f.
4.31:   562 f.
4.38:   561 f.

Theocritus
Idylls
7.83–9:   105
12.11:   99
22.94:   330 n. 20
24.1:   307
24.3–10:   307 f.
24.11–27:   308
24.34–59:   309
24.60–92:   310
24.103–140:   311

Theognis
39–40:   124 f.
53–54:   125
237–252:   257 f.

Theon
Progymnasmata (Spengel)
76.20–25:   54
80.16–20:   55 n. 32
86.9–87.12:   53 n. 25
86.32:   53 n. 26
93.5–94.11:   54 n. 30
94.12–95.2:   54 n. 31
119.23:   59 n. 43

Thucydides
1.20 ff.:   49 ff.
2.77.4–6:   170 f.
6.8:   169
6.15.4:   166 n.45
6.24.3:   166 f.
6.33–41:   167
6.46:   169
6.54–9:   166 n. 46
7.70.7:   121 f.
7.75.6 f.:   165 f.

Timotheus
Persae(PMG)
791 col. iv.150–61:   23 n. 16
Scylla (PMG)
793:   23 n. 16

Velleius Paterculus
2.50.1–2:   511 f.

Virgil
Aeneid
2.2:   226 f.
2.313:   58 n. 42
3.121–3:   557
5.362–484:   321 ff.
5.421–23:   330 f.
5.437–42:   333 f. n.28
5.465–67:   331
5.477–84:   332
5.563–5:   324
Eclogues
6.45–6:   114 n. 66

Xenophon
Anabasis
1.1.4:   474 f.
1.2.2:   456
1.2.3:   460 f.
1.3.13–4:   476
1.4.7:   455 f.
1.7.9–10:   474
2.2.1:   468 f.
2.4.15–22:   465 ff.
2.4.27:   474
2.5.25–6:   470
2.5.28:   469
2.5.31:   459 f.
2.5.33:   462 f.
2.6.21–9:   469 f.
2.6.28:   470 f.
3.1.30–31:   457 f.
3.1.47:   458 f.
3.2.25–6:   477 f.
3.3.1–4:   465 ff.
3.3.5:   462
3.3.20:   471 f.
5.1.2:   478 f.
6.5.24:   99
Hellenica
3.1.2:   452
Hieron
6.1–3:   263

Lightning Source UK Ltd.
Milton Keynes UK
UKHW021951100521
383482UK00006B/51

9 783110 482362